CAMBRIDGE LIBRARY COLLECTION

Books of enduring scholarly value

Religion

For centuries, scripture and theology were the focus of prodigious amounts of scholarship and publishing, dominated in the English-speaking world by the work of Protestant Christians. Enlightenment philosophy and science, anthropology, ethnology and the colonial experience all brought new perspectives, lively debates and heated controversies to the study of religion and its role in the world, many of which continue to this day. This series explores the editing and interpretation of religious texts, the history of religious ideas and institutions, and not least the encounter between religion and science.

The Short Journals and Itinerary Journals of George Fox

This volume brings together three journals of George Fox (1624–1691) the founder of the Religious Society of Friends. It was edited by Norman Penny and first published in 1925 to mark the tercentenary of Fox's birth. The Short Journal, dictated by Fox during his detention in Lancaster prison (1663–64), records Fox's missionary wanderings and the persecutions he faced between 1648 and 1663. The Itinerary Journal, compiled by John Field, contains an account of Fox's missionary work, church organisational activities and family life from 1681 to his death in 1690. The Haistwell Diary, written by Fox's companion Edward Haistwell, records Fox's activities between 1677 and 1679, including his missionary journey across the length of England and his missionary voyages to Holland and North Germany. The collection is a key source for those studying Fox's life and thought or the history and origins of the Quaker movement.

GW00771260

Cambridge University Press has long been a pioneer in the reissuing of out-of-print titles from its own backlist, producing digital reprints of books that are still sought after by scholars and students but could not be reprinted economically using traditional technology. The Cambridge Library Collection extends this activity to a wider range of books which are still of importance to researchers and professionals, either for the source material they contain, or as landmarks in the history of their academic discipline.

Drawing from the world-renowned collections in the Cambridge University Library, and guided by the advice of experts in each subject area, Cambridge University Press is using state-of-the-art scanning machines in its own Printing House to capture the content of each book selected for inclusion. The files are processed to give a consistently clear, crisp image, and the books finished to the high quality standard for which the Press is recognised around the world. The latest print-on-demand technology ensures that the books will remain available indefinitely, and that orders for single or multiple copies can quickly be supplied.

The Cambridge Library Collection will bring back to life books of enduring scholarly value (including out-of-copyright works originally issued by other publishers) across a wide range of disciplines in the humanities and social sciences and in science and technology.

The Short Journals and Itinerary Journals of George Fox

EDITED BY NORMAN PENNEY

CAMBRIDGE
UNIVERSITY PRESS

CAMBRIDGE UNIVERSITY PRESS

Cambridge, New York, Melbourne, Madrid, Cape Town, Singapore,
São Paolo, Delhi, Dubai, Tokyo

Published in the United States of America by Cambridge University Press, New York

www.cambridge.org
Information on this title: www.cambridge.org/9781108015325

© in this compilation Cambridge University Press 2010

This edition first published 1925
This digitally printed version 2010

ISBN 978-1-108-01532-5 Paperback

THE SHORT JOURNAL AND ITINERARY JOURNALS OF GEORGE FOX

CAMBRIDGE UNIVERSITY PRESS
LONDON : FETTER LANE, E.C. 4

NEW YORK : THE MACMILLAN CO.
PHILADELPHIA : THE FRIENDS' BOOK STORE,
304 ARCH STREET
BOMBAY
CALCUTTA } MACMILLAN AND CO., Ltd.
MADRAS
TORONTO : THE MACMILLAN CO. OF
CANADA, Ltd.
TOKYO : MARUZEN-KABUSHIKI-KAISHA

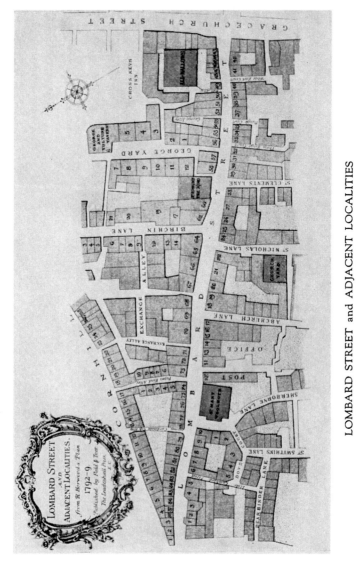

LOMBARD STREET and ADJACENT LOCALITIES
(From the original in the Guildhall Library, London)

THE SHORT JOURNAL AND ITINERARY JOURNALS OF GEORGE FOX

In Commemoration of
THE TERCENTENARY OF HIS BIRTH
(1624—1924)

Now first published for
FRIENDS' HISTORICAL ASSOCIATION
PHILADELPHIA, PENNSYLVANIA

EDITED BY
NORMAN PENNEY, LL.D., F.S.A.

WITH AN INTRODUCTION BY
T. EDMUND HARVEY, M.A.

CAMBRIDGE
AT THE UNIVERSITY PRESS
1925

Uniform with this volume

THE JOURNAL OF
GEORGE FOX

EDITED FROM THE MSS. BY
NORMAN PENNEY, F.S.A.

WITH AN INTRODUCTION BY
T. EDMUND HARVEY, M.A.

In two volumes. Royal 8vo.
With four plates. 40s. net

CAMBRIDGE
UNIVERSITY PRESS

PRINTED IN GREAT BRITAIN

PREFACE

THE plan to publish the original of the Short Journal of George Fox as an appropriate commemoration of the three hundredth anniversary of his birth had its origin in Philadelphia. The idea was brought before the Friends' Historical Association, and at once aroused interest and approval. A Committee was appointed to mature the project, and the plan gradually expanded to include the Itinerary Journal and finally the Haistwell Diary. This has made it possible to bring together in one volume the important documents which underlie the Great Journal. The present volume will thus be an admirable supplement to the two volumes which gave to the world George Fox's Journal (Cambridge Edition) in its original form. Norman Penney, LL.D., F.S.A., Consulting Librarian of Friends' Reference Library at Devonshire House, Bishopsgate, London, and Editor of the above-mentioned Cambridge Edition of the Journal, was asked by the Philadelphia Committee to do the editorial work now happily brought to completion.

There have been many fitting commemorative events and activities during this tercentenary year, but it is safe to predict that nothing has been done which will give more satisfaction to those who come after us than will the publication of these quaint narratives of travels and sufferings.

On behalf of the Committee,

RUFUS M. JONES,
Chairman.

HAVERFORD COLLEGE,
PA., U.S.A.

TABLE OF CONTENTS

PREFACE. By RUFUS M. JONES, LITT.D., LL.D. . . . v

INTRODUCTION. By T. EDMUND HARVEY, M.A. . . . ix

EDITOR'S INTRODUCTION xxi

KEY TO ABBREVIATIONS xxxi

EXPLANATION OF SIGNS xxxiv

I. THE SHORT JOURNAL 1

II. THE ITINERARY JOURNAL 73

III. THE HAISTWELL DIARY 223

NOTES 275

INDEX 383

LIST OF ILLUSTRATIONS

Lombard Street and Adjacent Localities, from a
  plan of 1792—9. . . . . . . *frontispiece*

A Page of the Short Journal . . . . *to face p.* 1

A Page of the Itinerary Journal . . . . *to face p.* 75

A Page of the Haistwell Diary . . . . *to face p.* 225

INTRODUCTION

THE student who is engaged upon the study of the life of George Fox must be grateful to the Friends' Historical Association, of America, for making available the new material which Dr Norman Penney has edited, and that the task has been entrusted to one so uniquely qualified for it.

The original documents now for the first time printed form part of the manuscript treasures of the Friends' Reference Library at Devonshire House, Bishopsgate, and have been consulted occasionally by Quaker historians, but with the publication of this volume a wider world has now access to information which adds to our knowledge of Fox and helps to complete the record given in the Cambridge Journal.

The Short Journal has a special interest of its own as being a sort of preliminary draft of the greater work, made under difficult conditions, since, as the writer tells, it was written during his long imprisonment in Lancaster Gaol (in 1663—64). The original faded manuscript is a frayed oblong volume, once a child's copy book, the first four pages of which had been filled by copies of texts from the first chapter of the Gospel of John. George Fox usually preferred to dictate, as we know, rather than to write himself, and only a few lines on the manuscript are in his own hand, but this little volume must be either the original Journal dictated by him in prison, or a copy made later under his care at Swarthmoor Hall, the child's writing being probably that of one of Margaret Fell's younger daughters.

The Short Journal is much less full than the Great Journal, and shews less attention to chronology, but here and there it supplies details and little touches which we are glad to have. Fox's opening words explain that it is a record of "some of his sufferings for preaching the truth," and the narrative commences abruptly with an incident at Mansfield not recorded in the Great Journal, and then passes to his first imprisonment at Nottingham (in 1649) and thereafter tells the story of his missionary wanderings and the hardships and persecutions which he had to face, up to his imprisonment at Lancaster in 1663.

Among the new material we may note the opening narrative, the account of the healing of a woman who was believed to be possessed, and a number of brief summaries of Fox's addresses in the various churches in which he spoke. We note that on two occasions before a message of protest he speaks of something "striking at his life"; in one case the sight of the great steeplehouse at Nottingham ("when I spyed it a great Idol and Idolatrous Temple") and in another the sound of a church bell has the same effect. At other times he tells how, when bruised and bleeding from the blows of his assailants, his spirit was "revived again by the power of God."

When his companion Thomas Aldam is arrested and a warrant against himself is not delivered by the friendly constable, he quaintly records: "And I saw a vision a man and two Mastiffe doggs and a Bear, and I passed by them and they smiled upon mee." We get a vivid picture of him at Mansfield Woodhouse, seated in the stocks while the people threw stones at him, bruising head and arms and body, till he is "Mazed and dazled with the blowes." Then he is liberated amid the threats of the people and we cannot wonder that when taken to a friendly house he tells us: "I was so bruised when I was cold that I could not turn mee in my bed, and bruised inwardly att my heart, but," he adds, "after a while the power of the Lord went through mee and healed mee, that I was well: Glory to the lord for ever!" Once again he is stoned through the streets of

Bosworth, and in several other passages we are given details of hard usage that are not recorded elsewhere.

Amidst this suffering there came moments of exaltation: "In Warwickshire in Adderstonne when I was two miles of it the Bell runge upon a Market day for a lecture, and it struck at my life, and I was moved to go to the steeple house, and when I came into it I found a man speaking: and when as I stood among the people the glory and life shined over all, and with it I was crowned, and when the priest had done I spake to him and the people the truth and the light which lett them see all that ever they had done, and of their teacher within them and how the lord was come to teach them himself, and of the seed Christ in them; how they were to mind that, and the promise that was to the seed of God within men, which is Christ; and it set them in a Hurry and under a rage and some said I was madd, and spoke to my outward Relacions to tye mee upp, and sett them in a rage but the truth came over all; and I passed away in peace in the power of the lord God, and the truth came over all and reached the hearts of many people."

As we read this narrative we can picture the scene in the church: the rapt look on the young stranger's face as he felt the reality of that Light of God within the soul whose messenger he was, and we can understand how some of the scandalized onlookers took him for a madman.

Two other passages may be set beside the narrative of Fox's examination at Lancaster Sessions in the Cambridge Journal, as an instance of the use of a phrase which must have deeply offended the orthodox of the day. He had been speaking words of warning to some fellows drinking in an ale-house in one of the North Yorkshire dales, and adds: "And the next morning I was moved to tell the man of the house that I was the sonne of God and was come to declare the Everlasting Truth of God, and did declare the truth to him and them."

The second passage relates his examination before the magistrates, previous to his being committed to prison at Carlisle and explains the reference in the Great Journal to his being generally supposed to be about to suffer the death penalty, doubtless on the charge of blasphemy:

"And they asked mee if I were the sonne of God, I said yes: They asked mee if I had seen Gods face, I said yes. They asked mee whether I had the spirit of disserning, I said yes. I disserned him that spoke to mee. They asked mee whether the Scripture was the word of God; I said God was the word, and the Scriptures were writeings; and the word was before writeings were; which word did fulfill them."

In one other passage somewhat earlier in Fox's narrative he records an incident at Kendal where we may feel the prophetic exaltation of spirit is very marked: "And I went into Kendale Markett and spoke to the People at the Markett time. I had silver in my pockett and I was moved to throw it out amongst the people as I was going up the street before I spoke, and my life was offer'd upp amongst them, and the mighty power of the lord was seen in preserving, and the power of the lord was so mighty and so strong, that people flew before and runne into the shopps, for fear and terror took hold upon them; I was moved to open my mouth and lift upp my voyce aloud in the mighty power of the lord; and to tell them the mighty day of the lord was coming upon all deceitfull Merchaundize and wayes, and to call them all to repentance and a turning to the lord God and his spirit within them for it to teach them and lead them...."

Other passages shew Fox, in calmer mood, with spirit sensitive to the inward condition of those amongst whom he passed: "And then I was moved to passe towards the South, and go through many townes and I felt I answered the witnesse of God in all people though I spoke not a word." He frankly notes in one place that his mission found far less response in the South of England than in the North:

"I passed into sussex and surrey and Hampshire and Dorsestershire when there were but few convinced and some place none at all," while he speaks of Cornwall as "a dark countrey."

There are one or two interesting cases of premonition of impending danger, as when he avoids an ambush of armed men near Sedbergh, being "Moved to passe over another way over a water, not knoweing outwardly of them," and when the day before his arrest by the constables at Swarthmoor in 1660 he tells us that he felt "somthing of darkness in the house before they came in, of somthing of a great darkness."

(In the Great Journal he simply says: "And I had a sense of the thinge before hande.")

In singling out these passages we must not forget the rest of the amazing narrative of hardship, toil and suffering, borne without flinching. We see him again and again beaten, stoned, and thrown to earth "mudded and bloodied," as he says in another place; suffering repeated imprisonments in crowded, dark and verminous dungeons, loathsome with unspeakable filth; and if there are sometimes touches of hardness as he writes of some of his persecutors, we have to remember that he is writing in prison, the darkness of the future lit up only by the light of his unconquerable faith.

A little before the close of the narrative we have a vivid picture of Fox's appearance at Lancaster Sessions, greeting his judges as he is called to the bar by an unwonted benediction of peace, but declining to remove his hat, which the Chairman bids the officers remove. "And so a pretty space wee looked att one another, till the power of the lord God arose over all." And so the trial commences and Fox is committed to prison, "where now I am with 8 more."

The Itinerary Journal brings us into a different atmosphere and almost into another world.

Less than twenty years separate the narratives but in that

time England has changed; the tense religious fervour of the Commonwealth has given place to the reaction of the Restoration. The Conventicle Acts have filled the gaols with Quaker prisoners, and the long years of persecution have steadied and sifted the Quaker fellowship, which has now a definite Church organization of its own, linking together hitherto isolated meetings in groups, and these groups in yet wider ones, with a yearly meeting for the whole country. George Fox too has changed with the years. We see him active still, despite failing strength, but moving over a more limited area, and engaged largely in building up existing Quaker meetings, in visiting the sick, advising on matters of Church organization and in other ways fulfilling many of the functions of a bishop of the primitive Church. Here unfortunately we are dealing, not with George Fox's own detailed narrative, but with a bare summary, of which the first few pages only appear to have been actually dictated by Fox himself. The reader must fill in by the light of other material the scanty outline, in order that it may be properly understood. At first sight the long list of places and persons visited and of meetings held seems unattractive, but it throws light at many points on the activities of Fox's closing years. The Itinerary Journals were made full use of by Thomas Ellwood in editing the Great Journal but while throwing the narrative into the first person he omitted many details and these we are now able to have before us.

Once or twice in later pages the first person singular recurs, a noteworthy case being the vivid picture of George Fox speaking at the Savoy meeting in 1683: "And as I was speaking in the power of the Lord the people were transported and the Lord's power was over all, and of a Suddain the Constables and the people came in like a Sea...." In Ellwood's edition of the Journal there is a characteristic modification of this passage, which there reads: "Now as I was speaking in the power of the Lord, and the people

were greatly affected therewith, on a sudden the constables,
with the rude people, came in like a sea...."

We find Fox's time now occupied not only with religious
meetings, or with the business of the Quaker Church, and
important colonial matters like the affairs of New Jersey,
but with visits to individual Friends: he goes one day to
visit " a woman at Ellington not well in her mind," another
day to Jane Bullock's school. He goes to talk over difficulties
about a broken marriage engagement, and at another time
settles a quarrel between servants. Visits are recorded to an
old Quaker gardener 92 years of age, to "old Mary Strut
who was muddled in mind," and to an old man who had
broken his leg. His interest in education is seen by repeated
visits to different schools; he goes to view a house at Chiswick
where it is proposed to start a women's school, and later twice
revisits the school itself. We see him several times meeting
with Friends from Holland and on another occasion going to
see "some Germaine friends that were goeing to pensilvania." Much time is given to the business of the Society
of Friends both in the meetings at "the Chamber," the central
office of the Society, at the Meeting for Sufferings and in less
formal gatherings of leading Friends. He even finds time to
go to see a passage by the meetinghouse in Long Acre about
which there is some dispute with a neighbour; and on another
occasion he goes to visit the young Quaker innkeeper at the
White Lion Tavern, "he being but a new beginner, to Advise
him," following up his good counsel by dining at the inn.
Later we see him conferring with some peer or member of
parliament, or going over to Westminster to help the efforts
made by his fellow Quakers to obtain effective legislative
safeguards for liberty of conscience.

Those wonderful piercing eyes of his were now it seems
less strong than of old, for we find him going on one occasion
"to the spectacle makers." He moves about repeatedly from
house to house, as he visits different meetings, now and then

going for much longer visits to the Essex country house of William Mead, the son-in-law of his wife, and sometimes for similar but shorter visits to Kingston, where lived another stepdaughter Margaret Rous. We see him "light out of the Coach at the shop of the seedsman in Bishopsgate St.," whose place of business must have been a Quaker house of call.

His physical strength was failing for most of his many journeyings are now made by coach, and often a coach is used when quite short distances of under a mile have to be covered. But occasionally he is able still to ride on horse-back, though not as of old. Thus in 1686 occurs the entry, "he went from thence...to Ed Mans at Ford Green miles 3 on horse back & with him Mercy Bentall & Walther her husband & prissila Heart went on foot," from which we may picture the slow pace at which he rode. At intervals he is able to go short distances also on foot, though the fact that a journey of as much as a mile on foot is once or twice recorded in the Journal shews how great an effort it must have been. Exposure to wind and weather, and ill usage at the hands of the angry mob, and those long years of hard imprisonment were now making their effects felt. But still he continues to move about upon his work. Only as time passes the entries become more frequent which tell of his having to lie down upon a couch or a bed to rest in the course of the day's labours.

In 1687 on one occasion we find him attending the early morning meeting of ministering Friends at the Chamber and staying on there instead of proceeding to the neighbouring meeting for worship, while William Penn and George Whitehead come in to visit him after the meeting in Grace-church Street is over.

In 1688 we find him having to leave a First-day meeting for worship before the close on account of increasing weakness, and at the general meeting of Friends in 1690 he leaves the meeting after speaking and has to lie down at a Friend's house.

In the winter and spring of 1689—90 we find him spending over five months with his son-in-law William Mead in Essex, but during the whole time, out of the nineteen meetings he attends, sixteen are in William Mead's house, where he is visited by many friends, and we may picture him busy, as so often, in dictating letters and messages to Friends near and far; his correspondence going out to the Quaker colonists in America and to the groups of Friends in Holland and in other parts of the Continent of Europe. Many of these writings of his later years were printed after his death in the two folio volumes of Epistles and Doctrinals.

The later pages of the Itinerary Journal give us now and then brief headings of the subject matter of George Fox's sermons, but even a full transcript would hardly convey to us the message as it must have come from that patriarchal figure to the friends who loved and revered him. To realize this we need to read William Penn's picture of Fox's ministry recorded in the Preface to the first edition of the Journal. Very often, though by no means always, he seems to have been the only speaker: on such occasions we read repeatedly of his "going to prayer" after preaching and then before the close of the meeting "speaking a few words to the people" by way of dismissal.

Another and more intimate type of meeting is represented in such a record as that at the beginning of the 1686 Journal:

"The 7th of the 1st mo: being the 1st day of the week he had a meeting att Edw: Manns with some friends that were come to see him & after some time sitting in Silence he went to prayer and soe Concluded the meeting."

The Journal records Fox's presence also at the great gatherings of Friends held at longer intervals, like the yearly meetings; in 1687 we find him attending a "generall meeting of men friends in the Ministry at the Bull and Mouth," which lasted "from Early in the morning till towards the 12th hour," Penn, Barclay and other eminent Ministers taking part, besides Fox: "all that declared & prayed were said to be 23," so that we cannot wonder that he left the meeting "being weary," and lay down upon a bed, before going to a business meeting later in the afternoon. Until the accession of James II, all these meetings were held under the shadow of the danger of arrest, and the frequent entry that the meeting was held "within doors" recalls the fact that often the authorities closed the meetinghouses and posted constables to guard them.

Frequent as the entries in the Journal are, they omit some material, dictated or written by Fox himself, which Ellwood has made use of; an instance of this is to be found in a folio page preserved at Devonshire House amongst the few leaves known as the "foul copy" of the Journal. The whole of one side of this page is a journal narrative, entirely in Fox's writing, describing vividly a meeting held in 1683 in the yard of Gracechurch Street meetinghouse, when the constables had closed the meetinghouse and hindered "john tisa[1]" from speaking, but when Fox himself intervenes most effectually and after his words of exhortation and prayer the constable cannot refrain from expressing his approval and even praying for a blessing upon Fox and his people.

Public opinion was doubtless slowly changing towards a friendlier attitude, which prepared the way for the coming of the Act of Toleration a few years later.

During all these years Fox is living for his work, moving from house to house continually, with no permanent resting place, and only at long intervals able to be with his wife: but the record makes us realize the wealth of friendship that was his, as we read of the many homes thrown open to him,

---

[1] Probably John Tyso (*c.* 1626—1700) of London. [ED.]

and the way in which his presence is sought, whether it be
when he is called out into the country, a ten miles' journey,
to visit a sick woman and bring her refreshment of spirit,
or to pass the night at the house of another Friend on her
deathbed, or when his help is needed in lesser cares and
troubles.

We get but the briefest glimpses of Fox's family life, but
we can see what a welcome guest he was in the homes of
his wife's married daughters, and note how he is called from
London to Kingston on several occasions to the sick beds of
his wife's grandchildren, to whom he was deeply attached.

The intense affection which Fox inspired may be seen
again and again in letters and documents written by his
contemporaries, though he himself is so reserved in expressing
his personal feelings that we do not at first realize this
tenderer side of his nature, to which the devotion of his
friends bears witness.

The last of the three documents now printed we owe to
the care of Fox's faithful attendant Edward Haistwell, a
young Friend who writes of him as "my dear master." He
gives us detailed notes of the long journey made by Fox in
1677 across England from Swarthmoor Hall to the South,
holding meetings as he went, and of his missionary voyage
in company with William Penn, Robert Barclay, George
Keith and a group of other Friends to Holland and North
Germany. This narrative has been made full use of by
Ellwood in preparing the first edition of Fox's Journal, but
it is satisfactory to have it as it was actually written, rather
than in the form in which it hitherto was known to us, where
the account has been put by Ellwood into Fox's own mouth.

Some day, perhaps, similar manuscript volumes to these
may come to light giving us itinerary notes for the years
1678—1681, and for the year 1682, but the material here

available helps us, in a way that has never before been possible, to fill in the background of that inimitable picture of George Fox which William Penn has drawn, which, better than any modern writer's words, reveals to us the man himself, as his friends beheld him, and the love that he inspired in others and still inspires to-day.

T. EDMUND HARVEY.

LEEDS, ENGLAND.

EDITOR'S INTRODUCTION

THE volume now in the hands of the reader consists of three sections:—I. The Short Journal. II. The Itinerary Journal. III. The Haistwell Diary.

I. THE SHORT JOURNAL.

This is a manuscript of 126 oblong pages measuring 8 inches by $6\frac{1}{2}$ inches (see illustration). It is endorsed on the last leaf: "a short jornall of gff never wer printd of some short things from ab^t y^e year 1648 to King Charles y^e 2^d Dayes," the first eight words being written by George Fox. Below is the following: "N^o (g) n° 1, 13, A 1648," which was doubtless some guide to the use of the manuscript in the preparation of the first edition of the Journal of George Fox shortly after Fox's death[1]. The handwriting is believed to be that of Henry Fell, who, though probably not a relative of Judge Fell, was "Judge ffells clark," according to a paper, in D, written by Richard Richardson, second clerk to Friends from 1681 to 1689. In volume i. of the Cambridge Journal, page 469, it is stated that Fell frequently wrote letters for Margaret (Fell) Fox, some of which, with some of his own letters, preserved in D, bear a close resemblance to the style of writing of the Short Journal. Fell was a preacher as well as a scrivener, and when in Norfolk he was arrested as a "vagrant," and sent home with the following pass:

Burrow of Thetford

Henry ffell an Idle vagrant person & a seducer of the people, a very suspitious Jesuited deluder & one who denyeth ye Oath of Alleageance & Supremasy, a man of middle statur of some thirty yeares of Age, with browne Curled haire, was this 28 day of May in ye twelfe yeare of his Maties raigne of England &^{c}. openly whipped in Thetford affores^d, according to Law, for a wandering Rogue, & is

[1] For evidence of such use of the MS. see pp. 298, 301, 304, 342, 345, 354, 366, 372.

assigned to pass from pish to pish by yᵉ officers thereof the next straight way to
Ulverstone in Lancashire, where as he confesseth he last dwelt, & he is Lymited
to be at Ulverston afforesᵈ with in 20 dayes next ensuing the date hereof at his
pill given under my hand & seale of office, the date above sᵈ

JOHN KENDALL
mayor

To the Constables of Croxton & to all other
Constables & other officers whom these presents may concerne for yᵉ due execution herof

From a facsimile in D, original endorsed by George Fox: "a uen cry after h
fell 1660 norfolk". See note 48. 2.

There is no indication, in this section of the book, of the
personality of the writer. There are signs of the Journal
having been written up at various times; the whole bears
evidence of having been copied from other papers. The
pages have headings: "The Commonwealthes Dayes," "In
the Protectors dayes," "In Olivers Time," "In the Kings
Time." There are very few corrections. W. C. Braithwaite
writes: "The Short Journal is defective in chronological
sequence in some details, though the general arrangement
of the sections follows the order of Fox's travels. It has the
appearance of being an abridgment for the purpose of bringing all his sufferings together" (*Beginnings of Quakerism,*
1912, page 536). Reference to pages 10—13, 24—26, 47,
60 will indicate sufferings described in greater length than
before printed. Other variations from the hitherto published Journals of George Fox include: more detailed reports
of sermons (pages 1, 3, 6, 9, 12, 13, 17—20, 30, 34, 41);
some excess in record of numbers (pages 18, 35, 51, 54, 62;
see note 45. 2); and many statements and incidents of
interest (pages 2, 11, 13, 14, 17, 20, 21, 23, 27—29, 31,
32, 36, 37, 39, 42, 43, 58, 60, 64, 65, 68; see Introduction).
It is not known when this manuscript first became part of
the Friends' Reference Library (D).

There is also in D another seventeenth-century writing
covering the same ground as the Short Journal and following it closely. It is comprised in seventy-six folios, enclosed

in a much soiled paper cover overrun with figures, and is entitled: "This is a Book of some of the Travells and passidges of G ffs." It is represented by the letter A. See footnotes. In D are modern copies of the Short Journal— B is a copy made by Emily Jermyn about 1866, and C is a copy made by Ellen M. Dawes in 1906. Another Jermyn copy is in the Library of Haverford College, Pennsylvania.

II. THE ITINERARY JOURNAL.

This is contained in two small books, each measuring 6 inches by $3\frac{3}{4}$ inches. The first book, bound in vellum with metal fastener on side, has 468 pages; and book two, bound in rough leather with clasps, has 191 pages, through the whole of which runs a worm-hole. These are doubtless the "Little Jornall Books," mentioned by Fox as available for a Journal of his life and sufferings. The first volume is prefaced as follows: "A Jornall of {Some of} ye Meetings and Travills of G ff & other passages Beginning 1681 & Continued to ye 28 :6: mo: 1687. The year 1682 is wanting." The title of the second volume runs: "A Jornall of the Travells of G: ff. and the Meetings hee hath been att &c: {from y^e 23 :4: mo :} in y^e Year: 1688: {to y^e 13: of y^e 11: mo : 1690 : on wch hee Dyed}." Attached to a blank leaf is the following: "Haveing Read G: ff Journall from the 23^d $\frac{4}{mo}$ 1688 To the 13th $\frac{11}{mo}$ 1690 on which day he dyed finde it mentiond, y^e severall places where he lay, & severall meetings he had bin att & hints of his declareing: severall docktrins & exhortations, & passages betweene frinds to be mentioned in a generall way. BENJ : ANTROBUS."

Between the two books there is a break of nearly ten months; the movements of George Fox during this time are outlined in note 182. 2. These little books have been in the Reference Library for many years. Extracts from them appeared in *Friends' Quarterly Examiner*, January,

1918, under the heading: "George Fox as Home Mission Worker." See *Second Period of Quakerism*, by W. C. Braithwaite, 1919, p. 433.

Though in diary form these books were composed from earlier documents and notes of travel, and not by daily or regular entry of events. A document of eleven pages, brown with age, is in D, endorsed: "A Jornall y^e foul Coppy 1682 $\frac{11}{\text{mo.}}$ 14. The substance in y^e Journall, laid by." From the 11th of the First Month, 1682/3 (see page 77), to the end of the first paragraph of page 81, the "foul Jornall" and the Itinerary Journal follow one another closely. Matter not in the latter appears in the first six pages of the former. On the last page of the former is the account of the Ringwood incident, given on pages 79 and 80; its presence here serves to explain its inclusion in the Itinerary Journal, the copyist having included the last page without consideration of the nature of its contents. See note 79. 7.

The writer of the Itinerary Journal, or perhaps it would be better to describe him as copyist, was, in all probability, John Field, of London (see note 112. 3), the handwriting closely resembling Field's autograph in letters and other documents in D (see illustration). We are told in *The First Publishers of Truth* that Field "seems to have assisted in some way with the entry of Sufferings on the official records" (page 157 n.). Endorsements to a letter in D, dated 1693, were made by Benjamin Bealing (Recording Clerk) and John Field. It may be that about this time Field wrote the two little books. It is to be feared that we must remain in ignorance of the personality of the annalist if we regard John Field as the copyist only. The original writer associates himself at times with the events recorded by the use of the word "we" (pages 97, 100, 105, 116, 188 ("our")). Other appearances of the first person are: "I think" (page 162), "as I take itt" (page 165), "my Master" (page 131, and compare "my dear Master" of the Haistwell Diary, page 273), and "that Night my ffather Came to visit us at Hartford" (page 216).

This Journal supplies many dates omitted from the Journal of George Fox as first published—the sneer of Thomas Carlyle is not applicable to the Itinerary Journal: "George dates nothing and his facts everywhere lie around him like the leather parings of his old shop" (*Cromwell's Letters and Speeches,* part x.). Yet the writer has not been very successful with his dates, as may be seen by reference to the following pages: 97, 146, 166, 186, 187, 204, 209, 216, 220, 302, 303, 305, 308, 311, 316, 342.

These books throw a flood of light upon the last few years of the life of George Fox, spent principally in and near London. The change from the work of the evangelist in earlier years (often viewed as the work of his life-time), to that of the pastor or bishop of an active settled Church, is noteworthy, and is pictorially pourtrayed in the difference between the mystic of thirty represented in the frontispiece to vol. i. of the Cambridge Journal and the Lely portrait of Fox as a statesman some 25 years later, reproduced in vol. ii. The reader will find evidence of this change by reference to notes 80. 8, 100. 5, 201. 1.

Though far away from his northern home at Swarthmoor, and seeing his wife only twice (page 313), George Fox was within reach of two homes of his wife's children, Rous at Kingston and Meade at Gooseyes, and at these homes he was a frequent and welcome visitor. He had no home of his own in the London area (page 295); there is an inserted reference to "his house" on page 174, but this statement is balanced by that on page 87, where, "'being a Lodger,' said Justice Guy, 'I cannot come by his fine'." However, many houses were opened to him and a warm welcome extended. Rebecka Travers expressed the feelings of many when she wrote: "I was never better pleased with my house then when hee was in It" (page 312). There are records in the

Itinerary Journal of some sixty of the houses of his friends where he was entertained over night more or less frequently, and on one occasion he "lodged at one of ye worlds house" (page 208). One wonders how arrangements beforehand for nights at so many different homes could have been made, but probably such were not required by either visitor or visited. In Tudor times night garments were not worn and the custom of "the naked bed," referred to by Pepys, May 21, 1660, and explained by his editor, H. B. Wheatley: "It was formerly the custom for both sexes to sleep in bed without any night linen," still lingered throughout the seventeenth century. (In *The Yea and Nay Academy of Compliments*, 1770, a scurrilous piece aimed at early Friends, page 80, we read: "We were conducted to our lodging, caps and neck-cloths being brought into the chamber"; perhaps the otherwise uncovered parts only being provided with night-wear. In his *Christian Progress*, 1725, page 393, George Whitehead tells us: "On 1st days I took my night caps in my pocket when I went to meetings.") Fox also frequently dropped in to a midday dinner, which was the only meal eaten in common during the day. (Supper is mentioned only twice in this volume (pages 110, 238) and breakfast not at all.) Dinners were important functions—Pepys's menu, on one occasion, consisted of "oysters, a hash of rabbits, a lamb, a chine of beef, a dish of roasted fowl, tart, fruit and cheese," which he considered "noble and enough"! (*Diary*, January 13, 1662/3; Wheatley, *Pepysiana*, 1899, page 95). But Fox was too busy, at times, to undertake a full meal, and would merely "Eate Something" (pages 133, 137, 143) and pass away. In any case he was "very temperate, eating little and sleeping less, though a bulky person."

Though constantly speaking in the meetings he attended, Fox was thoughtful for the service of others and frequently gave an opportunity for his companions to speak before he rose (see pages 105, 114, 120, 127, 139, 145, 163, 171, 185,

195, 216 and elsewhere). Occasionally he spoke first (pages 96, 98). The statement in an early letter could only have referred to the beginnings of his work in London: "Here are in the City many precious Friends and they begin to know George...and one thing they all take notice of that if George be in the company all the rest are for the most part silent." His frequent procedure was to "Declare a pritty long time & go to prayer & after a short testimony conclude the Meeting." We read of nothing to justify the statement of ex-Quaker Francis Bugg (1640—1727): "We have for many years observed, unless it be very lately amended, that when G. F. is minded to speak first in a Meeting, he will soon begin, and when he hath ended his speech, though the Meeting be not half spent, yet he goes out: likewise if he intend to speak last, he very seldom comes into a Meeting until it be half spent, as if he was above the state of waiting or receiving Benefit by others Preaching, which manifests his Singularity" (*The Painted Harlot Both Stript and Whipt*, 1683, preface, p. 3). We read little of silence in the meetings. At the Sunday Morning Meeting of Ministers, there was a period of silence (pages 142, 170, 174) before a vocal prayer and before Ministers "took thier Motions to ye severall meetings" (page 175), and also at private gatherings (pages 132, 137, 159).

George Fox served the metropolitan Church with ceaseless energy, but the terrible sufferings of his earlier life, added to the constant activity of later days, wore him out, and he died, at the age of sixty-six, a few days after attending at Gracechurch Street Meetinghouse, where he "Declared a Long time very pretiously & very audably, & went to prayer" (page 222). His remains were laid to rest in Bunhill Fields Friends' Burialground in the presence of some four thousand Friends, amid "many tender hearts and watery eyes and contrite spirits."

A prince and a great man was fallen in Israel.

III. THE HAISTWELL DIARY.

The third manuscript has only recently been acquired by the Reference Library. The little volume was in the possession of the Forster family for many years and came into possession of Friends from the library of William Edward Forster (1818—1886) on its dissolution in 1922. It has been thought well to add it to the two Journals, though somewhat out of order in point of time. It is known as the Haistwell Diary (though coming under the general term of Itinerary Journals, as on the title-page of this volume), having been written out fair, from earlier documents, by Edward Haistwell (c. 1658—1708/9, see note 116. 2 and Index), who was George Fox's amanuensis and who recorded the movements of "his Esteemed and welbeloved Friend (and Master)" from early in 1677 to the middle of 1678, during a part of which time they travelled together in Holland. This Diary is written, in an excellent hand, in an oblong book of 180 pages measuring $7\frac{7}{8}$ inches by 3 inches (see illustration), the cover having once been a portion of an illuminated missal for the service of the Mass, words and music, doubtless of much earlier date than the book.

The Diary was in the hands of the committee (see note 222. 4) appointed to prepare the Journal of George Fox, first published in 1694, corrections being made (see pages 229, 233, 236, 241, 244, 250, 251, 259) and passages crossed through (see pages 241, 243, 244, 247, 256, 257 and notes 243. 2, 257. 4) while in the hands of this committee. The period covered is represented in the Journal of George Fox, bi-centenary edition, 1891, volume ii. pages 255—330, for which it serves as a valuable background, but many more dates are given and some incidents described more fully, as, for example, the visit to Worminghurst, the work of Fox in London, and his visit to Lady Conway. There are some seventy-seven names which have not before appeared in the various texts of the Journal. At the close of the Diary occur the words, in another hand: "See large Journal, p. 821"— a reference not now understood. At intervals in the Diary there are lines of shorthand, and at the end of the manuscript, apart from the conclusion of the narrative, there is a page of shorthand. Attempts have been made at the British Museum in London to decipher this; and the Keeper of Manuscripts, having very kindly given attention to the matter, expresses the view that with time and patience it might be read, despite the use of many arbitrary abbreviations.

For an article on the Diary see volume xix. of *The Journal of the Friends' Historical Society.*

Edward Haistwell tells us (page 273) that he left his dear Master on Midsummer Day, 24th of the Fourth Month (June), 1678 and went to London, his Master passing to Ford Green, to the house of his friend, Edward Mann. Original records for the next three years are, at present, lacking, but from the Journal, bi-centenary edition, we may fill in the blank. Fox, after spending some time in London (volume ii. page 326), went to Hertford and there wrote letters dated 10th and 11th of the Fifth Month. Thence he visited many Meetings in the Midlands, George Whitehead sharing in the service a few days on his way to Westmorland. By stages, including a visit to John Gratton in Derbyshire, he arrived at Swarthmoor Hall in the Seventh Month and remained there till early in the First Month (March), 1679/80. Being moved of the Lord to travel into the South again (volume ii. page 343), he left his retreat at Swarthmoor and journeyed through the counties to London, arriving in time for the Yearly Meeting of 1680. This annual gathering over, and a few weeks spent in London, he turned southward into Surrey and Sussex and undertook other southern towns till the winter of 1680—81 which was spent in London. Short visits into Essex and North Middlesex occupied his time till the Yearly Meeting of 1681, and not long after that event the record of his stay at Worminghurst in Sussex with William Penn (volume ii. page 358) links the story of his life with the opening of the Itinerary Journal (page 75).

THE EDITOR desires to express his appreciation of the courtesy of the Royal Insurance Company, Limited, of London, also of the Guild-hall Librarian, in giving permission to reproduce the block printed as frontispiece to this volume.

He also wishes to acknowledge the frequent and valuable assist-ance of the Librarians of the Friends' Reference Library, Bishopsgate, London, during a period of many months.

KEY TO ABBREVIATIONS

Compare the Cambridge "Journal of George Fox," vol. i. p. 391, vol. ii. p. 372.

A = Ancient copy of The Short Journal of George Fox, written in the seventeenth century. In D.

A. R. B. MSS. = A collection of 250 original letters of early Friends, from 1654 to 1688, so named because worked over by Abram Rawlinson Barclay for his Letters, 1841. In D.

Abraham MSS. = A collection of letters in the possession of Miss Emma C. Abraham, of Swarthmoor Hall. Thirty of these MSS. are dated between 1658 and 1699. For a *précis* of this collection see *Jnl. F. H. S.* xi.

B = Modern copy of The Short Journal of George Fox, written from the original by Emily Jermyn, *c.* 1866. In D.

Barclay's Letters = Letters, etc. of Early Friends, illustrative of the History of the Society from nearly its Origin to about the Period of George Fox's Decease, edited by Abram Rawlinson Barclay. London, 1841.

Beginnings = The Beginnings of Quakerism, by William C. Braithwaite, B.A., LL.B. London, 1912.

Biog. Memoirs = Biographical Memoirs : being a Record of the Christian Lives of Members of the Society of Friends, 5 vols. The first vol. was printed (London, 1854), the remainder are in MS. in D.

Bristol MSS. = A collection of letters and documents relating to the early Friends, four vols. in D, and one vol. in Bristol. For a *précis* see *Jnl. F. H. S.* ix.

Bulletin F. H. S. Phila. = Bulletin of Friends' Historical Society of Philadelphia, beginning 1906. The name was changed in 1923 to Friends' Historical Association.

C = Modern copy of The Short Journal, written from original by Ellen M. Dawes, in 1906. In D.

Cal. S. P. Dom. = Calendar of State Papers, Domestic Series, preserved in the Public Record Office, Chancery Lane, London. A volume of Extracts Relating to Friends, from 1654 to 1672, appeared in 1913.

Camb. Jnl. = The Journal of George Fox, edited from the MSS. by Norman Penney, 2 vols. Cambridge, England, 1911.

Camb. Text = The text of The Journal of George Fox printed at the Cambridge University Press, England, in 1911.

Christian Progress = The Christian Progress of...George Whitehead—life and works. London, 1725.

Collectitia = Collectitia : or, Pieces, Religious, Moral, and Miscellaneous, adapted to the Society of Friends, compiled by William Alexander. York, 1824.

D = The Reference Library of the Society of Friends, at Devonshire House, Bishopsgate, London. Established 1673.

D. N. B. = Dictionary of National Biography, edited by Leslie Stephen, 68 vols., 1885—1904 and later volumes. London.

Ell. Text = The Journal of George Fox, edited by Thomas Ellwood. First published, London, 1694. The quotations are taken from the eighth or bi-centenary edition. London, 1891.

Encyc. Brit. = The Encyclopædia Britannica, 11th ed. Cambridge, 1910–11.

Extracts from State Papers = Extracts from State Papers Relating to Friends, 1654—1672. London, 1913.

F. P. T. = The First Publishers of Truth, being early Records (not previously printed) of the Introduction of Quakerism into the Counties of England and Wales. London, 1907.

F. Q. E. = Friends' Quarterly Examiner, beginning 1867. London.

First-days Meetings = First-days Meetings Supplied by Friends in the Ministry in and about London, 1682—4. Original MS. is in Friends' Library, 142 N. Sixteenth Street, Philadelphia, Pa. Copy is in D. See Books of Ministering Friends.

Fox, *Epistles* = A Collection of many Select and Christian Epistles...written on Sundry Occasions by...George Fox. London, 1698.

Gent's Mag. = The Gentleman's Magazine. Extracts referring to Friends appear in *Jnl. F. H. S.* xiii. xv. xvi. A run of the Magazine from 1731 to 1868 is in D.

George Fox Note Book = A folio memorandum and scrap book, paged according to the first edition of The Journal of George Fox. In possession of the Editor.

Great Journal = The Great Journal of my Life, Sufferings, Travills and Imprisonments, by George Fox, printed *verb. et lit.*, and published by the University Press of Cambridge, England. See Camb. *Jnl.*

Hist. Soc. Pa. = The Historical Society of Pennsylvania, located at 1300 Locust Street, Philadelphia, Pa. Founded 1824.

Jaffray, *Diary* = Diary of Alexander Jaffray, Provost of Aberdeen...with Memoirs of the Rise, Progress and Persecutions of...Quakers in the North of Scotland. Aberdeen, 1856. 3rd edition.

Jnl. F. H. S. = The Journal of the Friends' Historical Society, beginning 1903. London.

Kelsall, *Diaries* = The Diaries of John Kelsall, of Wales (*c.* 1683—1743), 8 vols. 1722—1743. Original in D, also a copy.

London Friends' Meetings = The London Friends' Meetings, shewing the Rise of the Society of Friends in London. Compiled by William Beck and T. Frederick Ball. London, 1869.

M.M. = Monthly Business Meeting of the Society of Friends. See vol. ii. p. 406.

Myers, *Narratives* = Narratives of Early Pennsylvania, West New Jersey and Delaware, 1630—1707, edited by Albert Cook Myers. New York, 1912.

Old Lombard Street = Old Lombard Street: Some Notes prepared by the Royal Insurance Company, Limited, on the occasion of the opening of their new building in Lombard Street, London, May, 1912.

Pease MSS. = A collection of ancient Quaker MSS., presented to D by the exors. of Mrs Thomas Pease, of Bristol, 1922.

Penna. Mag. = The Pennsylvania Magazine of History and Biography, beginning 1877, issued quarterly. Philadelphia, Pa.

Piety Promoted = Piety Promoted in a Collection of Dying Sayings of the People called Quakers. London, 1701—1829 and a volume published in Philadelphia in 1890, with memoirs 1779—1839.

Premonitory Extracts= Premonitory Extracts; selected from various Authors of the Religious Society of Friends, by Gawen Ball, M.D., 1819. Not published.

Q.M. = Quarterly Business Meeting of the Society of Friends. See vol. ii. p. 406.

Registers = All reference to Registers in the Notes are to the digested copy from original books (now in Somerset House, London), of births, marriages, and burials of Friends of Great Britain from about 1650 to the present time, kept at Friends' Central Offices in London.

Reynolds MSS. = A folio volume containing copies of about one hundred letters of various dates. In D.

s.p. = sine prole, without issue.

Second Period = The Second Period of Quakerism, by William C. Braithwaite, B.A., LL.B. London, 1919.

Sewel, *Hist.* = The History of the Rise, Increase, and Progress of the Christian People called Quakers...by William Sewel. First written in Dutch, Amsterdam, 1717, and translated by the author into English. London, 1722, and later edd.

Smith, *Adv. Cata.* = Bibliotheca Anti-Quakeriana; or a Catalogue of Books Adverse to the Society of Friends, compiled by Joseph Smith. London, 1873.

Smith, *Cata.* = A Descriptive Catalogue of Friends' Books...compiled by Joseph Smith, 2 vols. London, 1867, with Supplement, 1893.

Suff. = A Collection of the Sufferings of the People called Quakers from 1650 to 1689, compiled by Joseph Besse, 2 vols. London, 1753.

Swarth. Account Book = The Household Account Book of Sarah Fell, of Swarthmoor Hall, edited from the original MS. in D by Norman Penney. London, 1920.

Swarth. MSS. = A collection of about fourteen hundred original seventeenth-century letters, papers, etc., once preserved at Swarthmoor Hall. In D.

Tercent. Text = The Journal of George Fox: a Revised Text, prepared and edited by Norman Penney, in commemoration of the tercentenary of the birth of George Fox. London, 1924; also in Everyman's Library, no. 754.

Thirnbeck MSS. = A collection of twenty-eight letters and papers, dated 1654—1700, once in the possession of Wilfrid Grace of Bristol, presented to D by his widow in 1923. For a *précis* of this collection see *Jnl. F. H. S.* ix.

Thurloe Papers = A Collection of State Papers, made by John Thurloe (1616—1668), Secretary of State, edited by Thomas Birch (1705—1766, ex-Friend), 7 vols. London, 1742. See *Jnl. F. H. S.* viii.

Vol. i., and Vol. ii. = The two volumes of The Journal of George Fox. Cambridge, England, 1911.

Watson MSS. = A volume of copies of letters of early Friends, written by Samuel Watson (d. 1708). In D.

Waymarks = A publication with that title, edited by John E. Southall. Vol. i. 1902, vol. ii. 1903, all issued. Newport, Mon.

West Answering = The West Answering to the North in the fierce and cruel Persecution of...George Fox, Edward Pyot and William Salt at Launceston. London, 1657.

Whiting, *Memoirs* = Persecution Expos'd, in some Memoirs relating to the Sufferings of John Whiting and many others...Quakers, by John Whiting, of Somerset. London, 1715.

Y.M. = The Yearly Meeting of the Society of Friends in Great Britain, etc., usually called "London Yearly Meeting." See vol. i. p. 462, vol. ii. p. 406.

Y.M. Epistles = Annual address of London Yearly Meeting to its members, and others, consisting of reports of the proceedings of the yearly gatherings and Christian exhortation. From 1681 to the present annual epistles have been sent out—244 in number.

EXPLANATION OF SIGNS

Words omitted from all previous editions of The Journal of George Fox are, in many places, enclosed in brackets, thus: [a dark Countrey].

Interlineations by contemporary hands are enclosed in braces, thus: {y^e 5th day}.

Parentheses are reproduced as in the original, thus: (being a Persecutor).

I
THE SHORT JOURNAL

"Its larg to declare the workes and wonders of y^e lord god and the preservation of mee through all, by his mighty hand and power but I saw I was in his hand."

Page 35.

A Page of The Short Journal

I

THE SHORT JOURNAL

[1]GEORG FOX So Called of the World but the world knows neither him nor his {new} name, Here are some of his sufferings y^t hee hath sufferred by the world and their Professors, Priests & Teachers; For preaching the truth Christ y^t never ffell nor will fall nor chang but ends all the changing figures and Types and shadows in Adam in the fall, Christ y^t never fell nor Never will fall.

[In Mansfield there came a Priest who was looked upon to bee above others, and all y^t profest themselvs above the priests went to hear him and cryed him upp, I was against their going, and spoke to them ag^t their going; and asked them if they had not a Teacher w^{t}hin them The Anoynting to teach them; And why would they go out to man.

And then when they were gone to hear him I was in a sore travell and it came upon mee that I was Moved to go to the steple house to tell the people and ye priest and to bidd them to cease from man whose breath was in their Nostrils, and to tell them where their Teacher was, w^{t}hin them, the spirit and ye light of Jesus, And that How God y^t made the world doth not dwell in Temples made w^{t}h hands and many other things concerning the truth I spake to them...^{a} they were pretty Moderate to hear ye truth, whereby after...^{b} wrought upon.

First I was imprisond in Nottingham for speaking to a priest in ye Steeplehouse for] as I passed to Nottingham as I looked upon ye Town, The great steeplehouse [struck att my life when I spyed it a great Idol and Idolatrous Temple;] And so I went to the Meetting and after a while I went to the Steeplehouse[2]; as I was Moved I spake to the priest, and ye priest said y^t the Scriptures were the touchstone and Judg and were to try all doctrines and appease and to end

^{a} Edge of first leaf worn away. A has *and*
^{b} Edge of first leaf worn away. A has *many were*

Controversies att which sayings of his I said y^t the Scriptures were not ye Judg, but ye holy ghost y^t gave them forth
was the Judg and Toutchstone: for the pharisees had the
Scriptures and ye Jewes and professors, but the Controversies
are not ended then after they had mee before the Maior and
Aldermen who sent mee to prison; a pittifull stinking place,
[where the wind brought all the stench^a of the house of office
in ye place,] where ye stench^a of ye place was in my throat and
head many dayes after, and then in ye Evening I was brought
to the Sheriffs[1] house, and the sheriffs wife said y^t salvation
was comed to her house; and all their family was wrought
upon by ye power of ye lord; And they beleeved in the truth
and this being ye first day of ye week; the next Seaventh
day ye Sheriffe himself spake the truth in a paire of slippers
in ye market amongst the people, and his family; very many
others being wrought upon.

The Maior and some of ye Aldermen caused mee to be
sent to another prison where I was kept till I was sett...^{b}
Liberty. [when I was a prisoner in the same place there
came a woman...^{c} to the prison and two w^{t}h her and said y^t
shee had been possessed two and thirty years[2]. And the
priests had kept her and had kept fasting dayes about her,
and could not do her any good, and shee said the lord said
unto her arise, for I have a Sanctified people, hast and go to
them for thy redemption draweth nigh, and when I came
out of prison I bad friends have her to mansfield, and at that
time our meettings were disturbed by wild people, and both
them and the Professors and priests said y^t wee were false
prophets and deceivers and y^t there was witchcraft amongst
us, and the poor woman would make such a noyce in roaring
and Sometimes lying along upon her belly upon the ground
and w^{t}h her spirit and roaring and voyce, and would set all
friends in a heat and sweat. And I said all friends keep to
y^r owne, lest y^t which is in her gett into y^u and so she
affrightend the world from our meettings; and then they
said if that were cast out of her while she were w^{t}h us, and
were made well then they would say y^t wee were of God;
this said the world, and I had said before y^t shee should be
set free; and then it was upon mee that wee should have a

---

^{a} A: *strength* ^{b} Edge of leaf worn away. A has *att*
^{c} Edge of leaf worn away. A has *to mee*

meetting at Skekbey at Elizabeth Huttons[1] house; where wee
had her there; and there were many friends almost overcome
by her w^{t}h ye stink y^t came out of her; roaring and tumbling
on the ground; and ye same day shee was worse then ever
shee was, and then another day wee mett about her; and
about ye first hour ye life rose in friends, and said it was
done, and shee rose upp & her Countenance changed and
became white and before it was wanne and earthly, and she
sat down at my thigh as I was sitting and lift up her hands
and said ten thousand praise the lord and did not know
where shee was and so shee was well[2], and wee kept her
about a fortnight in ye sight of ye world and shee wrought
and did thinges, and...^{a} sent her away to her friends,
And then the worlds professors, priests & Teachers never
could call us any more false prophetts deceivers, or witches
after, but it did a great deal of good in ye Countrey among
people in relačon to ye truth and to ye Stopping the mouths
of ye world and their slandrous Aspersions.]

2^{ly} And in Lecestershire as I was passing thorow the fields
I was moved to go to Lester and when I came there I heard
y^t there were many to preach and it was so, and I was moved
to go among them, and after I had heard severall speak, and
at last a woman asked a question. And the priest in ye pulpit
said I permitt not a woman to speak in ye church, though hee
had before given liberty for any to speak; and then I stood
upp and spake and said dost thou call this mixt multitude
a Church; [and then I spoke how y^t the Church was in God
the father of our lord Jesus Christ; and what the woman
was y^t was not to speak, and w^t the woman was y^t might
prophecy and speak, and it broke them all to peeces and
confused them, and they all turned ag^t mee into Jangling
and they broke upp and came to a house from the steeple
house, & ye truth set them all in a heat and scatterd them
from the house and steeple house and the power of ye lord
came over them all, and the truth.]

3^{ly} In Darbyshire at Chesterfield where I was moved of
the lord by his power to go to ye steeplehouse and when I
had spoken w^t was upon mee to speak they put mee forth
of ye steeple house and ye Maior sent for mee [and after some
speech w^{t}h mee about comeing to ye steeple house and when

^{a} Edge of leaf worn away. A has *then wee*

it was said to him whether was it better to obey god or man
Judg yee, and ye Apostles sufferred for declareing ag^t y^e
Temple, and did bring people to Christ from ye Traditions]
and so hee caused ye watchmen to put us out of ye Town
about ye eleventh hour of ye night.

And the priest[1] preached of mee y^t I was taken up into y^e
clouds wth a whirlewinde, and I was found full of gold &
silver, upon which my outward friends sent for mee and I
wrote to them and they shewed it to ye priest, and hee said
any man might write, but where is ye man. And they sent
to mee ag^n and I went, and when I came into Darbyshire I
had a discourse of the thinges of God wth them, and they
acknowledged ye truth most of them and one said hee had
been a professor forty years & hee had not tasted of ye love
of God So much for his heart was opend wth it.

Then wee passed through friends to Darby Town, and
after I had visited friends; The next morning the Bell did
ring, and I asked y^m what it rung for, and they said it was
for a Sermon; and it struck at my life and then I was moved
to go and two others wth mee to ye steeple house and when
ye priest had done I spoke to him and the people [of the truth
and the day of ye lord and the light wthin them and the
spirit to teach and lead them to God] and after a while they
haled mee out and had mee before Collonels and Justices
and Priests, and the Examination held from ye first houre
until the Ninth houre. And I told them y^t God was power
and a Consumeing fire, and not for them to dispute of him,
for all their preaching, sprinkling, sacraments would never
sanctifie a man, nor their readings or expoundings; And
they said was I sanctified, and I said yes. And they said
had I no sin. I said no Christ had taken away my sin.
And then they made a Mittimus, and sent mee and another[2]
to ye house of Correction; and the other did not prove
faithfull but made for his liberty and gote out of prison, and
then the priests, Justices, professors, and people were in a
rage and said y^t I was a deceiver and a false prophet and a
seducer; And then the lord open to mee if all forsook mee my
spirit doubled to mee[a], and y^t I was a king sett for ye defence
of ye faith y^t giveth victory, and ye hope y^t purifieth as hee
was pure, and ye beliefe y^t passed from death to life in w^{ch}

[a] Vol. I. p. 3. Ell. text: *was strengthened*

condemnaͨon is not. And all other hopes, faiths, beleefs, y^t doe not give victory and purifieth and passeth out of death to life, Judg and deny. And great disputes I had wth all sorts of people; and as I preached down sin the priests raged^a and preached up sin; And the Goaler and ye Justices were in a rage ag^t mee, and ye lord smote ye Justices and ye Goaler That the Goaler came trembling up to mee, and said y^t hee had done mee wrong and had spoken ag^t mee and hee would speak to them[1].

And hee told his wife y^t hee saw the day of Judgment & hee saw mee there and was afraid of mee, for hee had done mee wronge And so hee was like the Goaler in ye Acts y^t came to the Apostles and he must lye wth mee hee said, and hee went to ye Justice y^t first called us Quakers whose name was Bennet[2], and told him y^t hee was willing to keep mee, but not as a prisoner, for hee did beleeve y^t the plagues would never depart from his house as long as hee kept mee a prisoner; and the Justice said hee beleeved the same; and y^t I was the honestest man amongst them all; and hee y^t had got his liberty y^t was Imprisoned wth mee, they said hee was a knave and they wondred at him y^t hee did not stand to his principle; [and the poor man was in trouble a great while before hee returned to ye power of God againe.]

Then they gave mee liberty more then I had, and y^t I might walk a little upp and down, and then they thought I would have gone away; and then one night they had mee before the Commissioners; and would have had mee to take upp Arms and to bee a Soldiour and I told them I stood in that which took away the occation of warrs and fightings; and They in a rage sent mee away wth the Goaler and bid him put mee in the dungeon, where hee did in a low place in the ground and lousey, and there I was kept a great while; [and then I was taken out and put in ye high Goale, and there I was kept till I was sett freely at liberty; who had been kept a year wthin three weeks, in four prisons and the house of Correction, and at ye Town prison house and the Countrey Goale and dungeon and this was in 1650 in the 30th of ye moneth called October[3] in the Common wealths dayes and then the light and truth and glory of ye lord flowed & spread abroad.]

^a A: *cryed*

4ly In yorkshire I was moved to go to Beverley and upon
the 7th day at night I came to an Inne very wett, and the
next day being ye first day I went to ye steeple house as
I was moved of ye lord and when the priest had done I spake
to him, and the people [of ye truth of God and the day of ye
lord and the light of Christ within them and of ye spirit
and of God's teaching by the spirit, and yt God yt made ye
world did not dwell in temples made wth hands;] and the
Major came to mee, [and took mee by the hand] and reasond
moderately wth mee; and so after a while I passed away;
and they reported yt a spirit had been there, for they were
in an amazement; I came suddenly and so passed away
suddenly; yt when I came a great way off yt was ye report
amongst ye great ones.

And in the afternoon I went about 3 miles off Beverley
and there went into ye steeple house and when the priest
had done I spoke to him, & ye People largly and they were
moderate and many heard the truth gladly; and desired
mee to give them another meetting; and so ye truth had its
passage.

And then I was moved towards ye lands end in Holderness
and as I went I spake thorow the townes and by ye sea side,
and to people in ye fields of ye day of ye lord yt was comming
upon all ungodlyness and unrighteousnesse, and how yt
Christ was come to teach his people himself and as I was
preaching and speaking through a town called Patrington
And as I passed down the town I was moved to bidd people
to repent & fear the lord and come off all their false Teachers
for ye day of ye lord was comming upon all sin and wickednes,
and the priest being in ye town street and hearing mee and
as I went down ye street I spake to ye people, and some
heard and others said yt I was madd, and it began to be
dark, and I being thirsty I desired drink or milk and meat
& saying yt I would pay them for it, and they would not,
and then I passed out of ye Town, & some followed mee, and
asked mee*a* some questions about outward things*a*, and I bad
them fear the lord [and prize their time for I saw their
question was tempting,] and they left mee and so I passed on
and lay out all ye night.

And when ye day brake I walked when I could see my

a...a Vol. I. p. 30: *what news?*

way and passed towards a Town, and in yᵉ way there came
a man after mee wᵗʰ a great staffe when it was hardly light
and hee went wᵗʰ mee to yᵉ town and raised the town and
the Constables upon mee, hee having a warrant yᵗ they had
made at Pattrington and the Constables brought mee wᵗʰ
staves to Pattrington where I had a great service wᵗʰ priest
and people the whole town in a manner being upp & they
sent mee to a Justice, and when I came near the Justices
house, there came a man to mee and asked mee if I were yᵉ
man yᵗ was apprehended and I said I was; and he said for
my sake hee was there, and went before mee to yᵉ Justice,
and when I came to yᵉ Justice, he bid mee put off my hat,
and I said did it trouble him, and yᵉ man yᵗ spake to mee
on yᵉ way told him it was tenderness*a*. And I took it of in
my hand and said to him doth this trouble thee; and I put
it on again, and bid him mind the witness of Christ the light
in him yᵗ sheewed him his sinns and his evill deeds yᵗ hee
had done, and he confessd to yᵉ truth and I was sett at
liberty; and I went back wᵗʰ yᵉ man yᵗ said hee was there
for my sake to Pattrington for hee lived there; and the next
first day I had a great meetting at his house in yᵉ after noone
where many of yᵉ Countrey was gathered and many were
convinced, and in yᵉ forenoone I went to yᵉ steeplehouse and
spake to yᵉ priest and people and they were pretty moderate
and a great many were convinced in yᵉ Countrey.

And I was moved to go to yᵉ formost town in Holdernesse, and spake through the Town three times; and then
the officers put mee forth of yᵉ Town and People had a report
yᵗ I would never come into Bedd nor Towns; and as I passed
out of that Countrey I came to an Ale house; and I desired
Lodging and other necessary thinges, and they would not
Except I would go to yᵉ Constable[1] and I passed away and
lay out all yᵉ night.

[2]And from the forementioned Town wᶜʰ I had passed
through in Holdernesse 3 times; I was moved to go to a
steeplehouse in Yorkshire[3], and when the priest had done I
spake to him and the people, and they were all light, and
after I had spoken to them the truth, I sleighted their light
spirits, and there came at night the heads of yᵉ Town where
I lay and was convinced of yᵉ truth and there was a priest

a Vol. I. p. 31: *my principle*

convinced[1] and after there was a Rantor[2] that was to dispute
w^{t}h mee who was mightily looked upon by ye People in the
Countrey, and when he came he said it was shewed to him
y^t I should bee sitting in a chayre and it was so, and y^t he
should bow down to the ground before mee and hee did so,
before ye people and priests; and the first words I was moved
to say to him was repent thou [Swine and] Beast, and he said
it was Jealousie, and I asked him what was the ground of
Jealousie, and the ground of a heathen in man, and give
mee account of thinges in the body before wee discourse of
thinges out of the body; and they were all amazed and
astonished, and the truth came over all, and the witnesse of
God answered and their wisdome confounded.

And when the meetting was broken upp the next morneing
one Priest Levens[a3] that was there desired mee to go alone
w^{t}h him for hee had some questions to aske mee, So I took
his Brother [William Ratliffe][4] w^{t}h mee, and so he asked mee
somethings and I answered him but his intent was to have
taken away my life and have murdred mee alone, for after he
had parted w^{t}h mee hee met w^{t}h a priest in a rage, and broke
his cane upon the ground in madnesse, and said if ever hee
mett mee hee would have my life, and hee would give his
head if I were not knocked down within a moneth, but truth
came over all; and there was another priest sent to dispute
w^{t}h me under a cover, hearing I was to go out of y^e
Countrey; and when I came he gote away and would not
be seen; and so truth came over his head and the people
came to see it, and his folly.

In Yorkshire there was a Justice[5] very loving and said his
house was myne and I was moved to go to the steeplehouse
and hee went w^{t}h mee in the fields and he said in himself If
I spoke they would put mee to him, and there came a Captaine[6] a friend and went w^{t}h mee, and ye Justice went back,
and I had a brave service w^{t}h ye priest and people, and the
truth came over all in laying open the false Teachers and
priests, and the truth and the true Teachers, and the light
and the spirit of Christ in them, and y^t God y^t made y^e
world dwelt not in temples made w^{t}h hands, but their bodyes
were the temples of ye holy ghost.

And in the afternoon I was moved to go to another

[a] Vol. i. p. 23: *Scotch Preist*

steeplehouse and there when I came ye Priest was preaching, and was bidding ye People to come without money and w^thout price, and hee had three hundred pounds a year of them, and so I said to him did hee bid them come w^thout price and had hee so much a year and took tyth of them; come down thou hyreling; and hee fled away, and I had a fine time to speak ye truth to ye People and they received it, and did not oppose but it came over all and I passed away.

And I was moved to go to [Stokslye][1] steeplehouse, and when ye priest had done I spoke to him as I was moved and to ye people the truth of God, and they were moderate and I lett them see their true Teacher, [and how that their Teacher was found in the stepps of the false teachers, and how ye lord was com'd to teach his people himselfe, and ye light which Christ did enlighten w^thall they might come to in y^mselves, and so by it come to Christ; so when wee were gone out of the steeplehouse into ye street, the priest sent for mee to his house, and I sent to him and bad him to come into ye street among ye People to try his ministry and himself, and it was in the snow in the winter, and hee did not come] and so I passed away in ye truth y^t reacheth in all hearts.

And I was moved to a steeple house which James Nayler was a member of[2] and when I came into it the priest was preaching and when hee had done, I spake to him; and hee and the people bad mee come up to him, and I went up to ye pulpitt, and beganne to speak to him, and ye People thrust mee out of ye doore and chancery and haled and pulled mee upp and down and cryed for ye stocks and threatned mee wth them, and this was ye greatest professor in yorkshire[3], but ye truth came over all and a great service was y^t day of the truth there and at a meetting not farre off.

I was moved to go to Moten[4] steeple house in yorkshire upon a lecture day, the day when ye Markett was, and ye priest was preaching to about a dozen people, and when hee had done there came another priest and would have had mee to go upp into ye pulpit and I denyed it, and this priest went to ye other priest & asked him for my going upp into ye pulpitt and he said yes I might, and then the priest came to mee ag^n and would have had mee to go into ye pulpitt, and because I would not some of the people beganne to call mee a deceiver and then began to bee a Tumult; I stood upon a seat and cryed for Audience and spake to them freely many hundreds of people there was and a great service for ye truth there was of openning the truth and speaking it to them and largly and letting them see the true teacher the spirit of God and the light in them selves, and the false teachers w^thout them for their ends meanes, and money and the truth came over all, and wee passed away peaceably in the truth of God answereing the witness of God in all.

And then I was moved to go to Doncaster steeplehouse and was moved to speak the truth both to ye priest and people where they plucked mee out beating mee and throwing mee down and bruised mee sore & then had mee before ye Maior and other officers, and after they had threatned mee they sett mee at liberty, and said If I came againe my blood bee upon my owne head, and turned mee amongst ye rude multitude who stoned us, and there was a Bayliffe y^t took mee into his house, & ye rude people broke his head, y^t ye blood runne down his face, and about his house the rude people waited; [and hee was lott I told him y^t ventured himselfe and took us into his house from ye rude multitude.] And when wee went out of ye Town they stoned us a great way out of ye Town some friends being wth me.

And I was moved to go to Tickell in Yorkshire, and when friends was in ye meetting and fresh and full of ye life and power of God I was moved to go to ye steeplehouse, and ye priest had done & I went upp among them in the chancery, and was beginning to speak, and they beat mee about ye head, y^t I was all bloody, and it runne of mee in the steeple house, and then they cryed take him out of the Church, and they punched mee and thrust mee out, and beat mee sore wth Books fists and sticks and threw mee over a Hedg into a close and there beat mee, and then threw mee over ag^n and then beat mee into a house punching mee into a house, and through the entry; and there I lost my hatt and never had it ag^n there they ston'd and beat mee along sorely Blooded and bruised; and then I went into a friends house, and ye priest beheld a great part of this his peoples doings, and then in o^r friends yard I spake the truth to them priest and people [they being in the street and I in ye friends yard on

a wall my spirit being revived ag^n by the power of God, for
through their bruiseing, beating, blooding, stoning and
throwing mee down, I was almost mazed, and my body sore
bruised but by ye power of the lord I was refreshed ag^n to
him be ye glory and so I passed away.]

And after I had been at Tickell steeple already spoken of
I was moved to go to warnsworth steeplehouse, & some friends
followed mee, and they went into ye steeple house And
Thomas Aldam[1] went in to his seat and ye Priest said hee
would catechise him and beganne to speak to him, and they
shutt the door and kept mee out, and then they open'd the
doore, and I went in, and ye Priest lost his matter and said
what come you hither for, and hee asked ag^n the same
question, And then hee said hee would prove us false prophets
in the 7° of Mathew, and 24° of Mathew, and hee could
not go on; but asked ag^n what came wee thither for, and all
this time I was silent and said y^t a question being asked it
might be answered, [and he said did I come to catch and
then I beganne to speak forth the truth amongst y^m and of
ye false prophetts & how hee was in ye stepps of them, & I
held forth Christ,] and they thrust mee out and shutt y^e
steeplehouse door, [and I staid in ye steeplehouse yard till
they came forth and then I beganne to speak to ye priest
and people the truth and how hee was in the footstepps of
ye pharisees] & ye priest shook mee & ye people beat mee, and
threw clods at mee and struck mee wth their crabb tree staves,
and threw mee about, and the Justice gave forth a warrant
for mee & Thomas Aldam; And they took Thomas their
towns man; and I saw a vision [a man and] two Mastiffe
doggs and a Bear, and I passed by them and they [smiled
upon mee^a.]

And the warrant was for all westrydeing to take mee, and
the Constable saw mee and did not take mee; and hee went
wth Thomas to york prison; and as they went they came to
a place where I was and staid y^t night & ye next dayes
meetting, and after I passed wth the Constable and Thomas
towards the prison and the Constable said hee had a warrant
for mee to take mee and hee had seen mee before and did not
take mee For hee was loath to trouble honest men; [and hee
had ye warrant in his pocket and desired mee y^t I should

^{a} Vol. I. p. 37: *doe mee noe hurte*

not tell any one y^t he saw mee, and I told him I could not
lie and so wee parted,] And hee went wth Thomas Aldam to
york prison [where they kept him two years, and this was
in the Common wealths dayes.]

And I was moved to go to Mansfield wood house steeple
house on a first day out of ye meeting in Mansfield in
Nottinghamshire and when the priest had done I began to
speak the truth to them in the steeple house of Mansfield
woodhouse a mile from Mansfield; and ye People fell upon
mee wth their fists Books and wthout Compassion or mercy
beat mee down in ye steeplehouse and almost smoothered
mee in it being under them, and sorely I was bruised in y^e
steeplehouse & threw mee ag^t ye walls and when y^t they
had thrust and throwen mee out of ye steeple house when I
came into ye yard I fell down being so sorely bruised and
beat among them and I gote up ag^n and then they punched
and thrust and struck mee upp and down, and they set mee
in ye stocks & brought a whipp to whipp mee but did not,
[and as I satt in ye stocks they threw stones at mee, and my
head Armes, Breast, and shoulders and Back and sides were
so bruised Mazed and dazled wth ye Blowes, and I was hote
when they put me in ye stocks,] and then they came and
took mee out to a great mans house, [and Examined mee
and I reasoned wth them of ye thinges of God; and of God
and his teachings, and Christs, and how y^t God y^t made the
world did not dwell in Temples made wth hands, and of
divers thinges of the truth, I spake to them,] and then they
set mee at liberty, and a great deale of rude people was
ready to fall upon mee [wth staves, but ye Constable kept
them of, and when they had set mee at liberty they threatned
mee wth pistols, if ever I came againe they would kill mee
and shoutt mee; and that they would carry their pistols to
ye steeple house and wth threatning I was freed, & when
I was passing along ye fields friends mett mee, and I was so
bruised when I was cold y^t I could not turn mee in my bed,
and bruised inwardly att my heart, but after a while the
power of ye lord went through mee and healed mee, y^t I was
well Glory to ye lord for ever, and this was in Nottinghamshire
in the Common wealths days.]

And in Lecestershire I was moved to go from a meetting
and other friends to Bagath steeple house, and some they

lett in, and mee they kept out, and they shutt the doors, and shut others out besides many of their owne people, and when they had their sermon as they called it they oppened the door, and I went in and began to speak ye truth to them, [and they heard mee a while and then after a while they rushed mee out, and I spoke to them in ye steeple house yard the truth of God, and they had much ado to hold their hands of mee and us, and there wee had good service and the truth came over all, and so wee passed away.]

And I was moved to go to Boseth[1] steeplehouse in Lecester-shire on a lecture day being ye market day; and I spake to the priest and people [in ye steeple house and yard of ye truth and light w^thin them to guide them to Christ from sinne, and the Clerk bid us go out of ye steeple house for hee was to locke ye door and when wee were in the Markett friends asked where was ye place to try the ministers but in ye steeplehouse, and bid them to come forth and prove their call and ministry, and the people of the town and Markett fell upon us and stoned us very sore and abused us hundreds of them wth stones a great way out of the town that it was a wonder y^t wee escaped wth our lives and so passed away in the truth of God, to the shame of both priests and professors for there were many their;] and friends had but litle harme.

And in Warwickshire in Adderstonne [when I was two miles of it the Bell runge upon a Market day for a lecture, and it struck at my life and] I was moved to go to ye steeple house, [and when I came into it I found a man speaking; and when as I stood among ye people the glory and life shined over all, and wth it I was crowned, and when the priest had done I spake to him and ye people the truth and ye light wch lett them see all y^t ever they had done, and of their teacher w^thin them and how the lord was come to teach them himself, and of ye seed Christ in them; how they were to mind that, and ye promise y^t was to ye seed of God w^thin them wch is Christ, and it set them in a Hurry and under a rage and some said I was madd, and spoke to my outward Relaçons to tye mee upp, and sett them in a rage but the truth came over all; and I passed away in peace in ye power of the lord God, and the truth came over all and reached in ye hearts of many people.

And in Darbyshire] I was moved to go to a steeplehouse
on a markett day being yᵉ lecture day, and when the priest
had done I spake to him and the people, [of yᵉ truth and
the light, and] of yᵉ day of yᵉ lord, [and of Gods work in
them, and the truth in them, and the spirit] and the teacher
wᵗhin them, and of their teachers wᵗhout them, And how yᵗ
the priest had said that the people loved to have it so In
Jeremy the 5° but he left out the priests preached for Hire
and bear rule by their meanes and yᵉ People love to have it
so, [and when I told the priest of his wronging the Scriptures
and yᵗ hee did not speak it all, for if hee had, it had been
his own Condic͂on, and he fled away, and yᵉ people fell upon
us and put us out and so wee passed away in the truth.

And at a Sessions in Yorkshire¹ held in yᵉ steeple house,
there being a great free School house hard by it: And in it
wee had a meetting where there were many priests and
professors, and many of them disputeing and reasoneing wᵗh
mee; and the truth came over all & answered all, and there
was an Old man a priest² convinced yᵗ when the people came
to him, and told him to take his Tyth, he denyed it, and
said he had enough, and there were four chiefe Constables
convinced then and there the priests and people were very
loving, and I was desired of them to many places; and yᵉ
Old man yᵉ priest went upp and down wᵗh mee to many
steeple houses and the people would ring the Bells when
wee came into a town thinking I would speak, and the truth
spread and I spoke in many steeplehouses, but I did not
come into their pulpitts, [and some places where the priests
were paid, they fled away from the town when as I came to
it and the people would break open the doors If I would go
into yᵉ steeplehouse if yᵉ Churchwardens would not open it,
but I would not let yᵐ but spake to yᵐ in yᵉ yards, or any
where the truth of God and in love it was received, and
many Justices were loving in Yorkshire, and the truth
spread.]

And in Yorkshire, there I had a meetting in a place called
Hightown³ which the next day there plotted together a
Company of people to destroy mee, and they yᵗ were wᵗh
mee, and there came the next day a man wᵗh a Pike and
sword and a Pistol and a crook to have plucked us out of yᵉ
meetting house where wee had been to have destroyed us but

wee were gone hardly a quarter of an hour before away out
of the house before they came rageing; and ye man y^t had
ye sword y^t should have murdred us hee had kild one man
before, but wee were gone; I lay out all y^t night, and in a
wood & it being a great raine, wee were very wett; [but there
were few friends but ye truth gote over all, & by ye power
of ye lord wee escaped, out of ye murtherous hands, glory to
ye lord god for ever.]

At Twicrosse in Lecestershire I was moved to go to see
a great man y^t was sicke, & after I had spoke to him in his
bed, and ye power of ye lord entered him that hee was loving
and tender, and I left him and came down among the family
in the house, and spake a few words to ye people [y^t they
should fear the lord and repent and prize their time & the
like words] and there came one of his servants wth a naked
sword and runne at mee ere I was aware of him, and sett it
to my side, and there held it, and I looked up at him in his
face and said to him alack for thee its no more to mee then
a straw, and then hee went away in a rage, wth threatning
words and I passed away, and ye power of the lord came
over all, & his master mended [according to my beliefe and
faith y^t I had seen before,] and he then turned this man away
that runne at me wth ye sword.

[I was moved to go from a Meetting in Nottinghamshire
to a steeplehouse, and when ye priest had done, I spake to
him & ye People, and the priest went away, but ye people
staid and heard ye truth declared to them till it was w^thin
the night and I was moved to kneele down in ye steeple
house and pray among ye people and there came a woman
and kissed the crown of my head when I was praying in the
dark behind mee, and shee was one of ye world, and there
combined together a Company of men to hale mee out, and
they did for there were many then y^t had a love to the truth,
but it was well and the truth came over all, and it made
them to love it the more, and wee had a meetting in y^t
town, and so I passed away in the truth of God and y^t was
over all.

I was moved to a steeplehouse on a lecture day at
Nottingham, where there were many priests; and when hee
y^t was speaking had done, I spake to them and the people,
and called them off their worshipps and temples and teachers

to ye Anoynting w^{t}hin them, and to look at the temple of God in themselves and to worship God in the spirit, and had a great reasoning w^{t}h the people and passed away and the truth came over all and went to ye priests house, where there was another priest and had a great dispute w^{t}h them about sprinkling children & other thinges concerning the truth, w^{c}h came over all their heads and so I passed away.]

There being warrants all over ye west Rydeing to take mee and the Constable having the warrant in his pockett told mee of it, and said y^t hee could take mee but hee was loath to trouble mee, and hee stayed w^{t}h mee at a meetting, and after I passed away Northwards, and there were no friends, and sometimes I laid out all night though in ye winter season, and I came in my travels to a house being weary; and bid the woman bring mee some meat & milke or creame if shee had any, and shee said shee had none, I was moved to aske her for it though I did not matter for it, and there was a litle child laid his hands on a churne in which there was a great deale of creame, and plucked it down before my face, and it runne like a poole in the floore of ye house, and ye woman fell a Blessing her, and beatting the child[1]; and so I passed away being at night in ye winter three or four dayes before y^t time called Christmas when it did snow and blow and so was out all ye cold night, and this was in Yorkshire. And thus the truth brought ye truth to light.

And I was moved to go into ye North, and as I passed through ye towns I bid the People repent for the mighty day of ye lord was comeing upon all sin and wickedness and so I passed on and came to an ale house where I staid all night, and ye lord opened to mee that hee had a great people in ye north, w^{c}h I saw by a river [y^t parted two Counties[2]], how they came forth in shineing white rayment, and so I gave forth pap^{rs} to that Countrey for the Ale wife woman to disperse which shee did which astonished people and admired them, and shewed them to people in the Markett, which made them to beleeve the truth, and then I passed away, and came to a house, and the man would have given mee money, [and I was moved to shake my hand at it and bidd him mind the lord, and Christ the teacher in him, for hee was comeing to bring them off of all ye worlds teachers, and the lord would teach his people himselfe.]

And so I passed away being among ye fell Countreys, and
lay out all night, and a stranger, and so ye next day I passed
upp to a Market town[1], upon a Markett day, and spoke to
ye people and bid them repent, [and take heed of deceitfull
merchandize;] and worshipp God in the spirit and truth and
so I passed away upp winsadayle, and declared the truth
through all ye townes as I went, and people took mee for a
madd man and distracted and some followed mee and
questioned wth mee and was astonished & there followed
mee a Schoolemaster and gote mee into a house and thought
I had been a young man y^t was gone away distracted y^t was
gone away from my parents and thought to have kept mee,
but they being astonished at my answers and the truth I
spoke to them they could not tell what to say, and would
have had mee to have staid all night, but I was not to stay
but passed away [and wandred in ye night.]

And at last I came to an alehouse where there was some
fellows drinking [and I walked up and down in ye house and
after a time they beganne to drink to mee and then I spake
to them the truth and warning them of ye mighty day of y^e
lord y^t was comeing and bid them take heed to that w^ch
sheewed them sin and evill in their hearts upon wch one rose
ag^t mee wth a clubb, and so they held one another, and then
they were quiet,] I walking out as to have gone to have
lyen all night at doores; and hee y^t would have strucke mee
followed mee [and so I was moved to come into ye house ag^n
and so staid there all night, and the next morning I was
moved to tell ye man of ye house y^t I was ye sonne of God[2]
and was come to declare ye Everlasting Truth of God, and
did declare the truth to him and them, and so hee had mee
down amongst some professors who after I had declared
truth to them and they received it, and they directed mee
to other professors.]

And then I came to one Bousfields [in Gasdaile][3] who
received[a] where there were many convinced, and from thence I
was directed to Gervase Bensons[4] where there was a meetting
of professing people; and I lay at Richard Robinsons[5] and
speaking to him hee was convinced, and ye next day being
the first day of ye week[6] I went down to ye meetting, where

---

[a] Vol. I. p. 41: *hee & severall more received mee*

they were generally convinced y[t] day, and generally received Truth, and came to y[e] teacher w[t]hin them Christ Jesus.

Presently after there was a great fair to be at Sedbury[1], near Gervase Bensons where many young people came to be hyred and I went through the fair and spake, and then went into y[e] steeple house yard, [and gote upp by a tree] and spoke to y[e] people largly, many Professors and priests being there; and to bring them off of their teachers to Christ their Teacher, and to come off, of their worshipps to worship God in the spirit, and to come off, of their Churches to the Church in God, and had no opposition, but only one Cap[t] which said the steeple house was the Church, which I told him y[t] was a place of lime and stone and wood, [for the Church was in God as in Thess. 1. and 1.[a]] and so after had some few words hee passed away, and the truth came over all, and many were satisfied concerning it; and when I was passing away, one priest said to y[e] people I was distracted, his mouth being stopped by y[e] power of God for opposeing, y[t] was onely his cover to y[e] People, and so I passed away and had some other meettings upp and down in that Countrey, where divers were Convinced and received the Truth.

And then I came to fforbank Chappel[2], where there was a great meetting of y[e] sober people, of y[e] Countrey and severall speakers, where some moderate people desired mee not to speak unto y[e] speakers because they were something contrary to y[e] world, and there were many sorts of people there, and so not to speak to them in y[e] steeplehouse; and indeed there was nothing upon mee to speak to them; and so afterward when y[e] meetting was done in the forenoone, I went upon the hill in the afternoone; and y[e] people came to mee for the steeplehouse would not hold them in y[e] morning & some ould men went into y[e] steeplehouse as being a strang thing for a man to speak out of y[e] steeplehouse; and so after a while I beganne to speak to y[e] People and all quiet, and y[e] greatest part of a thousand people [were convinced] that day.

So I passed away and y[e] week following I had a meetting at Preston Chappell[3] where there were many convinced and so I went into y[e] steeplehouse and I told them I did not hold up those places, but to bring off, of such thinges [to the church in god, and to worshipp God, in the spirit and truth, y[t] people

[a] A: *1 Thess : 1 : and : 1 :*

might come off, of their false worshipps and off of their false
teachers, and teachers to yᵉ church in God, and to bee taught
of Christ, and to come off of their days and tymes & sprinkling
infants and their other ceremonies, to Christ the light and
spirit wᵗhin them, and so after the truth was fully declared
to them I passed away; and there was a generall Convincement.]

And then I passed to Kendall[1] where I had a meetting in
the Mout hall peaceably and quiet where the truth was received by many, and then I passed to underbarrow[2] where
there were many professing people.

And the word of the Lord came to mee yᵗ I might appoynt
a meetting in the steeplehouse at underbarrow, and some was
for it and some was agᵗ it, but at last I prevailed to have a
meetting there and had a larg meetting, and the priest came
and all was quiet, and truth received in love by many, And
from thence I passed to Newton[3] where there were many
professors which received truth.

And then I was moved to go to [Stable[4]] steeple house, and
after when the priest had done I spoke and they Hurried
mee out, all was on a fire; and they took mee and threw mee
over a grave yard wall, but I received no harm and there
I spoke the truth to them.

And from thence I came to Swarthmoore[5] which when I
came there the priest of ulverston[6] followed and said as I said
deceitfully, which was a Rantor, and had liberty to do any
thing, who professed Christ highly in words, but was neither
comed unto yᵉ law nor John, and could witnesse neither in
the truth, nor as being in either of them.

And then I passed to ulverston steeple house in yᵉ week
day and spoke when the priest was silent, how hee was a
Jew yᵗ was one inward, and hee was not a Jew yᵗ was one
outward, but hee was one yᵗ was one inward that was of yᵉ
spirit; and so how they might come out of their outward
Ordinances and traditions of men to yᵉ light of Christ Jesus,
which hee had enlightned them; and they plucked mee out
of their steeplehouse, and so after a time when they had
thrust mee out I passed away.

The next first day I went to Aldingham steeplehouse, and
after yᵉ priest had done, I spoke to yᵉ People [the Gosple,
yᵉ truth yᵉ light of Jesus Christ in their owne hearts, which

2—2

he had enlightned y^m y^t they might all come to, y^t lett y^m see, all y^t ever they had done and said and acted, and y^t would bee their teacher when they were about their labours.] The priest told mee Mathew, Mark, Luke and John was ye Gosple, I told him ye Gosple was the power of God.

And then I passed the afternoone to Ramside[1], where ye priest of ye parish had given notice of my coming there, and a Commendation of ye truth, which after he received, and forsook his place, and there was a great meetting, abundance of people, and heard truth willingly.

Then I came to Swarthmoore ag^n. And from thence to Dalton steeplehouse another first day; when the priest had done, I spoke ye truth to ye people largly,[and the people grew Brutish, and fell of ringing the Bells, but the truth came over all.]

And I went after to Wanys steeplehouse, an Island[2], when the priest had done I spoke {the truth} to ye People, to come off all false teachers to Christ Jesus w^thin them, ye light the true teacher. And so people being rude after a while wee passed away, and in ye afternoon wee went up ag^n and ye Priest hid himself in a corn land hearing wee were coming, and so wee passed away in the truth over all.

And a meetting was appoynted at a Chappell a little beyond Gleaston[3] where there was never priest preached in it, where wee had a brave meetting where there were many convinced.

Then I was moved to go to [Cartmell steeplehouse[4], when the priest had done] I spake to [him and] the People largly of ye light and truth and truth in their own hearts to mind and there they might find their teacher to come out of all the teachers of ye world for the lord was comed to teach people himselfe.

And then I was moved to go to Lyndell[5] steeple house wch when the priest had done I spake to him and the people [the truth and the spirit and ye word of God was in their hearts that they might all come to, and that they might know the lord God at hand and so to come out of all ye false Teachers & Hyrelings y^t sought for their gaine & means from their quarter.]

Then I was moved to appoynt a meetting in a steeple house yard beyond y^t where there was a great meetting and severall contenders and one of ye priests convinced, and many con-

tenders there were, but truth came over all, and the
Contenders mouths stopped.

And then I was moved to go to [Hawton[1]] steeplehouse
upon a first day and after ye priest had done I spoke to him
and the people the truth [and how they might come out of
all their false wayes worshipps & teachers for the lord was
comeing to teach his people himself by his spirit and by the
word in their hearts.]

And then I was moved to Lancaster to speak in y^e
Markett att ye Cross ye truth in all peoples hearts, to come
off all deceitfull wayes and merchandize, &, to come to that
in their hearts y^t brought them to speak truth and do truth
one to another, and to lay a syde all deceitful merchaundize
for ye day of ye lord was comeing upon all ungodlynesse and
wickednesse of men. And then upon the first day I went to
ye steeple house and spoke to ye priest & people when hee
had done. And then I had a meetting in ye street afterward
and truth was largly spoken forth that day to ye people
where they might find their teacher w^{t}hin them, and not to
go to the hyrelings and false teachers w^{t}hout y^m which taught
for the fleeze and the woole and made a prey upon them.

And then I was moved to go againe into Westmerland
[where I had several larg meettings abundance convinced.]
And I went into Kendale Markett and spoke to ye People
at ye Markett time, [I had silver in my pockett and I was
moved to throw it out amongst ye People as I was going up
the street before I spoke, and my life was offer'd upp amongst
them, and the mighty power of ye lord was seen in p^{r}serving]
and the power of ye lord was so mighty and so strong, y^t
people flew before^a [and runne into ye shopps for fear and
terror took hold upon them, I was moved to open my mouth
and lift upp my voyce aloud in the mighty power of the
lord; and to tell y^m the mighty day of ye lord was coming
upon all deceitfull Merchaundize and wayes, and to call y^m
all to repentance and a turning to the lord God, and his
spirit w^{t}hin them for it to teach them and lead them and
tremple^b before ye mighty God of heaven and earth, for his
mighty day was comeing; and so passed through the streets,
and when I came to ye townes end, I gote upon a stumpp]

^{a} Vol. i. p. 53: *flew like chaffe before mee into there houses*
^{b} A: *tremple* altered to *tremble*

and spoke to ye people, and so ye People begane to fight some
for mee, and some against mee, and so after a while I passed
away w^thout any harme.

And then I came to Lancashire ag^n and the priest[1] of
Cartmell had sent mee a challendg, And so I went into his
steeplehouse and when hee had done I spoke to him but hee
gote away And they took mee and drew mee out of y^e
steeplehouse after I had spoke a few words to them and
when I was forth they tooke mee and threw mee down, and
many wranglings and Contendings they had I went upp to
the priests house and would have had him come out, but hee
would not, and so I spoke to ye people the truth of God and
so passed away, [letting y^m see where there teacher was, and
how they might know the power of ye lord in their hearts
to cease from men whose breath was in their nostrils, and
to looke unto the lord Jesus Christ their teacher and salvation and so passed away.]

Then I passed to [Silverdale[2]] and had a meetting of
friends in the Evening where there came a priest wth a
pistell [and other men wth Armes,] and so ye priest intending^a
in tending to come into ye house in the night, to light a pipe of
Tobacco, [but his intend was to have done Mischiefe wth his
pistell to mee, he being a desparate fellow] but ye man of y^e
house kept him out.

Then I came to [Katenbourough[3]] where there was a
meetting of friends in the Evening, [which I felt the time of
the meetting swords and pistols about mee, and all y^e
meetting while looking when as they should come in; they
lying in waite not farre off which I felt.] So after when the
meetting was done and friends almost gone away and past,
I passed away from the house to another friend's house, I
was no soon^r gone out of the house, but p^rsently they came
in wth naked swords, disguised men, which cutt and hacked
at {friends w^th} naked swords and put the candles forth and
friends was faine to take upp stools {and chairs} to defend
themselves and plucking friends that were there forth of
the house and abuseing y^m and cutt the chairs and stooles
which friends held up to defend and save themselves w^thall;
they lying in waite in ye way wch way I might passe, but I
was moved to passe another way. So they missed of mee,

---

^a This apparent duplication appears in B but A has *intending* only.

both in the house and in ye way through the hand of y^e
lord.

And when I was passing away att [halton] steeplehouse
aforesaid, after I spoke to ye people, and priest there came
a man^a to mee and said hee would runne mee thorow w^{t}h his
rapiour if hee were hanged for it w^{t}hin an houre, yet the
mighty hand of ye lord god delivered mee from them all,
and the truth came over the heads of y^m all.

And then I went upp to Swarthmoore ag^n over ye sands[1]
and went to ulverston Steeplehouse as I had done severall
times, and so upon a lecture day I went into ye steeplehouse
it being ye Markett day and when the priest had done I
spoke and there were many priests there [and one^b was
bitter^c and spoke to mee and asked mee If I had the spirit
of discerning, I told him I had, w^{c}h made him to tremble,]
the power of ye lord God being so mighty and powerfull
amongst them which made him so to tremble that hee
confessed y^t hee was afraid, y^t the steeple house should
have fallen upon his head, and so ye mighty power and
dread of ye lord God came over all, [y^t answered the witness
in many, and ye graves opened and ye dead heard the voyce
of God].

And then another Lecture day I was moved to go upon
a Markett day to Ulverston steeplehouse againe upon a
Lecture day, and many people resorting thither and professors and friendly people [to heare mee, and Quœried if I
would bee there,] and so when the priest had done I beganne
to speak as at other times, And there was one Sawrey[2] called
a Justice came to mee [and took mee by the hand and asked
mee if I would speak, and I said yes,] and he said If I would
speak according to scripture I should speak, and I told him
I would and give him Scripture for what I said; and I had
something upon mee to y^t the man had been speaking to;
vizt the priest of the town called Lampett[3], and he told mee
I should not speak; and then ye rude people [said to y^e
Justice, give him us, and hee did, and they] fell upon mee
w^{t}h staves and fists and Books, and fell upon mee and
knocked mee down ^{d}and tumbled mee over their sides^d and

---

^{a} Vol. I. p. 53: *a doctor whoe was soe full of envy*
^{b} Vol. I. p. 54: *preist Bennett* ^{c} A: *better*
^{d}...^{d} Vol. I. p. 57: *& people tumbled over there seates for feare*

many people was tumbled down [and knocked down and the
Justice and the priests among them].

And then the Justice said among ye rude people give him
mee, and then hee took mee from amongst them and lett
mee out of ye steeple house, and four Officers and Constables
hee gave mee to them, to have mee to ye town to whipp mee,
so some ledd mee by the shoulders and some by ye hands,
and some by ye Armes and shooke mee by ye head, and ledd
mee through mire and dirt and water, and some gote staves
and some gote hollow bushes and some gote willowes, and
some gote hedg stakes, and so they ledd mee till they came
to a Common and many friendly people their heads were
broken that day & the blood runne down their faces, and
then the constables took mee and gave mee a wisk over the
shoulders w^{t}h their willow rods, and thrust mee amongst
abundance of rude people, which fell upon mee w^{t}h their
hedg stakes and batts and staves, and struck at mee as hard
as ever they could stricke, my head, my armes, my back, [and
it was a great while before they beat mee down upon the
wett common w^{c}h was a great while before I fell, and there
I lay a pretty space upon the wett beat and bruised,] and
then the power of the lord went thorow mee, and refreshed
mee and healed mee and strengthened mee and I was moved
to stand up in it in ye mighty power of ye lord God among
all ye rude multitude, and stretched out my armes over them
in the power of the lord God and bid them stricke ag^n and
there came a man w^{t}h a Ruler and gave mee a blow over
my hand, y^t I could not stirre it, no manner of way, but it
stood out as it was, and the people cryed hee hath spoyld
his hand for ever, for having any use of it, [and the skin
was struck of my hand and a litle blood came,] and I looked
at it, and a love went towards it, and so afterward the
power of ye lord passed through it, and it was as well as it
was before, and I had never another blow afterward and
others came to mee and said if I would give them money,
they would preserv mee from the multitude; but I denyed
them; [And they said If I came into the town ag^n they
would kill mee.]

So I was moved to passe upp into ye town, and through
the Markett, and there mett mee a man w^{t}h a rapyer and
told mee he was my servant, and was greeved to see ye abuse

y^t was offered to mee, and of their bad behaviour to mee; So hee passed upp the street w^{t}h mee; and as I was going some of ye Market people was strikeing up of friends heeles; And so I turned mee about, and ye man had drawen his naked rapier and was running at them y^t abused the friendly men; so I stepped to ye man and clapped my hand upon the rapiour; and bad him put upp his rapiour if hee went along w^{t}h mee, and so not long after seven men set upon y^t man and beat him cruelly for drawing his rapour.

So this Justice Sawrey and Lampett was the begining of all ye persecution in the north of England, and raising & casting of false reports and reproaches upon honest people, and casting all manner of evill reports upon truth. And then I went up to Swarthmoore hall where they were dressing of many friendly peoples heads, who had their blood drawen of them y^t day through the persecution.

And then I was moved to go at this side of Wainey, where wee had a meetting, and in the evening there came a man who bound himselfe w^{t}h an Oth y^t hee would shoot mee w^{t}h a pistol; many people being in the fold, and the people of ye house went forth, and after a while I walked forth, The power of ye lord was so mighty to ye chaining of them in ye yard; y^t ye man of ye house being a professor was so tormented and terrifyed y^t hee went into a Cellar [to his prayers; and after I went into ye house when truth was come over them, and there was a Rawe man of ye house, seeing the truth had come over hee fell to speaking and lett upp their spirits. And so I walked out of ye house into ye yard ag^n and fell a speaking, and then the fellow drew his pistoll, and some held him, and some carried mee away, and so through the power of ye lord God I escaped.]

And the next day I went over into the Isle of Wanney, to James Lancasters[1], [hee being a friend and his wife being an Enemy to truth had gathered a Company of rude fellows^a as fishermen & ye like,] w^{t}h their fishing poles and the like fell upon mee, as soon as I was com'd to land and beat mee down to ye ground, [and bruised my body and head and all over my shoulders and back,] y^t when I was sencible againe, I looked up and a man was lying over my shoulders and a woman was throwing stones at my face, and so I gote up

^{a} Vol. I. p. 60: *there rusht out about 40 men*

[and I could hardly tell whether my head was cloven to peeces it was so bruised, nevertheless I was raysed upp by ye power of God,] and they beat mee wth their fishing poles into ye sea; and thrust mee into ye sea [a great depth. And thought to have sunke mee down into ye water, and so I thrust up amongst y^m ag^n.

And then they tumbled mee in a boat,] and James Lancaster went wth mee and carryed mee over the water and when I came to ye town where the man had bound himself wth an Oath to shoot mee, all ye town rose upp ag^t mee. Some wth muck forks, and some wth flayles and forks, and cryed knocke him in ye head. I should not go through ye town, and they called for a Cart, to carry mee to ye grave yard, and cryed knock him in the head, but they did not but guarded mee a great way wth their weapons but did not much abuse mee, and after a while left mee; so when I came to some water I washed mee, I was very dirty and much bruised; and then came to a friends house about three miles from y^t place[1]; [where I washed mee; they call the place Ramside where the friend lives; and I desired to have a litle bear^a I should go to bed and when I was in bed I could turn mee no more then a sucking child, I was so bruised,] and so then they sent for mee wth a horse to Swarthmoore; and the stumbling of ye horse in giving mee a litle shake did mee more hurt then all ye blowes.

So I came to Swarthmoore at Judg ffells[2]; who was mighty serviceable to truth, & so warrants was graunted out for mee by Sarrew when Judg ffell came home for his Cruelty I appeared before him and the Justices at Lancaster where ^btwo priests and a schoolmaster^b had sworne falsly ag^t mee which appeared ag^t mee before ye Justice, and another priest one Marshall[3] which was their Orator and so when they were Confounded, and their lies brought to nought, and truth cleared itselfe, and abundance of ye sober people of ye Countrey were gathered there and they heard my accusers; and they heard mee make a defence, and answered my accusation; and cleared myself from them all; and so when all was cleared one of ye Justices said I might speak to ye people; and so I began to speak of ye spirit of God; y^t it should be ye leader of all people into all truth, according to Christs promise and

^a A: *beare*   ^b...^b Vol. I. p. 62: *two preists sonns & a preist*

doctrine, & priest Jacon[1a] said the letter and the spirit was inseparable then answere was made to him; then every one y^t had ye letter had ye spirit and so ye truth came over all; and the priests fled away; and it was a day of Joy and rejoyceing to his people; and one of ye Justices[2] s^d hee never saw such a day in his life for hee had been sick, and y^t day hee was made whole; [and Judg ffell was made very serviceable to truth for his understanding being open and most of his family came into truth.]

The Priest of Lancaster did write a petition ag^t mee to ye parliam^{t3} [and one had said hee had been in heaven and was dead and was alive and hee had heard the voyse of God, and thus their Ignorance of the Scriptures appeard which speaks of such thynges of ye saintes, and the Sonne of God, and such as satt in heavenly places in Christ Jesus; and such as had been dead, and were made alive in Christ Jesus, and were perfect in Christ Jesus, and so wee gote ye petition and answered it, and sent it to ye parliament, before theirs was sent up; and the Priests when they should have sent it upp, it would cost y^m so much money, when the time came of sending it upp, that they did not send it upp, because it would cost so much money.]

Then I was moved of ye lord to go into Cumberland [where I saw the sparks of life rose before I came into it, and a Multitude of people the lord had there,] so I went to Boutle steeplehouse upon a first day; the priest of the parish hearing of my Coming, hee had gott another to help him, [and so I was moved to speak in his time[4], he utterred such wicked thinges, and therefore for ye truths sake I was moved to speak to him If I had been Imprison'd for it;] and so they halled mee out and People was mighty rude, and one gave mee a blow upon the wrist [w^{t}h a great Hedg stake, yet I felt no harme,] hee might have broken my wrist to peeces; but ye power of ye lord bare all off, and so the Constable being a sober man, he rescued mee out of their hands, and would have sett a fellow y^t struck [into the stocks, but ye rude people rescued him out of his hands,] and so hee went a litle way w^{t}h us, and so I told him hee might go a litle way on w^{t}h us, to ye house where wee lodged[5], and there lay a Company of rude people in ye way to have done us a mischiefe.

[a] A, C: *Jacor*

And in ye afternoone I was moved to Come up ag^n to y^e
Market Crosse; and there satt mee down wth my friends
about mee, and so at last friends were all moved to go into
ye steeplehouse, and then it came to mee y^t I might go in;
and so when I came in, the Priest was preaching, and all y^e
Scriptures y^t hee spake were of false Prophetts and deceivers;
and Anti-Christs, hee brought them and threw them upon
us: I satt mee down and heard till hee had done, [though
several friends spoke to him in his time;] so when he had
done I beganne to speak to him, and hee and the people
beganne to bee rude, and the Constable stood upp and
charged peace amongst them [in ye name of ye Commonwealth,] and all was quiet, and I took his Scriptures that
hee spoke of false Prophetts and Anti-Christs and deceivers
and threw them back upon him; and lett him see y^t hee was
in the very stepps of them; and hee beganne to oppose mee,
I told him his glasse was gone his time was out; the place
was as free for mee as for him; [and hee accused mee y^t I had
broken ye law in speaking to him in his tyme in the Morning,
and I told him hee had broken ye law then in speaking
in my tyme;] And so I called all people to ye true teacher;
out of the hyrelings such as teach for ye fleece and makes a
prey upon the people; for ye lord was com'd to teach his
people himself by his spirit & Christ saith learn of mee; I
am ye way which doth enlighten every man y^t cometh into
ye world, y^t all through him might beleeve; and so to learn
of him who had enlightned them who was ye light, and so
had a brave meetting in ye steeplehouse, and the priest of
ye parish fomed [like a pigg] through rage and madnes, but
ye truth and the power of ye lord God came over all their
heads.

A day or two after they had a plott ag^t mee, a Company
came wth swords; and a litle boy wth a rapour, and came
into ye house where I was; I was just gone out of it into
ye fields, though I saw them when I was in the fields, but
they came not to mee, and they had intended to have sett
ye Boy on to have done Mischiefe, & to have murdred;
but ye lords hand prevented them and stopped them; and
though others came to do us a Mischiefe, but one held
another, and so through the power of ye lord wee passed
over them.

And then I passed away to another steeplehouse neare
Cockermouth where I had appoynted a meetting; where
people having notice of it, and had not seen mee before, y^t
there came above a thousand people which was like a horse
faire; and they were gote into a Tree to heare and see, and
so a Professor asked mee If I would go into ye Church as
hee called it, and I said yes; and so I went in & people was
gote up into ye pulpitt when I was gote in, though I told
him I denyed all such places, but denyed them all, for y^e
Church was in God, and so let y^m see and so lett y^m see^a,
all their temples, and all their Rudiments, and their Teachers,
and then oppened the parables which Christ spoke unto y^e
world, & brought them to ye light which Christ had enlightned them w^thall w^thin themselves; wth y^t they might
see his parables and Christ y^t spoke y^m forth; and to w^t
nature they were spoken in man, and brought y^m to ye true
teacher in y^mselvs, for the lord was come to teach his people
himselfe, Which generally they received this doctrine, and
most was there convinced that day, ye meetting very peaceable, and so I spoke about three hours and broke up the
meetting in peace.

And there followed mee an old professor praysing mee
and the doctrine; [though his spirit was like a steeple.] And
so I turned to him and bid him fear the lord; and there was
a priest[1] said I should not Judg; and there were 4 priests
came when the meetting was done, and one of them fell into
dispute, and one of their mouthes was quickly stopped, after
hee was proved by Scripture y^t hee was found in ye stepps
of ye false Prophetts and shutt out from the true, hee was
quickly gone. And then there was another who had three
steeplehouses[2], who was of y^t parish hee fell to disputeing &
wrangling and contrary to ye witnesse of God in his own
conscience; in so much as his own people rose ag^t him his
own hearers; but at last they fled and people passed away
greatly satisfied and rejoyced in it.

And the first day after I passed to Cockermouth steeple
house in ye forenoone, and when ye priest[3] had done being a
great parish I spoke to him & the people and proved him in
ye stepps of all ye false Prophetts and hyrelings; and so hee
said y^t I said hee was an Hyreling, and so fled his way, and

^a This repetition appears in A, B, C.

left his flock; and severall soldio^{rs} were wth mee; wch were
convinced at ye meetting before, and ye people was rude and
they cryed they had ye law on their side, wch silenced y^{e}
people, & so truth was declared to ye people, and all was
quiet; and one man said there was no learned man to dispute
wth mee there, I told him I came not to dispute but to
declare truth to them, [that they might come out of all the
false Teachers, Shepherds wayes and to bee taught of god
who was come to teach his people himselfe, and to bring them
out of all false wayes and teachers and that they might come
off all false wayes and worshipps, and to bee guided by the
spirit of God in themselves to God who was a spirit; for y^{e}
mighty day of the lord was Comming upon all sin and wickednesse; and so had a larg time to declare the truth and the
light of Christ in their hearts; and the word that letts them
see their thoughts and their words that Divides asunder y^{e}
p^{r}tious from the vile.]

And so past away in peace to another steeplehouse some
two miles of from the Town; and being a thirsty I spyed a
Brooke I went down to drinke; and being hote as I came
back, I mett ye priest of ye parish, hee asked mee whether
I had any thing to say to ye people that day; and If I had
hee would neither oppose mee in word nor thought, so I told
him oppose if hee would I had something to speak to y^{e}
people; and how hee had made a foole of himselfe, and had
spoken contrary to ye witnesse of God in his Conscience two
or three dayes before, [for hee being the same priest of that
steeplehouse where I had spoken before the other day and
also in this, and hee knew that the people was taken wth
truth in the Countrey, and they would have comed to have
heard mee rather then him.]

And so I went upp to the steeplehouse, [being a great
place and a great people.] And a professor came to mee
and asked mee if I could go into ye Church as he cald it, and
I said yes, it being hote wthout there being no place to
Command a people thereabouts; I went into ye steeplehouse,
and the priest did not go into his pulpitt, and when the
people was gathered I beganne to speak, I had free liberty
to speak the truth to them all, [and all was quiet and
peaceable not a word was utterd neither in nor out of the
steeplehouse in opposition;] I spoke the truth to them some

houres, and brought them to see where the rest was and the
first stepp of peace, every one being enlightned wth Christ,
the peace, the rest, being turned every man and woman by
the light, from the sin and from the evill wth the light w^ch
comes from Christ, they standing still in it and beleeveing
in it, they come to Christ from whence the light comes there
rest and their peace; and they receiving ye light they receive
Christ; and hee gives them power to become the sonnes of
God and this would bring them into unity wth ye sonne and
wth ye father; and beleeveing in the light wherew^th Christ
hath enlightned them, w^thall they would become children
of ye light and ye day, and so openned the earthly parables
wch Christ had spoken in ye Earthly nature in man, and lett
y^m see all their traditions, & their false wayes and worshipps
and their false teachers together wth their Maintenance; w^ch
was Contrary to Christ and the Scriptures and so brought
them all to the true teacher the lord and Christ, who was
comed to teach his people himselfe, and his great day was
comeing and how they might find their teacher w^thin, [when
they were in their labours and in their beds,] and their was
a generall Convincement that day many hundreds of people;
and so I passed away in peace; and truth came over all
deceit and wickednesse.

And I had some other meettings in the Countrey and had
one at [Wiggin] Crosse¹; where there were many convinced
and some disputes there were but truth came over all.

And I poynted another meeting in ye steeplehouse yard²
where there were some disputes but truth came over all.

And so I passed to Carlisle Citty, which upon the seventh
day I went into ye Markett which some bad fellowes had
Combined together to do mee a Mischiefe, but I stood a topp
of ye Crosse in the middle of ye Markett and said ye mighty
day of ye lord was upon all deceit & ungodlinesse and wickednesse; and lay away all their deceitfull Merchandize; and
keep to yea and Nay in their Communications & spoke the
truth to them as I passed along the streets; and so a
Multitude of people followed mee, [and so there was a friend
led mee to his owne house.]

And so I went into the castle & spoke amongst the
soldio^rs the truth, and at a Meetting at the same friends
house, where many soldiors were Convinced, Baptizts &

others and great disputes I had wth some of them and there
was one Old Man which was the great opposer which was
called a Deacon amongst ye Baptizts; and hee desired mee
not to pierce him wth my eyes, full hee was full of deceit,
and I fastned myne eyes upon him; and another lieutenant
a Baptizt came [wth a rapour in his hand] hee came in hast;
and hee asked mee w^t must bee damned, and I told him that
was spoke in him, and so I oppend to him ye Election and
reprobation [wch stood in two seeds and two Births, & it
astonished him] and said y^t they never heard ye like before
in their lives and they received truth gladly.

Then the next first day I went into ye steeple house; and
when ye priest had done I began to speak, and ye Magistrates
desired mee to go my waies; and desired mee not to speak,
and so I spoke on a few words to ye People, and a great
tumult there was in the steeple house after a while; and a
mighty power of ye lord god there was y^t made people to
Quiver & Tremble, y^t it shooke them againe, that some
thought the very steeple house had shaken; and an uproar
there was in the Citty; y^t soldiours came into ye steeple
house y^t fetched ye other soldiours out of ye steeplehouse y^t
was wth mee which had been convinced, wch kept the rude
people off mee, and the Magistrates wives rushed through
the soldiours, to pluck mee by ye haire of the head[1], and then
when the souldiors came to call away the other soldiours;
they plucked mee down; and would not lett mee stay^a
amongst ye rude Multitude; and stones flew about and
cudgells in ye steeplehouse and about it; and w^thout in the
streets, and swords drawen and the Governour came down
to appease the people; and there came the same Leiutenant
the Pasture of the Baptizts [that came before wth his rapour
in his hand] and took mee out of the crowd into his own
house.

And so in the afternoone, hee offered upp his meetting to
declare the truth among them; and all was peaceable and
they all heard truth gladly, and so the second day the
Magistrates sent for mee; and I went upp to them to y^e
Town Hall, the streets being all in an uproar, and one sware
one thing and another sware another thing ag^t mee. [And
they asked mee if I were the sonne of God, I said yes: They

^a A: *Stand*

asked mee if I had seen Gods face, I said yes. They asked mee whether I had ye spirit of disserning, I said yes. {I disserned him that spoke to mee.} They asked mee whether the Scripture was ye word of God; I said God was the word, and the Scriptures were writeings; and ye word was before writeings were; wch word did fulfill them.]

And so they sent me to prison^a; and so I told ye Goaler I could pay him no fees, I would neither eat his meat nor lye in his Bed; [and so I satt up all night,] and continued there a litle time, and so ye Assizes came and when the Assizes was there came abundance of contenders & priests to mee and most of ye gentry of the Countrey to dispute, & there came one about ye tenth houre of ye night and plucked mee upp and down the roome; the very priests when they could gett no hold of my words for the truth did Convince them, and was like a fire upon their heads and in their hearts, the word of truth; and they all looked that I should have been put to death that Assize; for it was their generall talke both amongst the Gentry and ye priests; and they had gotten a Jury of purposse, and mighty looking there was for mee to have been brought forth; and much waiteings there was by the Countrey people, and so w^n the time, they were so confounded amongst themselves; they had not power to bring mee forth before them the lord had confounded them.

Then they cast mee into ye dungeon amongst the theeves and Mosse Trooppers; where ye men & women was all put together; where they had never a house of office where they could go to ease themselves; and there was one woman almost eaten to death wth lice; and there I was kept a good while and many friends came to visite mee, and they abused them pittifully and one Collonell Bensons wife[1] was moved to come, and was to eate no meat but what shee was to eate wth mee, and the Goaler brought a fidler into ye prison to play thinking to cross mee, and hee strucke mee, and I was moved to sing in ye power of ye lord god over him; and made the fidler sigh and give over his fidling; and so past away wth shame; and so p^{r}sently after I was sett att liberty[2].

And I was moved to go to a steeplehouse where I had had the great meetting near Cockermouth where I beganne before ye priest wch was ye same priest aforementioned[3] y^t said hee

^{a} Ell. text adds *as a Blasphemer, an Heretick and a Seducer* (I. 169).

would not oppose mee in word nor thought, but hee did then and so wee continued reasoning and disputeing all day long from morning untill night, and so hee passed his way and the truth of God came over all, and a good day it was, and so I had many meettings upp and down the County.

And then I passed into Northumberland where I had great service for y[e] truth there and had many meettings. And then into Bishoprick [where there were few steeplehouses but friends were moved to go to them, Nay I may say few in England but friends were moved to go to them to warn them of y[e] mighty day of y[e] lord, to tell them where their true teacher was, and a great people there was convinced, and brought to their teacher and out of the false worshipps to worshipp god in y[e] spirit and truth w[ch] the divell is out of; and came to own the light of Christ Jesus w[ch] hee had enlightned them w[th]all; w[ch] lett y[m] see all the evill deeds they had done; and all the evill thoughts they had thought; and all the ungodly words they had spoken, and that was y[e] light which Christ had enlightned them w[th]all w[ch] is Christ the great Prophctt, w[ch] tells every one all y[t] ever they have done.]

And I went to Newcastle, for there are many professors who had reported y[t] Quakers would fly like butterflies, they would not come to great Townes, So when I came there I sent for them being some of them the Aldermen of y[e] Town; but they would not come at mee so I went to one of their houses; whose name was Thomas Ledger[1]; and reasoned wth him, [and he said the Scriptures was above y[e] spirit and was above angells, and was the word of God; and I told him y[e] word was god and the spirit gave forth Scriptures and y[t] hee must know in himselfe both the word and spirit w[ch] reconciles to y[e] Scriptures to god & to one another; and that hee must know it in his heart and mouth w[ch] divides his good words from his bad and his good thoughts from his bad,] and so I passed away after I had a meetting wth friends and had spoken in their streets[2]; [and so I had great meettings upp and down in y[e] Countrey and many friends went to steeplehouses, and was sore abused, but truth was sett over all.

And then after I was moved to come into Westmerland where there was great meettings of such as were convinced

of ye lord and a beliefe in his Everlasting truth; and so as
I was passing to a Meetting near Sedbury there lay a Company of men in ye way at a Bridg at an Ale house w^{t}h
weapons to have done mee a Mischiefe, but I was Moved to
passe over another way over a water, not knoweing outwardly
of them and so some of them came to a meetting rudely, but
ye truth of ye lord y^t answers ye Witnesse of God in all
people, came over all, and they passed away w^{t}hout doing
mee or friends any hurt, and so then] friends had a meetting
not farre off y^t place[1] ye next first day where there was
about a thousand people and most convinced of the truth
of God, and some rude fellows had combined together, and
one[2] came w^{t}h a rapour; and so people being so many they
kept him of from rydeing among ye People to mee; and
which way hee rode friends kept together y^t hee could not
break in to mee, but truth came ov^r all and hee passed
away: and there was a gallant meetting & ended in peace;
[and its larg to declare the workes and wonders of ye lord
god and the preservation of mee through all, by his mighty
hand and power but I saw I was in his hand.

And then I was moved to passe towards the South, and
go through many townes and felt I answered the witnesse of
God in all people though I spoke not a word; and so I came
upp into yorkshire where I had been formerly a matter of
two years after I had been there; and this was in the dayes
of ye Protector; and the other before was most of it in the
Common wealths time; & so] friends y^t was convinced of the
truth having notice of my comming having a meetting at a
place called Sinderley[3] w^{c}h was Judged to bee about two
thousand people and one half & all peaceable and quiet; [and
so I passed upp and down ye most part of yorkshire, peaceably and quietly, where there were many thousands of
people Convinced of ye truth of God & came to know theire
teacher; and commonly where I had meettings upon the
first day the priests fled their parish, though I went not to
ye steeplehouse.]

[*In the Protectors Dayes*]

And then I was moved to come down to Hallifax, where
there was a great meetting some 3 miles out of it many
hundreds of people and ye Butchers of Hallifax had bound

themselves wth an Oath y^t they would kill mee; and they came to ye meetting and was very rude and desperate, but the presse of ye people was so great y^t they could not gett into mee and they bore friends out of their very places where they stood through their violence, and so ye man of ye house [1] wch was a friend being of repute amongst men, stood upon friends shoulders, and desired them y^t would not be quiet to go out of his ground; and they shouted for a great time, and said they would make it a Common^a, and so I was moved to stand out and friends about mee which was like a ringe; and said if there were any man y^t had reason or understanding of ye thinges of God lett him come in unto mee; and never a one would, and so ye truth came over them; and o^r meetting broke upp very well; and so they passed away missing their end; but ye Judgment of ye lord fell upon some of them, for one of them had kild a man and a woman y^t had bound himself to kill mee and severall of them perrished sadly, one used to hold out his tongue at friends when they went by them, and hee dyed wth his tongue hanging out of his mouth [below his chinne; And another dyed eaten to death wth lice; and sad ends came to them, and truth came over all.]

And so then I passed into Darbyshire, where there was fine meettings of friends, and there upon the night there combined together a Company of men and a great mans [2] Bayliffe, and hee came wth a sword in the night, and hee came to fetch mee out of ye house and they had an intent to have done mee Mischiefe, but there being severall friends, and their Neighbours y^t knew them, though they did violence and some abuses; yet truth came over them all by ye power of ye lord wee escaped them; for they had an intent to have taken mee away in the night to have done mee a Mischiefe.

And then I passed into Nottinghamshire and Lincoln-shire where there was brave meettings of friends and truth honourable; & so past upp into Lestershire, where there was great meettings; and so went to my Native town where my relations lived at a place called Drayton of ye clay [3]; haveing sent before of my Comming, hee^b gote another

---

^a Vol. I. p. 148 adds *& yelled & made such a noise as if they had beene come to a beare beatinge*

^b Ell. text: *Nathaniel Stephens the priest* (I. 200).

priest to help him and sent for mee ; where many of the
Countrey was gatherd, y^t I might come to ye steeplehouse,
for they could do nothing till I came ; Now I had not been
there of three years ; neither did I know of their gatherring
[as Outwardly;] and so I went up wth severall other friends,
and desired the priest to come out of their steeplehouse and
they did, and so wee had a great dispute ; and they carried
themselves uncivill ; and so I told them when the meetting
was ended, that I should bee there y^t day seaventh day.

And so when the day came there was seven priests were
gatherd wth a great people from severall parts of ye Countrey,
and I was Moved to go upp and stand upon a place in y^e
steeple house Yard ; and I sent for them out, and some of
them cryed heare mee and some of them fledd away when
I spoke to ye people so the Priest past away and so I told
them I never came to a place where there were so many
priests and none would stand so they came againe ; and the
people tooke mee upp in their Armes into ye steeplehouse
porch to carry mee into ye steeplehouse ; and the door being
locked, and the priest following ; people tumbled down upon
heapps, and I under them, [then they cryed for the clerk to
come to open the door,] so I gote from them [and leaped
through the Barrs and gote to ye place where I spoke before,]
and beganne to speak and they took mee upp againe and
carried mee and sett upp something under the steeplehouse
wall ; And the priests gathering about mee crying Argument argument, which I told them I denyed all their
voyces ; but stood still a while, and looking upon the great
concourse of people ; I told them I denyed all their voyces ;
for their voyces were the voyce of a stranger, and they bid
mee prove it which I did ; and then the priest thrust mee
down again from ye place where I stood among the people ;
which I drew Back ; feeling ye power of ye lord god go over
the people, and them both.

When I was gotten to ye place where I could Command
ye people I beganne to speak ; and told them if they had
patience and would own the Scriptures and give audience I
would shew them Scripture, and give them scripture ; why
I did deny those teachers, and the teachers of the world ;
and why I left them which I said I would ; and so I had
time enough and declared the truth freely to them ; and so

openned through the prophetts; and lett them see the steps
of the false Prophetts wch they were in wch the true Prophetts cryed ag^t such as stood for the fleece, and sought for
their gaine from their quarter, and bare rule by their meanes
and sought for the fleece and cared not for ye flock, Jer. 23.
and Jer. 5. Esa. 56. Ezek. 34. and Micha 3. and other places.
And also how they were in ye steps of ye Pharisees w^ch
Christ cryed against, Covetous, loving honour, called of men
master, stood praying in ye Synagogues: And loved saluta-
tions and greettings in ye Marketts, and went in long robes
and other Markes by wch they might see themselves; and
in ye stepps of the false Apostles. They were covetous for
filthy lucre, lovers of money, minders of earthly thinges; and
here all people might see the whole traine of them.

And so after a great while I had largly declared to them
where they were I spoke to their Consciences, the truth in
their hearts the light of christ Jesus, within them, by which
they might come to God; and so when I had done one of the
priests said, hee would go read those Scriptures that I had
quotted; and so hee began the 23 of Mathew^a, and read
more against themselves; then I had spoken; and so I bad
ye people take Notice; and so I answerd their questions;
and so broke upp; and so ye truth of the lord came over all.
And I told ye People I should bee there that day seventh
night againe; and then they gote a Company of soldiours,
And so I was moved to poynt the meeting att my outward
Relations house or ground; and when the Soldio^rs came they
could not take mee; and the priest sent for mee to come to
another close y^t the soldiours might take mee away; y^t they
might have ensnared mee. And presently after I went into
ye Countrey; and the Soldio^rs came to a meetting; which I
told one of them y^t was the head of y^m I should answere for
friends, they knew mee I was their countrey man.

So I went before Collonel Hacker [1]; and hee putt mee into
ye Marshalls hands the next Morning; and sent mee away
to London, to Oliver the Protector; and so then they kept
mee a prisoner att ye Mermaid in chearing crosse untill I was
brought before him. And after I was brought before him, hee
was pretty moderate, and said hee wished mee no more hurt

---

^a A, B, C read *Mathew.* Camb. text (vol. I. p. 156) and Ell. text (I. 204)
read *Jeremiah*

then his owne soul, which I said if hee did; hee went ag^t his own Soul; and so bidd him hear the voyce of God and harden not his heart; for that kept him from hardnesse of heart; and hee said it was true. And then I opened to him the false teachers; and lett him see where wee differd from all ye teachers of ye world; and from their worshipps; and where the true teacher and the true worshipp was; where all might come to the true teacher w^{t}hin them and the spirit, and so hee sett mee at liberty & said I might go where I would, and so the truth passed over all and spread mightyly. One great opposition it had through ye priests, professors and lawyers; but ye power of ye lord god and ye truth confounded them all, and none was able to stand before it.

And then I passed into Kent and Sussex, & Surrey and Middlesex, where I had great large meettings; and sometimes great contention w^{t}h the Professors of Scriptures w^{t}hout the life of it, but truth stopped their mouths, and came over; the truth y^t answers that of God, in all men and women; which multitudes came to look in to their own houses and to find their teacher, and the lord at hand; w^{c}h they looked to bee farre from them; though prisons and bonds were threatned.

Then I was moved to come to london ag^n [and truth had great wrestling with all bad spirits, such as had great proffessions and lived not in ye life of truth. And such as had Notions, and sometimes had had tendernes but it was hardned w^{c}h they wrestled ag^t the life. but ye life y^t comes over all came over.]

So then I passed into Northfolke, and Suffolk where I had brave meettings; where there was an Independant Justice in a town where I had spoken; where there were many sober people; hee could not tell how to take mee y^t hee might ensnare mee, but he sent forth a Hue and cry after mee and another friend that was w^{t}h mee[1] that there was a house broken on ye seventh day at night, this hee did in his wickednesse though hee was a great professor; and so they seised upon us after ye meeting was done, and came after us five miles; and had us the next day before a justice. And so there were severall friends y^t had been w^{t}h us upon the first day meetting w^{c}h cleared us before ye Justice where wee were the seventh day. And so this Justice was madd

because hee could have nothing ag^t us; who did confesse
that wee were not such men; and was sorry y^t hee had no
more ag^t us.

And so wee passed away to lin where wee had a fine
meetting where severall were convinced. And so upp into
Cambridgeshire where wee had a fine meetting[1]; where there
were severall hundreds^a, where there was three or four priests
and all was quiet but one; and truth answered to that of god
in all, and came over and was honourable in the hearts of
people; and so after ye meetting was done I passed to Cambridge; and when I came there the people and schollers
abused friends much in ye streets; and the town was all in
an uproar hearing of my comeing to the town; And there
was an Alderman[2] who was a friend; and hee came to the
Inne to us; and the people thronging upp into ye very
chamber door in the Inne, and so after a while it being in
ye Evening; I passed through all ye Multitude, but they did
not know of mee; and had a sweet heavenly meetting in his
house.

And the next day past away upp into Hardfordshire and
so to london where I had many and great meettings; [and discourse and dispute w^{c}h were larg to tell of; and all ye bad
spirits rose against truth but ye truth is y^t w^{c}h answers y^e
witnesse of God in all.]

And then I came down into Bedfordshire, and Buckinghamshire, and Northamptonshire and Lestershire; where the truth
spread mightily; and multitudes of people flocked to ye truth
and to hear it; and severall snares there were, but the power
of ye lord passed over them; And in Lecestershire where the
priests had been so madd against mee, there was one priest
[wise^{b3}] which had a great deale of men, many were flocking
about his men; and none did meddle w^{t}h mee at that time.

I passed to Esom where the Magistrates had many
friends in prison, and hearing of mee, they made a paire of
stocks, a yard and an halfe high, and a trapp door to sett
them in; purposely they said for mee; but I came into y^e
Town and had a brave meetting; and the next morning I
passed away; and some of them followed mee; but I had
visited ye prisoners and was upon horse back; and seing them

---

^{a} Vol. I. p. 189: *a multitude of people*
^{b} C has *wife*, altered to *wise*

come up the street as I was passing away wth severall other
friends.

So wee past to Worster where wee had a fine meetting,
and in the evening as I came down ye street there was an
uproar made in ye street and people Hurryed after us into
ye Inne, yet wee received no hurt it was a mighty deliverance.

And so then we came to warwicke, in the Evening wee
had a meetting^a, and as I was passing away in comes y^e
Bayliffe of ye Town wth other officers and took us to the
Inne; [And they were not to passe away till they had Orders
from him;] So then the next morning as I went forth of the
town I went to speak to ye Bayliffe; after hee had sett
friends at liberty; and the Town rose upp against us in y^e
open street, and one laid hold upon my horse bridle; my
horse being a stronge horse turned his head, and turned y^e
man under his feet; [and so hee hung upon ye Bridle, and
so there came another man or two to throw stones at my
face; and so hee was stopped, and was made to loosse the
other mans hands; y^t hunge at ye horsse bridle;] and so as
wee rode through ye streets people fell upon us wth Cudgels
and stones and throwing at us and much abused us; and so
when wee were Ridden quite thorow ye Markett, I was moved
of the lord to go back ag^n into ye street [to offerr up my life
among them,] and said to friends who ever found fredome
might follow mee, and so I passed upp the street and people
fell upon mee wth their Cudgels and abused mee and strucke
mee [and threw the horsse down yet by ye power of ye lord
I passed thorow them; and called upon the town and shopp
keepers & told them of their Immodest state;] how they were
a shame to Christians and the profession of christianity.

And so past away and came into Coventry; [and so into
Dentry¹ where I had some jangling with priests; and every
where the priests and people and professors opposed our
doctrine wch was and is y^t every man y^t cometh into ye world
is enlightned wth the light of christ; wth which they might
see their sinnes, when they turned ag^t this light w^thin; they
first turned against it their own particulars; and then keeps
people from it in the generall, and then becomes darker and
harder then ever they were; and losses both truth sence
and reason in the matter of true reasoning and disputeing.]

^a Vol. i. p. 198 adds *att a widow womans house*

And so I passed to london, and after a litle time in visiteing friends I passed into sussex and surrey and Hampshire and Dorsestershire [when there were but few convinced and some place none at all.]

And so passed upp to Plimouth and so upp into Cornwell; [through many desperate services and great oppositions, but through the power of ye lord god came over all.]

And so came into Cornwell [a dark countrey] where wee had a meetting[1]; and many priests and professors came; and one priests mouth was stopped, wee made him confesse hee was a states minister sent by them and not by Christ; but truth was received by many; and so wee passed on as farre as Market Jew[2] and had a good service in many places in publishing the truth; [And so when wee came thither in ye Evening; I heard one say that those men should be examined before they go away Therefore I was not to go away till I was examined;] so in ye morning the Maior and ye Aldermen sent for us by the Constables to go to the Town Hall; So wee asked for their warrant and they had none upon wch wee did not go; at last they sent a Mace for us; and so at last one of us went; and had good service amongst them; and brought ye truth over all; and so when wee were freed wee passed away.

And then I gave forth a pap^r to bee delivered among ye People a litle beyond Markett Jew; concerning that Christ was ye light of ye world and hee was their teacher, and they were to learn of him, and hear him; and come to the lord [which was a paper to ye Conditions of y^t dark people;] and so a friend gave it y^t came after mee; and hee told mee and as soon as hee had given it I felt wee were as taken prisoners; [but he should have given it mee before he gave it abroad. But I saw it would bee well; for if I fell upon that bad nature, I should crush it and make the good to come forth.]

The Paper was to one Justice Sillis[3] Clerke, which went before us to the town, wee lodged in the town, so I walked down to the sea, where they were shooing my horse; and w^n I came back all ye town was upp in an uproar; and they were Haleing of friends before ye Justices; and were pressing horsses to go into ye Countrey after us; and so wee went into ye Justices house, and had a great deale of discourse of the thinges of god. And yet hee was light and vaine; And so hee made a Mittimus and sent us to prison the next morning w^{t}h a party of horse and so being ye Markett day at St Ives, wee had good service to speake the truth amongst them.

So they carried us w^{t}h a party of horse to Redruth y^t night; and the next day being the first day; wee were not very willing to travaile; So one friend gote from the soldio^{rs}; & went to ye steeplehouse[1], and so after the steeple was done wee had a fine meetting w^{t}h ye people; but ye Soldio^{rs} were angry and then after a while wee passed; Some of ye people were satisfied. And after I was gone a litle way out of the Town; I was moved to go back ag^n to speak to ye People; and ye Souldio^{rs} were very desperate w^{t}h their pistols and swords [but the truth brought all under; for they rode after mee w^{t}h their pistols and they rode and I rode; and I discharged my selfe and when I had done I passed w^{t}h them.]

And then wee passed to Pendinniscastle to ye Governour[2] where wee staid all night at ye town neare unto it; where the Constables and ye people of ye town came to us and many were convinced; and people generally loving towards us. And there was a plott among some bad spirits to have done us a mischiefe; and about ye eleaventh houre of ye night a friend[3] was moved to shutt ye door where ye souldio^{rs} had put us; and ye next morning in comes a fellow and runnes upon mee; and fell a strikeing; and thought to have throwen mee down; but I stood still; and called for ye soldio^r y^t Commanded the party[4]; and asked him if he would own it; and hee said hee would; hee would own him to abuse us, upon which wee sent for the constable y^t was loving; and desired him to read his Order for his was to conduct us safely; and hee said hee would sufferr us to bee abused; w^{c}h was below men; And so the Constable and sober people wished us not to go along w^{t}h him to ye Governour, for the Governour was not at home; but wee passed, and so Desbury[5], w^{c}h was one of ye lord leivtenants in Oliver time; Severall knew mee & had mee to him, [but he being a hard hearted man sleigted us.]

So wee passed on wth ye souldiors y^t night, and so when wee came to an Inne, hee y^t said hee would tollerate y^t man to abuse us; hee putts mee into ye roome where there was a man wth a Naked rapyer in his hand: And so as soone as I was in ye Inne I turned mee about and called upon the Commander and asked him what hee meant by that; And hee desired mee to hold my tongue for if I spoke to him, they all could not rule him. I said dost thou put mee into a Roome wth a man y^t cannot be ruled, wth a Naked rapiour.

And so the next day at night wee came to ye prison at Lansõn and so the was there nine weeks till ye sessions under a very bad Goaler who much abused us; And when the Assizes came wee were brought before ye Judg[1]: and a great concourse of People there were gathered together to hear our Tryall; the noyce of Quakers being a strang thing unto them; And so when wee were brought before him to ye Barre; hee looked upon us, and wee stood still, wth o^r hatts on; And hee asked ye Goaler whether wee were prisoners. And hee said yes; and hee bid us put off o^r hatts; and then the Goaler took off our hatts, and gave them to us, and wee put them on againe[2]. And hee bidd us putt off our hatts And I bidd him shew mee a law y^t Commanded it; or where any of ye people of god or heathens; Moses or Nebuccadnezar Commanded any to put off their hatts in their Courts that were brought before them. And hee bidd the Goaler take us away; hee would firk[a] us.

And then hee bid him bring us upp againe; and hee bidd us put off our hatts, and I asked him for a law againe; and he told mee hee did[b] carry his law books upon his Back; and I bidd him tell where it was written y^t men should put off their hatts; when they were called into courts &c. for that was an honour below; and hee asked mee, where they had hatts or wore hatts from Moses to Daniel shew me a Scripture. I said in Daniel the three children was cast into ye fire wth their coates, hosen and hatts, [and you may see Nebuccadnezar was not offended att their hatts,] and hee bidd take us away againe And so put us among theeves; And then caused us to bee brought upp againe; and an Inditement was brought against us for wearing our hatts before him; and so wee cryed to have our Mittimus read in y^e open court; y^t wee might know what wee had lyen in prison for

---

[a] A: *firke*; B: *fine* altered to *sink* and then to *firk*; C: *firk* inserted in original blank. *Encyc. Dict.*:=to beat, whip, correct, punish.
[b] Vol. I. p. 212: *I doe not carry* The negative is omitted from A, B, C.

all that nine weeks; And so hee would not suffer it. So I
bid a friend read it upp; and hee said hee should not; hee
would see whether hee or I were master; And so the friend[1]
read y^e Mittimus upp aloud, and overcame them all in ye open
court.

And the Justice y^t sent us to prison whose name was
syley said in ye open court y^t I had struck him; and I
asked him where—hee said in ye castle yard. I asked who
was by; hee nodded att another Justice, but hee said nothing.
hee had mee in ye castle yard, and said how do you Sir,
and I bad him take heed of hypocrisie and deceit, and y^t
was the thing hee called strickeing, for the other was wickednes in him and then the same Justice said y^t I went aside
wth him, and told him I could raise [four hundred[2]] men in
a dayes warning; hee had a witness of it; and said how
serviceable hee might bee to mee: Then I desired him to
come off of ye Bench seing hee was an accuser; and stand
wth mee, wch I appeale to them all whether this man if it
were so were faithfull to his trust; to send me wth his
mittimus to prison for good behaviour, wch If I put in
Suertice then had I been gone and also hee said to ye Judg
y^t hee would^a us out of ye Countrey if I would
have gone; So by y^t they might all see how his words
savourd, and none of them beleeved him.

And so they sent us to prison againe; and kept us a great
while; and ye Goaler put us in Doomsdayle[3] because wee
would not satisfie him in his oppression; and give him his
rate for Dyet, and put the theeves over o^r heads. and in y^e
place called doomsdaile a nasty stinking place, where there
was not a house of office; nor chimney; and stray like
Chaffe; wee might have gone a topp of our shooes in water
in some places of it, & made morter wth our shooes in other
places of it; and wee gote a litle strawe one night to burn
in ye Roome to take away the smell. And the head Goaler
came among the theeves over our heads and stamped w^th
his foot and stick; and poured out Excrements in a Chamber
pott upon our heads; and quenched out our fire; and wee

---

^a Three letters were written and crossed out and a blank left after them.
The letters were, probably, *hav* A has *y^t he would out of ye Countrey*;
B and C have a space between *would* and *us*. Vol. I. p. 214: *woulde have
aided him* and p. 215: *would feigne have had him*

could not have liberty to cleanse the prison; it was called doomsdaile, because many received their end there and dyed in it and wee were kept a great while prisoners in that Town and castle I think a great part or ye most part of a year; And att last our abuses came to London to White hall; So one Densbury aforementioned came up to examine o^r abuses; and a while after wee were sett at liberty.

And as wee were passing to ye prison ye man y^t did abuse mee near pendinnis castle; wch hee y^t was commander of ye party owned ye action of abuseing of us; ye Noyce of y^t went up to white hall and an Order was sent down to Examine y^t matter, & ye man was much rebuked by ye Justices and the Governour and left open to ye law to be punished which was a mighty service for truth; for before it was a hard thing for a friend to speak in a town, markett or steeple house; which y^t gave way for all they being a desperate people; for they cryed all who durst meddle wth them, seing ye powers had owned them.

And when I was in prison there being abundance convinced; ye noyce was y^t none was able to speak to us one word for ten^a; severall came to dispute wth us; there came an officer, and being a bad contender and vaine disputer; his mouth was shutt on a sudden y^t hee could not speak nor able to open his mouth; and another who was a Justice[1] came full of words to dispute and hee was so full of words there was no roome to speak to him; it was said to him; was hee never at Schoole; did hee never know w^t belonged to a question and answere, & would hee hear nothing; they said hee was a Collonel; And so what ever hee was it was said to him hee did not do that wch became Civillity; And so he was desired to hold his peace [or see if hee could hold his peace a litle while till truth were spoken to him; and then the light were spoken of to him, wch lett him see his sinfull life y^t hee had lived in, and his words and his wayes, y^t would bee his teacher to lead him from them, if hee minded it; and his condemnation if hee acted ag^t it. And if hee had any thing to speak hee might speak] and hee was strucken dumb and his mouth was shutt, and hee cast his head upp and down and his face sweld, and hee

---

^a Vol. I. p. 225: *y^t ye Judge & Justices was not able to aunswer us one worde in 12*

could not speak for a good space, his face was as red as a
Turkey.

We had liberty to walk a litle way of the prison, and I
was laid down in a slumber and I felt somthing stricke at
my body; and I gote upp and struck at it againe wth y^e
power of ye lord, yet it was compassing about mee; so I
went up into ye prison and about ye eleaventh houre at night
ye head Goaler came and told us hee had gote a man to dispute wth us, wch was a plott. And so the next morning I
told ye under Goaler that their plott was discovered; for
when hee told mee hee had gote a man to dispute, I felt
what it was y^t struck att my body though I kept it w^thin
my selfe, and had not spoken of it. Neverthelesse I went
to ye place where ye dispute was to bee and there was none
appeared; and so I went into ye head Goalers; I told him
his plott was discovered; and so hee being eating meat hee
wrung his hands and gote from ye table, and threw his napkin away in a rage, so I went up into my Roome and when
I was there the fellow y^t I should have disputed wth all
called mee down, I went to ye head of ye staires, being then
put upp into a chamber; and the Goalers wife was upon
the staires betwixt mee and the man; he having his hand
behind him, I asked what hee had in his hand; hee was
very loath to lett mee see, so I bidd him pluck his hand
from behind him, why did hee hold it behind him, So hee
took it from behind him; and hee had a naked knife; for
hee had threatned before how hee would cutt my flesh; [So
truth came over, and many Miracoulous deliverance I had
wch would make a great volumn if they should be declared.]

Friends coming to visite us the Maior being a bad man; hee
would search ye women to their very head cloaths, being a
drunken bad man and loose; his condition was written, and
a friend went out of ye townes end wth it in his pocket w^ch
was the maiors bad life; the friend coming into ye town
againe hee searched ye friends pockett and found it; w^ch
was his own condition and bad life; and so y^t stopped him
for searching of friends any more after hee saw his own
Condicõn[1].

And after wee were sett att liberty wee passed to Exeter
where wee had many fine meettings. And then to Bristol,

where there was a great meeting upon the first day, many
thousands of people, and I had not been there before ; and
there was a bad man[1] y[t] did intend to make a Tumult in
ye Citty having form[rly] made disturbance amongst friends
meettings ; and hee having encouragement from some badd
people in y[e] town to do the same, that they might have had
some occation ag[t] our meetting ; So we went into an Orchard ;
where the bad man came, where I stood up and looked upon
the people and spoke never a word ; and yet this man said
I affirmed y[t] w[ch] I could not make good ; and so shamed
him selfe before all y[e] people, and was a shame to y[e] very
worst of people, and so truth came over all and y[e] wicked
lost his end ; and then I passed through the Countrey
through friends to London.

And in these dayes which was in y[e] dayes of y[e] Protector ;
hee gave forth an Oath of Abjuration to bee taken w[ch] the
bad Justices made use of ag[t] friends, knowing friends could
not sweare, and cast many into prison by it. [And also a
proclamation ag[t] vagrants[2] and Sturdy Beggars hee gave
forth w[ch] bad Justices made use of and took friends some
wth 40 and 50 pounds a year and whipped them as Sturdy
Beggars, and vagrants w[ch] were Sober people and feared
the lord god and chargeable to no man. And also y[e] many
petitions there was against us by y[e] priests and professors
to the Protector and Parliament but all could not do, the
truth came over all, and dayly spread, for they were like
unto y[e] task masters of egypt, and after a tyme being at
London and wth Oliv[r] the protector was moved to speak
wth him.]

I was moved to pass upp and down the Countrey to visite
friends ; and y[e] priests where I came and had meettings
they would have fled and so I was moved to pass back
againe to Exeter[3] where friends came out of Cornwell to
meett mee where wee had a meetting ; and some of y[e]
Magistrates came down, but I was passed away before. And
great threatnings there was after me.

And before as I passed up into Cornwell at Absom[4] there
wth much ado I escaped out of y[e] Town the people was
madd and y[e] Magistrates and so I went from Exeter to
Sommersetshire, at a meetting where there was a thousand
people.

And after I had been at Bristol I passed into wales [into every County in wales[1], when I came to Kardigen I lodged at a Justices house and had a brave meetting at a great house in y[e] Town; So wee came into Kardiken; and being upon a Markett day friends spoke in the Markett, and all the Town was in an uproar, but wee passed quietly out of y[e] Town after I had spoken the truth among them.]

So wee came to Tenby where a Justice[2] received mee into his house, and another friend[3] wth mee; And the Maior[4] and his wife came to y[e] meetting; and was convinced; and the friend went to y[e] steeple house y[t] was wth mee, to speak the truth to y[e] priest and people; and y[e] Governour cast him into prison; and the next day hee sent his Marshall for mee to come before him, having gotten another Justice; and so y[e] Maior and y[e] Justice y[t] were convinced went upp to him; and I went after. So I asked him hee were the governour; and wherefore hee cast the friend into prison, And hee said for standing wth his hatt upon his head when the minister[5] and y[e] people sung: And I told him had not the priest two capps upon his head, and if the friend should should[a] cutt off the Brim of his hatt; then hee would have but one, for the Brim was to save the Raine off his neck and shoulders; & hee cryed away wth these frevolous thinges; And then I asked him why hee imprisoned the friend for frevelous thinges, So I bidd him mind the light in his conscience wch lett him see the evill deeds hee had done, and y[t] would bee his teacher or his condemnation, if hee hated it, and so hee began to dispute about election and Reprobaçon, so I was moved to tell him y[t] hee was in the reprobation; at which hee stormed; and threatned hee will keep mee fast untill I prove that. I said I would prove y[t] quickly if hee would hold his tongue. So I asked him whether that malice, envy, passion, hast, foolishness; whether were they in y[e] Election or in y[e] Reprobation. And hee said it was in the reproba- tion, And so I asked him if y[t] were not his condition and hee confessed it was. So I lett him see how y[e] Election and reprobation stood in y[e] two births; and so brought[b] moderate, And the other Justice loving. And so hee freed mee and my

[a] This repetition appears in B and C; in A the second *should* is inter- linear.
[b] The writer of A first wrote *him* and then erased the word.

friend out of prison; and hee proved moderate, and ye other
Justice y^t hee had to have helped him proved loving, and
shouked mee by ye hand; And ye Governour would have
had mee to have dined wth him. So wee passed away[1] to
Hartford west, where wee visited friends. And to Pembrook
where wee had a meetting, being a fair. And the fair time
was in Hartford west and friends, and spoke in ye market.

So wee passed away to [Kirnarven;] where the friend
spoke in ye town y^t ·was wth mee [and was cast into prison
for bidding them repent & fear the lord. And many came
down to mee to ye Inne; So after when the friend when^a
sett att liberty] wee passed on to ye next County; & so the
friend y^t was wth mee spoke in ye streets, and they put
him out of ye towne but they were pretty moderate. And
wee had some discourse wth ye priests and people of ye truth
and so passed away.

And then wee came to [Merrannishire;][2] where wee had a
great meetting ye friend spoke in ye street; and there came
two priests and fell a disputeing in welsh before abundance
of people. And said y^t ye light spoken of in John which
doth enlighten every man y^t commeth into ye world was a
created light and made and a Naturall light, and a Naturall
Conscience. And I said y^t unto them y^t ye created or made
light was ye Sunne & ye Moone and ye Starres, and ye light
wch Christ had enlightened y^m w^thall was y^t which lett y^m
see their sinnes; the same would lett y^m see their salvation.

So wee passed to Braknock town; and ye friend spoke in
ye street, and I was walking a litle forth wth another friend[3],
and when I came into ye street, ye streets were in an uproar;
and ye street where I was, so I went and discoursed with y^e
people, and after some time when they had heard ye truth I
passed away; but ye street continued in an uproar about an
hour and one halfe; and some y^t had been Magistrates
shoutting amongst them; and setting on the people to shout,
And they had a Plott amongst them together wth the woman
of ye Inne, to have had us out of y^t roome where wee were,
wch wee had taken upp; into another Room to have supped,
a great Hall. And so I looked at ye Room, and perceiving
the plott, I bid ye woman bring our meat into o^r own chamber,
for there was a table sufficient; and chuse her whether she

^a A and B have *when*; C has *when* altered to *was*

would bring it or not then shee wished us out of her house,
and wee told her wee had taken a house of her and grasse,
and so when they could not by any meanes to get us out
then they came by flattery; but the lord prevented their
mischiefe for they had in intend to have murdred us; And
so ye next day wee passed away.

And wee had a meetting Ratnelshire; where wee had
many thousands of people[a]; And there were priests and many
of Gentry of ye Country came and many were satisfied and
convinced concerning truth, and it was reported If I had had
another meetting half ye Countrey would have comed in they
were so taken with ye truth.

So wee passed into Blew Morrice; and when wee went to
our Inne; the friend spake in ye streets, and hee was cast
into prison; and they said they were seeking of mee, but
did not come to ye Inne; and ye next day hee was sett at
liberty; And so wee had a fine time being ye Markett day,
I spoke amongst them the truth largly.

And so came into Cheshire[1] where wee had a meetting
about thre thousand[b] 3000 people and all quiet.

And so came into ye North through friends meettings and
so passed through Lancashire and Cumberland; and into
Scotland[2] through friends; and when I came a matter of four
score miles into Scotland, the priests petitioned ye Counsell;
and ye cry was among them all was undone. And so when
I came upp into Edenbourough; having been in severall
parts of ye Nation y^t the people was so bad they would
hardly give us lodging for our money. So when wee came
to Edenbouroug an Order was graunted out from ye Counsell
sitting in ye Parliament house for mee to appear y^t day
seventh night and so I did; and the door keeper took off
my hatt. And when I came before them I said peace be
amongst y^u. They asked mee w^t I came for into y^t nation;
I said to visite ye seed of God which had long lyen in death
and bondage; and to ye intent y^t people might come into y^e
spirit of God y^t gave forth ye Scriptures wch they professed;
and y^t in ye spirit they might have all[c] unity wth god and

---

[a] Vol. I. p. 273: *meetinge like a leager for multitudes*
[b] A: *threthousand people*; B has *thre thousand* inserted; C reads as
original.
[c] A omits *all*

ye scriptures and wth one another and bid them waite in the
fear of God to receive his wisdom by which all thinges were
made and Ordred y^t wth that they might bee Ordred to
Gods glory; and Order all things y^t God had given them
under their hands wth his wisdom to his glory. So they
desired mee to go out and then they called mee in againe;
and told mee I must depart the Naçon wthin seven dayes.
I asked them wherefore; and what was the cause, and they
desired mee to wthdraw; and I desired them to hear and
give mee a reason and the cause why; and they would not.
And I told them Herod heard John Baptizts; And Pharoah
heard Moses.

And so the door keeper took mee out; and y^n I was moved
to pass upp and down the Nation and came to Glascoe;
where there was many people gone to see a horse and a man
runne[1], where I had brave service in speaking the truth
among them and so wee passed to Johnstonns[2], where wee
were banished out of the town; and guarded out by souldiours,
being taken out of a friends house[3]; which the soldiours were
greeved, and they said they had rather have gone to Jemaica[4].
And then wee came to another Markett town, where there
were some friends where wee appoynted a meetting in the
towne hall; And to crosse us the Magistrates appoynted a
meetting; and so wee had it att ye Crosse in the Markett
day. And so truth had a good savour, though some were
rude. So I came to Leith And so to Edenbourough; where
I heard there were Warrants graunted out for mee, for the
seaven dayes were long past.

So after I had been at Edenbourough I passed againe just
by the place where I was Banished; which when I came
their some of the officers were astonished; and ye guards did
not question mee. And when I was off that Burden I passed
away. And so I came back againe to Edenbourough where
I had a brave meetting the first day; And all quiet and none
of ye guards questioned mee there neither. I was moved to
ride quite through the town over their guards And I saw I
went over their very Musketts, cannons; pistols, pikes, &
very sword ends.

And so the next day I passed away towards Dunbarr; and
w^n I came wthin sight of ye steeple house a great way off
it struck at mee y^t I should have a meetting the next day

in ye steeple house yard, [Many friends were wth mee that were turned out of ye Army.] And so I went upp into ye steeple house yard, there was one of ye chiefe men in ye town walking in the steeple house yard; And I sent a friend to tell to him there would bee a meetting of ye people of God wch ye world calls Quakers in the steeple house yard the next Morning by ye Ninth hour; And hee said the Lecture would bee by nine. And said wee should have it sooner. And so wee bid him give Notice and hee did. And the next Morning wee had a brave meetting, wch lasted till after ye lecture was done; And so ye priest heard a while & some professors disputed; but truth came over all; So wee passed away [in ye truth and escaped imprisonment into England] to Barwick; [And so it would bee larg to declare all ye service y^t was in Scotland; and ye sufferrings & ye service[1].]

When I came into Scotland many being convinced of truth & severall disputes there were wth ye priests. And they gave forth an Order[2] to bee read in the steeple house wch was curssed bee hee y^t denyed ye sabboth day. And all ye people was to say amen. And curssed was hee y^t said hee had a light from Christ y^t would lead him to salvation. And lett all ye people say amen. And curssed bee hee y^t said faith was pure. And lett all ye people say amen. And by this they manifested their darknesse for faith is pure and purifies. And Christ ends the Jews sabboth and this is denyed in all Christendom in words and practice, and Christ doth enlighten every man y^t Commeth into the world to salvation or Condemnation if hee hate it. And also ye priests of Scotland principle was that God had Ordained the greatest part of men and women ^a of ye world^a for hell lett them pray or do all that ever they could do, w^thout any cause lesse or more or fault in the creature; God had Ordained them for hell; & God had Ordained a number of Men and Women for heaven, lett them sin or do whatsoever they could do they should bee saved; And to prove it was in Jude of Ould were they Ordained for this condemnation. And all may read that Scripture and see whether there was not a fault and a cause in man wherefore God did condemn him for it sayes they were ungodly men; and denyed God and ye lord Jesus Christ y^t bought them and turned his grace into wantonnesse; and

^a...^a A omits *of ye world*

went in Cains way which was murder; and Balaams way
from the spirit, which taught ye people to Committ fornica-
tion, And in Cores way which gainsayed the law. And was
clouds w^{t}hout raine, and wells w^{t}hout water, and were twise
dead, And plucked up by ye roots; And yet these priests
could see no cause why this people should bee condemned.
And them y^t do sin and do unrighteously there Righteousnesse shall bee remembred no more, and if they sin wilfully
after they receive the knowledg of ye truth there remaines no
more sacrifice for sin. [And this corrupt doctrice is spread
over all Scotland and most part of England. And the grace
of God which brings salvation which hath appeared to all
men w^{c}h taught the saintes to live righteously and soberly &c.^{a}
This grace if it bee minded and regarded to teach them, and
its teaching it will bring every man to salvation. And this
was in Oliver Protectors dayes.]

And I passed to England and upp and down the Nation a
great part of ye Nation to London and Bedfordshire; [where
I had a matter of three or four Thousand people.]^1

So went upp to London and the sufferrings of friends in
England, Scotland and Ireland and beyond seas was sent
to Oliver Protector and ye Parliament to see y^t they might
bee warned; and y^t they might not do such thinges, for
if they did the Judgments of ye lord might come upon
them; and severall times friends were moved to go to
offerr upp their bodyes for mee (when I was in prison)^2 to
the Protector; and wee were moved to warn them of y^e
Judgments of ye lord God; And another tyme a matter
of two hundred were moved to offer upp themselves to
ye parliament, for to go into the Nasty holes and prisons.
And so would have had ye parliament to have taken their
bodies y^t the other might be released; to stay the Judgment
of God from comming upon them which was in love to god
to the brethren and to them. And so they sent friends away
and threatned them; and said Quakers should not meet;
and w^{t}hin two or three dayes; ye Parliament was Broken
upp and they did not meet. Then many disputers and many
unclean spirits turned ag^t ye truth and runne out which
was generally against friends and mee but the seed of God
came over all, which seed was the first and the last. [And

^{a} A: *& this grace*

then the Protector dyed. And then his sonne Richard was called Protector in whose dayes there was great sufferrings; and many Imprisonments but truth gote over all, and sufferings were laid upon him and his Councell and Parliament.

And then another Parliament gote upp and Richard Cromwell was put out, and all ye parliaments y^t gote upp one after another upon them all ye sufferrings of ye people of God was laid, in all ye Dominions. And then the Committee of safety[1] gote upp; and all ye parliaments were turned out, in whose dayes still wee sufferred by them, & many Imprisonments and sufferrings were laid upon their heads and they fell.] And ye parliament gote upp again and sufferings were laid upon them wch were upp and down in ye Nation. And all manner of evills and abuses were cast upon us by priests & Professors, and threatnings and flatteries and temptations to ye honours of ye world by preferments, till at last ye Conclusion was amongst them y^t wee were a people beyond all professors, which could not bee gained by gifts nor preferments wch all others could[2].

I had form^rly a meeting in Wales[3] where there were many Teachers, Baptizts and two Priests and a great dispute. And the Bayliffe of ye Town came upp; and there mouths had been stopped for two or three houres. And then one priest[4] said ye light y^t wee spoke of was Naturall created & made. And I bid all people take out their Bibles for I would make ye Scriptures bend him [though hee did not matter of ye spirit] So I asked him whether the light wherew^th Christ had enlightned every man y^t commeth into ye world; whether y^t were a made or created light or not. And hee said yes. And ye priest runne so farre out at last y^t hee said Christ and God was Naturall and created. for I shewed them y^t ye light y^t John spoke of was spirituall and not created; for it was ye word and ye word was god. And hee was light, and so ye truth came over all and their mouthes stopped, and ye good in ye hearts of people was gladed and truth came over all; and wee passed.

Then I came into Yorkshire where there were many Thousands of people ^a came to a meetting^a. In those dayes Lambert was upp[5]; the power was quarrelling one wth another

yet oʳ meettings were preserved though they came[1] wᵗh a
troope of horse to our meetting and trumpetts sounding and
rode upp just to mee as I was speaking; hee yᵗ did Command
them; So I and wee Moderated yᵉ mans spirit; [& told
him our meetting was made acquainted a great while before
and it was in no hurt to yᵉ powers;] and perswaded him to
bee quiet; and if hee had any Jealousie search every man
and woman; Or and if hee would not tarry himself, leav half
a dozen to see the Order of oʳ meetting; and so hee did he
said he had comed eight and twenty miles; and we bid them
go into the house to refresh themselves, and they did. And
oʳ meetting was preserved in the power of yᵉ lord God, and
friends parted in yᵉ truth and yᵉ power of yᵉ lord God
over all.

[And so I passed through friends into yᵉ North through
meettings. And this was the third time I had been most
part about yᵉ Nation.

And in the dayes of Oliver and his sonne Richard and yᵉ
Parliamᵗˢ if I or friends had been moved to go into a steeple
house and looked in any of yᵉ priests faces their mouthes
would have been stopped; they would have gone away the
power of yᵉ lord was so over them and they would have
comed down out of the pulpitt in many places and many
times they would have done so. The power of God would
have gone so over them they being so full of deceit, yᵗ it
would have choaked them.]

[*In the King's Tyme*]

And when I came down into yᵉ North I passing through
Lancashire when I had been [about a Moneth] at Swarthmoore and yᵗ awayes [after King Charles was comed in to
England] one called Justice Porter[2] wᵗh four or five more of
yᵉ Magistrates gave forth a warrant to the chiefe Constable
I feeling somthing of darkness in the house before they
came in of somthing of a great darkness. And so yᵉ chiefe
Constable came the next day after I had felt yᵗ wᵗh three
or four more private Constables; pretending to search the
house for Armes So I was going forth of yᵉ house and
called for a friend but hee did not come. So I went back
againe to call him and so mett yᵉ Constables coming down

ye stayres; and he asked mee my name; and I told him
and hee said I was ye man they look^d for. And they took
mee to ulverston, and when they brought me thither they
gloried much, and said they did not beleeve y^t a thousand
men should have taken^a, and so they kept mee at a Constables
house, & sett fifteen or sixteen men to watch mee all night;
their foolishnes and wickednes was so great; that they were
affraid I would have gone upp the Chimney And so I satt
upp all night; and they would hardly lett any friends come
to mee to bring mee necessarie things; And so ye next
morning the Town was upp and a matter of thirty horse
went along wth mee; and they sett mee upon a poor little
horsse with a Halter upon his head and sett mee upp behind
ye Saddle; after they had taken my knife from mee; So
they made ye horsse to kick; which I gote off again and told
them they should not abuse ye creature; And then they
lifted mee upon him againe. And after a while they lett
mee ryde upon another [of a friends;] and so led mee a matter
of sixteen miles to Lancaster in an halter without any Brydle,

And so brought mee to Justice Porter; who made mee a
Mittimus & sent mee to prison And how that I should not
bee delivered but by king and parliament quite out of any
Course of law or Goal delivery; [hee being a slanderous bad
tongued man] put in the Mittimus how y^t I and my faculty
was an Enemy to ye king. And I and my faculty^b was im-
brewing the whole kingdome into blood and raising a New
warre. which wee and o^r principles were knowen to ye nation
to bee peaceable; [and so I was kept in prison from May
day till towards Michaelmas,] Then I was had upp to
London.

And porters charge to the Goaler was to put mee in
to a dark house, and lett none come to mee; [but who
brought mee a little meat.] And so I was sent upp to
London And the Sheriffs and ye Bayliffs were so brought
down by ye power of God that they lett mee go upp w^th
two friends[1], and had meettings in ye way as I went; And
when I came to London they were burning ye Bowels^c of

---

^a Vol. I. p. 359 adds *mee*
^b That is, *company* as in vol. I. p. 375, and *Friends* in Ell. text (I. 485).
For *faculty* see vol. I. pp. 365, 366.
^c A omits *Bowels*

some that they had put to death And so I went to yᵉ Judg¹
and hee was putting on a redd Gown and was to sitt uppon
ᵃsome yᵗ was to dyeᵃ; and so bidd us come another tyme and
so wee went another tyme And when I came to him againe
hee called for yᵉ chiefe Justice of England² and so they read
my Mittimus, How yᵗ I and my faculty was raising a New
warre and embrewing yᵉ kingdome into blood and an Enemy
to yᵉ king And they lift upp their hands I told them I
was the man and I was as Innocent and pure as a child
concerning these thinges. & was it a like thing that I and
my faculty should bee raiseing a new warre to embrew the
Nation into blood and an Enemy to yᵉ king. and yᵉ sheriffs
and Justices and Officers of Lancashire sent mee upp hither
a matter of two hundred Miles, wᵗʰ two of my own faculty,
and so they called for yᵉ Goaler of yᵉ kings to take mee into
Custody & bring mee to morrow into Westminster hall; for
there they said they had more strength And so they bid
yᵉ Goaler not put mee into prison; and hee told them hee
had no where else to putt mee all was so full they told him
hee should not put mee there, they told mee If I said I
would appeare at Westminster hall to Morrow about yᵉ
tenth hour they beleeved I would not tell a lie And so I
told them I should If the lord permitted and so parted And
yᵉ next day I appeared there about yᵉ time [and so I was in
a topp of yᵉ board where the parchments lyes] And friends
that went along wᵗʰ mee delivered in their papers to them.

    And they read the charg against mee [and there was no
accusor appeared when they had read the charg] I streatched
forth my hands and said I was yᵉ man yᵗ the charg was agᵗ
but I was innocent and pure as a child, for I never learned
yᵉ postures of warre, and I loved all men; I was Enemy to
no man; and was it a likely thing yᵗ I should bee sent upp
by two of mine own facultie a matter of two hundred miles
by yᵉ Magistrates and Sheriffs and Officers of Lancashire yᵗ
should bee such a man yᵗ would Imbrew the whole kingdome into blood and Raise a New warre, were the Majes-
trats of Lancashire faithfull to their trust in doing such a
thing; I had need to have had two or three troopes of
horsse if I had been such a man. I told them I was Inno-

ᵃ...ᵃ Vol. I. p. 365: *some more of ye kinges Judges*

cent and pure concerning all such thinges wch were charged against mee; they asked mee whether I would travers or file it I told them they were Judges and understood my cause lett them do w^t they would. And then they put it to the king and the Councell; which presently after ye King graunted forth a warrant to one Judge Mallard[1] to sett Georg ffox att full liberty; for him to graunt forth another warrant for ye same which was done wch was of a mighty service to truth which came over all lyars and slanderrers and y^t day the power of ye lord God went over all and a great service for ye truth it was. Though many bad spirits gote upp and some was madd att my releasement; but ye truth and power of God went over all bad spirits and shined over them all.

And then an Order was Comming out for our liberty and through some bad spirits it was stopped againe and then the fift Monarchy people[2] rose and made an insurrection in London [a matter of thirty of them;] which caused the traine bands and souldiors to arise; both in ye Citty and Countrey; through wch cause our friends meettings was broken upp; and many Thousands were Imprisoned both in Citty and Countrey. [And many dyed in prison; they being so thronged upp,] And I was taken prisoner in that time. a party of horse came where I lodged and knocked at ye door [and ye maid asked who was there. and they said a friend;] and she oppened ye door, & they rushed into the house [as though they would have broken all to peeces, and runne upp and down ye Roomes;] and one laid hands upon mee, and asked mee for pistols; which I asked him if hee did not know our principle for our weapons were spirituall our principles were peaceable and so he told them I was one of the heads of them and they took mee prisoner, and there was a man of ye house[3] said I should not go away y^t night but said I should come in the morning that had some power amongst ye souldio^{rs}. And so I continued there that night till ye next morning about the tenth houre, there came a foot Company to search the house for the meetting being the first day And friends were gathering; And so one of them whipped out a sword; and held it upp before mee.

And so they took mee away [prison^r to Scotland guard[4]] to Whitehall, before the troopers were come for mee. and I

had a good service amongst ye soldiours; though they were
rude and Wild for a while. [And so when the steeple house
preaching was done, the officers came to mee and asked mee
If I would take ye oath of Allegiance; and I told them I
never took oath in my life And] they asked mee what I
was; and I told them a preacher of Righteousnesse [and so
preached the Gosple unto them which was peaceable; that
they should love one another And I asked them when would
they break their swords into plowe shares, and their spears
into Prunning hookes. And I asked them what they did
wth all their carnall weapons and swords by their sides, and
when would they break them to peeces, and come to y^e
gosple, of peace; and so after a while they sett mee at liberty
& threatned mee, and so] I spoke to ye souldio^{rs} in ye guard
and passed away.

And two y^t were officers ffollowed mee and so I asked
them to lett mee go into ye prison to see some friends and
they would not. So I went to ye Captaine of ye guard
my selfe, and asked him and hee lett mee go, and when
I was amongst them I looked out towards the house where
I had been taken where the meetting was; and they sent
a party of Musquetteers to seek mee in the meetting, and
so they sent three tymes while I was in that house amongst
ye prisoners And so those two officers y^t I asked to go up
to see the prisoners they sent a party of Musquetteers to y^e
prison; and said all y^t was not prisoners might come forth.
And so I asked ye soldiours whether I might [go forth and
whether I might] stay and they said I might stay and so
they missed of their prey. And so then I went upp into
ye Citty. [And men being all upp in an uproar, men could
hardly walk in ye streets, so ye next first day I and another
friend was going to a meetting and soldio^{rs} had just been
there, and the doors were shutt upp. And so went to another
meetting; and there ye souldio^{rs} had just broken upp that
meetting also and friends was gatherd againe. and I staid
a good while in the meetting; and friends were all refreshed
and well; I staid a good while, and went to another meetting and so the souldio^{rs} came soon after I was gone and
took friends: and great work had ye souldio^{rs} made wth
their swords, but the truth came over all. And severall
friends were cutt and wounded abroad. And in that day

driven like sheep by souldio^{rs} into Dungeons and bad prisons]
and then a proclamation was given forth from ye king y^t
all friends should be sett at liberty without paying y^e
Goalers fees.

And all our persecutors both priests and Magistrates and
other officers in the Common wealthes dayes came to be
turned out of their places by ye king but who turned to
them, and so it came upon them what wee had prophecyed
long before, of ye mighty day of ye lord y^t was comeing upon
Magestrates and priests and Army and Officers.

[And wo bee to the Teachers and wo bee to ye priests;
wch was cryed both in townes Marketts high waies courts
and in the dayes of their prosperity they cald us fooles and
Imprisoned us and beat us and abused us; but ye word of y^e
lord wch was spoken unto them came upon them all; wch some
came to poverty; and some runne into other Countreys; and
all turned out of their places except it were such as turned to
them and this was fulfilled in o^r dayes; wch was prophecyed
unto them to ye eyes of Thousands of the prophets of God
and spirituall men and women.]

And then after I was moved to go Bristol and through
friends in the Countrey and when I came to Bristol the
Magistrates were something in a rage; and a friend[1] being
wth mee it was upon him to speak in ye meetting; I bad
him either go before mee or after mee, it was upon him to
go before mee and when hee was speaking I sitting by him,
in comes some of ye officers and after some words plucked
him down, and called for the other stranger. that was wth
him, y^t was mee; and so I sitting still, they took ye friend
away [and after they had examined him and bid him appear
the next day; hee came into ye meetting againe; So hee
stood upp and cleared himselfe.] And when hee had done
I was moved to stand upp in the power of ye lord. and
there was a brave meetting, and ye life and truth came
over all and so parted in peace. And my friend being
cast into prison fell sick but after a great while recovered.

The next day after ye meetting they raised the traine
band and said They would hunt mee out and they would
have mee. And so ye next first day, the traine Bands being
upp diverse friends came to mee and said I would bee taken
to day and desired mee not to go to the meeting except I

were eternally moved of God, for it was past their reason
but I should bee taken. [and they would not have mee
taken for they would glory too much If I were taken.] And
so I sent friends away to ye meeting to tell mee how thinges
were and they mett mee and told mee and said the souldio^{rs}
were com'd and they were gone to ye Baptizts meetting;
and the Independants, [& they could know the time when
to come to the Quakers, for it was before our meetting begunne and was full.] So I went upp into ye meetting which
astonished friends to see mee come in and ye power of ye lord
god rose over all; [and So while they were att their dinners
and Examineing other men; for our meetting being kept
till the fift hour ye day before; and there usuall time was
to break it upp about the third houre,] and so when I had
cleared my selfe; and the truth was over all; and all fresh
and ye life upp in all I was passing away out of ye meetting
being a mighty full hote meetting So I was passing away
& I was moved to go back againe and speake a few words,
& stood upp and told them that they might see there was
a God in Izraell y^t could deliver.

So friends cryed as I passed away and said Georg the
officers are comeing, are comeing^a; So ye meetting broke upp
in peace; and friends was sett over all their heads, and
none was taken, [wch after they roared and raged, and
Spies was out to watch for mee.]

The next first day I had a meetting in the Countrey;
[and two other friends went up into ye meetting in Bristol
intending to speak] and the soldiours besett the house round,
there being severall doors and then went up and then they
said they would be sure to have mee. And they kept that
day [five hundred] friends prisoners in ye meetting place in
a rage when they missed mee. [And they kept them till the
seventh or eight houre at night; and they sent for their
suppers into ye meetting place; and then they sett them
at liberty; only those two y^t intended to speak were kept
prisoners[1]; and they queried of them which way I was gone.
The Maior would faine have spoken with mee, and said I
had been too Cunning for them; and How might they send
after mee into ye Countrey; and so the truth came over
all.]

^{a} A has no repetition of the words *are comeing*

And I came through friends upp to London So after I had been a while at London, I passed through ye Countrey to Lecestershire[1] and after a time Coming into a friends house at Swanton in the night there came a man called a lord[2] wth many Armed men wth swords and pistols in a very rude manner crying make fast the doors. So I was siting in the hall wth two friends and another friend y^t was in ye house and they examined them takeing their names and the lord himself was ready to strick them wth his pistols and there was one man's name was ffaux. And the lord bad him sett down his name ffox ; I being in the next Roome, I heard him they being so Greedy for mee. at last they sent for mee wth two soldiours. And so when they brought mee before the lord they asked mee my name, I told them my name was George Fox wch astonished them, and said I was innocent and pure and knowen over the Nation ; ay says hee all ye world over ; and what did they to come wth their pistols in that manner, for wee were gentle & Innocent and hee held upp his pistols and said hee would make mee gentle. And so hee Commanded a guard upon us, and bid them look to us but hee said hee could hardly trust ye guard with mee, but said hee would take mee along wth him.

And so the next morning wee were had upp to him and hee asked us whether wee would swear, I told him I never took Oath in my life[3], [and I would not swear my Coat were my owne ; nor swear if a man took it off y^t hee took it The Standers by said would I not do so and I said no, but I could say hee was ye man, but wee kept to Christ's doctrine which Commands us to keep to yea and nay in all our Communications. if hee or his Bishopps or Priests would prove y^t Christ and ye Apostles Commanded y^t the people should sweare after they had Commanded and taught they should not sweare and give us Scripture for it, wee would not stand long about it, wee would swear.] And so hee made a Mittimus and sent mee and severall other friends to prison men and women to Lester prison and being a matter of Nine^a So it was because wee would not sweare and how y^t wee were to have a meetting for hee could not prove it to bee a meetting wch was contrary to ye law. And so friends rode along through many townes wth open Bibles[4] in their hands,

^a Vol. II. p. 14: *five*

a and *b* one wth a spining wheele in her lapp *b* it being in harvest
time. as they went wth their open Bibles in their hands *a*
they cryed prisoners for the Lord Jesus Christ; which
astonished the Countrey people & it had an effect upon
their hearts. And so wee were kept in ye prison till the
Sessions.

And when the Sessions came wee were brought before
the Justices and they asked mee whether I would take the
Oath of Allegiance I told them I never took an Oath in
my life and called for my Mittimus to bee read before y^e
people wch they would not and desired Justice of them, and
if I had transgressed do Justice upon mee. If I were wrong
Imprisoned do me Justice. & then they put the Oath to mee
I told them if they would prove y^t the Apostle Commanded
to swear after they had denyed it I would. [I called for my
accusers and said Paul was brought before the Judgment
seat as I was and hee had his accusers face to face, but
where was myne. They told I was an Enemy to the King,
I told them I was cast into a Dungeon fourteen years since
because I would not take upp armes and bee a captaine ag^t
the King.] And so they tooke mee away and the power of
the lord came over them all. and after they had Examined y^e
rest of friends; the Justices whisper'd together; and bid the
Goaler take us away; and so ye Goaler brought us away;
and almost all ye people followed us out of ye Court, and it
was a mighty day for the truth. And so when I came into
the Goalers house The Goaler said Gentlemen you are all
sett at liberty and y^u know I must have my fees but give
mee what y^u will, [which a great service to ye truth it was.
And the Sessions was just like a meetting truth had such
an operation in peoples hearts.]

And then I was moved to passe through friends into
severall Counties and so into Cambridgshire and into ye Isle
of Ely [to Stoak[1] where wee had a great generall meetting
where the souldiours intended to come hearing of mee but
by ye power of ye lord, was stopped & so I passed on through
chatridge where there was a warrant out for friends and
strangers and strangers that came to ye Towne] So after I

---

a...*a* These words are omitted from A.

b...*b* Vol. II. p. 14: *ye two women carryd wheeles one their lapps to spinn
in prison*

had visited friends passed away to a meetting of friends in the ffen countrey and from thence to linne; and the Maior hearing of mee sent an officer and ye next morning I passed away a little before they came and when I was upon horseback I felt something of ye darkness y^t was upon mee for they gloryed at hearing of mee, as though they had had mee.

And so passed towards Norwitch where meettings were troublesome by some y^t were in power, but our meettings came over all. And so passed through Suffolk and into Essex and Bedfordshire and Herdfordshire through friends where meettings were peaceable and so up to London.

And after I had staid there awhile visiteing friends passed down into Kent and when I had visited friends and been at their meetings So ye last meetting was at Tenterdaine, [two friends[1] was moved y^t was w^{t}h mee to go one to ye Independant meetting and the other to the Baptizts to declare truth to them and so when the meetting was almost done being many of ye world there Some of their friends whispered to them to go out of ye meetting because ye souldio^{rs} were comming; but they would not go but fare as wee fared they said] and when ye meetting was done, I was passing into a field down comes a captaine w^{t}h a Company of Musquetteers and sent a Company to mee and stopped ye rest of friends and had mee to their Capt and so when hee came into ye yard he called and asked which was Georg which was Georg ffox; I told him I was ye man; and hee came to mee and told mee hee would secure mee & put mee amongst ye Souldiours, and took some other of the friends upp to ye town prisoners to ye Goalers house, and after a while called mee upp and Examined mee why I came thither to make a disturbance and said there was a law which was ag^t Quakers meettings made onely ag^t them. I told him I knew no such law, and he brought out the law that was made against Quakers and others. And I told him y^t was against such as were a terror to ye kings subjects and were Enemies and held dangerous principles; ffor wee held truth; and our meettings were peacable; and they knew their neighbours were peaceable people. And wee loved all people, and wee were Enemies to none, And they told mee I was an Enemy to ye king. I told them I had been cast into Darby Dungeon because I would not take upp Armes against him [fourteen years ago] about Worster fight. And was brought up by Collonell Hacker to London, as a Plotter to bring in king Charles; and was prisoner to London; and kept there till I was sett at liberty by Oliver the Protector, Though o^r Principles were peaceable. And they asked mee whether I was im-p^rsoned in the time of the Insurrection, I said yes I had been Imprisoned[a]; [b]and I had been sett att liberty by ye kings own word before[b]. And so spoke to them of their Conditions to live in ye feare of God, and to bee tender towards their Neighbours that feared god and mind gods wisdom by which all thinges were made & created; y^t they might come to receive it, by which they might come to Order all thinges to Gods Glory by ye wisdom by which all thinges were made. And y^t by it they might bee Ordred. And so they called upp the other two friends y^t was with mee, and they asked them from whence they came and they told them they came along wth mee.

And they said it was ye Maiors pleasure y^t wee should bee all sett at liberty and many words wee had of the truth, & they were brought pretty moderate and so wee passed away in ye truth & in the power of the lord which fredome was a great service to truth for at first they demaunded bond of us for o^r appearance at ye sessions; but wee denyed all being Innocent and peaceable. So wee passed on through Sussex and Surrey visiteing friends there and Hampshire where severall friends were Imprisoned. And so having a Meetting att Ringwood in Hampshire[1] ye Souldiours hearing of it, they raised the traine Bands; and came upp to the house hearing of my name; but they came before ye meetting was begunne; I being walking in the backsyde; one of ye world came to a friend y^t was wth mee and beckened to him and told him the traine Band was Comming to break upp our meetting and so o^r friend desired mee to walke a litle aside and after a while they would bee gone for our meeting did not begin till [c]after ye twelft houre[c] and then it was the tenth and so I walked over ye Hedg and I had no sooner passed over the close but it was spread over wth Soldio^rs and made a great noyce. And p^rsently they went their wayes and takeing some few friends along wth them and some they mett

---

[a] A: *been before*   [b]...[b] These words are omitted from A.
[c]...[c] Vol. ii. p. 24: *about ye 11th houre*

in the lanes. And so then after wee had a brave meetting; after they were gone and so there comes a man and looked into yᵉ meetting; I being speaking away hee goes into the town and gives the souldiours notice againe. The town being a mile and a halfe off it was a pretty while before they could come, So wee had a brave meetting, and departed in quiet and peace; but they came upp after like madd men wᵗh their swords, but I was gone and most of friends before they came, wᶜh made them in a pittifull rage. They took in all about sixteen and sent to prison.

And so I passed up into Wiltshire and there were enquiries made after mee after yᵉ meetting was done.

And then into Dorcestershire and Devonshire and Cornwell where meettings were quiet and peaceable. But in Tiverdon they had intended to have had mee in prison and had spoken to some of our friends as favouring of them that they should be their prisonʳˢ but our meetting was broken up before they came so wee passed to another town where wee had a great generall meetting where they had sorely persecuted friends and carried them by carts from Justice to Justice[1] and sent them to prison yet by the power of the lord god wee gote through all and friends were refreshed. And so wee came throrow Somersetshire by friends and then afterwards to Bristol; which after wee had visited friends there and in Wiltshire passed into Glostershire where meetings were larg and peaceable.

And wee passed into Wales [to Pontamile and when the meetting was done The next morning wee passed early away] To another meetting some Ten miles off in the Middle of yᵉ meetting Comes a Bayliffe to take upp the speaker[2] [and said they had been searching for yᵉ speaker at the house which I came from yᵗ morning and so the woman of the house took him in.] So when yᵉ meetting was done I passed away and hee was in yᵉ yard and Bowed to mee but said nothing to mee and the Countrey was in a great rage; and att night they came And shott off a pistoll or gunne against the house but did no hurt. And then I passed to Rosse and had a Meetting. And then to herdford and after I had visited friends there Wee passed upp into Wales againe and on the first day wee had a great meetting and on the third day wee had another meeting up in Wales and after

ye meetting was done wee passed away towards the third
day meetting and so when wee came to the meetting a noyse
was amongst friends y^t ye watches were sett and they had
taken some friends y^t were comming to the meetting, and
so I was moved to passe another way, and so missed them.
and so after ye meetting was done wee passed away peaceably and those friends were sett at liberty y^t were taken
upp by the watchmen being neighbours. So wee came into
England where wee were taken Notice of in a great town
in a faire day but wee escaped and by the power of the
lord wee came over. And I heard that Herford^a Magistrates were greeved because they missed mee. And so wee
passed through worstershire and into yorkshire & visited
friends.

And so into Bishoprick where o^r meettings were very
peaceable; but some Magistrates were ag^t mee, which had
taken some papers to mee. They threatned mee and said
if they could catch mee they would tye mee to a stake and
burne mee. So after I had visited friends I passed into
westmerland. And so from ye meeting in Westmerland I
passed to Swarthmoore, in Lancashire. And a Noyce being
of ye plott, I wrote papers to cleare friends of that thing and
sent them to the Magestrates and to ye king and the Councell
to take off Jealousies out of their minds concerning friends.
And so I was moved to go into westmerland, and there they
sought after mee when I was gone the Magistrates did. And
from thence I passed into Northumberland. And while I was
gone away they searched their house at Swarthmoore hall
for mee, yea to the very Trunks and Boxes. and so when
I came into Cumberland there was halfe a crown a day[1] and
a Noble given to men to take upp speakers meettings it
being the Sessions Tyme. [and great floods.] none came to
our meettings but they were peaceable, but after wee were
gone they were in a rage that they had missed their price
of mee.

And there was one ffleeming[2] a Justice for Cumberland
and Westmerland had given forth a warrant to take mee,
and any man y^t could should have five pound for his labour.
[hee sett mee att a higher rate then Christ who was sold
for thirty peeces of silver.] This same Justice had given

A : *Hearford*

forth a warrant to search and break up friends meettings
which the Constables hunted upp and down from meetting
to meetting. And as I went into Westmerland, Middleton[1]
a Justice sent two men to a meetting to breake it upp; but
it was broken upp before they came, and so they missed it.
And this ffleeming a heady man enraged other officers. So
they came to a meetting where friends were that they
searched under their beds for mee and I was not there.

So w[n] I came to Swarthmoore againe Collonel Kirbey[2] had
sent for to seek mee by Soldio[rs], and the Constables came to
seek for mee. I went upp to Collonel Kirkbey if hee had any
thing to say to mee I was comed to visite him. and when
I came to him he told mee hee had nothing against mee ;
and told mee If I would stay at Swarthmoore, and not keep
great meettings and not many strangers, none should meddle
with mee. I told him our meettings were peaceable and
wee had the word of the king for o[r] meettings & his speech
and declaration concerning Tender Consciences and for them
that lived peaceably ; should not bee called in question for
matter of Religion, and he knew his neighbours were peaceable. and so many of y[e] Gentry of y[e] country being there,
it was of Good Service. and so I passed from him and left
him seeming loving. and so came to Swarthmoore and so
after a little while the Deputy Leivtenant[3] of y[e] County sent
for mee to Hoolker Hall and Examined mee and asked mee
whether I owned the Battle door, and the Languages y[t] were
in it. I told them yes. And they asked mee If I could
understand languages I said sufficient for my selfe, and said
salvation did not lye in the tongues they were a lowe thing.
And what were so many tongues in matter of salvation for
the many tongues beganne att the confution of Babell. And
so they asked mee if I had heard of the Plott ; I told them
I had heard the noyce of such a thing of one which had
heard it from the Sheriffe of yorkshire[4], but I know no friend
y[t] was in any such thing but only I heard of such a thing,
I had written against all such plotters and all such thinges,
and I had sent them pap[rs] ag[t] such thinges and so they
were in a rage, and cryed make a Mittimus. And Preston
said hee would have an Independant, a Quaker, an Anna-
baptizt and a Presbyterian to Interpret y[t] Scripture w[ch]
said, woe be to the Scribes and Pharisees Hypocrites[5]. I

told him I would do it quickly for yᵉ Jews they had the
Law and would not do it; the Wo was unto them the
Christians they have Christs words and yᵉ Apostles which
saith love Enemies and love one another. Now judg yoʳ
selves in this case*a*. and then they gave Order that I should
appear att the Sessions which I did, and wⁿ I came there
they called mee to the Barre. And I said peace be amongst
them twice. And the Clerk of the peace cryed peace to all
yᵉ Court, in pain of Imprisonmᵗ and so the Chayre man asked
mee If I knew where I was and I told him yes, & said It
may bee it was the not putting of my hatt yᵗ troubled him
and that was not*b* the honour yᵗ came down from God, that
was a low thing I hope hee looked not for yᵗ. And hee said
hee looked for that too, and bid them take off my hatt, wᶜh
they did.

And so a pretty space wee looked att one another, till the
power of the lord God arose over all. and then one of them
asked mee if I heard of the plott, I told him in the same
manner as I did to yᵉ Deputy Leivtenants before. But I
knew no friend nor no one in it. They asked mee why I did
not declare it to yᵉ Magistrates. I said I had written to yᵉ
Magistrates and to yᵉ king also agᵗ Plotts. And wee were
peaceable. And they told mee yᵗ I had been in Westmerland.
I told them and in Cumberland too to declare agᵗ plotts. And
they asked mee if I did not know of a law agᵗ Quakers
meettings. I said there was a law yᵗ took hold of such yᵗ were
a terror to yᵉ kings subjects; and such as held dangerous
principles; And were Enemies to yᵉ king. It was truth yᵗ
wee held, and were Enemies to no man but loved all men.
And did not meet to terrify people the law was good in it
selfe yᵗ was made agᵗ those yᵗ did terrify people and were
Enemyes to yᵉ king and held Dangerous principles.

They asked mee if I would take the Oath of Allegiance[1].
I told them I never took Oath in my life. I could not swear
this was my coat; if a man took it, I could not sweare that
hee was the man. They asked mee if I *did my self*c to
bee a Quaker*c*. I told them Quakeing and trembling at yᵉ
word of God I owned according to yᵉ Scriptures but for yᵉ
word quakeing it was a Nickname given to us by Justice

---

a A: *cause*   *b* A omits *not*
c...c Thus A, B, C. Vol. II. p. 47 has *would own him self*

Bennett, y^t cast mee into a Dungeon because I would not take up armes ag^t the king and bee a Capt. so they asked mee If I would sweare; and they gave mee the Book and I took it and was turning to a place y^t was ag^t swearing and they took it from mee ag^n and bidd mee say after the Clerk So I told them if they would prove y^t Christ and ye Apostles Commanded to sweare after they had forbidden it, give us Scripture for this. and wee should sweare. It was Christs Command y^t wee should not swear. but if I could take any Oath I would take that. I told them o^r Allegiance did not lie in Oaths but in truth and faithfullnes. for they had Experience enough of mens swearing first one way and then another and breaking their Oaths but o^r yea was o^r yea, and o^r nay was o^r nay. And so they cryed take him away Goaler. And so I bid them take Notice it was in obedience to Christs Commands y^t I sufferd.

And so I was sent to prison where now I am w^{t}h 8 more[1].

This of ye following two first pages must be placed about ye middle of ye Book.

In the dayes of Oliver as I went into Portsmouth [ye guard bid me stand and light off my horsse where I was never unhorssed before and the Capt of ye guard proved to bee a friendly man] and they had mee before the governour to ye governours house; and one friend went in and spoke to him, and was not willing y^t I should go in because my name was so knowen. So after some time w^{t}h him^a wee were sett att liberty and had a fine meetting in the town and so passed away[2].

Another tyme when I came to Manchester where wee had a meetting and people threw water and stones and dirt at us. and at last (the Sessions being in the Town) people were very rude in the meetting and some runne to the Sessions and told them upon which they sent a Company of Officers and halled mee out of ye meetting into the Sessions house before the Justices[3]. And after some debate w^{t}h them for they were all so rude I did not know who were Justices att the first. So I asked w^{c}h were the Justices. and I called for Moderation and Civillity And Justice I own and so after

^{a} A: *mee*

some discourse wth them, they caused the Constables to take mee away and they kept mee in an Inne, and stayed wth mee about an houre, And came no more to mee. And so none coming to mee the next morning I went to the Constables house and hee had no further Order wth mee nor concerning mee. And so the next day I passed away in the truth of God over all.

The priests and Magistrates were in a rage at Lancaster ag^t mee, and enflamed the Judges When they came y^t one of ye Judges stept up in open court in a rage against mee and was sending for a warrant into ye Countrey for mee and one west[1] wch was Clerk [of ye Crowne Office and Justice of peace and Quorum;] stept up in the open Court before ye Judg and said y^t hee would offerr upp body for body and his estate for mee. and so stopped the Judges mouth wch was of great service and came over the Countrey and the same night I came to the Towne before ye Judges were gone but they were so stopped that they had not power to send for mee & thus the truth of God came over all [And the priests and Magistrates & wicked professors lost their end and this was in the Common wealth days].

II
THE ITINERARY JOURNAL

"Though the Lord had provided an outward habitation for him [Swarthmoor Hall], yet he was not willing to stay at it, because it was so remote and far from London where his service most lay. He stayed there and thereaways till he finished his course and laid down his head in peace."

From the conclusion of a sketch of the life of George Fox, by his widow. See Ell. text, II. 519.

A Page of *The Itinerary Journal*

II

THE ITINERARY JOURNAL

A Jornall, for y[e] year : 81 :

From London G: ff: came 20: miles to Rigate to friend Blotts[1] between 10: & 11: hour in y[e] night. And next day he went 20 miles to W[m] Pens house where there was a great meeting.

And from thence 9 miles to Horsam and there I met with many friends.

And from thence 6 miles to Humphrey Killingbancks[2] house. And from thence to Panes place[3] where there was many hundreds of people, and many of y[e] world at a meeting and all very quiet.

And from thence I passed to Worminghurst to W[m] Pens about 15: miles where I had a meeting.

And from thence I went out of our way to London 43 miles—117 miles this Journey. G: ff: was at Devinshire house[4] and Spittlefields[5] at 2 great meetings of a day & very precious.

And next day I was at Gracious[6] and y[e] Lords power was over all in that meeting.

And at a very Large meeting at a marriage at Horslydowne[7] and the people were affected where y[e] true marriage was distinguished from y[e] worlds.

G: F: went 6 miles to Edmonton and had 2 meetings there. I passed from Edmonton to Mary peningtons[8], 21: miles.

And ffrom thence to a meeting that was Large 27 miles backward & forward.

And from thence I passed to Hegaroll[9] where there was a very Large meeting & in my goeing & comeing I visited a man and a woman friend y[t] was ill and this was about 16: miles. and y[e] Lords power was over all in these meetings & they were very powerfull.

And from London to Edmonton 6 miles and from thence to a meeting that was precious 5 miles backward & forward y[e] 18th day 6 mo: 1681.

And I went to Charley Wood[1] meeting on ye 6 day after there was a very Large meeting & ye Lords presence was amongst us, wch was 8 miles backward & forward.

And on ye 20: day 6 mo: there was a very Large meeting at Rosells^a[2] and ye Lords power was over all and y^t day I travelled 7 miles.

And from thence to Wickam I went to an Inn and soe to ye meeting & Lay at John Archdales[3] house wch was 5 miles and from thence to Torvell Heath 8 miles to a precious meeting.

And from thence to Hendan^b 4 miles where friends came to see us.

And from thence to Reddin 6 miles to an Inn and soe to ye monthly meeting & then to ye weekly meeting and on ye 1st day at Reddin : G: ff: had 2 Large meetings and ye Lords power was over all ye bad and answered ye good.

And from Reddin to Ore 12 miles ye 3^d day we had a very Large meeting.

And from thence to Wabro^c (on ye 4 day we had a Large meeting & ye glory of ye Lord was over all) in Oxfordshire 11: miles, many friends came, some out of Barkshire, Buckinghamshire and Hampshire.

And ffrom thence to Elmer in Buckinhamshire :12: miles where we had a gloryous meeting on ye 1st day of ye 7th mo:

And from thence to Mary Peningtons :11: miles ye 2^d of ye 7 mo: 1681: Mil: 137:

On ye first day I went 6 miles from Mary Peningtons to Charle Wood monthly meeting wch was very precious.

ffrom Mary Peningtons to :T: Elets^d[4] backward & forward 6 miles where there was a monthly men and {womens} meeting and very Large & quiet & ye Lords presence was amongst them ye 5th of ye 7th mo:

And from thence to Watford to a meeting on ye 5th day :8: miles, & on ye 6 day there was a marriage and ye meeting was very Large & ye Lords power was over all.

And ye next day 8 miles to Uxbridge where friends Came to see me.

---

[a] *Rosells* is crossed through and *Jordens* substituted.
[b] *dan* crossed through and *ly* inserted.
[c] *Wabro* crossed out and *Warborow* inserted.
[d] *Elets* corrected to *Ellwoods*

And the next day I went 4 miles to Longford to a Large precious meeting where the Lords presence was.

And from thence to Stanes 4 miles.

And from thence to Sunbary 6 miles.

ffrom thence to Kingston 4 miles where I had 2 meetings and ye Lords presence was in them.

And from thence to Wa...ser[1] 5 miles where there was a precious meeting. And from thence 3 mil: to Hamersmith where there was a Large blessed meeting at a Buryall.

And from thence to Kingsington 2 miles or a mile & ½ Miles Journey.

And from thence to James Beeches[2] 3 miles where there was a gloryous meeting.

And from thence to John Elsons[3] att ye peel 2 Miles; where there was a Gloryous meeting.

And from London to Gooseys to Wm Meads[4] 13 Miles;
The whole Journey 210: miles[5]. ~

Here followeth a Jornall of the Meetings :G: F: hath Been att &c Anno domini 1683

Att Kingston ye 11th of ye 1st mo:[6] as I went to ye meeting I mett ye Chief Constable, & he was pritty Civill & he had Sett ye watchmen to keep us out of ye meeting but they Let friends have two fforms to Sitt upon in ye high way and we had a very precious meeting in ye Street and ye Lords presence was with us and Soe parted in peace. ~

And ye 16th day after I wentt to ye Bull and mouth[7] in London and ye Constables kept the meeting out in ye Street and made a great Bussell when any fri^d Spoke, & att Last I spoke & told y^m heaven was Gods throne and Earth was his footstool & would they not let us Stand upon Gods footstool to worship & Serve ye Liveing God, & many other words I Spake and they were quiett, & then we broak up our meeting in peace. ~

And on ye 18th of ye 1st month I was moved to goe to gracious street meeting & they set a guard y^t kept us out in Lumber street {&} another at Gracious street gate, & kept us out in ye Street & I stood upon a Chair and spoke Largely to ye people many weighty truths & opened ye principles of truth to them concerning of Magistrates and concerning ye Lords prayer and there ^a were thousands^a of people, and professors, and very quiet and none disturbed us, but we parted in peace & ye Lords power was over all.

And ye 19th day I went to Guilford where I visited friends and from thence to Wm Pens about 50 miles from London & we went almost 10 miles about, ye wayes being bad, and on ye 22^d day I had a very blessed meeting there amongst friends and quiet.

And on ye 25th day of ye 1st month 1683[1] James Claipole[2] was mighty sick of ye stone y^t he Could neither Lye nor Stand he was in such extreamity of ye Stone y^t he Cryed out like a woman in travell and I went to him & Spoke to him and was moved to Lay my hand upon him & desired ye Lord to rebuke his Infirmity and as I Laid my hands upon him the Lords power went through him & his wife had faith & was sensible of ye thing & he presently fell of a Sleep & presently after his Stone came from him like dirte & soe then he was presently well, formerly he used to lye a month or 2 weeks of the Stone, as he said, but ye Lords power in his time soon gave him ease y^t he came ye next day 25 miles in a Coach with me, & ye Same 25th day I went to a meeting from W : Pens, where there was a Large meeting & ye Lords presence was amongst us & it was quiet.

[And ye 26th day I came to Henry Guils[3] 25 miles and staid there a pritty while, and then he went to widdow Smiths[4] betwixt 4 & 5 miles & there I had a Large blessed meeting, on ye 28th day & ye Lords presence was amongst us, and from thence I came 15 miles to Kingston.]

And on ye 1st day of ye 2^d month I went to ye meeting at Kingston where they kept us forth of doors, two watch-men & a Constable it was the monthly meeting day, & pritty Large & many of ye people of ye world were there & all very quiet & ye Lords blessed presence was amongst us blessed be his name for ever.

:G: ff: was at Spittlefields ye 29th day of Aprill^b where there was a gloryous blessed meeting and many professors & friends and very peaceable and many things were opened to them to their great Satisfaction, & ye meeting was for

---

^a...^a Altered to *was a great multitude*
^b *Aprill* altered to *2 : mo :*

Largeness Like a yearly meeting, and yᵉ Lords power and truth was over all.

And after :G: ff: came out of yᵉ Country he was at the Peel¹ yᵉ 15ᵗʰ of yᵉ 3ᵈ mo: where there was a blessed meeting peaceable and quiet within yᵉ doors.

And yᵉ 20ᵗʰ of yᵉ 3ᵈ mo: he had a meeting at the Savoy² where there was many proud people³ besids friends & yᵉ Lords power was over all that they were all very quiet, and mighty affected with the truth and yᵉ Love of it wᶜʰ overcame them.

And the 23ᵈ of yᵉ 3ᵈ mo: :G: ff: was at Gracious Street where yᵉ meeting was kept within the doors, & it was Large & yᵉ blessed presence of the Lord was in the meeting, & gods power & Seed reigned over all, blessings & praises and glory & honour to his name over all for ever, and the meeting was very quiet and friends & people Satisfied besids many other meetings that he was at in London that were peaceable & quiet.

And on the 27ᵗʰ of yᵉ 3ᵈ mo: G: ff: was on yᵉ forenoon at a meeting near Lumberstreet⁴.

And on the 2ᵈ day being the 28ᵗʰ of yᵉ 3ᵈ mo: G: ff: was at the same meeting of Sufferings⁵ on the forenoon, And at Horslydowne on yᵉ after noon where yᵉ meeting was interrupted.

And on the day following being yᵉ 29ᵗʰ of the 3ᵈ mo: G: ff: was at the aforsᵈ meeting of Sufferings in Lumberstreet.

And the 30ᵗʰ of yᵉ 3ᵈ mo: G: ff: was at Gracious Street where the meeting was kept {with}in the doors and it was an exceeding Large meeting & very peaceable. On the same day in the after noon he was at the meeting of Sufferings, And he went from thence to another meeting of busyness⁶ the same night.

A Short account of yᵉ persecutors of Ringwood in Hampshire

There was a meeting intended by yᵉ people of god Called Quakers at pullner⁷ in yᵉ parish aforesᵈ in yᵉ year 1663 on yᵉ Last day of yᵉ 3ᵈ mo: before yᵉ meeting was gathered and yᵉ hour was come that yᵉ meeting was appointed John

Line[1] Constable came with John Streat[2] Captaine of ye train bands with Souldiers & took 17 men and after those men were hailed away there was a meeting held by :G: ff: The known persecutors were Tho: Blackherd[3] Warden, John Line Constable, John Streat Captain and it is observed by many people that ye Evident hand of god ffell upon them, all these were wealthy men & many did observe that the Just hand of god was ag^t them, as did plainly appear by their own confession as alsoe by ye wasteing of their outward Estates, the above said John Line Constable carryed these men to prison and when they were brought before the Judges of the Assyzes he took a false oath ag^t them who were innocent for wch they were fined & kept prisoners more than 10 years John Line Constable dyed in ye year 1682 A Sad spectacle to behold he grievously rotted away alive & soe dyed his wife alsoe (being a persecutor) after the same manner or the Like example & those things are Generally known by ye neighbourhood and witnessed by the sufferers (viz) Tho: Manner, Martin Bence, James Millar, Ed: Pricket Philip Bence &c.[4] This John Line did confess y^t he never prospered since he Laid hands on the quakers witnessed by John Chater who heard him speak ye words wth severall others & wished he had never medled with them and said he never prospered since in ye presence of Eliz: Benester, & said he was sory he had a hand in persecuteing ye Quakers and alsoe that he would never meddle with them more and said that he thought ye hand of ye Lord was ag^t him for it.

The 31st day of ye 3^d mo: G: ff: appointed a meeting in ye morning concerning busyness at Sam: Boultons[5].

On ye 6th day being ye 1st of ye 4th mo: G: ff: had a meeting about ye 5th hour in ye morning at Wm Crouches[6], with some ffriends from Scotland Ireland Holland ffreezland Dansick & America.

On the same day :G: ff: had a meeting at Ben: Clarks[7] about busyness.

And afterwards ye same day he had a meeting wth the phisitians at James Wasses[8].

He had alsoe ye same day 2 meetings at Rich: Richardsons[9] Chamber[10] about busyness.

On ye 2^d day being ye 4th of ye 4th mo: G: ff: was at ye morning meeting[1] in Lumberstreet & alsoe he was at another appointed at ye same place in the after noon Concerning of busyness.

On ye 31st day of ye 5th 83, I was at ye peel meeting & it was in ye house quiet[2], And a Little before ye Justices & chief Constable had broaken up the meeting there and were very bad to friends but that day there was a gloryous meeting blessed be the Lord.

And on the 5th day of ye 6th mo: 83: I went to Gracious street meeting[3] & 3 Constables were in ye meeting house, & ye Watchmen they kept ye door in Lumberstreet and ye meeting was in the Yard & when I had spoken about 3 quarters of an hour one of ye Constables came & took me by ye hand & said I must come downe, & I desired him to be patient & after I had spoken a while to ye people he had me into ye meeting house, & I asked them if they were not weary of this work, & one of them said indeed they were & they Let me goe into Mary ffosters house[4] and when ye meeting was done (for one spoke^a after I was taken away & prayed^b) the Constables said to some friends wch of them would pass their words y^t if they were questioned I should appear, & friends said there needs no such things ffor :G: ff: was a publick man & well known in ye Citty and he would neither shrink nor fly, & soe the Constables did not come into ye Chamber to me, but went their wayes and Left me at Liberty.

[And on ye 23^d of ye 7th mo: ye Constable y^t pluckt :G: ff: downe made a confession & said y^t day 7 weeks he had pluckt :G: ff: downe when he was speaking and since he had kept his bed within 4 dayes & he could hardly walk over ye room & his wife was Sick at present & he had a pain in his back shoulder and Arme ever since & he was Loath to have been there but y^t he was forced and did not Like y^t work and Some friends told him that he might hurt his back or shoulder by thrusting amongst ye people and not by takeing hold of :G: ff: but ye Constable answered & said he was smote and struck at ye heart before he Laid hands of :G: ff: to take him downe, & soe ye Constable seemed to be penitent

---

^{a} Altered to *prayed* ^{b} *& prayed* crossed out.

and sory, y^t he was brought into such a work & did not Like it, & told the people what misery and trouble he had been in since for meddleing with friends.]

And on ye 9th day of ye 6th mo: on ye 5th day of ye week :G: ff: was at ye Savoy where there was a precious meeting and quiet within ye doors.

And on ye 12th day of ye 6th mo: being ye first day of ye week :G: ff: was at ye meeting at Westminster[1] wch was Large & precious within ye doors & ye Lords power was over all and all ye Loose spirits were bound by ye power & spirit of ye Lord.

And on ye 16th of ye 6th mo: being ye 5th day of ye week :G: ff: was at a meeting at Devinshire house and ye meeting was within ye doors and it was a precious meeting & quiet and ye Lords presence was amongst us.

And on ye 18th of ye 6th month :G: ff: was sent for 10 miles into ye country to see Mary Wooley[2] y^t was sick & she was refreshed with ye power of ye Lord where on ye 19th day being ye 1st day of ye week many fri^{ds} met him at her house.

And on ye 20th of ye 6th mo: being ye 2^d day of ye week :G: ff: came to Devinshire house meeting being a 2 weeks men and womens meeting[3]. And after ye meeting was done some friends were desired to goe to ye major[4] who had sent to prison :19: friends from Devinshirehouse on ye 1st day of ye week being ye 19th day of ye mo: and ye major set them at Liberty at night after friends had spoken to him.

And ye 21st of ye 6th mo: being ye 3^d day of the week :G: ff: went to the 6 weeks meeting[5] at Devinshire house.

The 29th day of ye 6th month being the 4th day of the week :G: ff: was at Gracious street meeting where there came in severall malicious people. ye meeting being in ye house & these malicious people talked one to another & staired up & downe ye meeting and at Last they Spoke one to another & one of them went away & ye other called him againe and he went away again and I felt a body of darkness & a desire rise in me, for ye Lord to Cheain them I did believe they were going for some officers and I felt ye Lords power went over them & did cheain them & ye glory-ous Life of ye Lord rise & was over them all & we had a

gloryous blessed meeting & quiet & as :G: ff: went downe
yᵉ Street he met a couple of proud men in Lumberstreet &
one of them said it was a quaker & they stood about half a
dusen or more together & as :G: ff: went by, O Said they
had we but a warrant now soe great was their Envy but yᵉ
Lords power was over them all.

And then I went about : 12: miles into yᵉ Country and
staid a week.

And yᵉ 9ᵗʰ of yᵉ 7ᵗʰ mo: being yᵉ 6ᵗʰ day of yᵉ week :G:
ff: was at 2 meetings at Ratliff¹ in yᵉ meeting house & yᵉ
meetings were very Large & many professors were at them
& yᵉ Liveing presence of god was manifest amongst us to
his glory & praise, & besids many other meetings and publick
meetings :G: ff: was at.

On yᵉ 11ᵗʰ of yᵉ 7ᵗʰ mo: being yᵉ 3ᵈ day of yᵉ week :G:
ff: was at a meeting at yᵉ peel where there was a very Large
meeting within the doors & very peaceable & quiet, without
yᵉ Least disturbance.

On yᵉ 12ᵗʰ of yᵉ 7ᵗʰ mo: being yᵉ 4ᵗʰ day of yᵉ week :G:
ff: was at the monthly meeting at Bullon mouth wᶜʰ was
peaceable & quiet & wᵗʰin yᵉ doors at yᵉ same day he went
to visit yᵉ prisoners at yᵉ Counter and at Newgate yᵗ were
cast in for meeting together to worship god, and some by yᵉ
Byshops writts.

And on yᵉ 14ᵗʰ of yᵉ 7ᵗʰ mo: being yᵉ 6ᵗʰ day of yᵉ week
:G: ff: was at the meeting of sufferings where there was
many grievous Sufferings read yᵗ came out of many parts of
the nation.

And on yᵉ 15ᵗʰ day of yᵉ mo: being yᵉ 7ᵗʰ day of yᵉ week
G: ff: came to Dolston. And on the 17ᵗʰ day he went to yᵉ
womens School at Shackellwell² to visit them, where he had
a meeting.

The 26ᵗʰ day of yᵉ 7ᵗʰ mo: G: ff: went to Gracious street
meeting wᶜʰ was within the doors where yᵉ Liveing presence
of yᵉ Lord was amongst friᵈˢ and a gloryous meeting it was &
yᵉ Lords power was over all & did cheain all yᵉ wicked spᵗˢ
& it was peaceable, & many were reacht with yᵉ Lords
truth & the meeting ended peaceable.

And after :G: ff: had a Little meeting about busyness &
then he went to yᵉ monthly meeting yᵉ same day. The 30ᵗʰ
of yᵉ 7ᵗʰ mo: being yᵉ 1ˢᵗ day of yᵉ week :G: ff: was at

Wheeley street[1] where there was a very great meeting & very peaceable without doors in ye street.

The 1st day of ye 8th mo: G: ff: was at a quarterly men & womens meeting at Bullon mouth where it was kept very quiet and peaceable.

And on ye 2^d of ye 8th mo: being ye 3^d day of the week :G: ff: was at a Six weeks meeting at Bullon mouth where it was held very quiet & peaceable.

And on ye 6th of ye 8th mo: being ye 6th day of ye week :G: ff: was at ye meeting of Sufferings.

The 7th of ye 8th mo: being ye first day of ye week :G: ff: was at ye Savoy meeting[2], it being upon him to goe thither, & it was very larg and many precious things were opened to ye people and many professors were there and they were turned[a] to ye Sp^t of god wch ye Lord had poured upon them soe y^t all by ye Sp^t of god might know ye Scriptures y^t were given forth from ye Sp^t of god & by ye Sp^t of god might know god, & X^t y^t god had sent wch was eternall life to know and by ye Sp^t they might all come into X^t their sanctuary who destroyes ye devill ye destroyer & his works and bruises ye Serpents head for X^t was their Sanctuary who was their Saviour y^t Saved them from ye destroyer and X^t did baptize them with ye holy ghost & fire & throughly purge his flower & burn up their chaf with unquentiable fire y^t is sin & Corruption wch is got into man and woman by their transgression and X^t gathereth his wheat into his Garner soe all you that are baptized with X^{ts} Baptisme your wheat is in gods Garner, and noe spoiler can get into Gods Garner there to meddle with ye wheat though they may be permitted to meddle or make a noise with ye outward goods & ye platters & Coates, & as I was speaking in ye power of ye Lord ye people were transported & ye Lords power was over all, And of a Suddain ye Constables & ye people came in like a Sea & one of ye Constables s^d come downe, & Laid hands on me & I said to him art thou a Xtian we are Xtians & he had me by ye hand & was very fierce to pluck me downe and I spoke to ye people y^t ye blessings of god might rest upon all and still ye Constable bid me come downe, [& I said to him then Let me take my hat, & he said you may take your hat & I said how can I take my hat

[a] The word *turned* is crossed out and *directed* written over it.

& thou holdest me by ye hand, then Let my hand goe y^t I may take it and when I had taken it he plucked me downe,] & bid another with a staff take me & put me into prison & they Carryed me to another officers house y^t was more Civell and when they brought in 4 more they had taken of friends, & I was very weary and in a great Sweat Severall friends came to visit us in ye Constables house and I bad them all goe their wayes lest ye Constables & Informers should stop them.

And then ye Constables had us almost a mile to Justice [Guies^1 in Kings street in Bloomsbury] a fierce passionate man & he asked me my name and when I had told him the Clark wrote it downe and ye Constable told the Justice y^t I had preached in ye meeting and the Justice asked me whether I did preach & said did not I know y^t it was contrary to the Kings Laws to preach in such Conventicles y^t were contrary to ye Littergy of ye Church of England, and when I thought that he would have sworne some ag^t me I said let noe man swear ag^t me for it is my principle not to swear and therefore I would not have any man to swear ag^t me.

And ye Justice said did not I preach in ye Conventicle or meeting & I said that I did confess w^t god & X^t had done for my soul & did praise god, & I thought y^t I might have done it in the streets & in all places (viz) praise god & confess X^t Jesus, And this I was not ashamed to confess & this was not contrary to ye Littergy of ye Church of England. And ye Justice said against such meetings as were contrary to ye Littergye of the Church of England & I said I knew noe such Laws ag^t our meetings, but if ye Justice did mean y^t Conventicle Acte concerning such y^t did meet to plott & contrive & to raise insurrection ag^t the King, we did abhorr all such Actions and we were noe such people nor did we own our Selves such a people as that Acte was ag^t for we had nothing but Love and good will to ye King & all men upon ye earth & ye Justice asked me whether I had been in orders & I said noe never & then ye Justice took ye Law books & searched for Laws ag^t us & bid his Clark to take ye rest of their names but he found noe Laws ag^t us and then when y^t they had taken their names ye Clark sware ye Constable, & some of ye prisoners said

take heed what thou swearest, for he took them in yͤ Entry
& not in yͤ meeting Lest he was perjured, but yͤ wicked
Constable swore that they was in the meeting and then yͤ
Justice said yͭ there was but one witness & yͤ friends were
discharged but he would send me to Newgate & I might
preach there he said And I said to him could he in his Conscience send me to Newgate, for praiseing god and for confessing Xͭ Jesus and I felt my words touched his conscience,
& he cryed Conscience, Conscience, and soe he bad yͤ Constable take me away & he would make a Mittemus to send
me to prison when he had dined, & I said I desired his
peace & yͤ good of his family and that they might be kept
in yͤ fear of yͤ Lord if it was his will and passed away &
two friends passed their words to the Constables & they
took them that I should come to yͤ Constables house yͤ
next morning at eight of yͤ Clock.

And I and ffriends did goe next morning according to yͤ
hour. And yͤ Constables said that he went to yͤ Justices
after he had dined for the Mittemus, And yͤ Justice bad
him come againe after yͤ evening Service & he went & yͤ
Justice said to him at yͤ night yͭ he might Let me goe & soe
yͤ Constable said yͭ I was discharged[1] but yͤ Justice said
that if he did bring me again before him he would send me
to prison & soe being discharged I told yͤ Constable that he
had yͤ face of a man & I would not have him to be an Informer & that he should not have sworne agͭ friends, & soe
he promissed to doe soe noe more, & soe I passed away and
I told yͤ Constable yͭ he might have Let one Clark an Oxfordshire man have gone away (& not Carryed him before a
Justice) when I desired him but he would not but yͤ Justice
set him at Liberty with yͤ rest of friᵈˢ.

But when we were Carryed before yͤ Justice with yͤ Constables Shad yͤ wicked Informer[2] who had broken prison at
Coventry and was burned in yͤ hand at London he went up
to yͤ Justice & said to yͤ Justice yͭ he had convicted us of
yͤ 22ᵈ of King Charles, & yͤ Justice said what you convicte
them yes said Shad I have convicted them & you must convicte them according to yͭ Acte & yͤ Justice was Angry
with him & said you teach me what are you Ile convicte
them upon a riot said yͤ Justice soe yͤ Informer went away
from yͤ Justices house in a fret, Soe they were Confounded

& the Lords power came over them & we were set at Liberty.

And ye Justice asked Guil: Laty[1] ye next day if he would pay 20£ for :G: ffs: fine he said noe then saith he I am disappointed for he being a Lodger I cannot come by his fine and he being brought before me & of ability himself I cannot Lay his fine on any other.

[Then saith he I must have him brought before me again & I must send him to prison but y^t he could not doe for he had bid ye Constable discharge him ye night before wch accordingly ye Constable had done, & :G: ff: was gone into ye Citty, & ye Constable was very glad of it for he told ye Justice he was very Loath to Carry him to prison, wch made him soliscit ye Justice for to have him discharged.

The Justice spoke alsoe of fineing the meeting house but : J : V :[2] desired him not to doe soe seeing there was noe Information ag^t it. *And besids we had accomodated ye Kings Guards with ye use of it in the time of their necessity (when ye Late plott was discovered) there being not room enough for them in the Savoy upon request made to our friends, they gave them Liberty to Lodge there*[b] upon Condition they might have ye use of it in ye time of their necessity & they stayed about 5 weeks and when they went away they delivered the house up to us againe, when he heard this he spoke noe more of fineing the House*[3].]

ffrom the 10th of the 8th mo: 1683 being ye 4th day of ye week till ye 19th of ye said mo : G : ff: was at ff: Camfields[4] about busyness at the Sessions.

And on ye 21st of ye 8th mo: being ye 1st day of ye week :G: ff: was at Bullon mouth[5] where there was a very great meeting & very peaceable & quiet & kept with in the meeting house soe that the people were Soe refreshed with ye Lords power they were Loath to goe away.

On ye 25th of ye 8th mo: being ye 5th day of ye week :G: ff: went to Kingston in a Coach[6], & ye same day ye officers were very rude and did [nip &] abuse friends & drove them out of ye meeting place.

---

[a] ...[a] These words, occupying twenty lines in the MS., have a heavy line drawn diagonally through them.

[b] At this point four or five words have two thick lines drawn through them and cannot now be read.

[^aOn ye 1st day after fri^{ds} goeing about ye 10th hour kept their meeting till ye 11th being pretty quiet there being one Civill Constable & ye headborrow, but as they were passing away Eager ye Apothecary & a great Company following him were very fierce & threatened what they would doe but did nothing they being departed before they came^a.

On ye 1st day ffollowing being ye 4th of ye 9th mo: they were very bad with friends at ye same place and did greatly abuse them.

On ye 5th day following being the 8th of ye 9th mo: at ye aforesd place at Kingston ye Constable Lane was very bad to friends & put some of ye women into ye ditch and greatly abused ye rest of friends.]

On the 14th day of ye 9th mo: being ye 4th day of ye week :G: ff: was at Gracious street meeting where there was a very Large meeting & very peaceable and kept within doors.

On ye 16th of ye 9th mo: being ye 6th day of the week :G: ff: was at the meeting of Sufferings in Lumberstreet where there was Supposed to be an Informer watching and gazeing at ye windows in 3 King Courte.

On ye 18th of ye 9th mo: being ye 1st day of ye week :G: ff: was at Wheeley Street where there was an exceeding Large meeting & very peaceable and quiet & kept within the doors.

On ye 20th of ye 9th mo: being ye 3^d day of the week :G: ff: was at the 6 weeks meeting at the Bullon mouth.

And ye day ffollowing being ye 4th day of the week :G: ff: was at a meeting about busyness, at John Vaughtons.

The 22^d of the 9th mo: being the 5th day of ye week :G: ff: was at ye Savoy meeting where it was very quiet an peaceable within ye doors.

The 23th of ye 9th mo: being ye 6th day of the week :G: ff: was at ye meeting of Sufferings in Lumberstreet. And the next day he had a meeting about busyness at Samuell Boultons.

And on the 25th day of ye 9th mo: being the 1st day of ye week :G: ff: was at Horslydowne meeting where it was alsoe kept very quiet and peaceable within the doors.

On the 27th of ye 9th mo: (:G: ff: was at a meeting at Devinshire house) being ye 3^d day of ye week.

^a...^a This paragraph has a line drawn through it.

On ye 30th of ye 9th mo: being ye 6th day of ye week :G: ff: went to Abiah Roberts[1] at New Chappell in Essex where he had a meeting on ye 1st day after, being ye 2^d of ye 10th mo: and on ye 3^d day after he came to Jo: Bulls[2] at Miles end, And on the 4th day to Mary Stotts[3] at Dolston, And on ye 10th of ye 10th mo: (G: ff: had a meeting at Jane Bullocks at Shackelwell[4]) being ye 1st day of ye week.

And on the 14th of ye 10th mo: G: ff: came to London, And ye next day being ye 7th day of ye week he was sent for to Kingston to see young Margret Rouse[5] who Lay very Sick.

On ye 25th day of ye 10th mo: being {y^e 5th day} of ye week :G: ff: was at ye 6 weeks meeting at Bullon mouth.

On ye 28th day of ye 10th mo: being ye 6 day of ye week :G: ff: was at ye meeting of Sufferings in Lumberstreet:

And on ye 30th day of ye 10th mo: being ye 1st day of ye week :G: ff: was at Rattliff meeting both fore noon & after where there was very Large meetings both fornoon & after in ye meeting house & very peaceable.

And on the 2^d of ye 11th mo: being ye 4th day of ye week :G: ff: was at Gratius street meeting where it was kept very quiet & peaceable with in ye meeting house.

And on ye 4th of ye 11th mo: being ye 6th day of ye week :G: ff: was at ye meeting of Sufferings.

And on ye 6th of ye 11th mo: being ye 1st day of ye week :G: ff: was at Westminster meeting where it was very quiet & Large.

And on ye 2^d day of ye week being ye 7th day of ye mo: G: ff: was at a meeting about busyness Atte Bullon mouth.

And on ye 3^d day of ye week being ye 8th day of ye mo: G: ff: went to George Wattses house at Enfield[6] where he had a meeting on ye 1st day following being ye 13th of ye 11th mo: & ye next day he came to London.

And on ye 20th of ye 11th mo: being ye 1st day of ye week :G: ff: was at ye Savoy meeting where it was kept within ye doors pritty Large and Quiet.

The 15th of ye 12th mo: being ye 6th day of ye week he was att ye meeting for Sufferings in Lombardstreet. ~

On ye 17th of ye 12th mo: he was att ye peel where it was Kept with in ye meeting house very quiet and peaceable.

On ye 18th of ye 12th mo: being ye 2^d day of ye week he was att the morning meeting in Lombardstreet.~

On ye 22^d of ye 12th mo: being ye 6th day of ye week he was att the meeting for Sufferings in Lombardstreet.~

On ye 24th of ye 12th mo: being ye first day of ye week he was att wheeler Street where ye meeting was very Large & Quiett with in doors.

Besides many other meetings not hear Sett downe.~

Here ffolloweth a Jornall of the meetings :G:ff: hath been att &c. Anno domini 1684.~

The 7th of ye 1st mo: being ye 6th day of ye week he was att ye meeting for Sufferings in Lombard street.~

On ye 9th of ye 1st mo: being ye 1st day of ye week he was att ye meeting att Rattliff where it was very quiett & in ye meeting house he declared there a pritty time & afterwards went to prayer[1]. ~

The 13th of ye 1st mo: being ye 5th day of ye week he was att the meeting att Devenshire house where he declared it was very quiett and within doors.~

And on ye 14th of ye 1st mo: being the 6th day of ye week :G:ff: was at ye meeting of Sufferings in Lumberstreet.

And on ye 16th of ye 1st mo: being the 1st day of ye week :G:ff: was at Westminster where it was very quiet & peaceable within ye meeting house.

And on ye 21st day of ye 1st mo: being ye 6th day of ye week :G:ff: was at ye meeting of Sufferings in Lumberstreet.

And on ye 23^d of ye 1st mo: being ye 1st day of ye week :G:ff: was at ye peel meeting where it was very large and peaceable and within the meeting house.

The next day he went to visit a woman at Ellington[2] not well in her mind.

And on the 28th of ye 1st mo: being ye 6th day of ye week :G:ff: was at ye meeting of Sufferings in Lumberstreet.

On ye 30th of ye 1st mo: G:ff: was at ye Savoy where there was a Large meeting & peaceable within ye meeting house.

On ye 31st of ye 1st mo: being ye 2^d day of ye week :G:ff: went from ye Savoy to ye quarterly meeting at Devinshire house wch was very Large & quiet And ye next day (he came downe to Ed: Mans[1] where severall friends met him) being ye 1st day of ye 2^d mo: & ye 3^d day of ye week.

And on ye 2^d day after being ye 7th of ye 2^d mo: G: ff: went up to London to ffrancis Camfields to meet friends y^t attended on ye Sessions where friends Cast ye Informers.

And on ye 4th day after being ye 9th day of ye mo: G: ff: went to ye monthly meeting at Bullon mouth.

And ye next day being ye 5th day of ye week :G: ff: went to Newgate to visit ye prisoners.

And on ye 6th day being ye 11th of ye 2^d mo: G: ff: went to ye meeting of Sufferings in Lumber street.

And on ye 7th day being ye 12th of ye 2^d mo: G: ff: went to :M: Stotts where many friends came to him.

And on ye 4th day after being ye 16th of ye 2^d mo: G: ff: and some friends went up to Jane Bullocks School and from thence he came ye same day to Ed: Mans at Edmonton & on ye 5th day after he had a meeting with friends y^t awayes, about their Sufferings. being ye 17th of ye 2^d mo:

And on ye 21: of ye 2^d mo: being ye 2^d day of ye week :G: ff: went from Ed: Mans to Enfield. Miles :2:

And on ye 4th day after being ye 23^d of ye 2^d mo: G: ff: returned from thence to Ed: Mans again at fford Green. Miles :2:

And on ye 30th of ye 2^d mo: being ye 4th day of ye week :G: ff: came to London in ye Coach. Miles :9:

And on ye 2^d day of ye 3^d mo: being ye 6th day of ye week G. ff: went about ye 12th hour in a Coach to ye Savoy about some busyness. And came ag^n to ye meeting of Sufferings in Lombard street.

And on ye 4th day of ye 3^d mo: being ye 1st day of ye week :G: ff: was at ye after noon Meeting at Rattlif where it was very Large and peaceable within ye meeting house.

And on ye 5th day of ye 3^d mo: being ye 2^d day of ye week :G: ff: was at Wm Meads to see his wife y^t Lay in[2] where he had a Meeting with ye Women in ye Morning & after y^t he went to ye 2^d dayes morning meeting he had alsoe after y^t {at} a Meeting at Wm Crouches in Crown Courte wth some Dutch fri^{ds}, And towards night he had a meeting at Benjemin Antrobuses[3].

On ye 9th of ye 3^d mo: being ye 6th day of ye week :G: ff:

was at yᵉ meeting of Sufferings in Lombardstreet & yᵉ next day he was about busyness at yᵉ Chamber.

And on yᵉ 11ᵗʰ of yᵉ 3ᵈ mo: being yᵉ 2ᵈ day of yᵉ week :G: ff: was at Wheeleystreet meeting where it was very Large & peaceable within yᵉ doors.

And on yᵉ 12ᵗʰ of yᵉ 3ᵈ mo: being yᵉ 2ᵈ day of yᵉ week :G: ff: was at yᵉ morning meeting in Lombardstreet.

The 14ᵗʰ of yᵉ 3ᵈ mo: being yᵉ 4ᵗʰ day of yᵉ week :G: ff: went to ffrancis Camfields to Look after friends busyness at yᵉ Sessions, at Hixes Hall[1].

The 15ᵗʰ of yᵉ 3ᵈ mo: being yᵉ 5ᵗʰ day of yᵉ week :G: ff: had a meeting about busyness at Sam: Boltons in Lombardstreet.

And on yᵉ 16ᵗʰ of yᵉ 3ᵈ mo: being yᵉ 5ᵗʰ day of yᵉ week :G: ff: was at yᵉ meeting of Sufferings in Lombardstreet.

The 18ᵗʰ of yᵉ 3ᵈ mo: being yᵉ first day of yᵉ week :G: ff: was at the Morning meeting in Lombard Street. at yᵉ Chamber.

The 19ᵗʰ of yᵉ 3ᵈ mo: being yᵉ 2ᵈ day of yᵉ week :G: ff: was at yᵉ 2ᵈ dayes meeting in Lombard street. And on yᵉ afternoon he was at a meeting appointed about busyness with wᵗʰ yᵉ Country friends and others at Ben: Antrobus's.

The 20ᵗʰ of yᵉ 3ᵈ mo: being yᵉ 3ᵈ day of yᵉ week :G: ff: was at a meeting appointed about busyness at yᵉ Chamber in Lombardstreet.

And on yᵉ 21ˢᵗ of yᵉ 3ᵈ mo: being yᵉ 4ᵗʰ day of yᵉ week :G: ff: was at a meeting appointed about busyness at George Barrs[2] on yᵉ forenoon, & on the afternoon he had a meeting with some friends about busyness at Ben: Antrobusses.

And on yᵉ 22ᵈ of yᵉ 3ᵈ mo: being yᵉ 5ᵗʰ day of yᵉ week :G: ff: had a meeting on yᵉ forenoon with friends about busyness at Benjemin Antrobuses & {another} on yᵉ afternoon at Alexander Parkers[3].

And on the 23ᵈ of yᵉ 3ᵈ month: being yᵉ 6ᵗʰ day of yᵉ week :G: ff: had a meeting in yᵉ morning about busyness, And he was at yᵉ meeting of Sufferings in the afternoon.

And on yᵉ 24ᵗʰ of the 3ᵈ mo: being yᵉ 7ᵗʰ day of the week :G: ff: had a meeting about busyness at Nathaniell Braceys[4] (in the forenoon) in Lombardstreet.

And on yᵉ 26ᵗʰ of yᵉ 3ᵈ mo: being yᵉ 2ᵈ day of yᵉ week :G: ff: was at the Morning meeting in Lombardstreet.

The 27th of ye 3^d mo: being the 3^d day of ye week :G: ff: went to meet with Some ffriends at Martha ffishers[1] at the Savoy about Busyness.

And on the 30th of the 3^d mo: being the 6th day of the week :G: ff: was at the meeting of Sufferings in Lombard-street[2].

And on the 29th of ye 7th mo: {& 2^d day of ye week} G: ff: was at the Morning meeting in Lombardstreet. And on the afternoon he was at the quart: mens & womens meeting at the Bullon Mouth where it was very Large and peaceable. And from thence he went to George Watts where at night he had a meeting with Ed: Byllings & George Hutchison and Tho: Budd about New Jarceys[3] busyness.

And on the 30th of ye 7th mo: being ye 3^d day of ye week :G: ff: :G: ff: had a meeting about Henry Hopes[4] Son & Ben: Furley[5] at George Watts.

And on the 1st of ye 8th mo: being ye 4th day of the week :G: ff: had a meeting with Wm Kent[6] & Charles Bathurst[7] &c at the same Place besids busyness that he had at ye same place wth many others y^t came to him whilst there.

And on ye 2^d day of the 8th mo: being ye 5th day of ye week he Lay at Sam: Boltons where he & :G: W: & :A: P: had a meeting with Samuell concerning him & Mary Pen-nington[8]. And alsoe a meeting concerning them agⁿ ye next morning being the 3^d of ye 8th mo: & 6th Day of ye week. And on ye after noon he was at ye meeting of Sufferings. And afterwards he went to Benjemin Antrobusses where Rowland Vaughan[9] was to meet him about busyness & did*a*.

And ye next Day being the 4th of ye 8th mo: & 7th day of ye week :G: ff: had alsoe busyness with Rowland Vaughan about Distresses made at Swarthmoor.

And on ye 1st day of the week being ye 5th of ye 8th mo: :G: ff: was not very well & unfit to goe forth soe he had Mark[10] to write some things for him at Benjemin Antrobuses.

And on the 6th of ye 8th mo: being ye 2^d day of ye week :G: ff: staid at Benjein Antrobuses by Reason of ye Sessions at Guild Hall.

a Margin: *meetings this week were : 7 :*

And on ye 7th day of ye 8th mo: being ye 3^d day of ye week :G: ff: went to ffrancis Camfields to Speak with fri^{ds} concerned at ye Sessions at Hixes Hall. And on ye after noon he was sent for again to a meeting at Benjemin Antrobuses about a Difference betwixt fri^{ds} of New Jarcey & Ed: Byllings.

And on ye 8th of ye 8th mo: being ye 4th day of ye week :G: ff: went to ffrancis Camfields again about ffriends Busyness at Hixes Hall.

And on the 9th of the 8th mo: being the 5th Day of ye week :G: ff: was Sent for again from thence to Benjemin Antrobuses, to a meeting about new Jarceys busyness in ye morning and another in ye afternoon.

And on ye 10th of ye 8th mo: being ye 6th day of ye week :G: ff: was at ye abovesd meeting of busyness at Ben: Antrobusses in the morning & at ye meeting of sufferings in ye afternoon.

And on the 11th of ye 8th mo: being ye 7th Day of ye week :G: ff: was at ye above said meeting about new Jarceys busyness At the Chamber in Lombard street in the morning. And another at ye same place about ye same busyness in ye afternoon betwixt ye 9th and 10th hour at night^a.

And on the 12th of the 8th mo: being the 1st Day of the week :G: ff: being wearyed ye Day before at ye abovesd meeting about Jarceys busyness he staid all the day at Ben: Antrobuses & had Mark to write for him on the afternoon.

And on the 13th of the 8th mo: being the 2^d day of the Week :G: ff: was at the 2^d Dayes meeting in Lombard-street. And at night he went to ye Savoy.

And the next Day being the 14th of ye 8th mo: & 3^d day of ye week he had busyness with severall ffriends there.

And the next Day being the 15th of ye 8th mo: and the 4th Day of ye week G: ff: had a meeting wth Ed: Byllings & some other ffriends at ye 3^d hour on ye afternoon about new Jarceys Busyness at Samuell Boltons.

And on the 17th of the 8th mo: being the 6th Day of the week :G: ff: was at the meeting of Sufferings.

And on the 19th of the 8th mo: being ye 1st Day of the week he was at Wheeley street meeting where there was a

^{a} Margin: *meetings this week were : 7:*

very good meeting & very Large and peaceable with in the Doors[a].

. And on y[e] 20th of y[e] 8th mo: being y[e] 2[d] Day of y[e] week he was at the 2[d] Dayes morning meeting in Lombard street.

And on y[e] 21st of y[e] 8th mo: being y[e] 3[d] day of y[e] week he had a meeting of busyness at y[e] said Chamber in Lombard street.

And on the 23[d] of y[e] 8th mo: being the 5th day of the week :G: ff: had a meeting on y[e] forenoon & another on the afternoon about Edward Byllings busyness till about the 9th hour at night.

And on the 24th of the 8th mo: being the 6th Day of the week he was at the Meeting of Sufferings. And after that he had a meeting with a few friends about busyness at Nat: Braceyes.

And the next Day being the 25th of y[e] 8th mo: & 7th Day of y[e] week :G: ff: had a meeting with : W: P: & R Vickridge[1] about Richards own Busyness. And on the after noon he had a meeting wth Severall friends about busyness at the 7th hour at night both the meetings were at the Chamber[b]. And from thence he went to Benjemin Antrobuses at night. Where the next Day being the 26th of the 8th mo: & 1st Day of y[e] week he had Mark to write for him to y[e] King of Denmark & the Duke of Halstine[2] from about y[e] 11th hour of y[e] Day till 9 at night.

And on y[e] 27th of y[e] 8th mo: being y[e] 2[d] Day of the week he went from thence to the morning meeting in Lombard street. And on the afternoon he went to Martha ffishers at y[e] Savoy where he had busyness with some fri[ds].

And on the 30th of the 8th mo: being y[e] 5th Day of y[e] week he was at a meeting appointed about {y[e]} busyness of Mary Penington & Samuell Bolton at Benjemin Antrobuses.

And on the 31st of y[e] 8th mo: being y[e] 6th Day of y[e] week he had a meeting with some ffri[ds] at Benjemin Antrobuses in the morning about young Margret Drinkells[3] busyness. And on the after noon he was at the meeting of Sufferings.

And on the 7th Day being the 1st of the 9th mo: he went to Mary Stotts at Dolston[c].

[a] Margin: *meet: this week were :5:*
[b] Margin: *y[e] meet: G: ff: hath been at this week were :8:*
[c] Margin: *meet: this week were 4*

And on the 2^d Day morning being the 3^d of ye 9th mo: he Came from thence to ye Morning meeting in Lombard street. And on ye afternoon he Came from thence to Martha ffishers at ye Savoy to meet with some fri^{ds} about busyness.

And on the 5th of ye 9th mo: being the 4th Day of ye week :G: ff: went to ye quarterly meeting at Westminster and it haveing continued till about ye 7th hour at night he afterwards took Coach to Sam: Boltons.

And on the 6th of ye 9th mo: being ye 4th Day of ye week :G: ff: was at a meeting appointed about Margret Drinkells and her Daughters busyness at ye Chamber in Lombard street.

And on ye 7th of ye 9th mo: being ye 6th Day of ye week :G: ff: was at ye meeting of Suffering.

And on ye 8th of ye 9th mo: being the 7th Day of ye Week he went to Thomas Coxes[1] at ye White Lion in White Chapell to Look after ffri^{ds} Sufferings[a].

And on ye 9th of the 9th mo: being the 1st Day of ye week :G: ff: was at the Peel meeting where he declared & went to prayer & another fri^d declared after him, and then ye meeting haveing continued about 3 hours was after wards Ended without ye Least Disturbance. And afterwards Rol: Vaughan being appointed met :G: ff: on the after noon at John Elsons with some other friends about busyness of Ann Heleys[2] at Henden.

And the same Day at night he had a meeting with a young woman that friends had trouble with at the peel.

And on ye 10th of ye 9th mo: {being ye 2^d Day of ye week} he was at the morning meeting in ye Lombardstreet.

And on ye 11th of ye 9th mo: being ye 3^d Day of ye week :G: ff: went from Benjemin Antrobuses to Martha ffishers at ye Savoy, to speak with Rolland Vaughan & some others about busyness and haveing staid there all night he came ye next Day from thence to Ben: Antrobuses ag^n where he had busyness with some ffriends. And on ye after noon he went to ye Bullon Mouth monthly meeting where it was kept very peaceable & after ye meeting was Ended he came from thence to Ben: Antrobuses again where he staid all that night.

And on ye 13th of ye 9th mo: being ye 5th Day of ye week he went from thence to Laurans ffullers[3] about busyness

[a] Margin: *meet: this week were :5:*

where we dined & after a while he went from thence to {visit} Rebecah Traverses[1] and haveing Staid a While there we went from thence to ffrancis Camfields, where he Staid all that night.

And ye next Day being the 14th of ye 9th mo: & ye 6th Day of ye week he had a meeting at ffrancis Camfields about Widdow Healeys busyness of Henden on the forenoon. And on ye afternoon he went from thence to ye meeting of Sufferings till ye 6th hour at night. And after it was Done he went to Wm Meads where he Staid all night.

And on ye 15th of ye 9th mo: being ye 7th Day of ye week he went to Thomas Barkers in Seizing Lane[2] to visit Margret Rouse & her Children[a]. And haveing staid a while there & Dined we went from thence to Edward Bathursts[3] where John Hutson[4] Cobler met him about his busyness of being distrained upon to ye value of 20^lb for a fine of 10^lb & haveing staid there a while he went from thence to Ben: Antrobuses where he staid all y^t night.

And on the 16th of the 9th mo: being ye 1st Day of ye week he had Mark to write for him most of ye Day at Ben: Antrobuses.

And on ye 17th of ye 9th mo: being ye 2^d Day of ye week he was at ye 2^d Dayes morning meeting. And on the afternoon he was at a meeting appointed at George Barrs about Ed: Byllings & friends of New Jarceyes busyness till ye 10th hour at night, where he Lodged y^t night.

And ye next night being the 18th of ye 9th mo: & 3^d Day of ye week he had a meeting at Marg^t Drinkells about her Daughters busyness where he alsoe Lodged that night.

And on ye 19th of ye 4th mo: & ye 9th mo:[b] & ye 4th Day of ye week He Lay at Wm Meads his wife[5] being come up to London & gone thither that night.

And on ye 20th of ye 9th mo: being ye 5th Day of ye week he was at Wm Meads all that Day and night.

And on ye 21st of the 9th mo: being ye the 6th Day of ye week he was at ye meeting of Sufferings in Lombardstreet & went to Wm Meads againe at night.

And on ye 22^d of ye 9th mo: being the 7th Day of the week he was at the Chamber again about busyness on the forenoon[c].

---

[a] Margin: *meet: this week were :8:*
[b] A mistake in copying.   [c] Margin: *meet: this week were :5:*

And on the 23^d of the 9th mo: being ye 1st Day of ye week :G: ff: was at Wm Meads where he & :M: ff: had Mark to write for them part of the Day.

And on the 2^d Day being ye 24th of the 9th mo: he was at ye morning meeting at ye Chamber. And afterwards went to Ben: Antrobuses where he had busyness with Some ffri^{ds}, & from thence he went to the Savoy to Martha ffishers. And the next Day being ye 25th of ye 9th mo: & 3^d Day of the week he went from thence to ye Six weeks meeting at Bullon Mouth & from thence we went to ffrancis Camfields where he Dined, and afterwards went from thence to Mar: ffishers at the Savoy againe.

And on ye 26th of ye 9th mo: being ye 4th Day of ye week he was at ye Savoy.

And on ye 27th of ye 9th mo: being ye 5th Day of ye week he went from thence to Ben: Antrobuses where he staid all night, & had busyness with Several fri^{ds}.

And on the 28th of ye 9th mo: being the 6th Day of the week he went from thence to the meeting of Sufferings in Lombard Street.

And after it was done about ye 7th hour at night he went to Nat: Braceys about Busyness with some fri^{ds} where he Lay y^t night.

And on ye 29th of ye 9th mo: & the 7th Day of ye week he went from thence to ye Chamber about busyness, And from thence to Wm Meads where we Dined, And afterwards went from to his wife at Martha ffishers at ye Savoy^a.

And on ye 30th of ye 9th mo: being ye 1st Day of ye week he was at ye meeting at ye Savoy held in ye yard and Entry where he Declared & went to prayer & Geo: Watt Declared after him and then ye meeting Ended without any Disturbance, by the officers.

And on ye 1st of the 10th mo: being ye 2^d Day of ye week he went from ye Savoy to the 2^d Dayes morning meeting in Lombardstreet. And after that he had a meeting at Nat: Braceys about busyness. And afterwards he went to John Plants[1] in Spittlefields where he Lay y^t night by reason of busyness y^t he had wth Abraham Goedowne[2].

And ye next Day being ye 2^d of ye 10th mo: and 3^d Day of ye week he went from thence to ye 6 weeks meeting at

---

^{a} Margin: *meet: this week were :3:*

Devenshire house, & went from thence to Wm Meads at night.

And on the 4th of the 10th mo: being ye 5th Day of ye week he had busyness at ye Chamber most of ye Day^a.

And on ye 5th of ye 10th mo: being ye 6th Day of ye week he had busyness at ye Chamber on ye forenoon & was at ye meeting of Sufferings there in ye afternoon till ye 7th hour at night & after it was done he went from thence to Wm Meads to Lodge.

And on ye 6th of ye 10th mo: being ye 7th Day of ye week he had Alsoe busyness at ye Chamber most of the Day.

And on the 7th of ye 10th mo: being ye 1st Day of ye week :G: ff: was at Wm Meads & had Mark to write for him most of ye Day.

And ye next Day being the 8th of the 10th mo: & ye 2^d Day of ye week he went from thence to ye morning meeting. And from thence he went to Nat: Braceys where he had appointed to meet with Some fri^{ds} about New Jarceys proprietours busyness. And from thence he went to Benjemin Antrobuses {to meet with some friends &} to know how things went wth fri^{ds} at ye Sessions at yield Hall^1, where he Lodged all night.

And on ye 9th of ye 10th mo: being the 3^d Day of ye week he went from thence to ffra: Camfields to meet with fri^{ds} concerned at ye Sessions at Hixes hall.

And on ye 10th of ye 10th mo: at night he went from ffra: Camfields to William Meads.

And ye next Day being ye 11th of ye 10th mo: & ye 5th Day of ye week he came from thence to the Chamber about busyness and there Sent for Samuell Bolton & had a meeting with him about {his} busyness & Mary Peningtons.

And on the 12th of ye 10th mo: being ye 6th Day of ye week he was at ye meeting of Sufferings, & afterwards went from thence to Wm Meads, where he Lodged y^t night.

And on ye 13th of ye 10th mo: being ye 7th Day of ye week he had busyness at ye Chamber most of ye Day & alsoe appointed to meet :G: W: there about some pticular busyness^b.

And on ye 14th of ye 10th mo: being ye 1st Day of ye week

^{a} Margin: *meet: this week were :6:*
^{b} Margin: *meet: this week were :7:*

he was at ye forenoon meeting at Devinshire house where it was very large & peaceable without ye Doors.

And on ye 15th of ye 10th mo: being ye 2^d Day of ye week he was at ye 2^d Dayes morning meeting at the Chamber in Lombardstreet.

And on ye 17th of ye 10th mo: being ye 4th Day of ye week he and :G: W: went to Ratlif to speak with Justice Smith[1] & Lay all night at Ja: Struts[2].

And the next Day being the 18th of ye 10th mo: & ye 5th Day of ye week he came from thence to Thomas Coxes And from thence to Wm Meads where he Lay that night.

The next Day being the 19th of ye 10th mo: and ye 6th Day of ye week he was at ye meeting of Sufferings & went to Wm Meads at night.

And on the 20th of ye 10th mo: being ye 7th Day of ye week he & :M: ff: & :S: ff:[3] went in ye Coach to John Rouses[4] at Kingston. And we staid there from the 20th of the 10th mo: till ye 19th of ye 11th mo: (ie) a mo: Dureing wch time :G: ff: had a meeting in the evenings at John Rouses for ye most part thrice in ye week the meetings while he staid there were about :10: or :12:

And on the 6th Day being ye 23^d af ye 11th mo: :G: ff: was at ye meeting of Sufferings.

And on ye 25th of ye 11th mo: being ye 1st Day of ye week he was at Ben: Antrobuses where he had Mark most of ye Day & was busyed in Reading of books to be printed.

And on ye 26th of the 11th mo: being ye 2^d Day of ye week he was at ye 2^d Dayes morning meeting.

And on ye 28th of ye 11th mo: being the 4th Day of the week he had busyness at the Chamber in ye morning. And afterwards went to Rowland Vaughans about his own busyness[5]. And from thence he went to visit Wm Penn at his lodgings, at Chering Cross[6]. And from thence he went to ffra: Camfields where he staid that night.

And ye next Day being the 29th of ye 11th mo: & ye 5th Day of ye week he went from thence to visit Giles Pettyplace[7] in Hatton Garden who had not been very well, And from thence he went to ye monthly meeting at John Elsons where he staid that night.

And ye next Day being the 30th of ye 11th mo: & 6th Day

of yᵉ week he went from thence to yᵉ meeting of Sufferings.
And from thence to Wᵐ Meads*ᵃ*.

And yᵉ next Day being yᵉ 31ˢᵗ of yᵉ 11ᵗʰ mo: & yᵉ 7ᵗʰ
Day of yᵉ week :G: ff: went from thence to Bednall Green
to Visit Mary Stott.

And on yᵉ 2ᵈ of yᵉ 12ᵗʰ mo: being yᵉ 2ᵈ Day of yᵉ week
he went from thence to yᵉ 2ᵈ Dayes morning meeting.

And on yᵉ 6ᵗʰ of yᵉ 12ᵗʰ mo: being yᵉ 6ᵗʰ Day of yᵉ week
he was at yᵉ meeting of Sufferings and from thence he went
to Wᵐ Meads.

And on yᵉ 7ᵗʰ of yᵉ 12ᵗʰ mo: being yᵉ 7ᵗʰ Day of yᵉ week
he had busyness with some friends at yᵉ Chamber*ᵇ*.

And on yᵉ 8ᵗʰ of yᵉ 12ᵗʰ mo: being yᵉ 1ˢᵗ Day of yᵉ week
he was at Ben: Antrobuses where he Appointed severall friᵈˢ
to meet him.

And on yᵉ 9ᵗʰ of yᵉ 12ᵗʰ mo: being the 2ᵈ Day of the week
he was at yᵉ morning meeting on yᵉ forenoon and at night
he had a meeting with severall friends about Drawing up a
Paper to yᵉ King[1] at Ben: Antrobuses from about yᵉ 5ᵗʰ hour
till near yᵉ 10ᵗʰ.

And on yᵉ 10ᵗʰ of yᵉ 12ᵗʰ mo: being yᵉ 3ᵈ Day of yᵉ week
at night he was with some friends about yᵉ aforesᵈ busyness
at yᵉ Chamber.

And on the 11ᵗʰ of yᵉ 12ᵗʰ mo: being yᵉ 4ᵗʰ Day of yᵉ
week he had a meeting with some friᵈˢ at Martha ffishers
at yᵉ Savoy.

And on yᵉ 13ᵗʰ of yᵉ 12ᵗʰ mo: being yᵉ 6ᵗʰ Day of yᵉ week
:G:ff: was at yᵉ meeting of Sufferings and went from thence
to Wᵐ Meads where he lay yᵗ night.

And on yᵉ 14ᵗʰ of yᵉ 12ᵗʰ mo: being the 7ᵗʰ Day of yᵉ
week he mett :G: W: & ffra: Camfield at Laurance ffulloes
about busyness And after some time Staying there he went
from thence to John Elsons where he Staid yᵗ night*ᶜ*.

And yᵉ next Day being yᵉ 15ᵗʰ of yᵉ 12ᵗʰ mo: and yᵉ 1ˢᵗ
Day of the week he was at the Peel meeting where after he
had Declared a Considerable time and Gone to prayer the
meeting Departed in peace it being very*ᵈ* and kept within

ᵃ Margin: *meet: this week were :3:*
ᵇ Margin: *meet: this week were :3:*
ᶜ Margin: *meet: this week were :7:*
ᵈ Perhaps, *Large* omitted.

the Doors. And a while after ye meeting was done he went from thence to George Watts where he Lodged that night.

And ye next morning being ye 16th of ye 12th mo: & 2^d Day of ye week he had a meeting at the same place about the aforesaid Paper to be presented to King James.

And the next Day being the 17th of ye 12th mo: & ye 3^d Day of the week he went from thence to ye Six weeks meeting at Bullon Mouth. And from thence he went to Ben: Antrobuses where he Staid that night.

And on ye 20th of ye 12th mo: being ye 6. Day of ye week he was at ye meeting of Sufferings. And from thence he went to Wm Meads where he Lodged y^t night.

And ye next Day being ye 21st of ye 12th mo: & 7th Day of ye week :G:ff: & :M:ff: and Thomas Lower[1] and his wife[2] took Coatch to Kingston where they staid till ye 25th of ye 12th mo: being ye 4th Day of ye week where on Wm Mead & his wife goeing to visit John Rouses family Carryed a Coatch to bring them back and haveing come to London :G:ff: went the same night to ffra: Camfields it then being ye Sessions time at Hixes Hall to see what became of friends that were to appear there.

And ye next Day towards night he went from thence to Ben: Antrobus's.

And ye next Day being ye 27th of ye 12th mo: and ye 6th Day of ye week he went from thence to ye meeting of Sufferings, And from thence to Wm Meads.

And the next Day being ye 28th of ye 12th mo: and ye 7th Day of ye week he went from thence in the morning to a meeting appointed at Wm Crouches for Ed: Byllings about his busyness in West Jarcey. And haveing Staid Dinner there he afterwards went from thence to visit Mary Stott at Martha Hulls[3] at Beddnall Green and staid there till ye 2^d of ye 1st mo: being ye 2^d Day of the week.

A Jornall of ye meetings G : ff hath been at ffor ye year 1685

On ye first of ye first mo: being ye first day of ye week G ff was at Mary Stots at Bednall Green.

The next day being ye 2^d of ye 1st mo: & 2^d day of ye week he took Coach from thence to ye 2^d days morning meeting in 3 King Court in Lombardstreet & {went} to W: Meads at night.

The next day being ye 3^d of ye 3^d mo: & ye 3^d day of ye week he went from thence to W: Ps at Chering Cross & afterwards Crossed ye water to Wm Berkits[1] where he dined & from thence he returned to M: ffs: againe at ye Savoy.

The next day being ye 4th of ye 1st mo: & ye 4th day of ye week he went from thence to B: As: where he dined & afterwards went from thence to A: ps where he had a meeting with W: P: & Ed: Billings about New Jerceys busyness from thence he went to W: Ms where he staid y^t night.

The next day, being ye 5th of ye 1st mo: & 5th day of ye week he went to visit Ann Traverse[2] at Newington where he staid y^t night.

The next day being ye 6th of ye 1st mo & ye 6th day of ye week he went from thence to visit ye prisoners at ye Marshals[3] & from thence he went to the meeting for Sufferings. & from thence to W: Ms at night.

The next day being ye 7th of ye 1st mo: & 7th day of ye week he went from thence to ye Chamber about busyness & from thence to G: Ws where he lay that night.

And ye next day being ye 8th of ye 1st mo: & 1st day of ye week he went from thence to ye forenoon meeting at Devenshire house where he declared a pritty time & after that went to prayer & when he had done ye meeting departed it was very Large and peaceable within ye Doors, & from thence he went to G: Ws again where haveing staid a little while he went from thence to Mary ffosters and ffrom thence to W: Ms where he staid y^t night.

And on ye afternoon of ye 8th of ye 1st mo: & 1st day of ye week ye Informers and Soldjers & Constables Came & disturbed ye meeting at Devenshire house & took about 30 ffri^{ds} & Carryed before ye Major[4] & ye Informer and some of ye officers went to G: Ws house and said there used to be a meeting there & swore that they would break open ye door but ye people Came & fell soe on ye Informer y^t she[5] went away soe ye doors was not broken open.

The next day being ye 9th of ye 1st mo: & ye 2^d day of ye week he went from thence to ye 2^d dayes meeting & ffrom thence to B: As: where he staid y^t night.

The next day being ye 10th of ye 1st mo: and ye 3^d day of ye week he went from thence to ffra: Camfields to a meeting appointed about a difference betwixt Jo: Roose & Jo: Bell-hous[1] where he staied y^t night.

And on ye 11th of ye 1st mo: & ye 4th day of the week he went from ffra: Camfields to visit a fr^d y^t Lay sick in Hounds-dick a prisoner of New Gate & afterwards went from thence to A: ps where he dined from thence he went to the Chamber & from thence 2 W: Ms where he staid that night.

And ye next day being ye 12th of ye 1st mo: & ye 5th day of ye week he went from thence to the Chamber about busyness & from hence to A: ps: where he & his wife & Tho: Lower & Jo: Rowse &c were Invited to a dinner, & on ye afternoon he went to ye Chamber againe to a meeting appointed about busyness & from thence he went to John Osgoods[2] about some busyness & from thence to W: Ms where he staid y^t night.

The next day being ye 13th of ye 1st mo: and ye 6th day of ye week in ye morning he went from thence to ye Chamber & from thence to Nat: Braceys where he was invited to dinner & afterwards from thence to ye meeting for Sufferings & from thence to Nat: Blands[3] & from thence to W: Ms againe where he staid that night.

And ye next day being ye 14th of ye 1st mo: & ye 7th day of ye week he went from thence to ye Chamber againe about busyness of fri^ds & from thence to A: ps where haveing staid a while he went from thence to B: As: where he staid that night[a].

The next day being ye 15th of ye 1st mo: & ye 1st day of ye week he not being well & unable to goe to a meeting he had Mark to write for him at ye before said place B: As: & towards ye Evening he went from thence to W: Ms where he staid y^t night.

The next day being ye 16th of ye 1st mo: & 2^d day of the week he & W: M & his wife & T: Lower & M: Rowse & S: ff: took Coach with M: ff: & M: L: to ye swan with 2 Necks in Lad Lane[4] to see y^m take Coach to New Castle & soe for Swarthmoor ~ & from thence G: ff took Coach to ye 2^d dayes meeting in Lombardstreet & from thence to Nat

^a Margin: *meetings he was at this week were 4:*

Blands & from thence to another meeting with W: P & Ed:
Byllings & some others about New Jerceys busyness & from
thence to See Samuell Bolton who was sick and from thence
to B: As: where he lay y^t night.

The time :M ff: staid at & about London was from ye 19th
of ye 9th mo: to ye 16th of ye 1st mo: wch is 16 weeks & :3:
dayes. ~

The next day being ye 17th of ye 1st mo: & ye 3^d day of
ye week he staid at ye above said B: As: y^t day & at
night.

The next day being ye 18th of ye 1st mo: & ye 4th day of
ye week he went from thence to Ed: Mans in Geo: yard &
some other fri^{ds} there about^a & afterwards to y^e seedsmans
in Byshopgate street & soe to y^e Coach y^t Carryed him to
Bridgits at South Street Miles :9:^{b}

And y^e 26th of y^e 1st mo: being y^e 5th day of y^e week he
went from thence to Ed: Mans at fford green in a Coach
Mi: 1—$\frac{1}{2}$.

And on y^e 29th of y^e 1st mo: & y^e 1st day of y^e week he
had a meeting there where there were alsoe G: W: A: p
Rich^d pinder[1] &c. & G ff declared a pritty time & afterwards
went to prayer and after he had done y^e meeting departed.

And on y^e 7th of y^e 2^d mo: being y^e 3^d day of y^e week he
went from Ed: Mans to Widdow Dryes[2] at Enfild where
haveing staid till ye 12th of ye 2^d mo: being ye 1st day of y^e
week towards night he went from thence to G: Wats at y^e
Chase Side who with ffra: Camfield Came from London with
an Intent to get him thither. ~

On ye 18th of ye 2^d mo: being ye 7th day of ye week he
went from :G: Ws: to Tho: Hearts[3] where he dined &
T: Robison[4] alsoe, & haveing staid a while there we went
from thence to Tho: Bennets[5] at Walthum Abbey miles 3
where we staid y^t night.

The next day being ye 19th of ye 2^d mo: & ye 1st day of y^e
week he went from thence to ye meeting at ye said towne &
T: R: alsoe where was alsoe Ben: ffreeman[6] & Eliz: Bathurst[7]
who all three haveing Declared he stood up & declared &
afterwards went to prayer & then spoke a few words to y^e
people & when he had done ye meeting departed it was very

---

^{a} Margin: *remained at London 18 Day's*
^{b} Margin: *remained at South gate 7 Dayes & 8: nights*

Large and peaceable within ye doors & Continued from about
ye 12th hour till betwixt ye 2^d & 3^d.

The next day being ye 20th of 2^d mo: & ye 2^d day of y^e
week he went from Tho: Bennets to Tho: Hearts againe in
a Chariot mil 3 where he appointed to meet Robt Barkley[1]
he dined there & staid y^t night.

The next day being ye 21st of ye 2^d mo: & ye 3^d day of y^e
week he went from thence to G: Watts again where on y^e
1st day ffollowing being y^e 26th of y^e 2^d mo: he had a meeting^a.

The next day being y^e 27th of y^e 2^d mo: he went from
thence to Bridgits at South Street, againe miles :3 : where
haveing staid from y^e 27th of y^e 2^d mo: till y^e 9th of y^e 3^d
mo: he went from thence to Ed: Mans at fford green againe
in a Coach :M: 1$\frac{1}{2}$.

And on y^e 10th of y^e 3^d mo: being y^e 1st day of y^e week
he was at y^e meeting at Winzmerhill[2] where after G: W:
Geo: Watt & James park[3] had declared he stood up & declared a pritty while & after wards went to prayer & then
spake a few words to y^e people & when he had done y^e
meeting departed it was very Large and peaceable within
ye doors, ffrom thence he went to Ed: Mans at ffordgreen
againe. ~

And on ye 14th of ye 3^d mo: being ye 5th day of ye week
he went from thence to Bridgits at South Street againe to
be blooded with horse Leaches.

On ye 16th of ye 3rd mo: being ye 7th day of ye week Ed:
man bringing 2 horses brought him from thence to his house
at ffordgreen ag^n where on ye next day being ye 17th of y^e
3^d mo: & ye 1st day of ye week many fri^{ds} Came to visit him.

On ye 20th of ye 3^d mo: being ye 4th day of ye week he
went from thence in a Coach to London Miles :9 : he Lighted
out of ye Coach at ye Seeds mans in Byshopgate street &
haveing staid a while there, he went from thence to A: ps:
where he dined & from thence to B: As: where he staid y^t
night. The time he Remained in the Country {was} from
ye 18th of ye 1st mo: to ye 20th of ye 3^d mo: y^t is about :9 :
weeks.

The meetings he was at in ye Country were :4 : {besids
other small meetings of busyness.}

And ye next day being ye 21st of ye 3^d mo: & ye 5th day

^{a} Margin: *Remained at G: Ws :5: days & :6: nights*

of y[e] week he staid at y[e] befores[d] place where several fr[ds] Came to him he alsoe staid there at night againe.

The 22[d] of y[e] 3[d] mo: being y[e] 6th day of the week he went to y[e] meeting of Sufferings w[ch] held from between y[e] 3[d] & 4th hour till about y[e] 7th from thence he went to Jo: Elsons where he staid y[t] night.

The next day being the 23[d] of y[e] 3[d] mo: & 7th day of y[e] week after dinner he went from thence to Jo: Dewes[1] about some busyness goeing from thence he afterwards took Coach to Josiah Ellises[2], & afterwards went to M: ffs where he staid that night.

The next day being y[e] 24th of y[e] 3[d] mo: & y[e] 1st mo: & y[e] 1st day of y[e] week he was at y[e] meeting at y[e] Savoy where after Tho: Robinson had declared he stood up & declared & afterwards went to prayer & then spake a few words to the people & after he had done y[e] meeting departed, It was pritty Large in y[e] yard and with out any Disturbance.

And on y[e] 25th of y[e] 3[d] mo: being y[e] 2[d] day of y[e] week he went from M ffs to James Beeches at Westminster where he met W: P: G: W: R: Barkley &c about fr[ds] busyness the parliament being then sitting, from thence he went by water to Josiah Ellises & from thence to M: ffs where he staid that night.

The next day being y[e] 26th of y[e] 3[d] mo: & y[e] 3[d] day of y[e] week he went from thence to :B: As: where he dined & afterwards went from thence to y[e] Chamber to meet with some fr[ds] there, about drawing up fr[ds] Sufferings & Laying them before y[e] King & parliament, from thence he went to :B: As: againe at night. ~

The next day being y[e] 27th of y[e] 3[d] mo: being the 4: day of y[e] week he was alsoe about y[e] befores[d] busyness forenoon & after at y[e] Chamber where he alsoe appointed some fri[ds] to meet him, & went to B: As: again at night. ~

The 28th of y[e] 3[d] mo: being y[e] 5th Day of y[e] week he went from thence to a meeting appointed about y[e] 10th hour in y[e] morning at ffra: Camfields Concerning Widdow Helays busyness at Henden, & haveing dined there he afterwards went to philip ffords[3] to Speak with him about some busyness, and from thence to Ed: Dyheys[4] to Speak with Charles

Marshall about some busyness & from thence to :B: As: where he staid y^t night. ~

And ye next day being ye 29th of ye 3^d mo: & ye 6th Day of ye week after dinner he went to ye meeting of Sufferings, & about ye 7th hour he went from thence to Sam^{ll} Boltons where he staid a little in ye Shop & went from thence to :B: As: where he staid y^t night.

The 30th of ye 3^d mo: & ye 7th day of ye week he went from thence to ye Chamber about busyness where haveing staid till about ye first hour he went from thence to A: ps: in George Yard who had invited him to dinner & afterwards he went from thence to ye Chamber againe to look after fri^{ds} Sufferings where there Came to him John Bowlrun[1] a north Country fr^d who had busyness wth him & about ye 6th hour he went from thence to S: Boltons where haveing staid a while in ye Shope there came to him Leonard ffell[2], & staying a little Longer they went to B: As: where they {both} staid that night.

The meetings he was at this week were 5: one publick & 4 ab^t busyness &c.

The 31st of ye 3^d mo: being ye 1st day of ye week he was at B: As: & had Mark on ye forenoon & R Richardson both forenoon & after till ye 4th hour with him about busyness relateing to fri^{ds} Sufferings &c[3] there Came many other fr^{ds} to visit him & y^t had busyness with him he alsoe staid there ag^n that night.

The next day being the {1st of y^e} 4th mo: & 2^d day of ye week he went from ye befores^d :B: As: to ye 2^d days meeting at ye Chamber where Andrew Sowl[4] was sent for to print {a} paper of fr^{ds} Sufferings to Lay before ye King & part^{mt} ag^t ye 5th hour in ye Evening, from thence he & R: Barkley went to Nat: Blands where they dined & afterwards went from thence to ye Chamber ag^n about Busyness from thence he went to Geo Wats to visit ye Dutch fr^{ds} pet: Hendrick[5] & ffrancis Mungumtongrum[6] where he staid y^t night.

And ye next day being ye 2^d of ye 4th mo: & ye 3^d day of ye week haveing staid Dinner at ye befores^d place he afterwards went from thence to a meeting appointed about ye 5th hour at night about laying fr^{ds} Sufferings before ye King

& parliam^t, & from thence he went to :B: As: Where he staid y^t night & several fr^{ds} Came to him.

The next day being ye 3^d of ye 4th mo: & ye 4th day of ye week he went from thence to James Beeches at Westminster to meet with some fr^{ds} appointed to spread papers of fr^{ds} Sufferings in ye parliam^t house &c and from thence he went to ye monthly meeting at Westminster & from thence to :M: ffs: at ye Savoy where he staid y^t night, & had busyness with Ro{w}land Vaughan. ~

The next day being ye 4th of ye 4th mo: & ye 5th day of ye week he went from thence to ye Chamber about busyness, from thence to Wm Crouches & from thence to ye Chamber ag^n & afterwards to B: As where he staid that night and several fr^{ds} Came to him.

And ye next day being ye 5th of ye 4th mo: & ye 6th Day of ye week after dinner he went from ye befores^d place to ye meeting of Sufferings & afterwards to B: As againe where he staid y^t night & several fr^{ds} Came to him. ~

On ye 6th of ye 4th mo being ye 7th day of ye week he went from thence to ye Chamber where he mett several fr^{ds} about busyness of fr^{ds} & haveing staid till ye 2^d hour he went from thence to Wm Tilebyes[1] where he dined & afterwards went to ye Chamber again where he likewise mett some fr^{ds} about busyness & towards night he went from thence to B: As ag^n where several fr^{ds} Came to him :

The meetings he hath been at this week were :6: One mo^{ly} meeting and ye 2^d Dayes meeting & {y^e} meeting for Sufferings & 3 about other Concerns.

And ye 7th of ye 4th mo: & 1st day of ye week he went from :B: As: to ye 1st days morning meeting there being many Country fr^{ds} in ye Citty Come up to ye yearly meeting[2] where haveing staid till near ye 12th hour with W: p: & G: W: &c. he went from thence to S: Boltons to see M: Rowse & from thence to :B: As: againe where several fr^{ds} Came to him.

The 8th of ye 4th mo: being ye 2^d day of ye week he was at ye General meeting of fr^{ds} in ye Ministry at ye Chamber which held from about ye 8th hour till ye 10th where :W: P & several others haveing declared he stood up & declared &

afterwards went to pray^r & after ye meeting was done he went from thence to N: Braceys where he was invited to a dinner with ye Dutch fr^{ds} & from thence to a meeting appointed at :B: As: ab^t ye 2^d hour concerning ye General sufferings of fr^{ds} where he stayd that night.

The 9th of ye 4th mo: & ye 3^d day of ye week he went from thence to Daniell Whirley's[1] in George Yard to a meeting appointed about ye 9th hour Concerning the General Sufferings of fr^{ds} wch Continued till about ye 1st hour & after ye meeting was done he haveing dined there afterwards went to Geo: Barrs where haveing staid some time he afterwards went to :B: As where staid y^t night.

The next day being ye 10th of ye 4th mo: & ye 4th day of ye week he went to George Barrs where he had Mark to write things relateing to ye yearly meeting & after dinner he was at a meeting appointed there with some fri^{ds} about fr^{ds} Sufferings where he staid y^t night. ~

The next day in ye morning being ye 11th of ye 4th mo: & ye 5th day of ye week he went from thence to Nat: Braceys to another meeting appointed about fr^{ds} Sufferings & after dinner he went to ye Chambcr where he alsoe mett some ffr^{ds} & writt several Letters in Answer to ffr^{ds} beyond ye Seas[2] & goeing from thence he afterwards went to :A: ps: in George Yard where he Supped & afterwards went to :B: As: where he staid y^t night & several fr^{ds} Came to him.

The next day being ye 12th of ye 4th mo: & 6th day of ye week ab^t ye 12th hour he went frō thence to Geo: Watts where he was invited to dine with ye Dutch ffr^{ds} & several others from thence he went to ye meeting of Sufferings & afterwards to B: As where he staid y^t night & several fr^{ds} Came to him. ~

The next day being ye 13th of {4th mo: &} ye 7th day of ye week he went from thence to ye Chamber ab^t busyness of fr^{ds} where he was till ab^t ye 3^d hour & afterwards went to Tho: Coxes in a Coach & haveing staid there a while he went from thence to Mary Stotts at Bednall Green. ~

The meetings this week were :8: y^t he was at, ye Gener^{ll} meeting of fr^{ds} in ye ministry at ye Chamber ye meeting for Sufferings & others appointed about ye General Sufferings of ffr^{ds} &c.

On ye 14th of ye 4th mo: being ye 1st day of ye week he was at ye above said place M: Stotts where there came to visit him Robt Barkley Charles ffloyd[1] & several others.

The next day being ye 15th of ye 4th mo: & ye 2^d day of ye week he went to ye 2^d days morning meeting at ye Chamber where he alsoe had busyness after ye meeting was done till near ye 3^d hour, and from thence he went to Dan: Whirleys Shop where he staid a while with Charles ffloyd & R: Davis[2] & afterwards went to B: As where he stayd a pritty while with some fr^{ds} & afterwards went to M: ffs at ye Savoy where he stayd that night.

The 16th of ye 4th mo & ye 3^d day of ye week he went from thence with T Robinson & Jo: Vaugton in a Coach to Ja: Beeches 1 Mile, & from thence he & T: R: took Coach to Gravill pitts[3] about 3 Miles where haveing stayd ab^t 4 hours he went from thence to Kingsington on foot ½ Mile where he & T: R took Coach to Josiah Ellises & from thence he went to M: ffs: where he stayd y^t night.

The next day being ye 17th of ye 4th mo: & ye 4th day of ye week he dined at ye beforesaid place & towards ye evening went from thence to B: As: in a Coach where he stayd y^t night.

The next day being ye 18th of ye 4th mo: & ye 5th day of ye week haveing stayd dinner at ye aboves^d place he afterwards went to ye Chamber & Came to B: As again y^t night.

The next day being ye 19th of ye 4th mo: & ye 6th day of ye week he went from thence to ye Chamber & afterwards goeing from thence, he went to Mary ffosters where he dined, from thence to N: Blands & from thence to ye meeting for sufferings & ffrom thence to John Etridges[4] where he stayd that night.

The next day being ye 20th of ye 4th mo: & ye 7th day of ye week he dined at ye aboves^d place & afterwards went from thence to ye seeds mans in Byshopgate-street & took Coach for South Street[5] & Called upon Mary Wooley & Bridgit & Mary Stott & her Grand Child (who went with them to their house at South Street) at Charles Bathursts at ye Signe of ye 3 Sugar Loaves without Byshopgatestreet.

The meetings he was at this week were :2: ye 2^d dayes meeting & ye meeting for Sufferings.

The time he stayd in ye Citty was from ye 20th of ye 3^d mo: till ye 20th of ye 4th mo: wch is a month. ~ ~

And haveing stayd at Southstreet from ye 20th of ye 4th mo: till ye 9th of ye 5th mo: {& 5th day of ye week} y^t is 2 weeks & 4 dayes (where for 2 first dayes many fri^ds Come to visit him & alsoe several on ye weekdayes,) he went from thence to Ed: Mans at fford Green in a Coach where on ye 7th day night there Came to visit him James Hardin[1] of Jamaica & other two from Road Island & John Elson & his wife who stay{d} till 2^d Day.

On ye 19th of ye 5th mo: being ye 1st day of ye week G: W: & his sister & some others Came to visit him at Ed: Mans where he had a very good meeting with fri^ds & E: Ms ffamilly on the forenoon & haveing declared a pritty time he afterwards went to prayer & then spoke a few words ^a to ye people^a & soe Concluded ye meeting.

The 20th of ye 5th mo: being ye 2^d day of ye week he had a meeting with Ed: Bylings & Tho: Bud & Tho Heart about New Jarceys busyness.

The next day, haveing stayd from ye 9th till ye 21st of ye 5th mo: and 3^d day of ye week he went from thence to Geo: Watts at Enfield & with him Ed: Man on horse back where he had not been Long before there Came to visit him Ed: Billings & Michell Russell[2].~

The 26th of ye 5th mo: being ye 1st day of ye week he had a meeting at G: Ws (where there was also A: p: & Tho: Robinson, who were Come to visit him) he declared there & afterwards went to prayer & then Spoke a few words to fri^ds & when he had done ye meeting departed^b.

And on ye 3^d day ffollowing being the 28th of ye 5th mo: he went from thence to Widdow Dryes where he stayd y^t night.

The next day being ye 29th of ye 5th mo: & ye 4th day of ye week he was at ye monthly meeting there, it was very Large severall Strangers being there as B: A: Jo: ffield[3] & Jo: Vaughton who Came to visit him he declared (a pritty time touching a marriage between Alice at Ed: Mans and Tho: Bowls[4] y^t was Layd before fr^ds) to the Glading of fr^ds

---

^a...^a These words have a line through them.
^b Margin: *stayd at G Watts 7 days*

there Generally, he Lay that night at Tho: Hearts & stayd there till ye 3^d of ye 6th mo: y^t is 5 nights.

The 3^d of ye 6th mo: being ye 2^d Day of ye week he went to Widdow Dryes ag^n where he stayd till ye 6th of ye 6th mo: being ye 5th day of ye week where B: A: &c^a Came to visit him & ye same day haveing dined at Tho: Hearts he afterwards went to Ed: Mans & ye befors^d fr^{ds} with him on horse back^b.

Where haveing stayd from y^e {6th} of ye 6th mo: & 5th day of ye week till ye 12th of ye same being ye 4th day of ye week (in which time severall fr^{ds} Came to visit him) he took Coach ffrom thence to London Miles :9: he lighted out of ye Coach at ye Seedsmans in Byshopgatest^t & went from thence to ye Chamber on foot where he had busyness from ab^t ye 1st till ye 3^d hour from thence to Nat: Blands where he stayd a little from thence to S: Boltons shopp where stayd a little from thence to B: As: where he stayd y^t night.~

He Remained in ye Country 7 weeks & 3 Dayes In wch time he had :4: meetings 2 meetings on ye 1st Days a mo^{ly} meeting & one about other busyness {besids other sev'all meetings.}

The next day being ye 13th of ye 6th mo: & 5th day of ye week he also stayd at ye same place (where severall ffr^{ds} had busyness with him). ~

The next day being ye 14th of ye 6th mo: & ye 6th day of ye week he went from thence to ye Chamber & from thence to Wm Crouches where he with some other ffr^{ds} dined & from thence he went to ye Chamber ag^n to ye meeting for Sufferings wch Continued from between ye 4th & 5th hour till ye 7th & from thence he went to B: As: ag^n where he stayd y^t night.~

The next day being ye 15th of ye 6th mo: & 7th day of ye week he went from thence to ye Chamber & afterwards he & :A: p: went by Water to Widdow Grooms^1 at Rattlif where he stayd that night.

---

^{a} *Richard p* was written above the line and crossed through. The inclusion of Richard Pinder's name was, presumably, incorrect.

^{b} Margin: *went to Ed: Mans Miles 3*

The next day being ye 16th of ye 6th mo: & ye 1st day of ye week he went from thence to :A: ps: Lodgings at his Sisters & from thence to ye forenoon meeting at Rattlif & after a Woman ffr^d & Rodger Langworth[1] had declared he stood up & declared a pritty time & afterwards went to prayer & after wards ye meeting ended it was Large and peaceable within ye doors & after ye meeting was done he went to Ja: Strutts & on ye afternoon he went to ye meeting again at ye same place, where he declared a pritty time & afterwards went to prayer & afterwards ye meeting ye departed It was alsoe very Large & peaceable within ye doors & afterwards he went to Ja: Strutts ag^n where he stayd that night.~

And ye next day being ye 17th of ye 6th mo: & ye 2^d day of ye week he went from thence to ye 2^d days meeting at ye Chamber where he stayd from ab^t ye 10th to ye 2^d hour & went to B: As: towards night where he Lodged.

The next day being ye 18th of ye 6th mo: & ye 3^d day of ye week he went from thence to N: Braceys & from thence to John Cashamers[2] y^t were goeing to pensilvania & from thence to ye Chamber & afterwards to :N: Bs: where he stayd y^t night.

The next day being ye 19th of ye 6th & ye 4th day of ye week he went from thence to Mary ffosters & from thence to ye meeting att Gracius Street where after a ffr^d had declared he stood up & declared a pritty while & then went to prayer & afterwards ye meeting departed very peaceably being within ye doors soe when it was ended he went from thence to Mary ffosters againe where fr^{ds} Came to him & haveing stayd a while there he went from thence to Nat: Blands where he dined & afterwards to B: As: where he stayd y^t night.

The next day being ye 20th of ye 6th mo: & ye 5th day of ye week he went from thence to ye peel & visited severall ffr^{ds} as he went amongst ye Rest ffrancis Camfields with whom he dined, And haveing stayd that night at John Elsons, And dined there ye next day being ye 21st of ye 6th mo: & ye 6th day of ye week he afterwards went to ye meeting for Sufferings at ye Chamber wch Continued ffrom ab^t ye 4th to ye 7th hour, ffrom thence he went to :B: As: where he stayd that night.~

The next day being ye 22^d of ye 6th mo: & ye 7th day of
ye week he had a meeting with severall ffriends ab^t drawing
up Certificates to present to ye Cheif Justice ab^t fr^{ds} Clear-
ness in ye West from ye Rebellion[1], &c and after he had dined
there he went from thence to philip ffords & ffrom thence
to Marabella ffarnboroughs[2] where he stayd a while in y^e
shop & from thence to Jo: Dewes where haveing stayd a
while he went from thence to Rolland Vaughans & he not
being within he went from thence to ye Spectacle makers
where haveing staid a while he went from thence to Martha
ffishers at ye Savoy all ye way on foot where he stayd that
night.

The meetings he was att this week were 6: 3 publick
meetings, ye 2^d Days meeting ye meeting for Sufferings &
one ab^t other Concerns.~

The 23^d of ye 6th mo: being ye 1st day of ye week he was
at ye meeting at ye Savoy where he declared & afterwards
went to prayer & then spake a few words to ye people &
afterwards ye meeting departed; it was very large & peaceable within ye yard It was said ye officers Came afterwards
to the yard but finding noe meeting there they passed away
againe.
    The next day being ye 24th of ye 6th mo: & ye 2^d day of
ye week ab^t ye 11th hour he & Edward Brooks[3] went from
thence to Wm Beeches[4] where after they had stayd a while
they took Coach 3 Miles to Richard Kertons[5] near Hollons
house beyond Kingington to see W: P: but he not being at
home Ed: Brooks went away ag^n but :G: ff: stayd that night
at Rich: Kertons & ye next morning :W: P: Called to see
him there, being then goeing from home & invited him to
goe to his house & stay till he Came againe & dine with him
who did accordingly, & after dinner :W: P: goeing from home
ag^n he stayd till he Came back at ye 8th hour at night &
then W: P: sent his Coach with him to Rich: Kertons.
    The next morning being ye 26th of ye 6th mo: & ye 4th day
of ye week he went from thence with :W: P: & his wife in
their Coach to their Lodgings at Chering Cross Miles :3: &
from thence he & Guly: Penn[6] went to visit Widdow Berkit[7]
beyond ye Water but She was not at home Soe haveing

stayd a while they went from thence to her Sisters where they stayd & dined & afterwards Crossing ye water ag^n he went to Josiah Ellisses & from thence to M: ffs: where he stayed that night and fri^{ds} Came to see him.

The next day being ye 27th of ye 6th mo: & ye 5th day of ye week he went from thence to :B: As: in a Coach where he stayd y^t day & many fr^{ds} Came to him there ab^t busyness & to visit him.~

The next day being ye 28th of ye 6th mo: & ye 6th Day of ye week he went from thence to ye Chamber ab^t busyness & alsoe stayd ye meeting for Sufferings till ye 7th hour at night. & afterwards went to :B: As: where he stayd y^t night.

The next day being ye 29th of ye 6th mo: & ye 7th day of ye week he went from thence to Ed: Mans Warehouse in George Yard {&} afterwards to ye Chamber where he had busyness till ab^t ye 12th hour and from thence he went to Nat: Braceys where he Dined & afterwards went to ye Seedsmans in ByshopGatestreet where he and Walther Newbury[1] & his wife & Ed: Haistell[2] took Coach 9 Miles to Ed: Mans at ffordgreen beyond Edmunton.

The meetings he was at this week were 2: a pub: meeting & ye meeting for Sufferings.~

The next day being ye 30th of ye 6th mo: & ye 1st day of ye week he went from thence to ye meeting at Winsmorhill where he declared a pritty time & afterwards went to prayer & after that Spake a few words & when he had done ye meeting departed being very Large & peaceable within ye doors & Continued till ab^t ye 2^d hour from thence he went to Rich: Chairs[3] where fri^{ds} Came to him & afterwards he went from thence to Ed: Mans againe.

The 2^d of ye 7th mo: being ye 4th day of ye week he went from Ed: Mans to Bridgit Ostens at South Street & haveing gone ab^t a quart^r of a Mile from thence on foot we mett with B: A: & Wm Bingley[4] on horse back who were Comeing to visit him & goeing a little furthur Jo: plant over took us with a horse for him to ride upon from E: Ms: thith^r a Mile & $\frac{1}{2}$.

The 4th of y^e 7th mo: being y^e 6th Day of y^e week he went from thence in a Coach to London Miles :9: & Lighting out

of y^e Coach at Devenshire Buildings he went from thence
to :G: Ws: to see his wives Sister who Lay Sick, & from
thence to y^e seedmans in Byshopgate street & from thence
to George Yard & goeing to Dan: Whirleys he dined there
& afterwards went from thence to ye meeting for Sufferings,
wch Continued {till} ab^t the 7th hour at night, & afterwards
he went to :B: As: where he stayd y^t night.

He remained in the Country 5 Dayes & a night. ~

The next day being ye 5th of ye 7th mo: & ye 7th day of y^e
week severall ffri^ds Came to See him at :B: As: & ab^t ye 11th
hour he went from thence to the Chamber where he mett
with some fr^ds ab^t busyness from thence he went to Nathan:
Braceys where he dined & afterwards had a meeting with
several fr^ds there ab^t busyness & Lay there that night. ~

The meetings he was at this week were :4: one in y^e
Country, ye meeting for Sufferings and two about other
Concerns. ~

The 6th of ye 7th mo: being ye 1st day of ye week he went
from thence to ye Chamber ab^t ye 11th hour where he stayd
most of ye afternoon about fr^ds busyness from thence he
went to Ja: Wasses & after a while from thence to B: As:
where he stayd y^t night.

The next day being ye 7th of ye 7th mo: & the 2^d Day of
ye week he went from thence to ye monthly meeting at y^e
Chamber where he declared twice & afterwards went to
prayer & then Spake a few words to ffr^ds & after he had
done ye meeting departed it was {pritty} Large & peaceable
& afterwards visiting some fri^ds there ab^t he went to B: As:
where he had appointed to meet wth some fr^ds ab^t Reading
a Book of Ben: Linleys[1] in {answer} to ye Separates[2] (at
York) where he stayd y^t night.

The next day being ye 8th of ye 7th mo: & ye 3^d day of y^e
week he stayd at B: As: most of ye day where severall fr^ds
Came to him & towards night he went to Han: Marshals[3] &
philip ffords & afterwards took Coach to Jo: Elsons where
he stayed y^t night.

The next day being ye 9th of ye 7th mo: & ye 4th day of y^e
week haveing stayd dinner at ye befores^d place he afterwards
went from thence to ye monthly meeting at ye Bull & mouth

where there was a pritty Large & peaceable meeting within yᵉ doors, it continued from about yᵉ 4ᵗʰ hour till yᵉ 7ᵗʰ at night & after yᵉ meeting was done he went from thence to M: ffs at yᵉ Savoy.

The next day being the 10ᵗʰ of yᵉ 7ᵗʰ mo: & yᵉ 5ᵗʰ day of yᵉ week he went from thence to Josiah Ellises where haveing stayd a while he and Tho: Robison went beyond yᵉ Water to Wid: Berkits where he stayd that night.

The next day being yᵉ 11ᵗʰ of yᵉ 7ᵗʰ mo: & yᵉ 6ᵗʰ day of yᵉ week he went from thence to Cupit Stares on foot from thence he Crossed yᵉ Water to yᵉ 3 Cranes in Kingstreet from thence he went on foot to :B: As: where he dined & afterwards went from thence to yᵉ meeting for Sufferings wᶜʰ Continued till yᵉ 7ᵗʰ hour & after it was ended he went to B: As: where he stayd yᵗ night. ~

The next day being yᵉ 12ᵗʰ of yᵉ 7ᵗʰ mo: & yᵉ 7ᵗʰ day of yᵉ week he went from :B: As: to yᵉ Chamber abᵗ busyness, & from thence to Edward Bathursts in George Yard where he dined & afterwards took Coach with Mary Stott to Charles Bathursts at Epin fforest.

The Meetings he was at this week were :3: two monthly meetings & the meeting for Sufferings.

The 14ᵗʰ of yᵉ 7ᵗʰ mo: being yᵉ 2ᵈ day of yᵉ week he went from thence to Ham Mile 1½ on foot with Charles Bathurst & his wife & daughter Eliz: &c to visit George Ayres[1] & his wife where they dined but George was not at home Soe haveing Stayd a pritty while there they took Coach back again for Charles Bathursts but yᵉ Coach horses tyreing they were forced to goe about half yᵉ way on foot. ~

The next day being yᵉ 15ᵗʰ of yᵉ 7ᵗʰ mo: & yᵉ 3ᵈ Day of yᵉ week he writt a Generall Epistle to ffriends[2]. ~

The 19ᵗʰ of yᵉ 7ᵗʰ mo: & 7ᵗʰ day of yᵉ week he went from thence to James Mathews[3] at plasto on foot Mile :1:½ where he Stayd that night. ~

The next day being yᵉ 20ᵗʰ of yᵉ 7ᵗʰ mo: & yᵉ 1ˢᵗ day of yᵉ week he was at yᵉ meeting there where after three friᵈˢ had declared he stood up & declared a pritty while & afterwards went to prayer & then spake a few words to yᵉ people & when he had done yᵉ meeting departed It was a very

good meeting & very Large & peaceable within ye doors, &
after he had stayed a while at Ja: Mathews he went from
thence with Lady Lawson[1] in a Coach to Charl: Bathursts
againe where he Stayd y^t night & ye next day. ~

The next day being the 22^d of ye 7th mo: & ye 3^d day of
ye week he went from thence to Bows on foot ab^t 3 Miles &
visited ffr^ds as he went along at Stradford & Bows & haveing
Stayd a while at R: Richardsons he took Coach from thence
to Tho: Coxes where he Stayd that night. ~

He Remained in the Country :9: dayes & :10: Nights.

The next day being ye 23^d of ye 7th mo: & ye 4th day of
ye week he went from thence to ye Chamber ab^t busyness &
afterwards to :B: As: where he Stayd y^t night.

The next day being ye 24th of ye 7th mo: & ye 5th day of
ye week he haveing dined at ye befores^d place he went from
thence to ye Chamber ab^t fr^ds busyness & from thence he
went to B: As: againe where he Stayd that night. ~

The next day being ye 25th of ye 7th mo: & ye 6th day of
ye week he went from thence to ye Chamber ab^t busyness &
afterwards Stayd ye meeting for Sufferings till ab^t ye 7th
hour, from thence he went to Nat: Braceyes where he stayd
y^t night.

The next day being ye 26th of ye 7th mo: & 7th day of y^e
week he went from thence to ye Chamber ab^t busyness &
afterwards haveing visited Severall fri^ds at night he went
to Margret Drinkells. ~

The meetings he was at this week were :2: one publick
meeting in the Country & ye meeting for Sufferings besids
other Concerns.

The next day being ye 27th of ye 7th mo: & ye 1st day of
ye week he went from M: Ds: to ye meeting att Wheeler
Street where after Tho: Robinson had declared he stood up
& declared ab^t an hour & afterwards went to prayer & then
Spake a few words to ye people & when he had done the
meeting departed it was a very Good meeting Large &
peaceable within the doors & afterwards Calling at 2 or 3

places as he went a long he went to :B: As: where he Stayd
y^t night.

The next day being ye 28th of ye 7th mo: & the 2^d day of
ye week he went from thence to ye 2^d dayes meeting at y^e
Chamber & after y^t haveing stayd most of ye day ab^t other
busyness he went to B: As: againe where he Stayd y^t night.

The next day being ye 29th of ye 7th mo: & ye 3^d day of
ye week he went from thence to ye Chamber where he stayd
ab^t ye busyness of fri^{ds} sufferings most of ye day & went to
:B: As: ag^n at night.

The next day being ye 30th of ye 7th mo: & ye 4th day of
ye week he went to ye Chamber again where he was most of
ye Day ab^t ye busyness of fr^{ds} Sufferings & went againe to
:B: As: at night. ～

The next day being ye 1st of ye 8th mo: & ye 5th day of y^e
week he went from thence to ye Chamber again where on y^e
forenoon he had a meeting with :W: P: & some others ab^t
fri^{ds} sufferings &c & afterwards dined with :W: P: & Dan:
Whrleys & from thence to ye Chamber againe where he
stayd till night ab^t fri^{ds} sufferings, from thence he went to
S: Boltons where he & G: W: stayd a while & had busyness
with :S: B: afterwards he took Coach to ye peel where he
stayd y^t night.

The next day being ye 2^d of ye 8th mo: & ye 6th day of y^e
week after dinner he went from thence to ye Chamber ab^t
fr^{ds} Sufferings & afterwards stay^d ye meeting for Sufferings
wch Continued till ab^t ye 7th hour & after ye meeting departed he went from thence to :B: As: where he stayd y^t
night. ～

The next day being ye 3^d of ye 8th mo: & ye 7th day of y^e
week he went from thence to ye Chamber ab^t busyness &
towards night he went by Water to James Strutts at Rattlif
where he Stayd that night. ～

The meetings he was at this week were :4: a publick
meeting ye 2^d days meeting & one ab^t other Concerns ～ {& y^e
meeting for Sufferings}. ～

The 4th of ye 8th mo: & ye 1st day of ye week he was at y^e
fornoon meeting at Ratliff where after Tho: Whitehead[1] a
Country fr^d had declared he stood up & declared a pritty

time & afterwards went to prayer & then spake a few words
to yᵉ people & when he had done yᵉ meeting departed it
was very Large and peaceable within yᵉ doors. He was
Likewise at yᵉ afternoon meeting at yᵉ same place where he
declared a pritty Large time & afterwards went to prayer
& then spake a few words to yᵉ people & after he had done
yᵉ meeting departed it was Large & peaceable within yᵉ
doors. ~ from thence he went to Ja: Strutts againe where he
stayd that night.

The next day being yᵉ 5ᵗʰ of yᵉ 8ᵗʰ mo: & yᵉ 2ᵈ day of yᵉ
week he went from thence to yᵉ 2ᵈ dayes monthly morning
meeting at yᵉ Chamber where he afterwards stayd most of
yᵉ Day from thence he went to :B: As: where he stayd yᵗ
night.

The next day being yᵉ 6ᵗʰ of yᵉ 8ᵗʰ mo: & yᵉ 3ᵈ day of yᵉ
week he went from thence to yᵉ Chamber againe where he
was most of yᵉ day about busyness of friᵈˢ Sufferings, & in
yᵉ Evening he took Coach from thence to :G: Watts where
he stayd that night. ~

The next day being yᵉ 7ᵗʰ of yᵉ 8ᵗʰ mo: & yᵉ 4ᵗʰ day of yᵉ
week he went to visit John Elson & severall frᵈˢ thereawayes
& went to G: Ws: again to dinner & alsoe stayd there yᵗ night.

The next day being yᵉ 8ᵗʰ of yᵉ 8ᵗʰ mo: & yᵉ 5ᵗʰ day of yᵉ
week he went from thence to :B: As: where he Stayd dinner
& afterwards went to yᵉ Chamber abᵗ friᵈˢ Sufferings & Came
to B: As: againe at night.

The next day being the 9ᵗʰ of yᵉ 8ᵗʰ mo: & yᵉ 6ᵗʰ day of
yᵉ week he went from thence to yᵉ Chamber abᵗ yᵉ busyness
of friᵈˢ Sufferings & afterwards he went from thence to Ed:
Bathursts where he dined & from thence to yᵉ meeting for
Sufferings & from thence to Wᵐ Meads where he stayd
that night. ~

The next day being the 10ᵗʰ of yᵉ 8ᵗʰ mo: & the 7ᵗʰ day
of yᵉ week he went from :W: Ms: to yᵉ Chamber again abᵗ
busyness & on yᵉ afternoon he went by Water to Horsly
downe & from yᵉ Water Side to Ann Traverses {on foot}
where he stayd yᵗ night. ~

The meetings he was at this week were :4: two pub:
meetings a monthly meeting & a meeting for Sufferings.

The next day being ye 11th of ye 8th mo: & ye 1st day of ye week he went to ye meeting at Horsly downe where (after :T: R: he stood up and declared a pritty Large time & afterwards went to prayer & then spake a few words to ye people & when he done ye meeting departed it was very Large & peaceable within the doors. & after ye meeting he haveing stayd a little at James parks & ffri^{ds} Come to see him he afterwards went from thence to Hen: Snooks[1] where haveing stayd ab^t an hour he went from thence to N: Bracyes where he stayd y^t night.

The next day being ye 12th of ye 8th mo: & the 2^d day of ye week he went from thence to ye 2^d dayes meeting & at noon he went to Nat: Braceys ag^n where he dined & afterwards went from thence to ye quart^{ly} men & womens meeting at Devenshire house & after the meeting was Ended he went to :G: Ws: ab^t busyness with him & Gilbert Latye & from thence to :B: As: where he stayd y^t night.

The next day being ye 13th of ye 8th mo: & ye 3^d day of ye week he went from thence to ffran: Camfields to inquire after fri^{ds} busyness at ye Sessions at Hixes hall where he staid that night. ~

The 14th of ye 8th mo: & ye 4th day of ye week he went from thence to M: Meakins[2] & visited John Stapler[3] & some other fr^{ds} in ye way, from thence Calling at Nick: Coopers[4] a Shoe Maker by ye way he went to John Elsons at ye peel where he stayd that night. ~

The next day being ye 15th of ye 8th mo: & ye 5th day of ye week he went from thence to ffra: Camfields where he was invited to dinner from thence he went to :B: As: where he stayd y^t night. ~

The next day being ye 16th of ye 8th mo: & ye 6th day of ye week he went to ye Chamber ab^t busyness from thence to Nat: Bracyes where he dined & from thence to ye meeting for Sufferings from thence to Dan: Whyrleys to speak with :W: P: & from thence to Nathan: Blands & afterwards to W: Ms: where he Stayd that night. ~

The next day being ye 17th of ye 8th mo: & ye 7th day of ye week he went from thence to ye Chamber where he was most of ye day ab^t busyness & afterwards went to Nat: Bracyes where he Stayd y^t night.

The meetings he was at this week were : 5 : a publick meeting ye 2^d dayes meeting a quart: meeting {of men & women} ye meet: for Sufferings besids other Concerns.

The next day being ye 18th of ye 8th mo: & ye 1st day of ye week he went from : N : Bs: to ye morning meeting at ye Chamber where he stayd ye forenoon & afterwards went from thence to : B : As: where he stayd y^t night.

The next day being ye 19th of ye 8th mo: & ye 2^d day of ye week he went from thence to ye 2^d days meeting at the Chamber & afterwards (Calling at severall fr^{ds} houses there abouts) he went to : B : As: where he had busyness with : G: W: & afterwards went from thence to : M : ffs: at the Savoy where he staid y^t night. ~

The next day being ye 20th of ye 8th mo: & ye 3^d day of ye week he went from thence to : W. Ps: at Chering Cross & visiting John Collits[1] wife Tavern Keeper at ye Bulls head at Chering Cross & some other fr^{ds} by ye way he went to : M : ffs: again where he stayd y^t night. ~

The 21st of ye 8th mo: being ye 4th day of ye week he stayd at : M : ffs: ~

The next day being ye 22^d of ye 8th mo: & ye 5th day of ye week he took Coach with Ann Traverss & her daughter & Nathaniell Willmour[2] from thence to Chisick to See after a house for a Womens School Miles : 6 : from thence to peter princes[3] at Hamersmith where haveing Stayd a little they went from thence to see ye house where Wm Lodington[4] dwelt from thence to y^e Goat Inn where they dined from thence : G: ff: went (in y^e Coach y^t carryed Ann Travers &c. to London) to Wid: Symmons[5] where he stayd that night. ~

The next day being y^e 23^d of y^e 8th mo: & y^e 6th day of y^e week towards night he went from thence to petter princes on foot ab^t $\frac{1}{4}$ of a mile in a great Storm of Rain Lightening & Thunder. ~

The next day being y^e 24th of y^e 8th mo: & y^e 7th day of y^e week he was alsoe at : p: ps:

The next day being y^e 25th of y^e 8th mo: & y^e 1st day of y^e week he went from thence to y^e meeting at Hamer Smith where he declared a pritty Large time & afterwards went to prayer & then spake a few words to ye people & after he had done ye meeting departed and after a while he went from thence with John Osgood to his house at Moatlack by Water where he stayd y^t night.

The next day being ye 26th of ye 8th mo: & ye 2^d day of ye week in ye afternoon pet: prince went with a boate to bring him into his house at Hamer Smith ag^n where he stayd that night.~

The next day being ye 27th of ye 8th mo: & ye 3^d Day of ye week he he went from thence to ye Broom house by Water a Mile to see an old man a fr^d 92: years of age a Gardiner there where haveing stayd a while he went from thence to Chelsey by Water : 1 : Mile, ~ to Wm Kemps[1] where he stayd y^t night. ~

The next day being y^e 28th of y^e 8th mo: & y^e 4th day of y^e week he went from thence nigh Rich: Kertons on horse back and with him Wm Kemp but a gate being fastened they walked up to y^e house a little way on foot and haveing stayd a while there he went from thence to John Kertons[2] {at Gravill pitts $\frac{1}{2}$ a Mile on foot} (Calling to see his two brothers in y^e way hard by) where he stayd y^t night. ~

The next day being y^e 29th of y^e 8th mo: & y^e 5th day of y^e week he took Coach from thence to James Beeches at Westminster Miles : 3 : where haveing Stayd ab^t 2 or 3 hours disided a difference betwixt two of ye Servants he took Coach from thence to Josiah Ellises, Where haveing stayd a little he went from thence to Wm Beeches & from thence to :M: ffs: at the Savoy where he stayd y^t night. ~

The next day being ye 30th of y^e of ye 8th mo: & ye 6th day of ye week he took Coach from thence to Bow Lane and went to philip ffords where haveing stayd a little he went from thence to :B: As: where he dined & afterwards went to ye meeting for Sufferings wch Continued till ab^t ye 7th hour at night, from thence he went to Wm Meads where he stayd that night. ~

The next day being ye 31st of ye 8th mo: & ye 7th day of ye week he went from thence to ye Chamber about busyness & in ye afternoon he went to Nat: Blands where he dined & afterwards to :B: As: where haveing stayd a while he took Coach to M: ffs: at ye Savoy where he stayd that night. ~

The meetings he was at this week were :2: a publick meeting in ye Country & ye meeting for Sufferings. ~
Remained in ye Country a week.

The 1st of ye 9th mo: being ye 1st day of ye week he was at ye meeting at ye Savoy where he declared a pritty time & afterwards went to prayer & then spake a few words to ye people & when he had done ye meeting departed it was pritty Large & peaceable in ye yard & Entry but mostly in ye Entry being a Rainy day & continued till between ye 11th & 12th hour he afterwards went to :M: ffs: againe where he stayd that night & many fr^{ds} Came to visit him. ～

The next day being the 2^d of ye 9th mo: & ye 2^d day of ye week he took Coach from thence to ye 2^d days monthly meeting at ye Chamber where he declared twice & went to prayer & afterwards ye meeting departed, there were a great many fr^{ds} of ye Ministry & it continued from ab^t ye 9th to ye 11th hour, he stayd there afterwards till betwixt ye 1st & 2^d hour & then went to Nat: Braceyes where he dined & in ye evening went from thence to B: As: where he stayd y^t night. ～

The next day being ye 3^d of ye 9th mo: & ye 3^d day of ye week he stayd there most of the day where many fr^{ds} Came to him & in the Evening he took Coach from thence to John Elsons at ye peel where he stayd that night & ye next day. ～

The day following being ye 5th of ye 9th mo: & ye 5th day of ye week he went from thence Calling to see severall fr^{ds} by ye way to John Thorps[1] where he was invited to dinner & Tho: Robinson, & from thence Calling to see some other fr^{ds} by ye way he went to B: As: where he stayd y^t night.

The next day being ye 6th of ye 9th mo: & ye 6th day of ye week he went from thence to ye Chamber ab^t ye business of fr^{ds} Sufferings & afterwards stayd ye meeting for sufferings till ab^t ye 7th hour and afterwards went to :W: Ms: where he stayd y^t night.

The 7th of ye 9th mo: & ye 7th day of ye week he went from thence to ye Chamber and afterwards took Coach to see M: Wooley and Bridgit who was Sick but Bridgit was gone into ye Country & after a while he went to Tho: Coxes on foot & from thence he took Coach to Mary Stots at Bednall Green.

The meetings he was at this week were /3/ a publick meeting ye 2^d days meeting & ye meeting for Sufferings.

The 12th of ye 9th mo: being ye 5th day of ye week he took Coach from M: S's: at Bednall green to George Yard in Lombardstreet, & from thence {he went} to the Chamber about busyness & in ye evening to :B: As: where he stayd that night.

The next day being ye 13th of ye 9th mo: & ye 6th day of ye week after diner he went from thence to ye meeting for Sufferings wch Continued till ye 7th hour & afterwards he went to :W: Ms: where he stayd y^t night. ∼

The next day being ye 14th of ye 9th mo: & ye 7th day of ye week he went from thence to ye Chamber about busyness & from thence to Dan: Whirleys where he dined {& writ a Letter} & from thence to Wm Crouches and from thence to take water to Ratlif & from thence to James Struts where he stayd y^t night. ∼

The next day being the 15th of ye 9th mo: & ye 1st day of ye week he went to ye forenoon meeting at Rattlif where he declared a pritty time & afterwards went to prayer & when he had done ye meeting departed being very large & peaceable within ye doors & afterwards he went to :J: S's: ag^n On ye afternoon he was Likewise at ye meeting at ye above s^d place where he declared a pritty time & afterwards went to prayer & then spake a few words to ye people & when he had done ye meeting departed being very Large & peaceable wthin ye doors, & afterwards he went to :J: S's: ag^n where he stayd y^t night. ∼

The next day being ye 16th of ye 9th mo: & ye 9th mo: & ye 2^d day of ye week Susanah ffell & Bethiah Rouse[1] Came to J: Struts Early in ye morning in a Coach to ffetch him to goe to Kingston being sent for thither to see young Margret Rouse who was very sick in whose Coach he went to ye 2^d {day's} meeting in Lombardstreet & from thence {he went} to Nat: Braceys where he dined & afterwards had a meeting ab^t busyness & stayd there that night. ∼

The next day being ye 17th of ye 9th mo: & y^e {3^d day of y^e} week he took Coach to Jo: Rouses at Kingston to see young Margret Rouse who was very sick.

Remained at John Rouses from ye 17th of ye 9th mo: to ye 28th of ye 10th mo: (viz) 6 weeks wanting a day in wch time he had 2 evening meeting on first day nights with John Rouses familly & severall fr^{ds} Came to see him. ∼

On ye 28th of ye 10th mo: & ye 2^d day of ye week he went
from thence to Ann ffielders[1] and after a while went with her
by Water to John Osgoods at Motlack^a where he stayd that
night. ~

The next day being ye 29th of ye 10th mo: & ye 3^d day of y^e
week he was invited to ffr^d Muckleys[2] to dinner & stayd at
Jo: Osgoods ag^n y^t night. ~

The next day being ye 30th of ye 10th mo: & ye 4th day of
week he went from thence to Ann Traverses by Water at
Chizwick Miles :1: Early in ye morning She being but in
Removeing thither. ~

The 1st of ye 11th mo: being the 6th day of ye week in y^e
forenoon he went from Antraverses to see Christopher Ward[3]
where haveing stayd a while he went from thence to peter
pri{n}ses where he stayd that night. ~

The 3^d of ye 11th mo: being the 1st day of ye week he was
at ye meeting at Hamersmith where after Jo: Vaughton had
declared he stood up & declared a pritty Large time & afterwards went to prayer & then spake a few words to ye people
& when he had done ye meeting ended being pritty Large
and peaceable within the doors & afterwards he went to
peter pri{n}ses again where he stayd that night & severall
ffr^{ds} Came to see him. ~

The 4th of ye 11th mo: being ye 2^d day of ye week he went
from thence by water with Antraverse to widdow Berkits
where he dined & from thence to the quart^{ly} meeting att
Devenshire house^b & from thence he took Coach with George
Watt to B: A's: where he stayd y^t night.

The next day being ye 5th of ye 11th mo: & ye 3^d day of y^e
week he went from thence with G: W: in a Coach to Rolland
Vaughans at ye Temple ab^t busyness & from thence to M: ffs
at ye Savoy where he stayd that night. ~

The next day being ye 6th of ye 11th mo: & ye 4th day of y^e
week he went from thence to ye quart^{ly} meeting at Westminster wch Continued from ab^t ye 3^d to ye 7th hour at night
& from thence he took Coach to :M: ffs: at ye Savoy ag^n
where he stayd that night. ~

The next day being the 7th of ye 11th mo: & ye 5th day of
ye week he went from thence to Rolland Vaughans & from

---

^{a} Margin: *ab^t Mil :12:* ^{b} Margin: *Miles :6:*

thence visiting some other fr^{ds} by the way he went to B: A's: where he stayd y^t night & severall fr^{ds} came to visit him. ~

The next day being the 8th of ye 11th mo: & ye 6th day of ye week haveing dined at ye aboves^d place he went from thence to ye meeting for Sufferings wch haveing Continued till about ye 7th hour he afterwards went to W: Ms: where he staid that night. ~

The next day being ye 9th of ye 11th mo: & ye 7th day of ye week he went from thence to ye Chamber where he stayd till about ye 2^d hour frõ thence he went to visit Wm Tilbeys & R: Whitpains^1 & from thence to Nathaniell Braceys where he staid y^t night.

The meetings he was at this week were :4: a publick meeting 2 quart^{ly} meetings & ye meeting for Sufferings.

The next day being ye 10th of ye 11th mo: & ye 1st day of ye week he went from thence to ye morning meeting at ye Chamber & from thence to ye meeting att Gracious street where he declared a pritty Large time & afterwards went to prayer & after he had done it being almost the 11th hour ye meeting departed being very Large and peaceable within ye doors & afterwards he went to Mary ffosters where many fr^{ds} Came to him & haveing stayd there till ye Evening he went from thence to Nat: Blands & from thence to Nat: Braceys again where he stayd y^t night.

The next day being ye 11th of ye 11th mo: he went from thence to ye 2^d dayes morning meeting at ye Chamber from thence he went to James Wasses where he dined & in ye Evening he went to another meeting of twelve appointed at Nat: Braceys & afterwards from thence to B: As': where he stayd that night. ~

The next day being ye 12th of ye 11th mo: & ye 3^d day of ye week he went from thence to ffrancis Camfields to see after fr^{ds} busyness at ye Sessions at Hixes Hall where he stayd that night. ~

The 13th of ye 11th mo: & ye 4th day of ye week he went from thence to James^a Mathews & John Elsons & to ff Camfields ag^n to dinner where he alsoe stayd y^t night.

The next day being ye 14th of ye 11th mo: & ye 5th day of

^{a} Altered from *John*

yᵉ week after dinner he went to Bengemin Antrobuses where he stayd yᵗ night.

The next day being yᵉ 15ᵗʰ of yᵉ 11ᵗʰ mo: & yᵉ 6ᵗʰ day of yᵉ week he went from thence to George Yard & haveing dined at Edward Bathursts he afterwards went to yᵉ meeting for Sufferings & from thence to :W: Ms: where he stayd yᵗ night. ~

The next day being yᵉ 16ᵗʰ of yᵉ 11ᵗʰ mo: & yᵉ 7ᵗʰ day of yᵉ week he went from W: M's: to the Chambʳ abᵗ busyness where he stayd till abᵗ yᵉ 1ˢᵗ hour, from thence he went to George Yard & afterwards to Tho: Coxes where he dined & after a while took Coach to Mary Stotts at Bednall Green[1], where yᵉ next day G: W: Came to visit him and some other frᵈˢ. ~

The meetings he was at this week were 5: a publick meeting, yᵉ 1ˢᵗ dayes morning meeting, yᵉ 2ᵈ dayes morning meeting, yᵉ meeting of twelve & yᵉ meeting for Sufferings. ~

The 20ᵗʰ of yᵉ 11ᵗʰ mo: being yᵉ 4ᵗʰ day of yᵉ week he took Coach from Mary Stots abovesᵈ to yᵉ George in Corn{e}well & soe went to Ed: Mans in Georgeyard & afterwards to yᵉ Chamber & on yᵉ afternoon he was at a meeting there abᵗ distributeing to yᵉ Necesity's of poor Sufferings frᵈˢ in Every County ~ & afterwards at another meeting att yᵉ same place abᵗ Sam: Boltons & Mary peningtons busyness wᶜʰ Continued till abᵗ yᵉ 7ᵗʰ hour, from thence he went to W: Ms: where he stayd that night. ~

The next day being yᵉ 21ˢᵗ of yᵉ 11ᵗʰ mo: & yᵉ 5ᵗʰ day of yᵉ week he went from Wᵐ Meads to yᵉ Chamber & afterwards went to Ben: Antrobuses where he dined, & sent for a {great} Docter that Came from poland[2] & had discourse with him, he alsoe stayd there that night and severall frᵈˢ Came to him. ~

The next day being yᵉ 22ᵈ of yᵉ 11ᵗʰ mo: & yᵉ 6ᵗʰ day of yᵉ week he went from thence to Ed: Mans & Dan: Whirleys in George yard & from thence to yᵉ Chambʳ abᵗ busyness & afterwards stayd yᵉ meeting for Sufferings till betwixt yᵉ 7ᵗʰ & 8ᵗʰ hour from thence he went to Ben: Antrobuses where he stayd that night. ~

The next being ye 23^d of ye 11th mo: & ye 7th day of y^e
week in ye forenoon he went to ye Chamber where he stayd
till betwixt ye 1st & 2^d hour & afterwards took Coach to visit
Mary Wooleys where he dined and afterwards went to Abra:
Godownes & through their house to visit Sam: Walldenfield[1]
& his wife & afterwards went to Mary Wooleys ag^n & from
thence to Marg^t Drinkells & from thence to :G: W^s: where
he stayd y^t night.

The meetings he was at this week were 3—1 ab^t busyness
& ye meeting for Sufferings & ye 2^d days meeting. ~

The next day being ye 24th of ye 11th mo: & ye 1st day of
ye week he went from :G:W^s:above s^d to ye morning meeting
at ye Chamber where after ye meeting was done he writ a
paper to ye King of poland & ab^t ye 1st hour he went from
thence to Mary ffosters where he staid ye afternoon & from
thence he went to ye Chamber ag^n and from thence to
George Barrs where he stayd y^t night. ~

The next day being the 25th of ye 11th mo: & ye 2^d day of
ye week he went from thence to ye 2^d dayes meeting at y^e
Chamber & from thence ab^t ye 1st hour to Nat: Braceys
where he dined & afterwards went from thence to Benjemin
Antrobuses where he stayd that night, & severall fr^{ds} Came
to him.

The next day being ye 26th of ye 11th mo: and ye 3^d day
of ye week he took coach frõ thence to Rolland Vaughans
ab^t busyness & from thence he went on foot to Martha
ffishers at ye Savoy & towards night he went from thence
to visit some fr^{ds} there ab^t & Came to M: ffs: ag^n where he
stayd that night & also fr^{ds} Came to visit him.

The next day being ye 27th of ye 11th mo: & ye 4th day of
ye week he Stayd ye forenoon at M. ff: till :G: W: and
Gilbert Latey Came frõ Whitehall who had been ab^t fr^{ds}
Sufferings & after dinner he took Coach from thence to John
Elsons where he stayd night {& was at ye mo: meeting
there}. ~

The next day being ye 28th of ye 11th mo: & ye 5th day of
ye week he alsoe stayd at John Elsons where several fr^{ds}
came to See him.

The next day being ye 29th of ye 11th mo: & ye 6th day of

the week he went from thence to Tho: Scots & from thence
to ffranc: Camfields where he was invited to dinner & from
thence to yᵉ meeting for Sufferings att yᵉ Chamber & after
it was done he went to W: Meads where he stayd yᵗ
night. ∾

The next day being yᵉ 30ᵗʰ of yᵉ 11ᵗʰ mo: & yᵉ 7ᵗʰ day of yᵉ
week he went from thence to yᵉ Chamber abᵗ busyness & abᵗ
yᵉ 1ˢᵗ hour he went to Dan: Whyrleys where he dined &
afterwards went from thence to yᵉ seedsmans in Byshopgatestreet where G: Wat was to meet him & there to take
Coach to Geo: Watts house at Enfield Miles : 10:

Stayd at G: Ws: abovesᵈ from yᵉ 30ᵗʰ of yᵉ 11ᵗʰ mo: to yᵉ
8ᵗʰ of yᵉ 12ᵗʰ mo: viz: 8 dayes where on the 7ᵗʰ of yᵉ 12ᵗʰ
mo: being yᵉ 1ˢᵗ day of yᵉ week several friᵈˢ Came to see
him & he had a meeting. ∾

The 8ᵗʰ of yᵉ 12ᵗʰ mo: being yᵉ 2ᵈ day of yᵉ week he went
from Geo: Watts to Widdow Dryes & with him Geo: Whitehead[1] (who Came on first day to see my Master) where he
stayd that night but G: W: went to Ed: Mans. ∾

Stayd at Widdow Dryes & Tho: Hearts abᵗ night for
night from yᵉ 8ᵗʰ of yᵉ 12ᵗʰ mo: till yᵉ 16ᵗʰ of yᵉ same {viz}
8ᵗʰ dayes where on yᵉ 1ˢᵗ day being yᵉ 14ᵗʰ of yᵉ 12ᵗʰ mo:
severall frᵈˢ Came to see him.∾

And on yᵉ 16ᵗʰ of yᵉ 12ᵗʰ mo: being yᵉ 3ᵈ day of yᵉ week
he went from thence viz Tho: Hearts to Ed. Mans at fford
Green miles 3 on horse back & with him Mercy Bentall &
Walther[2] her husband & prissila Heart went on foot. ∾

On yᵉ 21ˢᵗ of yᵉ 12ᵗʰ mo: being yᵉ first day of yᵉ week he
had a meeting att Ed: Mans with his familly & others yᵗ
were come to see :G: ff:ᵃ where he declared a pritty while
and afterwards went to prayer & after spoke a few words to
friᵈˢ & then Concluded yᵉ meeting.

On the 24ᵗʰ of yᵉ 12ᵗʰ mo: and yᵉ 4ᵗʰ day of the week he
went on horse back with Ed: Man from thence to yᵉ mo:
meeting at Tho: Hearts at Enfieldᵇ where he declared twice
a pritty time & afterwards went to prayer and after some
other frᵈˢ had declared he declared agⁿ there was a very
good meeting & Large friᵈˢ being there from Walthum &
Southstreet & other places; it Continued with busyness
too frõ abᵗ yᵉ 12ᵗʰ hour till yᵉ 3ᵈ/, & afterwards haveing

ᵃ Altered to *him*   ᵇ Margin: *Miles /3/*

stayd dinner there he went back ag^n with Ed: Man to his house at fford Green^a.

Stayd at Ed: Mans from ye 16th of ye 12th mo: being ye 3^d day of ye week to ye 26th of ye same being ye 6th day of the week wch is 9th days & one day where on he went to ye mõly meeting att Enfield & Came back ag^n att night in wch time severall fri^{ds} Came to visit him. ∼

The 26th of ye 12th mo: being ye 6th day of ye week he went from thence to Bridgitt Austells att Southstreet where he stayd till ye 5th of ye 1st mo: being the first mo: viz: 6: dayes: ∼ in wch time A: p: and severall others Came to See him. ∼

On ye 5th of ye 1st mo: and ye 5th day of ye week he went thence to Edward Mans againe where he Stayd till ye 9th of ye same being ye 3^d day of ye week viz /4/ dayes in wch time Severall fri^{ds} Came to See him.

ffinis.

Here ffolloweth a Jornall of the meetings &c :G: F: hath been att Anno domini 1686: ∼

The 7th of ye 1st mo: being ye 1st day of ye week he had a Meeting att Edw: Manns with some fri^{ds} that were come to see him & after some time sitting in Silence he went to prayer and soe Concluded the meeting. ∼

The 9th of ye 1st mo: being ye 3^d day of ye week he took Coach from Ed: Mans to his Warehouse att London in George Yard in London Miles :8: ffrom thence he went to ye Chamber where he stayd till towards night and afterwards took Coach to ffrancis Camfields where he stayd y^t night & was at a meeting appointed there ab^t Cotten Odes[1] sons busyness of marriage.

He remain in ye Country in all from ye 30th of ye 11th mo: to ye 9th of ye 1st mo (viz) 5 weeks and 2 dayes, in wch time he was at 4 meetings, ye monthly meeting at Enfield, & 3 meetings on ye first dayes with their famillyes (& others

^{a} Margin: *Miles /3/*

that Came to see him) where he remained. Travelled in y^e
Country Miles :30:~ Besids other Little meetings ab^t
busyness.

The next day being the 10th of ye first mo: & ye 4th day
of ye week he sent for Cotten Oddes ag^n ab^t ye same busyness & also had busyness with severall other fri^{ds} & after
Dinner he went from thence to Benjemin Antrobuses where
he stayd y^t night & severall fri^{ds} Came to him. ~

The next day being ye 11th of ye 1st mo: & ye 5th day of y^e
week he stayd there & severall fr^{ds} Came and had busyness
with him.

The next day being the 12th of ye 1st mo: and ye 6th day
of ye week he went from thence to some fri^{ds} houses in
George yard & afterwards to N: Blands where he Eate
something to dinner & afterwards to ye meeting for Sufferings wch Continued from betwixt ye 3^d & :4: hour till near
y^e /6th/ frõ thence he went to W Meads where he stayd y^t
night.

The next day being ye 13th of ye 1st mo: & 7th day of y^e
week in ye morning he went to ye Chamber ag^n ab^t busyness where he stayd till ab^t ye 3^d hour from thence he went
to B: Antrobuses & after a while he & T: Robison took
Coach from thence to Martha ffishers at ye Savoy where he
stayd that night. ~

The 14th of ye 1st mo: being ye 1st day of ye week was at
ye meeting at ye Savoy, where after Tho: Robison and Gilbert
Latye had declared he stood up and declared a pritty time
& afterwards went to prayer & after he had done ye meeting
departed there was a very good meeting & Large & peaceable in the yard. ~

The next day being ye 15th of ye 1st mo: & 2^d day of y^e
week he went from thence to ye 2^d dayes meeting at y^e
Chamber where he alsoe Continued till towards ye Evening
& afterwards went to B: Antrobuses where he stayd y^t
night ~ & severall fr^{ds} Came to him.

The next day being the 16th of ye 1st mo: & ye 3^d day of
ye week he went from thence to Rowland Vans at ye temple
there to meet G: W: and Gilbert Latye &c ab^t fr^{ds} busyness
with ye Atturney Generall[1] from thence to Elyas Syms[2] where
he dined & afterwards went to R: Vans ag^n & from thence

to Ben Antrobuses (where he had appointed severall fr^{ds} to meet him ab^t goeing to ye Atturney Generall in ye Country) & stayd there y^t night. ~

The next day being ye 17th of ye 1st mo: & the 4th day of ye week he was at another meeting appointed there at ye 10th hour ab^t ye befores^d busyness of going to ye Atturney Generall & ab^t noon he took Coach with Mary Elson from thence to her house at ye peel in St John Street where he stayd y^t night & ye next day. ~

The 19th of ye 1st mo: & ye 6th day of ye week he went from thence to ye Chamb^r & after a while from thence to Nathan^{ll} Braceys where he dined & from thence to ye Chamb^r agⁿ to ye Meeting for Sufferings wch continued till ye 6th hour thence he went to W: Meads where he stayd y^t night. ~

The next day being the 20th of ye 1st mo: & ye 7th day of ye week he went from thence to Wm Crouches in Crown Courte to speak with Steven Crisp[1] & ab^t ye 9th hour in ye morning he took Coach thence to John Rowses at Kingston he being sent for thither to see Nat: Rowse who was sick of ye small pox, Miles :10:

The meetings he was at this week were :6: a publick meeting ye 2^d days meeting ye meeting for Sufferings and 3 ab^t other busyness relateing to fr^{ds} Sufferings.

Remained at John Rowses at Kingston frõ ye 20th of ye 1st mo: till the 29th of ye same; viz :9: day's.

The 29th of ye 1st mo: being ye 2^d day of ye week he went from thence to ye Water side on foot one Mile, thence he took water to John Osgoods at Mortlack Miles :10: where haveing stayd ab^t an hour he afterwards went to Ann Traverses at ye school at Cheeswick one mile where he stayd that night. ~

The next day being ye 30th of ye 1st mo: & ye 3^d day of ye week in ye afternoon he went from thence to Ann ffielders at Hammersmith :1: mile on foot where haveing stayd ab^t 2 hours he took water from thence to Salsbury Change Miles :8: thence he went to Josiah Ellises, & thence to M: ffs: at ye Savoy where he stayd y^t night.

The next day being ye 31st of ye 1st mo: & ye 4th day of ye week he went from thence ab^t ye 6th hour in ye morning to

visit one Sr Wm Coddrington[1] who had been Govern^r of
Barbadoes at his Lodgings over ag^t ye Scoth Arms, ag^t
St James Square in pall Mall on foot where haveing stayd
a while he went thence to ffri^d Hulls[2] Grosser, thence to ffri^d
Winingtons[3] in^a Street where G: W: & Gilb^t Latye
Came to him & they all 3 dined there & afterwards going
thence G: W: went towards the Citty & G ff: & G Latye
Called at fri^d Collits keeper of ye tavern at ye Bulls head at
Chering Cross {& to visit a fr^{d}ly man} a Chiurgion a little
above Chering Cross and afterwards Came to :M: ffs: at y^e
Savoy ag^n where he stayd y^t night. ~

The 1st of ye 2^d mo: being ye 5th day of ye week he went
from thence to Ben: Antrobuses where he dined & afterwards
went to a meeting appointed at ye Chamb^r wch Continued
till after ye 6th hour he afterwards went to Dan: Whirleys
where he stayd a while in ye Shope & spake with some fr^{ds}
thence he went to :B: As: ag^n where he stayd y^t night. ~

The next day being ye 2^d of ye 2^d mo: & y^e & ye 6th day of
ye week he went to ye Chamber ab^t busyness & ab^t noon he
went thence to visit Nathan: Brasy who was very sick where
he eate some thing & afterwards went to ye Chamber ag^n
to ye meeting for Sufferings wch Continued till ab^t ye 6th
hour and after it was done he went to B: Antrobuses ag^n
where he stayd that night:~

The next day being ye 3^d of ye 2^d mo: & ye 7th day of y^e
week he went thence to ye Chamber ag^n to a meeting appointed ab^t busyness and betwixt ye 1st and 2^d hour he went
thence to Wm Crouches to meet with John Rowlif[4] a dutch
fri^d where he dined thence he went to John Ettridges &
afterwards went with :A: p: by water to Widdow Grooms
att Rattlif where he staid that night. ~

The meetings he was at this week were :3: ye meeting
for Sufferings & :2: ab^t other busyness.

The next day being ye 4th of ye 2^d mo: & ye first day of
ye week he went thence to ye forenoon meeting at Rattlif
where after other two fri^{ds} had declared he stood up & declared a pritty time & afterwards went to prayer and soe
concluded ye meeting, it was a very good meeting Large &

^{a} There is a blank left in the MS.

peaceable within the doors from thence he went to fr^d John Sellwoods a Brewer hard by & on ye afternoon he went thence to ye meeting at ye same place ag^n where he declared a pritty Large time and afterwards went to prayer and when he had done ye meeting departed, it was a very good meeting and Likewise Large and peaceable within ye doors. thence he went to Widdow Grooms ag^n where he staid that night.~

The next day being the 5th of ye 2^d mo: & ye 2^d day of ye week he went from thence ab^t ye 7th hour in ye morning wth A: p: & Richd Mew[1] by water to ye Citty & soe to Wm Crowches to meet J: Rowlif ye dutch ffri^d ab^t busyness & afterwards he went thence to ye 2^d dayes meeting at ye Chamb^r, & on ye after noon he went thence to visit Nath: Bracy who was sick & in a Short space after he was with him dyed, thence he went to Mary ffosters where he was to meet Jo: Elson ab^t busyness & there dined, thence he went to Wm Crowches ab^t busyness with Jo: Rowlif aboves^d thence he went to the Chamb^r ag^n & after a while to B: As: where he stayd y^t night. ~

The next day being ye 6th of ye 2^d mo: & ye 3^d day of ye week he went from thence to a meeting appointed ab^t busyness at ye Bull & Mouth and from thence to ffrancis Camfields where he dined and thence to Charles Marshalls in Aldersgate Street, thence to visit Eliz: ffullove[2] who was sick & afterwards to Geo: Barrs in Gracious street where he stayd y^t night. ~

The next day being ye 7th of the 2^d mo: & ye 4th day of ye week he went to ye meeting at Gracious Street where after two other fr^{ds} had declared he stood up & declared a pritty Large time & afterwards went to prayer, & then exhorted ye people in a few words and when he had done ye meeting departed it being ab^t ye 11th hour it was a very good meeting Large & peaceable within ye doors, thence he went to M: ffosters thence to Hen: Goulneys[3] where he dined thence to ye Chamb^r ab^t busyness, & towards ye evening he went thence to Ezek: {Woolyes} where he stayd y^t night.

The next day being ye 8th of ye 2^d mo: & ye 5th day of ye week after dinner goeing from thence he went to ye Chamb^r where he sent for Wm Crowch & Richd Whitpain to speak with John Bringhursts[4] wife ab^t John Blaklains book thence

he went to Wm Crowches thence to Richd Whitpains ab^t y^e
said busyness where he stayd y^t night. ~

The next day being ye 9th of ye 2^d mo: & the {6th day of
y^e} week he went thence to Wm Crowches to speak with
John Rowlif & his wife dutch fr^{ds} thence he went to y^e
Chamber where he had busyness till ab^t ye first hour &
afterwards went to Eliz: Bracys where he eate something
thence to ye meeting for Sufferings wch Continued till ab^t
ye 6th hour thence to Wm Crowches to see the dutch fri^{ds}
thence to Wm Meads where he Stayd that night. ~

The next day being the 10th of ye 2^d mo: & the 7th day of
ye week he went thence to ye Chamb^r where he had busyness
till the 1st hour & afterwards went to Tho: Coxes & thence
took Coach to Mary Stotts at Beddnall Green where ye next
day he writt a Letter to fri^{ds} at East & West Jarcey &
pensilvania ab^t Tho: Buds Book^1 y^t it might be Called in ag^n
&c and at night desireing y^t ye familly might Come and sit
together he after a while went to prayer & soe Concluded
ye meeting. ~

The 12th of ye 2^d mo: & ye 2^d day of ye week he took Coach
from ye abovesaid Mary Stots to George yard thence he went
to ye 2^d dayes meeting wch Continued till ab^t ye 1st hour
thence to B: As: where he stayd y^t night. ~

The 13th of ye 2^d mo: being ye 3^d day of ye week he went
thence to ffran: Camfields, & after a while he went thence
to the Kings head {to meet some fr^{ds}} y^t were Concerned at
ye Sessions at Hixes hall ab^t Appeals &c. thence he went to
ffranc: Camfields to dinner & alsoe G: W: & A: p: thence
he went to ye Kings head ag^n on ye afternoon to meet fr^{ds}
ab^t ye aboves^d busyness & afterwards went to ffrancis Camfields ag^n where he stayd y^t night.

The next day being ye 14th of ye 2^d mo: & ye 4th day of
ye week he went thence to ye Kings head ab^t ye aboves^d
busyness to ffri^{ds}, there & Returned to ff Camfields ag^n ab^t
noon where he dined, & afterwards went to ye aboves^d place
ag^n to meet fri^{ds} ab^t ye said busyness and afterwards went
to John Elsons where he staid y^t night. ~

The 15th of ye 2^d mo: being ye 5th day of ye week in y^e
morning after he had Compleated busyness with severall
fri^{ds} y^t Came to him, he went to ye Kings head ag^n to meet
fr^{ds} ab^t ye prementioned busyness at the Sessions & Came

to John Elsons to dinner in ye afternoon he went forth ag^n &
returned to John Elsons where he staid y^t night. ~

The next day being ye 16th of ye 2^d mo & ye 6th day of y^e
week in ye morning he went thence to ye Kings head ag^n
where he mett a great many ffr^{ds} ab^t ye aboves^d busyness at
ye Sessions & ab^t ye 10th hour he took Coach from thence
to B: As: where haveing Staid till after ye first hour he went
to ye Chamb^r ab^t busyness & alsoe stayd ye meeting for
Sufferings wch Continued till ab^t ye 7th hour & haveing stayd
there till towards ye 8th hour he afterwards took Coach to
ffranc: Camfields where he staid y^t night. ~

The next day being ye 17th of ye 2^d mo: & ye 7th day of
ye week he went thence to ye Kings head but there being
noe ffr^{ds} Come he went to John Elsons & after ye fr^{ds} were
Come together at ye Kings head he sent for John Edge to
him ab^t busyness, and ab^t ye 11th hour he and Mary Elson
& Marabella ffarnbora & her daughter took Coach thence to
Anthony Elwoods[1] in Grays Inn Lane in Holbourn where
haveing Stayd a Little till John Elson Came to them they
all /5/ took Coach thence to visit Widdow Healah at Henden
ab^t /7/ miles from the Citty where they Stayd y^t night. ~

The meetings he had & was at this week were /9/ a ffamilly
meeting, ye 2^d dayes meeting ye meeting for Sufferings & 6
ab^t fri^{ds} busyness at ye Sessions at Hixes hall.

The next day being ye 18th of ye 2^d mo: & ye 1st day of
ye week he was at ye meeting at Henden where after John
Elson & another fri^d had declared he stood up & declared a
pritty Large time & afterwards went to prayer and then
spake a few words in Exhortation to ye people & w^n he had
done ye meeting departed, there was a very good meeting &
pritty Large (and peaceable with in ye doors) many Londoners
being there, thence he went to Widdow Helahs againe where
he staid y^t night.

The next day being ye 19th of ye 2^d mo: & ye 2^d day of y^e
week haveing ordered ye same Coach y^t brought them to
Come for them ag^n ab^t ye 4th hour in ye afternoon they took
Coach thence to John Elsons where he Stayd y^t night. ~

The next day being ye 20th of ye 2^d mo: & ye 3^d day of y^e
week he went thence to y^e :6: weeks meeting at ye Bull &

Mouth (wch was to have been ye 3^d day before but was deferred because of ye Sessions at Hixes Hall) ye meeting Continued till ab^t ye 2^d hour & after it was done he went to visit Job Netherwoods[1] wife who was Sick & desired to see him Where haveing stayd a Little he after went to Geo: Watts where he was Invited to dinner thence he took Coach to ye Chamber {to a meeting apointed but was dismist} & afterwards went to B: Antrobuses where he stayd y^t night.~

The next day being ye 21st of ye 2^d mo: & ye 4th day of ye week he went thence to ye Chamb^r where he Continued most of ye day & afterwards went to :B: As: where he Stayd y^t night.

The next day being ye 22^d of ye 2^d mo: & ye 5th day of ye week he went thence to philip ffords where haveing stayd a while he went thence to Abell Wilkisons[2] thence to John Dues ab^t busyness where haveing Stayd a while & afterwards visited some other fr^ds in ye afternoon he went to B: As: where he staid that night. ~

The next day being ye 23^d of ye 2^d mo: & ye 6th day of ye week he went thence to ye Chamb^r in forenoon & stayd ye meeting for Sufferings wch Continued till after ye 6th hour thence he went to Wm Meads where he stayd y^t night.

The next day being ye 24th of ye 2^d mo: & ye 7th day of ye week he went to ye Chamb^r ab^t busyness where Stayd a while he afterwards took Coach to Martha ffishers at ye Savoy to a meeting appointed there ab^t ye 10th hour Concerning fr^ds Sufferings where he stayd y^t night. ~

The meetings he was at this week were 4: a publick meeting a :6: weeks meeting ye meeting for Sufferings & a meeting appointed ab^t fr^ds sufferings.

The next day being ye 25th of ye 2^d mo : & ye 1st day of ye week he was at ye meeting at ye Savoy where after 2/ other fri^ds had declared he stood up & declared a pritty Large time & afterwards went to prayer and then exhorted ye people in a few words & when he had done ye meeting departed, it was a very good meeting & very Large and peaceable in ye Yard & Entry.~ and in ye afternoon :G: W: and John Edge[3] mett him there ab^t fr^ds busyness & after y^t he writt a Letter to Wm Dewsbury[4] at Warrwick.

The next day being ye 26th of ye 2^d mo: & ye 2^d day of ye week in ye morning he went thence to R: Vans to a meeting appointed there with some fri^{ds} ab^t fri^{ds} Sufferings in York-shire for their Release thence Calling on Severall ffr^{ds} by the way he went to Benjemin Antrobuses where he stayd that night. ~

The next day being the 27th of ye 2^d mo: & ye 3^d day of ye week in ye forenoon he went thence to ye Chamb^r to a meeting appointed ab^t delivering Barbadoes Sufferings[1] to ye King where he stayd till ab^t ye 3^d hour & afterwards went to Ezek: Woolyes where he stayd y^t night. ~

The next day being ye 28th of ye 2^d mo: & ye 4th day of ye week he went thence to ye Chamb^r to another meeting appointed ab^t ye prementioned busyness of Barbadoes where he was most of the Day & in the Evening went to Geo: Barrs where he Stayd that night. ~

The next day being ye 29th of ye 2^d mo: & ye 5th day of ye week in the morning he went thence to ye Chamb^r ag^n to a meeting appointed ab^t ffri^{ds} of Midlsex Sufferings thence he went to James Wasses where he dined & afterwards went to ye Chamb^r ag^n & in ye evening went to B: Antrobuses where he stayd y^t night. ~

The next day being ye 30th of ye 2^d mo: & the 6th day of ye week he went thence after dinner to ye meeting for Suf-ferings at ye Chamber wch Continued till ab^t ye 6th hour & afterwards went to Wm Meads where he Stayd that night.~

The next day being ye 1st of ye 3^d mo: & ye 7th day of ye week in ye morning he went to ye Chamb^r ab^t busyness where he stayd till ab^t ye 3^d hour and afterwards went to Geo: Barrs where he staid y^t night & writ some thing to ye Magistrates &c. in Christendome to be printed. ~

The meetings he was at this week were /6/ a publick meeting, ye meeting for Sufferings and 4 ab^t other busy-nesses. ~

The next day being ye 2^d of ye 3^d mo: & ye 1st day of ye week he went from Geo: Barrs to ye morning meeting & thence to Gracious Street meetings. where after Charles Marshall & ffranc: Stamper[2] had declared he stood up and declared a pritty large time & afterwards went to prayer &

after he had done ye meeting departed it was a very Large meeting & peaceable within ye doors, thence he went to Mary ffosters where Severall ffr^{ds} Came to him, & haveing Stayd dinner there he went thence to ye Chamber again ab^t busyness where he stayd till ab^t ye 6th hour, thence he went to Geo: Barrs ag^n where he Stayd that night. ~

The next day being the 3^d of ye 3^d mo: & ye 2^d day of ye week ab^t ye 6th hour in ye morning he went to ye Chamb^r ab^t busyness & alsoe staid ye monthly meeting at ye Chamb^r where he declared & afterwards went to prayer & when he had done ye meeting departed^a haveing continued ab^t half an hour^a thence he went to B: Antrobuses where he dined & afterwards took Coach to Rowland Vans where he mett G: W: & R: Barkley {& other fri^{ds}} who went to ye Atturney Generalls ab^t ye Release of fri^{ds} at Bristoll thence he went to M: ffishers at ye Savoy where he stayd y^t night.

The next day being ye 4th of ye 3^d mo: & ye 3^d day of ye week he took Coach with Bridgit Austill thence to Bow Lane, and went to Philip ffords ab^t busyness with him thence he went to B: Antrobuses where he stayd y^t night.

The next day being ye 5th of ye 3^d mo: & ye 4th day of ye week he went thence to the Chamber ab^t busyness and ab^t noon he went to Ezek: Woolyes where he dined & afterwards took Coach with Mary Wooly & Bridgit Austill thence to South Street miles :9: ~

Remained at Bridgitt Austills from ye 5th of y^e /3^d/ mo: to y^e /14/ of ye same being ye 6th day of ye week (viz) :8: days in wch time severall fri^{ds} Came to See him.

And on ye 14th of y^e /3^d/ mo: & ye 6th day of ye week haveing dined at Bridgitt Austells he went thence to Ed: Mans att ffordgreen on horse Back a mile & ½ where he Staid till ye 19th of ye same mo: & ye 4th day of ye week /viz/ 5 dayes where alsoe Severall fri^{ds} Came to visit him, Remained in ye Country in all 13: dayes.

The 19th of ye 3^d mo: and ye 4th day of ye week he took Coach thence to Byshopgatestreet in London Miles :8: & Soe went to ye Seeds mans where he Stayd a while and

^{a}...^{a} These words are heavily erased.

afterwards went to ye Chamber ab^t busyness where haveing
stayd :2: or :3: hours he afterwards went to :B: As: where
he Stayd that night & severall fri^ds had busyness with him.

The next day being ye 20th of ye 3^d mo: & ye 5th day of y^e
week he went thence to philip ffordes ab^t busyness with him
thence to Ed: Dyleys where he had busyness with a Country
fri^d in ye Shop thence to B: As: ag^n where he dined & afterwards went to John Elsons where he Stayd that night.~

The next day being ye 21st of y^e /3^d/ mo: & y^e :6: day of
ye week he went thence visiting severall fri^ds by ye way he
went to Laurens ffulloves where he dined thence to B: As:
where haveing Stayd a while in ye Shope he afterwards went
to ye meeting for Sufferings wch Continued till ye 6th hour
thence he went to Eliz: Braseys where he had a meeting
with Robt Barkley & severall fri^ds about busyness & Stayd
that night. ~

The next day being ye 22^d of ye 3^d mo: & ye 7th day of y^e
week he went thence to ye Chamber where he had a meeting
with many Country fri^ds & stayd till after ye 1st hour thence
he went to Dan^ll Skin{n}ers[1] where he was invited to dinner
& afterwards went to ye Chamber again, where he likewise
mett Severall country fri^ds and haveing Stayd till towards
ye 7th hour he went to Eliz: Braseys where he also had busyness with Country fri^ds and afterwards went to Wm Crouches
to Some fri^ds there & came to Eliz: Braseys again where he
Staid that night[a]. ~

The next day being ye 23/ of ye 3^d mo: & the 1st day of y^e
week he went thence to ye morning meeting at ye Chamber
where sitting some time in Silence he went to prayer & fri^ds
afterwards devided themselves to each meeting and haveing
staid there till ab^t ye 1st hour went thence to Mary ffausters
and ab^t ye 5th hour he went to ye Chamber ag^n and writt a
paper Concerning marriage[2] thence he went to Eliz: Braseys
where he Stayd y^t night. and Severall fri^ds Came to him. ~

The next day being ye 24th of ye 3^d mo: & ye 2^d day of y^e
week he went thence to ye Generall meeting[3] of ffri^ds in y^e
ministry at ye Chamber ab^t ye 8th hour in ye morning where
he declared a pritty time & after him R: Barkley & :W: P:
& :6: or :7: more & afterwards he went to prayer and after

[a] Margin: *ye meetings he was at this week were /4/ ye meeting for Sufferings, :1: ab^t oth^r Concerns :2: wth Country friends:*

he had done fri^{ds} (haveing appointed another meeting ab^t ye 2^d hour att ye Bull & Mouth) departed ye meeting haveing Continued frõ ab^t ye 8th hour till towards ye 10th itt was a very good meeting and many fri^{ds} of ye Ministry were there thence he went to B: As: where many fri^{ds} Came to him & he dined & ab^t ye 2^d hour he went thence to ye meeting appointed att the Bull & Mouth ab^t ye Generall Sufferings & Concerns of fri^{ds} wch Continued till ab^t ye 7th hour thence he went to :B: As: againe where he Stayd y^t night & many fri^{ds} Came & had busyness with him.

The next day being ye 25th of ye 3^d mo: & ye 3^d day of ye week in ye morning many fri^{ds} Came to him there and ab^t ye 9th hour he went thence to ye Chamb^r to a meeting there ab^t ye Generall Sufferings of fri^{ds} &c where he stayd till ab^t ye 12th hour thence he went to B: As: where he dined & many fri^{ds} Came to him, thence ab^t y^e /2^d hour or near ye 3^d he went to ye Bull & Mouth to a meeting appointed there ab^t ye generall Sufferings of fri^{ds} &c where he Stayd till ab^t ye 8th hour thence he went to Widdow Brasyes where he Stayd that night.

The next day being ye 26th of ye 3^d mo: and ye 4th day of ye week ab^t ½ an hour after 8th he went to ye meeting at Gratius Street where after W: P: R: Barkley & ab^t :7: or :8: more had declared he stood up & declared a pritty large time & afterwards went to prayer & y^n Spake a few words ag^n & after he had done ye meeting departed it was a very good meeting, peaceable & Exceeding large ye meeting house and a great part of ye yard being filled with people ~ thence he went to Mary ffausters where he dined & many fri^{ds} Came to him & ab^t ye 2^d hour he went thence to a meeting appointed ab^t the Generall Sufferings of fri^{ds} at John Etridges wch Continued till betwixt ye 8th & 9th hour, & Stayd there that night.

The next day being ye 27th of ye 3^d mo: & ye 5th day of ye week in ye morning G: W: & Gilbert Latye Came to him there ab^t busyness & after a while he went thence to ye Chamber (where Severall fri^{ds} mett ab^t busyness) & Stayd there till the afternoon thence he went to Ed: Bathursts to see Mary Stott where he Eate Something & afterwards went to B: As: where he Stayd that night and severall fri^{ds} had busyness with him.

The next day being ye 28th of ye 3^d mo: & ye 6th day of y^e

week Severall ffri^{ds} in Like manner Came to him there &
after dinner he went to the Chamber ab^t busyness and Stayd
alsoe the meeting for Sufferings wch Continued from ab^t y^e
3^d till ye 6th hour & afterwards went to :B: As: againe
where he Stayd y^t night, and severall fri^{ds} Came and had
busyness with him.~

The next day being ye 29th of ye 3^d mo: & ye 7th day of
ye week he went thence to ye Chamber agⁿ to a meeting
appointed there att ye 10th hour ab^t the Generall busyness
of fri^{ds} thence ab^t noon he went to Widdow Braseys where
he dined & went thence to ye Chamber againe and after a
Little time went & took Coach from Gratius Street to Mary
Stots att Beddnall-green where he stayd y^t night.

{And ye next day being ye 30th of ye 3^d mo: & 1st day of
ye week he writ an Epistle there to ye generall meetings &
severall fri^{ds} came to visitt him.}

And ye next day being ye 31th of ye 3^d mo: & ye 2^d of y^e
week ab^t ye 9th hour he took Coach thence to George Yard
in Lombardstreet, thence he went to ye morning meeting
at ye Chamb^r and ab^t ye 2^d hour he went thence to W^m
Crowches ab^t busyness with Steven Crisp, thence he went
to ye Chamber again & in ye Evening he went to :B: As:
where he Stayd y^t night, and a great many fri^{ds} Came to
him.

The next day being ye 1st of ye 4th mo: & ye 3^d day of
ye week he went thence to ye Chamber where :G: W: Gilbert
Latye & severall other fri^{ds} mett him ab^t busyness, & ab^t y^e
1st hour he went thence to Widdow Braseys where being
very weary he Lay downe upon ye Cooch to rest him &
afterwards haveing Eate something went to ye Chamber agⁿ
to a meeting appointed ab^t drawing up ye grievances made
by Informers & betwixt the 6th & 7th hour he went thence
to :B: As: where he stayd awhile in ye Shope thence to
John Elsons where he stayd that night.~

The next day being ye 2^d of ye 4th mo: and ye 4th day of
ye week being very weary he stayd there y^t day to rest
him.

The next day being ye 3^d of ye 4th mo: and ye 5th day of
ye week he took Coach thence to ye Chamber where he mett
some ffri^{ds} ab^t busyness & afterwards went to Natt: Blands
where haveing rested him a Little on ye Cooch he went

to ye Chamber where he Likewise {had} busyness wth fri^ds & in ye Evening he went to :B: As: where he Stayd y^t night. ~

The next day being ye 4th of ye 4th mo: and ye 6th day of ye week haveing dined att ye aboves^d place he afterwards went to ye Chamber where he stayed the meeting for Sufferings wch Continued till betwixt y^e :6: & :7: hour thence he went to :B: As: againe, where he stayd that night. ~

The next day being the 5th of ye 4th mo: & ye 7th day of ye week thence he went to ye Chamber ag^n ab^t busyness and ab^t noon he went to Mary ffausters where he rested him awhile upon ye bed being weary & not very well, and haveing dined there, after ye 4th hour he & Edw: Bourn[1] went by water to Ann Traverses at Cheeswick Miles :9:

The Meetings he was att ye week before this, being ye generall meeting time were :10: the first dayes morning meeting ye Generall meeting of fri^ds in ye Ministry ye 4th dayes meeting att Gratius Street the meeting for Sufferings ye other :6: mostly ab^t ye General Concerns of fri^ds besids almost Continued busyness wth Some or other fri^ds of more particular matters: ~

The meetings he was att this week were :5: ye 2^d days meeting a meeting appointed ab^t ye grieveances made upon fri^ds by Informers, ye meeting for Sufferings & :2: ab^t other busyness, besids other particular Concerns as before with fri^ds y^t have Come to him:

The next day being ye 6th of ye 4th mo: & ye week he went by water thence to ye meeting att Hamersmith where after Ed: Bourn & and G: W: had declared he Stood up & declared a pritty Large time and afterwards went to prayer & then Exhorted ye people in a few words & when he had done ye meeting departed it was a very good meeting & Large many Londoners being there & severall y^t were not fri^ds, and afterwards (haveing Stayd a while there & severall fri^ds Come to him) he went to visit ye Gardiners wife who Lived att ye meeting house who haveing broak her Leg Lay very Lambe & weak and after a while went to Antraverses againe.

The 13th of y[e] 4th mo: and y[e] 5th [a] day of y[e] week he went thence to y[e] meeting at Hammersmith againe where after Ed: Bourn and some other fri[ds] had declared he stood up & declared a pritty Large time & afterwards went to prayer & when he had done y[e] meeting departed it was a very good meeting pritty Large & peaceable severall Londoners being there and afterwards haveing Stayd a pritty while in y[e] Gardin & fri[ds] Come to him he visited y[e] Lame[b] fri[d] of y[e] house he went to Ann Traverses ag[n] by water. ~ Mile :1:

The 15th of y[e] 4th mo: and y[e] 3[d] day of y[e] week he went to London and with him Edw: Bourn who accompanyed there 2 or 3 dayes & Ann Traverse, Miles :9: he went on shore at Salsbury Change & went thence to Josiah Elises & after a while to Martha ffishers where he Stayd y[t] night. :~

Remained att Ann Traverses att Cheeswick from y[e] 5th of y[e] 4th mo: and 7th day of y[e] week till y[e] 15th of y[e] said mo : & 3[d] day of y[e] week (viz) :9: dayes in w[ch] time Severall fri[ds] visited him :

The 17th of y[e] 4th mo: and y[e] 5th day of y[e] week he went from Martha ffishers to Bow Lane in a Coach and soe went to philip ffords ab[t] busyness with him ; and ab[t] y[e] 1st hour he Came to : B: As: where not being well he Lay downe to rest him & afterwards G: W: Comeing to him they sent to W[m] Ingram[1] and W[m] philips[2] to meet them there at y[e] 7th hour ab[t] busyness relateing to George Coales Estate[3], he alsoe Stayd there that night.

The next day being y[e] 18th of y[e] 4th mo: & y[e] 6th day of y[e] week in y[e] forenoon he went to y[e] Chamber ab[t] busyness and Stayd y[e] meeting for Sufferings which Continued till y[e] 5th hour thence he went to widdow Braseys where severall fri[ds] mett ab[t] busyness of going to y[e] Mayor[4] &c and he Stayd there that night: ~

The next day being y[e] 19th of y[e] 4th mo: and y[e] 7th day of y[e] week he went from thence to y[e] Chamber ag[n] ab[t] busyness and ab[t] y[e] 11th hour he took Coach from Gratius Street to Mary Stotts at Bednall green where he Stayd that night.

---

[a] Should be *1st*   [b] Corrected from *Lambe*

The meetings he was att this week were :4: a publick meeting att Hamersmith ye meeting for Sufferings & :2: ab^t other Concerns:

Stayd att Mary Stotts att Beddnall green from ye 19th of ye 4th mo: being the 7th day of ye week till ye 5th of ye 5th mo: being ye 12th day of the week (viz) 15/dayes in wch time severall fri^{ds} Came to visit him & that had busyness with him.

The 5th of ye 5th mo: & the 2^d day of ye week he and Edw: Bourn took Coach thence to Lombardstreet thence he went to ye 2^d dayes morning meeting att ye Chamber & in ye afternoon he went to B: As: to hear how things went with friends at ye Sessions att Guild hall where he stayd y^t night and severall fri^{ds} Came and had busyness with him:

The next day being the 6th of ye 5th mo: & the 3^d day of ye week he went to John Mathews[1] att the Kings head att Smithfield Barrs to Look after friends Busyness att ye Sessions att Hixes Hall thence he went to visit John Staploes thence to another fri^{ds} hard by thence to visit Geo: Watts who was not well thence to ff Camfields where he stayd y^t night.

The next morning he had busyness with 2 ffri^{ds} that he had appointed to meet him there, & afterwards went to John Mathews thence to John Elsons where he had busyness with some fri^{ds} about ffriends busyness at ye Sessions where he stayd y^t night & ye next day being ye 8th of ye 5th mo: and ye 5th day of ye week & likewise had busyness wth severall fri^{ds} y^t tended {at} ye Sessions &c And in ye after noon was att ye quarterly meeting there where after severall other fri^{ds} had declared he declared a pritty time itt was a very good meeting and pritty Large. ～

The next day being ye 9th of ye 5th mo: & ye 6th day of ye week he took Coach thence to ye Chamber where he had busyness and stayd ye meeting for Sufferings till almost ye 6th hour & afterwards went to Ben: Antrobus's where he stayd y^t night.

The next day being the 10th of ye 5th mo: & ye 7th day of ye week after he had dined he went to ye seeds mans in Byshop

gatestreet in order to take Coach to Edw: Mans att ffordgreen beyond Edmonton, Miles /8/:

The meetings he was att this week were /3/ y[e] 2[d] dayes
meeting & y[e] {meeting for Sufferings & a} quarterly meeting
at y[e] peel besides other busynesses as 3 dayes Looking after
friends busyness at y[e] Sessions &c. ~

The 18th of y[e] 5th mo: being y[e] first day of y[e] week he
went in James Lawryes[1] Coach to visit Ann Whitehead[2] who
Lay very Sick at Southstreet & came back in y[e] Coach ag[n]
to Edw: Mans y[t] night, Miles /3/ backward & forward.

The 26th of y[e] 5th mo: and y[e] 2[d] day of y[e] week he had
ordered y[t] James Laweryes Coach Coms for him againe to
Carry him to Southstreet to visit Ann Whitehead who Lay
on her Death Bed and ffinding her soe very weak he stayd
with Tho: Coxes y[t] night and ab[t] y[e] 10th hour att Night
went thither again to visit her & to speak some thing that
Lay upon him to her, & ab[t] y[e] 3[d] hour in y[e] morning she
departed. ~

The next day being y[e] 27th of y[e] 5th mo: & y[e] 3[d] day of
y[e] week he went thence in y[e] afternoon to Edw: Mans ag[n]
(with severall women fri[ds] y[t] Came to see Ann Whitehead)
in the Coach. ~

The next day being y[e] 28th day of y[e] 5th mo: & y[e] 4th day
of y[e] week he went from Edw: Mans on horse back to
Widdow Dryes att Enfield Miles 3: thence to y[e] monthly
meeting att Tho: Hearts where he declared a pritty time
& after him John Crook there was a very good meeting &
pritty Large & afterwards he went to Widdow Dryes where
he stayd y[t] night.

Remained att Edw: Mans ab[t] /16/ dayes in w[ch] time many
fri[ds] Came almost daily to see him:

The 30th of y[e] 5th mo: being y[e] 6th day of y[e] week in y[e]
afternoon he went thence to Geo: Watts on horse back to
speak wth John Crook where he stayd that night and y[e] next
day towards Evening he went on horse back wth Thomas

Heart & Gariot Roberts[1] who were Come to see him to :T:
Hs: & thence to widdow Dryes Where he stayd y^t night:

The 1st of ye 6th mo: being ye 1st day of ye week he &
some att Thomas Hearts & Wm Shewins[2] took Coach to
Winsmer hill {meeting} where after Geo: Watts & John
Crook had declared he stood up & declared a pritty Large
time & afterwards spake a few words in Exhortation to y^e
people & when he had done the meeting departed, t'was
a very good meeting, Large & peaceable within the doors,
thence he went to R. Chaires where many fri^{ds} Came to him
and after a while took Coach thence to Enfield againe and
went to Widdow Dryes where he stayd y^t night, ab^t :6:
Miles backward and forward:

The 8th of ye 6th mo: & ye 6th mo: & ye 1st day of ye week
he went with some of Wm Shewins ffamilly in a Coach to
ye meeting att Walthum Abey where after Geo: Whitehead
had declared he stood up & declared a pritty time & afterwards went to prayer & then Spake a few words in Exortation to ye people & when he had done ye meeting departed
'twas a very good meeting and pritty Large & peaceable
with in ye doors thence he went to Tho: Bennets where he
stayd y^t night and severall fri^{ds} Came to him.

The next day being ye 9th of ye 6th mo: & ye 2^d day of y^e
week he took Coach thence to Tho: Hearts att Enfield and
with him Tho: Bennett and his wife & Young Margret
Rowse where he mett with Alexand: parker and Geo:
Whitehead they dined there & afterwards he went to Widdow Dryes where he stayd that night:

The 13th of ye 6th mo: & ye 6th day of ye week after dinner
att Thomas Hearts he took Coach to Edw: Mans att fford-
green about Miles :3:

Stayd att Widdow Dryes att Enfield from the 28th of y^e
5th mo: being ye 4th day of ye week to ye 13th of ye 6th mo:
being ye 6th day of ye week save a Night att Geo: Watts &
a day & a night att Tho: Bennets att Walthum Abey wch is
in all ab^t :15: Dayes in wch time he dined severall times
att {Wid: Dryes &} Tho: Hearts :2: or :3: times att W^m
Shewins, once att Geo: Watts:

The 20th of ye 6th mo: being ye 6th day of ye week in y^e

afternoon Bridgit Austill and Mary Wooly fetched him with a Coach to their house at Southstreet*a*. Stayd att Edw: Mans from ye 13th of ye 6th mo: till ye 20th of ye same /viz/ :7: dayes.

The 29th of ye 6th mo: being ye first day of the week he & Mary Wooly & Bridgit Austill took Coach to ye meeting att Winsmerhill*b* where after George Whitehead had declared he declared a pritty large time & afterwards went to prayer & then Exhorted ye people in a few words & when he had done the meeting departed 'twas a very good meeting pritty Large & peaceable within ye doors, thence he went to Richd Chairs where he stayd a while & many fri^ds Came to him thence he went in ye Coach to Edw: Mans where he stayd y^t night haveing busyness there with Geo: Whitehead:

The next day being ye 30th of ye 6th mo: & ye 2^d day of ye week he went on horse back to Bridgit Austills att South Street againe*c*.

The first of ye 7th mo: being ye 4th day of ye week John Clause ye Dutchman[1] Came to visit him there

The 2^d of ye 7th mo: & ye 5th day of ye week he & John Clause took Coatch to London; to Byshopgatestreet & thence {he} took Coach to Benj: Antrobuses*d* where he stayd y^t night:

Remained att Bridg^t Austells from ye 20th of ye 6th mo: till ye till ye 2^d of ye 7th mo: save one day on wch he was at ye meeting at Winsmerhill {meeting} & lay att Edw: Mans y^t night, wch is :11: Dayes.

Remained in ye Country from ye 10th of ye 5th month to ye 2^d of the 7th mo: (viz) :7: weeks & :4: dayes in wch time a great many fri^ds Came to visit him and that had busyness with him, he was at 4: meetings in ye Country ye monthly meeting att Enfield a publick meeting att Walthum Abbey & 2 att Winsmerhill: and travelled to and again in ye Country about :45: miles:

a Margin: *Miles :1: ½:*   *b* Margin: *Miles /1/½*
c Margin: *Miles 1: ½*   *d* Margin: *Miles :9:*

The 3^d of ye 7th mo: being ye 6th day of ye week he went
to the Chamber where he had busyness & alsoe stayd y^e
meeting for Sufferings & afterwards went to Eliz: Braseys
where he stayd y^t night:

The next day being ye 4th of ye 7th mo: and ye 7th day of
ye week he went thence to the Chamber ag^n & in ye afternoon took Coach to Ezek: Wooleys[1] where he stayd y^t night:

The next day being ye 5th of ye 7th mo: & ye first day of
the week he went to the meeting att WheelerStreet where
he declared a pritty {Large} time & afterwards went to
prayer & when he had done ye meeting departed, it was a
very good meeting, Large & peaceable wthin ye doors, and
afterwards he went to Ezek: Wooleyes where he stayd that
night:

The 6th of ye 7th mo: & the 2^d day of ye week he went to
ye monthly morning meeting att ye Chamber where haveing
stayd till ab^t noon he went to Edw: Bathursts to speak with
Mary Stott and dined there & afterwards went to Benj: Antrobuses where he stayd that night:

The 7th of ye 7th mo: being ye 3^d day of ye week he went
thence to Edw: Haistwells where haveing stayd a while he
went thence to the Chamber & haveing stayd till ab^t y^e
2^d hour he went thence to Daniell Whirleys and afterwards
to Wm Crowches {&} thence to Eliz: Braseys widdow where
he stayd y^t night:

The 8th of ye 7th mo: & ye 4th day of ye week he went
thence to ye meeting att Gratius Street where after John
Vaughton and a Lestershire ffri^d had declared he stood up
and declared a pritty Large time and afterwards went to
and then exhorted ye people in a few words and when he had
done ye meeting departed, itt was a very good meeting Large
& peaceable within ye doors & haveing stayd a while att
Mary ffausters and in George Yard he & Alexand: parker
afterwards took Coatch with Geo: Watts (who had Invited
them to Dinner) to his house and afterwards he went to John
Elsons where he stayd that night:

The next day being ye 9th of ye 7th mo: & ye 5th day of
ye week he stayd there alsoe.

The 10th of ye 7th mo: & 6th day of ye week he went thence
after diñer to ye meeting for Sufferings & afterwards went to
Benjamin Antrobuses where he stayd y^t night.

The next day being ye 11th of ye 7th mo: & ye 7th day of
ye week he went to ye Chamber ag^n ab^t busyness & visiting
some fri^{ds} there aways afterwards went to Ben: Antrobuses
where he stayd y^t night:

The meetings he was att this week were :4: ye 2^d days
monthly Meeting at ye Chamber ye meeting for Sufferings &
2 publick meetings, besids other particular Concerns wth fri^{ds}
y^t have Come to him.

The next day being the 12th of ye 7th mo: & ye first day
of ye week in ye afternoon he went to ye meeting att ye Bull
& Mouth where after Tho: Robison had declared he stood up
& declared a pritty Large time & afterwards went to prayer
and then spake a few words in Exortation to ye people and
afterwards ye meeting departed, & he went to Edw: Brushes[1]
where haveing stayd a while he went thence to John Dues
where he stayd a while & afterwards went to Benj: Antrobuses where he stayd y^t night, and severall ffri^{ds} Came to
him. ~

The next day being ye 13th of ye 7th mo: & ye 2^d day of y^e
week he went to ye 2^d dayes morning meeting & in the —
noon to ye 2 weeks meeting (att Devenshire house) of men
& women, ye Womens meeting was very Large {&} ye mens
alsoe he declared there a pritty time & after the meeting was
done he and Marg^t Rowse took Coatch to Benj: Antrobuses
where he stayd y^t night.

The next day being ye 14th of ye 7th mo: & the 3^d day of
ye week he stayd att B: As: y^t day & had busyness with
Tho: Lower who was Come out of Cornwall &c And at night
took Coatch to John Elsons where he sent for ye Lesťershire
fri^{ds} y^t were come to London ab^t their Sufferings to meet him
there the next morning:

The next day being ye 15th of ye 7th mo: & ye 4th day of
ye week aft^r busyness had with the Lesťershire ffri^{ds} & others
y^t came to him he went to Widdow Braseys where he had
busyness with W: p: &c and afterwards went to ye Chamber
ab^t busyness & afterwards took Coatch to Mary Wooleys in
Spittle ffields where he stayd y^t night:

The next day being ye 16th of ye 7th mo: & ye 5th day of
ye week after dinner he took Coatch to Lombardstreet thence

he went to ye Chamber to meet some there who not accordingly Comeing itt was deferred till ye 10th hour ye next day at ye Chamber, soe after busyness had some time there visiting some fri^{ds} in George Yard he went to B: As: where he Stayd y^t night & severall ffri^{ds} Came to him:

The next day being ye 17th of ye 7th mo: & ye 6th day of ye week he went to ye aboves^d meeting of busyness att ye Chamber with Gari^t Roberts &c and afterwards went to Walther Bentons in George Yard where he dined and thence went to ye meeting for Sufferings att ye Chamber wch Continued till after ye 5th hour & after it was done he went to :B: As: againe where he Stayd that night:

The next day being ye 18th of ye 7th mo: & ye 7th day of ye week he went thence to Martha ffishers att ye Savoy on foot and visited severall ffri^{ds} by ye way amongst ye Rest Rolland Vaughan whom he dined:

The next day being the 19th of ye 7th mo: & ye first day of ye week he was att ye meeting att ye Savoy where after two fri^{ds} had declared he stood up & declared a pritty Large time & then went to prayer and afterwards ye meeting departed. itt was a very good meeting Large and peaceable in the yard: ~

The meetings he {had &} was att this week were :7: a publick meeting ye 2^d dayes morning meeting ye men and womens two weeks meetings, ye meeting for Sufferings and :2: ab^t other busyness.

The next day being ye 20th of ye 7th .mo: & ye 2^d day of ye week he & W^m penn & Tho: Lower dined att Gilbert Latyes & he alsoe Staid at Martha ffishers y^t night:

The next day being ye 21st of ye 7th mo: & the 3^d day of ye week in ye morning he took Coach to Martins where he visited severall fri^{ds} att ye Bull & mouth and thereaways and thence visited John Dues and Marabella ffarnborahs and afterwards went to :B: As: where he stayd y^t night. and sent for ye Lestershire fri^{ds} to meet him there that were Come up ab^t their Sufferings:

The next day being ye 22^d of ye 4th mo: & the 4th day of ye week he appointed ye Lestershire ffri^{ds} to meet him there ag^n Early in ye morning and severall more ffri^{ds} Came to him there and afterwards he went to ye Chamber ab^t busyness and went to :B: As: ag^n in ye Evening where he stayd y^t night:

The next day being ye 23^d of ye 7th mo: & ye 5th day of ye week thence to Nat: Willmer where haveing Stayd a while he afterwards went to ye Chamber ab^t busyness & near ye 2^d hour went to Nat: Blands where he dined:

The next day being ye 24th of ye 7th mo: & ye 6th day of ye week he went to ye Chamber and was at ye meeting for Sufferings {there} in the afternoon & towards night went to Benjemin Antrobuses where he stayd y^t night:

The next day being the 25th of ye 7th mo: & ye 7th day of ye week he went to ye Chamber ag^n ab^t busyness & in the Evening went to Eliz: Brasyes Wid: where he stayd that night:

The meetings this week y^t he was at were :4: a publick first days meeting ye meeting for Sufferings & /2/ ab^t busyness besids more pticular matters wth fri^{ds} that Came to him:

The next day being ye 26th of ye 7th mo: and the first day of ye week went to ye Chamber where he stayd ye forenoon and in ye afternoon went to Devenshire meeting where he declared a pritty Large time and then went to prayer and afterwards ye meeting departed; itt was a very good meeting, Large, and peaceable within the doors, and after many fri^{ds} had Come to him in ye Little Roome in a short time in went thence to Geo: Whiteheads & thence to Tho: Coxes where he stayd y^t night & had discourse with a great Docter of phis:[1] y^t night & ye next morning who was very ffriendly and Glad of ye opportunity with him.

The next day being the 27th of ye 7th mo: & ye 2^d day of ye week in ye morning he went thence to ye 2^d dayes morning meeting att ye Chamber; and afterwards went to Edw: Hs'^{a} where he & Tho: Lower & Alexand^r parker & Tho: Robison dined, & afterwards he went to Ben: Antrobuses where he stayd y^t night:

The next day being the 28th of ye 7th mo: & ye 3^d day of

^{a} First written *Haistwells*

ye week he went to y^e :6: weeks meeting att ye Bull and
Mouth and afterwards went to Geo: Watts where he dined
thence he went Rebec. Traverse & retured to Geo: Watts
ag^n and thence to John Elsons where he stayd y^t night:

The next day being the 29th of ye 7th mo: & ye 4th day of
ye week he was att ye monthly meeting there where he declared a pritty time, there was a very good meeting and
Large he alsoe stayd there that night:-

The 30th of ye 7th mo: & ye 5th day of ye week in ye forenoon he took Coach to Bow Lane & went to philip ffords ab^t
busyness where he dined and afterwards went to Ben:
Antrobuses where he Stayd that night:

The next day being ye first of ye 8th mo: & ye 6th day of
ye week he went to ye Chamber ab^t busyness & in ye afternoon was att ye meeting for Sufferings there, and att night
went to Eliz: Braseys where he Stayd y^t night:

The next day being ye 2^d of ye 8th mo: and ye 7th day of
ye week he went thence to ye Chamber ab^t busyness, &
between ye 3^d and 4th hour he and Tho: Lower took Coach
from Wm Meads in ffancy Street to his house att Gooseys in
Essex ab^t 13: miles:

The meetings he was att this week were 5: a publick
meeting on ye first day ye 2^d days meeting, y^e :6: weeks
meeting, a monthly meeting & ye meeting for Sufferings.

The next day being ye 3^d of ye 8th month & the first day
of ye week he went thence ab^t a mile on horse back to a
meeting att one John Hardins where he declared a pritty
Large time & when he had done went to prayer & then
spake a few words in Exortation to ye people, and haveing
done ye meeting departed there was a very good meeting &
Large (there being severall from London and Else where) itt
Continued from ab^t ye 12th to ye 2^d & afterwards went to
Wm Meads ag^n and John Elsons & his wife and severall others
went from ye meeting & dined there:

And haveing stayd att Wm Meads till ye 6th of ye 8th month
and 4th day of ye week he and Tho: Lower took Coach y^e
same day thence to Wm Meads att London[a] where he dined
& afterwards he went to the Chamber ab^t busyness &

[a] Margin: *Miles /13/*

afterwards went to Ben: Antrobuses & thence took Coatch to John Elsons where he stayd y^t night.

Remained in ye Citty from ye 2^d of ye 7th mo: till ye 2^d of ye 8th mo: y^t is a Month.

The next day being the 7th of ye 8th mo: & the 5th day of ye week Calling on severall fri^{ds} by the way he went to visit Eliz: ffullove {who was not well} where he dined and afterwards went to Benjemin Antrobuses where he stayd that night and had appointed Tho: Lower to meet him there and severall other fri^{ds} Came to him:

The next day being ye 8th of ye 8th mo: & ye 6th day of ye week in the forenoon he went to ye Chamber about busyness, & Stayd the meeting for Sufferings and after y^t another meeting att ye same place & afterwards went to :B: As: again where he stayd y^t night.

The next day being ye 9th of ye 8th mo: & the 7th day of ye week he went to ye Chamber againe and afterwards went to Mary ffausters where he dined and thence went to take water to Mary Birkets[1] near Lamboth Miles /2/ where he stayd y^t night:

The next day being ye 10th of ye 8th mo: & ye first day of ye week he went thence to ye meeting att Westminster where after Tho: Robison had declared he stood up and declared a pritty time and afterwards went to prayer and haveing done the meeting departed, itt was a very good meeting Large & peaceable wthin the doors there was many of ye world there and severall papists one or all of wch were said to belong to the popes Nuncio, and haveing Stayd a while and visited ye old Woman James Beeches Wid: he afterwards went towards Martha ffishers on foot but a Little beyond Westminster accedentally mett with a Chariot wch Carryed him & Gilbert Latye & Martha ffisher to ye Savoy:

The 11th of ye 7th mo: & ye 2^d day of ye week he took Coatch to ye 2^d dayes morning meeting att ye Chamber and ab^t noon he went to widdow Braseys, and thence to ye quarterly mens & womens meeting at Devenshire house and declared there. the womens meeting was Exceeding Large the mens Large also and both very quiet and peaceable thence he went to Ezek: Wooleys where he stayd that night:

The next day being the 12th of ye 8th mo: & ye 3^d day of ye week he took Coach to ffra: Camfields to Look after fri^{ds} busyness att the Sessions att Hixes hall but he & his ffamilly being out of towne he went to Jacob Camfields[1] where he dined & afterwards went to John Elsons where he stayd y^t night and ye next day to Look after fri^{ds} busyness at ye Sessions att Hixes hall as aboves^d:

The 14th of ye 8th mo: being ye 5th day of the week in ye morning there came severall fri^{ds} to him thither as John Tayler[2] John Blaklaine[3] Rich^d pinter &c and after a while he went thence to Ben: Antrobuses where he stayd y^t night and ye aboves^d fri^{ds} & Geo: Whitehead & a Welch fri^d & Came to him thither: ~

The next day being ye 15th of ye 8th mo: & ye 6th day of ye week John Blakelain had busyness with him there in ye forenoon & W^m pen & severall others Came to him there and after dinner he went to ye meeting for Sufferings to ye Chamber wch Continued till ab^t ye 6th hour & thence he went to Benjemin Antrobuses ag^n where he stayd y^t night:

The next day being ye 16th of ye 8th mo: & ye 7th day of ye week in ye forenoon he went to Tho: Coxes where he dined and afterwards took Coatch to Mary Stots att Beddnall Green:

The meetings he was att this week were :5: a publick first days meeting ye quarterly men & womens meetings ye 2^d dayes meeting & ye meeting for Sufferings besids Looking áfter fri^{ds} busyness att ye Sessions and other particular Concerns with ffri^{ds} y^t Came to him: ~

Stayd att Mary Stotts from ye 16th of ye 8th mo: till ye 21st of ye same wch is 4: dayes in wch time many fri^{ds} Came to visit him & y^t had busyness with him:

The 21st of ye 8th mo: and ye 5th day of the week he took Coatch to Lombardstreet & went to ye Chamber and after busyness had there some time he afterwards went to Benj: Antrobuses where he Stayd y^t night:

The 22^d of ye 8th mo: and ye 6th day of ye week after dinner he went to ye meeting for Sufferings wch Continued till towards ye 7th hour thence he went to Wm Meads where he stayd that night:

The next day being ye 23^d of ye 8th mo: & ye 7th day of ye week in ye morning he went to ye Chamber ag^n ab^t busyness and stayd there till after ye first hour & afterwards visited some fri^{ds} not fur from thence & in ye afternoon took Coatch to John Elsons where he stayd that night:

The 24th of ye 8th mo: and ye 1st day of ye week he was att ye peel meeting where after John Elson had declared he stood up & declared a pritty Large time & afterwards went to prayer & after he had done George Watt declared a small time & he haveing done ye meeting departed 'twas a very good meeting Large and peaceable within ye doors and after ye meeting many friends Came to him & he alsoe stayd att John Elsons y^t night.

The next day being ye 25th of ye 8th mo: & ye 2^d day of ye week he took Coach to ye 2^d days morning meeting att ye Chamber where he stayd till ye afternoon, and towards night went to Ezek: Wooleys where he stayd that night:

The next day being ye 26th of ye 8th mo: & ye 2^d day of ye week he visited some friends there aways and afterwards took Coatch to Geo: Watts in Aldersgatestreet and thence he went to ffrancis Camfields where he stayd that night:

The next day being ye 27th of ye 8th mo: & ye 4th day of ye week he went to Geo: Watts where he was invited to dinner & afterwards went to Benj: Antrobuses where he stayd that night:

The next day being ye 28th of y^e {8th mo: & 5th day of y^e} week he went to ye Chamber ab^t busyness & in the afternoon went to Edw: Hastells where he stayd some time & in the Evening went to Benj: Antrobuses where he stayd that night:

The next day being the 29th of ye 8th mo: & ye 6th day of ye week ye Mayer show [1] being that day he stayd till noon to still ye people that went thither to see itt & thence went to ye Chamber and stayd ye meeting for Sufferings there and afterwards went to Wm Meads where he stayd that night:

The next day being the 30th of ye 8th mo: & ye week he went thence to ye Chamber ab^t busyness & haveing stayd there till about ye 1st hour afterwards went to philip ffords

where he & severall other friends were invited to dinner &
afterwards went to Eliz: Brasyes wid: where he stayd y^t
night:

Y^e meetings he was att this week were :3: a publick meeting on ye 1st day ye 2^d dayes meeting & ye meeting for Sufferings besids other particular Concerns wth friends y^t have
come to him:

The next day being ye 31st of ye 8th mo: & ye 1st day of
ye week he went to ye meeting att Gratius street where after
/2/ others had declared he stood up and declared a pritty
{large} time and afterwards went to prayer & w^n he had done
ye meeting departed itt was a very good meeting Large &
peaceable within ye doors thence he went to Mary ffausters
where many friends Came to him and afterwards he Lay
him downe on ye Bed being wearyed & not very well thence
he went to Eliz: Brasyes where he stayd that night and
severall fri^{ds} Came to him:

The next day being ye 1st of ye 9th mo: & ye 2^d day of
ye week he went to ye 2^d dayes morning meeting and in
ye afternoon took Coatch to Tho: Coxes and after a while he
& Edw: Bourn took Coatch to Mary Stots at Bednall Green
where he stayd till ye 5th of ye 9th mo: in wch time severall
friends Came to visit him and on ye 5th day night Causing
the ffamilly to be Called together after sometime Sitting in
Silence he went to prayer Edw: Bourn was alsoe there.

The 5th of ye 9th mo: being ye 6th day of ye week he took
Coach thence to ye Change & soe went to B: As: where he
dined & severall fri^{ds} with him & afterwards went to ye meeting for Sufferings wch Continued till ab^t ye 6th hour & thence
he went to Wm Meads where he stayd that night:

The next day being ye 6th of ye 9th mo: & ye 7th day of y^e
week he went to ye Chamber ag^n to a meeting appointed
there ab^t fri^{ds} Concerns & ab^t ye 1st hour he went thence to
Dan^{ll} Quares[1] & thence to Benj: Antrobuses and towards
night he went to ye Savoy & went to Martha ffishers where
he stayd that night^a:

The next day being ye 7th of ye 9th mo: & ye first day of
ye week he was att ye Meeting att ye Savoy where he de-

---

^{a} Margin: *ye meetings he was at this week were /4/*

clared a pritty Large time & afterwards went to prayer &
when he had done ye meeting departed it was a very good
meeting Large & peaceable in ye yard & Entry:

The next day being ye 8th of ye 9th mo: & ye 2^d day of y^e
week he stayd att ye said place:

The next day being ye 9th of ye 9th mo: & ye 3^d day of y^e
week he took Coatch thence to Rowland Vañs ab^t busyness &
after a while took coatch to Ben: Antrobuses where he dined
& afterwards went to Eliz: Brasyes Widd: where he stayd that
night.

The next day being ye 10th of ye 9th & ye 4th day of y^e
week he went thence to ye meeting att Gratius street where
after another friend & W^m pen had declared he stood up to
declare but was p^rvented att y^t time by one Nath: Coalman[1]
a separate who interposed & after N Coalman, had done he
had a pritty time in declaration and afterwards Concluded
ye meeting wth prayer itt was a very good meeting Large &
peaceable w^thin ye doors thence he went to Mary ffausters
when W: pen & G: W: and severall other fri^ds Came to him
& after a while he went to Theoder Eglestons[2] where he
dined & John Tayler & John Blakelaine and severall others
and afterwards went to visit Eliz: Bland[3] who was sick &
thence to Eliz: Brasys where he stayd that night:

The 11th of ye 9th mo: & ye 5th day of ye week in y^e
morning he took Coatch thence to Tho: Coxes Daughters[4]
marriage att Devenshire House where after Geo: Whitehead
had declared {he stood up} a pritty time and opened things
in Relation thereto very plainly {&} after him Alexander
parker went to prayer & when he had done they took Each
other & then John Vauton declared a while & after him W^m
pen then ye Certificate being Read ye meeting after departed
there was a very great meeting aboundance of the worlds
people being there, thence he went to Geo: Whiteheads
where he stayd a while and severall friends Came to him, &
after a Short time he took Coatch wth the Marryed people to
Southstreet, Miles :9:

The meetings he was att this week were /3/ a publick
meeting on ye first ye 4th days meeting, & att a marrage on
ye 5th day besids other particular busynesses with friends that
Come to him:

Stayd att Southstreet from ye 11th of ye 9th mo: to ye 21st of ye Same viz :10: dayes: in wch time severall fri^{ds} Came to see him^a:

The 21st of ye 9th mo: & ye first day of ye week he took Coatch thence to the meeting att Winsmer hill Mile 1½ where he declared a pritty {large} time and afterwards went to pray^r and then Exhorted ye people in a few words and when he had done ye meeting departed, itt was a very good meeting Large & peaceable within the doors thence he went to Richd Chaires where he stayd a while & afterwards took Coach to Edward Mans att ffordgreen where he stayd y^t night:

The 24th of 9th mo: being ye 4th day of ye week he took Coatch to ye monthly men & womens meeting att Tho: Hearts att Enfield, he declared a pritty time in ye mens meeting & then went to prayer & afterwards went into ye womens meeting where he alsoe declared, there was a pritty many friends att ye meeting he stayd att Tho: Hearts y^t night & ye next day and night:

The 26th of ye 9th mo: & ye 6th day of ye week he dined at Wm Shewins and stayd there y^t night

The next day being ye 27th of ye 9th mo: & ye 7th day of ye week he dined att Tho: Hearts againe & stayd there that night:

The next day being ye 28th of ye 9th mo: & ye first day of the week he took Coatch with Wm Shewins & Thomas Hearts to the meeting att Walthum Abbey where after John ffield had declared he stood up & declared a pritty Large time & went to prayer & after he had done ye meeting departed itt was a very good meeting Large & peaceable within the doors, Thence he went to Tho: Bennetts where where many friends Came to him & he stayd that night:

The first of ye 10th mo: being ye 4th day of ye week he was att there weekly^b meeting att Walthum Abbey where he declared a pritty large time & afterwards went to prayer & then declared a Little while againe and when he had done the meeting departed itt was a very good meeting and peaceable within the doors, & afterwards he went to Tho: Bennets againe where he stayd that night:

^{a} Margin: *stayd att Bridgitt Austill's att Southstreet :10: dayes*
^{b} Altered from *monthly*

The next day being ye 2^d of ye 10th mo: & the 5th day of
ye week he went to their monthly {men & womens} meeting
att widdow Tylers[1] where he opened severall things to them
Relateing to truths affairs &c and afterwards went to y^e
womens meeting:

The next day being ye 3^d of ye 10th mo: & ye 6th day of y^e
week early in ye morning he & Eliz: Bennet[2] & widdow Tyler
took Coatch thence To Geo: Barrs near Berry Street in
Edmunton _pish where he dined and after took Coatch to
Edw: Mans (where he stayd that night) att ffordgreen ab^t
7: Miles from Walthum Abbey:

The 5th of ye 10th mo: being ye first day of ye severall
friends Comeing to visit him he had a meeting att Edw: Mans
where after Geo Whitehead had declared he declared a
pritty time & afterwards went to prayer & then declared a
little while againe & when he had done ye meeting departed,
itt was a very good meeting:

The 10th of ye 10th mo: being ye 6th day of ye week Bridgit
Austell brought a Coatch to Carry him to her house att
Southstreet: Mile 1½:

Stayd att Edw: Mans from ye 3^d of ye 10th months to y^e
10th of ye same mo: viz :6: dayes & :7: nights.

Stayd att Bridgit Austells att southstreet from ye 10th of
ye 10th month till the 15th of ye same in wch time severall
friends visited him there:

Remained in the Country from ye 11th of ye 9th mo: &
5th day of ye week till ye 15th of ye 10th mo: being ye 4th day
of ye week wch is 5: weeks wanting a day in wch time he had
many Visiters travelled ab^t :34: Miles in ye Country & was
att :8: meetings ye meeting att Winsmerhill ye men &
womens monthly meeting att Enfield ye first days meeting
att Walthum Abbey, ye weekly meeting and their Men &
Womens mo^ly meeting (I think) itt fell out to be their
Quarterly meeting too & a meeting on ye first day att Edward
Mans:

The 15th of ye 10th mo: being ye 4th day of ye week he
took Coatch thence to London Miles :9: he went out of y^e

Coatch att ye half Moon in Byshopsgatestreet and thence
went to Jacob ffranklaines[1] att ye white Lion Tavern in Cornwell he being but a new beginner to Advise him &c he dined
there, and afterwards went to ye Chamber and towards night
to B: As: where he stayed that night:

The next day being ye 16th of ye 10th mo: & ye 5th day of
ye week after Dinner he went to ye Chamber & Came to B:
As: again where he stayd that night:

The next day being ye 17th of ye 10th mo: & ye 6th day of
ye week he went thence to ye meeting att ye Bull and Mouth
where he declared a pritty Large time & afterwards went to
prayer & after he had done ye meeting departed, itt was a
very good meeting Large and peaceable within ye doors thence
he went to ffranc: Camfields where he dined and afterwards
took Coatch to ye Meeting for Sufferings att the Chamber
where haveing stayd till ab^t ye 7th hour he afterwards went
to Wm Meads where he stayd that night:

The next day being the 18th of ye 10th mo: & ye 7th day
of ye week he went to ye Chamber ag^n and afterwards went
to visit Eliz: Bland & Martha ffisher who was not well &
afterwards went to James parks where he stayd that
night[a]:

The next day being ye 19th of ye 10th mo: & ye first day
of ye week he was att ye meeting att Horsly downe where
after some other fri^ds had declared he stood up & declared a
pritty Large time & went to prayer and afterwards ye meeting departed, itt was a very Good meeting Large and peaceable within ye doors, thence he went to James parks ag^n
where many fri^ds Came to him & he stayd there that
night:

The next day being ye 20th of ye 10th mo: & ye 2^d day of
ye week he went to ye 2^d dayes morning Meeting att y^e
Chamber & afterwards went to :B: As: where he stayd that
night:

The next day being ye 21st of ye 10th month and ye 3^d day
of ye week he went to the 6th weeks meeting att ye Bull &
Mouth and afterwards went to John Dues where he dined &
thence he went to :B: As: & thence he went to Widdow
Brasyes where he stayd that night:

The next day being ye 22^d of ye 10th mo: & ye 4th day of

---

^a Margin: *ye meetings he was at this week were |2|*

11—2

ye week he went to Gratius street meeting where after
another fri^d or 2 had declared he stood up & declared a pritty
time & then went to prayer & afterwards the meeting
departed itt was a very good meeting large & peaceable
within the doors thence he went to Mary ffausters she being
sick & visited her thence to Henry Goulneys where he dined
& afterwards went to B: As: where he stayd y^t night^a:

The next day being ye 23^d of ye 10th mo: & ye 5th day of
ye week in ye afternoon he not being well took Coatch to
Mary Stotts att Bednall Green where he writt severall things
& stayd there till ye 3^d day following being ye 28th of ye Sayd
mo: where upon he took Coatch to Tho: Coxes & haveing
stayd dinner there he afterwards took Coatch to ye peel
meeting where after 2 other fri^{ds} had declared he stood up &
declared a pritty Large time & then went to prayer & afterwards ye meeting departed itt was a very Good meeting
large & peaceable within the doors, he alsoe stayd there
that night:

The next day being ye 29th of ye 10th mo: & ye 4th day of
ye week he was att ye monthly meeting att ye peel where he
declared twice 'twas a very good meeting & Large & Continued till pritty Late in ye night, he alsoe stayd there that
night:

The next day being ye 30th of ye 10th mo: and ye 5th day
of ye week he was Invited to dinner at ffrancis Camfields
where after haveing dined he afterwards went to B: As:
where he^b

The next Day being ye 31st of ye 10th mo: and ye 6th day
of ye week severall fri^{ds} Came to See him there & after
dinner he went thence to ye meeting for Sufferings att y^e
Chamber wch Continued till between ye 6th & 7th hour thence
he went to Wm Meads where he stayd y^t night:

The meetings he was att this week were :3: ye 3^d days
meeting att ye peel, ye monthly meeting there & ye meeting
for Sufferings.

---

  ^{a} Margin: *he was att :3: meetings this week 1 on ye 1st day ye 2^d days
meeting & ye 4th days meeting*
  ^{b} The writer has begun the record of the next day at the head of the page,
without finishing the previous day's account.

The 1ˢᵗ of yᵉ 11ᵗʰ mo: being yᵉ 7ᵗʰ day of yᵉ week he went
from W: Meads to yᵉ Chamber abᵗ busyness where hee staid
till yᵉ afternoon & afterwards went to Nat: Blands & att
night to Eliz: Braseys where he stayd that night:

The next day being yᵉ 2ᵈ of yᵉ 11ᵗʰ mo: & the 1ˢᵗ day of
yᵉ week he went to yᵉ morning meeting at yᵉ Chamber and
afterwards went to yᵉ meeting at Gratius street where after
another friᵈ had declared he stood up and declared a pritty
Large time and afterwards went to prayer & when he had
done yᵉ meeting departed 'twas a very good meeting Large &
peaceable within yᵉ doors thence he went to Michell Russells
where he dined & stayd that after noon with his wife & sister
they being in trouble for their Mother Mary ffauster who was
lately deceasedᵃ: (and as I take itt) stayd att El: Braseys
{agⁿ} yᵗ night:

The next day being yᵉ 3ᵈ of yᵉ 11ᵗʰ mo: & yᵉ 2ᵈ day of yᵉ
week he went to yᵉ 2ᵈ days monthly meeting of friᵈˢ in yᵉ
ministry att yᵉ Chamber where he declared a prity Large
time and afterwards yᵉ meeting departed there was a pritty
many friᵈˢ, & a very good meeting and in yᵉ afternoon hee
went to yᵉ Quarterly men & Womens meeting att Devenshire house to the Womens meeting first & yⁿ to yᵉ Mens
meeting where hee declared a pritty time and some friᵈˢ
after him & after they had done & their busyness were Compleated the meeting departed, and afterwards he & some
other Select friᵈˢ had another meeting in the same place
abᵗ Mark Swanner & R Richardson wᶜʰ Continued till late
in the night & afterwards he took Coatch to B: As: where
he stayd that night:

The next day being yᵉ 4ᵗʰ of yᵉ 11ᵗʰ mo: & yᵉ 3ᵈ day of yᵉ
week in yᵉ morning severall friᵈˢ Came to visit him there, &
abᵗ noon he went to patience Ashfields[1] & thence went to
take Boat to Ann Traverss att yᵉ womens school att Cheeswick abᵗ :9: Miles.

The 6ᵗʰ of yᵉ 11ᵗʰ mo: & yᵉ 5ᵗʰ day of yᵉ week he went
by water to the Monthly meeting att Ham̃ersmith 1: Mile
where he declared a pritty while and went to prayer & then
spoke a few words, & after he had done yᵉ meeting went
upon their busyness there was a very good meeting & a
pritty many friᵈˢ & after yᵉ meeting was done & friᵈˢ

ᵃ Margin: *to Comfort yᵉ afflicted*

mostly gone he went to Ann Traverses again by water
:Mile /1/ [a]
The 9th of y[e] 10[th][b] mo and y[e] 1st day of the week he took
water to y[e] meeting att Hamersmith where he declared a
pritty time & went to prayer & afterwards y[e] meeting departed 'twas a very good meeting pritty large & peaceable
& after y[e] meeting was done and many fri[ds] Came to see
him in y[e] ffri[ds] house Adjoyning to y[e] meeting house he went
by water to Ann Traverses again Miles :1:
The 12th of y[e] 11th mo: & y[e] 4th day of y[e] week John
Kertons wife fetched him in a Coatch to their house att
Gravell pitts, Miles :3:
The 15th of y[e] 11th mo: being y[e] 7th day of y[e] week in y[e]
afternoon he took Coach thence to James Beeches att Westminster where he stayd that night:
The next day being y[e] 16th of y[e] 11th mo: & y[e] 1st day of
y[e] week he was att y[e] meeting att Westminster where after
John Vauton had declared he stood up & declared a pritty
Large time & went to prayer and afterwards y[e] meeting [c]
departed there was a very good meeting large and peaceable
within y[e] Doors & many of y[e] worlds people there and haveing stayd a while above Stairs and many ffri[ds] Come to
him afterwards he went to James Beeches again where he
stayd that night:
The next day being the 17th of y[e] 11th mo: & y[e] 2[d] day
of y[e] week in y[e] morning ffrancis Dove[1] fetched him thence
to his house in Lesterfields with a Coach where he dined &
afterwards went to Tim: Emersons[2] hard by & thence took
Coach to visit Edw: Brooks &c. & Came to Tim: Emersons
again att night & haveing stayd there till towards y[e] 9th
hour & severall fri[ds] come to him, some ab[t] busyness he
afterwards went to ffrancis Doves where he stayd that
night:
The next day being y[e] 18th of y[e] 11th mo: & y[e] 3[d] day of
y[e] week after severall ffri[ds] had Come to visit him there he
went to view y[e] passidge into the meeting place att Long
Acre w[ch] was then in Debate betwixt fri[ds] & y[e] Man of y[e]
house he haveing altered y[e] passidge thence he went to visit
y[e] ffri[ds] att y[e] purl house. thence to visit W[m] Beech who was

[a] Margin: *ye meetings he was at this week were :7:*
[b] Should be *11th*   Margin: *Stayd in y[e] Country 10: days*

sick & thence to M: ffishers at ye Savoy where he stayd y^t
night & severall fri^ds Came to him:

The next Day being ye 19th of ye 11th mo: and ye 4th day
of ye week in ye afternoon he took Coach to John Elsons
where he stayd that night & severall ffri^ds Came to him:

The next day being ye 20th of ye 11th mo: and ye 5th day
of ye week in ye afternoon he took Coach to B: As: where
he staid y^t night & he & G: W &c. had a meeting with
Sam^ll Bolton about Contract of Marryage between him &
Sarah ffreckelton[1]:

The next day being ye 21st of ye 11th mo: and ye 6th day
of ye week in the afternoon he went to ye meeting for
Sufferings att ye Chamber wch Continued till towards ye 7th
hour thence he went to Wm Meads where he stayd y^t
night:

The next day being ye 22^d of ye 11th mo: & ye 7th day of
ye week he went to ye Chamber ab^t busyness where he
stayd till ab^t ye 1st hour & afterwards took Coach to Tho:
Coxes & thence to Mary Stots at Bednal Green where he
stayd that night:

The meetings he was at this week were 3 a publick
meeting ye meeting for Sufferings & one ab^t other busyness.

Stayd att Mary Stots at Bednall Green from ye 22^d of y^e
11th mo: & ye 7th day of ye week to ye 28th of ye same & y^e
6th day of the week:

The 28th of ye 11th mo: & ye 6th day of ye week he took
Coach thence to Tho: Coxes where he stayd a while &
thence took Coach to ye Chamber in Lombardstreet ab^t
busyness & stayd the meeting for Sufferings till after y^e
6th hour thence he went to Wm Meads where he stayd y^t
night:

The next day being ye 29th of ye 11th mo: & ye 7th day of
ye week he went to ye Chamber ab^t busyness where he stayd
till pritty Late in ye afternoon & afterwards went to Eliz:
Brasseys wid: where he stayd that night:

The next day being ye 30th of ye 11th mo: & ye 1st day of
ye week he went to ye morning meeting at the Chamber
where he declared of several things to fri^ds in the Ministry

there mett together; & after the ffri^{ds} were departed he went to ye meeting at Gratius street where, after two fri^{ds} had declared he stood up and declared a pritty Large time & afterwards went to prayer & when he had done the meeting departed itt was a very good meeting Large and peaceable & held till after ye 11th hour thence he went to Michell Rusells where he stayd & dined and afterwards went to Eliz: Braseys Wid: where he Lay downe on ye Cooch awhile being weary and in ye Evening severall fri^{ds} Came to visit him there & he stayd there y^t night.

The next day being ye 31st of ye 11th mo: and ye 2^d day of ye week in ye morning he went to ye 2^d days morning meeting att ye Chamber and stayd there ab^t other busyness till pritty late in ye afternoon and afterwards took Coach to Mary Wooleys in spittle fields where he stayd y^t night.

The next day being the 1st of ye 12th mo: & ye 3^d day of the week he took Coach thence to George Yard & went to Daniell Whirleys ab^t busyness with him & thence he went to ye Chamb^r where he stayd till late in ye afternoon & afterwards took Coach to B: As: ab^t busyness where he stayd a little while & took Coach to Eliz: Braseys wid: and afterwards went to Wm Meads where he stayd y^t night.

The next day being ye 2^d of ye 12th mo: and ye 4th day of the week towards ye 9th hour in ye morning he & Marg^t Rouse and her daughter Marg^t took Coach to their house att Kingston Miles :10:

A Jornall of the meetings : G: ff: hath been at &c~ Anno dom: 1687:

The 13th of the 1st mo: being ye 1st day of ye week he went to ye meeting att Kingston on horse back ½ a mile where he declared a pritty Large time & after went to prayer and yⁿ declar'd agⁿ a Little time and after he had done ye meeting departed itt was a very good meeting and peaceable within ye doors thence he went to Steven Hoberts[1] and visited Ruth Lilly[2] who had Lodgings there^a and after a while went to John Rowses again on horse back Mile ½:

---

^a Margin: *Visit ye sick*

Stayd att Kingston at John Rowses from ye 2^d of ye 12th
mo: and 4th day of ye week to ye 18th of ye 1st mo: & 6th day
of ye week wch is, 6 weeks and two Dayes; in wch time many
fri^{ds} Came to visit him there[1]:

The 18th of ye 1st mo: being the 6th day of ye week he
walked on foot to ye water side Mile /1/ & there took boat
to Ann Traverses at the school at Cheeswick Mi: /11/ where
he stayd y^t night:

The next day being the 19th of ye 1st mo: and ye 7th day
of ye week he went by water thence to the Salsbury Change
& soe went to Josiah Elises & after a while to Martha
ffishers where he stayd that night & severall fri^{ds} Came to him:

The next day being ye 20th of ye 1st mo: & ye 1st day of
ye week in ye Morning G: W: A: P: & John Elson &c Came
to see him and were at ye meeting at ye Savoy where after
George Whitehead had declared he stood up and declared
a pritty Large time & after wards went to pray^r and then
exhorted ye people in a few words & haveing done ye meeting
departed it was Large and peacable in ye yard and afterwards many fri^{ds} Came to Visit him at Martha ffishers:

The next day being ye 21st of ye 1st mo: & ye 2^d day of y^e
week severall fri^{ds} Came to see him there & towards y^e
Evening he went to John Elsons where he stayd y^t night:

The next day being ye 22^d of ye 1st mo: and ye 3^d day of
ye week he was at ye meeting at ye peel where after two
other fri^{ds} had declared he stood up & declared a pritty
Large time & afterwards went to prayer & when he had
done ye meeting departed it was a very good meeting Large
and peaceable within ye doors, he stayd att John Elsons y^t
night where severall fri^{ds} visited him:

The next day being ye 23^d of ye 1st mo: & ye 4th day of
ye week he went to ffrancis Camfields where he was invited
to Dinner thence to visit Rebecah Traverse and afterwards
went to :B: As:, where he stayd that night:

The next day being ye 24th of ye 1st mo: & ye 5th day of
the week he stayd att B: As: where severall fri^{ds} Came to
visit him:

The next day being ye 25th of ye 1st mo: & ye 6th day of
ye week he went to ye Meeting for Sufferings att ye Chamber & att night went to Wm Meads:

The next day being ye 26th of ye 1st mo: & ye 7th day of ye week he went to ye Chamber about busyness where he stayd till ye afternoon & afterwards went to Nath: Blands where he dined & afterwards to Eliz: Braseys where he stayd y^t night:

The Meetings he was at this week were :3: two publick meetings & ye meeting for Sufferings besides other busyness with fri^{ds} y^t Came to him:

The next day being ye 27th of ye 1st mo: and ye 1st day of ye week he went to ye morning meeting of ministering ffri^{ds} at ye Chamber where after sometime waiting he went to prayer & afterwards ye meeting departed thence he went to ye meeting at Gratius Street where after G: W: had declared he stood up & declared a pritty Large time and afterwards Concluded ye meeting with pray^r thence he went to Michell Russells where many fri^{ds} Came to him, he stayd diñer there & afterwards went to B: As: where he stayd y^t night: ~

The next day being ye 28th of ye 1st mo: and ye 2^d day of ye week he went to ye 2^d days meeting at ye Chamb^r & in ye after noon took Coach to Mary Stots at Bednal Green where he stayd that night & ye next day:

The next day being the 30th of ye 1st mo: and the 4th day of ye week he took Coach to Spitle fields to visit Mary Wooly & Bridg^t Austell where he dined and afterwards took Coach to B: As: where he had busyness wth severall fri^{ds} & stayd there y^t night & ye next day:

The next day being ye 1st of ye 2^d mo: & ye 6th day of ye week he went thence to ye Chamber ab^t busyness, thence to John Osgoods where hee dined & afterwards went to ye meeting for Sufferings & after the meeting was done he went to Edw: Haistwells & after awhile to :B: As: where he stayd that night:

The next day being ye 2^d of ye 2^d mo: & ye 7th day of ye week he went thence to ye Chamber again where he had busyness with severall ffri^{ds} in ye after noon he & James parks took Coach to Tho: Coxes where they dined thence he & J: p: & A: parker took Coach to Ratlif & went to Robt Scotins^{a1} where he stayd y^t night:

---

^{a} Margin: *about Miles |2|*

The meetings he was at this week were 4: ye first days morning meeting ye publick meeting at Gratius street ye 2^d days meeting & ye meeting for Sufferings besids other particular Concerns with fri^ds that Came to him:

The next day being ye 3^d of ye 2^d mo: & ye 1st day of ye week he went to ye morning meeting at Rattlif where after :A: p: had declared he stood up and declared a pritty time & afterwards Concluded ye meeting wth prayer; 'twas a very good meeting Large & peaceable & Continued till ab^t ye 12th hour thence he went to a ffri^ds a Brewer hard by where he dined & afterwards went to ye afternoon meeting at ye same place where after :G: W: had declared he stood up & declared a pritty Large time & went to prayer & after declared a little time & w^n he had done the meeting departed; it was a very good meeting & Exceeding Large; thence he went to Robert Scotins again where he stayd y^t night and severall ffri^ds Came to him:

The next day being ye 4th of ye 2^d mo: & ye 2^d day of ye week he went to visit Martha Dry[1] at Wappin who was not well part of ye way on foot & part by water and visited old Mary Strut who was muddled in mind & severall others by ye way and he stayd at fri^d Dryes that night:

The next day being ye 5th of ye 2^d mo: and ye 3^d day of ye week he went thence to visit John Patron[2] on foot & thence took Coach to George Yard in Lombard street & went to ye Chamber about busyness where he stayd some hours & went thence to James Wasses & thence to ye Chamber again & afterwards took Coach to George Wats where he stayd that night:

The next day being ye 6th of of ye 2^d mo: & ye 4th day of ye week in ye afternoon he went thence to John Elsons, & was at their meeting for the Collection where he spoke a pritty time and after went to prayer it was a very good Meeting; & he stayd there that night:

The next day being ye 7th of ye 2^d mo: & ye 5th day of ye week he had a meeting {there} ab^t Wm Brigins[3] & Cottin Oades & after he took Coach to :B: As: where he stayd y^t night:

The next day being ye 8th of ye 2^d mo: and ye 6th day of ye week in ye after noon he went to ye Chamber where he

had busyness & stayd yᵉ meeting for Sufferings & in yᵉ
Evening went to Eliz: Braseys where he stayd that night:
The next day being yᵉ 9th of yᵉ 2d mo: & yᵉ 7th day of yᵉ
week he went to yᵉ Chamber where he stayd abt busyness
till yᵉ afternoon & thence went to Theodr Egglestons where
he dined & :W: P: Came & had busyness with him there
thence he went to yᵉ Chamber agn & afterwards took Coach
to Ezek: Woolyes where he stayd yt night:

The meetings he was at this week were :5: two publick
meetings at Ratlif a Collection meeting at yᵉ peel, yᵉ meeting for Sufferings & another abt a difference betwixt two
ffrds.

The next day being yᵉ 10th of yᵉ 2d mo: & the first Day
of the week he went to yᵉ Meeting at Wheelerstreet where
after another ffrd had declared he stood up and declared a
pritty Large time & afterwards went to prayer & then spoke
a few words in Exhortation to the people & when he had
done yᵉ meeting departed, it was a very good meeting Large
& peaceable, afterwards he went to Ez: Woolyes again where
he stayd that night:
The next day being the 11th of yᵉ 2d mo: & yᵉ 2d day of
yᵉ week he took Coach to yᵉ 2d Dayes morning meeting at
yᵉ Chambr in 3 King Courte in Lombard street & after had
busyness with :W: P: &c at yᵉ said place, and afterwards
went to Edw: Haistwells in Scotch yard & after a while to
B: As: where he stayd yt night:
The next day being yᵉ 12th of yᵉ 2d mo: & yᵉ 3d day of yᵉ
week after diñer he went to yᵉ Chamber about busyness & after
he had stayd some time there he went to Edw: Bathursts
about busyness & afterwards went to Eliz: Braseys where
he stayd that night:
The next day being yᵉ 13th of yᵉ 2d mo: & yᵉ 4th day of the
week he went to yᵉ meeting at Gratius Street where after
two other ffrids had declared he stood up & declared a pritty
Large time and afterwards went to prayer & when he had
done yᵉ meeting departed, it was a very Good meeting &
very Large & several great persons, one said to be a Lord &
another a Knight there, & many other people of yᵉ world,
thence he went to M: Russells where hee dined thence to

Visit Eliz: Bland & Martha ffisher her mother & afterwards
went to B: As': where he stayd that night:

The next day being the 14th of ye 2^d mo: & ye 5th day of
ye week in ye afternoon he was att a meeting appointed att
ye Chamber ab^t some ffri^{ds} Sufferings in England & Beyond
Seas ab^t Wills & for not swearing &c: wch Continued till
night, thence he went to Eliz: Braseys where he stayd that
night:

The next day being ye 15th of ye 2^d mo: & ye 6th Day of
ye week in ye forenoon hee went to ye Chamb^r about busyness & went thence to Theod^r Eglestons where he dined,
and afterwards went to ye meeting for Sufferings at ye beforesaid place & thence he went to Wm Meads where he
stayd that night:

The next day being ye 16th of ye 2^d mo: and ye 7th day of
ye week ab^t ye 9th hour in ye morning he took Coach with
Wm Mead to his house Called Gooseys in Essex about :13:
Miles:

The meetings he was at this week were :5: a publick
meeting at wheelerstreet ye 2^d Dayes meeting ye 4th Dayes
meeting att Gratius street a meeting appointed about fri^{ds}
Sufferings & ye meeting for Sufferings; besids other busyness
at ye Chamber & with ffri^{ds} {have} Come to him:

And on ye first of the 3^d mo: being ye first day of ye week
B: A: & his wife and several others Came to visit him and
towards ye 12th hour he went on horse back with Wm Mead
&c to ye Meeting att John Hardins, Mi: ½: he declared there
a pritty Large time and after went to prayer and then in a
short Exhortation to ye people Concluded ye meeting it was
a very good meeting & Large ffri^{ds} from London & several
parts being there and after a while he went to Gooseys
again, and a Great many ffri^{ds} frõ London who dined there
and went away y^t night.

Stayd att Gooseys from ye 16th of ye 2^d mo: to ye 4th of
ye 3^d mo: wch is 2 weeks & :3: dayes in wch time many fri^{ds}
visited him[1]:

The 4th of ye 3^d mo being ye 4th day of ye week he took

Coach from Gooseys to {his house at} London Miles : 13:
thence he went to Eliz: Braseys wid: where he had busyness
wth some fri^{ds} and afterwards went to B: As where he stayd
that night:

The next day being the 5th of ye 3^d mo: & ye 5th Day of
ye week he stayd at B As and severall fri^{ds} Came to him
there:

The next Day being ye 6th of ye 3^d mo: & ye 6th day of y^e
week he was at ye meeting at ye Bull & Mouth where after
James parks had declared he stood up and declared a pritty
large time and afterwards Concluded ye meeting wth prayer
it was a very good meeting & Large, thence he went to
Laurance ffulloves where he dined & thence to visit Eliz:
Grise alias Gotherby[1] who was sick thence he went to the
meeting for Sufferings at ye Chamber & afterwards to Eliz:
Braseys wid: where he stayd y^t night:

The next day being ye 7th of ye 3^d mo: & ye 7th day of y^e
week he went to ye Chamber againe where he had busyness
a good part of y^e day & after visiting some ffriends there
awayes went to Eliz: Brasyes againe where he stayd y^t
night:

The meetings he was at this week were : 3: a meeting in
y^e Country a weekly meeting at y^e Bull & Mouth & y^e
Meeting for Sufferings besids other busyness with ffriends at
y^e Chamber &c.

===

The next day being y^e 8th of y^e 3^d mo: & y^e first day of y^e
week he went to y^e morning meeting at y^e Chamber where
there were severall ffriends & after some time sitting went
to prayer he stayd there y^e forenoon & in y^e afternoon went
to y^e meeting at Devenshire house where after R Barkley had
declared he stood up & declared a pritty Large time & afterwards went to prayer and after he had done ye meeting
departed it was a very good meeting {&} Large thence he went
to Marg^t Drinkwells where he stayd y^t night:

The next day being ye 9th of ye 3^d mo: & ye 2^d day of y^e
week he went to ye 2^d Days meeting at ye Chamber & afterwards went to B: As: where he stayd y^t night & severall
ffriends Came to him:

The next Day being ye 10th of ye 3^d mo: & the 3^d day of

the week he went to the Chamber ab^t busyness & afterwards
went to Wm Meads where he stayd that night:
The next day being the 11th of ye 3^d mo: & the 4th day
of ye week hee went to the meeting att Gratius street where
after Jasper Bat[1] had declared he stood up & declared a pritty
Large time & afterwards Concluded ye meeting with prayer
thence hee went to Michell Russells where many ffriends
Came to him thence he went to Henry Goulneys & afterwards
took Coach with Geo: Watts to his house in Aldersgatestreet
where he dined thence to ffrancis Camfields where he stayd
y^t night:
The next day being the 12th of ye 3^d mo: & ye 5th day of
ye week in ye after noon hee went to John Elsons where hee
stayd that night:
The next day being the 13th of the 3^d mo: & ye 6th Day
of ye week severall Country friends Came to visit him there
and afterwards took Coach to the Chamber & stayd the
meeting for Sufferings and thence went to another meeting
at Wm Crouches and afterwards to Wm Meads where he
stayd y^t night:
The next day being ye 14 of ye 3 mo: & ye 7th day of
ye week in the forenoon he went to ye Chamber about busyness & in ye afternoon he went to Eliz: Brasyes where he
stayd that night & many ffriends Came to him:

The meetings he was at this week were :6: ye morning
meeting of ffriends in ye ministry at ye Chamber a publick
meeting at Devenshire house, ye 2^d dayes meeting at y^e
Chamber, ye 4th dayes meeting at Gratius street ye meeting
for Sufferings & another meeting ab^t busyness, besides other
busynesses with ffriends y^t have Come to him & at ye Chamber:

The next day being the 15th of ye 3^d mo: & ye 1st day of
ye week he went to ye morning meeting at ye Chamber
where there was a Great Many Country ffriends he went to
prayer there & afterwards they took thier Motions to y^e
severall meetings he stayd there ye forenoon & after the
meeting at Gratius street W: p: & G W: &c Came to him
to ye Chamber againe thence he went to B: As: where he

stayd that night & many Country ffriends Came to visit him
wch were Come up to ye generall meeting:

The next day being ye 16th of ye 1st mo: & ye 2^d day of y^e
week in ye morning he went to ye generall Meeting[1] of
friends in ye Ministry at ye Chamber where after some other
ffriends had declared he stood up & declared a pritty time &
afterwards went to prayer & then declared againe & afterwards went thence to Eliz: Braseyes Wid: where being very
weary & willing to Lay downe upon ye Bed, but had noe
sooner Lay downe then he was moved to Rise & goe to y^e
meeting againe furthur to declare what was upon him, twas'
a very Large meeting he afterwards went to B: As: where
he dined with many more Country ffriends he being weary
Lay downe some time to Rest him, and ab^t ye 3^d hour took
Coach to ye Generall meeting of Busyness held at ye Bull &
Mouth twa's a very Large meeting & Continued till ab^t y^e
6th hour thence he took Coach to B: As again where he stayd
y^t night:

The next day being the 17th of ye 3^d mo: & ye 3^d day of
ye week he went to ye Generall meeting of Men fri^{ds} in y^e
Ministry at ye Bull & Mouth twas a very Large meeting &
Continued till ab^t ye 6th hour thence he took Coach Where
after a great many ffri^{ds} had declared he stood up & declared a pritty time tooching diverse things and afterwards
Leaving ffr^{ds} to Clear y^{m}selves went to Edw: Brushes where
being weary he Lay downe upon ye Bed the meeting Continued from Early in ye morning till towards ye 12th hour
in wch time declared G W: A p: Steven Crisp R: Barkley
Ambros Riggs[2], Sam^{ll} Watson[3] W: p: Charles Marshall Edw:
Bourn John Graton[4] Cha: ffloyd G: ff: Geo: Mires[5] W^m
Bingley Robt Lodge[6] Jasp^r Bat ffra: Stamper & another
ffriend prayed and there were severall other fr^{ds} that declared all that declared & prayed {were said to be} 23:
thence he went to ffra: Camfields & dined at his Sons &
afterwards took Coach to ye Generall meeting for Busyness
appointed at Devenshire house wch Continued for some
hours & afterwards took Coach to Eliz: Brasy's wid: where
he stayd y^t night.

The next day being ye 18th of ye 3^d mo: & ye 4th day of
ye week he went to ye meeting at Gratius street where after
Tho: Gilpin[7] Geo: Myres G: W: John Bolron &c had

declared he stood up and declared a pritty Large time & afterwards went to prayer & when he had done ye meeting departed, It was a very good meeting, and very Large ye meeting and Gallerys being filled & ye yard very ffull there was two great psons from ye Courte there & severall of ye world; it Continued from ab^t ye 7th hour to ye 12th or after thence hee went to Hen: Goulneys where being weary he Lay down upon the Bed, he dined there & afterwards went to a meeting at ye Chamber for ye drawing up the acknowledgments of ye Generall assembly to ye king and afterwards went to Eliz: Brasyes wid: where he stayd ye night and several fri^ds Came to him:

The next day being ye 19th of ye 3^d mo: & ye 5th Day of ye week ab^t the 7th hour he took Coach to a Meeting appointed ab^t ye Generall busyness of fri^ds at Devenshire house there was alsoe another meeting above Stares with some Choice ffri^ds ab^t busyness; ye meeting Continued till about noon thence he took Coach With W: p: who had Invited him to dine with him att Dan^ll Whirleys and afterwards he went to B: As: where he stayd y^t night and severall fr^ds Came to visit him:

The next day being the 20th of ye 3^d mo: & the 6th day of ye week he went to ye Chamber ab^t busyness & afterwards to Nat: Willmers where he was Invited to diñer & W: p: & a great many Country ffri^ds thence he went to ye meeting for sufferings at ye Chamber wch was Large and afterwards went to Wm Meads where he stay y^t night:

The next day being ye 21 of ye 3^d mo: and ye 7th day of ye week he went to ye Chamber againe to a meeting appointed about the 7th hour about drawing up ye yearly meeting paper and Looking after ye Records[1] &c and in ye afternoon he was at another meeting at ye said place about ye Like busyness till ye evening & then went to Eliz: Brasyes where he stayd y^t night & several fr^ds Came to him:

─────────────────────────────

The Meetings he was at this week were :11: ye first dayes Morning meeting at ye Chamber ye Generall meeting of fri^ds in ye Ministry at ye Chamber ye General meeting of Men ffriends in ye Ministry at ye Bull & Mouth, ye 4th days meeting at Gratius street ye meeting for Sufferings & 6 ab^t

ye Generall Concerns of ffriends: besids {other} busyness'
with ffri^{ds} y^t have Come to him:

The next day being ye 22^d of ye 3^d mo: and ye first day
of ye week haveing got a Cold & great horstness he stayd
there that Day where many ffri^{ds} came to visit him:
    The next day being ye 23: of ye 3^d mo: & the 2^d day of
ye week he was at ye 2^d Dayes morning Meeting at y^e
Chamber where there was many Country ffri^{ds}, he dined at
Edw: Bathursts and afterwards had busyness with ffri^{ds} at
ye Chamber till ye Evening thence he went to Eliz: Brasyes
where he stayd y^t night & severall fri^{ds} visited him:
    The next day being ye 24th of ye 3^d mo: and ye 3^d day of y^e
week he went to ye Chamber againe where he had busyness
wth several Country fri^{ds} & in ye afternoon went to B: A's:
where he stayd y^t night & several ffriends visited him:
    The next day being ye 25th of ye 3^d mo: & ye 4th day of
ye week he stayed at B As, and several ffri^{ds} visited him
there y^t night:
    The next day being ye 26th of ye 3^d mo: and ye 5th day of
ye week in ye afternoon he went to ye Chamber where he
had busyness with severall ffriends & afterwards went to
Eliz: Brasyes where he stayd y^t night:
    The next day being ye 27th of ye 3^d mo: & ye 6th day
of ye week he and Leo: ffell took Coach to Edw: Mans
near Winsomer hill :Miles :8: {he not being well and much
wearyed out at ye yearly meeting}:
    The 5th of ye 4th mo: and ye first day of ye week he went
to the meeting at Winsmerhill where after Edw: Bourn had
declared hee declared a pritty Large time & after went
to prayer and then declared a few words in Exhortation to
ye people & when he had done ye Meeting departed it was
a very good meeting & Exceeding Large thence he went to
Richd Chaires & thence took Coach with Mary Wooly &c to
Edw: Mans againe:

Stayd at Edw: Mans from ye 27th of ye 3^d mo: & ye 6th day
of ye week to ye 10th of the 4th mo: & the 6th day of ye week,
y^t is 2 weeks in wch time he was frequently visited by very
many ffriends.
    The 10th of ye 4th mo: and ye 6th day of ye week in y^e

afternoon he was fetched in James Laivryes Coach to Bridg^t
Austells at Southstreet.

The 19th of ye 4th mo: & ye first day of ye week he had a
meeting there where he declared a pritty Large time &
afterwards went to prayer & y^n Exhorted fri^ds in a few
words and w^n he had done ye Meeting departed {itt was a
verry good meeting &} there was a pritty many fri^ds, their
household & Scholars & from T: Coxes & Lodgers in y^e
towne:

The 26th of ye 4th mo: and ye first day of ye week he &
Mary Wolly & Bridgit Austell and Ann Cox [1] &c. took Coach
to Geo: Bars att Berrystreet ab^t Miles :3: where he had
appointed a meeting where after Edw: Bourn had declared
he declared a pritty time & afterwards went to prayer and
then Exhorted ye people in a few words & when he had
done ye Meeting departed itt was a very good meeting &
there was a pritty many ffri^ds there & about ye 5th hour he
took Coach to Edw: Mans where he stayd y^t night and Leo:
Fell & Ben Antrobus met him there and pritty many fri^ds
Came a Long with him from ye meeting:

Stayd att Bridgit Austells att Southstreet from ye 10th of
y^e of ye 4th mo: to ye 26th of ye Same & ye first day of y^e
week y^t is :2: weeks & a Day in wch time many fri^ds Likewise
visited him there:

The 29th of ye 4th mo: & ye 4th day of ye week he went
from Edw. Mans to ye mo^ty men & Womens meeting att
Eliz: Dryes wid: at Enfield he declared a pritty while
among^st ye Men ffri^ds & afterwards went to ye Womens
Meeting—there was a pritty Many fri^ds there & a very good
meeting he dined at Eliz: Dryes and afterwards went to
Tho: Hearts where he stayd that night:

The 2^d of ye 5th mo: & ye 7th day of ye week in ye morning he and Tho: Heart & his wife pricilla took Coach to
Henry Stouts [2] at Har{t}ford Miles :11: where he stayd
that night:

The next day being ye 3^d of ye 5th mo: & ye first day of y^e
week he went to ye Meeting at Hartford where after Tho:
Burr [3] had declared he stood up and declared a pritty Large
time and afterwards went to prayer and after that declared

a Little while ag^n & w^n he had done ye meeting departed itt was a very good Meeting & very Large: thence he went to Henry Stouts againe where being weary & not very well after {y^e meeting} he Lay downe a while upon ye bed:

The next day being ye 4th of ye 5th mo: & ye 2^d day of ye week hee went to their Quarterly Mens and Womens meeting at Hartford he declared a pritty time in ye mens meeting & after he had done Leaveing y^m to their other Busyness went to ye Womens Meeting: there was a very good meeting and a pritty many ffri^{ds} thence he went to Henry Stouts ag^n: Stayed at Henry Stouts :3: Dayes:

The 6th of ye 5th mo: & ye 4th day of ye week he & Tho: Heart & his wife to Coach from H: S's to Tho: Bennets at Waltham Abby Miles :9: where he stayd y^t night: but T: H: & his wife went away in a Little time:

The 10th of ye 5th mo: & ye first day of ye week he was at ye meeting att Waltham Abby where after Alexand: parker & John Crook had declared he stood up & declared a pritty Large time & went to prayer & afterwards ye meeting departed itt was a very good meeting and very Large & many of ye worlds people were there: thence he went to Tho: Bennets againe where many ffri^{ds} Came to him:

The next day being ye 11th of ye 5th mo: & ye 2^d of ye week hee took with Eliz: Bennet & Wm Bakers[1] wife &c. to Geo: Watts to att Enfield to make up a differrence betwixt ffra: Camfield's wife & his daughter & Son in Law Wm Baker and Returned to Tho: Bennetts againe^a y^t night^b:

The 13th of ye 5th mo: being the 4th day of ye week ab^t ye 5th hour in y^e morning he & Eliz: Beñet & Wid: Tyler: & Wm Baker & his wife took Coach to Wm Meads at Gooseys ab^t 10: Miles & Tho: Bennet Rid they went away again y^t night but G: ff: stayd:

The 24th of y^e 5th mo: and y^e first day of y^e week he went on horse back to y^e Meeting at John Hardins Miles 1$\frac{1}{2}$ he declared at y^e meeting a pritty Large time, & went to prayer & y^n declared againe a little time & after he had done y^e meeting departed it was {a very good meeting} pritty Large & a many of the world there: thence he went to W: Ms again & some other fri^{ds} who dined there:

^{a} Margin: *Miles to & ag^n /6/*
^{b} Margin: *stayd at T: Benets about 6: Day's*

The 31st of ye 5th mo & ye first day of the week he &
S Mead & R Barkley who Came over night to visit him &
Bethiah Rouse went in a Coach to ye Meeting at Wanstead
W M & J Rowse Rid on horse back he stayd at Lady Lawsons & another fri^{ds} house sometime & after went to y^e
meeting where after 2 other fri^{ds} he stood up & declared
a pritty large time & went to prayer & y^n in a few words
of Exhortation &c to ye people Concluded ye Meeting it was
a very good meeting Large & many of ye world there: thence
he went to Lady Lawsons againe where he stayd a while
& many fri^{ds} came to him & afterwards he took Coach to
W: Meads againe^a:

The 7th of ye 6th mo: & ye first day of ye week he & Sarah
Mead and Bethiah Rowse went in a Coatch to Barkin Meet-
ing W: M went on horse Back: he spoke there a pritty
Larg time & went to prayer and after with a few words in
way of Exhortation &c Concluded ye Meeting. it was a very
good Meeting and Large thence he went to a ffri^{ds} house
hard by & after awhile they took Coach back again to
Gooseys^b:

The 14th of ye 6th mo: & ye first day of the week he went
on horse back to ye Meeting att John Hardins where he
declared a pritty Large time & went to prayer & after
with a Brief Exhortation &c to the people, Concluded y^e
Meeting; It was a very good Meeting, Large, & had Many
of ye world there: & some fri^{ds} from London: thence he
went to Gooseys ag^{nc} & John Elson & his wife went thither
alsoe who were Come to visit him & stayd there till y^e
afternoon next day:

The 21st of ye 6th mo: and ye first day of ye week Wm Mead
had the Coatch to Carry him & S: M & B: R: to ye Meet-
ing att Wanstead: W: M: Rid on horse Back he stayd at
Lady Lawsons and another ffri^{ds} house some time & after
went to ye Meeting where after John Boweter[1] he stood up
& declared a pritty Large time, and went to prayer, &
then in a few words of Exhortation &c. Concluded ye Meeting: itt was a very good Meeting and Large; thence he
went to Lady Lawsons ag^n where many ffri^{ds} Came to him

^{a} Margin: *about 16 Miles thither & back*
^{b} Margin: *Miles to & again about :14:*
^{c} Margin: *Miles to & ag^n /3/*

& after a while they took Coach to visit M Stott at Cha:
Bathursts house upon the forest a Mile from Wanstead &
after a Little while took Coach thence to Gooseys:

The 28th of ye 6th mo: & ye first day of ye week they had
ye Coach ag^n to Barkin Meeting: he declared there a pritty
Large time & y^n went to prayer and after with a few
words by way of Exhortation &c. Concluded ye Meeting, it
was a very good Meeting & Large & several of ye world
were there: thence he went to a ffri^{ds} house hard by and
after a while they took Coach back again to Gooseys[a]:

The 4th of ye 7th mo: being ye first day of ye week he
went on horse back to ye Meeting at John Hardins where he
declared a pritty Large time & after went to prayer & then
after in a few words of Exhortation to ye people Concluded y^e
Meeting: it was a very good Meeting & Large & many of the
world were there, thence after a while he went to Gooseys
ag^n:

Stayd att Wm Meads from ye 13th of ye 5th mo: {& 4th of
ye week} to ye 8th of ye 7th mo: & ye 5th Day of ye week: w^{ch}
is :8: weeks & :2: days in wch time he was at 7 Meetings 3
at John Hardins 2 at Wanstead & 2 at Barkin: and had
Many visiters Came to him whilest at Goosey[1]:

Stayd in ye Country from ye 27th of ye 3^d mo: & ye 6th
Day of ye week to ye 8th of ye 7th mo: & ye 5th day of y^e
week: viz: ab^t :15: weeks: in wch time he had very many
visiters & was at :16: meetings[b]2:

[a] Margin: *Miles to & ag^n /14/*
[b] Here ends the first extant volume.

A Jornall of the Travells of G : ff: and the Meet-
ings hee hath been att &c {from ye 23 : 4 : mo:
in ye Year 1688: {to ye 13 : of ye 11: mo: 1690:
on wch hee Dyed:}

The 23^d of ye 4th mo: and ye 7th day of ye week in y^e
Morning he & E B took Coatch to W: Meads at Gooseys in
Essex Miles :13:

The Meetings hee was att this week were /5/ two publick
Meetings at ye park a Meeting with ffr^{ds} of ye 2^d Dayes
Meeting at the Chamber, y^e :6: weeks Meeting & ye Meeting
for Sufferings besides almost continued Busyness with ffriends
& in truths Concerns:

The 24th of ye 4th mo: & ye first Day of ye week hee was
att ye Meeting belonging to Gooseys where after E B he
stood up & Declared a pritty Large time & went to prayer
and after he had done ye Meeting departed, there was a
pritty many people there & were pritty attentive: thence he
Rid on horseback to W Ms againe[a]:

The first of ye 5th mo: & ye first Day of ye week he went
to ye Said Goosey Meeting again on horse back where after
E B and John Butcher[1] he Stood up & Declared a pritty
Large time and went to prayer & after he had done y^e
Meeting Departed, itt was a very good Meeting & pritty
Large, The people attentive & pritty tender:

The 8th of ye 5th mo: & ye first Day of the week he went
to Goosey Meeting on horseback where he Declared a pritty
Long time and opened many things to ye people[2] touching y^e
time ye Gospell was first preacht to Abraham: what Manner
of Men ye Lord Chosed for prophets and to Declare himself
by, to ye people, as Jerimiah a Childe Amos a Herdman &c
~ there Cry ag^t ye hyreling priests & such as Bare Rule by
their Meanes: ~ The Abolition of that priesthood wch took
Tythes & Maintenance, by Christs offices &c: with many

[a] Margin: *Miles to & ag^n /1/*

other things & after went to prayer, & when he had done y^e
Meeting Departed, itt was a very good Meeting & pritty
Large, ye people Ready to hear, and Some pritty much
tendered; thence he went to W: Meads againe:

The 15th of ye 5th mo: & y^e {1st} Day of ye week he went
ag^n with W: p: & his wife who were Come to W Ms the
night before, in their Coatch to ye Meeting; at Gooseys
where after John Rouse & John Elson & another ffri^d and
W P had declared he Stood up & declared a pritty time
opening Many things to ye people, Concerning preaching y^e
Gospell; ye Election of ye prophets: ～ Their Messuadge
Concerning the priests, ～ The Abollition of that priesthood
that Received Maintenance; the offices of Christ {&c} to y^e
Refreshment of many there, and after he had done he Concluded ye Meeting with prayer, It was a very Large Meeting
there being a great Many friends from London & a great
Many {of ye worlds} people from ye Adjacent places & after
a while he took Coatch to W Ms ag^n where W P & his wife
& Son[1] & a great many more friends Dined & after went away
that Night.

The 22^d of ye 5th mo: & ye first Day of ye week, he went
to Goosey, Meeting on horse back where after John ffield &
John Butcher had declared he in a Short testimony opened
Severall things to y^m well Defineing between ye Worlds
Teachers & such as are Sent of God and withall Laying
before y^m what they had to Undergoe by ye Worlds people
after Convincem^t as Lies, Slanders, Evill Speakings Defame-
ings, &c: and the Growth & Strength Wittnessed und^r these
Callumnyes, as they Remaine ffaithfull, and after Concluded
the Meeting (with prayer); itt was Large, and ffriends
departed with much Refreshm^t & Satisfaction thence hee
went to W: Ms: ag^n & severall more fri^{ds} who Dined there:
& went away y^t Night:

The 29th of ye 5th mo: being ye first Day of ye week he
went to Goosey Meeting on horse Back where hee Declared
a pritty time & opened many things very well to ye Great
Satisfaction of ye Meeting then he went to pray^r & after
hee had done ye Meeting Departed, thence he went to W
Ms againe:

The 2^d of ye 6th mo: being ye 5th day of ye week hee & S
M & S ff & Mary Wallingfield[2] took Coatch to ye Monthly

Meeting at Barkin hee was both att ye Men & Womens
Meeting: & they Came back again that Night^a.

The 5th of ye 6th mo: & ye first Day of ye week hee Went
to Goosey Meeting where after another ffr^d or two he Declared a pritty time & opened many things to ye great Satisfaction of the Meeting & y^n went to pray^r & after in a few
Words Cõmending y^m to ye Grace of God &c Concluded y^e
Meeting; he after went to W Ms and Many other ffr^{ds}:

The 12th of ye 6th mo: & ye first Day of ye week he went
to ye Meeting att Gooseys where after Isabell Yeamans[1] &
W: M: he Stood up & Declared touching Christs Parable of
ye Plough, & ye Sower, & ye Seed upon different Grownds, &
severall other things with their Spirituall Applycation to y^e
Great Satisfaction of ffriends, then he went to pray^r & after
hee had done ye Meeting Departed, itt was a very Good
Meeting & Large, thence hee went to W Ms ag^n where alsoe
went Many other ffri^{ds}:

The 19th of ye 6th mo: & ye first Day of ye week he was
Likewise att Goosey Meeting where after B: A: he Stood up
& Declared a pritty Large time and opened Severall things
to ye Refreshm^t of ffriends & when he had done went to
pray^r and afterwards the Meeting Departed thence he went
to W: Ms: again where alsoe went many other ffri^{ds}:

The 22^d of ye 6th mo: being ye 4th Day of ye week in the
Morning hee took Coatch thence to Tho: Bennets at Waltham
Abbey ab^t Miles 10: and in ye afternoon, was at their weekly
Meeting where he Declared a pritty Large time & w^n he
had done went to prayer & afterwards the Meeting departed
in much tenderness:

Stayd att Gooseys from the 23: of the 4th mo: & the 7th
Day of ye week to ye 22^d of ye 6th mo: & ye 4th Day of y^e
week (viz) 8: weeks & 4 Dayes) In wch time many ffri^{ds}
Visited him there, & he was att :11: Meeting :9: att
Goosey & ye Men & Womens Monthly Meeting att Barkin:

The 26th of 6th mo: and ye first Day of ye week hee took
Coatch from Waltham Abbey, to Hodgdon Meeting & wth
him Eliz: Bennet &c: the Meeting was att an Inn where
after Marabella ffarnbora hee Stood up & Declared a pritty

^{a} Margin: *ab^t Miles /9/ to & ag^n /18/*

Large time touching ye Meanes how all Might feel the Lords
Drawings to his Son.—The Largeness of ye Lords power
who hath Measured the Waters in the hollow of his hand
and Metted out heaven with a span and Comprehended the
Dust of ye Earth in a Measure and Weighed ye Mountains
in Scales & ye hills in a Ballance &c—The Reason why Sons
Daughters hand Maids &c doe not Wittness ye Lords Spirit
poured upon y^m &c:—The Difference between ye true peace
& ye Worlds peace.—And ye historicall Belieff & ffaith & y^e
true Belieff and ffaith—The Church of Christs being Cloathed
wth the Sun & haveing ye Moon Under her ffeet[1]—The Cross
of Christ, & what itt was—The true Mother Church her
Antiquity above the false Sectarian Churches Set up according to ye Various Change of Governm^{ts} &c: When he had
done he went to pray^r & after with a few Words of Admoni-
tion to Adhere to ye Lords Counsill &c, Concluded ye Meeting,
wch was very Large and ffriends Departed in Much tenderness &c—thence after a while that he had Layd downe &c,
being weary hee took Coatch to Waltham Abbey againe,
Miles /6/

The 28th of ye 6th mo: being ye 3^d Day of ye Week he
took Coatch to Geo: Bars & with him Eliz: Bennet &c:

The 2^d of ye 7th mo: being ye first Day of ye week he took
Coatch to Waltham Abbey Meeting but being Weary he
Lay down at Tho: Bennets & Rested him, & thence went to
ye Meeting, where after A P: he Stood up & Declared opening Many things to y^e Great Refreshment of friends, he after
went to prayer & w^n he had done with a few Words in Exhortation to ffri^{ds} concluded y^e Meeting: he went thence to
T: Bs: againe & after took Coatch with Pricilla Heart to
their house att Enfield ab^t Miles :4:

The 5th of y^e 4$^{th\,a}$ mo: & y^e 4th day of y^e week he went
thence and with him Wm Shewin in a Coatch to Edw: Mans
ab^t Miles :2: $\frac{1}{2}$:

The 6th of y^e 4$^{th\,a}$ mo: and y^e 5th day of y^e week he was at y^e
Burying of a Woman ffri^d at Winsmore hill when hee opened
Severall things pertinent to Such an Occasion with Admo-
nitions to a Godly Life &c: he after went to prayer & w^n he
had done y^e Meeting departed & they went to Bury y^e
Deceased fri^d thence he went to E Ms againe in ye Coatch:

^{a} Should be *7th*. The margin has also *4th mo:*

The 9th of ye 7th mo: & ye first Day of ye week he went to ye Meeting at Enfield & with him Richard Sutton[1] a Barbadoes friend & his daught^r &c Miles /2/ where he Declared a pritty Large time touching Divers things as Outward Offerings & Sacrifices in ye time of ye Law &c.—Moses Chair —The priesthood that Received Maintenance of Tythes in ye Time of ye Law & their Abolition by Christ, & ye Law that upheld them—Election and Reprobation &c—to ye great Satisfaction of ffriends he afterwards went to Prayer & then wth a few Words to ye people Concluded ye Meeting, which was Large, thence he went to Edw: Mans where he Stayd^a &c:

The 11th of ye 6^{th b} mo: & ye 3^d Day of the week he went from thence to Southgate in a Coatch^c & with him Richd Sutton a Barbadoes ffriend, &c:

The 16th of ye 7th mo: & ye first Day of ye week hee had a Meeting att Bridget Austells where hee Declared a pritty time touching the three that Bear Wittness in heaven & ye three that bear Wittness on ye earth with many other things & after went to pray^r and wⁿ he had done with a few words to ye above said Matter Committing them to ye Lord Concluded the Meeting:

The 23^d of ye 7th mo: & ye first day of ye week he went in ye Coatch to Winsmor hill Meeting^d Where after A: P: had declared he Stood up & Declared a pritty Large time touching purification—Belieff—The true Mother and ye false, And Christs parable of ye Tares Sowne among ye Wheat or Good Seed by the Enemy while ye Men Slept with many other good things & after went to prayer and wⁿ he had done wth a Short Exhortation: & Desires that the Blessings of ye Lord Might Rest upon them Concluded the Meeting wch was Large; thence he took Coatch to E: Ms where hee Stayd that Night:

The 25th of ye 7th mo: & ye 3^d day of ye week hee and A: P: took Coatch to White Heart Court in Grace Ch: street, London^e, and went to Hen: Gouldneys where he Stayd that night:

---

^a Margin: *Miles /2/*   ^b Should be *7th*. The margin has *6th*
^c Margin: *Mile 1/½*   ^d Margin: *Mile ab^t 1−½*
^e Margin: *ab^t Miles /9/*

Stayd in ye Country after our Comeing frõ Gooseys from ye 22^d of ye 6th mo: & ye 4th Day of ye week to ye 25th of ye 7th mo: & ye 3^d Day of ye week /viz/ :5: weeks wanting a Day:

Stayd in all in ye Country from ye 23^d of ye 4th mo: & ye 7th Day of ye week to ye 25th of ye 7th mo: & ye 3^d Day of the week /viz/ 13 weeks and three Days, in wch time he {had many visiters &} was att :18: Meetings :15: publick Meetings: the Men & Womens Meeting at Barkin & a Burying at Winsmerhill : {& was taken to & ag^n ab^t 96 Miles:}

The Next Day being ye 26th of ye 7th mo: & ye 4th Day of ye week hee went to Gracious street Meeting where after John Vaughton hee Stood up & Declared a pritty Large time opening Many things to ye Refreshm^t of ffriends there, when he had done he went to pray^r & afterwards ye Meeting Departed, wch was Large {y^ir was also of ye worlds people there} thence he went to Hen: Gouldneys ag^n & in ye afternoon went to B: As: where he Stayd that night & ye Next Day:

The Next Day being ye 28th of y^e {7: mo: & 6: day} week in ye afternoon he went to ye Meeting for Sufferings wch Continued till pritty Late in the Evening, and afterwards he went to W Ms where hee Stayd that night:

The Next Day being ye 29th of ye 7th mo: & ye 7th Day of ye week in the Morning he went thence to ye Chamber where he had busyness most of ye Day and after went to Henry Goldneys where he Stayd that Night ; and Severall ffri^ds Came thither to visit him:

The next Day being the 30th of ye 7th mo: & ye first Day of ye week he went to Grace Ch: street Meeting where after ffra: Stamford &c had declared he Stood up & Declared a pritty Large time & opened Many things to the Great Satisfaction of Many there, and w^n he had done hee went to prayer, and afterwards ye Meeting Departed, itt was Large & there was of the World's people there; thence he went to Michell Russells where being Weary he Lay downe to Rest him upon their Couch and afterwards went to Henry Goldneys ag^n where he Stayd that Night:

The next Day being ye first of ye 8th mo: & ye 2^d Day of

the Week he went to ye Monthly Meeting at ye Chamber
& after itt was done took Coatch thence with ffra: Camfield
to his house where he Stayd that Night, and ffri^ds Came to
Visit him.

Stayd att ffr: Camfields till ye 5th of ye 8th mo: & ye 6th
Day of ye week whereupon in ye afternoon he went to y^e
Meeting for Sufferings & after itt was done went to W. Ms
where he Stayd that Night:

The Next Day being ye 6th of ye 8th mo: & ye 7th day of
ye week he went to Henry Goldneys where he Stayd till y^e
afternoon, and took Coach to John Elsons at the Peel in S^t
John Street; where hee Stayd y^t Night:

The Meetings he was at this week were :3: Grace Ch:
Street Meeting ye 2^d Days Mo^ly Meeting & ye Meeting for
Sufferings:

The Next Day being ye 7th of ye 8th mo: & ye first Day
of ye week he was at ye Peel Meeting where after B A he
stood up & Declared a pritty Large time & opened Many
things to ye Great Reffreshm^t of frid^s and afterwards Concluded ye Meeting wth pray^r itt was Large and ffri^ds Departed in Much tenderness he Stayd at J Es: that Night:

The next Day being ye 8th of ye 8th mo; & ye 2^d Day of
ye week hee & John Elson & Mary his Wife took Coatch to
ye Quarterly Meeting att Devensh^re house he went and
Declared in ye Womens Meeting first & after Came to y^e
Mens Meeting where he Spoke severall things to y^m by
Way of Counsill & went to pray^r & then after a very Sweet
Testimony to ffri^ds Left ye Meeting to be Ended by y^m &
not being well took Coatch to B As, where he stayd that
Night till ye 5th Day being very weakly in wch time many
ffri^ds Visited him:

The 11th of ye 8th mo: being ye 5th Day of ye week he
went to Hen: Goldneys where he Stayd that night:

The next Day being ye 12th of ye 8th mo: & ye 6th Day of
ye week hee went to the Meeting for Sufferings, and after
itt was done hee Went to W: Meads where hee Stayd y^t
Night.

The Meetings hee was att this week were /4/ ye Peel

Meeting; ye Quar^{tly} Mens & Womens Meeting & the
Meeting for Sufferings:

Staid att Wm Meads house at London from ye 12th of y^e
8th mo: & ye 6th Day of the week to ye 2^d of ye 12 mo: & y^e
7th Day of ye week viz /16/ weeks

The 2^d of ye 12th mo: & ye 7th Day of ye week he went
with W M & his ffamilly in ye Coatch to Gooses Miles /12/.
The 3^d of ye first mo: & ye first day of ye week he was at
Gooses Meeting where he Declared touching severall things
to ye Refreshment of ffriends and went to prayer and when
he had done being weakly he went forth of ye Meeting which
was Continued by Benj: Antrobus & W M &c. and after
some time Concluded it was pritty Large severall from
London being there.

Staid at Gooses from ye 2^d of ye 12th mo: and 7th Day of
ye week to ye 18th of ye first mo: & ye 2^d day of ye week
viz :6: weeks and 2 Dayes in wch time many friends Came
to Visit him and he writt a great deal touching many
things[1].

The 18th of ye 1st mo: & ye 2^d Day of ye week he took
Coatch with W M to his house at London Miles /12/ where
he Stayd that Night & Many ffriends came to see him.
The next Day being ye 19th of ye first mo: & ye 3^d Day of
ye week he took Coach to Ja: Beetches at Westminster their
to Meet with friends ab^t their Busyness wth ye parliam^t[2] he
stayd there y^t night; And ye Next day being ye 20th of y^e
first mo: & ye 4th Day of ye week in ye morning he went to
ye Chamber y^t fri^{ds} had taken adjoyning to Westminster
hall where he stayd till pritty late in ye after noon and after
went to Ja: Beetches again where he staid that night.—
And ye Next Day being ye 21st of the first mo: & ye 5th Day
of ye week in ye Morning he had a great Deal of Discourse
with Sr Robt Knaper[3] a Parliament Man at I Bs & after
went to ye said Chamber of fri^{ds} near ye parliam^t house
where Many ffriends came to him & he had discourse with
one Honeywood a great Man & two parliam^t Men Majour
Manley & Dutton Colt ye Busyness with ye Latter was

about a friends Apprentice that had made Complaints to
ye said Dutton ag^t his Master   Cleared himself to ye Satisfaction of ye parliam^t Man^a and in ye afternoon, he took
Coach to B A's where he stayd that night.

And ye next day in the afternoon he took Coach to y^e
Chamber where he was at ye Meeting for Sufferings w^ch
Continued till ab^t ye 6th hour & after went to W Ms: where
he staid that Night.

The next Day being ye 23^d of ye first mo: & ye 7th Day of
ye week in ye afternoon he took Coach to Josiah Ellises
where hee stayd that Night at ye Golden Key at ye Savoy.

The next Day being ye 24th of ye 1st mo: & ye 1st Day of
ye week he was at ye Savoy Meeting where after G W: he
stood up and Declared touching severall things to ye great
Satisfaction of friends & then went to pray^r & after he had
done ye meeting departed, he stayd at Josiah Ellises that
night where many ffriends came to him:

A Jornall of ye Travells of G∶ff∶ And the Meetings hee hath been att &c in ye year 1689

The 25th of the first mo: & ye 2^d Day of ye week he took
Coach from Josiah Elises to B A's where he staid a while
& in ye afternoon took Coach thence to ye Quarterly Men &
Womens Meeting at Devenshire house where he declared
several things Admonition-wise & after he had done went
among ye Women where he alsoe Declared & w^n ye meeting
had done ab^t ye 6th hour he took Coach to W: Ms: where he
stayd y^t Night:

The 26th of ye 1st mo: and ye 3^d Day of ye week in y^e
Morning he took Coach thence to friends Chamb^r in palace
yard near ye parliam^t house where many friends came to
him & in ye afternoon he went to Ja: Beetches where he
stayd that night.

The 27th of ye first mo: & ye 4th Day of ye week Sr Robt
Knaper came to him there & they had Discourse together
and afterwards he went to ye ffriends Chamb^r near ye parliament house where many ffriends came to him and L^d
Carbery[1] came to see him & had discourse with him, & in y^e

---

^a Margin: *ye apprentices Complaint heard and found unjust* afternoon he & G W took Coach to ffr: Doves in Martins Lane Nigh Charing Cross where he stayd y^t night.

The next Day being ye 28th of ye first mo: & ye 5th Day of ye week he went to ye said Chamber of ffriends near ye parliam^t house where severall fri^{ds} came to him Majour Manly alsoe came to him there & had discourse with him, afterwards he took Coach to B As where he staid y^t night.

—The next day being ye 29th of ye first mo: & ye 6th Day of ye week in ye afternoon he went to ye Meeting for Suffer{i}ngs & afterwards to W Ms where he staid that Night.

The next Day being ye 30th of ye first mo: & ye 7th day of ye week he took Coach to ffr: Camfields where he staid that Night.

The Meetings he was at this week {were (4)} the Savoy Meeting ye Quarterly Men & Womens Meeting & ye Meeting for Sufferings Besides friends Busyness wth the parliam^t &c:

Stayd at ffr: Camfields ye first & 2^d Day:

The 2^d of ye 2^d mo: & ye 3^d Day of ye week in ye afternoon he took Coatch to Hen: Goldneys (& with him ffr : Camfield) where hee stayd y^t night:

The next day being ye 3^d of ye 2^d mo: & ye 4th Day of ye week he went to ye Meeting att Gracious Street & after S: Crisp & W Penn had Declared he stood up and Declared a pritty time how ye Lord spoke to Adam & Eve in paradice & to Noah & ye prophets &c in ye old testament and how God speaks now by his Son in ye new & Concerning such as doe not hold Christ their head & ye two Suppers &c to ye great Satisfaction of ffriends and afterwards & when he had done ye Meeting Departed which was very Large thence he went to Henry Goldneys againe being weary & very weak, and W P & his Wife & severall other ffriends Came to visit him there thence he took Coach to B A's where he stayd y^t night & ye next.

The 5th of ye 2^d mo: & ye 6th Day of ye week in ye afternoon he went to ye Meeting for Sufferings & afterwards to W: Ms: where he stayd that Night.

The Meetings he was at this week were /2/ the weekly

Meeting at Gracious street and yᵉ Meeting for Sufferings,
Besides other Busyness with ffriends and in Truths Concerns.

The 6ᵗʰ of yᵉ 2ᵈ mo: & yᵉ 7ᵗʰ Day of yᵉ week hee took
Coach to John Elsons where he stayd that night.

The next Day being yᵉ 7ᵗʰ of yᵉ 2ᵈ mo: & yᵉ first Day of
yᵉ week he was at yᵉ peel Meeting wᶜʰ he Continued mostly
himself alone in Declaration touching Diverse things, & in
prayer & after with few Words by Way of Exhortation &c.
all to yᵉ great Satisfaction and Establishing of ffriends and
then after John Elson had Spoke a few Words yᵉ Meeting
Departed which was Large.

The next Day being yᵉ 8ᵗʰ of yᵉ 2ᵈ mo: & yᵉ 2ᵈ day of yᵉ
week he alsoe Stayd at John Elsons.

The next Day being yᵉ 9ᵗʰ of yᵉ 2ᵈ mo: & yᵉ 3ᵈ Day of yᵉ
week he took Coach thence to yᵉ 6 weeks Meeting at yᵉ
Bull & Mouth & thence took Coach to B As where he stayd
that Night & yᵉ Next Day & yᵉ Day ffollowing.

The 12ᵗʰ of yᵉ 2ᵈ mo & yᵉ 6ᵗʰ Day of yᵉ week he took
Coach to Westminster hall to see after ffriends Busyness
with yᵉ parliament & in yᵉ afternoon went to Ja: Beetches
where he stayd yᵗ Night.

The next Day being yᵉ 13ᵗʰ of yᵉ 2ᵈ mo: & yᵉ 7ᵗʰ Day of
yᵉ week he went to friends Chamber near yᵉ parliament
house agⁿ to see after friends Busyness and in the afternoon
Crossed yᵉ Water with G W to Elinʳ Birkits where was
alsoe Ste: Crisp who both viz he & S C: stayd there that
Night:

The Meetings he was at this week were /2/ the peel Meeting & yᵉ :6: weeks Meeting.

The next Day being yᵉ 14ᵗʰ of yᵉ 2ᵈ mo: & yᵉ first Day of
yᵉ week he Crossed yᵉ Water again & went to Westminster
Meeting where after S C he stood up & declared a pritty
Large time Opening many things to ffriends Concerning
Grace, ffaith & worship &c, and when he had done went to
prayer and afterwards yᵉ Meeting departed wᶜʰ was Large,
thence he went to James Beetches where he stayd that
Night:

The next Day being ye 15th of ye 2^d mo: & ye 2^d Day of ye week in the morning he went to fri^{ds} Chamber near ye parliam^t house to see how ffri^{ds} Busyness went on there & in ye afternoon took Coach to ffra: Doves where he stayd y^t Night:

The next Day being ye 16th of ye 2^d mo: & ye 3^d Day of ye week he went again to see after ffriends Busyness with ye parliam^t & in ye afternoon to ffrancis Doves againe where he stayd that night:

The next Day being ye 17th of ye 2^d mo: & ye 4th Day of ye week he went again to see after ffriends Busyness with ye parliam^t & in ye afternoon took Coatch to B A's where he stayd y^t night & ye next Day & ye Day ffollowing & many ffri^{ds} Came to him there.

The next Day being ye 20th of ye 2^d mo: & ye 7th Day of ye week he took Coach thence to Southgate to Bridg^t Austins Miles /9/

The 21st of ye 2^d mo: & ye first Day of ye week he had a Meeting there among ye Children her Scholars where was alsoe Tho: Cox & his wife & G Roberts &c, he Declared there Concerning several things and went to prayer & after with a few Words of Advice &c, Concluded ye Meeting.

The 28th of y^e 2^d mo: & y^e first Day of y^e Week hee writ an Epistle to Peter Hendricks at Amsterdam & ffri^{ds} at Danstsik who were under great persecution & a paper to y^e Magistrates their persecutours[1].

The first of y^e 3^d mo: & y^e 4th Day of y^e week he took Coach to Edw: Mans Mile 1—$\frac{1}{2}$:

Stayd at Southgate from y^e 20th of y^e 2^d mo: to y^e first of y^e 3^d mo: viz. 10: Dayes.

The 5th of y^e 3^d mo: & y^e first Day of the week he was at the Meeting at Winsmerhill where after G W: he stood up & Declared touching various things & went to prayer & after hee had done y^e Meeting departed thence he took Coach to E: Ms againe where he stayd y^t night:

The 14th of ye 3^d mo: & ye 3^d Day of ye week he took Coach to London ab^t Miles /9/ to B A's where he stayd y^t night:

Stayd at E: Ms ab^t /12/ Dayes:

Stayd in ye Country from ye 20th of ye 2^d mo: & ye 7th Day
of ye week to the 14th of ye 3^d mo: & ye 3^d Day of ye week
(viz) :3: weeks & a day.

The 15th of ye 3^d mo: & ye 4th Day of ye week pritty many
friends Mett there ab^t Reading & fitting their Amendments
upon ye Bill of Indulgence[1], stayd at B: A's: y^t night & y^e
next Day.

The Day ffollowing being ye 17th of ye 3^d mo: and ye 6th
day of ye week many fri^{ds} Came to him there & in ye afternoon hee went to ye Meeting for Sufferings & after to W M s
where he stayd that Night.

The next Day being ye 18th of ye 3^d mo: & the 7th Day of
ye week he went to ye Chamber where pritty many friends
Came to him: & in ye afternoon he went to W M s againe
where he writt an Epistle to ye Yearly Meeting paper[2] &
stayed there y^t Night & ye next Day:

The next day being ye 20th of ye 3^d mo: & the 2^d Day of
ye week he went to ye Generall Meeting[3] of ffriends in y^e
Ministry at ye Bull & Mouth where after several other ffriends
he Declared Concerning the Universal Spirit and ye Love of
God & severall other things to ye tendering & great Refreshment of ffriends, and after he had done being weak he went
forth to a ffriends Room y^t Lives in ye Meeting house &
thence took Coatch to B: As where he stayd a while & in
ye afternoon took Coach to ye Generall Meeting appoynted
ab^t Busyness of ye Sufferings of fri^{ds} &c: & after it was done
took Coach to Wm Meads where he stayd that night.

The next Day being ye 21st of ye 3^d mo: & ye 3^d Day of
ye week in the Morning he took Coach to ye Generall Meeting of ffriends in ye Ministry at wheelerstreet where he
Declared a pritty time Concerning ye Light—Belieff; Resurrection—ye Spirituall plow & several other things, and
after he had done being Weakly he went forth to a ffriends
house where friends usually goe after Meeting & thence
took Coach to Ezek: Wooleys where being weary hee Lay
downe to Rest him, & in ye afternoon took Coach to y^e
Bull & Mouth to ye Generall Meeting ab^t busyness where
he bore his testimony agst Tythes, & that ffri^{ds} keep to
their testimony in ye Non-payment thereof & of their Rise
and time w^n first paid in England &c, and after ye Meeting

was done wch was very Large he took Coach to B: As:
where he stayd that Night & many friends came to visit
him there:

The next Day being ye 22^d of ye 3^d mo: & ye 4th day of y^e
week he was att ye General Meeting ab^t Busyness appoynted
at ye Bull & Mouth where he had a short testimony by way
of advice to ffri^{ds} touching several things & after went to
B A's where he stayd that Night:

The next Day being ye 23^d of ye 3^d mo: and ye 5th Day of
the week in ye Morning he took Coach to ye General womens
Meeting at Devensh^r house where he Bore a very fresh
testimony touching ye great Extent {& incomprehensibl-
ness} of ye Lords power who {hath} Measured ye water in
ye hollow of his hand and Metted out heaven wth ye Span
& Comprehendes ye Dust of ye Earth in a Measure & weighed
ye Mountaines in Scales &c. and several other things & after
he had done Leaving ye Meeting to be Concluded by y^e
Women he took Coach to W M's where he stayd that
Night:

The next Day being the 24th of ye 3^d Mo: & y^e & ye 6th Day
of ye week in ye afternoon he went to ye Meeting for Sufferings at ye Chamber and afterwards took Coach to B A's
where he stayed that Night; & ye next day & ye day ffollowing. and many friends Came to visit him there[1].

The Meetings he was att this week were :7: the Generall
Meeting of ffriends in ye Ministry ye 2^d Day Morning at
Bull & Mouth & ye 3^d Day Morning at Wheelerstreet & 3
General Meetings ab^t Busyness ye 2^d 3^d & 4th Days in y^e
afternoons att ye Bull & Mouth; ye Womens Meeting on
5th Day Morning at Devensh^r house, & ye Meeting for Sufferings on ye 6th Day att ye Chamber besids Busyness with
ffri^{ds} y^t almost Continuedly Came to him:

The 27th of 3^d mo: & ye 2^d Day of ye week he went to y^e
Morning Meeting at ye Chamber & in ye after-noon went to
BA's where he stayd y^t Night.

The next Day being ye 28th of ye 3^d mo: & ye 3^d Day of
ye week in ye Morning he took Coach with Margret Rowse
& her Daughter Ann to their house at Kingston & with
him Mary Lower & her Daughter[2] Miles :10:

The 14th of ye 5th mo: & ye first Day of ye week Ben:
Antrobus & his wife & sister & a Coachfull of friends Coming
from London to see him he went in there Coatch to y^e
Meeting att Kingston where after Benj: Antrobus he stood
up & declared a pritty Large time & went to prayer & after
with a few words Exhortation—wise &c Concluded y^e
Meeting wch was pritty Large & fri^{ds} in much tenderness
& ffreshness.

The 11th of ye 6th mo: & ye first day of ye week he went
to Kingston Meeting againe wch hee Continued in Declara-
tion and prayer there was a very good meeting & pritty
Large after the Meeting was done he went to ffr: Holdens[1]
where he stayd that Night & ye next day.

And on ye 14 of ye 6th mo: & ye 4th day of ye week hee
went to John Rowses.

The 8th of ye 7th mo: and ye first Day of ye week he went
to Kingston Meeting where he declared a pritty Large time,
Concerning Tythes,—& ye Gospell preached before ye Law
& againe by X^t Jesus and his Apostles, & the Apostacy from
itt sence their Dayes with many other things to the Edifying
& Strengthening of ffriends & yⁿ went to prayer and after
with a Short testimony to friends to keep good order in
their ffamillyes among their Children & Servants &c Concluded ye Meeting thence he went to ffr: Holdens where hee
stayed that Night & ye next Day & ye Kings Chirurgion[2]
Came to him there & he had some Discourse with him.

And the next Day being ye 10th of ye 7th mo: & ye 3^d day
of ye week hee & Ann Rowse & Margery Lower went by
Water to Cheezwick ab^t Miles /11/ and Called at John
Osgoods at Mortlack by ye way where he stayd a little while.

Stayd att Kingston from ye 28th of ye 3^d mo: & ye 3^d Day
of ye week to ye 10th of ye 7th mo: & ye 3^d day of ye week
wch is /15/ weeks in wch time he was at 3 Meetings there
& many fri^{ds} Came to see him & some great people of y^e
World.

The 15th of ye 7th mo: & ye first day of the week he went
by water to ye Meeting at Hammersmith where after Ch:
Marshall & another friend he stood up & Declared a pritty
time & Inlarged pritty much on ye parable of ye Rich Man

& Lazerus[a], applying it to y[e] papists how unlike they were
to pray people out of purgatory w[n] ffather Abraham said
there was such a Gulff fixt between y[m] that there was noe
passing from him to y[e] Rich Man nor from y[e] Rich Man
to him Soe that he could not send Lazerus wth soe much
Water as would Lay on y[e] Top of ffinger to Coul his
Tongue & many other things he opened to y[e] Confirmation of ffriends & when he had done went to pray[r] and
afterwards y[e] Meeting Departed. It was a very good Meeting and Large & many of y[e] Worlds people there he afterwards went to Sarah Robins[1] ag[n] where he stayd that Night
& y[e] next day. being y[e] 10th of y[e] 7th mo: and y[e] 2[d] Day of
y[e] week in y[e] afternoon went by water to London & stayd
at B As that night & y[e] next day.

Stayd in y[e] Country in all ab[t] 16 weeks & was at
4 Meetings:

The next day being y[e] 18th of y[e] 7th mo: & y[e] 4th Day
of y[e] week he went to Gratious Street Meeting where after
some others hee stood up Exhorting to bee attentive to
Christs Drawings & to hold him y[e] head—and many other
openings hee had Concerning various things as eating of y[e]
feast of Unleavened Bread at y[e] passover not y[e] Leavened
Bread of Sowreness, Malice and hatred & Concerning y[e]
ffeast of Trumpets & y[e] ffeast of Tabernacles & Green Boothes
—and y[e] Gospell—& who were y[e] Sons of God &c—and after
Concluded the Meeting with pray[r]. Thence he went to
Henry Goldneys & in y[e] afternoon took Coatch to John
Elsons where he stayd that Night & y[e] next day.

The next Day being y[e] 20th of y[e] 7th mo: & y[e] 6th Day of
y[e] week hee took Coatch to y[e] Meeting for Sufferings at y[e]
Chamber and after itt was done hee went to W Ms where
he stayd that Night:

The next Day being y[e] 22[d] of y[e] 7th mo: & y[e] first Day of
y[e] week he went to Grace Ch: street Meeting w[ch] after 2 or
3 Women &c he Continued in Declaration, touching y[e] passover of Unleavened Bread with many other things as before
Mentioned on y[e] 4th Day & then went to pray[r] & after y[e]

---

[a] Margin: *y[e] parable of Dives & Lazerus*

Meeting departed thence he went to Henry Gouldneys &
thence in ye afternoon to see Nathaniell Willmour & his
ffather who were lame and thence to B: As: where he stayd
that Night & till 6th Day next.

The 27th of ye 7th mo: & ye 6th Day of ye week in ye afternoon he went to meet W: P: who was y^n under ye Messin-
gers hand in picadilly[1] & after went to ffra: Doves in Martins
Lane near Charing Cross where he stayd that night & friends
Came to him:

The next Day being ye 28th of ye 7th mo: & ye 7th day of
the week he took Coatch to Josiah Ellises at the Savoy
where he stayd y^t Night.

The next Day being ye 29th of ye 7th mo: & ye first Day
of ye week he was at the Savoy Meeting where after John
Vaughton he stood up & declared a pritty time touching y^e
heads Mentioned in ye two Meetings before & Divers other
things to ye Refreshm^t of friends & w^n done went to prayer
and afterwards ye Meeting departed.

The next day being ye 30th of ye 7th mo: & ye 2^d Day of
ye week he took Coatch to B As: where he stayd that
night:

The next day being ye first of ye 8th mo: and ye 3^d Day
of the week in ye afternoon hee took Coatch to John Elsons
at ye peel where he stayd y^t night: & ye next day was at y^e
Quarterly Collection Meeting att ye peel and the next day
att a Marryage at ye said place where he opened things to
that purpose both out of Scripture & hystory & Left itt to
be further Concluded.

The 6th of ye 8th mo: & ye first Day of ye week he was
at ye Peel Meeting where he opened a great many things
profitable for ye Instruction & Edification of friends & went
to prayer & after he had done ye Meeting departed.

The next Day being ye 7th of ye 8th mo: and ye 2^d Day of
ye week in ye afternoon he took Coatch and with him Jo:
Elson and Mary from their house to ye quarterly Meeting at
Devensh^r house & spake both among ye Mens and Women
& after ye the Meeting was done took Coatch to W Ms
where he Stayd y^t night and the next day in ye after noon
went to ye Chamber and thence to B As where he stayd y^t
night:

The 11th of ye 8th mo: and ye 6th Day of ye week in y^e

afternoon hee took Coatch and with him B A & Joan Cook[1]
to Br: Austills at Tatnam High Cross Mil :5:

Stayd at London from ye 16 of ye 7th mo: to ye 11th of y^e
8th mo: viz: 3 weeks & 3 Dayes:

The 13th of ye 8th mo: & ye first Day of ye week he had a
Meeting there where after Joan Cook he declared a pritty
time Concerning ye Birth temporal and Spirituall, & ye Body
before & after Conception according to ye saying of David
Before I was Conceived in ye wombe all my Members were
written in a Book—And Concerning ye several Estates of
Man Children Youth & old Age and w^t Required of each
state as their Duty to God, &c, and went to prayer and
after with a few words Admonitory—wise Concluded y^e
Meeting.

The 16 of ye 8th mo: and ye 4th day of ye week he took
Coatch to Edward Mans near Winsmorehill, Mil :4:

The 21st of ye 8th mo: & ye first day of ye week he was at
Winsmorhill Meeting where after G W hee stood up & De-
clared a pritty time Concerning gathering together—Outward Sanctuaryes. Concerning Tythes & w^n first paid in
England—Tythes as being Called of Men Masters & L^d
Bishops &c & how Contrary to ye scriptures—And ye ffeast
of ye Passover with unleavened Bread {&c} and w^n he had
done went to prayer and afterwards wth a Short Testimony Concluded ye Meeting & thence took Coatch to Edw:
Mans ag^n.

The 22^d of ye 8th mo: and the 3^d Day of ye week {Tho:
Heart} fetched him wth a Coatch thence to his house at
Enfield.

The 24th of ye 8th mo: & ye 5th Day of ye week hee was att
their Weekly Meeting att Wm Shewins where hee Declared
a pritty Large time Concerning Divers things and went to
prayer and after with a Short Testimony Concluded the
Meeting

The Next Day being ye 25th of ye 8th mo: & the 6th Day
of ye week hee went in ye Coatch to Edw: Mans again &
with him Tho: heart from his house.

The next Day being ye 26th of ye 8 mo: & ye 7th Day of

ye week hee took Coatch thence to Br: Austells att
Tatnam high Cross ab^t Miles four where he stayd that
night:

The next Day being the 27th of ye 8th mo: & ye first Day
of ye week hee had a Meeting att Br: Austells, and Declared
a Long time how Adam & Eve Eating brought Death &c—
& Concerning ye Law & how Christ Abollished Tyths Offerings Sy^r: places White Coates & Black Coates with all y^e
outward Types and Ceremonyes in ye old Testam^t—Concerning Circumcission and Baptisme—Of the Sight he had
in his Youth how Blessed a thing itt was for people to be
brought to that wch would never Deceive y^m—The Rich
Man & Lazerus & Abraham his Calling Abraham ffather
and Abraham him Son his Desiring Abraham to send
Lazerus with as much water as would Lay of ye Typ of his
finger Abrahams Denyall telling him of ye Gulf fixt betwixt y^m {viz betwixt heaven & hell} he then desires him
y^t he would send Lazerus to his 5 Brethren to forwarn y^m
that they might Repent & Ecape y^t place of Torment—
Abraham Still Refuseth & Referreth y^m to Moses & ye prophets to hear y^m wch shews hee was of ye Stock of ye Jews
& there fore professedly Religious Yet Abraham who was
ye father of ye ffaithfull Could not help him not with soe
much water as would Lay on ye Tipp of a finger to Cool his
Tongue &c, Which is alsoe an Argument ag^t ye papists
Purgatory & praying from ye Dead—How there was noe
Condemnation before Transgression—{Concerning Keeping}
The ffeast of the pass over with unleavened Bread not y^e
Unleavened Bread of Malice Envy & hatred wch is to be
purged out &c—Concerning ye Gospell—ffaith--And Grace
of God which brings Salvation &c Its Sufficiency &c hee
after went to prayer & w^n done with a short Testimony,
Committing y^m to ye Grace & Word of ffaith & power &c,
Concluded ye Meeting : & ffriends Departed in a good Sense
of what they had heard, ye Meeting was Large their being
many from London The Earle of Ancram[1] & his Nephew
and two Neeces were alsoe there & very attentive The
Earle & his Nephew and Neeces Dined att Bridgitts and
G ff had a great deal of discourse wth y^m both before & after
the Meeting:

The 1st of ye 9th mo: & ye 6th Day of the week hee took

Coach thence to London to B As where he stayd that Night:

Stayd in ye Country from ye 11th of ye 8th mo {& :6: day of ye week} to ye first of ye 9th mo: & ye 6th day of ye week /viz/ :3: weeks: in wch time he was at :4: Meetings:

The 2^d of ye 9th mo: & ye 7th Day of the week he took Coatch to Ri: Cooks[1] at ye Swan without Bishopsgate where he stayd y^t Night.

The next {day} being ye 3^d of ye 9th mo: & ye first day of ye week he was at ye Meeting at Devonshire house wch he Continued himself alone, he declared a pritty time Concerning ye Salvation of God—the true Tabernacle wch God hath pitched & not Man—The Jews dwelling in green Boothes—The feast of ye pass over with unlevened Bread and many other weighty things; w^n done went to prayer & after wth a Short testimony Concluded ye meeting one passage not unremarkable was said to fall out at this said meeting (viz) two Women that had been at variance & in Enemity Each ag^t other a long time while Gff was declaring Concerning ye feast of ye passover with unleavened Bread & having ye old Lump of Leaven purged out they were soe smitten & humbled through ye power of his Ministry that they were observed much to Eye one another in the time & w^n ye meeting was done takeing one another kindly by ye hand &c they made fri^{ds} thence he went to Ri: Cooks again where he staid that night:

The next day being ye 4th of ye 9th mo: & ye 2^d day of ye week he took Coatch to the Morning meeting at ye Chamber & in ye afternoon to B As where he staid that Night:

The next day being ye 5th of ye 9th mo: & ye 3^d day of ye week he took Coatch to ye 6 weeks meeting at Devonshire house & after it was dark took Coatch to B As againe where he stayd y^t night

The next Day being ye 6th of ye 9th mo: & ye 4 day of ye week he took Coatch to ffra: Doves in Martins Lane near Charing Cross where he stayd y^t night: & there Came unto him G W: G Latye & J Etheridge acquainting him what they had done in fri^{ds} Busyness with ye parliam^t.

The next Day being ye 7th of ye 9th mo: & ye 5th day of y^e

week he took Coatch to ye Savoy Meeting where he spake
a Long time Concerning ye Dry Bones spoken of in Ezekiel
which though Dead from an Inward Sense & feeling yet
Could speak &c : and many other weighty things & w^n he
had done went to prayer & after with a short testimony
Concluded ye Meeting wch was pritty large and fri^ds departed
in a good sense of w^t had been spoke he Lay at Josiah
Elises y^t night; & ye next day took Coach to B As where
he stayd that Night & ye next Day & ye Day ffollowing:

The next day being ye 11th of ye 9th mo: & ye 2^d Day of
ye week he went to ye morning Meeting at ye Chamber
where after Busyness was done he went to prayer & y^e
Meeting departed & in ye afternoon he went to B As againe
where he staid that Night & ye next day & severall fri^ds
Came to him:

The next Day being ye 13th of ye 9th mo: & ye 4th Day of y^e
week he took Coatch to Grace Ch: street meeting where he
declared a pritty Large time touching many weighty Matters
& went to prayer & after he had done ye Meeting departed
thence he went to Henry Goldneys where many fri^ds Came
to him & he staid that night.

The next Day being ye 14th of ye 9th mo: he went to W Ms
where he stayd y^t night & ye next day—& ye Day following
being ye 16 of ye 9th mo: & ye 7th Day of ye week he took
Coatch with W M to Gooses Miles :12:

Staid in ye City from ye 1st of ye 9th mo: to ye 16 of y^e
same viz ab^t 15 Dayes:

The next Day being ye 17 of ye 9th mo: & ye first Day of
ye week he had a meeting with W Ms ffamilly at his owne
house where he declared a pritty time & went to prayer &
after he had done ye meeting departed:

The 24th of ye 9th mo: & ye first Day of ye week he had a
Meeting again with W Ms familly where he opened many
things—Concerning Christianity & ye persecution of y^e
Christians 300 years after Christ—Christ ye Substance y^e
End of all figures and Shadows &c in ye old testam^t—the
Lost peece of silver found by Lighting ye Candle & ye pearl
in ye field &c—Concerning Swearing—And ye Saboth w^n
first given & how long after Adam: viz ten Generations
from Adam to ye fflood ten Generations from ye old world

to Abraham and thence to ye promiss 70 years from thence
to ye Children of Israel Coming out of Egypt 430 years
then ye Saboth was given wch may be ab^t 1600 years from
Adam—The Jews priests Lips were to preserve peoples
knowledge not ye Gentiles—The Righteousness of the Law &
ye Righteousness of ffaith—Concerning Belieff—The priests
Compared with Babilons Merchants Building up & throwing
downe all in Confusion &c—What work ye Apostles had to
preserve people in Christ after Conviction—And after went
to prayer & when hee had done ye Meeting departed.

The 8th of ye 10th mo: & ye first Day of ye week he had a
Meeting againe at W Ms where he opened divers things
touching ye Law in ye old testam^t—the Manifestation of y^e
Spirit of God—The Reproaches to bee undergone by y^m y^t
Come to Receive ye truth and the victory ye Lord gives
over y^m all—Concerning offering Insense—And how y^e
Lord provideth for such as trust in him &c—and went to
prayer and afterwards with a short testimony Concluded
ye Meeting.

The 15 of ye 10th mo: & ye first day of ye week he was at
a Meeting again att W Ms where he bore a Sweet testimony
Concerning abiding in ye vine &c. and went to prayer, and
ye Meeting afterwards Ended:

The 29th of ye 10th mo: & ye first Day of ye week he was
at ye meeting again at W Ms where he declared a Long
time—how the inward Strength was to be Renewed /viz/ by
waiting upon y^e Lord—Concerning y^e observation of Dayes,
Contrary to Christs Coñand—of y^e outward Churches &c,
and their Rise &c, viz from y^e papists whose Mark they Bear
viz y^e Cross on y^e Steeples, when done he went to prayer
& after with a Short testimony Concluded y^e Meeting:

The 6$^{th\,a}$ of y^e 11th mo: & y^e first day of y^e week he had a
Meeting in W Ms ffamilly where he declared a pritty time
& went to prayer & afterwards y^e Meeting Ended:

The 20$^{th\,b}$ of y^e 11th mo: & y^e first Day of y^e week he had
likewise a Meeting att W Ms where he declared touching
many mighty things & went to prayer and afterwards with
a Short testimony Concluded y^e Meeting:

The 26th of y^e 11th mo: & y^e first day of y^e week he had
a very good Meeting in W Ms ffamilly where he declared a

---

^{a} Should be *5th* ^{b} Should be *19th*

Long time of many particulars & went to prayer & after
wth a Short testimony Concluded ye Meeting:

The 9th of ye 12 mo: and ye first day of ye week he had
a Meeting in W Ms ffamilly where he opened many things,
how ye Kingdome of God {standeth} not in Words but in
power—John ye preparer of ye Way, since John ye Kingdome of God preached & men press into it—ye offering of
Insense—The Abolition of Tythes &c in ye old Testam^t—
How Christ makes all things new—How God would have
all to Come to ye knowledge of ye Truth & be Saved—The
Kingdom of God attained through many tribulations—How
by ye Word of Gods power all things are upheld & by it doe
Consist &c, and then went to prayer & afterwards with a
short testimony Concluded ye Meeting:

The 16th of ye 12th mo: & ye first Day of ye week he had a
meeting in W Ms ffamilly where he declared a pritty time,—
of ye particulars as follow—How ye Children of god are
taught by him—Mans happyness in paradise—The foundation & Rise of Sin The Promiss Concerning Christ—How
ye Seed of ye Woman should Bruise ye Serpents head &c
& went to prayer & afterwards wth a short testimony Concluded ye Meeting:

The 23^d of ye 12th mo: & ye first Day of ye week he went
in W: Ms Coatch to Gooses publick Meeting where after
W M: B A: & another he Declared touching ye Nameing of
Dayes after the heathen Gods &c—perfection—purgatory—
The Ministry of ye true Sanctuary wch God hath pitcht &
not Man, with many other things to ye greatly affecting of
ffri^ds & after Concluded ye Meeting with prayer:

The 2^d of ye first mo & ye first day of ye week he had a
Meeting in W Ms ffamilly again where he Declared a Long
time & went to prayer & after with a Short testimony Concluded ye meeting:

The 9th of ye first mo: & ye first day of ye week at y^e
Meeting in W Ms ffamilly he had likewise a Large Declaration & went to pray^r & after with a short testimony Concluded ye Meeting:

The 16th of ye first mo: and ye first day of the week hee
went in ye Coatch to ye publick Meeting at Gooses where
after Robt Langhorne[1] he declared a pritty time & went to
prayer & afterwards ye Meeting departed, it was Large &

many of ye worlds people there who were very Sober & attentive:

The 23^d of ye first mo: and ye first Day of ye week hee had a Meeting in W Ms ffamilly where hee Declared many pretious things & went to prayer and after with a short Testimony Concluded ye Meeting:

A Jornall of ye Travells of G: ff: and the Meetings hee hath been att &c, Anno Dom: 1690:

The 30th of ye 1st mo: & ye first day of ye week hee had a Meeting in W Ms ffamilly where he Declared a pritty time & went to prayer and afterwards ye Meeting departed.

The 6th of ye 2^d mo: & ye first day of ye week he was at Gooses publick Meeting where after John Butcher he Declared a Long time touching many particulars & went to pray^r & afterwards ye meeting departed thence he went back again in W Ms Charat where alsoe went many other fri^{ds}:

The 13 of ye 2^d mo: & ye first day of ye week he had a Meeting in W Ms ffamilly where after M ff his wife & W M he declared a Long time & went to prayer & after with a short testimony Concluded ye meeting:

The 20th of ye 2^d mo: and ye first day of ye week he had another Meeting in W Ms ffamilly where after W M he declared a Long time of many particulars & went to prayer & after wth a Short testimony Concluded ye meeting:

The 21st of ye 2^d mo: & ye 2^d Day of ye week he went in W Ms Charat to his house at London /Miles 12/ where he stayd y^t night:

Stayd at W Ms at Gooses from ye 16 of ye 9th mo: to ye 21: of ye 2^d mo: 90: viz 22 weeks, in wch time many friends visited him there & he was at /19/ Meetings :16: in W M ffamilly & :3: in ye publick meeting house[1].

The next day being ye 22^d of ye 2^d mo: & ye 3^d day of ye week he went to ye six weeks meeting at Devenshire house

wch Continued till ab^t ye 2^d hour & afterwards he went to
H. Goldneyes where he stayd y^t night.

The next day being ye 23^d of ye 2^d mo: and ye 4th day of
ye week he was at ye meeting at Grace Ch: street where he
Declared a Long time & Concluded ye meeting wth prayer
thence he went to Henry Goldneys ag^n where he stayd y^t
night:

The next day being ye 24th of ye 2^d mo: & ye 5th Day of
ye week in ye morning he went to a meeting appointed at
the Chamber from ye Six weeks Meeting, after it was done
he went to Theoder Eglestons & in ye afternoon took Coach
thence to Br: Austills at Tatnum high Cross:

The Meetings hee was at this week in London were /3/
a publick Meeting, ye Six weeks Meeting & a Meeting appoynted from thence:

The 27th of ye 2^d mo: and ye first Day of ye week he had
a Meeting at B: Austils at Tatnam high Cross where he
declared a Long time of many particulars, viz how they y^t
wait upon ye Lord Renew their Strength—Christ given for
an Ensigne[1] to ye Gentiles who is ye Captain of their Salvation, therefore Exhorted y^m to stand to their Colours &
Ensigne—How people become Leaky vessels viz by not
giving attention to ye Light—And how vessels y^t hold y^e
Living water viz by yielding obedience to Christ who saith
all yee y^t are thirsty Come take of ye Water of Life freely,
without Money & without price—Balaam who Loved y^e
Wages of Unrighteousness reproved by his Dumb Ass, Ap-
plyed to ye Balaams & Asses of our own Age viz {y^e priests} y^e
Magistrates & y^m under their Authority as ye Ass was under
Balaams:—How Natural Artes & Sciences and all outward
Learning & know Ledge may be bought for money but the
Gift of God is not to be purchased &c. he afterwards went
to prayer & w^n done with a Short testimony Advizing to
wait on ye Lord for their Strength who is able to make y^m
wiser than all their Teachers &c Concluded ye Meeting:

The 30th of ye 2^d mo: & ye 4th Day of ye week he took
Coach thence to London and went to W Ms where he stayd
y^t Night.

The next Day being ye first of ye 3^d mo: & ye 5th Day of

ye week he took Coach to B: As: where he stayd y^t night.
and several fri^{ds} Came to him:

The next day being ye 2^d of ye 3^d mo: & ye 6th Day of y^e
week he went in John Rouses Coach to W Ms: and thence
he went ab^t ye 11th hour with his wife & Bethiah and Ann
Rouse in their Coach to their house at Kingston. Miles : 10 :

The 11th of ye 3^d mo: & ye first day of ye week he went
in John Rowses Coatch to Kingston Meeting where after
John Rouse he Declared a Long time touching many weighty
things & went to prayer & after with a Short testimony
Concluded ye Meeting: he thence went to see Ruth Lilly
& after Returned in J: Rs: Coach to his house:

The 16th of ye 3^d mo: & ye 6th day of the week he & his
wife & J R & his wife went in their Coach to ye Watermans
thence he went by water to Sarah Robbins at Cheeswick
Miles /11/ where he staid till 2^d Day but Lodged at one of
ye worlds house that was her Neighbour:

The 18th of ye 3^d mo: & ye first Day of ye week he went
by Water to Hamersmith meeting Mile /1/ where he De-
clared touching heathenisme & Jewisme—The Original of
Languages—The Gospel preached to Adam, Abraham & y^e
Apostles & Since in these Last dayes—Touching Balaam
who Loved ye Wages of unrighteousness & his Ass Con-
gruing wth ye priests & people of our Age who Received y^e
Wages of unrighteousness of ye people & w^n their Eyes Came
to be opened & they see over y^m & Reprove y^m as Balaams
Ass did his Master & doe not give y^m their Wages then
worse than Balaam they Cast y^m in prison &c—Alsoe touching Simon Magus who thought ye Gift of God was to be
bought for Money & ye State of ye formal Xtians who give
Money to ye priests to preach to y^m &c—And went to prayer
—And after had a short testimony touching ye Minister of
ye true Tabernacle wch God hath pitcht & not man and when
he had done went to ye fri^{ds} house & Ri: Amon[1] Concluded
ye Meeting:

Staid at Kingston from ye 2^d of ye 3^d mo: to ye 16th of y^e
same mo: viz two weeks (& was at there Meeting once) &
several fri^{ds} Came to see him there:

The 19th of ye 3^d mo: & ye 2^d Day of ye week he took
Coach from Cheezwick to Ja: Beeches att Westminster ab^t

/5/ Miles where he staid y^t Night & ye next day being ye 20th of ye 3^d mo: & ye 3^d day of ye week he took Coach to ffr: Doves in Martins Lane & in ye afternoon took Coach to Josiah Elises at ye Savoy where he stayd y^t night.

The next Day being ye 21st of ye 3^d mo: and ye 4 day of the week he went on foot thence to B As there being never a Coach to be had because t'was y^e fast Day. he staid at B As y^t night & y^e Day following being y^e 23 of y^e 3^d mo: & y^e 6th day of y^e week he went thence to y^e meeting for Sufferings & after to B As againe where he staid y^t night, & y^e next day And y^e Day following being y^e 25th of y^e 3^d mo: & y^e 2$^{d\,a}$ Day of the week he went to y^e Bull & Mouth Meeting wch he Begun & ended himself alone^b (t'was in y^e afternoon) in Declaration & prayer & a Short testimony to fri^{ds} The Meeting was Large & many fri^{ds} went away seemingly in a good sense of w^t they had heard thence he went to B As againe where he stayd that Night:

The 26th of ye 3^d mo: & ye 2^d day of ye week he went to ye 2^d Days morning Meeting at ye Chamber & afterwards to B As againe where hee staid that Night:

The 27th of ye 3^d mo: & ye 3^d Day of ye week towards Evening he went to John Elsons^c where he stayd that Night.

The next Day being ye 28th of ye 3^d mo: & ye 4th Day of ye week he was at their Monthly Meeting at their Mo^{ty} Meeting at ye peel:

The next Day being ye 29th of ye 3^d mo: & ye 5 Day of ye week he was at a Marryage at the peel where he opened several things Relating there to:

The next Day being ye 30th of ye 3^d mo: & ye 6th Day of ye week he went thence to ye Meeting for Sufferings & afterwards to B: As: where he stayd that night:

The next Day being ye 31st of ye 3^d mo: & ye 7th Day of the week in ye Evening he went to Josiah Ellises at ye Savoy where he stayd that Night:

The next Day being the first of ye 4th mo: & ye first Day of ye week he was at the Meeting at ye Savoy where after Jasper Bat & another ffriend he Declared a Long time touching several perticulares to ye tendering of fri^{ds} & went to prayer & after he had done ye Meeting departed:

---

^{a} Should be *first* ^{b} Margin: *Kept ye meeting alone*
^{c} First written *Josiah Ellises* and altered to *John Elsons*

The next Day being ye 2^d of ye 4 mo: & ye 2^d Day of y^e
week he took Coach to ye 2^d days Meeting at ye Chamber
& after to B As where hee stayd that night:
The next Day being ye 3^d of ye 4th mo: & ye 3^d Day of y^e
week he went to ye Six weeks meeting at ye Bull & Mouth
& after to B As where^a fri^{ds} Came to him:
The next Day being ye 4th of ye 4th mo: & ye 4th day of
ye week in ye afternoon he went to ye Chamber ab^t Busyness & after to W Ms in his Coach y^t was sent for him:
The next Day being ye 5th of ye 4th mo: & ye 5th Day of
ye week he went to ye Chamber ab^t Bussyness where he was
part of ye Day & Returned to W Ms at Night. where many
fri^{ds} came to him:
The next Day being ye 6th of ye 4th mo: & ye 6th Day of
ye week he went to ye Chamber againe in ye forenoon & in
ye after noon was at ye Meeting for Sufferings there & after
went to W Ms where he stayd y^t night & many fri^{ds} Came
to him there:
The next Day being ye 7th of ye 4th mo: & ye 7th Day of
ye week he went to the Chamber againe where he was a
great part of ye Day & many Country fri^{ds} Came thither
he after went to W Ms where he staid that Night & many
fri^{ds} Came to him:

The Meetings he was at this week were 4: the Savoy
Meeting ye 2^d Dayes Meeting ye six weeks Meeting & y^e
Meeting for Sufferings:

The next Day being ye 8th of the 4th mo: & ye first Day
of ye week he went to ye Morning Meeting at ye Chamber
where was many Country fri^{ds} & after it was done he went
to B As where he stayd y^t night:
The next Day being ye 9th of ye 4th mo: & ye 2^d Day of
ye week he was at ye General Meeting[1] of fri^{ds} in ye Ministry
at ye Bull & Mouth in ye forenoon where he Declared
touching severall things & went to prayer: he was like wise
at ye General Meeting of Busyness there in ye afternoon, &
after went to W Ms where he staid y^t Night:
The next day being ye 10th of ye 4th mo: & ye 3^d Day of
ye week he was at the General Meeting of fri^{ds} at Wheeler
street where he Declared touching severall things—as ag^t

^{a} *many* written and erased.

ye ffashions of ye World; —going without Aprons[1] &c.—y^e
feast of Trumpets—ye feast of ye passover & ye paschy Lamb
—The ffeast of Tabernacles—The Resurrection &c, and after
he had done not being able to stay any Longer he went out
to ye friends house & after took Coach to Ezek: Wooleys
where he Lay downe on ye Bed & in ye afternoon took Coach
to ye Generall Meeting of Busyness at Devenshire house,
and after it was done he took Coach to B As where he stayd
that night:

The next Day being ye 11th of ye 4th mo: & ye 4th Day of
ye week he was at ye 4th Day of ye week^a he was at Grace
Ch: street Meeting where he declared touching Severall
things—as, ye Seed: Reprobation—ye Gospell—And other
Mentioned in ye Beforesd Meeting &c: And when done not
being Able to Stay any Longer went to Henry Goldneys &
Lay on ye Bed & in ye afternoon took Coach to ye Generall
Meeting for Bussyness at ye Bull & Mouth where hee Advised
touching severall things & went to prayer & after ye Meeting
was done took Coach to W Ms where he Stayd y^t Night:

The next Day being ye 12th of ye 4th mo: and ye 5th Day
of ye week he went to ye General Womens Meeting at y^e
Bull & Mouth where after he had borne a Short Testimony
among y^m he Left y^m & Came to Edw: Bruches & after a
while took Coach to B As where he stayd y^t Night & many
fri^{ds} Came to him there.

The next Day being ye 13th of ye 4th mo: & ye week^a he
went to ye Meeting for Sufferings & after to W Ms where
hee stayd that night:

The next Day being ye 14 of ye 4th mo: & ye 7th Day of
the week he went to ye Chamber where there Came several
fri^{ds} & after went to B As where he stayd that Night & y^e
next day & many fri^{ds} Came to him there:

The Meetings he was at this week were /9/ ye first Day
Morning Meeting, the Generall Meeting of fri^{ds} in ye Ministry at ye Bull & Mouth ye Generall Meeting at Wheelerstreet /3/ Generall Meetings ab^t ye Nationall Busyness,
the 4th Dayes Meeting at Grace Ch: Street, the Generall
Womens Meeting & ye Meeting for Sufferings, besides much
other Busyness with ffriends:

---

^{a} This is as written without correction.

Some of y^r heads upon wch G ff Spoke at ye Yearly Meetings, in ye Year 1690:

How ye Lord is turning ye Moon ye Changable World into Blood & ye persecuting Sun into Darkness before ye Lords Day & Sun of Righteousness appears:

The Tree of Knowledge of Good & Evill Eve saw it was good for food, there was ye Lust of ye flesh & pleasant to ye Eye there was ye Lust of ye Eye, & to make wise there was ye pride of Life, And John saith for all that is in ye world the Lust of ye Eye ye Lust of ye fflesh & ye pride of Life is not of the ffather but is of ye world & if any Love ye world ye Love of ye ffather is not in y^m:

And now Consider are you not in ye Lust of ye Eye ye Lust of ye flesh & pride of Life wch is not of ye father & are not you Brittle & peevish w^n you are told of these things wch are not of ye ffather but of ye world &c: with many other heads of wch a Manuscript is Made:[1]

The 16th of ye 4th mo: & ye 2^d day of ye week he went to ye morning Meeting at ye Chamber & after went to W Ms where he staid y^t night.

The next Day being ye 17th of ye 4th mo: & ye 3^d Day of ye week he went to ye Chamber where he had Busyness, & many fri^{ds} Came to him he after went to B: As where hee stayd that night:

The next Day being ye 18th of ye 4th mo: & ye 4th Day of ye week he went to ye Chamber to a Meeting appoynted there ab^t Busyness in ye afternoon & after went to W Ms where he staid that night:

The next Day being ye 20th of ye 4th mo: & ye 6th Day of ye week he went to ye Chamber ab^t Busyness in ye Morning and stayd ye Meeting for Sufferings in ye afternoon & afterwards went to W Ms again where he staid y^t Night.

The next Day being ye 21st of ye 4th mo: & ye 7th Day of the week he went to ye Chamber again ab^t Busyness & after went to B As where hee staid that Night & the next Day:

The Meetings he was at this week were /3/ the 2^d Days Meeting, a Meeting ab^t Busyness & ye Meeting for Sufferings besides much other Busyness Relating to ye truth:

The Day following being ye 23^d of ye 4th mo: & ye 2^d Day
of ye week he went to ye Morning Meeting at ye Chamber
& after went to W Ms where hee staid that Night:

The next Day being ye 24th of ye 4th mo: & ye 3^d Day of
ye week he took Coach to B As where he staid that Night:

The next Day being ye 25th of ye 4th mo: & ye 4th day of
ye week he took Coach to ye Chamber ab^t Busyness and
after went to W Ms where he staid y^t night:

The next Day being ye 26th of ye 4th mo: & ye 5th Day of
ye week in ye Morning he went to the Chamber ab^t Busyness & in ye afternoon was at a Meeting there ab^t W Kents
Busyness & after went to W Ms where he stayd y^t night:

The next Day being ye 27th of ye 4th mo: & ye 6th Day of
the week he went to the Chamber ab^t Busyness & in y^e
afternoon was at ye Meeting for Sufferings & after went to
W Ms where he Stayd that night.

The next Day being ye 28th of ye 4th mo: & ye 7th Day
of ye Week after visiting severall fri^{ds} he went to Richard
Cooks att ye Swan Inn without Bishopsgate where he staid
that night:

The next Day being ye 29th of ye 4th mo: & ye first Day
of the week in ye afternoon he went to Devenshire house
Meeting & after B A & S C he stood up & Declared a pritty
time & went to prayer & after with a Short Testimony Concluded ye Meeting wch was Large: thence he went in John
Rouses Coach to W Ms where he stayd that night.

The next Day being ye 30th of ye 4th mo: & ye 2^d Day of
ye week M ff his wife took Coach thence on her Journey
towards the North^1 & Tho: Lower and his wife & children
& after they had done he took Coach to B As where he staid
that Night:

The next Day being ye first of ye 5th mo: & ye 3^d Day of
ye week towards Evening he took Coach to John Elsons
where he stayd y^t night: & ye next Day & was at their
Quarterly Meeting for Collection:

The next Day being ye 3^d of ye 5th mo: & ye fifth Day of
ye week he went {p Coatch} to a Meeting at ye Chamber
ab^t Wm Kents Busyness & after went to B As where hee
stayd y^t night:

The next Day being ye 4th of ye 5th mo: and ye 6th Day
of the week in ye Morning he took Coach to Brig^t Austills

at Tatnum high Cross, & with him Ann Cox where he stayd
y^t Night :

The 6th of ye 5th mo : & ye first day of ye week he was at
ye Meeting there where he Declared a great while & went
to prayer, & ye Meeting after departed :

The 9th of ye 5th mo : & ye 4th Day of ye week he took
Coach to Edw : Manns near Winsmoorhill ab^t Miles : 4 :

The 13th of ye 5th mo : & ye first Day of ye week he took
Coach thence to ye Meeting at Enfield where he Declared a
Long time Concerning Christ ye Ensigne & Captain of Sal-
vation how he had stood by friends in all their persecutions
& Sufferings therefore Exhorted to stand by him & hold him
there head—And ye priests who say they watch for peoples
Souls wch they Confess is Imortall to present y^m before God
{&c} yet Say there is noe having ye holy Ghost & ye holy
Spirit as ye Apostle had while on this side ye Grave, with
many other things & went to prayer & after with a Short
Testimony Concluded ye meeting wch was Large, he after
took Coach to Tho : Hearts where he staid y^t night :

The 16th of ye 5th mo : & ye 4th day of ye week ffr : Camfield fetched him in a Coach to his house at Tiballs^a where
he Remained for some time :

The 20th of ye 5th mo : & ye first Day of ye week he went
in a Coach to ye Meeting at Chesson where after some other
fri^{ds} he had a Large testimony & went to prayer & y^e
Meeting after Departed thence hee went to ffr : Camfields
againe^b.

The 29th of ye 5th mo : & ye 3^d Day of ye week he went
thence on horse back to Tho : Bennets at Walthum Abbey ;
Mile : 1 :

The 30th of ye 5th mo : & ye 4th Day of ye week he was at
their Meeting at Walthum Abbey where after G W T : Bur
he stood up & Declared a pritty Large time touching how
Ishmael was not to be heir of ye promiss—Isaac in whom
the Seed was to be Called Borne to Abraham & Sarah {his
wife} in their old Age Even when they were past Strength,
And ye Apostle saith when they were yet without strength
in Due time Christ Dyed for ye Ungodly &c :—Inward and
Spiritual Sacrifices—Christians to sing^c in Hymes, psalms,

* Margin : *Miles /3/* ^{b} Margin : *forward & Backward Miles /2/*
^{c} Altered from *Concerning singing*

& Spiritual Songs, not David's psalms made Meter by
Hopkins & Starling[1] after the Manner of ye priests—Christ
given for a Covenant to the people & an Ensigne to y^e
Nations &c—and went to prayer & after wth a Short Testimony Concluded ye Meeting.

The 3^d of ye 6th mo: & ye first Day of ye week he was at
ye Meeting ag^n att Walthum Abbey where he Declared a
Long time of many particulars & went to prayer & after
with a short Testimony Concluded ye Meeting wch was
Large, thence he went to Tho: Bennets where he staid y^t
night:

The next Day being ye 4th of ye 6th mo: & ye 2^d Day of
ye week he went from thence p Coach to Geo: Barrs; miles
/5/ where he Remained some time:

The 10th of ye 6th mo: & ye first Day of ye week he went
in a Coach to Enfield Meeting where he Declared a Long
time distinguishing betwixt y^e Worlds peace wch Christ
Came to Break & the heavenly peace wch he brought—
When done he went to prayer & y^e Meeting after departed
wch was Large, he went that Night to Edw: Mans p Coach:

The 17th of y^e 6th mo: & y^e first day of y^e week he went
to Tatnum Meeting at $Bridg^t$ Austels where after G W hee
Declared a pritty time & went to prayer & y^e Meeting after
departed: wch was Large:

The 23^d of y^e 6th mo: & y^e 7th Day of y^e week he took
Coach to Edw: Mans att ffordgreen, where he staid that
night:

The next Day being y^e 24 of y^e 6th mo: & first Day of
the week he went to Winsmorhill Meeting where he Declared a Long time touching several pticulars to ye much
Reaching & affecting of fri^{ds} & went to prayer & after wth a
short Testimony Concerning ye vine: how as a Branch Cut
of from ye vine cannot Live noe more Can Man Separated or
Cut of from Christ: Concluded ye Meeting: wch was Large
thence he went p Coach to E: Ms: againe:

The 31st of ye 6 mo: & ye first Day of ye week he went in
a Coach to Waltham Abbey Meeting & with him E: M: &
his Wife & G W & his wife: after G W: G ff Declared a
pritty Long time & went to prayer and after with a short
Testimony Concluded ye meeting thence he went to Thomas
Bennets where hee staid that Night:

"The next Day being ye 25th of ye 6 mo: John Elson & his wife & ffra: Camfield Came to him there & he went with ffrancis thence to his house at Tibalds on his horse:"

The 5th of ye 7th mo: he took Coach from Tiballs to Henry Stouts at Hartford, Miles :8:

The next Day hee visited ffr: plumstead[1] & several fri^{ds} in ye Towne & went to Hen: Stouts againe that Night my ffather Came to visit us[b] at Hartford & staid all night at Ri: Thomases.[2]

The next Day being ye 7th of ye 7th mo: and ye first Day of ye week he was at their Meeting where he Declared a Long time & went to prayer & after with a short Testimony Concluded ye Meeting:

The next Day he Appoynted a Meeting with some of ye antient friends ab^t something he had in his Mind to Speak to y^m:

The next Day being the 9th of ye 7th mo: & ye 3^d Day of ye week he took Coach to Tho: Dockreas[3] at Ware & with him Henry Stout Miles :2:

The next Day, being ye 10th of ye 7th mo: & ye 4th Day of ye week visiting some ffri^{ds} & Tho: Burrs by ye way he went to their Meeting where after Tho: Robison hee Declared a Long time & went to pray^r & after with a short Testimony Concluded y^e Meeting he after went to Tho: Dockreas ag^n where he staid that Night:

The 12th of y^e 7th mo: & y^e 6th Day of y^e week he went to Tho: Burs and thence took Coach to Geo: Barrs in Berry-street, Edmunton ab^t Miles /13/ where he staid that Night:

The 14 of y^e 7th mo: & y^e 6$^{th\,c}$ Day of y^e week some ffri^{ds} went to visit him & he went thence in their Coach to Edw: Manns in y^e afternoon ab^t Mile :1:

The 21st of y^e 7: mo: & y^e first Day of y^e week he was at Winsmorhill Meeting where after 2 other fri^{ds} had a few words he Declared a Long time & went to prayer & after with a short testimony Concluded ye Meeting thence he went to Edw: Mans and after took Coach with Bridg^t Austill to her house at Tatnum Miles /4/

---

[a]...[a] This paragraph appears to be out of order and should be read prior to the previous paragraph.

[b] Margin repeats this interesting statement: *my father Came to visit us that night*   [c] Should be *first*

The 28th of ye 7th mo: & ye first Day of ye week he was at Tatnum Meeting where he Declared a pritty time & went to prayer & after wth a short testimony Concluded ye Meeting {w^{ch}} was Large many London^{rs} being there:

The 30th of ye 7th mo: & ye 3^d Day of ye week he took Coach thence to Jacob ffranklins att London {& thence to Henry Goldneys} where he staid y^t night:

Staid in ye Country from ye 4th of ye 5th mo: & ye 6th Day of ye week to ye 30th of ye 7th mo: & ye 3^d Day of ye week viz 12 weeks & ab^t 5 Dayes: in wch time he was at :14: Meetings & many fri^{ds} Came to visit him.

The first of ye 8th mo: & ye 4th Day of ye week he was at ye Meeting at Grace Ch: street where after Ben: Brown[1] a Yorkshire ffri^d and Ch: Harris[2] a Separate he Declared a pritty Long time & went to prayer & after ward ye Meeting broke up thence he went to Henry Gouldneys & after to B As where he staid that night.

The Day ffollowing being ye 3^d of ye 8 mo: & ye 6th day of ye week he went thence to ye Meeting for Sufferings and after it was done he took Coach to John Elsons where he staid that night.

The 5th of ye 8th mo: & ye first Day of ye week he was at the Peel meeting where after John Heart[3] a Notinghamshire ffriend he stood up & Declared a Long time & went to prayer & afterwards ye Meeting broke up wch was Large & ye people went away very tender & sensible:

The next Day being ye 6th of ye 8: mo: & ye 2^d Day of ye week he went to ye Quartly Men & Womens Meeting at Devenshire house where he had a testimony at y^m both & after went to G Ws where he staid that night:

The next Day being ye 7th of ye 8th mo: & ye 3^d day of ye week he was at ye 6 weeks meeting at Devenshire house & after took Coach to B As where he staid that Night:

The 10th of ye 8th mo: & ye 6th Day of ye week he went to the Meeting for Sufferings & after it was done he went to Michel Russels where he staid y^t night:

The next Day being ye 11th of ye 8th mo: & ye 7th Day of the week he was most of ye Day at ye Chamber ab^t Bussyness of sending Books Beyond the Seas & after went to Henry Goldneys where he staid y^t night.

The next Day being ye 12th of ye 8th mo: & ye first Day of Grace Ch: street Meeting where after S C: he stood up & Declared a pritty time & after Concluded ye Meeting with prayer wch was Large & ye people very sensible he after went to Henry Goldneys ag^n where he stayd y^t night:

The next Day being ye 13th of ye 8th mo: & ye 2^d Day of ye week he went to ye 2^d Days Meeting and after to B As where he staid y^t Night:

The next Day being ye 14th of ye 8th mo: & ye 3^d Day of week he took Coach to Josiah Ellises where he staid that night:

The next Day being ye 15th of ye 8th mo: & ye 4th Day of ye week he took Coach to {Westminster & went to} Ja: Beeches^a where he staid that night: & ye Earle of Carbery Came & gave him a visit there of 2 or 3 hours: he staid there also ye next Day & Sr Robt Knapper Came to visit him several times whilst there

The next Day being ye 17th of ye 8th mo: & ye 6th Day of ye week he went to ffr: Doves in a Coach where he staid that Night:

The 18th of ye 8th mo: & ye 7th Day of ye Week he went thence in a Coach to Ja: Beeches again where he staid that Night where ye Earle of Carebery gave him another visit of an hour or two and also Sr Robt Knaper

The next Day being ye 19th of ye 8th mo: & ye first Day of ye week he went to Westminster Meeting where he declared a long time & after Concluded ye Meeting wth prayer wch was Large & fri^ds departed in a Good sense, thence he went to James Beeches where he staid that night: {S^r Robt Knaper was wth him a great while y^t night:}

The next Day being ye 20th of ye 8th mo: & ye 2^d Day of ye week he took Coach to Edw: Brookes in Bloomsbery where he staid that night:

The next Day being ye 21st of ye 8th mo: & ye 3^d Day of ye week he met some friends appoynted to tend ye parliam^t Men at ye Coffy house[1] where friends used to be Joyning to Westminster Hall & after took Coach to ffr: Doves where he staid some time and there Came to him G W & James Parks

^a Margin: *to Speak wth some of ye parliam^t men Concerning fri^ds:*

who took Coach with {him} thence to B As where he staid
that night & ye next day & ye Day ffollowing:

The 24th of ye 8th mo: & ye 6th Day of ye week he went to
ye Meeting for Sufferings & after to Hen: Goldneys where he
staid y^t night:

The 25th of ye 8th mo: & ye 7th Day of the week after
visiting several fr^{ds} there awayes he took Coach to Marg^t
Drinkwells in Bishops gatestreet where he staid y^t night:

The next Day being ye 26th of ye 8th mo: & ye first Day of
ye week he was att Devensh^r house Meeting in ye afternoon
where he Declared a Long time & went to prayer & after wth
a short testimony advising to seek ye Kingdome of heaven
first & all other things should be added &c. Concluded y^e
Meeting wch was Large & friends departed very weighty &
sensible, he after went to Marg^t Drinkwels ag^n where he
stayd y^t night: & had discourse wth Joan perkins[1] son in law
ab^t Religion who Came with his mother to visit him:

The next Day he took Coach to ye 2^d Dayes Meeting &
after went to B: As: where he staid y^t night & ye next Day:

The 29th of ye 8th mo: & ye 4th Day of ye week he went to
a Meeting appoynted at ye Chamber ab^t Considering upon
drawing up ye Case of oaths to Lay before ye parliam^t &
thence he took Coach to James Beeches at Westminster
where he stayd y^t night: & ye next Day to Look after fri^{ds}
ab^t Clandestine marryages wch through defect in ye Drawing
up would have Comprehended fri^{ds}

The 31st of ye 8th mo: & ye 6th Day of ye week he went
thence to Westminster hall & thence took Coach to ffr: Doves
and after to B As: where he stayd y^t night & ye next Day
& ye Day following:

And ye 3^d Day of ye 9th mo: & ye 2^d Day of ye week he
took Coach thence & wth him Mary Antrobus to Bridget
Austels at ye Womans School at Tatnum high Cross Miles
/5/: where he Remained sometime:

Stayd at London from ye 30th of ye 7th mo & 3^d Day of
ye week to ye 3^d of ye 9th mo: & 2^d Day of ye week wch is a
Month & 5 Dayes:

The 9th of ye 9th mo: & ye first Day of ye week he was
at ye Meeting at Tatnum where after another ffri^d had a

short testimony he declared a long time very pretiously &
after Concluded ye meeting wth prayer:

The 15th of ye 9th mo: & ye 7th Day of ye week he took
Coach {thence} to Edw: Mans Miles 4 where he Remained
sometime.

The 16th of ye 9th mo: & ye first Day of ye week he went
in the Tatnum Coach to Winsmorhil Meeting where after
ffrancis Stamper he had a Large Declaration & very powerfull and went to prayer & after with a short testimony
Concluded ye Meeting thence he went p Coach to E: Ms
againe:

The 30th of ye 9th mo: & ye first Day of ye week he took
Coach & with him E Man & his wife to Enfield Meeting
where he Declared a Long time & went to prayer & after
with a short testimony Concluded ye Meeting wch was pritty
Large & thence took Coach to Thomas Hearts^a where he
stayed y^t night & ye next Day:

The Day ffollowing being ye 2^d of ye 10th mo: & ye 3^d Day
of ye week he went to William Shewins where he Continued
ye Rest of ye time att Enfield & on ye 5th Day was at their
Meeting at Wm Shewins where he Declared a pritty long
time & went to prayer & after with a short testimony Concluded ye Meeting.

The next Day being ye 5th 10: mo: & ye 6 day of y^e
week he took Coach thence to Bridget Austells at Tatnum
Miles 6:

The next Day being y^e :7: 10: mo: & ye first Day of y^e
week he was at ye Meeting there where after G W: he Declared a pritty time & went to prayer & ye Meeting after
departed

The 14th 10: mo: and ye first Day of ye week he took
Coach to Winsmor hill meeting where he Declared a pritty
Long time & went to prayer & ye Meeting after departed
thence he took Coach to Edw: Mans where hee stayd that
night:

The 17: of ye 10: mo: & ye first^b Day of ye week he took
Coach to Bridget Austels at Tatnam ~ ab^t Miles 4 where he
staid some time:

The 21st 10: mo: & ye first Day of ye week he was at
Tatnam Meeting where after ffra: Stamper he declared a

^{a} Margin: *Miles /2/* ^{b} Should be *4th*

pritty time & went to prayer & after with a short testimony
Concluded ye Meeting wch was Large:

The 28 of ye 10: mo: & ye first day of ye week he staid
at Tatnam & was at noe Meeting where some fri^{ds} Came to
visit him: The next Day he took Coach thence to Marg^t
Drinkwells at London & thence went to the Quarterly Mens
& womens Meeting at Devonshire house & had a testimony
in each of y^m thence he took Coach to B As: where he staid
that night:

The next Day being ye 30th of ye 10: mo: & ye 3^d Day of
ye week he went to ye Six weeks Meeting at Devonshire
house p Coach & after took Coach with Ann Cox to their
house where hee staid that Night:

The next Day he took Coach to ye 4th Dayes Meeting at
Grace Ch: street where after Charles Marshall &c he Declared a, pritty time very pretiously & Concluded ye Meeting
with prayer thence he went to Henry Goldneys where he
staid y^t night:

Staid in ye Country from ye 3^d of ye 9th mo: & ye 2^d Day
of ye week to ye 29th of ye 10: mo: & ye 2^d Day of the week
viz :8: weeks in wch time he was at :7: Meetings & many
fri^{ds} visited him

The 1st of ye 11th mo: & ye 5th Day of ye week he went to
Benjamin Antrobuses where he staid that night
The next Day he went to ye Meeting for Sufferings & after
to B As where he staid that night:
The Day following he took Coach to ffr: Camfields where
he staid that night:
The next Day being ye 4th 11th mo: & ye first Day of y^e
week he went to ye Bull & Mouth Meeting where he had
a Large Testimony & went to prayer & ye Meeting after
Departed wch was Large thence he went to ff Cs: againe
where he staid that Night:

The Meetings he was at ye Last weeke were 4: ye quartly
Men & Womens meeting ye Six weeks meeting Grace Ch:
street Meeting & ye Meeting for Sufferings; besides other
Bussyness Relating to fri^{ds} and Truths Concerns:

The 5th of ye 11th mo : & ye 2^d Day of ye week he took Coach to the 2^d Dayes Meeting & after went to B : As : where he staid y^t night : & ye next Day :

The Day ffollowing being ye 4th Day of ye week towards Evening he took Coach to ye peel & was at their Mo: Meeting he staid there that Night & ye next day :

The Day ffollowing he took Coach to ye Meeting for Sufferings & after went to B As where he staid that Night : The next Day being ye 7th of ye week he took Coach (towards Night) to Henry Gouldneys where hee staid that Night & writt an Epistle to ffriends in Ireland :[1]

The next Day being ye 11th of ye 11th mo : & ye first Day of ye week he was at Grace Ch : Street Meeting where he Declared a Long time very pretiously & very audably & went to prayer & ye Meeting after departed wch was Large thence he went to Henry Gouldneys and he said he thought he felt ye Cold strike to his heart as he Came out of ye Meeting but was pritty Cheary with fri^{ds} y^t Came to him there {& said he was glad he was at ye meeting now he was Clear} & after they were gone {he} Lay downe upon ye Bed (as he was wont to doe after a Meeting) twice & at his Riseings wch were but for a little Space he still Complained of Cold ye Latter time he was worse & groaned much soe that after a very little being much out of order he was forced to goe to Bed, and, in ab^t /2/ hours after his Strength failed him very much & soe he Continued Spending till ab^t half an hour & half a quarter after Nine on third Day Night & then departed this Life : after ye 3^d Dayes Illness : being ye 13th of ye 11th mo : 1690 :[2]

In his Illness hee used these words to some friends that Came to see him The Seed of God Reigns over all & over Death ittself ; & tho : hee was weak in Body yet the power of God is over all and Reigns over all disorderly Spirits ;

The 16th of ye 11th mo : & ye 6th Day of ye week he was Buryed from Grace Ch : street where there was a very Large Meeting the house & yard well peopled, & a great Many Testimonyes Borne Concerning him[3] aboundance of friends accompanyed him to ye Burying Grownd where alsoe Severall Testimonyes were Borne Concerning him[4] :36: ffriends all or Mostly Ministers were appoynted to Carry him to y^e Grownd :

III
THE HAISTWELL DIARY

"So here is A Brief Journall of G ff^s travells while I traveld with him in 1677 & 1678."

EDWARD HAISTWELL.

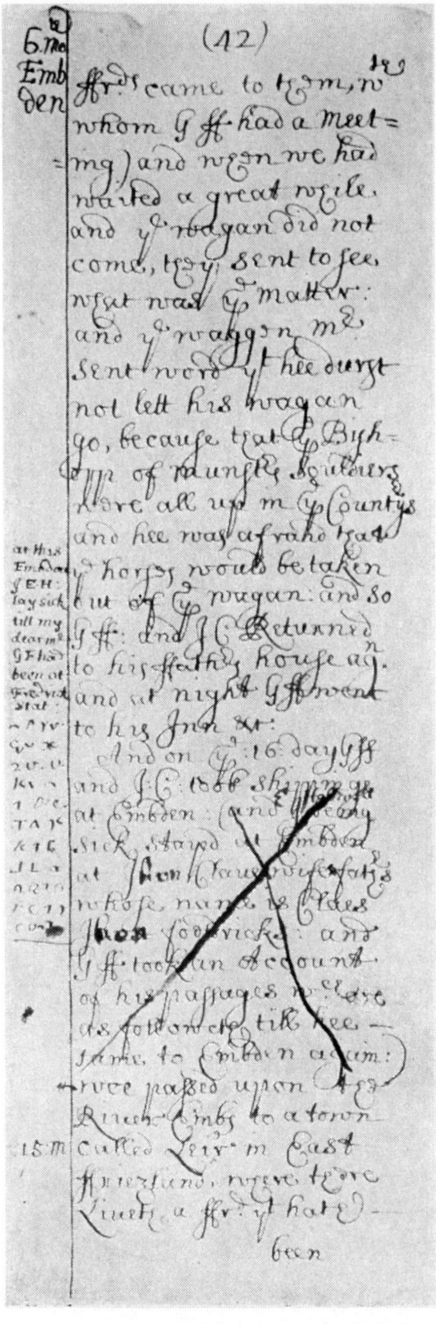

(42)

6 mo
Emb
den

ffrds came to them, wth
whom G ff had a Meet=
=ing) and when we had
waited a great while.
and ye wagan did not
come, they sent to see,
what was ye matter:
and ye waggon mr
sent word yt hee durst
not lett his wagan
go, because that ye Bish=
opp of Munster Souldiers
were all up in ye Countys
and hee was afraid that
ye horses would be taken
out of ye wagon: and so
G ff: and J C: Returned
to his ffathers house agn.
and at night G ff went
to his Inn &c:
And on ye 16 day G ff
and J C: took Shipping
at Embden: (and E H being
sick, stayed at Embden
at John Clauswife's fathrs
whose name is Claes
John Goodrick: and
G ff took an Account
of his passages wch are
as followeth, till hee
came to Embden again:)
wee passed upon the
River Embs to a town
called Leir in East
ffriesland, where there
Liveth a ffrd yt hath
been

at this Embden E H lay sick till my dear mr G F had been at ...

15 m

A Page of *The Haistwell Diary*

III

THE HAISTWELL DIARY

A short journall of G: F:ˢ Travells in the service of the Lord (with a short Relation of passages), since hee came from Swarthmoore on the 26ᵗʰ day of the first month: 1677.

After G: ff: had taken his leave of his ffamily and ffr^{ds} they parted in that Love which endures for Ever, his wife and Rachell F¹: with severall other ffr^{ds} accompanying him to Tho: Pearsons² at Powbanck:ᵃ where ffr^{ds} there greatly Rejoyced to see him; So on yᵉ 27: day G: ff: was at a Larg Meeting there, where he declared yᵉ truth: to the comfortinge and Refreshing of many there p^{r}sent &cᵇ:

And on yᵉ 28: day G: ff: and M ff accompanyed with severall ffr^{ds} passed from thence to Thomas Cam̃s³ at Cam̃sgillᶜ, where Robt Widders and his wife, and severall other ffr^{ds} was come to meet G ff: and to bee at the Meetinge the next Day, and there came severall ffr^{ds} to visit G ff: that night:

And so on the 29 Day there was a larg meeting in a Barn, where G ff Declared yᵉ truth some houres: having much discourse after yᵉ meeting with Gervase Benson: and severall ffr^{ds} of that Meeting, who at y^{t} time were not at unity with ffreinds of y^{t} Quart^{r}ly meeting, they belonged too, but severall tender hearted ffr^{ds} seeing their Error; gave forth Condemnations ag^{st} themselves:

And on yᵉ 30: Day Jnº Blaykling came thither for G. ff who with his wife and severall oth^{r} ffr^{ds} went along with him (visiting ffr^{ds} as they went) to his house at Draw-well in Sedberghᵈ : where there came severall ffreinds to visit G ff: y^{t} night: and on yᵉ 31 day also.

ᵃ Margin : *12 m*

ᵇ This abbreviation *&c.* appears frequently, but its signification is not clear. It has been omitted from the print.

ᶜ Margin : *6 m*   ᵈ Margin : *6 m*

And on ye 1st of 2th moth G ff: and M ff. went to y^e
Meeting at Brigflatts: and It being the first day of the
week there was ye most p^t of ffr^{ds} from ye severall Meetings
there abouts, as also a great Concourse of people, Insomuch
that It was thought there was :5: or 600: And at this
Meeting G ff declared ye Everlasting truth severall houres
to the Comforting and Refreshing, many ffr^{ds} there p^{r}sent,
and to ye drawing near; them y^t were affar off (to witt from
ye truth:) the meetinge done G ff. with his wife took Leave
of ffr^{ds} and Returned to J. B^s ag^n.

And on y^e 3 day G ff: and M ff: were at A Men & womens
Meeting at J: B^s: wch was very Large & precious.

And while that G:ff: did stay at J B^s. there came severall
ffr^{ds} out of Lancashire & Westmorland, and Yorkshire, to
visit him:

So on the 5: day G ff: had another Meeting at .J: B$'^s$:
where there was severall ffriends out of y^e Countrys w^{ch}
was come, in order to go to a Quart^{r}ly Meeting at Kendall
the next day: So on y^e 6 day 2^d moth after G ff had taken
his Leave of ffr^{ds} and ffr^{ds} of him, they parted in y^e unchang-
able Love of God: his wife and Rachell passed wth ffr^{ds} to y^e
Quart^{r}ly Meeting at Kendall:

And then G ff and Leo: ffell (who came ye day before in
order to go with G ff) passed from Jno Blayklings thorow
Sedbergh and Gasdaile, and into Wensydaile, visitinge ffr^{ds}
as they went, and L: ff: stayed at a place called the Haws,
where hee had a meeting in ye Evening, and G ff passed
further to Richard Robinsons[1] of Countersyde[a], where
severall ffreinds came to visitt him that night.

And on ye 7: day L: ff: with severall ffreinds came to
G ff at R. R^s and so G ff with severall ffr^{ds} passed from
thence over ye hills, where wee had much to do, to gett
thorow ye snow, and so passed to widdow Tennants[2] at Scarr-
house in Langstrothdaile[b], who greatly Rejoyced to see G ff:
there:

So on the 8: day being the first day of the week: there
was a Larg meeting, where G ff: declared the truth severall
houres. there was ffr^{ds} from severall parts, hearing of G ff
being there; vizt there was out of Wensydaile, & Litten-

daile & Bishopsdaile & Skipton & Coverdaile & from Kellet in Lancashi^r and from Sedbergh.

And on y^e :9 : day after G ff: had taken Leave with ffr^{ds} hee passed from thence with severall ffriends, thorow Bishopsdaile to Midlum, where wee dined at an Inn, & wee passed thence with Marmaduke Beckwith[1] to his house at Burton sup^r Our^a, where G ff stayed on ye 10 : day, and had much service amongst ffr^{ds} there: and Leo: ff: went to visit ffreinds in Bishoprick:

And on ye 11 : day G ff: with severall ffr^{ds} passed from thence thorow the Country (visiting ffr^{ds}) by Beedle, & northal^{r}ton, and so to Georg Robinsons[2] at Borrowby^b: and severall ffr^{ds} came to visit G ff that night.

And on ye 12 : day Leo: ff: and Rich: Watson[3] and severall ffr^{ds} Out of Bishopprick, and Ro: Linton[4] and some ffr^{ds} from New-Castle, (being in Bishoprick), came to Borrowby and there was a very Larg meeting y^t day at wch Meeting G ff declared severall houres, and ended ye Meeting in prayer; all beinge very peaceable: But not long after A Justice (who was Envious agst ffr^{ds}) hearing y^t G ff: had had a Larg meeting att Geo: Robinsons, hee troubled ffreinds, and putt them into ye Law: so ffr^{ds} appeared at ye Sessions, where ye Justice asked ffr^{ds} many ensnaringe Questions: amongst ye Rest., this envious Justice told ffreinds ^{c}that hee had heard that Geo ffox was at a Larg meetinge and they satt all silent and none spoke in ye Meetinge^c: (mark ye Cunningness of this Justice, y^t hee might gett his ends about, to ffine freinds.) But ffr^{ds} being ordered in the wisdom of God, did not Answer him according to his desire, and so they escaped his snare, and hee could gett nothing agst them, whereby hee might ffine them:

And on ye day aforesaid y^t G ff had ye Meeting at Geo: R:^{s} there was two ffr^{ds} y^t was come out of Ireland who after ye meeting was done at G R^s went about three Miles off; and had A meeting y^t night, for wch ye Justice plundred ffr^{ds} very sore Streaning y^{ir} goods: And so on ye 13 : day all being clear; G ff took Leave with ffr^{ds} and passed from thence accompanyed with severall ffr^{ds} (as Rich: Watson, and Robt Lodge, & some ffr^{ds} from York, who accompanyed

---

^{a} Margin: *16 : m* ^{b} Margin: *12 m*
^{c}...^{c} These words are underlined.

him thither) so wee passed thorow Thirsk, where G ff visited ffriends, and so to Isaac Lindleys[1], where we stayed y^t night^a.

And on ye 14: day G ff: and severall ffr^{ds} passed from thence (visiting severall ffr^{ds}) to York Citty, and G ff went to Tho: Waytes[2] where hee stayed y^t night.

And on ye 15: day (being the first day of ye week) G ff: went to ye Meeting, wch was Larg and peaceable:

And on y^e 16: day G ff: had two meetings at Jno Taylors house amongst ffr^{ds}.

And on y^e 17 day G ff: passed from J T.^{s} to Edw: Nightingailes[3] and Tho: waytes, to take his Leave wth them, and so passed from York accompanyed with severall, to William Sidells[4] att Todcast$^{r\,b}$ where G ff had A Meeting in y^e Evening:

And on y^e 18: day G ff & L ff: taking Leave with Edward Nightingaile & Rich Watson (who accompany them thith^r) and ffr^{ds} they passed from thence to Samuell Pooles[5] att Nottingley^c, who with his wife greatly Rejoyced to see G. ff: and on y^e :19: day there was a meeting:

So on y^e 20: day G ff: passed from thence thorow y^e Country to Henry Cookes$^{d\,6}$ where G ff had appointed a meeting to bee there y^t day, So y^e meeting being gathered when hee came there; hee went into y^e meeting wch was very Large, and serviceable, not only in respect to ffr^{ds} but also to other people, who were there.

And so from thence on y^e 21: day G ff passed by Doncast^r and so to Balby^e to Jno: Killams[7], where severall ffr^{ds} came to visit him, and on ye 22 day being ye first day of ye week, G ff was at ffr^{ds} meetings there: and L. ff: parted with G ff at H. C: and went to Thornton, where he was at ye meeting on ye 22: day.

And on ye 23: day L ff came to G ff at Balby and they passed from thence to Tho: Aldams[8], where they visited ffr^{ds} and Henry Jackson[9] and his wife came to G ff: there, who with Thomas Killam[10] accompanyed G ff to Thomas Stacys[11] at Ballowfield^f, who at that time was at differance wth ffr^{ds}

^{a} Margin: *9 m:*	^{b} Margin: *8 m*
^{c} Margin: *9 m*	^{d} Margin: *7 m*
^{e} Margin: *8 m*	^{f} Margin: *9 m*

and G ff and ye ffr^ds aforementioned had A meeting that
night concerning them^a:

And on ye 24: day G ff taking his Leave with Henry
Jackson & T K: and other ffr^ds hee passed from thence out
of Yorkshire to Jno ffrettwells att Stainsby in Darbyshire^b,
who with his wife and ffr^ds there wayes greatly Rejoyced to
see him there, It being ye Count^ry where G ff: had Lived
formerly, when truth first broke forth, and L: ff: passed
from G ff: at Tho: Stacys, and went to Shiffield, where hee
had a meeting y^t day:

And on ye 25: day (a meeting being appointed to be there)
ffr^ds from severall parts resorted to ye meeting and L ff w^th
severall ffr^ds from Shiffield came along with him: to y^e
meeting, the meeting done G ff took Leave with ffr^ds and went
that night to Skeggby^c, where severall ffr^ds came to visit him:

And on ye 26: day G ff: and L ff passed from thence
thorow the Country to Nottingham, to Jno Recles house^d
who when G ff first declared truth in that town, hee was y^e
Sheriff^e; and cast G ff in prison, at wch time hee was Convinced, and so Remaines a good ffr^d to this day^f and that
night G ff had a meeting there and also on ye 27: day G ff
had a publick Meeting at ffr^ds meeting place: wch was
peaceable.

And on ye 28: day G ff: (taking Leave with ffr^ds) passed
from thence accompanyed with severall ffr^ds to Jno: ffoxes^1 at
Wymeswould in Leicest^rshire^g (and L ff pased with severall
ffr^ds that night to Wm Smith's^2 at Syleby^h) and G ff: had a
meeting at J: ff^s: that night:

And on ye 29 day G ff: passed from thence to W: S: house
also, and it being ye first day of ye week, hee went to ffr^ds
meeting (wch was very Large, and the Townes people hearing
y^t G ff: was there many of them came to ye meeting and
heard ye truth declared peaceably: ye meeting done G ff:
Returned to W S^s where many ffr^ds came to visit them, (to
witt G ff & L ff).

thence G ff passed accompanied with severall ffr^ds to

---

^a Added in another hand: *& Reconciled y^m*   ^b Margin: *10 m*
^c Margin: *3 m*   ^d Margin: *12 m*
^e First written *mayor* and altered to *Sheriff* in another hand.
^f Inserted above the line: *& his familly*
^g Margin: *7 m*   ^h Margin: *4 m*

Leicester on y[e] 30: day: to Samuell Brownes[a1]: and there were many ffr[ds] out of y[e] Country, come to y[e] town that day: (to bee att A horse ffayr the next day:) and G ff had a meeting with ffr[ds] y[t] night.

So y[e] 1st day of y[e] 3: mo[th] being y[e] fayre day, severall ffr[ds] came to visit him. So in y[e] Evening G ff: passed with W[m] Wells[2] to his house at Knighton[b], and had a meeting there that night.

(And Leo ffell passed from G ff at Leicester: to Syleby again: and on y[e] 2: day passed to a men and Womens meeting at ......in y[e] vaile of Bever: and from thence to Clausson in y[e] Vaile, where hee had a meeting on y[e] 3: day thence passed after the meeting to Leicest[r] and on y[e] 4: day passed to a meeting at Little freatling, and on y[e] 5 day hee passed to Hinkley and on y[e] 6: day L ff mett G ff at Badseley.)

And from Knighton aforesaid, G ff passed on y[e] :2: day thorow Leicest[r] and so thorow y[e] Country to Swanington to Edw: Mugletons[3] house[c] where hee had A meeting y[t] night: and It being very Rainy weath[r] G ff: stayd there on y[e] 3[d] day:

And on y[e] 4 day G ff (accompanyed with severall ffr[ds]) passed thence to Samuell ffrettwells[4] att Hartshorne in Darbyshire[d] who wth his wife and ffr[ds] were glad that G ff was come to visit them: so hee had A meetinge there y[t] day.

And on y[e] 5: day G ff (accompanyed with S: ff) passed thorow y[e] Country to Henry Sidon's[5] in Badsley in Warwickshire[e]: where severall ffr[ds] came to visit G ff.

Thence Hee passed on y[e] :6: day being y[e] first day of y[e] week, to Badsley meeting[f], w[ch] was very Larg, and peaceable: there was a Justice who Lived not farr off: had threatned that he would come and break up y[e] meeting, but none did appeare to disturb, the meeting done G ff: went to a ffr[ds] house: (many coming to visit him) and in y[e] Evening took Leave with ffr[ds] and passed to Rich: Baals[6] at Whittenton[g], where severall ffr[ds] came to visit him.

[a] Margin : *5 m*	[b] Margin : *1 m*
[c] Margin : *12 m*	[d] Margin : *4 m*
[e] Margin : *10 m*	[f] Margin : *2 m*
[g] Margin : *2 m*	

Thence G ff passed on y[e] 7: day to Nathaniel Newtons[1] at Hartshill[a], where severall ffr[ds] mett G ff: with whom hee had good service.

And from thence G ff: & L ff: passed on y[e] 8: day thorow Non Eaton, & by high Cross & thorow Ulcetrop & Litterworth, and so to Jn[o] Eliots[2] at north Killworth[b] in Leicest[r]-shire, where ffr[ds] came to visit G ff y[t] night.

So from thence G ff: passed on y[e] 9: day: thorow Husband bozworth and Marsdon, & Harborrough: at w[ch] places G ff visited ffr[ds] and so passed to Tho: Allens[3] at Dingley (and L ff stayed at Harborrough, and had a meeting that night) and a meetinge was appointed to be at Dingley[c], on y[e] 10: day: wch was accordingly, and was very Large: and when G ff had declared y[e] truth some houres (viz[t]) opening to y[e] people how that Christendome, was gone from y[e] pure Religiõ: y[t] is undefiled, there was a man who in a furious manner; went out of y[e] meeting, crying, I deny It: the meeting being done: G ff: and L ff: passed with Thomas Charles[4] to his house at Adingworth[d].

And on y[e] 11: day, passed from thence to Northampton[e] to Benania Bradshaws[5] house, where severall ffr[ds] came to visitt G ff: y[t] night, and on y[e] 12: day G ff: went to Edw. Cowps[6], where severall ffr[ds] came to him, amongst whom hee had much service, and L ff passed y[t] day to Wellingborow, where hee was at ffr[ds] meeting on y[e] 13: day being y[e] first day of y[e] week: And G ff was at ffr[ds] meeting at Northampton y[t] day w[ch] was very Larg and peaceable.

And on y[e] 14: day aft[r] G ff had taken Leave with fr[ds] hee passed from thence, (accompanyed with E: Cowper) to James Brearlys[7] at Ony in Buckinghamshie[r][f] where he mett L ff) and severall ffr[ds] came to visit G ff y[t] night:

And on y[e] 15: day G ff passed from thence accompanyed wth severall ffr[ds] to Williã Richardsons[8] at Turvy in Bedfordshire[g]: where there was A meeting appointed to bee y[t] day: and there came ffr[ds] from severall parts to y[e] meeting, and It was very Larg. W[m] Dewsberry mett G ff there y[t] day: so y[e] meetinge being done, (and G ff had stayed a while w[th]

[a] Margin: *4 m*	[b] Margin: *15. m*
[c] Margin: *7 m*	[d] Margin: *3 m*
[e] Margin: *9 m*	[f] Margin: *7 m*
[g] Margin: *3 m*	

ffreinds) hee passed from thence wth W: D: to his sonn Jno: Rushes[1], at Kemston Hardick^a: where G ff stayed with Wm Dewsberry ye most part of ye 16 day.

So from thence G ff: & W D. and L ff: passed in ye Evening, thorow Amtill, and so to Tho: Gambells[2] at Pullockshill^b, where severall fr^{ds} came to visit them.

And from thence G ff: and L ff: passed on ye 17: day (W: D: accompanying them pt of ye way: and then they parted,) and G ff passed to Luton and from thence passed to Markett-Street^c to George Sawyers[3] att Markett street: And on ye 18: day (severall ffr^{ds} ffr^{ds} came to visit G ff:) and hee & L ff passed to Kensworth to a meeting wch was larg & peaceable, ye meeting done Returned to Market-Street ag^n and after they had stayd a while passed from thence thorow Redburne, and so to Edmond Howes[4] at St Albaines^d, where severall ffr^{ds} came to visit G ff.

And on ye 19: day after G ff had visited ffr^{ds} he passed from thence thorow South-Mims & thorow Barnett, where G ff visited ffr^{ds} and so passed to Ann Haylys at Guttershedge in Hendon in Middlesex^e.

And on ye 20: day being ye first day of ye week: there was a Larg meeting, being severall ffr^{ds} from London, as also Wm Mead, who not knowing of G ff^s being there greatly Rejoyced to see him: and after the meeting Tho: Rudyard[5] came to visit G ff and Returned to London ag^n: that night: and G ff stayed at Hendon on ye 21st day.

And on ye 22: day William Mead and his wife, & G. W^s wife & A P wife, came to Hendon In Wm Meads Coach for G ff: so he went along with them to Wm Meads house at Highgate^f: where severall ffr^{ds} from London came to visit him:

And on y^e :23: day G ff passed to London^g with Wm Mead & his wife: and It being ye 4 day of the week they went to ye meeting at Gracious Street: the meeting being done, and G ff had stayed a pretty while amongst ffr^{ds} at Gerrard Roberts, hee went to Jno Elsons, where many ffr^{ds} came to visit him:

^{a} Margin: *5 m*	^{b} Margin: *6 m*
^{c} Margin: *10 m*	^{d} Margin: *9 : m :*
^{e} Margin: *17 m*	^{f} Margin: *4 m*
^{g} Margin: *4 m*	

And on ye 24: day Wm Penn and severall ffr^ds came to
G ff there: and hee & W P. passed, to a meeting of suffrings
at Elis Hookes[1] house in Lumbard street: ye meeting done
G ff went to Edward Manns.

And on ye 25: day G ff: passed to another meeting at
Elis: Hooks ye meeting done Returned to E: M^s: ag^n.

And on y^e :26: day G. W: and A P: & W P. and Charles
Marshall: came to G ff att E M^s: so from thence G ff passed
to Jane Woodcocks[2] & Martha ffish^rs at ye Savoy: and on y^e
27: day being ye first day of ye week: G ff was at a large
meeting there:

And on y^e :28 day W P came to G ff, and they passed to
A mens meeting at E. H^s ye meeting done hee went to A
P^s: and aft^r a while Returned to E. H^s ag^n with severall
ffr^ds: and hee went that night to James Claypooles,

And on y^e :29: day aft^r severall ffr^ds had been with G: ff:
hee and Marg^t Rouse: took boat at London for Puttney,
and took horse there, and passed to Kingston^a to M R^s house,
and on ye 31st day: James Strutt, and Robert Linton and
Iss: Yeamans came from London to G ff and there was A
Meeting y^t day:

And on ye 1st of y^e :4: mo^th G ff and ye ffr^ds aforementiond
took boat at Kingston & passed to London^b: G ff went to
Gerard Roberts house where severall ffr^ds came to visit him,
So from thence hee passed to Edw: Mann's: and on ye 2^d
day G ff stayed at E. M^s and ffr^ds beinge come from all pts
of the nation and from beyond Seas, (in order to bee at y^e
yearly Meeting[3]) there came many to visit G ff: and he
stayed at E: M^s on ye 3rd day also.

And on ye 4: day G ff: went to a second dayes Meeting
at E: H^s and y^t night hee Returned to E M^s ag^n.

And on ye 5: day about y^e :4: hour in ye morning G ff
went to ye yearly meeting at Devonshire house: the Meeting
done hee went to Willm Welch[4] house, and in ye afternoon
(ye meeting being appointed to bee at ye Bull and Mouth)
G ff went to It: and at night when the Meeting was done:
hee went to Rebecca Traverse house:

And on y^e :6: day there came one Dr Moor[5] to dispute^c
with G ff: and after G ff went to a publick Meeting at y^e

---

^a Margin: *10 m*   ^b Margin: *20 m by wat^r*
^c First written *dispute* and altered in another hand to *discourse*

Bull & Mouth wch was Large and peaceable: the Meeting done G ff with severall ffr^{ds} went to Franciss Camfields, and y^t night hee passed to Wm Welches: where there was A meeting on y^e :7: day of ffr^{ds} Concerning R B: and W R:[1]

And on ye 8th day G ff: wth severall ffr^{ds} passed to James Claypooles and from thence passed with Wm Penn to A meeting of ffr^{ds} where there was some out of ye most Counties in the Nation: ye meeting done G ff: went to Jno Elsons:

And on ye 9 day after that hee had spent some time amongst severall ffr^{ds} there: hee went to Edward Manns where there was a Select Meeting: the meeting done G ff with severall ffr^{ds} took Coach and passed to James Strutts in Rattcliff and on the :10: day G ff went to ffr^{ds} Meeting wch was Large and peaceable: ye meeting done hee Returned to James :S: house ag^n where severall ffr^{ds} came to visit him that night:

And on ye 11: day G ff & severall ffr^{ds} took boat, & went to London; and G ff: went to ye 2: days meeting at E: H^s: ye meeting done he went to E. M^s.

And on y^e :12: day G ff: went to anoth^r Meeting at E: H^s: the meeting done hee went to Tho: Rudyards and aft^r he had spent some time wth ffr^{ds} hee passed to Jane Woodcocks & M ff^s:

And on y^e :13: day G ff went to visit Coll: Kirby[2] (who had been a psecuto^r of ffr^{ds}) and now he was very Loving to G ff: and then G ff Returned to J W & M ff^s ag^n where severall ffreinds came to him y^t day, about truths affaires.

And on ye 14: day G ff passed to a meeting at Ellis H: and after it was ended, hee went to E. M^s:

And y^e :15: day hee spent in ye service of truth amongst ffr^{ds}: and in ye Evening hee went to Wm Gosnells[3]: and then went to visit Councello. Corbett[4], who was very glad to see G ff: so hee Returned to E M^s ag^n.

And on y^e :16: day severall ffr^{ds} came to G ff: at E. M^s: and in ye Evening hee with severall ffr^{ds} went to Ann Traverse house at Horseley downe in Surry: and on ye 17: day (being ye 1st day of the week) G ff went to ffr^{ds} meeting wch was Larg and peaceable:

And on y^e :18: day G ff: passed from A: Traverses to y^e :2^d dayes meeting at E: H^s and when ye meeting was done hee went to Ezekiell Woolies, where severall ffr^{ds} came to him Concerning truths affaires.

And on ye 19: day G ff: took Leave of ffr^{ds} there and went to visit severall ffr^{ds} and passed to William Welch's where there came severall ffr^{ds} to visit him.

And on ye 20: day G ff and Jno: Burnyeat and severall other ffr^{ds} passed from London wth Willm Penn in order to go to his house: and as they went thorow Surry they hearing of a Quarîly meeting (not farr out of ye way) went to It: and after ye meeting was done they passed on their Journey to Willm Penns at Worminghorst^a in Sussex: where severall ffr^{ds} came to visit him.

And on y^e :24: day being y^e :1st day of ye week G ff: passed from thence to ffr^{ds} Meeting, and aft^r ye meeting Returned to W P^s. ag^{nb}.

And on ye 28: day G ff was at a Larg meeting at W: P:^{s} which was very peaceable.

And on ye 8th of ye 5th moth being ye 1st day of ye week: there was A meeting at W P:^{s} where there was many ffr^{ds} as also severall hundreds of people: at wch meetinge G ff: & Isaac Pennington[1], and Geo: Keith[2], & Jno Burnyeat & W P: declared ye truth, all being very peaceable.

(And ye week following W. P: and G K: & R Barclay & S: Smith[3]: had meetings up & down ye Count^{r}y amongst ffr^{ds} many people coming in to meetings Insomuch that ye Justices threatned to psecute ffr^{ds}) And on y^e :12: of ye 5: moth there was a Meeting at W P:^{s} where there was severall hundreds of people and ye Informers had told ffr^{ds} y^t they would come to ye meeting: and severall ffr^{ds} when they came to ye Meeting told G ff what ye Informers had said: and hee bidd them bee Chearfull, & not fear them so G ff walked into ye Garden, and when ye Meeting was settled: hee went Into ye meeting where severall ffr^{ds} did declare ye truth: aft^r whom G ff declared some houres : but no Informers did appear, and so ye Meeting ended in peace.

(And while G ff and Jno Burnyeat were at W P:^{s} they did Answer A book of one Roger Williams[4] of New England, Printed in 1676; which Book was writt agst G ff: and ffr^{ds}:)

And on ye 13: day G ff and J Burnyeat: taking Leave

^{a} Margin : *40 m* ^{b} Margin : *4 : m*

with W P:ˢ family, passed from thence with Stephẽ Smith
in order to go to his house: W. Penn accompanying G ff:
12: miles in his Coach, and then they took Leave: W P:
Returning home again, and G ff passing on to Stephẽ Smiths,
at Worpleton in Surry*a* where severall ffrᵈˢ came to visit him:
and on yᵉ 14: day also:

And on yᵉ :15: day being yᵉ first day of yᵉ week there
was A Larg meeting, where G ff: and J B: were, and when
ffrᵈˢ Meeting was done at Gillford (wᶜʰ was not farr from
thence) many came to visit G ff: and also on yᵉ 16: day.

And on yᵉ :17: day G ff: and J B: & S. Smith passed from
thence in order to go to Kingston, visiting Wᵐ Lilly[1] and
his wife, and ffrᵈˢ In the way, and so passed to Margᵗ Rous's
at Kingston: where G ff had much service amongst ffrᵈˢ:

And on the 18: day G ff: and J B, and severall other
ffrᵈˢ passed to Putney, and took boat there to London: G ff:
visiting severall ffrᵈˢ went yᵗ night to Jnᵒ Elson's: where
there came many ffrᵈˢ to visit him.

And on yᵉ 19 day G ff: passed to Edw: Manns: to prepare,
for his Journey Into Holland[2], and to put his Bookes and
Epistles, and things Concerning truths account in order
before hee went and there came severall ffrᵈˢ to visit him:

And on yᵉ :20: day G ff was at E Mˢ wᵗʰ severall ffrᵈˢ
Concerning truths affaires: and in yᵉ afternoone hee passed
to a Meetinge at wheeler Street: the meeting done hee
Returned with severall ffrᵈˢ to E Mˢ again, where many ffrᵈˢ
came to visit him, and take their Leave wᵗʰ him that night.

And on yᵉ :21ˢᵗ: day: G ff accompanyed wᵗʰ severall ffrᵈˢ
takinge Leave with ffrᵈˢ at London passed from thence
thorow yᵉ Country to Jnᵒ ffurlyˢ[3]: at Collchestʳ in Essex*b*.

And on yᵉ 22: day being yᵉ first day of the week G ff
went to ffrᵈˢ Meeting, wᶜʰ was Larg & peaceable: yᵉ Meeting
done Returned to J ffˢ: again, where there was A Larg
Meeting that night.

And on yᵉ 23: day G ff was at a Large womens Meeting
there:

And on yᵉ 24: day G ff accompanyed with severall ffrᵈˢ
{passed}*c* to John Vandewalls[4] in Harridge*d*, where severall
ffrᵈˢ came to visitt G ff yᵗ day:

a Margin : *20 : m*   *b* Margin : *43 m*
c Insertion in another hand.   *d* Margin : *18 m*

And on y^e :25: day W P: Jno: ffurly, Geo: Watts, and
W^m: Taylcoat^1 came to G ff: and Geo: Keith, and Robt
Barclay & G K^s wife^2, and Iss: Yeamans: and after Dinner
they went all to Meeting: where ye Lord by his overcoming
Refreshinge powe^r opened many mouths to declare and
minist^r his Everlastinge truth, and to prayse and glorify
him. the Meeting done they returned to John Vandewall's
where they took leave of ffr^{ds} there p^{r}sent, that is to say of:
Giles Barnadiston^3 Rob: Duncom^4: Geo: Wetherley^5: Sam:
Bolton, and Job: Bolton^6 wth others: who accompanyed them
or mett them there: and so ffr^{ds} went on board ye packett
boat about ye 9: hour in ye eveninge on ye 25: day afors^d
being ye 4: day of ye week: and sett sayle about ye 1st hour
in ye morning on y^e :26: day: and had a fair winde that day:
and y^e :27: day was clear & calme, till y^e :4: hour in the
afternoon, and then there was a fair fresh Gaile, wch carryed
the packett Boat to within one League of ye shoar, and then
It was calme ag^n so they cast Anchor y^t night: and they lett
down A little boat; & two men wch belonged to ye shipp
carryed W Penn, & R B: to Shoar, and so they went to y^e
Citty of Briell but It being in ye night the Gates were shutt,
y^t they could not gett in: and there being no houses wthout
ye Gate they went to a fish^{rs} Boat and Layd there till y^e
morning and they went into ye Citty, where they mett with
Benjamin ffurly and A. Sonnemans^7, & Simon Johnson^8: who
were come wth A Boat from Rotterdam to meet ffr^{ds}.

So that being y^e :28: day they afores^d drew Anchor in y^e
morning, and set sayle; and p^{r}sently wee mett A pleasure
boat and three young men y^t Lives wth B ff: coming to fetch
G ff and ffr^{ds} to Shoar, so they went to shoar, where ffr^{ds}
were waiting for y^m. So they went to ye Briell: and after
they had Refreshed themselves, took boat Immediatly for
Rotterdam where wee Arived about ye 11th: hour that day^a.
All being well praysed & honnoured bee the Lord, who
preserves all that truly feares him severall Dutch ffriends
came to visit them y^t day {at B. F^s:}

And y^e :29: day being ye first day of the week G ff and
ye ffr^{ds} y^t came with him were at two Meetings at B. ff^s:
house whith^r resorted a great Concourse of people: some of
them being of ye Considerablest note of the Citty, and they

^{a} Margin: *From England to Rott^{r}dam 96: m*

heard the truth declared peaceably: and as yᵉ English ffrᵈˢ
did declare, Ben: ffurly & Jnᵒ Claus did Interprett to yᵉ
Dutch people, and yᵉ meeting ended in peace: And 30ᵗʰ day
:G: ff: and W: P: and the rest of ffrᵈˢ spent in visiting ffrᵈˢ
and people, severall of ffrᵈˢ dined and supped at two great
mens houses, yᵗ day:—where they had good oppertunities,
for yᵉ service of truth:

And the 31: day G ff: passed from B: ffˢ: to A Sonnemans
and aftʳ dinnʳ G ff: Jnᵒ ffurly Wᵐ Penn, & Wᵐ Taylcoat
& Iss Yeamans: (and also Jnᵒ Roeloffs and Jan Claus who
came {from Amsterdam} on purpose to conduct them thither)
took boat there and passed to Delf Citty and walked thorow
yᵉ Citty, and took boat againe to Leiden Citty*ᵃ* and ffrᵈˢ
Lodged at an Inn yᵗ night:

And on yᵉ: 1ˢᵗ: of: 6ᵗʰ moᵗʰ: ffrᵈˢ took Boat and passed
to Harlem Citty*ᵇ*, where they went to a ffrᵈˢ house whose
name was Dirk Klasen[1], and after a while they went to yᵉ
meetinge (wᶜʰ G ff & W P had appointed) where yᵉ Lord
gave them a blessed oppertunity, not only with Respect to
ffrᵈˢ but many sober baptists, and proffessoʳs yᵗ came in, and
abode in yᵉ Meeting to yᵉ end: the meeting done ffrᵈˢ went
to Amstʳdam*ᶜ*, in Company with severall ffrᵈˢ of that Citty
and of Alkmaer: and G ff and W P: Jnᵒ: ffurly & W T. I Ŷ
went to Geertruyd Dirk-nieson's[2] where severall ffrᵈˢ came
to visit them yᵗ night.

And on yᵉ 2: day G. K. and his wife and R B. & B ff.
came to Amstʳdam: and It being yᵉ day of ffrᵈˢ generall
Meetinge there were severall ffrᵈˢ from Rotterdam, and out
of the Country, and G ff & W P were at yᵉ meeting: where
they opened many things to ffrᵈˢ concerning the good order
of yearly and Quartʳly & Monthly men and Womens meetings.
Jan Claus. & B ff. Interprettring to the people[3]:

And on yᵉ :3: day G ff: and yᵉ ffriends aforemetioned,
were at a Larg meeting at G. D: Nˢ: whither Resorted
severall sorts of professors, and heard the truth declared
peaceably, many things being opened yᵗ day Concerning
Salvation: B: ff: and J: C: Interpretinge.

And after yᵉ meetinge ffrᵈˢ went to Jnᵒ: Lodges[4]: and
Returned to G. D. Nˢ: where there was a more select meeting
then yᵉ day before:

ᵃ Margin : *18 m*   *ᵇ* Margin : *14: m*   *ᶜ* Margin : *9 : m*

And on y⁰ :4 : day ffrᵈˢ had anothʳ select meeting : att wᶜʰ
select Meetings G : ff : and ffrᵈˢ Established a yearly Meetinge,
and Quartʳly Meetings to bee at Amsterdam : and Monthly
meetings also. for ffrᵈˢ in Holland & ffriesLand.

And on y⁰ 5: day being the first day of y⁰ week there
was A Larg meeting, whithʳ resorted a great Concourse of
people : and that of severall opinions, as Baptists, Seekers,
Socinians, Collegions, & Brownists¹ att wᶜʰ meeting G ff :
W P: G K: R: B: declared the Everlasting truth opening
many things Concerning y⁰ Estate of man in y⁰ fall : as also
by what way man and Woman might come into y⁰ Restoration by Xᵗ Jesus yea even y⁰ mysterie of Godlyness, & y⁰
mystʳy of Iniquitty were Layd open : B ff and J C Interpret-
ting : so y⁰ meeting ended in peace.

(And on y⁰ :6 : day W P: G K: R B: B F: took leave with
ffrᵈˢ at Amsterdᵐ and sett forward {on} their Journey
towards Germany where they travelled many hundred mile,
and had good service for y⁰ Lord, as may be seen at Larg in
W Pˢ Journall²:) and that day G ff visited ffriends : and there
came three Baptists to discourse with him, so after they
had discoursed a little, they went away, being well Satisfyed :

And on y⁰ 7: day G ff: visited ffrᵈˢ : and that day hee
writt a Lettʳ to y⁰ Princesses Elizabeth³ᵃ which Isabell
Yeamans gave to her : when shee and Geo: Keithˢ wife went
to visit her.

And on y⁰ :8 : day G ff took leave wᵗʰ ffrᵈˢ and hee and
Jhon Claus (who was his Interpretʳ) took boat there and
passed to Buycksloott, thence to purmerent : and after they
had Refreshed themselves a little at an Inn : took Wagan
there and passed thorow y⁰ Beamstʳ to Alkmaer Cittyᵇ, to a
ffrᵈˢ house whose name is Willem Willems⁴, and G ff had a
meeting there yᵗ night.

And on y⁰ 9 day there was Anothʳ Meeting : and severall
proffessoʳs came to y⁰ Meeting, and all was peaceable : y⁰
meeting done G ff went to visit some ffrᵈˢ and then took
boat to Russlenborrow, and took boat there to —— thence to
Hoornᶜ y⁰ Chief Citty in North Holland, and went to an
Inn and lodged there yᵗ night.

ᵃ Here follows a line and a half of dashes.
ᵇ Margin : *30 : m*   ᶜ Margin : *14 m*

And on y^e :10: day G ff: and J : C: took wagan there and
passed thorow a Long town called the Streik, and so to y^e
Citty of Encusen^a: and took Shiping there at y^e :9th hour
that Morning for ffriezland: and passing by Staverin Citty
in ffriezland, and by Malquiring, and Hindalopen Landed at
Worckum^b before ye 2^d hour, and after wee had Refreshed us
a little at an Inn: took Wagan, and passed upon the high-
banck of ye ffrozen Seas, where two ffr^{ds} was coming wth a
Wagan to meet G ff and ffr^{ds} so wee passed together to
Mackum, where ffr^{ds} stayed A while at an Ale house, and
then went In the ffr^{ds} wagan to Harlingen ye Chief seaport
towne in ffriezland, and G ff: went to a ffr^{ds} house whose
name is Hesell Jacobs[1], where severall ffr^{ds} came to visitt him
y^t night:

And on ye 11: day G ff writt A pap to all y^t persecute ffr^{ds}
for not observing their fast dayes.

And y^e :12: day being the first day of ye week G ff went
to ffr^{ds} meeting, and there came many professo^{r}s to ye Meeting, and were very Civill: the meeting done G ff went to
H : J^s : ag^n : and there came a Calvinist to ask G: ff: some
Questions: and discourse wth him, and hee went away well
satisfyed: and then there came A preach^r of ye Collegions to
discourse with him, and hee was satisfyed also. And y^t night
G ff had a meeting with ffr^{ds}.

And on y^e :13: day after G ff had visited some ffr^{ds} and
all was clear, hee wth severall ffr^{ds} took boat: & passed
thorrow ffranceker Citty & so by Don-Rijp & Dinum to
Leuwerden^c, (wch is ye Chief Citty in ffriezland and y^e
place where ye Prince Liveth) and G ff went to Sijbran
Dowes[2] house y^t night:

And on ye 14: day before y^e :5: hour in ye morning, G ff:
and severall ffr^{ds} took Boat ag^n and passed to Dockum Citty,
and walked thorow ye Citty and took boat to Strobuss, w^{ch}
is ye outmost part of ffriezland, and when ffreinds had
Refreshed themselves at A Comisers house took boat there
and passed into Croning Land, and so to Groningen Citty
wch is the Chief Citty in the province, and one of ye Magistrates of that Citty came with us from Leeuwerden, and
G ff: had some discourse wth him, and hee was Loving. and
G ff and ffr^{ds} walked neare two Mile thorow ye Citty, and

^{a} Margin: *8 m* ^{b} Margin: *18 m* ^{c} Margin: *12 m* took boat for Delfsiell, and wee passed thorow a town called Appingdalem: (where there had been a great horse ffay^r y^t day, It being in ye Evening there came many drunken officers hushinge into ye Boat, and they being very Rude, G ff Exhorted them to fear ye Lord, and to take heed of Solomons vanities) and wee Landed att Delfsiel Citty, It is ye outmost fronteer place or Cijtadell of ye states of ye Low Countries It lyes upon ye River Embs: and as ffr^{ds} passed thorow ye Guards, they Examined Jhon Claus wheth^r or no G ff was not a Militia Souldie^r and hee told them no: and aft^r a few words ffr^{ds} went to an Inn It being y^e: 10: hour at night, wee travelled y^t day by draw Boat: 50: English miles.

And on ye 15: day ffr^{ds} took shipping there, and passed over ye River Embs to Embdon Citty^a, (being a place where ffr^{ds} have been cruely psecuted, and banished,) and G ff went to an Inn: where he stayed & dined, with some men y^t understood English: and he had a fine time wth them and they were Lovinge and Jan Claus went wth his wife to her ffath^{r}s, who Lives in ye Citty: and after diner G ff went thither they being desirous to see him: thence hee and J C walked thorow ye Citty to ye place where ye wagan should have mett them y^t they had hyred (so they went to an house, where severall ffr^{ds} came to them, wth whom G ff had a meeting) and when we had waited a great while and ye wagan did not come, they sent to see what was ye matter: and ye waggen m^r sent word y^t hee durst not lett his wagan go, because that ye Bishopp of Munst^{r}s Souldiers were all up in ye Count^{r}ys and hee was afraid that ye horses would be taken out of ye wagan: and so G ff: and J C Returned to his ffath^{r}s house ag^n and at night G ff went to his Inn^b.

And on ye 16: day G ff and J: C: took shippinge at Embden: ^{c}(and I being sick stayed at Embden at Jhon Claus wifes ffath^{r}s whose name is Claes Jhon foeldricks[1]: and G ff took an Account of his passages wch are as followeth till hee came to Embden again:)^c {&} wee passed upon the River Embs to a town called Lei{e}r in East ffriezland^d, where

---

^{a} Margin: *9 m*
^{b} Margin: *at this Embdon I E. H lay sick till my dear m^r G F had been at Fredrickstat:*
^{c}...^{c} This parenthetic sentence has been crossed through.
^{d} Margin: *15: m*

there Liveth a ffr^d y^t hath been banished from Embden; and
wee went to an Inn and hyred a Wagan and passed thorow
a princes Country to a Garrison town called Strikehusing^a,
where the officers Examined us: thence wee went to Deteren^b
where wee hyred anoth^r wagan, and passed thorow y^e
Country to anoth^r Garrison town where we were Examined,
and thence wee passed to Ape in ye King of Denmarks
Country: and when ye officers had Examined us, wee went
to an Inn, where wee Lodged that night: and this day wee
mett ye Earle of Oldenborrough[1], going to ye treaty of peace
at Lembachie:

And ye next day wee hyred a wagan, and passed thorow
ye Country to ye Citty of Olden borrough^c, (being a famous
great place latly burned downe, and but few houses stand-
inge), and we hyred a wagan in ye suburbs, and passed into
ye Citty where the Souldiers Examined us: and wee passed
thorow ye Country to Dellmenhurst^d: and after ye souldiers
had Examined us, wee went to a Burgamast^r who Kept an
Inn: and Lodged there that night: ^eand I (to witt G ff)^e
declared to him and ye people ye truth: and warninge them
of ye day of ye Lord.

And ye next day wee hyred a Wagan and passed to Breman^f
(wch is a Statly Citty) and after ye Souldiers and officers had
Examined us, wee went to an Inn at ye Signe of ye Swann,
where wee hyred A Wagan and passed to a wat^r at Overde-
lend^g, and took boat there to ffish^r hold^rh where hee spoke the
truth to ye people: Exhorting them to fear ye Lord: and
so wee hyred a wagan and travelled in ye Bishopp of Munst^rs
Country[2], to Clostersevei^i; (the people of this Country are
dark: and as I passed thorow ye Countrys, I declared y^e
Lords truth to them and warned them of ye great and
notable day of ye Lord: exhorting them to soberness & to
mind ye good sp^t of God:)

So It being night wee gott fresh horses to travell all
night, and wee sett forward, but when wee had gone a little
way, It was so dark and rained so exceedinge hard, y^t wee

---

^a Margin: *:12: m*   ^b Margin: *:8 m*
^c Margin: *24 m*   ^d Margin: *24 m*
^e...^e Altered to read: *and G ff*   ^f Margin: *7 m*
^g Margin: *6 m*   ^h Margin: *6 m*
^i Margin: *24 m*

turned back again, and went to an Inn and gott some fresh
strow and lay upon It till break of day: and then wee took
wagan, and passed thorow yᵉ Country to yᵉ Citty of Buxte-
hudeᵃ, where the souldiers stricktly Examined us twice (and
without yᵉ Citty there was a great fayr of sheep and Geese
on yᵉ first day) So after wee had dined wee took wagan, and
passed to A town where wee hyred a Boat and passed to
Hamborrough Cittyᵇ: and after wee were Examined wee went
to a ffrᵈˢ house It being yᵉ first day of yᵉ week, I had a good
& glorious Meeting: and there was a Baptist teacher and his
wife, and an Eminent man of Sweedland and his wife, and
all was quiett blessed bee yᵉ Lord: and his seed was sett over
all: ᶜAnd at Hamborrough there was A Woman that had
spoken agˢᵗ mee in Jnᵒ: Parrots¹ time, and shee hath been
plagued ever since, though shee never saw mee before: [and
shee likned her selfe like unto Miriam yᵗ spoke against
Moses²] and I doe beleive yᵗ yᵉ Lord will forgive herᶜ. And
Jan Claus went to hyre A wagan: and I had none but him
with mee then hee being my Interprettʳ And yᵉ next day
wee took wagan, and passed thorow yᵉ Country to Ellemen-
son, where wee dined at an Inn, and then took wagan, and
passed to a Garrison town of yᵉ K. of Denmarks: where yᵉ
officʳs Examined us: thence we passed by yᵉ monument of yᵉ
Earle of Ranseuny³: and so to yᵉ Citty of Itsehoᵈ: where wee
Lodged at an Inn yᵗ night: And I exhorted yᵉ people of yᵉ
house to soberness, and to mind yᵉ feare of yᵉ Lord.

And so wee hyred a wagan and travelled thorow the
Country to Hoghenhorne, and wee went to an Inn, where
wee dined wᵗʰ one of yᵉ Councell of ffredrickstat, and I
declared yᵉ truth to him, and yᵉ people and they were
Lovinge; thence wee passed thorow yᵉ Country to A River
called Hyder and took boat there and went to ffredrickstatᵉ
Citty: (where there is A fine Meeting of ffrᵈˢ) so wee went
to Willᵐ Pooles⁴, where severall ffrᵈˢ came to us: and wee
had a meetinge yᵗ night: (And this was yᵉ furthest place yᵗ
we did go {to} and wee were very weary, It having beene

ᵃ Margin: *24 m*   ᵇ Margin: *18 m*

ᶜ...ᶜ This sentence has been crossed through, and the words *And I...her*
have a further line through them; but in the margin are the words, in
another hand: *note this to stand*

ᵈ Margin: *·42 m*   ᵉ Margin: *44 m*

much Raine for severall dayes, and ye wagans were open, so that wee were wett thorow o^r Clothes: but ye Lord made all well blessed bee his name for Ever:

This Citty is in the Duke of Hollistyne Count^{r}y[1] and hee would have banished ffr^{ds} out of ye Citty[a] and Country, and sent to the magistrates of ye Citty to do ye same, but they said they would lay down their offices before they would do It, for they (meaning ffr^{ds}) had come to y^t Citty upon matter of Conscience, and not long after ye Duke himself was banished out of ye Citty & Country by the King of Denmark, and at p^{r}sent hee Remaineth at Hamborrough. and ffr^{ds} do enjoy their Liberty, and are of good Report amongst ye people: both in Citty and Count^{r}y: and at this Citty [b]I sett up[b] a men and Womens Monthly meeting[c]: and on the first day of ye week wee had A Meeting, and the Lords power, seed, and Life was sett over all; though there came Rough Spiritts, but the power of ye Lord bound all, and at y^t Citty I had A discourse with A Levite y^t was a Jew, and hee was much Confounded; in all that hee said, and was Lovinge: and I went to his house (where there was a Jew an Israelite and his family) and hee shewed me ye Talmud and many other Bookes: So after I had had another meeting wth ffr^{ds} wee left ffr^{ds} in good order and came away (and at this Citty there was a Baptist Priest[d] wch had Reproached and belyed ffriends: and Jan Claus and two other ffr^{ds} went to the house where hee Lodged and layd his Lyes & slanders upon his head to his shame, and to ye clearing of truth) All things being cleare wee took wagan and passed thorow ye Country[e] and Lodged at an Inn y^t night: I enquired of ye man if there were any tender people in ye town y^t feared God, or any that had A mind to discourse of ye things of God: but hee said, there were few in that towne.

And wee took Wagan there: and passed to Pennanbark, and went to an Inn, where wee dined and then tooke wagan againe and passed to Hamborrough[f]: and after ye Souldiers had examined us wee went to a ffr^{ds} house, and wee were

[a] The word *Citty* is struck through.
[b]...[b] These words are crossed through.
[c] Inserted in another hand: *was sett uppe*
[d] First written *Priest* and altered to *teacher* in another hand.
[e] Margin: *42 m*   [f] Margin: *44 m*

very weary being up those two mornings before the 3ᵈ hour, and till yᵉ 11ᵗʰ hour at night (And Jnᵒ: Hill[1] had been sick in a Ship bound for Amstʳdam 40 mile off Hamborrough, where hee had layd two weeks wayting for A winde, and he hearinge that I was in yᵉ Country was come thither to meet mee, and to go {a}long with mee): So yᵉ next day after wee came, wee had a very good meeting, and all was peaceable: the meeting being done I had a discourse with an Eminent man yᵗ was a Sweed (who was banished out of his own Country for his Religion) and after yᵗ I had a discourse wᵗʰ a Baptist; concerning Baptisme and Sacrament: And so all being clear, & ffrᵈˢ in good order the next day being yᵉ 31. of yᵉ :6: month I and Jnᵒ: Hill & J: Claus took boat at Hamborrow, and passed to A Custom house[a], and wee took boat agⁿ there to a Citty in yᵉ Duke of Lewenbrogs[2] Country[b] where yᵉ Souldiers Examined us, and then had us to yᵉ maine Guard, who stricktly Examined us, and when they see wee were no Souldiers, they were Lovinge: and then wee went to an Inn, and hyred a wagan, and travelled till yᵉ 11: hour at night: and in yᵉ way wee hyred a boy to guide us, yᵉ waters being out, and so we passed to a great watʳ and It being deep yᵉ man was fain to waid, and I drove yᵉ Wagan thorow, and then wee came to A Bridge, part of wᶜʰ yᵉ horses broke, & one of yᵉ horses fell Into yᵉ water and yᵉ wagan remained upon yᵉ part of yᵉ Bridg yᵗ was left: (It was yᵉ Lords mercy yᵗ yᵉ wagan did not Runn into yᵉ Brook) so after a while they got yᵉ horse out, and hee lay a while as if hee had been dead: but at last they gott him up, and putt him into yᵉ wagan, and Layd yᵉ planks over yᵉ brook and gott safe over: and after yᵗ wee came to a great watʳ where wee hyred two men to guide us thorow to the Bridge, and yᵉ water, being so deep and yᵉ Stream so strong yᵗ It carried one of yᵉ horses off his Leggs from yᵉ other, and hee was going down yᵉ stream, and I called to yᵉ Waggoner and to yᵉ men yᵗ held yᵉ wagan with Cords, that It went not down yᵉ Stream, to pluck yᵉ horse up to them; and so yᵉ wagenʳ plucked yᵉ horse to him, and hee Recovered his Leggs, and at length thorow much difficulty wee gott to yᵉ Bridge, It being in the night, and so wee passed to Bormorhaven[c], where yᵉ wagener dwelt: It being yᵉ 11ᵗʰ hour in yᵉ night: so wee gott A little

---

[a] Margin: *9 m*   [b] Margin: *9 m*   [c] Margin: *22 m*

strow and lay upon It till ye 4th hour in ye morning on y^e
1st day of y^e :7: moth and then wee hyred A wagan and
passed throw ye Country^a to—A markett town, and wee went
to an Inn and I declared ye Everlasting truth to them that
were at ye Inn: [and they were very Loving: Insomuch y^t y^e
Woman of ye house said, that ye words y^t I spoke to her:
shee could not forgett, if shee did not see mee again this
five yeares:] so wee took boat (and there being severall
people, I warned them of ye day of ye Lord y^t was coming
upon all flesh, and told them y^t God was come to teach his
people himselfe, and Exhorting them to Righteousness, and
to turne to ye Lord,) so wee passed in ye Boat aforesaid to a
town^b where wee hyred A Wagã: and went In it to the
Citty of Breman, where ye Souldiers & officers did Examin
us, and then wee went to an Inn, and Stayed a while (and
ye Lords power was over ye Citty, and his seed Reigned and
Reigneth, though my Spiritt suffred much in that place for
ye peoples sake) and there wee hyred a wagan and passed
thorow ye Count^{r}y to Keby^c, and wee went to an Inn, &
Lodged there y^t night: (& I spoke the truth to ye man of y^e
house and hee was Loving).

And on y^e :2: of y^e :7: moth: being ye first day of the
week at ye 5 hour in ye morning, wee passed to Oldenborgh
Citty, wch was a Lamentable sight to see such a great Citty
burned downe, so wee went to an Inn, and there was
Souldiers and people drinking and playing at Shuffleboard[1],
and ye Shopps were open & they were traiding one with
anoth^r though It was ye first day of ye week: and I was
moved to speak to ye people ye truth: and to warn them: of
ye Judgments of God: and they were Civill: but I was
burdened with their wickednes: and many times in mornings,
noons, & nights, and as I travelled, I spoke to ye people y^e
truth, and warned them of ye day of ye Lord, and Exhorted
them to ye Light, and sp^t of God.

And on ye 3: day wee hyred a boat, and passed out of y^e
K: of Denmarks Country, unto a princes Country[2], so we
came to a towne^d, and went to an Inn where wee hyred a
wagan, and we passed by ye princes Garrison who Examined
us, and after wee passed thorow many great Waters to Leier^e.

^{a} Margin: *18 m* ^{b} Margin: *6 m* ^{c} Margin: *16 m*
^{d} Margin: *8 m* ^{e} Margin: *12 m*

And on y^e :4th: 7th mo^th wee took boat at Leier about y^e
4 hour in ye morninge and came to Embden Citty^a againe
(where I left Edward sick:) thorow many difficulties, so I
and Jno: Hill went to an Inn, where wee dined: and after
dinner I went to ye march^t house where I left Edw: and had
a good meeting in ye family at night:

^bI take a Journall again as followeth^b.

On y^e :5: day G ff & Jno: Hill, and J: C: with severall
oth^r ffr^ds took Shipping at Embden, and passed to Delfsiel^c,
where ye Souldiers Examined G ff: and then had him up to
ye maine Guard and after they had examined him wee went
to an Inn, where we stayed a while: and there came a ffr^d y^t
Liveth at Delfsiel to visit G ff: they have banished him from
Embden often, and hee being a Gold smith had a house and
a shopp in ye Citty so hee went ag^n and at last after that
they had Imprisoned him and fedd him with Bread and Water,
they took his goods from him and banished him & his wife &
Children out of ye Citty[1], and ye friends afore mentioned took
boat and passed to Groningen Citty^d and walked about a
mile thorow ye Citty wth Cornelius Andries[2] to his house:
who hath suffred much Imprisonm^t, and banishm^t at Embden.

And on ye 6: day G ff: had a good meeting in ye Citty,
whith^r Resorted severall professo^rs and all was peaceable:
ye meeting done ffr^ds Returned to Cornelius house ag^n and
after they had Refreshed themselves a little took boat and
passed to Strobuss, and took boat there to Dockum^e, and
Lodged at an Inn y^t night.

And on ye 7: day in ye morning G ff: and ffr^ds took Boat
and passed to Leeuwerden^f ye cheif Citty in ffriezland: and
they went to A ffr^ds house where they mett with Thomas
Rudyard and Issabell Yeamans, who was come from Amsterdam to meet G ff: and there was a precious meeting y^t day
at Sybran Dowes house: and after ye meetinge G ff had some
discourse with some y^t were at ye meeting, who had been
formerly Convinced. (y^t day Jno: Hill went to Harlingen,

---

^a Margin: *15 m*   ^b...^b This is heavily scored through.
^c Margin: *9 m*   ^d Margin: *15 m*
^e Margin: *27 m*   ^f Margin: *12:*

and so to Amsterdam) and so G ff and ye ffr^ds stayed there y^t night:

And on y^e :8: day G ff: and T: R: and J Claus, and I: Y: took boat and passed down ye River to ye Lake of Hempen Sarmer, and so passed by ye Lake Lugmer, and so to a town called Anderiga, thence wee Sayled thorow ye Lake of Whispoole, so wee came to A towne called Gardick^a in the night, and went to an Inn.

And on ye 9 day being ye first day of the weeke, G ff was at ffr^ds meeting wch was very large many of ye townes people came in and were civill, ye meeting done, ffr^ds went to ye Inn, and Refreshed themselves a little, and then went towards ye Boat, and as they were going, severall of the townes people gathered together at A Bridg and G ff: declared to them the Lords truth, and they were Civill: and then ffr^ds passed Into ye Boat and came back again to ye Citty of Leeuwerden^b, It being ye 11: hour at night, ye Gates were shutt, so wee lay in ye boat till ye morning on y^e :10: day and then they went to ye Gate but there being a man Killed in ye City y^t night, It was long ere ye Gates were opened so y^t people could not pass in and out: so ffr^ds went to anoth^r Gate, and went In to the Citty to A ffr^ds house, and after they had Refreshed themselves took boat, and passed thorow ffrancker Citty to Harlingen^c to Hesell Jacobs house: where there came dear Wm Penn y^t night to G ff: who came from Amst^rdam on ye first day at night; after hee had been {at} a Larg Meeting there y^t day, being come two or three days before out of Germany.

And on y^e :11: day G ff: and W P: was at A men and womens meeting there, and settled one to bee every month: And after ye monthly meeting was done, there was A publick meeting, whither resorted severall Socinians, and Baptists and a Doctor; and A Priest ^dof physick^d: and after G ff had declared ye truth to ye people ye priest stood up & prayed to God to prosp y^t doctrine, and hee had heard nothing but truth; and hee being A Lutheran^e priest, was to preach that night at ye Steeplehouse; so hee went away, and made

---

^a Margin: *27. m*   ^b Margin: *27 m*   ^c Margin: *12 m*
^d...^d These words are crossed through. They should, doubtless, have followed the word *Doctor*
^e First written *Collegion*

a Short Sermon and came to ye meeting {place}^a ag^n but
when hee came ye meeting was done, all being very peaceable,
and so G ff and W P. & T R Returned to Hesell Jacobs
where at night G ff had A meeting with ffriends and the
Docto^r of phisick y^t was at the Meetinge came to discourse
with Wm Penn, wth whom hee had good Service: and y^e
priest sent wth the Docto^r to Rememb^r his Love to G ff: and
that hee might tell him that hee left preaching halfe an hour
sooner then hee used to doe, y^t hee might come to ye meeting
ag^n but It seemes since his hearers questioned him for what
hee had said in ye meeting, (some of them being there) but
hee stand{ing} by his words, they were not satisfyed: but
have complained to ye rest of ye priests of y^t Citty, and told
them what hee had said in ffr^ds meeting: who were to call
him and hear his Reasons.

And y^t night W P took leave with G ff and ffr^ds hee and
Jan Claus passed from Harlingen on ye 12: day, in order to
go to Leeuwerden to a meeting, and then travell into anoth^r
pt of Germany: to visit some tend^r people: And this day
after G ff: and T. Rudyard and I. Yeamans had taken Leave
wth ffriends took shipping there for Amst^rdam at y^e : 9th hour
y^t Morninge: and came to Harbour at Amsterdam^b, about the
first hour in ye night. but ye Gates being shutt ffr^ds lay on
board till ye morning: on y^e :13: day and then took Boat &
passed to Geertruyd Dirk-Niesons, where severall ffr^ds came
to visit G ff y^t day[1]:

And on ye 16: day being ye first day of ye week G ff was
at ffr^ds meeting and there came many to ye meeting, and were
very Civill, hearing ye truth declared severall houres by G ff:
and Jno Roeloffs did Interprett:

And on ye 17: day aft^r y^t Tho: Rudyard & Issabell Y. had
taken Leave wth G ff: and ffr^ds took boat for Rotterdam, and
then to go by ye packett for England[2]:

And on y^e :19: day G ff was at a Larg meeting, there
being severall professo^rs and all was peaceable.

And on ye 20: day G ff and severall ffr^ds tooke boat at
Amsterdam, and passed to Lansmeer in Water Land (in w^ch
towne there is above 100: Bridges) and G ff had a good
meeting there y^t day where there came severall professors,
ye meeting done G ff and ffr^ds Returned to Amst^rdam.

---

^a Insertion in another hand.   ^b Margin: *54 m*

And on ye 23 day being the first day of ye week G ff was at ye meeting, and there came many professo^{r}s and heard ye truth declared:

And on ye 25: day G ff: was at ffr^{ds} Mo^{ty} Meeting^1.

^{a}Here followeth a Relation of two meetings by G ff^{a2}.

On ye 26: day there beinge a fast thorow all ye provinces of Holland^b I was moved to stay A meeting the same day at Amst^{r}dam, whither resorted many great persons as also a great Concourse of people: and ye Lords power was over all: and I was moved to open to them y^t no man by all his witt and study, nor by Reading history in his own will, could declare or know ye generation of Christ, who was not begotten by ye will of man, but by ye will of God: and this was Largly opened. And then I did open to them ye true fast from ye false, shewing them y^t ye Christians Jewes, and Turks, were out of ye true fast: & fasted for strife and debate, and ye bands, and fists of Iniquitty was over them, and oppression; and with that they were smiteing one another: & ye pure hands were not Lifted up to God: and how that they did all appeare to men to fast, and did hang down their heads for a day like a Bull Rush. wch fast God did not accept, and in y^t state all their bones were dry, and when they called upon ye Lord hee did not Answer them, neither did their health grow, for they kept their own fast and not ye Lords, And therefore all were to come & keep ye Lords fast: & this with many other things were opened to ye astonishm^t of ye fasters. and all parted in peace, ye Lords power being over all.

And I having appointed a meeting at Harlem Citty to bee on ye 27 day I and Peter Hendrickz and Geertruyd Dirknieson took wagan and passed thither^c, where wee had A Blessed meeting, severall professo^{r}s and a high^d priest of ye Lutherans were at ye meeting: and ye priest sat and heard G ff declare some houres and then hee went away and said that hee had heard nothing but what was according to ye word of God: and desired that ye blessing of the Lord might

^{a}...^{a} These words are crossed through but the *Relation* follows.
^{b} *of Holland* is crossed through.
^{c} Margin: *9 m* ^{d} *high* struck out.

rest upon us and our Assemblies. Geertruyd did Interpret for mee, so yᵉ Meeting did end in peace and in yᵉ power of the Lord others Confessing to yᵉ truth, saying, they had never heard things so plainly opened to yᵉ understanding before.							G ff:

So G ff and ffriends went to Dirk Klasen's house, where they stayed that night:

And on yᵉ 28: day G ff and ffrᵈˢ took wagan to Amsterdamᵃ: to G: D: Nˢ: and yᵗ day there came a great high Priest; who had belonged to yᵉ Emperor of Germany, and anothʳ Germã Priest to speak with G ff: so after they had spoke wᵗʰ him hee declared yᵉ truth unto them (and they were tender) opening unto them how they might know God and Christ, & his Law & Gospell: and shewing them that they should never know It by Studying, nor by philosophy, but by Revelation, and Stillness in their minds by yᵉ spirit of God: and they were well satisfyed, & so passed away.

And on yᵉ 30 day being yᵉ first day of yᵉ week G ff: was at the meeting, and declared the truth some houres, severall professoʳs were at yᵉ meeting and were very Civill not Leaving the meeting till It was ended. and there was a Doctoʳ of Polland at yᵉ meeting who was banished out of his Native Citty for Religion, (and yᵉ Citty shortly after was burned) and after the Meeting hee came to G ff and hee had some discourse wᵗʰ him, and hee was very tender & loving.

And on yᵉ 3ᵗʰ: 8ᵗʰ: moᵗʰ: G ff was at ffrᵈˢ meeting, where hee declared yᵉ truth severall houres, and Jnᵒ Roeloffs did Interprett and the meeting ended in peace.

And on yᵉ :7: day being yᵉ first day of yᵉ week, W. Penn, G. Keith, Ben: ffurly, and Jan Claus, came to Amsterdam, (W P. having been travelling in Germany since hee parted wᵗʰ G ff at ffriezland aforementioned) and It being yᵉ first day of yᵉ week ffrᵈˢ had a Large Meeting, and all was peaceable.

And on yᵉ :9: day in yᵉ Eveninge ffriends had a dispute with one Gollanus, who is {one of}ᵇ yᵉ greatest Baptist in all Holland, and many professors were there.

And on yᵉ :10: day G ff: and W P: & G K. were at ffrᵈˢ Meetinge whither there resorted many hundreds of people,

ᵃ Margin: *9 m*					ᵇ Insertion in another hand.

and there were also at ye Meeting an Earle, & a Lord, & many Eminent persons, who were very Loving (and a Brother of one of ye Lords of ye states, Invited G ff to dinner, and hee had good service with them) and ye ffr^{ds} aforementioned declared in ye Meeting & B. F. & J: C: did Interprett and all was quiett till W P^a had ended ye Meeting, & then there were some priests y^t made an opposition, but W P. understanding stood up again, and answered them, to ye great satisfaction of ye people: who were much affected wth ye severall Testimonies, y^t they had heard declared: And after ye Meetinge there came severall professo^{r}s to G. D. N^s. wth whom G K & B ff: had much discourse in Latine: [And y^t day there was A Woman at ye Meeting, who had gone : 14 : Yeares on her hands, & her knees, and thorow ye wonderfull hand & Arm of ye Lord was this year^b Restored to her strength again, and can go very well: & It being such a miracle, y^t many people goes to see her: and after ye Meeting shee came to G ff: and since her Recovery, so many people going to se her, and shee not keeping Low in her mind, and in ye fear of ye Lord, was much runn into words, so G ff spoke much to her, Exhorting her to fear ye Lord, and telling her y^t if shee did not keep Low and humble before ye Lord, y^t shee would bee worse then ever shee had been, and ye woman was much tendered, & confessed to ye truth:]

And whilst G ff: was at Amsterdam hee writt severall Bookes[1] in Answer to Priests, and others to ye Clearing of truth, ye names to whom ye Answers are, Is as followeth: as also severall Lett^{r}s to ffr^{ds} and others. Y^e dates when they were written: Imprimus on y^e :18: day 7 moth G ff witt An Epistle to Friends at Danzik and on y^e :19: 7th month Hee writt A warning to ye Citty of Oldenborgh, It being lately burned down: and hee writt a warninge to ye Citty of Hamborrough: And on ye 21: of 7th moth G F writt an Epistle to ye Embassadours y^t were treating for peace at Nimwegen[2]. And on ye 29: day :7: moth G F gave forth a book to ye Magistrates and priests of Embden citty, shewing them their unchristianity in persecuting ffr^{ds} And on ye 1st: 4: & 5: & :6: days of ye 8th month G ff: gave forth Bookes in

---

^{a} The initials are written in the form of a monogram.
^{b} *this year* is crossed through.

Answer to Priests, and others, at Hamborrough, and Danzik:
to ye clearing of truth:

^aSo now I will proceed on ye Journall^a.

On ye 11: day of ye 8: month W Penn, and G. Keith had
a dispute again with Gollanus Abrahams[1], at Corneliss Roeloffs[2] house, and G ff was there, and many ffriends & professors: and Gollanus was much confounded, so after ye dispute
ffr^ds Returned to Gertruyd Dirknieson's, and ye most of
ffriends in ye Citty came thither, and G ff: and W P: took
their Leave with them:

And so they and B. ffurly took wagan and passed to Leiden^b
citty, to an Inn, where they Lodged y^t night, and ffr^ds mett
with a German y^t was partly convinced, and on y^e :12: day
hee Informed ffr^ds of an Eminent man y^t was enquiring after
truth: so ffr^ds went to him and G ff spoke to him, and hee
owned all y^t hee said, being a serious man: (And about 2 or
3: days after W Penn and B. ffurly, went to visitt another
Man who Liveth near Leiden, and hee hath been ye Generall
to ye King of Denmark, and hee & his wife are very Loving,
and Received ye truth with Joy:) so after ffr^ds had visited y^t
man aforesaid, they passed to ye Hage, wch is accounted y^e
greatest village in ye world, and ye Prince of Orange Court
is there, and ye two Dewitts[3] who were ye greatest common
wealths men in Holland, were Murdered there, and their
flesh was sold: so G ff and W P. and B: F: went to one of
ye greatest^c Judges[4] in Holland, and had pretty much discourse wth him, hee is a wise tender man, & after many
objections, & queries, hee was satisfyed, and they parted
with great Love; and then they went to speak wth some
other sober people, but they did not meet with them: so
ffr^ds took Wagan, and passed to Delf Citty, and there took
boat & passed to Rotterdam Citty^d to Benjamin ffurly's house,
and after supper W P. went to his Lodging at Areant Sonnemans:

And ye 13: day G ff: visitted ffr^ds in y^t place, And y^e
:14: day being ye first day of the week {G ff & W. P.} was
at ffr^ds Meeting at B. ff^s and they declared ye truth severall

---

^a...^a These words are crossed through.   ^b Margin: *25. m*
^c *greatest* crossed out.   ^d Margin: *18 m*

houres, and B F did Interprett: and there were many pro-
fesso^{rs} at ye meeting & all was peaceable.

And on ye 15: & 16: days G ff gave forth a book for
ye Jewes, for when hee was at Amsterdam, hee sent to them
to have A discourse wth them, but they refused. and there
came severall ffr^{ds} from Amst^rdam to take their leave wth
G ff & W P & G K. before they went to England.

And on y^e :17: & :18: G ff was at B F^s hearing severall
bookes and papers, wch hee had given forth (being Tran-
scribed) and on y^e :18: day at night W: P: came to G ff:
there, and ye King of Denmarks Resident[1] {came} along wth
him, W P: had visited him in Germany, so hee hearing y^t W P
was at Rotterdam, came to see him, being Convinced:

And on y^e :19: day G: F: and W P: & G K: and
Geertruyd Dirknieson, were at a large Meeting at B: ff^s:
where there was many ffriends, as also a great concourse of
people; and all was peaceable. and after ye Meeting was done
ffriends had a perticular Meeting.

And on y^e :20: day, G ff: passed from Ben: ffurly's about
ye 7th hour in ye Morning, to Symon Johnson's where W P
Mett him, and severall ffr^{ds} came to take their Leave wth
English ffriends:

And so G ff: & W P: and G. K., & Geertruyd & her
Children took boat there for ye Briell (in order to take
ye packet boat that day for England) being accompanied wth
Ben: ffurly, and Peter Hendrickz & Symon Johnson, &
Corneliss Roelofs & A Sonemans & his Brother[2], and the
Resident aforementioned and they arrived at the Briel about
y^e :11: hour, but ye packett being not come: ffr^{ds} went into
ye Citty to an Inn; and waited for It, but it not coming
before night ffr^{ds} Lodged at ye Inn's.

And on y^e :21: day being ye first day of ye week, G ff:
and W P: & G K and Geertruyd & her Children took Packett
Boat, being accompanied wth ye ffr^{ds} aforementioned, who
did not leave them till ye Shipp was under sayle {about y^e
10: hour} and so parted in Love and unity: and there was
about 60: passengers, in all[3]; and wee had Contrary winds,
and a great storm ye most pt of ye time, wee were at Sea &
ye Vessell was so exceeding Leaky, y^t two pomps went both
day & night, and 'tis beleived they pompt more water then
twice ye vessell full. But ye Lord alone who is able to make

ye stormy winds to cease, & ye Raginge waves of ye sea, to
bee calm, yea & to raise them, & stopp them at his pleasure,
hee alone preserved us, praised bee his name for ever: And
ffr^{ds} had a fine time on shipp board, wth a Collon[1] and severall
Eminent psons, who were very kind and Lovinge.

So wee arrived at Harrwich^a on ye 23: day about ye 7 hour
at night being :3 days and two nights at Sea: And ffr^{ds} went
to Jno Vande-Walls house: and aft^r supper W P. and G K.
went to Lodge at other ffr^{ds} houses and G ff: and ye rest
stayed at Jno V-W. So all ye ffr^{ds} y^t went over to Holland
wth G ff: were come to England again, (vizt) Jno ffurly
senior & William Taylcoat, & Robt Barclay, & George
Watts, & G. Keiths wife and Issabell Yeaman's, were all
come (at severall times) before.

And y^e :24: day W P & G. K. took horse & passed to
Collchester: and there being no Coaches att Harrwich, G ff
& ye rest wayted for one from Collchest^r to have gone y^t
day also: but there came none before night so G ff had
a meeting at J: V-W^s & about y^e :9: hour at night Jno
ffurly Junior[1]; came thither, who expected to have mett ffr^{ds}
as hee came: and hee went to ye post masters house, who
keeps Stage Coaches, and he being not at home, J: ffurly
spoke to his wife, who is an unreasonable woman[2], for hee
bidd her 40^s for a Coach to Collchest^r (It being but about :18
mile) & shee would not under :50^s: so hee came and
accquainted ffr^{ds} and afterwards went & bidd her ye same
mony again, before they sought for another Conveniency, but
shee Refused It: so then ffr^{ds} ordered a man to go in y^e
morning to a ffr^d about a mile & a halfe off: to desireing him
to come wth his wagan in ye morning, & they would Satisfie
him: so ffr^{ds} went to Bedd, and then this woman sent word
p two Messengers y^t shee would take their Mony. and to see
what time ye Coach must bee ready: so they sett down 7th
hour and ffr^{ds} gott ready in ye morning, (being ye 25 day)
and wayted Long at ye Fr^{ds} house, but ye Coach came not;
so they went severall times to know ye Reason, but could
gett no Answer till y^e :11: hour and then wth many excuses,
shee said y^t her man told her ye horses were not able: But
ffr^{ds} knew her design, It being A good wind for ye packett

^{a} Margin: *From Rotterdam 96: m*

boat coming in, shee expected passengers to London; and so thought to gett more gain:

And then G ff tooke horse to ye ffr^ds house aforementioned, & ye Rest of ffr^ds went on foot, and they hyred his wagan, and Layd some Straw in It, and so went to Collchest^r and in ye night ye post boy from Harwich overtook ffr^ds so they asked him if there were many passengers for ye Coaches, and hee told them there were but 6: and some of them took horse, so shee was right served for her Coveteousness & deceit. and friends gott very well to Collchester, many ffr^ds from thence came to meet them in ye way; W P: & G. K. had wayted for G ff: till y^e :4: hour in ye afternoon, and then passed away: and G ff went to Jno ffurly's senior, and Geertruyd Dirk-Nieson and her Children to Stephen Crisp's: ffr^ds Rejocying greatly to see them:

And ye 26 and 27: days G ff spent amongst ffriends in truths affaires.

And on ye 28 day being ye first day of ye week: ffr^ds from severall parts came to ye Meeting hearing of G. F^s being there, and It was thought (the meeting was so large) y^t there was about: 1000 people: and G ff declared ye truth severall houres, and all was peaceable, ye meeting donc hee returned to Jno Furly's again.

And on ye 29: day G ff: was at a larg men and Womens meeting there: ^aand after ye Meeting, and on ye 30: day G ff had meetings wth ffr^ds and people that were gone from fr^ds and there was :10: men and women y^t hath been gone from friends this many yeares, and G ff: Reconciled them to ffr^ds again^a.

And on ye 31: day G ff took leave with ffriends, all things being in good order, and passed from thence accompanied with Jno ffurly & Geo Weatherly thorow Colen, where they visited severall ffr^ds and so passed to Halsted to William Bunting's[1] house^b; where severall ffr^ds came to visit G ff y^t night.

And on y^e :1st of ye 9th mo^th there was a large meeting ffr^ds from severall pts being there, and G ff declared ye truth severall hours and after ye meeting returned to Wm Buntings, where there was A meeting y^t night.

^a...^a These words have two lines drawn through them cross-wise.
^b Margin: *10 m*

And on ye 2: of ye 9 mo^th after G ff had spent some time with ffr^ds hee took horse and passed from thence accompanied with Giles Barnidiston and John Child & his wife[1]: thorow ye Country by Brantree, where they mett Wm Bennett[2] and so passed together to Jno Child's house at ffellsted: where G ff stayed, and G B: and W B: passed on further to bee at A meeting ye next day.

And on ye 3 day severall ffr^ds came to visitt G ff.

And on y^e :4: day being ye first day of ye weeke G ff passed from thence to a monthly Meeting att Salling [and Gowen Lowry[3] & Samuell Newton[4] and Tho: Rudyerd came to him there, and a large & peaceable Meeting there was blessed bee ye Lord: ye Meeting done G ff passed to a ffr^ds house, whose name is Wm Crow[5], where hee stayed y^t night & G. L. & S. N. stayed there Likewise:

And on ye 5: day G ff and G. L. & S. N. passed to Jno Childs, and spent y^t day in ye service of truth.

And on ye 6 day G L and S N: passed to a Monthly meetinge at Steben: And G ff stayed at a men and womens Meetinge {there}.

^a And on y^e :7: day G ff: stayd at J: C^s: at a meeting, of some differences depending betwixt 2: ffr^ds.^a]

And ye 8th day G ff tooke leave with ffriends & passed from thence accompanied with Jno Child to Chelmsford, to a ffr^ds house: where G ff had a meeting y^t night: and there being many ffr^ds prisoners they came to ye meeting;

And ye 9: day G ff & :J: C: passed thorow ye Country to London, where ffriends greatly Rejoyced at G ff^s Returne: and hee went to E. Manns that night:

And y^e :10: day G ff stayed at E M^s where many ffr^ds came to visit him.

And ye 11: day being ye first day of ye week G F went to Grace-Church-Street-Meeting, where hee declared ye truth and ye glory of ye Lord Sorrounded ye meetinge and all was peaceable. praysed bee ye Lord.

And ye 12 day G ff passed to ye mens meeting at Elis Hookes house^b, & after ye meeting hee returned to E M^s And ye 13 day G ff went ag^n to E. H^s where hee gave forth severall Letters and Epistles to ffr^ds and at night hee passed

---

^a...^a This paragraph is crossed out.
^b The word *house* is struck through and *chamber* substituted.

to James Claypooles: And ye 14 day also hee gave forth severall paps to ffriends beyond sea: & severall ffr^{ds} came to visitt him: and at night hee and W P passed to Rebecca Traverse house, where there was a meeting y^t night: after which G ff returned with J: C to his house ag^n.

And ye 15 day G ff passed to E Hookes to ye meetinge of suffrings, ye meetinge done G ff & W P stayed there a while, and then G ff went to Job Boltons where severall ffriends mett him: and hee passed y^t night to Benjamin Antrobus house: And ye 16 day after G ff had spent ye fore noon in writinge about truthes affairs: hee passed to E H^s: to a meeting after which hee passed to Wm Penn at his Lodging at Wm Hages[1] (where they writt Lett^{r}s into Germany) and hee stayed there y^t night.

And ye 17 day after some time G ff went to B. Antrobus house, where hee stayed till night, and then went to visitt old Jno Bolton[2], and so went to Jno Elson's, where divers fr^{ds} came to visit him.

And ye 18 day being ye first day of ye week G ff was at ye meeting there, which was Large & peaceable, blessed bee ye Lord.

And ye 19 day after G ff had spent some time amongst ffr^{ds} hee passed to Devonshire house to a Womens Meetinge, after wch hee went to E M^s.

And ye 20 day G ff passed to a nother Meeting at Devonshire house: And then returned to E M^s where ffr^{ds} came to visit him.

And ye 21st day G ff went to Grace-church-street meeting, where hee declared some houres, and all was peaceable ye meeting done hee went to Gerrard Roberts where hee stayed with some ffr^{ds} till night, and then hee went to Tho: Rudyards, and went from thence accompanid with G. R. & T R to give Councelor Corbett a visitt, & so passed to Ben: Antrobus house where hee & W P & W G[3] had a meeting with Jno Raunce[4] & Charles Harris.

And ye 22 day hee passed to a meeting at E H^s: after which hee went (visitinge ffriends) to Jane Woodcocks & Martha ffishers, where there was severall ffr^{ds} (hearing of his comeing thither) came.

And ye 23 day G ff tooke Coach to E: Manns, and aft^r a while hee & Jno Osgood and ffra: Moore[5] & Tho: Rudyard

and severall other ffriends passed to Shakle-well, where they
had a meeting touching ye schoole for young women:

Y^e Meeting done G ff & friends returned to London & y^t
night G ff had a meeting at E M^s concerning ffriends suffrings—And ye 24 day[1] severall ffriends came to visitt G ff:
and y^t day hee passed to Ezekiell Woolies, And ye 25 day
(being ye first day) G ff went to ye meeting at wheelerstreet,
which was large & peaceable after which hee returned accompanied with Wm Mead and his wife & severall ffriends to
Ezekiell Woolies again.

And ye 26: day G ff passed to ye mens meetinge at E H^s
after wch hee and D. Barclay[2] went to E M^s and many fr^ds
came to him there.

And ye 27: day after G ff: had spent some time amongst
friends hee went to Ben: Antrobus house where G W & A P.
mett him: & they spent some time there in ye service
of truth. And ye 28 day G ff passed to a mens meeting at
E. H^s after wch hee went with Wm Mead to his house—and
after dinner hee Returned to a meeting at E: H^s: after w^ch
hee passed to Rebecka Traverse house to visit Tho: Moore[3]
& hee Lodged there y^t night.

And ye 29 day hee passed to a meeting at E H^s after which
he passed to E. M^s:—

And ye 30 day G ff went to Ben: Antrobus where G W
& W G mett him about Jno: Penymans[4] booke—And on y^e
: 1st day of y^e : 10 : month G W came to him Likewise and at
night G ff took Coach, and passed to James Strutts at
Rattcliff.

And on ye 2 of ye 10: mo^th (being ye 1st day) G ff was at
ye meeting at Rattcliff^a, where there was Wm Penn and W^m
Mead & A: Parker: & many ffriends from London, and all
was peaceable.

And ye 3 day G ff accompanied with James Strutt passed
to London, and after G ff had visitted severall ffr^ds hee passed
to E. M^s—and y^t night G ff & Isaac Pennington & Wm Penn
& severall ffriends had a meeting there concerning...........^b

And ye 4 day G ff went to Ann Traverse house at Horsley-
downe, & was at y^t meeting y^t day: & hee Lodged at A: T^s:

---

^a Margin: *2 m*
^b Originally dashes filled out the line, later the words *S Bolton & M : p :*
were written over the dashes. See 80. 5.

house:—And ye 5 day hee returned visiting fr^{ds} to B: Antrobus, where hee gave forth divers Lett^{r}s & Epistles to fr^{ds} in Jamaica & Nevis: & Maryland[1].

And ye 6: day G ff went to ye mens meeting at E: Hookes, after which hee went to James Claypooles, where severall ffriends came to him, and at night hee with W P passed to Ben: A^s: and y^t night G ff returned to J Claypooles ag^n.

And ye 7 day G W & A P & W G & W P: and divers ffriends came to him at J: C's: where he abode y^t day—And the 8 day hee passed from thence to Jane: Woodcocks & M: ffishers—

And ye 9 day being ye first day G ff was at ye meeting there:

And ye 10 day G ff went to ye mens meeting at E: H^s after wch he went to E M^s: And ye 11 day G ff passed to Ben: A^s thence to ffran: Camfields where W P & severall ffr^{ds} came to him. and that night G ff went to Jno: Elsons —And stayed there ye 12 day in ye service of truth—And ye 13 day G: ff passed to J: woodcocks and M F^s: where severall fr^{ds} mett him, and y^t night hee was at a meeting there—

And ye 14 day after he had spent some time amongst ffriends, hee took Coach & passed to Sarjeunt Birkets[2], where hee stayed y^t night.

And ye 15 day G ff passed to Jno: Rouse house at Kingston^a[3].

And ye 16 day being the first day of ye week G ff went to ffr^{ds} meetinge, after which hee returned to Ann ffielders: And ye 17th: day hee stayed there: and at night went to Jno Rouse's.

And ye 20 day G ff went to ffriends monthly meeting and after ye men & womens meeting: was done, there was a publick meetinge after which hee returned to Ann ffielders with Gilbert Laty, and y^t night Tho: Robertson[4] came to G ff: And ye 21st day G ff Returned to Jno Rouse's.

And y^e :25: day A. P. & G W: and W P: and G. R. & J. Claypool, & severall ffr^{ds} came to visitt G ff: And y^e: 26: day G ff & G W & his wife and A P. & Ezek: W: & his wife & J R: went to James Claypooles: and after dinner returned to J R^s again:

---

^{a} Margin: *10 m'*

And ye 30: day being ye first day of ye week G ff went to fr^ds meeting which was peaceable: & after ye meeting returned to A. ffielders, & so passed y^t night to Jn° Rouses: And so G ff stayed at Kingston :15: dayes and in y^t time his booke in Answer to Roger Williams was examined, & prepared ready for ye press. that being done on ye 31: day hee took Leave with Jn° Rouse family and ffriends in Kingston and passed away accompanied with Jn° Rouse thorrow ye Country to Longford^a, where there was A men and womens meeting After which G ff took horse and passed with severall ffr^ds to Uxbridge^b to Tho: Tanners^1 where many ffr^ds came to visitt him.

And on ye 1st of ye 11 ^mo: after divers ffriends had been with G ff: hee passed with severall to Chalfont in Buckinghamshire and they went to an Inn, and G ff went to visitt friends, and so took horse and passed to Isaac Pennington's at Amersham Woodsyde:

And on ye 2 day G ff and Isaac Pennington & his wife and Christo: Tayler^2 passed to Tho: Ellwoods att Hunger hill to a Mo^ly men & womens meetinge: after which they returned to I. P^s againe.

And on ye 3 day G ff and Isaac P. and his wife & Chris: T: passed to a meetinge at Amersham, where G ff: declared some houres, and all was peaceable after which they returned again^c.

And ye 4 and 5 days G ff stayed at I P^s and many ffriends resorted thither about truths Concerne.

And ye 6 day being ye first day of ye week G ff & Isaac P. and his wife passed to ye meeting at Jourdans where Alex: Parker mett them, and there was a blessed (large) meeting y^t day, ye meeting done they passed to I P^s again^d,

And that night Bray Doiley^3 came to Isaac's.

And ye 7 day they all passed to Tho: Ellwoods^e, where there was a meeting wth Jn° Raunce & Charles Harris concerning differences^4, and y^t night G ff lodged at Tho: Ellwoods and Isaac and his wife passed home: And ye 8 day Stephen Smith and Wm Penn came to G ff there, and they passed to Geo: Salters^5 at Hedgerly^f where there was a Large meeting y^t day and David Barclay & Jn°: Swinton^6 & Geo: Keith and

Issabell Yeamans mett G ff there: so ye meeting done G ff and severall ffr^ds passed to Henry Tradeawayes^a1 and ye 9 day I: Y: and G. K: tooke leave wth ffr^ds and passed to D B & J S: who were all going toward Scotland, so after G ff and A P: and W P & S S: & C T & I. P. had drawn up a pap to p^rsent to ye King^2 about ffr^ds affaires Alex: P: and W: Penn passed towards London, and all ye rest of ffr^ds passed to Wickham^b where they mett wth Geo: Whitehead & Wm Gibson and Wm Welch and there was A meeting that night, after wch ffr^ds went to their Inn again And ye 10: day ffr^ds had a private meeting wth Jno Raunce and C. Harris G ff Lodged att Jeremiah Stevens^3 y^t night.

And ye 11: day G ff tooke leave wth Isaac Pennington & his wife (who Returned homeward again) and G ff and S: Smith & John Archdale passed to Turvie Heath^c to Eliz: Wests^4, who being an old woman, was glad to see G ff, and there was A meeting y^t night: And ye 12 day G ff and Stephen Smith passed to Henly in Oxfordshire^d where they mett G Whitehead & W Gibson and Wm Welch & Chris: Tayler: and after G ff had stayed some time amongst ffr^ds hee and G W & W W passed to Tho: Curtis^5 house at Cassum^e And ye 13 day being ye first day of ye week they passed to ffr^ds meeting at Reading where they all declared ye truth ye meeting done ffr^ds passed to Geo: Lambells^6, and at night ye towne fr^ds resorted thither and there was A meetinge.

And y^e :14: day there was another Meeting concerning truthes affaires, and that day Wm Welch returned home, and G ff and G: Whitehead & Wm Gibson & C: Tayler passed thorow ye Country to Oar^f to Wm Austills^7: and y^e :15th: day G ff and ye ffr^ds passed to a meeting wch they had appointed, and they Lodged at W: A^s y^t night also: And y^e :16: day G W & W G passed to a meeting in ye Country after wch G ff and C T: passed thorow ye country to Bartholomew Mallins^8 at Lamben woodlands^g, where there was a meeting that day: And ye 17 day there was another large meeting after wch G ff: and C: Tayler accompanied wth severall ffr^ds passed to Marleborrough in Wiltshire^h, where they mett

---

^a Margin: *1 m*   ^b Margin: *7: m*   ^c Margin: *7: m*
^d Margin: *5. m*   ^e Margin: *8 m*   ^f Margin: *11: m*
^g Margin: *11 m*   ^h Margin: *6 m*

with G: Whitehead & W: G: and S: Smith and there was a
large meeting that night at Wm Hitchcocks[1].

And on ye 18: day after ffr^ds had much service in that
Towne they passed away to Calne^a to Israell Noyes[2] where
severall fr^ds came to visitt them y^t night: And y^e :19: day
after they had spent some time amongst friends, G W &
W G passed to the Devizes where they had a meeting y^e
next day, after wch G ff and C. Tayler & S: Smith passed to
widdow Hailes at Charlcott^b where Richard Snead[3] and
Laurence Steel[4] mett them: And ye 20 day being ye first day
of the week A large meeting was there, and many friends
having had notice thereof: Resorted thither, from the severall
meetings thereaways.

And ye 21st day R: Snead & C: Tayler passed to Bristoll
and G ff and S: Smith and Charles Marshall passed to
Chipingham^c to ye widdow Gouldneys[5], where G W: & W G:
mett them again, and they had a Large meeting there y^t
night. And y^e :22 day after ffriends had spent ye most part
of ye day in truthes affaires, they all passed to ye widdow
Wallis's[6] at Slattenford^d: where there was a meeting y^e :23:
day, many hundreds of ffriends being Resorted thither:

And ye 24 day G ff and G: W: & W G: and S: S: and
C: Marshall passed to Bristoll^e and G ff. went to Joan Hileys[7],
and ye rest went to other ffr^ds houses.

And ye 25: day severall fr^ds came to visit G ff And y^e
:26: day many ffr^ds came to visitt him also, and Jno: Story[8]
came to G ff: and y^t day G ff went to Rich: Sneads, where
many ffr^ds resorted thither and that night Wm Penn came to
G ff: And y^e :27: day being ye first day of ye week there
was severall meetings in ye Citty (being faire time) and in
the Afternoon G ff went to the meeting at Friers where hee
declared ye truth to ye great Satisfaction of Many ffr^ds G W
& W P and S S was at ye meeting also ye meeting done G ff
passed to Joan Hileys.

And y^e :28 day G ff passed into ye Citty to vissit fr^ds after
wch hee Returned to ye mens meeting at ffryers thence
passed to R. Sneads, & so to Tho: Jordans[9] where hee Lodged
y^t night:—

And ye 29 day hee spent in ye service of truth amongst

^a Margin: *12 m*   ^b Margin: *2 m*   ^c Margin: *4 m*
^d Margin: *5 m*   ^e Margin: *13 m*

ffr^{ds} & Lodged y^t night at R S and ye 30 day there being A
meeting appointed to bee at ffryers G ff & G W and W G
and W P: and C M and many other ffr^{ds} went thither; but
Wm Rogers & 12 more had sent a paper (or warrant) to
Jno Batho[1] to suffer no meeting to bee there y^t day, w^{ch}
accordingly he pformed thoug agst his mind; so ffr^{ds} being
deprived of ye meeting house they Returned to R: S^s: where
they had a blessed meeting: G ff Lodged there y^t night: and
ye 31: day G ff spent in ye service of truth amongst fr^{ds} &
y^t night he Lodged at Tho: Jordans:

And ye 1st of ye 12: moth after G ff had spent some time
among fr^{ds} there, hee passed to ye meeting at ffryers, w^{ch}
was large and peaceable—thence he passed to R: Sneads—
And y^e :2: day hee spent amongst fr^{ds} & lodged at R. S^s. y^t
night also And ye 3: day being ye 1st day of ye week G ff
went to ye meeting at Fryers, wch was very Large & peaceable thence he passed to Joan Hileys:—And ye 4 day G ff
went to A meeting at ffryers, appointed by Wm Penn &
Wm Rogers in order to putt an end to ye differences amongst
ffr^{ds} and ye 5th day there was anoth^r to ye same effect: but
no stopp was putt to the differences:

And ye 6 day G: ff spent wth ffr^{ds} and these nights he Lodged
at R S^s. And y^e :7: day G ff passed to Symon Clemence[2] to
A meeting there Relateing to ye differences & he Lodged
there y^t night: and ye 8 day G F passed thence to R: S^s:
where hee stayed y^t day—and ye 9: day also: and ye 10:
day hee passed to ye meeting att ffriers—thence hee passed
to Joan Hileys—

And ye 11: day G ff passed to ye mens meeting, where
W R: was very contentious & hee passed thence to Joan
Hiley's and ye 12: day hee stayed there also—and y^e:13:
day G ff passed to R. S: thence to Tho: Jordans where many
fr^{ds} came to him.

And ye 14 day G ff passed to ye men & womens meetings,
after wch hee passed to Charles Jones junior[3] thence to R: S^s:
and ye 15 day hee spent amongst fr^{ds} there, and at night
there was A meeting wth W R and ye 16: day G F: passed
to Charles Jones senior's[4] where hee & S: Smith and R: Snead
and his wife took horse and passed to Clarum^a, where they
were at A meeting on y^e :17: day and on ye 18 day they

^{a} Margin: *6 m*

Returned againe and went to Rich: Vickris house, thence
passed to the Womens meeting att ffryers, and passed thence
to Joan Hiley and y^e :19: day Wm Penn took Leave wth G ff
and fr^{ds} and passed away from Bristoll, having stayed some
time longer then hee Intended to have had J: S: to A
Publick meeting y^t they might have discoursed things, but
as long as W P stayed in Town hee would not come out, but
(as hee s^d) was {sick} at T G^s: so y^t day when W P was gone
G ff and G W went to ye meeting at ffryers; after wch they
passed to Tho: Jordans and y^e :20: day Gff took Leave wth
ffr^{ds} att ye Citty and passed to Rich: Sneads Country house^a,
where severall ffr^{ds} came to visitt him both that night and
y^e :21: day after which hee passed with S: Smith and
R Snead to Winterburne^b to Hezekiah Coales[1], where hee
had appointed severall suffring fr^{ds} to meet him, so hee and
S S: & R S: drew upp their suffrings to p^{r}esent to y^e
Judges.

And y^e :22: day G ff and S: Smith and R.: Snead passed
to Sadbury^c to Rich: Gabells[2], where there was a Large
meeting at ye meeting house y^t night.

And y^e :23: day G ff and R S: and S: S: passed thorow
ye Country to Tedbury Upton^d att Nathaniell Cripps, And
ye 24 day being ye first day of ye week G ff and S S & R S
and severall other ffr^{ds} passed to Nailsworth G ff went to
Robt Langleys^e[3], and a Larg meeting there was y^t day: and
S S: & R S: lodged at Rich: Smiths[4], and y^e :25: day they
stayed there and at Rich: Smiths, & G ff Lodged at R: L^s:
y^t night also and many ffr^{ds} came to visitt them.

And ye 26: day G ff: and S: S: and R. Snead passed with
fr^{ds} to ffinchcomb[5] to a Quartly meeting, where they had
good service; ye meeting done they returned to Rich: Smiths
at Nailsworth^f ag^n and the 27: day hee stayed there also, and
ye 28: day G ff & ffriends was at a Large meeting there and
ye 1st of ye 1st moth: G ff: and S. Smith & R. Snead passed
thence to Cyrencester^g to Rich: Townesends[6], and Gyles
ffetteples and ye 2: day Rich: Snead returned to Bristoll and
y^t day G ff went to Charles Marshalls thence to Gyles
ffetteples, where hee lodged and ye 3: day being ye first day

^{a} Margin: *1: m* ^{b} Margin: *5 m* ^{c} Margin: *5 m*
^{d} Margin: *11 m* ^{e} Margin: *3 m* ^{f} Margin: *10 m*
^{g} Margin: *8 m:*

of ye week G ff and S S: was at ffr^{ds} meeting wch was
exceeding Large and peaceable, and at night there was A
large meeting at Gyles ffetteples house: and ye 4: day G ff
wth divers ffr^{ds} passed to Charles Marshall^s & at night
returned to G. ff^s ag^n and on ye 5 day G ff and S: S: passed
away (vizt) G ff and Charles Marshall and Gyles in his Coach
to Cheltinham^a, where there was A Large meeting y^t day
and C M Rich: Townesend & Gyles returned back in y^e
Coach. and ffr^{ds} had another meeting at night and G ff & S S
lodged in towne.

And ye 6: day G ff and S S passed with Edward Edwards[1]
to his house at Stoak-Orchard^b, and many ffr^{ds} came to visitt
him that night and ye 7: day G F and S S passed to Tewx-
bury^c where there was A Larg meeting that day and G ff and
S S. lodged at Joshua Carts[2]; and ye 8 day they stayed
there in ye service of truth amongst ffriends and ye 9: day
G ff and S S (accompanied wth severall ffr^{ds}) passed to
Worcest^r Citty to Wm Pardoes[3], and ffriends was very glad
to see G ff there; and ye 10 day being ye 1st day of ye week
G ff & S S: were at ffr^{ds} meeting, wch was very Large and
peaceable:—ye meeting done G ff & S: S: & Edw: Burne and
Robt Smith[4] passed to Wm Pardoes, where many ffr^{ds} came
at night and ye 11th: day after G ff and S S had visited ffr^{ds}
they went to ye men & womens meeting, ye meeting done
they returned to W Pardoes ag^n and ye 12 day G ff wth
severall ffr^{ds} passed to Edw: Burnes, and abode there y^t day
about truthes concernes and G ff Lodged there and ye 13 day
G ff visited severall ffriends, and then passed to W P^s where
many ffr^{ds} resorted to him, and y^e :14 day G ff and S S:
passed to ye meeting where there came severall eminent
persons of ye Citty, who heard ye truth declared peaceably:
the meeting done G ff wth severall ffr^{ds} passed to Thomas
ffuckes[5], and at night passed to W P^s where many ffr^{ds} came
to take their Leave of him, and y^e :15: day G ff and S: S
took leave with ffr^{ds} at Worcest^r and passed accompanied
wth Edw: Burne to Pashur^d to Henry Gibbs[6], where there
was a good meeting that day: and y^e :16: day G ff and
S: S: & E. Burne passed with Jno: Woodward[7] to his house
at Evasham^e.

^{a} Margin: *12 mi* ^{b} Margin: *3 m* ^{c} Margin: *3 m*
^{d} Margin: *6 m* ^{e} Margin: *5 m*

and ye 17: day being ye 1st day of ye week G ff & S: S: & Edw: Burne passed to ye meeting, wch was very Large, there being ffr^{ds} from severall parts, out of ye Country, ye meeting done G ff returned to Jno Woodwards ag^n where there was A meeting at night and ye 18 day Stephen Smith tooke leave with G ff and passed from him after wch G ff & Edw: Burn and Wm Pardo passed with Geo: Keith to ye Lord Viscount Conoways[1] at Ragley in Warickshire^a to visit ye Lady: [and Van Helment[2] & ffr^{ds} there was very glad y^t G ff came.

And ye 19 day G ff and ffriends abode there and had 2 or 3 houres time wth ye Lady in her Chamb^r and the 20: day G ff and Edw: Burne passed to Jno Stanglys[3] att Cladswell^b, where G ff had appointed some ffr^{ds} to meet him, and at night Edw: Burn & Wm Pardo passed to Worcest^r] and ye 21: day Wm Dewsberry came to G ff where they abode y^t forenoone and then W D passed away, [after wch G ff returned to Lord Conway's^c, and there hee and G. Keith spent y^t afternoon in Answering pt of A German booke: and ye 22. day G ff and G K and Van Helmont were Answering part of a booke[4] wch ye priest of ye pish belonged to Ragley had put forth agst ffr^{ds} and ye 23: day they spent there in ye service of truth: and ye 24 day being ye first day of ye week G ff and G K and divers ffr^{ds} passed to ye meeting at Jno Stangleys, whither there resorted severall fr^{ds} from Worcest^r and out of ye Country round about, wch made ye meeting very Large: ye meeting done G ff returned to Ragley^d—and ye 25°: day G ff had 4 houres time wth ye Lady to her great Refreshm^t and Satisfaction & G ff was to pass away ye next day, but shee was very earnest for his staying, & was not willing y^t hee should go away, and y^t night Bray Doily came to G ff:—so ye 26 day^e G ff took leave wth ffr^{ds} & passed with G. Keith and B: Doily & Van Helmont to Stratford^f, and Lyted at an Inn and then went to Rich: Bromlys[5] where there was A Meeting y^t day. and G K & Van H: returned to Ragley]—and ye 27 day aft^r G ff had spent some time amongst ffr^{ds} hee and B: Doiley passed through ye Country visiting ffr^{ds} to Lamcoat^g to Willm Lucas[6] his house—and B:

---

^{a} Margin: *6 m* ^{b} Margin: *2 m* ^{c} Margin: *2 m*
^{d} Margin: *4 m:* ^{e} Margin: *1678* ^{f} Margin: *5 m*
^{g} Margin: *6. m:*

Doiley passed home y^t night; and y^e :28: day G ff stayed
there in truths service : and y^e :29: day being ye day of their
mo^{ty} Meeting G ff was there, and It was large & peaceable:
and Bray D & Edw: Vivers[1] & Jno Halford[2] mett G ff there
and when ye meeting was done & G ff had spent some time
amongst ffr^{ds} hee passed to Jno Halfords house at Armscott^a
(where hee was taken prisoner by Justice Parker in 1673:)
and ye 30^d: G ff and B Doiley & E: Vivers passed (visiting
ffr^{ds}) to Little Sibbard^b, to Joseph Harris[3] his house—and y^e
31^{day} being ye 1st day of ye week G ff passed to broad Sibbard, where unto there resorted many 100^s of people & y^e
meeting was in a Barne. ye meeting done, when G ff had
spent some time, among ffr^{ds} hee Returned to Joseph Harris.
And ye 1st of ye 2mo G ff & E: Vivers passed (visiting ffr^{ds})
to Nathaniell Balls[4] at North-newton^c and ye 2^d :2mo: hee
passed to Banbury^d, and went to the mo^{ty} meeting: ye meeting done hee passed to Edw: Vivers his house, where many
ffr^{ds} came to see him: and ye 3 day hee spent in visiting
ffr^{ds} about ye towne, and at night hee returned to Edw:
Vivers ag^n and ye 4 day he spent among Friends in y^e
service of truth and ye 5^d: G ff passed with Bray Doiley to
his house at Adderbury^e, where many ffr^{ds} came to visitt him,
and at night there was a blessed Meetinge and y^e :6: day he
stayed there. and ye 7^d being y^e first day of y^e week, he
passed to ffr^{ds} Meeting, wch was very large y^e meeting done
he returned to B Doiley's ag^n where divers ffr^{ds} came to visit
him : and y^e 8^d: G ff passed away from thence wth Bray and
severall other Fr^{ds} to Mary Hiorne's's[5] at Astropp in North-
amptonsh$^{r f}$ where there was A larg mo^{ty} meeting—and y^e
:9: & 10: days G ff abode there where many ffr^{ds} came to
visitt him: And y^e :11: day after G ff had spent y^e fornoone
amongst ffr^{ds} he passed with Bray Doileys through y^e
Country to Long Crendon to Wm Wests[6] in Buckingamsh$^{r g}$.
And y^e 12: day G ff & B D: passed away (visiting ffr^{ds}) to
Tho: Sanders[7] his house at Elmer^h; And y^e 13 day divers
ffr^{ds} came to visit him, after wch hee passed to Jno Whites[8]
at Meadle^i and y^e 14: day being y^e first day of y^e weeke,
G ff passed with ffr^{ds} to Jno Brown[9] his house at Weston

---

^{a} Margin: *2 m* ^{b} Margin: *6 m* ^{c} Margin: *3 m*
^{d} Margin: *2 m* ^{e} Margin: *3 m* ^{f} Margin: *2 m*
^{g} Margin: *14 m* ^{h} Margin: *5 m* ^{i} Margin: *2 m*

Turvill[a], where there was a larg meeting y[t] day, being ffr[ds] from severall parts.

And y[e] 15 day G ff and Bray D...[1] passed away to Cholsbury[b] to Robert Jones[2] his house, where they stay'd y[t] night: and y[e] 16: day there was a large meeting....and the 17: day G ff and B D passed to Chessam where they visited friends and from thence passed to Isaac Peningtons at Amersham woodsyde[c]....And y[e] 18[o]: day G F: stayed there, and Jn[o] Raunce & Charles Harris & severall oth[rs] came: and they had a meeting about some differances....and y[e] 19[d]: Bray D... passed away and G ff stayed there in y[e] service of truth.... And y[e] 20[d] G ff stayed there also, and about y[e] 11: hour at night W[m] Penn and Tho: Rudyard & Jn[o] Swinton...came to G ff there....And y[e] 21: day being y[e] 1st of y[e] week they passed away to y[e] meeting at Uxbridge, and G ff and Isaac Penington & his wife & family passed to y[e] meeting at Charlewood[d], y[e] meeting done he passed to Geo: Belch[3] his house where he stayed y[t] night; and y[e] 22[o]: day G ff passed with Edw: Vivers to his (wifes) house at Watford[e] where severall fr[ds] came to visit him.

And y[e] 23[d]: he stayed there...and y[e] 24[d]: there was a Larg meeting: and it being a fast day there resorted many to y[e] meeting....And y[e] 24[d] many fr[ds] came to visit G ff: ...and Leo: ffell came to him there...and there was a meeting in y[e] Evening...and y[e] 26[d]: G ff took leave with fr[ds] and passed with Edw: Vivers, and Samuell Bolton to Hemell Hempstead[f], where they visited ffr[ds] and Lodged at an Inn y[t] night...(and Leo: ffell returned from Watford to London wth Ben: Antrobus)...and y[e] 27[d] after G ff & E V & S B had spent some time among ffr[ds] they passed to Markett Street[g] to an Inn at George Sawyers, and fr[ds] came to visit them: And y[e] 28[o] day being y[e] 1st day of y[e] weeke G ff...passed to y[e] meeting w[ch] was very Large....y[e] meeting done they returned to their Inn ag[n] where fr[ds] came to visit them:... And the 29[d] G ff...passed to Luton[h] to visit Jn[o] Crook[4]... and at night they passed to St Albans[i] to an Inn. where fr[ds] came to visit them...and y[e] 30[d]: Edw: Vivers passed away, and G ff and S: Bolton passed to South Mims to

[a] Margin: *4 m*   [b] Margin: *4 m*   [c] Margin: *5 m*
[d] Margin: *4 m*   [e] Margin: *5 m*   [f] Margin: *7 m*
[g] Margin: *5 m*   [h] Margin: *3 m*   [i] Margin: *8*

Samuell Hodges[1], where they stayed some time and then
passed to Barnett[a] to Henry Hodge[2] his house, where fr^{ds} came
to visit them....And ye 1st day of ye 3mo: G ff and Sam:
Bolton were at A meeting there: And ye 2^d they passed
from thence to Ann Hayles at Hendon[b] where they mett
with Leo: ffell and y^t night L ff and S B passed to London:
And ye 3 & 4 days G ff abode there, writing, and severall
from London came to visit him....And ye 5^d being ye 1st day
of ye week, there was A Large Meeting and severall from
London was there: And ye 6^d G ff stayed there...and ye 7^d
he took Leave with ffr^{ds} there, and passed to Wm Mead his
house at Highgate: And ye 8da G ff took horse and passed
to London to ye Pewter Platter[3], and took Coach there and
passed to ye meeting in Gracious street ye meeting done he
stayed at Gerard Roberts some time, and passed thence to
Jno Elson's,...and ye 9° day G ff passed to Ben: Antrobus
where he spent some time amongst ffr^{ds} and then passed to
Jane Woodcock's and M ff^s where hee stayed y^t night: and
ye 10° day he stayed there in ye service of truth: And y^e
:11^d he passed down to Westminst^r Hall...and having spoke
wth some parliam^t men...he Returned to ye Savoy ag^n....
And the 12^d being ye 1st day of y^c week, hee was at the
meeting at ye Savoy, and in ye afternoone hee passed to A
meeting at Long Akers: the meeting done he Returned to
Jane W^s ag^n....And ye 13: day G ff passed wth G: Whitehead to Westminst^r to the Parliam^t house: after wch he
returned to ye Savoy to A womens meetings....And ye 14^d
after he had spent ye most of ye day among Friends: he
passed to Edw: Manns. And ye 15^d he passed to A meeting
at Elis Hookes's and then passed to visit ffriends, and at
night returned to E: M^s....and ye 16^d there came many to
visit him, and he passed to ye mens meeting at Elis Hookes
house & y^t night he passed to John Elson's, where he abode
y^t night, And ye 17°: day, after G ff had spent some time
among ffr^{ds} he passed visiting Friends to Edwd: Mann's And
ye 18^d there being many ffr^{ds} come out of ye country in order
to be at the Generall {Yearly} meeting[4]; hee spent y^t day in
ye service of Truth among them:...And ye 19^d being ye first
of ye week there being many Friends in ye Citty, hee abode
at Edwd Manns, and was at no meeting that day: And y^e

---

[a] Margin: *10 m*   [b] Margin: *6 m*

20: day G ff passed to the mens meeting at Elis Hookes
house: and after the meeting Hee passed to Ezekiell
Woolies, where hee abode that night:...And ye 21: day
being the day of ye generall meeting, he passed thence to
Wheeler street too It, and It was very Large, and glorious;
and many heavenly Testimonys were born to the Truth and
G ff^s was taken down in Caract^{r}s and afterwards writ out
at Length: And when this is writ out at larg It might
come in here............^{a}The meeting done he Returned to
Ezek: Woolies ag^n where he abode that night: And ye 22
day passed to Horsly-downe where there was A mens
Meeting concerning ye generall Afaires of Truth in ye nation
...The meeting done he passed to Ann Traverse house,
where he abode y^t night, and ye 23^d: passed thence to y^e
Savoy to Jane Woodcocks house, where there was anoth^r
meeting to ye same purpose: & G ff abode there y^t night,
and ye 24: day passed thence to ye Bull & Mouth where
there was anoth^r mens meeting...after wch he passed to
John Elson's: And ye 25 day passed thence to James Claypoole's to A meeting there, where many Testimonies were
given agst a spirit of division that was then in opposition to
truth, and G ff^s Testimony was taken down in Charact^{r}s
and is to come in here......^{a}the meeting done G ff passed at
night from James Claypooles to Edw: Mann's where he
stayed ye 26^d: being ye 1st of ye week and ye 27: day He
passed to ye mens meeting at Elis Hookes, ye meeting done
he passed to Alex: Park^{r}s, thence to Ben: Antrobus' where
he spent some time in ye service of truth: and then returned
to Elis's ag^n and so passed y^t night at Edwd Mann's: And
y^e :28°: & 29° days G ff stayed there, Answering A bad
book (in writing) agst Himself & ffriends[1], and ye 30^d in y^e
morning G ff passed to Georg yard, to Wm Penn...thence
to Tho: Rudyards, and so to Elis's to A meeting wch done
he passed to Jno Elson's...And ye 31st day he passed to y^e
Savoy to J: Woodcocks where many came to visit Him:

And ye 1st of ye 4° moth: G ff passed thence to Edwd Mann's
and aft^r he had stayed some time, hee took coach & passed
to Ratcliff^b to James Struts, where he abode y^t night, and
ye 2^d day being the first day of ye week G ff was at ffr^{ds}
meeting at Ratcliff, wch was Larg and peaceable: and G ff

---

^{a} There are no insertions at these points. ^{b} Margin: *2: m*

Lodged at James Strutt's y^t night: And ye 3^d: G ff returned
to London to Ezekiel's where he stayed ye 24° & 25: dayes,
and many Friends came to visit him: and ye 6: day he
spent there in ye service of truth amongst ffr^{ds} & at night
passed to Edwd Mann's:....And ye 7° day G ff passed to visit
ffr^{ds} in Citty, and y^t night he passed to ffra: Camfields
where he abode y^t night and ye 8 day G ff spent amongst
ffr^{ds} in ye service of truth, and at night he passed to Horsly
down to Ann Traverse house where he abode y^t night and
ye 9 day also wch was ye 1st of ye week and ye 10 day he
took Boat and passed to ye Savoy to J: Woodcocks and y^e
11° day G ff was at A meeting there about some difference
amongst some pticul^r ffr^{ds}...and at night Hee passed to
John Elson's...and ye 12^d hee spent there in ye service of
truth amongst Friends:...and y^e: 13:^{d} G ff passed into
Lumbardstreet where he spent some time amongst ffr^{ds} and
then passed to ye meeting of suffrings at Elis's ye meeting
done he passed to Edwd Manns....And ye 14^d: G ff passed to
Ben: Antrobus house where he writt somthing in Answ^r to
Ro W^s book^1...and y^t night he passed accompanied wth Jno
Burnyeat to ye Savoy to J Woodcock's, and ye 15: day there
was a meeting: and in ye aft^{r}noon G ff took Boat and
passed accompanied with Gibbard Laty and Tho: Dockry
to Kingston^a to Ann ffielders where he abode y^t night: And
ye 16:^{d} being ye 1st of ye week: G ff passed to ye meeting
wch was peaceable, ye meeting done He Returned to Ann
ffield^{r}s. And ye 17^d: after Hee had spent some time among
Fr^{ds} he took Boat and passed with G L and T D to London
to ye Savoy^b to J: Woodcocks, where G F Lodged y^t night:
And ye 18° day G F passed to ye 6 weekes Meeting at Bull
& Mouth, after wch he passed to George Watts house and
passed thence to Jno Elson's where he was at A meeting y^t
day...And ye 19° day aft^r hee had spent some Time among
ffriends he passed to Ben: Antrobus's thence to Tho: Rudyards, & y^t night he passed to Edwd Manns.

And ye 20:^{d} hee was Answering Lett^{r}s only in ye aft^{r}noon
he passed to ye meeting of suffrings and ye meeting done
Returned to Edw M^s ag^n where G W and W P and Ben:
ffurly came to visit Him, And ye 21st day after G ff had
spent some time amongst Friends He and divers other

^{a} Margin: *20 m* ^{b} Margin: *20 m*

Friends, passed down to ye wat^rsyde, and went a board
Jos: ffreemã[1] shipp, and dined on board...and y^t night G ff
returned to E M^s...And ye 22: day G ff having taken leave
of severall ffr^ds took Coach and passed wth Ezek: Wooly
& Tho: Dockry to Plasto^a to Solomon Eccles[2] house, where
they Lodged y^t night.

And ye 23° being ye 1st of ye week A great concourse of
Friends from London and out of ye Count^rys thereabouts,
resorted to ye meeting. and G ff & Alex: Park^r declared:
and ye meeting was peaceable:

And ye 24:^d (comonly called midsumer Day) I took Leave
wth my Dear & ever Loving M^r G: ff: and came to London,
and he passed (visiting ffr^ds) to Enfeild to Edwd Mann's
house there.

So here is A Brief Journall of G ff^s travells while I
traveld with him in 1677 & 1678[3].

^bSee large Journal, p. 821 ^b.

> ^a Margin: *4 m*
> ^b...^b These words are in another hand.

NOTES

For Key to Abbreviations see preliminary pages.
Where names in this volume appear in the Cambridge Journal, vols. i and ii,
with notes to them, reference only to such notes is given below.

PAGE NOTE

1   1   In the left hand margin, opposite the introductory paragraph appears in A: "3, 21 D Sup^r: ye Substans In ye Journall," and in B and C: "Pref to Controv. or the Vol. of Suff." The handwriting of the paragraph in A is that of Thomas Lower who wrote the dictated parts of vols. i. and ii. The word "new" in the second line was inserted by George Fox.

1   2   Fox would sometimes first attend the meeting of Friends and then leave it to go to the church (pp. 10, 12 (2), 15). As early as 1652 he wrote: "When there are meetings in unbroken places, ye that go to minister to the world take not the whole meeting of Friends with you... but let Friends keep together in their own meetingplace....And let three or four or six that are grown up and are strong (in the Truth) go to such unbroken places and thresh the heathenish nature" (*Epistles*, no. 14). Of the work in London Burrough and Howgill wrote (1655): "We get Friends on the first days to meet together in several places out of the rude multitude...and we two go to the great meeting place which we have...to thresh among the world" (Barclay, *Letters*, p. 27).
     Braithwaite, *Beginnings*, Index under "Threshing Meetings" and "Retired Meetings"; Beck and Ball, *London Friends' Meetings*, 1869, pp. 27, 32, 240; Fox, *Epistles*, no. 135—"good Plow-men and good Threshermen to bring out the wheat."

2   1   The sheriff of Nottingham was John Reckless. See vol. ii. p. 405. He was one of the "Dispersers of Quakers Books," 1664 (*Extracts from State Papers*, p. 228—*Cal. S. P. Dom.* 1664—5, p. 142).

2   2   In the Ell. Text (i. 45) there is a narrative of a "distracted woman" at Mansfield Woodhouse who "mended and afterwards received the truth." The two accounts may be reminiscent of the same event.

3   1   For Elizabeth Hooton see vol. ii. p. 463.
     Jones, *Quakers in American Colonies*, 1911; Braithwaite, *Beginnings*, 1912; *Extracts from State Papers*, 1913; Manners, *Elizabeth Hooton, First Quaker Woman Preacher*, 1914; Brailsford, *Quaker Women*, 1915.

3   2   There are numerous instances of remarkable cures effected through the instrumentality of George Fox. See Index, vol. ii. p. 511, col. 2, adding a reference to vol. ii. p. 342; see also Subject Index (*s.v.* Miracles) to the Ell. Text (ii. 587). Appendix B to Brayshaw's *Personality of George Fox*, 1918, should be consulted. The following is taken from a MS. in D (*Jnl. F. H. S.* xvi. 61): "His [Fox's] mother had a dead Palsy, and had little use of one side, and she often did fall down & then could not help herself, and had been so many years; and George Fox came to see her & at night she fell down, and he was moved to take her by the hand, and it immediately left her, and she arose, and could go about her business."
     For records of rapid recovery in Fox himself see pp. 11, 24, 26, 27.
     Bugg, *A Finishing Stroke*, 1712, pt. iii. p. 194; *Beginnings*, pp. 550, 551; Grubb, *Spiritual Healing among the Early Friends*, 1916; Dr H. T. Gillett on "Spiritual Healing," in *The Friend* (Lond.), 1924, p. 880.

PAGE NOTE

4   1   The priest was Nathaniel Stephens. See vol. i. pp. 394, 397.
        Edwards, *Fenny Drayton, its History and Legends*, 1923.

4   2   This was John Fretwell. See vol. i. p. 394, vol. ii. p. 314. In 1669
        he was evidently in good esteem again, as his name appears in a list
        of witnesses to a marriage (*Elizabeth Hooton*, 1914, p. 64), and in 1677
        Fox visited his wife and him (p. 229) but the name is omitted from
        Ell. Text (ii. 259), presumably because he had been a defaulter.

5   1   This was Thomas Sharman by name. Ell. Text (i. 523) inserts a
        letter from Sharman, full of warm feeling towards Fox. It is as follows:
        "Dear Friend: Having such a Convenient Messenger, I could do no
        less, than give thee an Account of my present Condition; remembring,
        that to the first Awakening of me to a Sense of Life, and of the Inward
        Principle, God was pleased to make use of thee as an Instrument:
        So that sometimes I am taken with Admiration, that it should come
        by such a means, as it did, that is to say; That Providence should
        order thee to be my Prisoner, to give me my first, real sight of the
        Truth: It makes me many times to think of the Jailer's Conversion
        by the Apostles. O happy George Fox! that first breathed that Breath
        of Life within the Walls of my Habitation! Notwithstanding my out-
        ward Losses are since that time such, that I am become nothing in
        the World; yet I hope, I shall find, that all these light afflictions,
        which are but for a moment will work for me a far more exceeding
        and eternal Weight of Glory. They have taken all from me: and now
        instead of keeping a Prison, I am rather waiting, when I shall become
        a Prisoner my self. Pray for me, that my Faith fail not; but that I
        may hold out to the Death that I may receive a Crown of Life. I
        earnestly desire to hear from thee, and of thy Condition which would
        very much rejoice me Not having else at present, but my kind love
        unto thee, and all Christian Friends with thee; in haste, I rest, Thine
        in Christ Jesus. THOMAS SHARMAN. Derby, the 22ᵗʰ of the 4ᵗʰ Month,
        1662."
        Hodgkin, *Quaker Saints*, 1917, pp. 87—95.

5   2   For Gervase Bennett, J.P., see vol. i. p. 394. His name appears in
        1659 among those of "persecutors of freinds yᵗ are Justices in Derby-
        shire" (*Extracts from State Papers*, p. 114—*Cal. S. P. Dom.* 1658—9).

5   3   October 30, 1650, was the date of the mittimus. The release took
        place towards the end of 1651. Ell. Text: "About the beginning of
        Winter, in the year 1651" (i. 77).

7   1   For the practice of a traveller presenting himself to the local con-
        stable before applying for lodgings see vol. i. pp. 17, 33. See p. 377.

7   2   At this point in the original there is a side-note: "Let this be read
        before coming to Doncaster." In response to this request we have
        altered slightly the order of the next few paragraphs as they appeared
        in the original.

7   3   This was Stathes, a place on the seacoast of N.E. Yorkshire. See
        vol. i. p. 22. Convincements in this district are mentioned in *F. P. T.*
        pp. 296, 297.

8   1   This was Philip Scarth. See vol. i. p. 400, vol. ii. pp. 107, 321.
        F. P. T. p. 296; *Beginnings*, p. 68.

8   2   This noted Ranter was Thomas Bushel (vol. i. p. 401), of whom
        nothing further appears. It is not known from whence the name came
        into the Ell. Text.
        There are two etchings by Robert Spence illustrating this occurrence.

8   3   For Priest Leavens see next note. More information respecting him
        is not at hand.

8   4   The name William Ratcliffe appears here only. Vol. i. p. 23 has "brother law of the Scotch preist" (Priest Leavens). The surname appears among Friends of N.E. Yorkshire—there was a William Ratcliffe living at or near Stathes whose name is associated with that of Philip Scarth (*F. P. T.* p. 296).

8   5   This Justice Hotham was, in all probability, Durand Hotham (1619 —1691), of Winthorpe, in Lockington parish, East Yorkshire. We have studied the work, *The Hothams*, by Mrs Stirling, 1918, but do not find much there respecting Durand Hotham, he being aside from the main line of descent. He was the fifth son of Sir John Hotham (1589—1645), governor of Hull, and younger brother of Captain Hotham who was executed on 1st January, 1644/5, "for betraying his Trust to ye State." "His brother (Mr Durand Hotham) immediately took the head up, wrapt it in a scarf and laid it together with his body in a coffin prepared for the purpose" (*The Hothams*, vol. i. p. 94). The next day his father was executed "for betraying his trust to the parl^t," despite the efforts of his son Durand "who had had legal training and conducted his father's defence with the greatest ability" (*ibid.* vol. i. p. 89). Durand Hotham aided in the management of the estate of his nephew, Sir John Hotham (1632—1689), second baronet, during his minority. He is also said to have translated into English a book written by his elder brother, Charles Hotham, rector of Wigan (1653—1662), third son of the first baronet and to have edited the writings of Boehme in 1654 (*D. N. B.*). Durand Hotham married Frances Remington, his first-cousin, in 1645, and they had eleven children who, according to the pedigree in *The Hothams*, "all died young." In the Lockington "Overseers Book," Durand signs as Justice of the Peace, from 1650 to 1661. The sympathy shewn to the Friends by this Justice may have aided in the opening and sustaining a meeting at Lockington, which place appears among the "Towns belonging to Meetings," in 1668 (*Jnl. F. H. S.* ii. 103). As Cranswick, a few miles north, was in the possession of the Hothams, Durand may have resided there also, as would appear from the reference to the Justice in association with Captain Pursglove of Cranswick. N.B. The identification of "Justice Hotham" with Sir John Hotham, second baronet, in vol. i. p. 400, is incorrect.

      Information from the Rev. Philip C. Walker, M.A., rector of Lockington and from Admiral Sir Charles Hotham, G.C.B., G.C.V.O., 1923.

      Sir John Hotham (1589—1645), the first baronet, married five times, his first wife, whom he married when he was eighteen, being Catherine "daughter of Sir John Rodes, of Barlborough, Co. Derby, the eldest son of Francis Rodes, Esq. of Great Houghton, Co. York" and ancestor of Sir John Rodes, the Quaker (d. 1743, see *A Quaker Post-Bag*, 1910).

      Captain Hotham (1611—1645), issue of his father's first marriage, married three times in his short life, his first wife being Frances, daughter of Sir John Wray of Glentworth (see Camb. *Jnl.* vol. i. p. 445).

      Sir John Hotham (1632—1689), son of Captain Hotham, married in 1650 Elizabeth, daughter of Sapcote, second Viscount Beaumont of Swords in the peerage of Ireland (see Camb. *Jnl.* vol. ii. p. 382).

8   6   This was Capt. Richard Pursglove. See vol. i. p. 399. Dr Hodgkin describes the incident of Pursglove entering the church "without a bande" (vol. i. p. 19) as "an interesting little detail in the history of costume" (*George Fox*, 1896, p. 60).

      There was a Friend named Richard Pursglove, resident in N.E. Yorkshire (*F. P. T.* pp. 293, 296, 297 n.; *Jnl. F. H. S.* ii. 101) W. C. Braithwaite writes: "Captain Richard Pursglove, of Cranswick was certainly a Friend" (*Beginnings*, p. 71).

9   1   The anonymity of vol. i. p. 22 is here removed. Stokesley soon became a Quaker centre, Richard Harpson being one of the local Friends in 1652 (*F. P. T.* p. 298, "Stouseley"). In 1668, "Stoxley" was one of the five Meetings which formed one Monthly Meeting (*Jnl. F. H. S.* ii. 75).

Jnl. F. H. S. vi. 146.

9   2   For James Nayler see vol. i. p. 398. He was a member of a Church near Wakefield (see vol. i. p. 37) of which Christopher Marshall was minister (vol. i. p. 402). Oliver Heywood (1630—1702), writing in his *Diaries* under date Sept. 15, 1678, of some dissension in the Church at Topliffe, describes it as "the first and greatest difference that hath arisen in that church since it was a church which is above 30 years, except James Naylour and other 3 quakers that turned off from them 27 years agoe, and were turned out of their communion" (*Jnl. F. H. S.* xviii. 88).

Jaffray, *Diary*, 3rd ed. p. 413 ; *Waymarks*, 1902, p. 21 ; *Jnl. F. H. S.* many volumes.

9   3   This was Christopher Marshall, mentioned in previous note.

9   4   That is, *Malton.* See vol. i. p. 25. "In all probability the form *Moten* was an attempt to represent the pronunciation of the name. Even to-day, in our dialect, you hear people refer to *Malton* as *Morten* or *Mawton*" (letter from Ernest E. Taylor, 1923). Here, in 1652, occurred the great awakening when "'the men of Malton' burnt their ribbons and other fine commodities 'because they might be abased by pride'" (*Beginnings*, p. 72).

11   1   For Thomas Aldam see vol. i. p. 402. The old meetinghouse at Warmsworth, near Doncaster, long unused, was re-opened for worship, in 1913, by a descendant of the Aldam family. In the Journal of James Thornton (1727—1794), an American preacher in Great Britain, we read, under date 5 viii. 1788 : "We rode to Wandsworth [Warmsworth] and lodged at the ancient seat of Thomas Aldam. Two of his great-granddaughters now live at it in great splendour. The meetinghouse built by their grandfather on a piece of ground which he gave Friends for that purpose, is a small, decent house" (Comly, *Miscellany*, vol. viii. (1836), p. 257). William Penn, in his Preface to the *Journal of George Fox*, gives the name *John* Aldam among those of the early Quaker worthies ; this should, probably, have been *Thomas* Aldam.

George Fox's Testimony to William Dewsbury in works of latter, 1689 ; MSS. in D.

13   1   That is, *Market Bosworth.* The priest was Nathaniel Stephens, according to Ell. Text (i. 48).

The other Leicestershire place mentioned was Bagath, that is, *Bagworth.* Several visits in this county here mentioned and in Ell. Text (i. 46—48) were probably recorded in the missing pages of the Camb. Text. See vol. i. pp. xxxiii, 1.

14   1   This meeting took place at Pickering. See vol. i. p. 26.

14   2   For Priest Boys see vol. i. p. 401. "A charming old man of whom we would fain know more" (*Beginnings*, pp. 68, 69 n., 76).

14   3   Hightown in Liversedge is in about the middle of the county of York. Liversedge belonged to Brighouse M.M., in 1668 (*Jnl. F. H. S.* ii. 34). See vol. i. p. 38. The conduct of the two women towards the travellers is in striking contrast. For Widow Green see vol. i. p. 402. Her opposition did not prevent the convincement of members of her family. There is an ancient burialground, called "Sepulchre Close," in

this neighbourhood, once belonging to the family of Green of Liversedge (MS. in D, written by Joseph J. Green—"The Family of Greene of Liversedge, and an Ancient West Riding God's Acre," with illustration of the Close).

16 1   This incident of the woman and the cream forms the subject of an etching by Robert Spence. See vol. i. p. 20.

16 2   Probably the river Lune, in that district dividing Westmorland from Yorkshire (Nightingale, *Early Stages of the Quaker Movement in Lancashire*, 1921, p. 10), or, possibly, the river Rawthey, a tributary of the Lune (*Beginnings*, p. 80). For the sounding of the day of the Lord on the summit of Pendle Hill see vol. i. p. 40.
Hodgkin, *Quaker Saints*, 1917, p. 123.

17 1   Said by some editors to be Hawes, a town situated at the head of Wensleydale, surrounded to-day by people of Quaker descent. See vol. i. p. 403.

17 2   For the expression "son of God" see vol. i. p. 425. It is interesting to notice that in A the words originally written were "ye Sonne of God," but at some later but early date a capital letter A has obscured the "y^e" and at the apex of the letter appears a small a. It will be seen that the reference here to the expression "son of God" is omitted from the Camb. and Ell. Texts (vol. i. p. 41; i. 111), as also the reference on pp. 32, 33, which is omitted from these Texts (vol. i. p. 116; i. 169). The Tercent. Text omits the expression entirely. See p. 27.
Hodgkin, *George Fox*, 1896, chap. vii.; *Beginnings*, pp. 53, 70, 107—109, 117, and in Index *s.v.* Blasphemy; Hirst, *The Quakers in Peace and War*, 1923, Appendix C.

17 3   For Major Miles Bousfield see vol. i. p. 403.

17 4   For Gervase Benson see vol. i. p. 403. This meeting of Seekers ("a seperate meetinge," vol. i. p. 42) was held on Sunday, 6th June, 1652. "This crowded fortnight was the creative moment in the history of Quakerism. In the freshness of his powers and of his experience Fox had a living message, which he uttered with prophetic authority, and both the message and the messenger answered the yearnings and the hopes of a strong community of earnest-hearted Seekers" (*Beginnings*, p. 86, and see Index *s.v.* Seekers).

17 5   For Richard Robinson see vol. i. p. 403.

17 6   This "first day of ye week" was Whitsunday, 6th June, 1652. Gervase Benson's home was Borrat. See vol. i. p. 404.

18 1   The fair at Sedbergh was held on the following Wednesday (Whit Wednesday). See vol. i. p. 42. The yew tree by which Fox overlooked his auditory was blown down in January, 1877. A portion of it is preserved in Brigflatts meetinghouse. There is a good account of Fox's doings at the fair in *F. P. T.* p. 243.
Beginnings, p. 83; Hodgkin, *Quaker Saints*, 1917, p. 133; there is a view of modern Sedbergh in Tercent. Text.

18 2   For Firbank Chapel see vol. i. p. 42. "A place of far-stretching views, high up the steep fell on the Westmorland side of the Lune. It was standing in 1837, but fell into ruins a few years later" (*Beginnings*, p. 84).
Thompson, *Sedbergh, Garsdale and Dent*, 1910, pp. 68—70 (first ed. is dated 1892).

18   3   That is, *Preston Patrick*. See vol. i. p. 405. Of the meeting here Thomas Camm (1641—1707/8) wrote: "A nottable day Indeede never to be forgotten by me, I being present at that meeting, a schoole boy, but aboute 12 years of age, yet I do still remember that blessed & gloryouse day" (*F. P. T.* p. 244).
        Beginnings, pp. 80—89 and see map at end.

19   1   "Kendal in the undeveloped rural North of the seventeenth century had, as an industrial centre, a much greater importance than it has to-day. The district of which it was the natural 'capital' was also the stronghold of the group of Seekers whose members were swept, whole-sale, into the early Quaker movement by Fox's preaching in the summer of 1652. Kendal therefore provided many of the leading preachers of Quakerism in the expansive period immediately following. It was hence that the fund was distributed which provided for the needs of these northern preachers in their travels and imprisonments (see *Jnl. F. H. S.* vol. vi.). One of the earliest General Meetings of the nascent Society was held at Kendal in 1661, and the town has been a strong Quaker centre to this day" (note by John L. Nickalls, B.A., 1923).
        Beginnings; *Second Period*; *F. P. T.*; Nicholson and Axon, *The Older Nonconformity in Kendal,* 1915 ; *Swarth. Account Book.*

19   2   For this visit to Underbarrow and incidents connected with it see vol. i. p. 45.
        F. P. T.

19   3   Vol. i. p. 46: "I came to James Taylors of Newton in Cartmell in Lancasheere." See vol. i. p. 406.

19   4   For Stable read *Staveley*, the home of Gabriel Camelford. See vol. i. pp. 46, 406—the Short Journal gives the name of the place and the Camb. Text the name of the priest. (So, piece by piece, we recon-struct the past.) The place-name is confirmed in Margaret Fox's Testimony to her husband in Ell. Text.
        Beginnings, p. 98; Nightingale, *Quaker Movement in Lancashire,* 1921, p. 16.

19   5   For Swarthmoor Hall see vol. i. p. 407, where the passing of the estate out of Quaker hands, in 1759, is noted. We are glad to place on record the return of Swarthmoor Hall, after 153 years of alienation, to the possession of the Society of Friends, by purchase, on 28th August, 1912, of "the Hall and about one hundred acres of land, jointly by representatives of the Society of Friends and by Emma C. Abraham, of Liverpool, a direct descendant of Margaret Fell, the sale price being £5,250" (*Jnl. F. H. S.* ix. 208 ; see also Crosfield, *Margaret Fox*, 1913, p. 261: "By deed of purchase certain members of the Society have the option of acquiring the Hall on the death of E. C. Abraham and her heir"; *Bulletin F. H. S. Phila.* iv. 147—149, v. 20—22, 25, 71). It will be noticed that the name is given throughout the Short Journal and in all the dictated parts of the Camb. Text as Swarth*moor.*
        The condition of the estate appears to have deteriorated soon after passing from the hands of its Fell descendants. In 1772 William Forster (1747—1824), of Tottenham, visited the district and reported : "The House is much come to decay...and the whole Estate much out of repair" (*Jnl. F. H. S.* xx. 31). The present owner is devoting much loving care to the home of her ancestors.
        Jnl. F. H. S. many vols. ; *Swarth. Account Book.*
        In the summer of 1652, Fox arrived at Swarthmoor Hall (vol. i. p. 47) and visited for some time in the district with sundry calls at the Hall till some date early in 1654, when he passed southward (vol. i. p. 142).

The next visit was a short one, at the close of the Welsh tour of 1657 (vol. i. p. 290). Another took place also in 1657 (a record of which is absent from the Cambridge Text owing probably to the loss of two leaves from the MS. (vol. i. p. 312 n.); it is mentioned in the Ellwood Text (i. 416). In the late spring of 1660, after long journeyings, Fox was once more at the hospitable home of Margaret Fell (vol. i. p. 358), but was not allowed to remain in peace more than a month (p. 56), being arrested and sent to Lancaster Castle. In 1663 two visits were paid in quick succession (vol. ii. pp. 35, 37), but about twelve years elapsed before he was again at the Hall, he having meanwhile married its mistress. On the 25th June, 1675, four months after liberation from Worcester Jail, to the joy of the whole family and household, he once again set foot in his northern home (vol. ii. p. 311). The account book of Sarah Fell gives some insight into his life during this respite from travel. On the 26th March, 1677, Fox left for further service, rested but not entirely recovered (Ell. Text, ii. 255). He was again at Swarthmoor in September, 1678 (*ibid.* ii. 335), remaining until early in March, 1679/80 (*ibid.* ii. 343), when his last visit came to an end.

Margaret Fox writes, in her Testimony to her husband: "Though the Lord had provided an outward habitation for him yet he was not willing to stay at it, because it was so remote and far from London where his service most lay."

Information from A. Neave Brayshaw, B.A., LL.B., 1923.

19   6   The priest of Ulverston was William Lampitt. See 23. 3.

20   1   The rector of Rampside was Thomas Lawson, who became a prominent Friend (vol. i. p. 408).

20   2   Walney Island is separated from the Furness district of Lancashire by a narrow strait. It is eight miles long and a mile wide. "From the Dalton Parish Registers we find that a Mr Soutwerke was minister of Walney between 1649 and 1657....Like other Lancashire ministers of the time he was a Presbyterian," quoted in *Jnl. F. H. S.* xix. 103. Mr Soutwerke's name also occurs in Kendall's *History of Northscale,* 1899. Vol. i. p. 49 has *Wana,* which points to the silence of the letter *l.* See *Swarth. Account Book,* p. 547.

20   3   This was the place called Dendron. In the *Victoria History of Lancashire* (viii. 327), it is stated that the chapel was built in 1642 by Robert Dickinson, citizen of London, who left £200 to be invested in land for a "sufficient scholar to read divine service there every Sunday and to teach school on week-days." The disturbed condition of the time probably interfered with the opening of the work in that place. In 1717 the chapel was used only as a school.

Information from John F. Curwen, F.S.A., 1923.

In M. Fox's Testimony to her husband, she states that he preached at "Dendrum" (Ell. Text).

20   4   The discourse here referred to, given in the Cartmel church, is connected in vol. i. p. 46 with the visit to an ale-house between the services in the church. Bennett was in charge at this time. See 22. 1.

20   5   The discourse delivered here at Lindale is referred to in vol. i. p. 47 simply as "what ye Lord commanded mee."

21   1   Here the name of the place is given (Halton on the Lune near Lancaster); in vol. i. p. 53 the name of the priest appears (Priest Whitehead). See vol. i. p. 409. The record of this visit has been divided and continues on page 23. The man of evil intent was a doctor according to the Camb. and Ell. Texts. In *Jnl. F. H. S.* iv. 152 it is stated, on the authority of Palmer, following Calamy, that Whitehead died in February, 1679, aged 73.

22   1   This was the Rev. Philip Bennett. He was the "bitter" priest of page 23. See vol. i. p. 410.

22   2   See vol. i. p. 61, where this incident is stated to have taken place at Yealand. Silverdale was in the compass of Yealand Meeting (vol. ii. p. 488).

22   3   According to vol. i. p. 103 the meeting was held at Thomas Leaper's, at Capernwray. The other Friend was Robert Widders, who lived near-by, at Kellet, both places being in N.W. Lancashire. Several places in the neighbourhood bear the name Caton.

Thomas Leaper, his wife Margaret, and daughter Esther, are mentioned in Nightingale's *Early Quaker Movement in Lancashire*, 1921, p. 112. Leaper's name also appears in a list of "disaffected," 1669— "the supposed disaffected are classed together—Recusant Papists, Ejected Nonconformists, and Proscribed Quakers" (*ibid.* p. 201).

For Robert Widders see vol. i. p. 395 and Nightingale, *op. cit.*

23   1   For a description of the Sands see vol. i. p. 415.

23   2   For John Sawrey, J.P., see vol. i. p. 408. In 1659 Sawrey is placed among the persecutors (*Extracts from State Papers*, p. 112—*Cal. S. P. Dom.* 1658—9, p. 360) and "Jon. Sawrey of Plumpton" is included in a list, dated 1669, of those disaffected and "to bee Searched for Armes and Amunition" (Nightingale, *Quaker Movement in Lancashire*, 1921, p. 203).

23   3   William Lampitt (vol. i. p. 407) was of Worcester by birth and graduated at St John's College, Oxford, in 1626. He described himself as "once minister and governor in Lunde Island." Prior to his living at Ulverston, he was minister at Aikton (Cumb.), from which position he was turned out in 1650 by Sir Arthur Haselrig because not properly appointed according to law. He was one of the Ejected in 1662, and "lived obscurely beyond the Sands and died in 1677." The Ell. Text states that Lampitt died while Fox was at Swarthmoor, in the previous year, 1676 (ii. 254). If 1676 is correct and the death took place in the earlier half of the year, the entry in the *Swarthmoor Account Book* may refer to his widow: "1676 July ye 20° To m° Rec^d fo^r A Cow bullinge of widdow Lampitts, 000 00 06" (see pp. 292, 406, 567).

Dr Nightingale writes of Lampitt: "William Lampit, the Ulverston minister, with whom Fox was now brought into contact, is a most interesting personality. From the very first Fox appears to have had the strongest aversion to him and there are few characters in his Journal against whom he indulges in more bitter and violent language" (*Quaker Movement in Lancashire*, 1921, p. 20). Lampitt is among the "disaffected" in 1665 (*ibid.* p. 203).

Nightingale, *The Ejected of 1662 in Cumberland and Westmorland*, 1911.

25   1   For James Lancaster see vol. i. p. 408. His wife's name was Margaret. Their home was Northscale, in the North of Walney Island.

Jnl. F. H. S. many reff.; Kendall, *History of Northscale*, 1899; *Swarth. Account Book*, p. 524.

26   1   This was Thomas Hutton of Rampside (vol. i. p. 411). He was one of the early preachers and travelled into Scotland and other parts (vol. ii. p. 331; *Jnl. F. H. S.* xii. 80), being supplied with ten shillings from Margaret Fell's Swarthmoor Fund for his journey northward (*Jnl. F. H. S.* vi. 51). He was, perhaps, the same as the Thomas Hutton mentioned in the *Swarth. Account Book*: "1678 Aug: ye 5° To m°

Rec^d from Edw : Brittaine y^t hee Rec^d of Tho : Hutton for carriage of a p^{cell} of his from London 000 00 02 " (two-pence !).

Nightingale, *Early Quaker Movement in Lancashire*, 1921 ; Emmott, *Short History of Quakerism*, 1923.

26 2 For Judge Fell see vol. i. p. 407. There is a view of the dining room at Swarthmoor Hall, and of the Judge's private room beyond, in an illustration to the Tercent. Text.

26 3 Dr William Marshall, of Lancaster. The brief note, vol. i. p. 412, can now be supplemented from *Lancaster Jottings*, 1915, quoted in *Jnl. F. H. S.* xiii. 170. Dr William Marshall (*c.* 1621—1683), probably the "Priest Marshall" of the various Texts, was presented to the "vicarage of Lancaster by George Tomlinson gent., the patron," probably the George Toulnson of vol. i. p. 411. In February, 1654/5, he married the daughter of Thomas Shaw, vicar of Aldingham, mentioned in vol. ii. p. 475. He had settled in London in 1669, in which year he was admitted to the College of Physicians. His home was "Nags Head Court in Gray's Church Street."

27 1 For Priest Jaques see vol. i. pp. 71, 412. John Jaques succeeded Richard Collingwood as minister of Bolton-le-Sands in 1644. He was a member of the classis in 1646, and in the same year received an augmentation of £50 from Sir Henry Compton's sequestered tithes (*Plundered Ministers Accts.* i. 22). He signed the Harmonious Consent in 1648. In 1649 his allowance was increased to £100. He was "approved of according to the ordinance for approbation of public preachers." Information from John F. Curwen, F.S.A., 1923.

27 2 The life-story of William West, colonel, justice, clerk of assize, coroner, mayor of Lancaster, Parliamentarian, clerk of the Crown office and justice of peace and quorum (p. 72), as given in the several Texts and elsewhere, is full of interest. He appears to have taken the position of Judge Fell, favourable to the Quakers but non-committal. West is placed among the moderate men of North Lancashire in a list prepared by George Taylor in 1659 (*Extracts from State Papers*, p. 112—*Cal. S. P. Dom.* 1658—9.

MSS. in D.

27 3 For a reference to the Lancashire Priests' Petition see vol. i. pp. 76, 413. The tract referred to on these pages bears the apposite title *Sauls Errand to Damascus with His Packet of Letters from the High-Priests against the disciples of the Lord*, etc., printed in 1653. The petition, prepared but never dispatched, was addressed "To the Right Honorable The Councel of State: The humble Petition of Several Gentlemen, Justices of Peace, Ministers of the Gospel, and People, within the County of Lancaster, whose names are subscribed [unfortunately the names are not given] Sheweth that George Fox, and James Nayler, are persons disaffected to Religion, and the wholesome Laws of this Nation ; and that since their coming into this country, have broached Opinions tending to the destruction of the relation of Subjects to their Magistrates, Wives to their Husbands, Children to their Parents, Servants to their Masters, Congregations to their Ministers, and of a People to their God : and have drawn much people after them ; many whereof (men, women, and little children) at their meetings are strangely wrought upon in their bodies, and brought to fall, foam at the mouth, roar, and swell in their bellies. And that some of them affirmed themselves to be equal with God, contrary to the late Act, as hath been attested at a late Quarter-Sessions holden at Lancaster in October last past ; and since that time, acknowledged before many Witnesses ; besides many other dangerous Opinions,

and damnable Heresies, as appears by a Schedule hereunto annexed, with the names of the Witnesses subscribed. [A list of six sayings of Fox, three of James Milner, and one each of Leonard Fell and Richard Hubberthorne, are given, without names of witnesses.] May it therefore please your Honours upon the consideration of the Premisses to provide (as your wisdom shall think fit) That some speedy course may be taken for the speedy suppressing of these evils. And your Petitioners shall ever pray, as in duty bound." Fox's answers occupied 12½ quarto pages, and Nayler's 4½ pages. There is an introductory address "To all that love the Lord Jesus Christ," beginning "Dear hearts!" and one "To the Contrivers and Subscribers of the Petition," beginning "Poor hearts." In the section "To the Christian Reader" there is a reference to the Seekers of the day—"many pretious Christians have, for some time past, forborne to concorporate in Parochial Assemblies, wherein they profess themselves to have gained little of the knowledge of Jesus Christ."

27   4   The first "Publishers of Truth" as they saw it went everywhere preaching the gospel of the light that lighteneth every man. Where men foregathered in the streets, in the churches, in the sports-field they delivered their message with boundless courage. This account of Fox's action in connection with the services in Bootle church (most of it peculiar to the Short Journal) illustrates his spiritual energy and also the difficulty of keeping it within legal bounds. In the less formal methods of the Commonwealth period, interruptions and discussions took place, until legal restrictions were imposed which permitted others present to speak *when the appointed preacher had concluded his discourse.* "Fox and his friends have often been censured for their disturbance of public worship. It can hardly be maintained that this censure is in every case undeserved. But the main weight of it falls to the ground in view of the usages of the age as respects the national places of worship. George Fox was sometimes apprehended and imprisoned for his discourses in the churches, but it is observable that on every occasion, so far as I remember, the offence alleged against him was the doctrine he preached, not the disturbance of the worship. There is ample evidence to show that in the Puritan epoch it was a common thing for laymen to speak in the churches, usually, though not always, after the minister had finished" (*John Stephenson Rowntree*, 1908, pp. 387 f.). Not all justices were prepared to issue warrants of arrest. On one occasion Gilbert Latey was apprehended and taken before a magistrate for objecting to some statements made in church; the magistrate said to the constable: "This man talks very rationally. I think you should not have brought him before me." The constable rejoined: "Sir, I think so too" (*Life*, 1707, pp. 24 ff., quoted in a note to Ell. Text, i. 102).

For instances of "Speaking in Churches," see vols. i. and ii.; *Christian Progress*, pp. 22, 23, 34, 35, 68, 70; *F. P. T.*; Ell. Text (1891); *John Stephenson Rowntree*, 1908; *Extracts from State Papers*, 1913, pp. 103, 203; *Jnl. F. H. S.*; *Beginnings.*

27   5   There are brief notices of Joseph Nicholson, of Bootle, in vol. i. p. 416 and *Swarth. Account Book*, p. 531. The visit of Fox to Nicholson in 1653 is also recorded in *F. P. T.* p. 33. A visit of Nicholson to New England is placed in 1655 (vol. ii. p. 331). A sum of two pounds was given him in that year from the Swarthmoor Fund towards his expenses (*Jnl. F. H. S.* vi. 50). In 1657 he was in Scotland and the same year saw his departure, with his wife, for New England (vol. ii. p. 336). In 1666 we read that they "went lately for Road Island" (*Jnl. F. H. S.* ix. 95). They were again in N.E. in 1675. Joseph Nicholson

was one of the many Friends who offered to lie "body for body" in the place of prisoners that they might have a little respite (*Beginnings*, p. 236). The *Swarthmoor Account Book* contains numerous references to his money-matters which were under care in his absence. A loan to him forms a subject dealt with in a letter from Sarah Meade to her mother in 1683: "Sist^r Susannah would have you call in y^t 40^li laid upon Jos. Nicholson land...for shee was never satisfied y^t y^t money should bee lent to him" (*Jnl. F. H. S.* xi. 165). In 1705 he received permission from Settle M.M. to engage in religious service in Warwickshire (MS. in possession of T. Edmund Harvey, 1923).

29   1, 3   This was George Larkham, M.A. (vol. i. p. 416).
Nightingale, *The Ejected of 1662 in Cumb. and West.* 1911.

29   2   This was John Wilkinson (vol. i. pp. 109, 111, 417). Of his "three or four steeple houses besides chapels," one only seems to be named, viz. Brigham. On p. 61 of *F. P. T.* it is stated he "had been a preacher amonge the independants"; on p. 70 we read: "He had been a teacher amongst ye Baptists."

31   1   That is, *Wigton* (vol. i. p. 417). The Camb. and Ell. Texts give no name to the "market town." *F. P. T.* tells us that there was a little company of Seekers here to whom the Quaker missionaries addressed themselves with good results (pp. 52—56).

31   2   Camb. Text adds: "Upon ye borders" of England and Scotland (vol. i. p. 114).

32   1   This incident is the subject of an etching by Robert Spence, reproduced as an illustration in Tercent. Text.

33   1   Dorothy Benson. See additional particulars respecting her in vol. i. p. 125.

33   2   The trial and imprisonment of Fox in Carlisle is an interesting episode in his life. This account should be read in connection with the narrative as given in the Camb. and Ell. Texts. "The Baptist Church, which then met in the Cathedral, went over *en bloc* to the Friends, including the 'Pasture'" (letter from Dr W. T. Whitley, hon. sec. Bapt. Hist. Soc., 1923). The "steeplehouse" was the cathedral church of St Mary (*F. P. T.* p. 30).

Moss troopers (vol. i. p. 125) were marauders who infested the mosses or borderland of England and Scotland previous to the union of the two Kingdoms. In *An Epistle to Friends*, by John Bellers, dated 1724, he writes: "The Northern Borders are a noted Instance of the good Effect that our Friends Labour of Love had among those Robbers call'd Moss Troopers that were there, so far to reform the Country (where they murdered as well as robbed) that the then Earle of Carlisle told King Charles the Second that the Quakers had done more to suppress them than all his Troups could do. I have been informed that Friends have or had a Meeting in the midst of that part of the Country." Lord Carlisle had been told by John Grave "that he might now take away his gallows, for truth had gott an enterance in the borders of England and would make them honest men," *circa* 1672 (*F. P. T.* p. 62, under heading Kirklinton).

Hodgkin, *George Fox*, 1896, p. 100.

33   3   This was John Wilkinson (29. 2). His church was at Brigham.

34   1   We have here, for the first time in any text of the Journal, the full name Thomas Ledgerd, confirming the identification in vol. i. p. 454. For the five priests of Newcastle who wrote against Friends see vol. i. p. 454.

The Guild of Merchant Adventurers of Newcastle in "An act passed in 1657 laments that 'in these late tymes (wherein iniquity abounds) wee finde, by woefull experience, a great apostacy and fallinge of from the truth to Popery, Quakerisme, and all manner of heresy and unheard of blasphemy and profainences.' Whereupon it was determined that 'no brother of this fellowshipp whatsoever shall from henceforth take any apprentice who in his judgment or practice is a popish recusant or Quaker, or any who shall not attend duely on his maister at the publicke ordinances.' For every offence against this act the master was to be fined 100 marks 'without grace or favour of court,' and the apprentice to 'lose what tyme he hath served and never enjoy any freedome of this fellowshipp'" (*Vestiges of Old Newcastle and Gateshead*, by Knowles and Boyle, 1890, p. 21).

Note by A. Neave Brayshaw, B.A., 1924.

34   2   The meeting was held at Gateshead, across the river Tyne from Newcastle. See vol. i. p. 311. It is said that the meeting was held in Pipewellgate at the Fountain Tavern, a building standing until the year 1906 (*Sketch of the Society of Friends in Newcastle and Gateshead*, 1899).

35   1   According to vol. i. p. 290 the meeting was held at John Audland's, at Crosslands, near Preston Patrick.

35   2   Vol. i. p. 291 gives the name—Otway—and at p. 450 there is a note respecting him—George Otway, brother of Sir John Otway.

35   3   Camb. Text has Senderland greene; Ell. Text (1694) has Synderhill green. The place is now "Cinder Hill," near Woodhouse, on the borders of Yorkshire and Derbyshire (vol. i. p. 422).

36   1   The Friend of repute who was owner of the ground where the disturbance occurred was Thomas Taylor of Brighouse. See vol. i. p. 148. To the account of the judgment on the man who put out his tongue at Friends, in the Camb. Text, is added here that the tongue hung out "below his chinne," which, though it may not be a physical impossibility, is surely an exaggeration.

36   2   The name of the great man does not appear. He is styled a Knight (vol. i. p. 150).

36   3   The dispute between Fox and the priests, at his native town, is given fully in Camb. Text (vol. i. p. 152) and in other Texts. There was plain speaking on one hand and rough handling on the other.

A little book on Fenny Drayton, by the vicar, Jenkyn Edwards, appeared in 1923. There is a view of the church as an illustration in the Tercent. Text.

38   1   Col. Francis Hacker, of Withcote Hall, Rutlandshire, is frequently mentioned in vols. i. and ii. The date of Fox's arrest was 11th February, 1654/5 (*Beginnings*). In 1660, at a meeting at Peterborough, George Whitehead was beset by a hostile crowd who "threw dirt and eggs (thought rotten). Next morning Isabel Hacker, the wife of Colonel Hacker, bestowed some labour to get out of my hair the dirt that was thrown at me" (*Christian Progress*, p. 232). Col. Hacker was "hanged and quartered," Oct. 19, 1660 (Pepys, *Diary*).

39   1   Fox's companion was Richard Hubberthorne (vol. i. p. 188). For Hubberthorne see vol. i. p. 410.

40   1   Vol. i. p. 189 gives "a tounde neer ye Ille of Ely caled Sutton." Fox was there again in 1661 (vol. ii. p. 9).

PAGE NOTE

40   2   The alderman who was a Friend would be James Blackley (vol. ii. p. 373). He is mentioned in *F. P. T.* (p. 13), and was closely connected with the sufferings of Friends in Cambridge (*Beginnings*, p. 296; Smith, *Cata.*). Blackley was deposed from his position in 1662.

           The kindly action here ascribed to the alderman is credited to the mayor in vol. i. p. 191. One of the Spence etchings represents the scene at the arrival of Fox in the university town.

           Christian Progress, p. 23.

40   3   A comparison of this sentence relating to Priest Wise with the paragraph respecting the death of the priest of Nuneaton (vol. i. p. 195) makes it possible that Wise was the priest whose benefice was so sought after. Enquiries kindly made by Rev. Jenkyn Edwards, rector of Fenny Drayton, however, have failed to discover the name of Wise in Nuneaton at this period.

41   1   Doubtless, *Daventry*, in Northamptonshire, not far from the Warwickshire border. Fox passed through Northants on his way to London (vol. i. p. 199). About this time Thomas Stubbs (d. 1673) was imprisoned for street preaching in Daventry (*Extracts from State Papers*, p. 9—*Cal. S. P. Dom.* 1655—6, pp. 64, 65).

42   1   This meeting was at the house of Edward Hancock at Menheniot (vol. i. p. 204).

           An early account of George Fox's entry into Cornwall is printed in *F. P. T.* p. 20. There is also a full account of the Friends' sufferings in the book *The West Answering to the North*, 1657.

42   2   Market Jew is now Marazion. The name Market Jew denotes "the market on the ridge of the hill" (Stone, *England's Riviera*, 2nd ed. 1923, p. 220).

42   3   For Peter Ceely, major and justice, see vol. i. p. 436. The other justice to whom Ceely referred (p. 45) was Captain Bradden (vol. i. p. 216).

43   1   This was William Salt. See vol. i. p. 208. The pamphlet *West Answering* gives an account of Salt's experience in a neighbouring parish to Launceston when he was in the church, where, when "one Tregosse, a youth, one of P. Ceelies sisters sons (it is said) had done reading his notes, papers and other services, shaking his gold ring on his finger, and his broad cuffes on his hands, like a lad acting in a stage-play" (p. 127), Salt began to speak and was turned out and imprisoned. This was, perhaps, the "younge silly preist" who offered to cut Fox's hair (vol. i. p. 207).

43   2   Captain John Fox was governor of the Castle (vol. i. p. 209).

43   3   Vol. i. p. 209 gives the name Edward Pyott. Salt and he were Fox's companions in travelling and suffering. We often wish we could visualize some of these early Friends—we are told in *West Answering* (p. 3) that Pyott wore spectacles—"the priest called Ed. Pyott Jesuit because he used spectacles." A spectacle maker is mentioned on p. 115. He with others was allowed to address the House of Commons against a bill which become known as the Quaker Act, of 1662 (*Christian Progress*, pp. 265, 269; *F. P. T.* (for the Act), p. 356).

           He signed the Fox-Fell wedding certificate, 1669.

43   4   Captain John Keate was the commander of the soldiers in charge of Fox. He is mentioned, but not by name, on pp. 44, 46. He was the "Clerke" to Ceely mentioned on p. 42. See vol. i. p. 437.

43   5   John Desborough was Cromwell's major-general for the Western Counties (vol. i. p. 437). He offered the prisoners that "if they would promise they would go to their own homes they might have their enlargement" (*West Answering*, p. 4).

44   1   The judge was Sir John Glynn (vol. i. p. 437). The scene in Court is the subject of an etching by Robert Spence, titled, incorrectly, "George Fox at Worcester," in the list of Spence etchings, 1918.

44   2   What has become known as "hat honour" will always be associated with Chief Justice Glynn, owing to the discussion between judge and prisoner in which Fox's knowledge of Scripture gave him the advantage. Reference to Biblical practice was, of course, beside the mark. The orthodox Quaker of that and later days would not honour man by removal of his hat but God only. For a full treatment of the subject see vol. ii. p. 482.
Besse, *Defence of Quakerism*, 1732, p. 230; *F. P. T.*; Graham, *William Penn*, 1917; Pepys, *Diary*; Stone, *England's Riviera*, chap. ix.

45   1   William Salt. See 43. 1. The name is omitted as Salt joined the Perrot party—"a bad spirit and creeper in darkness" (Swarth. MSS. iv. 128).

45   2   This is a question of 0's. Here it is stated that Fox had said he could raise *400* men; vol. i. p. 214 gives *40000* and p. 215 *ffoure thusande*; Ell. Text (i. 278) has *forty thousand*, also Tercent. Text (p. 125).
Numerical statements seem frequently excessive, see pp. 18, 35, 62, 75, 78.

45   3   For Doomsdale see vol. i. pp. 227 ff. See also a description of the place in the Tercent. Text, p. 128, where is reproduced Spence's etching of the prison scene. The name of the jailer is not found; the under keeper was Nicholas Freeleven. The three specially concerned in their dealings with the Quakers at Launceston were Thomas Gewen, recorder, Philip Pearse, mayor, and the keeper of the jail. The jailer, on one occasion, being disturbed at a meal, "gott uppe from ye table and strucke his napkin away in a rage" (vol. i. p. 230). For a note respecting the use of the napkin see Pepys, *Diary*, Oct. 29, 1663. The introduction of forks lessened the need for napkins.

46   1   This was Anthony Rouse (vol. i. p. 438), Justice and Colonel.

47   1   The mayor of Launceston who was tricked, and whose character was "bad" (vol. i. p. 236), was Philip Pearse (or Peare). He was in office in 1655—6. A contemporary document, dated January, 1656, refers to him as "Phillipp Pearse, gentleman and Maior of this towne." The mayor had no control over the prison. In fact, the jailer threatened that if he came there he would "put him by the heels." The pamphlet *West Answering* states: "Their Cloaths and pockets he searcheth, and rifles; he searcheth a womans head for letters, with his own hands, taking her fowl Cloathes out of her hat and searching them also" (p. 66).
Robbins, *Launceston Past and Present*, 1884, pp. 195—199; Peter, *Histories of Launceston and Dunheved* (the old name for Launceston), 1885, pp. 231, 289; information from Claude H. Peter, town-clerk of Launceston, 1924.

48   1   The "bad man" was Paul Gwin (see vol. i. p. 255).

48   2   For vagrancy see vol. ii. p. 485. A pass as outlined in this note would give a valuable general indication of the appearance of the person named. In D there is a facsimile of a pass for Henry Fell, 1660, and also a contemporary copy of one for William Simpson, 1657.
Christian Progress, pp. 103—108, 133; *Beginnings*, p. 445; Emmott *Short History of Quakerism*, 1923; *Jnl. F. H. S.* vi. 146.

48   3   This General Meeting (vol. i. p. 270) was held early in March, 1656/7, at the sign of the Seven Stars, an inn at the foot of the bridge connecting Exeter and St Thomas. The old inn disappeared about fifty years ago (letter from Francis W. Dymond, of Exeter, 1905).

48   4   Given as Apsum in vol. ii. p. 178. Absom was visited by Charles Marshall in 1671 (*Works*, 1704). The modern name is Topsham.

49   1   The route taken by George Fox in this tour in Wales in June and July, 1657, is not clear. The order of places visited differs here from that in vol. i. pp. 270—285. There is a brief sketch of this Welsh visit in *John Ap John and Early Records of Friends in Wales*, by W. G. Norris, 1907. We read: "In these travels in South Wales there seems to have been less desire on the part of the magistrates to imprison vindictively than to imprison and send away for the purpose of preserving the peace" (p. 9). Fox writes: "Wee were very weary with travaileinge soe hard uppe & downe in Wales & it was harde in some places to gette meate for our horses or our selves either in many places" (vol. i. p. 284, see pp. 278—280, 284).
"The History of the Quakers in Wales and their Emigration to America" was the subject of essays prepared for the National Eisteddfod of Wales, 1923. The prize was won by Rev. T. Mardy Rees, of Neath, whose valuable work is still in manuscript.

49   2   This Justice was probably Thomas Barrett. He was mayor of Tenby in 1665—6. Francis Gawler, in his *Record of Some Persecutions*, 1659, p. 21, states that a meeting, called by Elizabeth, wife of Thomas Holme, was held at Barrett's house in 1659.
See 49. 4.

49   3   This was John ap John. See vol. i. p. 422.

49   4   The mayors of Tenby were elected on Michaelmas Day, when the ex-mayor became the deputy and two aldermen were appointed to act as justices for the year.... Thomas Rogers was elected mayor at Michaelmas, 1655. He died in office (after 3rd January, 1656) and was succeeded by Thomas Barrett. Richard Barrowe was elected in 1656 and John Sayes in 1657. It appears that Barrowe was the mayor of Fox's visit. Information from David Salmon of Narberth, Pemb., author of *The Quakers of Pembrokeshire*, 1923. See 49. 2.

49   5   The "preist with two capps" was probably Edward Carner who held the living during the Commonwealth.
Salmon, *The Quakers of Pembrokeshire*, 1923.

50   1   Vol. i. p. 278 adds: "Soe I went backe to ye other Justices house & ye maior & his wiffe & ye Justice & his wiffe & diverse other freinds of ye tounde went abut halfe a mile with us to ye waters syde [the shore of Carmarthen Bay]: & there I was moved of ye Lord to kneele doune with y^m & pray to ye Lord to preserve y^m."

50   2   According to vol. i. p. 281 this occurred in the town of Dolgelly in Merionethshire, to which Fox and his fellow traveller "came doune" from Cader Idris, "a hill which they say was 2 or 3 miles high."
Beginnings, p. 78.

50   3   The other Friend was Thomas Holme (vol. i. p. 271). He is frequently mentioned in vols. i. and ii. There is an interesting reference to the spiritual fervour of Holme and his wife, Elizabeth, the expression of which did not meet with the approval of some of their friends, in vol. ii. p. 326. The short married life of these evangelists is dealt with fully in Miss Brailsford's *Quaker Women*, 1915, pp. 148—156. She styles

Holme "the excitable Apostle of South Wales." Thomas was supplied from the Swarthmoor Fund with "a paire of britches and showes" (*Jnl. F. H. S.* xix. 78, 79). With Thomas Castle Holme walked naked through the streets of Kendal "as a sign" (Fox, *Great Mistery*, 1659, p. 233). The subject of "going naked as a sign" is dealt with fully in vol. i. p. 462 and see references there.

51   1   This meeting was held at the house of William Gandy at Frandley. The date was the 28th June, 1657 (*Beginnings*, p. 349).

51   2   Fox entered Scotland on the 10th September, 1657 (vol. ii. p. 337).

52   1   According to vol. i. p. 304 this horse-and-man race took place at Stirling. Fox was at a race-meeting somewhat earlier (vol. i. p. 291).

52   2   St Johnstons was the early name for the town of Perth.

The "Market town" referred to as the next place visited was, probably, Dundee (as suggested by Dr Butler in his *George Fox in Scotland*, 1913, p. 39 n.). Alexander Parker went to the Cross, with a Bible in his hand, and spoke to the people, followed by Fox (vol. i. p. 305).

52   3   The "friends house" was that of Captain Davenport (vol. i. p. 307).

52   4   "Jamaica, with its deadly climate, had lately been taken by England from Spain, and it was at this time proving the grave of hundreds of English soldiers" (*Beginnings*, p. 352).

53   1   Fox's summing up of the results of his Scottish mission is given in vol. i. p. 310. His estimate of the future can hardly be said to have proved correct, cp. vol. i. p. 451: "Quakerism never took firm root in the soil of Scotland, despite much cultivation."

Another view of the religious condition of Scotland about the same period is given by James Kirkton in his *Secret and True History of the Church of Scotland from the Restoration to 1678*, 1817: "Then was Scotland a heap of wheat set about with lilies, or a palace of silver beautifully proportioned, and this seems to me to have been Scotland's high-noon" (quoted in Butler's *George Fox in Scotland*, 1913, p. 13).

53   2   For an amplification of these three "priests curses" see vol. i. p. 295; *Beginnings*, p. 351, quoting Fox's *Great Mistery*, 1659; Butler, *George Fox in Scotland*, 1913, p. 35.

54   1   This was, doubtless, the General Meeting at John Crooks' at Beckerings Park, held on the 31st May, 1658. Fox's address on the occasion appears in vol. i. pp. 317—323, see also pp. 428, 455, 456.

F. P. T. p. 6; *Jnl. F. H. S.* i. 41 n.; *Beginnings*, pp. 175, 185, 333, 353; *London Y. M. 1668—1918*, 1919, pp. 18, 145.

54   2   For the brotherly action of Friends in offering to take the places of others in prison see vol. i. p. 442. For an address to Friends on this subject see Ell. Text, i. 248, and consult *ibid.* pp. 44, 318 (this was Humphrey Norton), 439.

Brailsford, *Quaker Women*, 1915.

55   1   For the Committee of Safety see vol. i. p. 458.

Pepys, *Diary*, anno 1660; *Beginnings*, pp. 459, 466.

55   2   Similar words to these are put into the mouth of Cromwell on the occasion of Fox's first visit to Whitehall in 1654 (Ell. Text, i. 211, see i. 450).

55   3   This meeting took place at Leominster in Herefordshire in 1657 (vol. i. pp. 274—277).

PAGE NOTE

55   4   This "priest" was John Tombes. See vol. i. pp. 275, 448. *Beginnings*, p. 390.

55   5   There is a note on Major-Gen. John Lambert in vol. i. pp. 460, 462. The powers quarrelling one with another may refer to the strife between the Royalist Booth and the Parliamentarians (vol. i. p. 343).

56   1   This was the occasion of a meeting of Friends from all parts, met at Balby, in Yorkshire, in a great orchard belonging to John Killam. See vol. i. p. 353. This was one of the "yearly meetings" held in various parts of the country, before the governing body of Friends met regularly in London.
Jnl. F. H. S. ii. 61.

56   2   For Justice Porter see vol. i. p. 463. It is stated, vol. i. p. 361, that "when Margarett [Fell] went to London This Justice Porter aforesaid vapored y^t hee woulde goe & meete her in ye gappe." The gap was probably that part of the West Riding of Yorkshire known as the Aire Gap, where there is almost a complete break in the Pennine Range and where the rivers Ribble and Aire nearly meet, one flowing west and the other east.
Letter from F. H. Cheetham, of Southport, 1924.

57   1   According to vol. i. p. 364 these two companions of Fox on his three weeks' journey to London were Richard Hubberthorne and Robert Widders.

58   1   According to vol. i. p. 365 this was Sir Thomas Mallett.

58   2   The Chief Justice of the day was Sir Robert Foster. See vol. i. p. 365.

59   1   Judge Mallett's warrant for Fox's delivery is given in vol. i. p. 372. See 58. 1.

59   2   For particulars of the Fifth Monarchy rising and its effect upon Friends see vol. i. p. 468. The number of persons composing this outburst in London varies in different accounts thereof. Here it is said: "a matter of thirty"; in the State Papers Domestic (*Cal.* 1661, pp. 470, 471) we read: "Jan. 11. Fifty Fifth Monarchy men began the disturbance...in fighting with the troops thirty six were either taken or killed"; Emmott, following Braithwaite, gives "some thirty-five persons" (*Short Hist. of Quakerism*, 1923, p. 220). See also Pepys, *Diary*, Jan. 10, 1660/61; *Christian Progress*, p. 241.

59   3   More accurately, "a man in ye house," for "Esquire Marsh," out of love to Fox, had spent the night in the latter's lodgings. See vol. i. p. 387. For Richard Marche see vol. i. p. 465.

59   4   Scotland Yard is said to derive its name from a palace built near for the accommodation of Scottish kings visiting the southern metropolis.

61   1   This was Alexander Parker. See vol. ii. p. 19, and later note (92. 3).

62   1   The reference to the two Friends "who intended to speak" in a meeting in Bristol, and the statement that they two were detained after all the others had been liberated, have not appeared before. Were they introduced as a warning to Friends not to go to meeting "intending to speak," but to await, in the meeting, any intimation of a call to take vocal part?

63   1   The Camb. Text (vol. ii. p. 13) places the Leicestershire episode before the visit to Bristol (p. 19). The Ell. Text (i. 527) takes Bristol first.

PAGE NOTE

63   2   This was Viscount Beaumont, of Swords. See vol. ii. pp. 13, 382.

63   3   The deep-seated religious objection of Friends to take a judicial oath has been dealt with in vol. ii. p. 483.

63   4   For instances of the use early Friends made of the Bible in their work see vol. ii. p. 503, col. 2 (Ell. Text, ii. 588. 2).
F. P. T.; Emmott, *Short History of Quakerism*, 1923.

64   1   Stoke, in the Isle of Ely, has not been located; Chatridge is the modern *Chatteris*.

65   1   The companions of Fox at Tenterden were Thomas Briggs and John Moore (vol. ii. p. 23). For the former see vol. i. p. 413, and the latter see vol. ii. p. 386.

66   1   According to the later and fuller accounts given on pp. 79, 80, the date of this meeting in the parish of Ringwood was the last day of the Third Month (May), 1663.

67   1   There are several lively narratives of like conduct on behalf of Friends in demanding exact fulfilment of the warrants under which they were arrested. One occurred in 1662 (vol. ii. p. 14) and another is described vol. ii. p. 32. The following account is taken from the State Papers Domestic—*Calendar*, 1671, p. 419—a letter dated Yarmouth, August, 1671 : "* * He shewed them his warrant and required them to goe wth him they told him no, for the warrant required him to bring them before the Justice and therefore they would not goe upon wch the Constable gott a Cart, but they not being free to goe in of themselves the Constable with his assistance was forst to put them in, the first that were put in were so cross that they would lye at their length so y^t they could not Stow halfe of them where upon the Carter laid them one upon an oth^r, but this not being for theire ease they then Sett up, being brought to ye doore where the Justice was, they could not pswade them to come out of ye Cart, upon wch the Carter cast of the belly band of the ffiller, lifted up the tibbs of ye Cart and so threw them out altogeth^r at ye Carts arse, wch So cooled theire courage y^t coming before the Justice they all gave in theire names & were dismist for ye p^{r}sent" (*Extracts from State Papers*, p. 332). Tercent. Text, p. 213.

67   2   For this incident see vol. ii. p. 116, *anno* 1667.

68   1   A noble was a coin first issued *temp.* Edward III, worth about six shillings and eightpence.

68   2   For Sir Daniel Fleming see vol. ii. In *Jnl. F. H. S.* vii. 146, there is a copy of a letter from Fox to Fleming in 1663, with additions to the letter in Ell. Text, ii. 30 and Fox's own endorsement: "justes flimen Westmarland this filmon did presen one to death 1663 & flinnen his wife died & one of her childern & shee laft 14 moutherles childern a sad judgment upon an old percuter." Note the three different spellings of Fleming.

69   1   For Sir George Middleton see vol. i. p. 462. The incident, here connected with his name, may be the one recorded in vol. ii. p. 35

69   2   A note respecting Col. Richard Kirkby will be found in vol. ii. p. 390.

69   3   The discussion at Holker Hall with the Deputy Lieutenants is given at great length in the Camb. Text (vol. ii. pp. 39 ff.).
For a description of the *Battle-Door* see vol. ii. p. 379; *Jnl. F. H. S.* vi. 141, where it is said by Fox's opponent, Francis Bugg, that

" Eighty Pounds of mill'd money was paid by Gerard Roberts, besides a Dozen Bottles of Wine given by M: Fell, to hire some Jew to assist G. Fox in preparing the Hebrew Portion of the Battle-Door." Whiting, in his reply to Bugg, asks: " Was that any *Crime*?"

69   4   The high-sheriff of Yorkshire was Sir Thomas Gower and Fox's informant was Dr Hodgson. For these persons and note on the Plot see vol. ii. p. 391; Hirst, *Quakers in Peace and War*, 1923, pp. 71 ff.

69   5   This assertion of Justice Preston is given anonymously in an inserted document in the Camb. Text. See vol. ii. p. 44.

70   1   For a comprehensive paragraph respecting Quakerism and judicial oaths see vol. ii. p. 483. The painting by John Pettie of Fox's refusal of the oath, mentioned in vol. ii. p. 391, is now in the possession of Robert Leatham Barclay, of Bishop Stortford, Co. Essex.

71   1   This touching conclusion of the Short Journal must be read in connection with two inserted documents in the Camb. Text (vol. ii. pp. 48—52 and pp. 52—56). The first is headed: "An account of G: ffs: & others sufferings att Lancaster 1664." This gives brief statements of the reasons for commitment at the Lancaster Sessions in January, 1663/4, of Fox and the "8 more," and the second paper is a recital of their religious profession under fifteen heads. This paper is signed by George Fox and the eight—Thomas Waters, William Wilson, William Grave, John Stubbs, Thomas Chorley, Thomas Davenport, James Brown and Margaret Fell.

71   2   For this visit to Portsmouth see Ell. Text, i. 260, *anno* 1655.

71   3   For this disorderly meeting in Manchester see vol. i. p. 289, *anno* 1657.

72   1   This was Col. William West (27.2). This courageous speech is recorded in vol. i. p. 77, *anno* 1652.

75   1   The family of Blatt, of Reigate, was well known in early Quaker days. John was a tanner, of Red Hill (*Jnl. F. H. S.* i.) and Thomas was one of the " Dispersers of Quakers Books," 1664 (*Extracts from State Papers*, p. 229—*Cal. S. P. Dom.* 1664—5, p. 142). He was desired by Reigate Friends in 1687 to make enquiry *re* building land for a meeting-house (Marsh, *Friends in Surrey and Sussex*, 1886).

75   2   Humphrey Killingbeck lived at Twineham (*F. P. T.*) and was a member of Horsham M.M. (*Jnl. F. H. S.* iv.).
Penney, *My Ancestors*, 1920, pp. 35, 36.

75   3   Panes Place lies north of Hurstpierpoint in about the centre of Sussex.

75   4   For Devonshire House see vol. ii. p. 421. At this period Friends were in possession of "a substantial meeting house, with rooms for committees and caretaker, and with attics occupied by some poor Friends" (Penney, *Devonshire House*, 1920).
Sefton-Jones, *Old Devonshire House by Bishopsgate*, 1923.

75   5   The Meeting in the Spitalfields district East of London was held at Wheeler Street (84. 1).

75   6   Gracechurch meetinghouse was situated in White Hart Court which was entered from both Gracechurch and Lombard Streets. The house was built in 1668 on land cleared by the Great Fire and portions of the land were built on as residences by Gerard Roberts, Henry Gouldney and others; Tace Sowle had her bookshop here also. The

meetings were frequently visited by George Fox. His last sermon was preached here on Sunday, 11th January, 1690/91, and his funeral passed hence to the Bunhill Burialground on the 16th. The name appears also as *Gracious* and *Grasschurch.*

Gracechurch Street Meeting came to an end on the 28th May, 1862 (*Jnl. F. H. S.* xiv. 186).

75   7   The first meeting in the Horslydown district of Southwark was held in the garden of Mary Webb, widow, in Fair Street, *c.* 1655. In June, 1670, "the Quakers meeteing house is next to or adjoyneing upon the Martiall Yard att Horseydowne in Southwarke" (*Extracts from State Papers*, p. 312—*Cal. S. P. Dom.* 1670, p. 273), but in August of that year soldiers and carpenters pulled down the meetinghouse. In 1671 another was built, and another in 1739. In 1800 the house was sold. In the early period persecution was specially rife in this district. *London Friends' Meetings.*

The marriage here was, probably, that of Nathaniel Markes, of London, with Rebecca Chandler, of New Fish Street, London, 21 v. 1681.

75   8   These visits were paid at Woodside in the Chalfont country of Buckinghamshire. See Ell. Text, ii. 358. Mary Penington's death took place in the following year while on a visit to her daughter, G. M. Penn, at Worminghurst.

Camb. Text, vol. ii. p. 425; Penney, *Experiences in the Life of Mary Penington*, Phila. 1911.

75   9   Probably *Hunger Hill*, the home of Thomas Ellwood from his marriage in 1669 to his death in 1713. He wrote a poetical description of the route to be taken to reach his house (Graveson, *Hist. of Life of Thomas Ellwood*, 1906, p. 335). Fox "visited the men's and women's meetings at Hunger Hill," after his visit to Mary Penington (Ell. Text, ii. 358). Upperside M.M. was held at Hunger Hill for more than forty years. It is now known as Ongar Hill, near Beaconsfield, Co. Bucks.

76   1   Chorley Wood is in the county of Buckingham, in a district abounding in Friends at that time. The King's Farm, where William Penn's first marriage took place, was near here (*Jnl. F. H. S.* v. 55).

76   2   Russells is doubtless Old Jordans Farm, inhabited by William Russell (*c.* 1596—1683), who was succeeded by a son of the same name. Here, for many years, Friends of Chalfont, Rickmansworth and adjacent places met to worship, until Jordans meetinghouse was built in 1688. The farmhouse is now a Friends' hostel, and the district has again become peopled by Friends owing to the expansion of London. Russell's daughter Elizabeth was the first to be buried in the burialground, which contains the remains of William Penn and his two wives, several members of his family and other Friends, well known in England and America.

Littleboy, S., *Visit to the Grave of William Penn*, 1853; Littleboy, Anna L., *Jordans*, 1909, etc.; Warner, *Jordans, a Quaker Shrine*, 1921; many vols. of *Jnl. F. H. S.*; and plentiful reff. in print and MS.

76   3   John Archdale (d. *post* 1713) was a Buckinghamshire Quaker squire. In 1680 he became one of the proprietors of the Carolinas and in 1695 he became governor of the colony. In this position he "combined with singular felicity the firm requisites of the governor with the gentle and simple benevolence of the Quaker," quoted in an account at large of Archdale in *Quakeriana*, vol. i. (1894), pp. 36—40). In 1698 he was elected to represent Wycombe in the House of Commons, but was

not allowed to take his seat as his religious principles forbad the taking of the oath. There is now in the possession of E. Harold Marsh, of Tunbridge Wells, a letter, believed to be the original, written by John Archdale and presented to the Speaker, dated "9th 11 mo called Jan. 1698/9," explaining why he could not take the oath. Archdale's will is dated 1713 (copy in D).

D. N. B.; Jones, *American Colonies*, 1911; *Second Period*; *Jnl. F. H. S.* ii. viii. xiv. xix.; *Bulletin F. H. S. Phila.* iii. iv. vii.; MSS. in D.

76   4   For sketch of the life of Thomas Ellwood see vol. ii. p. 486.
          Beginnings; *Second Period*.

77   1   According to Ell. Text, ii. 359, this was Wandsworth.

77   2   James Beech, the younger, frequently entertained Fox in his home in Westminster, who on one occasion acted as peacemaker below stairs (p. 124), and on another met at his house William Penn, George Whitehead and Robert Barclay (p. 107). (How one would have enjoyed being there!)

          James Beech, Senr., of St Margaret's, Westminster, died 5 i. 1686, aged 65, of "Tyssick and rising of the lights." It was probably his widow who was visited by Fox (p. 156).

77   3   John Elson, of The Peel, Clerkenwell, is referred to frequently in vol. ii. (sometimes as John *Nelson*, see p. 433). Fox visited the Elsons on many occasions and over-nighted at The Peel. Private conferences were held there. J. and M. Elson also visited Fox at the homes of his friends. Having no home of his own, Fox's possessions had to be housed here and there among his London friends. We find that in his testamentary dispositions he mentions a great trunk at John Elson's, also saddle and bridle and other accoutrements for horse-riding (vol. ii. pp. 351 ff.).

          Swarth. Account Book.

          For Mary Elson, wife of John, of The Peel, see vol. ii. p. 493. In her Testimony to Anne Whitehead she writes: "Some twenty-seven years ago [*i.e. circa* 1659], it was my lot to meet her at Kingston, at the house of John Feilders, where we had a Meeting on the first day of the Week, and the Lord was pleased to seaze so upon me...through her Ministry... that I could set to my seal that it was the true and living way; which day is never to be forgotten with me" (*Piety Promoted by Faithfulness*, 1686, p. 19). George Fox left Mary Elson "a ginney & some of my books" (vol. ii. p. 361).

77   4   For William Meade see vol. ii. p. 420 and for his wife, Sarah Meade, see vol. ii. pp. 386, 485. At the "First Settling of the Meeting for Sufferings in London" in 1676 (MS. in D) Meade was appointed to represent Friends in Northumberland and Durham and also those in New England. In addition to his city-house in Fenchurch (Fanchurch, Fancy, p. 155) Street and country-house in Essex, he lived on one of the northern heights of Middlesex, at Highgate (p. 232). Fox was many times, for longer and shorter periods, at the houses of his step-son-in-law. Meade's coach was sometimes called a chariot (p. 206) or had he both means of conveyance? See 87. 6.

          In vol. ii. p. 420, it is stated on the authority of Smith, *Cata.* ii. 162, that Meade "lost his early love for Friends," but W. C. Braithwaite thinks this statement is "to be rejected" (*Second Period*, p. 207 n.). There was, however, some friction between William Penn and William Meade (*F. Q. E.* 1902, "George Fox's Writings and the Morning Meeting," p. 66; Crosfield, *Margaret Fox*, 1913, pp. 197, etc.).

77   5   For this journey see Ell. Text, ii. 358, 359.

PAGE   NOTE

77   6   This and several following paragraphs supply exact dates to the incidents recorded in Ell. Text, ii. 376—378.

77   7   The meetingplace known as the Bull and Mouth or, simply, the Bull, "formed part of an ancient Inn known by the sign of the Bull and Mouth, in Aldersgate Street. The room is described as holding 1000 persons, though that probably meant standing, inasmuch as forms for sitting were not anywhere much used at first. Over it were other rooms which Friends either sub-let or used for various purposes" (*London Friends' Meetings*, p. 134). This property, occupied since 1654, was destroyed in the fire of 1666 but Friends were back again in 1671, with a meetinghouse to hold a thousand, and with committee rooms over, and rooms above occupied by John Field for his school (*ibid.* p. 143), until they vacated in 1740. It is usually stated that Friends were squeezed out by the increasing business of a carriers' stopping-place ; apparently the new people called Methodists were accommodated here in 1744 (*London Directory*, 1744, p. 83).
        Pepys seems to have confused the Bull and Mouth with the Mouth Tavern, Without Bishopsgate, when writing: "I intended to have seen the Quakers, who, they say, do meet every Lord's day at the Mouth at Bishopsgate, but I could see none stirring, nor was it fit to aske for the place" (Oct. 2, 1664). Fox attended many meetings for worship here and also meetings for consultation (pp. 136, 143). He also visited Friends resident on the premises (p. 153). The Six Weeks Meeting (82. 5) was held here and several meetings at Y.M. time. The Meeting was also known as the City Meeting and London Meeting.
        Gilbert Latey, 1707, p. 10; *William Crouch*, 1712, p. 16; Barclay, *Letters*, p. 146; Bellows, *Survivals of Roman Architecture in Britain*, 1898.

78   1   The year 1683 began on this day. The heading of this section is placed a few days earlier, at the commencement of the First Month (March), as also those on pp. 90, 132, 168; the headings on pp. 191, 206 are accurately placed.
        For information respecting the Calendar see vol. i. p. xli.

78   2   James Claypoole (1634—1687) was a prominent London Friend. At the First Settling of the Meeting for Sufferings, 1676 (MS. in D), he was appointed London representative for Staffordshire and Derbyshire and also Ireland. He was also an active member of the Six Weeks Meeting and of the Meeting of Friends in the Ministry. His brother John married Elizabeth, daughter of Oliver Cromwell.
        James Claypoole emigrated to America in 1683 in the *Concord*, with his wife Helena, four sons and three daughters, besides five servants, his eldest son, John, having preceded him in the *Amity* in 1682 (*Jnl. F. H. S.* v. 159, see also pp. 53, 202). He became a "Merchant in Philadelphia and one of the Councel" (*ibid.* xix. 123).
        A Letter from Dr More relating...to the Province of Pennsylvania, 1687; Comly, *Friends' Miscellany*, vol. i. (1834), p. 45; *The Friend* (Phila.), vol. 27 (1854), p. 172; Newport, *Eudemon*, 1901, p. 513; Gummere, *The Quaker, a Study in Costume*, 1901, p. 146; *Jnl. F. H. S.* i. xii. xiii. xviii.; *Bulletin F. H. S. Phila.* iv. vi.; Camb. *Jnl.* vol. i. p. 457.

78   3   Henry Gill (—1708) was a "publick friend," living at Eashing, parish of Godalming, Co. Surrey, and a yeoman. In 1664 he married Martha Hatt, of "Redding," at John Lee's house at Guildford. He was committed to the White Lion Prison in Southwark in August, 1658 (see copy of the warrant in *Extracts from State Papers*, p. 76 and see also p. 54—*Cal. S. P. Dom.* 1658—9, pp. 162, 163), and he was in the Fleet Prison in 1659.
        F. P. T. p. 232.

78   4   Widow Smith was, doubtless, the widow of Stephen Smith, of Pirbright and Worplesdon. She was Susanna Purse (*c.* 1623—1693). See vol. ii. p. 446, where read "Alexandretta" in place of "Alexandria.'

79   1   "As early as 1656 Friends began to meet in that carpenter's yard [77. 3], and ever since upon that spot have they maintained, often in the face of bitter persecution, the Meeting known as The Peel" (vol. ii. p. 457). Peel Court is in St John Street, Clerkenwell. The minutes of Peel M.M. are extant (in D) for the whole of its period (1668—1860).

"The Meeting for the Collection" (pp. 171, 199, 213) was held quarterly. The minutes of the M.M. give particulars of amounts collected for poor Friends and disbursed, and the names of the persons helped. At times other business was taken up.

London Friends' Meetings, chap. xi.

George Fox attended several marriages at The Peel; the one mentioned on p. 199 was probably that of David Jones and Sarah, daughter of John Bletso, of Red Cross Street. Another is mentioned on p. 209 which was doubtless that of John Hopegood, of Old Bailey, a sawyer, and Anne, daughter of Thomas Swan, of Old Street. There was another wedding at The Peel two days before but Fox did not arrive in time for that event.

79   2   The authors of *London Friends' Meetings* have traced briefly the history of the Savoy Palace from its erection by Peter, Earl of Savoy, in 1245 to its reorganization as the Savoy Hospital, and abolition in the reign of Queen Anne. The principal entrance at the time of the Itinerary Journal opened onto the Strand and contiguous property was in the hands of William Woodcock, "between the great gate of Sommerset House and the Watergate," writes Richard Hawkins in his uncle's memoirs (*Gilbert Latey*, 1707, p. 8). Here a meeting was held till 1669, when a fire destroyed the property. On the site, Jane Woodcock, William's widow, in conjunction with Martha Fisher, built a meetinghouse, and also some dwellinghouses in which resided several Friends, forming a little colony of Friends similar to that on both sides of Lombard Street. The meetinghouse was at the rear of the other houses and there was "a passage four feet wide, leading to a stone staircase which terminated in a yard paved with stone" (*London Friends' Meetings*, p. 246), doubtless the yard and entry referred to on pp. 86, 98, 107, 115, 125, 139, 160, 169.

79   3   The expression "proud people" (pp. 79, 83) for non-Friends is unusual. The expression generally used in original documents is "world's people"; it occurs in the Camb. Text and in Tercent. Text. The earlier editions of the Ell. Text have "worlds people" but modified, in later editions, to "not Friends," "not in profession with us," "people of all sorts," etc. In the Itinerary Journal we have "one of ye world" (p. 66), "worlds people" (p. 160) and on one occasion Fox "lodged at one of ye worlds house" (p. 208). See pp. 65, 75, 78, 145, 160, 166, 180, 198.

The term " proud women," referring to women members of a congregation in Norwich, was used by George Whitehead (quoted in a MS. history of Friends in Norwich, written by Arthur J. Eddington, 1924).

Early Quaker historians were careful to note the presence of people of position at their meetings, *e.g.* "several papists one or all of wch were said to belong to the popes Nuncio" (p. 156), "great persons, one said to be a Lord and another a Knight" (p. 172) "great psons from ye Courte" (p. 177), "The Earl of Ancram & his Nephew and two Neeces" (p. 201). See also pp. 237, 243, 250, 252, 255, 266, 308; and Camb. Text of Fox's American journey.

79 4   "By name and reputation the best known thoroughfare in the world, ...associated with monetary dealings, and the spot chosen by the Goldsmiths for carrying on their craft and doing a large trade in money lending" (*Old Lombard Street*, 1912). In the first *London Directory*, dated 1677, there is a list of "goldsmiths that Keep Runing Cashes," most of them in Lombard Street.

79 5   A document has been referred to in these notes with the title : "The First Settling of the Meeting for Sufferings in London in the Fourth Month 1676—the names of the persons appointed to meet upon y^c account of Friends' sufferings, also the names of persons in ye country to whom they are to send upon any occasion of sufferings." The British Islands are divided into twenty-five sections and there are, in addition, appointments for Barbados, New England and New York, Virginia and Maryland, Nevis and the Leeward Islands, Jamaica, and also Holland (MS. in D). The first minute of the Meeting is dated 22 iv. 1676. The Meeting was held weekly at Three Kings Court, on the "6th day."

      It appears from the document mentioned above that about 70 Friends were members of the Meeting, all men ; perhaps the country correspondents might also attend. This has its bearing upon the size of the Chamber (80. 10). At the sitting of 14 vii. 1683 (p. 83) "there was many grievous Sufferings read y^t came out of many parts of the nation." On one occasion the Meeting was disturbed by the spying of an Informer (p. 88). George Fox was a constant attender down to four days before his death. William Penn wrote that Fox "would be sure to stir them up to discharge their duty especially in suffering cases...and endeavouring speedy relief....So that the Churches or any suffering members thereof were sure not to be forgotten or delayed in their desires if he were there" (Tercent. Text, p. xx). If absent, cases were at times postponed "till George comes."

      The Friend (Lond.), 1896, p. 678. The minutes of the Meeting, which is now held monthly, are in D.

79 6   The meetings for the consideration of questions of business attended by Fox were innumerable. He spent long hours at the Chamber and met Friends at private houses to consult on many themes. Friends often met quite early in the day. See Introduction.

79 7   It is not evident why this account of the meeting at Poulner, near Ringwood, is inserted at this place in the Itinerary Journal. The heading follows on without any break and the Journal is resumed with the addition only of the figures 1683. But here we have exact date. See p. 66 and vol. ii. pp. 24, 386. Ell. Text has part of this narrative within quotation-marks as though it had been taken direct from the narrative on p. 80.

      In commemoration of the tercentenary of the birth of George Fox (1624) a party of friends visited the farm at Poulner and held a meeting at Ringwood in May (3^d mo : O.S.), 1924, two hundred and sixty-one years after the meeting described here.

80 1—3   Neither the name of John Line, constable (—1682), nor the account of his horrible death, appears in the Camb. Text (vol. ii. p. 24), but we find both in the Ell. Text (ii. 5). Here, in addition, is mention of Mrs Line and other persecutors—wealthy men upon whom judgement fell in "ye wasteing of their outward Estates." There is an article on "Early Friends in Poulner, Hants," in *Jnl. F. H. S.* vii.

80 4   Joseph Besse records this event in his books of *Sufferings* (vol. i.
p. 234): "The last day of the month called May 1663, Philip Bence,
Martin Bence, James Miller, Edward Pritchett, being some of them on
the Road, some in a Friend's House, others in an Orchard, and some in
other Places near Ringwood, were taken up by an officious Constable
and committed to prison for supposed intention of holding meetings [!].
They were in close confinement about half a year and then by the
Gaoler's Favour they obtained some Liberty and were Prisoners
at Large several years and continued till released by the King's Letters
Patent in 1672." *Extracts from State Papers*, p. 344—*Cal. S. P. Dom.*
1671—2, p. 489.

80 5   Samuel Boulton (Bolton) was a London Friend and a Minister. As
"citizen and grocer" he married Hannah Polsted, at The Peel in 1668.
She died 20 viii. 1675, at the age of 26. We have hints here and there
(pp. 93, 95, 99, 129) between viii. 1684 and xi. 1685/6, of some difficulty
in the way of Boulton's proposed marriage with Mary Penington
(93. 8). It was evidently of long standing as in the Haistwell Diary,
under date of "3rd day of 10 month 1677," we read "y^t night G ff &
Isaac Pennington & Wm Penn & severall ffriends had a meeting concerning..." (p. 259). The blank at the end has been covered by another hand,
the same as the writer of the Itinerary Journal, with the words:
"S Bolton & M: p." Seven years later the matter was still *sub judice*
and continued till late in 1685, when these long and probably painful
discussions came to an end. The conclusion is outlined in the following
letter from Ambrose Rigge (MS. in D): "I understand y^t Samuell
Bolton and Mary Penington had even been at 2 meetings in order to
finish their intended Marryage and that he had ye Consent of her
parents & herself thereto & ye Consent of ye meetings, but haveing
seen a Letter under Samuell Bolton's hand wherein he freely gave it up
to her parents and Relations & they haveing given their Judgement a^{gt}
it, it wholly rests there & ye meeting hath nothing to doe with it as
I understand now, but I did not then when I writ to them. Witness
my hand this 15th of 11th mo. 1685/6, AMBROSE RIGGE." The M.M. at
Hunger Hill wrote, 7 ix. 1687, to S. Boulton respecting his engagement
to Mary Penington, implying that he had "at the same time an attach-
ment to another woman," name not given (MS. in D). In 1686 Mary
Penington had married Daniel Wharley (110. 1); why should not
the matter have been allowed to rest?

    The next episode in the personal affairs of Samuel Boulton is recorded
under date 20 xi. 1686/7: "G. ff. & G. W. &c. had a meeting with Sam^{ll}
Bolton about Contract of Marryage between him & Sarah ffreckelton"
(p. 167). Sarah Freckleton is named in Fox's testamentary dispositions,
c. 1688 (vol. ii. pp. 351, 489): "Sarah thou may give Sarah ffrecklton
half a Guiney for she hath been Serviceable to me, an honest Carefull
young Woman."

    This also failed to materialize, but we are glad to know that Samuel
found another wife at last in Prudence Wager, of Ratcliff, whom he
married at Liskeard in Cornwall in 1700, with the approval of the Two
Weeks Meeting in London. She was, perhaps, a daughter of Prudence
Wager, who married Alexander Parker (vol. i. p. 427).

    Christian Progress, pp. 423, 592; *Jnl. F. H. S.* v. 202; Minutes of
Morning Meeting, vols. i. and ii.

80 6   William Crouch (1628—1710) arrived in London from his Hampshire
home in 1646 and after his apprenticeship he settled at Spread Eagle
Court in Finch Lane, near Cornhill. He was a "citizen and upholder."
He became a Friend about 1656. He was burnt out in the Great Fire

of 1666 and for a while took refuge at Devonshire House, occupying, with other Friends, a part of the premises so called. On the rebuilding of the City, he settled in Gracechurch Street. Crouch married Ruth Brown (c. 1638—1710), one of the earliest of London converts. He was one of the early members of the Meeting for Sufferings. He assisted George Whitehead in obtaining relief for Quaker sufferers (*Christian Progress*, pp. 500 n., 526, 528, 531, 594, 595). His *Posthuma Christiana*, 1712, gives much information of Quaker doings in London.

For a recent history of the Fire see Bell, *The Great Fire of London in 1666*, 1920.

80   7   This was probably Benjamin Clark, the bookseller and printer of Friends' books, in George Yard. His name is connected with that of Andrew Sowle (108. 4) in minutes of the Morning Meeting (*Jnl. F. H. S.* xviii.) and elsewhere. Dunton, in his *Life and Errors*, 1705, p. 292, calls him "Thee and Thou Clarke." His business was taken over by Thomas Howkins in 1687.

Antiquarian Researches among the Early Printers and Publishers of Friends' Books, 1844; Plomer, *Dict. of Printers and Booksellers*, 1922, p. 71.

80   8   James Wasse (c. 1638—1712), "citizen & chirugeon," of London, married Mary Woodwarde in 1664. Several of their elder children were born in Houndsditch; in 1679, at the birth of another child, the residence is given as Clement's Lane. On Sunday, 9th September, 1683, with other Friends, he was taken from a meeting at Gracechurch Street but released later in the day. He died at Hackney and was buried at Bunhill Fields.

First-days Meetings, p. 133, MS. in D.

It would be interesting to know what Fox said to the "phisitians." He had probably a better estimate of the value of the doctor than he had in earlier days when he said it was opened to him "that the physicians were out of the wisdom of God by which the creatures were made and so knew not their virtues" (Tercent. Text, p. 17). That was in 1649 when he was twenty-five. Since which, association with Dr Edward Bourne, Dr Thomas Lower, the "great Docter from poland" (p. 129), the "friendly Chiurgion" (p. 135), the "great Docter of phis:" (p. 154), "ye Kings Chirurgion" (p. 197), Dr Samuel Browne (p. 230), "a Doctor of physick" (p. 248), and others, had doubtless modified his views of the profession.

80   9   Richard Richardson was the second Recording Clerk to Friends. See vol. ii. p. 498. His home was at Bow, East of London, where G. Fox visited him (p. 119) and his office was in Three Kings Court, off Lombard Street (see next note). He attended on Fox as his secretary (p. 108).

See note respecting Mark Swanner (93. 10).

80   10   The "Chamber" of the clerk to Friends was in Three Kings Court, a turning out of Lombard Street to the South (pp. 88, 103, 172). It is usually referred to simply as "the Chamber." The accommodation here must have been considerable—the Meeting for Sufferings (79. 5) was held here, also the Second Days Morning Meeting (81. 1), and, at Y.M. time, the General Meeting of Friends in the ministry (p. 109). George Fox was in constant attendance at the Chamber and spent very many busy hours in its precincts.

In the *London Directory* of 1677 other tenants of Three Kings Court are named.

When negotiations with Parliament were frequent and long it appeared necessary to have some business centre nearer than the Chamber in Lombard Street, so Friends took a chamber in Palace Yard adjoining Westminster Hall (pp. 190, 191, 193, 194)—"Westminster Hall, with its courts of law [see p. 58], and its stalls of booksellers, law stationers, sempstresses, and dealers in toys and small wares" (Wheatley, *Pepysiana*, 1899, p. 202). Near, if not the same place, was "yᵉ Coffy house where friends used to be Joyning to Westminster Hall" (p. 218).

81   1   The Second Days Morning Meeting, to give it its full name, was first held 15 vii. 1673, and the Meeting was last held 28 i. 1901. For many years it consisted of men Ministers only and one of its most important functions was the examination and approval or rejection of manuscripts proposed to be printed. When met on a Monday morning, the Ministers placed their names in books ruled for the various London and near-by country meetings, to indicate the places they felt inclined to visit on the following Sunday. Twenty-two folio volumes—*Books of Ministering Friends*—dating from 1699 to 1793, are extant in D, as are also the minutes of the Morning Meeting, in ten folios. See *F. Q. E.* 1897, pp. 254—259, 1901, pp. 325—329 ; *The Friend* (Lond.), 1901, pp. 442, 719 ; *Jnl. F. H. S.* i. 23. An index to vols. i. and ii. and an abstract of the minutes 1673—1700 are among MSS. in D.

There was a Sunday morning meeting of Ministers which Fox occasionally attended, in which were some periods of silence (pp. 109, 142, 170, 174).

London Friends' Meetings, pp. 336 ff.

81   2   In our days it seems incongruous to remark that a meeting was "in the house" and "quiet," but the reader of this Itinerary Journal will find occasions when meetings were disturbed and the houses emptied and closed. Kingston seems to have been one of the storm-centres (see pp. 77, 87, 88) though meetings there were, at times, "peaceable within yᵉ doors." In *London Friends' Meetings* we read : "The earliest history of the [Quaker] Church at Kingston is a story of persecution and violence. As late as 1685 we find the meetings broken up with brutal violence" (pp. 311 f.). Opposition lessened as time went on, and the last reference to disturbance of meetings that we have noticed, also at Kingston, took place on the 8th November, 1683 (p. 88) though, somewhat later, at the Savoy, "officers Came but finding noe meeting passed away againe" (p. 115). For a time we read that meetings were "large and peaceable within the doors," then the formula is shortened to "large and peaceable" and finally to "large" when the diarist or copyist first wrote "large and peaceable," crossed out the last two words, and inserted "&" before "large"—8 iii. 1687 (p. 174).

81   3   The account of this meeting at Gracechurch Street here given in the first person was doubtless the basis of the recital in the Ell. Text, ii. 387. The appearance of the first person may indicate an early autobiographical statement incorporated in the Itinerary Journal.

81   4   Mary Forster (*c.* 1619—1686) was the widow of Thomas Forster (112. 2); she lived near the Quaker centre in Gracechurch Street, and George Fox often stepped into her house after a Sunday morning meeting in White Hart Court, at times resting himself on a bed there. He visited her when sick (p. 164) and called soon after her death "to comfort the afflicted" (p. 165); she was the author of several pamphlets and wrote Testimonies to her husband (who died in 1660) and to Anne, wife of George Whitehead. She departed this life the 25th of Tenth Month, 1686.

82   1   As Friends spread toward the West from London City, meetings were opened in various places. Elizabeth Trott "gave up her house which was towards the end of the Pall Mall, near James's House, for a meeting, which in great measure was settled by Gilbert, who was a very constant attender" (*Gilbert Latey*, 1707, p. 59). On the decease of Elizabeth Trott in 1666, "Westminster being the residence of several Friends and a great concourse of people that way, Friends bought the Term of a lease of a House and Garden in the little Amberry, in Westminster...and the Meeting hath continued there ever since" (*ibid.* p. 65).

         William Crouch, 1712, p. 18; *London Friends' Meetings.*

         For this and the previous paragraph see Ell. Text, ii. 387. Two days later Fox wrote the epistle to " Friends and Brethren, who have received the peaceable truth," given *ibid.* ii. 388.

82   2   For Mary Woolley see vol. ii. p. 493. Her husband was Ezekiel Woolley (151. 1). She accompanied Fox on some of his visits and Fox visited her husband and her at their Spitalfields home.

82   3   The Two Weeks (or Fortnightly) Meeting was of early origin, being established within two years of the rise of Friends in London. It settled down as a meeting having special care of Friends' marriages in the London district. Men and women met separately.

         London Friends' Meetings, pp. 85—91.

82   4   The Lord Mayor for 1682—3 was Sir William Pritchard (*c.* 1632—1705). There is a considerable account of his year of office in *D. N. B.*

82   5   "The Six-weeks Meeting, as originally instituted in 1671, was a selected assembly of 'grave and antient' Friends (both men and women) chosen out of all the Meetings in the metropolis and its district, to whose management and control all matters affecting the common interest of these Meetings were committed, forming also a court of final appeal among them in all cases of difficulty that might arise. George Fox termed it, in after years, 'the prime meeting of the city'" (*London Friends' Meetings*, pp. 91—133). At its opening the Meeting consisted of 49 men and 35 women among them being George Whitehead, Alexander Parker, Gilbert Latey, Francis Camfield, William Crouch, William Meade, Rebecka Travers, Anne Whitehead, Mary Elson, Mary Forster, and Mary Woolley. It appears to have met generally at the Bull and Mouth, and acted in a more private capacity than the Two Weeks Meeting (82. 3). The "Meeting of Twelve" was a finance committee of the Six Weeks Meeting (? p. 128).

         Minute books are in D.

83   1   According to *London Friends' Meetings* (pp. 267—269) a meeting-house was built at Ratcliff about 1666, at the corner of Schoolhouse Lane and Brook Street. In 1670 Sir John Robinson, governor of the Tower, did his best (or worst) to scatter the Friends—forms and tables were taken away but Friends met to worship, standing. Friends' hats were swept off and thrown over an adjoining wall, "but neither the loss of their forms nor their hats could prevent Friends from meeting, so Sir John destroyed the house, yet Friends met upon the ruins and then restored their building," *ante* 1681. The visits of Fox to Ratcliff Sunday meetings, sometimes by water, were not infrequent and the meetings held were usually "large and peaceable within yᵉ doors." The one recorded here ("6ᵗʰ day" should be "1st day") is noted in *First-days Meetings*, p. 134. The considerable attendance of "professors" is also noted.

83   2   See 89. 4.

84   1   Wheeler Street Meeting in the Spitalfields district dates from a Meeting in a private house at the corner of Wheeler and Westbury Streets in 1656. When several London meetinghouses had been destroyed, Wheeler Street was saved by the clever and prompt action of Gilbert Latey who installed a tenant in the building (*Gilbert Latey*, 1707, p. 71; *London Friends' Meetings*, p. 163; vol. ii. p. 401). At one time a large Meeting met here but later the number diminished and in 1749 the meetinghouse tumbled down and the Meeting was given up. Westbury Street is now known as Quaker Street and here the Bedford Institute Home Mission Association has its head-quarters.

84   2   This Sunday at the Savoy is one of the few narrative portions of the *post*-1675 Ell. Text (ii. 390—393), omitting a personal touch and the name of the Justice concerned, and, as often, the exact date. This date seems correct, but the day of the month in the previous paragraph should have been "5th" instead of "6th."

85   1   Further information respecting Justice Guy, of King Street, Bloomsbury, is not forthcoming. The name is not given in the Ell. Text (ii. 391).

86   1   It is noticeable that there is no record of the imprisonment of Fox since his liberation from Worcester Jail in 1675, while many of his followers were suffering from close confinement in prison.

86   2   Gabriel Shadd was a very hardworking Informer. His name appears not infrequently in Friends' records. The minutes of the Meeting for Sufferings held 9 xii. 1682 contain: "The copy of Shads conviction & to be burnt in ye hand to be inserted in ye book by R^d R^{d}son & to pay 2s to Ben: Antrobus for Meet." A few days after this affair at the Savoy, Shadd was again at work, and with Yates, another Informer, caused distraint to be levied upon John Elson of The Peel (*Suff.* i. 457). In *First-days Meetings*, there are other notices of Shadd's activities. On the same day, apparently, as he stated that he had informed against Fox at the Savoy, he informed against Francis Stamper at Westminster, but he was equally unsuccessful as Stamper was released because no constable would swear against him. On the 14th of Eighth Month Shadd was again at the Savoy: "Informer Shadd came with Constables. Friends when asked for their names objected to Shadd (of his being burnt, etc.). They were taken and kept till night and then released because Shadd did not appear."
Christian Progress, pp. 521, 541, 596 (Dorothy Shadd).

87   1   There is a brief note respecting Gilbert Latey in vol. ii. p. 401. The service of this Friend during the period of the Itinerary Journal is described by George Whitehead in his Testimony: "He was for many Years my true companion in laborious Sollicitations in the late three Kings Reigns, before whom we divers times appeared and often attended in behalf of our suffering Friends." (From this it would appear that the "G. W." associated with Latey on pp. 122, 130, 133, 135, 143, 144, 202, was George Whitehead.) In the State Papers Domestic, 1670, Latey is described as "a great Ag^t of ye Quakers in ye Strand at ye Peacocke a Taylo^r near to Drury Lane" (*Extracts from State Papers*, p. 312—*Cal. S. P. Dom.* 1670, p. 299). Latey married Mary, only daughter of John and Ann Fielder (127. 1) of Kingston. He lived on the Fisher-Woodcock estate at the Savoy. Of their eleven children only two lived to man's estate. Latey signed the Testimony to George Fox (Ell. Text, ii. 525). He represented Cornwall and Devon at the first settlement of the Meeting for Sufferings, 1676 (MS. in D). In the *Life* of Latey, edited by his nephew, Richard Hawkins, and published in 1707 (reprinted 1821, etc.), there is a valuable record of the opening

of work on behalf of poor Friends undertaken by women (see vol. ii. pp. 342 ff.: Brailsford, *Quaker Women*, 1915, chap. xiii.; *Bulletin F. H. S. Phila.* iii. 150).

87   2   For John and Elizabeth Vaughton see vol. ii. p. 487. In the *Manuscripts of the House of Lords, 1695—1697*, issued by the Historical MSS. Commission in 1903, there is, dated 8 April, 1697, a petition *re* Tithes signed by Theodor Eccleston and John Vaughton, for the Friends, endorsed: "Offered by the Quakers and read and rejected." Vaughton was a very active Minister in the London district. With Whitehead he was concerned with the needs of about forty Pietists in England; he received money for them and paid them visits (*London Friends' Meetings*, p. 131).

In 1685 Vaughton was living at the Joyners Arms, Stanhope Street near New Market, within the verge of Westminster M.M., where Fox was a frequent visitor.

Christian Progress, pp. 595, 601, 635, 659, 671, 680.

87   3   This suppressed passage relating to the loan by Friends of the meetinghouse at the Savoy (79. 2) to the King's Guards is very interesting. The Ell. Text (ii. 393) omits all reference to the action of Friends. It is clear from the context that soldiers made use of Friends' property by the *favour* of Friends and not by *force*, and it is probably for this reason that the passage was struck through and some of it made illegible. In *First-days Meetings*, under date 1683, 4 mo. 28, we read: "Savoy, The Kings Guards (being doubled) took up their Quarters in ye meeting house." Some years later Friends were not so accommodating (or, should it be said, were more true to principles). The meetinghouses at the Park and the Savoy were *forcibly* taken by soldiery, and occupied for some years till a clearance was ordered by King James in 1686 (*Gilbert Latey*, 1707, p. 117; *Christian Progress*, pp. 614—618; Hirst, *Quakers in Peace and War*, 1923, p. 77). During this time meetings were held in the yard and entry (see 79. 2).

In 1745, at the time of the rebellion of the Young Pretender, the meetinghouse at Devonshire House became a guard room by *favour* of Friends of the M.M. (*London Friends' Meetings*, p. 169; Hirst, *Quakers in Peace and War*, p. 188 n.).

87   4   Francis Camfield (*c.* 1628—1708) had a house in the City and also at Theobalds (Tiballs), near Waltham Abbey (vol. i. p. 426), at both of which places he received and entertained George Fox. The town-house being near to Hicks Hall in Clerkenwell Fox frequently looked in there to be informed of magisterial decisions. Various consultations were also held at his residence. His daughter Hannah married William Baker (180. 1) at the Bull and Mouth in 1672. Jacob Camfield (157. 1) was a son (pp. 157, 176). Francis Camfield married Elizabeth Watts of Aldersgate Street in 1677 (*c.* 1632—1716). She was his second wife; his first wife, Patience, died in 1675. Wife, daughter and son-in-law appear on p. 180. There is a curious minute of the Meeting of Twelve dated 22 ix. 1680, which reads: "Agreed that Wᵐ Parker & John Edge do speake with ffran Camfield about yᵉ Damidg done at Bull & Mouth by his tobacco." Camfield is very frequently mentioned in *First-days Meetings* and in *Books of Ministering Friends*. He preached at the funeral of George Fox. A sermon of his at Gracechurch Street, 14 May, 1693, was printed, with others, in *The Concurrence and Unanimity of the People called Quakers*, 1711.

Y.M. Epistles, 1685, 1686; *Jnl. F. H. S.* i.

87   5   This meeting at the Bull and Mouth is referred to in Ell. Text, ii. 395, the wording here being taken into the Ell. Text.

87   6   As conveyance by road became easier owing to the improved condition of the streets, passage along the great waterway was less frequent,
to the lament of the watermen (107. 2). The hackney coaches were
being rapidly improved and glass coaches are mentioned by Pepys
(Sept. 23, 1667). Fox made frequent use of coaches and some of his
friends owned private vehicles or obtained such for his use.

Chariots also are referred to in the Itinerary Journal. William
Meade owned one (p. 106). This was a lighter carriage "made with
springs" (Pepys *Diary*, Sept. 5, 1665).

Fox went down to Kingston that he "might be free from interruptions, having several things to write" (Ell. Text, ii. 396). He wrote *The
Saints, their Heavenly and Spiritual Worship*, printed same year, also
letters to Friends in Maryland and Barbados (*Register of George Fox's
Letters*, MS. in D).

89   1   Abiah Roberts, of Newchapel, Essex, has not yet been identified. Fox
spent a week-end at his house and had a meeting on the Sunday.

89   2   In *London Friends' Addresses* (MS. in D) John Bull (*c.* 1646—1698)
is described as a "hosier at his warehouse in Throgmorton Street near
Barthelemew Lane, 1678." With other Friends he signed a petition to
Parliament on the question of sufferings for non-swearing, 1695
(*Christian Progress*, p. 647).

Suff. i. 462.

89   3   Mary Stott (—1688), widow of John Stott, lived at Dalston when
we first meet her in the Itinerary Journal. At the end of 1684 we find
her at Bethnal Green. Epistles of George Fox, dated from Dalston, were
probably written at the Stott home. One is mentioned in Ell. Text
(ii. 368) and another, *ibid.* ii. 396. See *Register of George Fox's Letters*
(MS. in D). In 1685 and later Fox's letters were written at Bethnal
Green and he was a frequent visitor at Mary Stott's here. The quiet of
her home in Bethnal Green was specially suited to letter-writing
(pp. 137, 144, 164). See 129. 1. Fox also met the widow Stott at the
house of her son-in-law, Edward Bathurst (97. 3). Some difficulty in
executing her will is mentioned in note 93. 6.

89   4   Jane Bullock was the principal of the Shacklewell School (pp. 83, 89,
91), at Hackney in North London, "sette uppe to Instruct younge
lasses & maydens in whatsever thinges was civill & usefull in ye
creation" (vol. ii. p. 119). In 1677 the school was said to be in a poor
way and more pupils were needed (*Second Period*, p. 528). George Fox's
meeting, if held on a First-day, must have been on the 9th, not the
10th, of the Tenth Month. At an earlier date the school was under the
care of the widow Stott (*London Friends' Meetings*, p. 360).

89   5   There is a note respecting Margaret Rous, daughter of John and
Margaret, in vol. ii. p. 422 (though it is probable that in the text
"younge Margaret Rouse" refers to the mother and not to the daughter).
In the Itinerary Journal "young Margret Rouse" doubtless refers to
the daughter.

89   6   George Watts (—1688) belonged to Peel M.M., living in the parish
of St Botolph, Aldersgate. He was a member of the Meeting for
Sufferings, representing Ely and Lincolnshire, in 1676. He accompanied
Fox to Holland in 1677 (p. 237) and 1684 (Ell. Text, ii. 397). See 93. 2. On
his return he entertained Dutch Friends at his house (p. 110). Fox was
frequently at his town-house and also at his country-house at Enfield.
John Gratton (*c.* 1641—1711/12) tells us in his *Journal*, p. 105, that
while he was in Derby Jail in 1684, he was the means of the conversion
of the jailer's eldest son and that, with the consent of the lad's parents,

Gratton took him to London and "placed him with an honest Friend, George Watts, where he did well," married, "and grew rich every way." Watts was doubtless referred to in the Itinerary Journal by his initials but it is difficult to state whether "G. W." refers to him or to George Whitehead. In *First-days Meetings* we read: "1683/4, 12 mo. 3, Grace-church Street. Kept out in Grace's street abo‍ᵗ half an hour, then permitted into yᵉ yard where ffrᵈˢ stood peaceably G. Watts declaring, & Marr. ffarmb. & G. Wᵗˢ praying yᵉ meeting ended, it being a very cold frosty morning, yᵉ Conᵇˡᵉˢ kept within yᵉ meetinghouse, having shut yᵉ doors, till ended" (p. 216). Fox wrote a Testimony to his friend.

MSS. in D, some relating to Friends on the European Continent.

90   1   Prayer almost invariably followed sermon in George Fox's vocal service in the meetings he attended, but we do not have any outline of the burden of it. Penn wrote: "Above all he excelled in prayer....The most awful, living reverent frame I ever felt or beheld, I must say, was his in prayer" (Tercent. Text, p. xix). The words of a prayer, written 17 ii. 1671, are given in Tercent. Text, p. 269. It was apparently usual for a prayer to follow a sermon. The collection of the sermons of Stephen Crisp, published in 1694, includes "his Prayer after every Sermon" and in the collection of sermons preached by fourteen Friends, 1688—1694, there follows a prayer after each sermon. These prayers seem much after the manner of the modern minister in the pulpit, not as usual in Friends' meetings to-day. They begin with such words as "Most Glorious Infinite Powerful Father" (Stephen Crisp), "Blessed God of Life" (Francis Stamper), "Most Glorious and Infinite God of Heaven and Earth" (William Penn). Charles Marshall's prayer contains about 2200 words (*Concurrence and Unanimity*, 1711). See 137. 1.

90   2   There is a place Ellington in Huntingdonshire North of London and another in East Kent South of London, but neither place seems to be near enough to London to make it likely that Fox visited it.

91   1   For Edward Mann see vol. ii. p. 422. The "several times" of this note, based on the Ell. Text, must be altered to "very many" consequent on the exploitation of the Itinerary Journal. The visits were paid at both Mann's warehouse in George Yard and his home at Ford Green. Elizabeth Mann must have had a busy time when Fox was there, as, for instance, when he spent sixteen days at the Mann home, "in wᶜʰ time many friᵈˢ Came almost daily to see him" (p. 148, see also pp. 178, 179, 233, 234, 236, 257—259, 272). Edward Mann represented North Wales in the Meeting for Sufferings.

Many references in vol. ii.

91   2   Sarah Meade's only child was Nathaniel (1684—1760). See vol. ii. p. 491, where it is stated that Sir Nathaniel Meade, knight, died "probably without descendants." More recent information does not support this supposition. In a pamphlet written by Henry J. Mead in 1918, it is stated: "Sir Nathaniel had two sons, Robert and William. Both died in infancy, and were buried at Romford. His widow, Martha, Lady Mead, died in 1779 and was buried at Romford." In 1920 Mr Mead wrote to the editor of *Jnl. F. H. S.*: "I have recently come across an entry in the Middle Temple Records shewing that Thomas Meade, son and heir of Sir Nathaniel Meade, was admitted a student of that Inn on 6th November, 1732....I had hitherto thought that the only children of Sir Nathaniel were two, who died in infancy." (*Jnl. F. H. S.* xvii. 130.) No further information is forthcoming.

Jnl. F. H. S. xi. xiii.

91   3   The Friend whose name or initials occur most frequently in the Itinerary Journal is, without doubt, Benjamin Antrobus (*c.* 1645—1715).

He was a linendraper at the Plough and Harrow in Cheapside. George Fox lodged at his house a multitude of times, and stored there some of his possessions—papers, chest "with some Gold in itt," a hundred pounds "which is for G ffs Dayly Charge" (vol. ii. pp. 348—352, 355—360). "B. A." was to assist in the collection of Fox's books and papers for printing and distribution. He suffered imprisonment in Newgate 1683—1685. He was a Minister and his name occurs frequently in *First-days Meetings.* The Y.M. of 1686, 1687 and 1688 appointed him, with others, to have charge of the accounts. Many consultations took place at the Plough and Harrow, some of a private character (*Jnl. F. H. S.* xii. 61). Though constantly mentioned, few particulars appear. He was twenty years younger than Fox. He wrote much halting verse, on a variety of subjects, *e.g.* A Complaint against New England Persecutors ; Concerning Persecution ; Concerning the Philosopher's Stone. He represented South Wales in the Meeting for Sufferings in 1676.

He is also frequently mentioned in the Haistwell Diary.

Mary Antrobus (*c.* 1650—1705) was Mary Burrell, of Greenwich, before she married Benjamin Antrobus in 1671. She accompanied Fox on some of his visits to the country, alone and with her husband and sister, and "a Coachfull of friends" (p. 197). Her shoulders must have borne most of the weight of G. Fox's entertainment, and that of others who came to see him at the Plough and Harrow, especially while her husband was in prison. Sometimes, however, the visits were apparently to the shop only, pp. 142, 144.

The names Joseph Antrobus and Elizabeth Antrobus appear among records in D.

92   1   "Hicks Hall was the Middlesex Sessions House in St John Street, Clerkenwell, named after Sir Baptist Hicks, one of the justices, afterwards Viscount Campden, at whose cost the Hall was built in 1612" (Wheatley, note to Pepys's *Diary*, Dec. 6, 1660). Fox often called at Francis Camfield's in order "to look after Friends busyness at ye Sessions," or "to see what became of Friends that were to appear there." At times also he waited for news at John Matthews's "att the Kings head att Smithfield Barrs" (p. 147). See Ell. Text, ii. 431.

92   2   George Barr (—   ) was resident in Gracechurch Street and also at Bury Street near Edmonton and was visited by Fox at both places. He was engaged in matters of finance (*Jnl. F. H. S.* xii. 123; *Y. M. Epistles,* 1686, 1687). Little is at present known of him outside the Itinerary Journal.

There was a George Barr (*c.* 1656—1722) of Stepney, broadweaver, who married Ann Comfort in 1670 and "died of age," in Gravel Lane, Houndsditch.

92   3   For Alexander Parker see vol. i. p. 427. There are many references to Parker in vols. i. and ii. but only slight intimation that he made his residence in London during his later days. John Whiting states that Parker settled in London soon after his marriage in 1669 (*Memoirs,* p. 185), but still travelled extensively in the ministry. His home was in George Yard where Fox and others frequently dined (pp. 104, 108) and on one occasion (the only mention of such in the Itinerary Journal) Fox "supped" at his house (p. 110). At Ratcliff Fox was at ": A : ps: Lodgings at his Sisters" (p. 114, see pp. 135, 136, 170, 171). Parker died in 1688/9 and was buried in Bunhill Fields (*London Friends' Meetings,* p. 331).

Christian Progress, pp. 299, 536, 546, 570, 572; many reff. in D in print and MS.

92 4   Nathaniel Brassey (*c.* 1646—1686) "was a goldsmith of Lombard Street. He was an active Friend and a Minister and a faithful testimony-bearer" (*Jnl. F. H. S.* xi. 169). G. Fox was constantly at his house and enjoyed his friend's hospitality and also that of his wife Elizabeth Brassey. Brassey was with Fox in Holland in 1684 and subsequently entertained some Dutch Friends (p. 110).

In a letter from Sarah Meade to Margaret Fox, dated 7 ii. 1686, we read: "wee heare y^t Nath: Brassey & his onely sonn [Nathaniel] are both to be buried this day, both in one Coffin; the Childe was a fine lively Childe about a yea^{re} & a qu^{r}te^r old & I did not hea^{re} but they were both well when wee came out of Towne—its a sickly time in these parts" (Abraham MSS., printed *Jnl. F. H. S.* xi. 169).

Upon the death of her husband Elizabeth Brassey continued to entertain Fox who was very frequently at her house for the night. In 1687 she married John Toovy and died in less than two months afterwards "of Colick."

93 1   Martha Fisher is mentioned several times in vol. ii. Her name is frequently associated with that of Jane Woodcock in vol. ii. and in the Haistwell Diary. George Fox was very frequently at her house and often lodged there. She occupied three chambers and a garret above the meetinghouse at the Savoy. She signed the Fox-Fell wedding certificate in 1669, in Bristol. Her daughter Elizabeth married Nathaniel Bland (104. 3).

93 2   The Y.M. was held on the 19th and 20th of the Third Month, but there is only a slight allusion to it on the 19th. Either chronicler or copyist has bungled in giving one day of the week to two successive days of the month! 3 mo. 16 was "6th day," the day on which the weekly Meeting for Sufferings was held.

George Fox, accompanied by Alexander Parker, George Watts and Nathaniel Brassey, and also by William Bingley and Samuel Waldenfield, left for his second visit to Holland on the 31st of the Third Month and returned on the 16th of the Fifth Month. "They travelled 772 milles, vizt in England 149, by sea Rivers & in Holland 612, had 18 Meetings...two Earles came to ye meeteing at Amsterdam & also seu^{r}all considerable psons came to seu^{r}all of ye meeteings" (MS. in D, printed *Jnl. F. H. S.* vi. 37). After resting in the country Fox returned to London on the 21st of the Fifth Month to meet some Friends who had come over from New Jersey on business (Ell. Text, ii. 397—404).

For Friends in Holland see vol. ii. p. 411; note 236. 2.

93 3   For the troublesome question of the ownership of West Jersey see vol. i. p. 452 and vol. ii. p. 434. The twelve proprietors of East New Jersey in 1682 were William Penn, Robert West, Thomas Rudyard, Samuel Groom, Richard Mew, Thomas Hart, Ambrose Rigge, Thomas Willcox, Hugh Hartshorne, John Heywood, Clement Plumstead and Thomas Cooper. A valuable document containing their signatures and seals is described in *Jnl. F. H. S.* xiii. 76. The award in this matter was signed by William Crouch, James Parke, Charles Marshall, Richard Whitpain, William Shewen, Thomas Hart, George Whitehead, and Charles Bathurst and copied by Mark Swanner, 8 mo. 1684 (*Case Put and Decided*, reprint of 1880, p. 10).

There are eight notices of Edward Byllinge (vol. i. p. 452), all connecting him with the "New Jarseys busyness." G. Fox had conferences at various houses with him, George Hutchinson, Thomas Budd, William Penn, and Thomas Hart, in 1684 and 1685. In addition to the references to Byllinge in Pepys's *Diary* (ed. Wheatley) and *Pepysiana*, 1899, there is a paper amongst the Pepys MSS. written by him "to friends and people of all sorts whatsoever," dated March 22, 1673/4, in which he refers to "debts having been run into by him and his late wife" and repents his part of it and hopes that "no reasonable nor tender hearted man or woman will not too far oppress with their tongues him that's already overwhelmed in sorrow, neither anyone charge this my miscarriage upon the principal people of God called Quakers, for their principle is holy and true and they are clear of these things" (*Hist. MSS. Commission, Report* xix.).

Extracts from State Papers, 1913—*Cal. S. P. Dom.* 1658—9, 1660—1, 1661—2, 1664—5, 1670.

93   4   "The Hopes of Amsterdam, and Deepdene, Dorking, were associated with the Gurnells, Harmans and Hoares. Thomas [? Henry] Hope, apprenticed to the Gurnells, became a millionaire" (notes by J. J. Green, to letter from Sir Eustace Gurney in *Jnl. F. H. S.* xviii.). The letter states that the second wife of Edmund Gurney (1723—1796) "was Anne, daughter of Hubert van Flierden, of Lynn, cousin of his first wife, Martha Kett, their mothers being sisters, daughters of John Hope, of Amsterdam." The Henry Hope mentioned here was doubtless of the same family. Benjamin Furly and George Watts were both connected with Holland.

In the life of Samuel Hoare (1751—1815) there is a note which states: "Mr Henry Hope of Amsterdam was apprenticed in 1754 to Gurnell, Hoare and Co., remained with the firm till 1760, and died in 1811, leaving a fortune of more than a million sterling." In the article in *D. N. B.* on Sir Thomas Hope (d. 1646) it is stated that his younger brother, Henry, settled in Amsterdam.

Jnl. F. H. S. xx. 113.

93   5   Benjamin Furly (1636—1714) "was one of the wealthy people who allied themselves with Quakerism in its early days. He was born at Colchester and began business life there" (full account of Furly in *Jnl. F. H. S.* xi. 62—73. A reference to his connection with the *Battle-Door* will be found in vol. ii. p. 379. Prior to 1660 Furly settled at Amsterdam, afterwards removing to Rotterdam. He corresponded with several men of note—Algernon Sidney, the third Lord Shaftesbury, and John Locke. His extensive library was sold by auction in October, 1714. Some of the books once belonging to Furly, sold by Jacob Claus to Thomas Story, were lost at sea (MS. in D). Furly was a son of John and Ann Furly. His father died in 1673, aged about 83. Another and elder son was John Furly (236. 3). Benjamin married twice; his descendants left Friends (*The Essex Review,* April, 1899—"The Furly Family of Essex"). He seems, for a time, to have had some sympathy with the Perrot Hat-schism (vol. ii. pp. 375, 482; *Collectitia,* 1824, p. 148).

Fell-Smith, *Steven Crisp,* 1892; *D. N. B.*; Learned, *F. D. Pastorius,* 1908; Macewen, *Antoinette Bourignon,* 1910; Myers, *Narratives,* 1912; *Second Period*; *Jnl. F. H. S.* iii. vi. vii. x. xvii.; MSS. in D.

93   6   William Kent (*c.* 1650—1720) was a son of Edward Kent, of Pavement, Oxfordshire. He married, firstly, Anne, daughter of Charles Bathurst, at Devonshire House, in 1679, and, secondly, Margaret Cole in 1684/5. He was a cheesemonger in Bishopsgate Street. There is a letter in D, from George Fox to William Meade, dated 8 xi. 1689/90, which refers to the will of Mary Stott (89. 3) and mentions William Kent and his brother-in-law Edward Bathurst. The matter is not stated very clearly, but evidently M. Stott left money to the poor, some of which was claimed by relatives or other legatees. Fox defends the claims of the poor.

93 7   The town-house of Charles Bathurst (*c.* 1626—1700) was at the sign of the Three Sugar Loaves, Without Bishopsgate, and his country-house was "at Epin florest" (p. 118). His first wife, Frances, and the mother of his children, died of cancer in 1675. Later he married Grace Hubbard (*c.* 1634—1703). A son, Benjamin, was apprenticed to John Mackett, "coatseller" of Aldgate Within, but died of small-pox in 1682 at the age of fifteen. Another son was Edward (97. 3) and there were daughters Elizabeth and Anne (105. 7). Charles Bathurst was a grocer and confectioner. Fox was a frequent visitor, in town and country. Bathurst was one who signed a certificate of the *bona fides* of George Whitehead, in 1680 (*Christian Progress*, p. 418). In 1692 he signed a paper entitled *The Doting Athenians Imposing Questions no Proofs*, in answer to statements respecting Friends which had appeared in *The Athenian Mercury*. Other Friends who signed were John Edridge, William Meade, Theodor Eccleston, William Ingram, William Crouch, George Whitehead, Walter Benthall and Thomas Barker, all of whom are mentioned in these notes. He wrote a brief and beautiful Testimony respecting his daughter Elizabeth (105. 7), in which he says, truly: "Deep Sorrows can make no long Discourses."
Jnl. F. H. S. v. 178, xi. 180.

93 8   Mary Penington was the only daughter of Isaac and Mary Penington (235. 1) and was at this time about twenty-seven years old. Her name appears four times in the Itinerary Journal, in connection with that of Samuel Boulton (pp. 93, 95, 99, 129). See 80. 5. She married Daniel Wharley, 9 iv. 1686 (110. 1), and died in 1726.

93 9   Rowland Vaughan was an attorney employed by Friends. He accompanied John Edge and George Whitehead on their urgent visit to the Attorney General (133. 1) and prepared warrants of liberation for signature (*Christian Progress*, p. 589, see also pp. 610, 612). His office was at the Temple.
MSS. in D.

93 10   "Mark" was Mark Swanner, assistant to Richard Richardson (80. 9), Friends' general secretary. He seems to have begun work in the Chamber early in 1684, to have received "30 lbs per year" (*Jnl. F. H. S.* i. 63), and to have removed into Hertfordshire early in 1688. Between these two dates we find him assisting Fox with his literary work. He evidently was not opposed to Sunday work, as when Fox was unable to get out to meetings, Mark was summoned to several houses to assist in writing and in reading books to be printed. On one occasion he wrote for both George and Margaret Fox (p. 98) and on another both clerks had to forgo their Sunday rest (p. 108). The salaries of the two clerks came up for consideration, "wch Continued till late in the night," attended by Fox and "other Select fri^{ds}" (p. 165). One would think that Fox might have been spared work of this kind. This conference is probably the one referred to in the history of the Devonshire House Reference Library (printed *Jnl. F. H. S.* xviii. 11), where Swanner's further work is described. He is called the "German friend." "Mark Shwaner" was in prison in Silesia in 1676 (Fell-Smith, *Steven Crisp*, 1892, p. 38). He appears to have been discharged from Friends' service in 1698 (*Jnl. F. H. S.* xviii. 13).

95 1   Richard Vickris (—1700), of Chew Magna, in Somersetshire, is noted as "the only case where sentence of death was passed upon a Friend in the mother country" (*F. P. T.* p. 360). He was only son of Robert Vickris, merchant and alderman, of Bristol and Chew Magna. He was sent abroad in the hope that his Quaker notions would be dis-

pelled, but while away he was much impressed with the errors of popery, and on his return he allied himself with Friends. He married Elizabeth, daughter of George Bishop, in 1671/2. He was often fined and distrained for meetings, imprisoned and abused. There is a long account of the trial in Whiting's *Memoirs*. The sentence was "That he should Conform, or abjure the Realm in three months, or suffer death as a Felon, without benefit of Clergy." A *habeas corpus* removed him to London where George Fox and William Penn had the interview here recorded. In the Ninth Month he was legally discharged by Lord Chief Justice Jeffreys on errors in the indictment. At the date of Whiting's *Memoirs*, Vickris was living at Chew with wife and ten children. Several articles are credited to him in Smith's *Cata*.

Whiting, *Memoirs*, pp. 89—91, 119, 120; *Jnl. F. H. S.* ix. xix.; *Second Period.*

Later. Referring to the above statement, based on *F. P. T.* p. 360, there is, in a recent pamphlet, written by Elizabeth B. Emmott, *Early Quakerism in Wales*, 1924, the following statement: "In 1676 the Judges declared in open Court at Bala that any Quakers who refused the Oath of Allegiance a second time would be proceeded against as traitors, the men to be hanged and quartered, and the women to be burned. Roland Ellis received this sentence at Dolgelly, but was allowed time to consider. He decided to emigrate to Pennsylvania."

95   2   During his continental travels in 1677 Fox was in the Duke of Holstein's country from which the Duke would have banished Friends had the magistrates agreed to do so (p. 244). Hearing that he had been scandalized by the preaching of Elizabeth Hendricks (108. 5), Fox wrote him a long letter, dated London, 26 viii. 1684, on the subject of women's preaching, which is given in full in Ell. Text (ii. 404—408). The duchy was situated on the borders of Sweden and Denmark. Christian Albert was probably the Duke written to. Apparently, later, the Duke liberated Friends from confinement—"At Dantzic there are now no prisoners; the Duke of Holstein has put forth a declaration for liberty of conscience" (*Y. M. Epistle*, 1692).

95   3   There is a slight notice of Margaret Drinkwell, Senr. (c. 1623—1695), in vol. ii. p. 385. We have not discovered the nature of the "busyness" in which mother and daughter are concerned. Fox visited Margaret Drinkwell at her house in Bishopsgate Street, parish of Shoreditch.

In the paragraph on p. 96, with the mention of M. Drinkwell, the day should be "5th" not "4th."

Jnl. F. H. S. xi. 150.

96   1   Thomas Cox (c. 1641—1711) was a wealthy vintner, of the White Lion, in Whitechapel, son of Thomas Cox, of Cheltenham. At the institution of the Meeting for Sufferings in 1676 Thomas Cox was appointed to act for Friends in Norfolk and Cambridge in conjunction with Clement Plumstead. George Fox was frequently at his house and took dinner with him from time to time and passed a night there. In 1686, 11th of Ninth Month, G. Fox attended the marriage of a daughter of T. Cox at Devonshire House and accompanied the couple to South Street, where it is probable that there was another Cox home. (Search has been made for a record of this marriage (160. 4) but it has not been found.) Cox's daughter, Christian, married Lascelles Metcalfe at Devonshire House in 1691. Thomas Cox heads the list of subscribers to a fund to assist William Gibson, c. 1725, with a donation of seven guineas (*Jnl. F. H. S.* i. 26). He witnessed the sealing by William Penn of a document in 1681 (vol. ii. p. 367). His wife is mentioned on p. 194, see 179. 1. In a letter from John Tomkins to Sir John Rodes,

1702, we read respecting a consignment of wine: "I did buy it of Tho:
Cox, and told him who it was for, and I beleeve he has taken care that
thou hast his best. It is covered with Canvas to prevent their taping
of it with pencers." Then follows a copy of Cox's bill for the wine—
twenty gallons, 2 casks, canvas and porterage £5. 15. 6. (*Quaker Post-
Bag*, 1910, p. 189).

"Thomas Cox, a Quaker, formerly grocer in Aldersgate street,...
very considerable fortune," died 13 May, 1739 (*Gent.'s Mag.*, quoted
Jnl. F. H. S. xiii. 28).

96   2   Ann Hayley, widow, of Guttershedge near Hendon, early opened her
house as a meetingplace for Friends. Ellwood reports two visits to her,
in 1677 and 1680 (Ell. Text, ii. 261, 345). We have no knowledge of the
"busyness" which called certain Friends together (pp. 96, 97, 107). In
1686 Ann Hayley lodged five Friends at her house—George Fox, John
and Mary Elson and Mariabella Farmborough, Senr. and Junr.
(p. 138).

96   3   Lawrence Fullove (*c.* 1626—1689) lived in the parish of St Alphage,
London Wall. He was one of the Friends sentenced to banishment to
Jamaica in 1664 and put on board the *Black Eagle* in August, 1665.
A storm drove the ship to the coast of Norway, but the prisoners were
not permitted to land. Eventually they reached Holland and were
two months on shore, and then returned to England. But of the fifty-
five put on board in the Thames twenty-seven only reached the Downs
alive. William Crouch prints a letter from Fullove from Amsterdam,
27 ii. 1666, to his uncle, Amor Stoddard, giving some account of their
adventures (*Posthuma Christiana*, 1712, pp. 89 ff.). In the history of
the Devonshire House Reference Library which appeared in volume
xviii. of the *Jnl. F. H. S.*, we are told of a search for lost records, and
that, at the Meeting for Sufferings, ix. 1689, "John Dew Acquaints the
meeting that a deal Chest with Writtings and Books of ffriends (Supposed to be the Chest soe much enquired after by ffriends) is now
found at Lawrence ffulloves. This Meeting Orders that the said Chest
and Writtings be sent to ffriends Chamber in Lombard Street." It may
be that to-day we benefit from the action of 1689 in centralizing records.
Suff. i. 406; Smith, *Cata.* i. 826. See 136. 2.

97   1   Rebecka Travers (1609—1688) was the wife and widow of William
Travers, tobacconist, at the sign of the Three Feathers in Watling
Street. She was educated in the Baptist Church but was convinced of
Quakerism by James Nayler, who, during a discussion, "putting his
hand over the Table, and taking her by the Hand, said, 'Feed not on
knowledge, it is as truly forbidden to thee, as ever it was to Eve. It is
good to look upon, but not to feed on, for who feeds on knowledge dies
to the innocent life'" (Whiting, *Memoirs*, p. 177). She became a prominent worker and writer. The Morning Meeting was held, at times, at
her house (*Jnl. F. H. S.* xviii. 2), and Fox was a frequent visitor; she
wrote, in an original letter in D (Swarth. MSS. i. 395), dated 5 ix. 1671:
"I was never better pleased wth my house then when hee was in It &
employed it for y[e] service of truth, or any of his." She was one of the
Friends of "London" M.M. appointed to see to the right conduct of
marriages (*Sundry Ancient Epistles*, p. 41, MS. in D), and was also a
prison-visitor—"Rebeck: Travers is gone towards Ipswich to see
p[r]soners" (Swarth. MSS. iv. 96). She had experience of prison-life. Her
writings in support of Quakerism were voluminous—"one Rebecca
Trewish in Watling streit is a wryter of books, and getts them
prented by Widdow Dover" (*Extracts from State Papers*, p. 230—*Cal.
S. P. Dom.* 1664—5, p. 148). Next to Margaret Fell and Dorothy

White, she appears to have been the most prolific woman Quaker writer (*Jnl. F. H. S.* x. 94). She wrote Testimonies concerning William Bayly, 1676, Susanna Whitrow, 1677, Alice Curwen, 1680, Anne Whitehead, 1686. In a tract, dated 1664, *This for all or any of those*, etc., she breaks out into verse, beginning:

"Things to come are here declared,
but blind men cannot see;
But as the World draws to an end
some shall remember me."

(We are trying to revive the memory of this good woman, but know not if the time be ripe therefor.)

William Travers (—*c.* 1663) is mentioned several times in Quaker books. He was one who offered to lie "body for body" (54. 2) in 1659, and Friends met at his house on business bent (*Hidden Things Brought to Light, or the Discord of the Grand Quakers* [Fox, Nayler and Perrot] *among Themselves*, 1678, pp. 9, 11). There was a son, Matthew, and a daughter, Rebecka, who married John Osgood (104. 2) in 1667. Rebecka Travers's sister, Mary Booth, lived also at the Three Feathers. George Whitehead lodged there during the year of the Plague (*Christian Progress*, p. 292). William Penn preached a sermon "upon occasion of the Death of Mrs Rebecca Travers, an Aged Servant of God, June 19, 1688" (*Concurrence and Unanimity of the People called Quakers*, 1694, pp. 73—77), but there is only a slight reference to R. T.

Vol. ii. pp. 412, 471; Penn, *Judas and the Jews*, 1673, p. 92; Sewel, *Hist. of Quakers*; *London Friends' Meetings*, pp. 92, 128, 129, 324, 351; *D. N. B.*; *Extracts from State Papers*, 1913; Brailsford, *Quaker Women*, 1915; *Beginnings*; MSS. in D.

97   2   The name of Thomas Barker occurs several times in *First-days Meetings* when he suffered imprisonment and fining for attendance at several of the London meetings. In *F. P. T.* (pp. 153—157, 361) there is a full recital of the trial of him and others at the Guildhall, 18 x. 1683, under the statute 35 Eliz., the Recorder, Sir Thomas Jenner, trying to prove that the meeting was a tumultuous one, despite the evidence of a witness that "they were Quiet, standing together even as Lambs." Barker was one of the London Friends appointed by Y.M. 1687 and 1688 to inspect the accounts relating to charitable affairs. "Thom. Barker, Seething Lane" appears in *The Little London Directory of 1677* (reprint of 1863 in D).

97   3   Edward Bathurst, son of Charles, had a house in George Yard. In 1682 he married Mary, daughter of John Stott, late of Black Eagle Street, Spitalfields, and his wife Mary Stott (89. 3). G. Fox frequently called in George Yard to see widow Stott and dined there from time to time; once it is said "he Eate Something" (p. 143) as if a hurried meal was taken.

97   4   John Hutson has not yet been identified. There was one of the name, a mariner, across the river, who died in 1698, aged 34. Anna Hutson's name is attached to a letter from the Women's Q.M. of London to Margaret Fox in 1695.

97   5   For Margaret Fox see vol. i. p. 407. Of her ten visits to London, two hundred miles from Swarthmoor, the eighth and ninth are recorded in the Itinerary Journal. In 1684—5 she passed sixteen weeks in the Metropolis (pp. 97, 104, 105). In Second Month, 1690, she suddenly appears before us at her husband's side at the Meade home and departs

again for the North two months later (pp. 206, 213). Writing of this
1690 visit, *c.* 1691, she tells us that "of all the times that I was at
London this last was most comfortable" (Ell. Text, ii. 519).

Crosfield, *Margaret Fox of Swarthmoor Hall*, 1913; *Quaker Women*, by
Mabel R. Brailsford, 1915; *Swarth. Account Book*, 1920; "Margaret
Fell, The Mistress of Swarthmoor Hall," by M. Ethel Crawshaw, in
The Holborn Review, July, 1924.

98	1	John Plant (*c.* 1648—1718), of Spitalfields and later of Bishopsgate, broadweaver, son of Humphrey Plant, of Fleet Street, married Elizabeth Broadbank, of the same, at Devonshire House, in 1683. Fox lodged a night at Plant's house as convenient for some business with Abraham Godowne. A son, Ezekiel, was drowned, "in Westminster liberty," in 1700, aged 17. At his death John is described as a vintner.

There was a John Plant, resident at Newbury, Berks (Besse,
Sufferings; *Jnl. F. H. S.* iv. 28).

98   2   The London Friends' Registers record the marriage of Abraham
Godowne, of Bishopsgate, and Jane Tomkins, at Westbury Street,
Spitalfields, in 1668. In 1674 was born a son, Abraham, his father
being described as "of Stepney, broadweaver." Abraham and Jane lost
by death a son Benjamin in 1672, another Benjamin in 1678, and
Isaac in 1680. Jane Godowne died of "a surfeit" in 1684, aged forty,
her husband surviving her.

99   1   As with the Sessions held at Hicks Hall in North London (92. 1), so
in connection with the Sessions held at the Guildhall in the heart of
the City, Fox was concerned to know the latest respecting the trials of
Friends and awaited news from the latter at the house of Benjamin
Antrobus in Cheapside hard by (pp. 93, 99, 147). There is a very
valuable manuscript in D, containing, among other references to London
sufferings, numerous references to Friends in Sessions Rolls preserved
in the Crypt of the Guildhall. The extracts were made by the late
Prof. G. Lyon Turner, and are dated 1662 to 1665. Attached to above is
a list of London Friends sentenced to transportation, 1664—1665, with
notes by William C. Braithwaite.

Four days afterwards Fox wrote an autograph letter to Friends
lying in Plymouth Prison, encouraging them to faithfulness (original
in D, see facsimile in *Jnl. F. H. S.* i.).

100   1   Was Justice Smith, of Ratcliff, mentioned here the same as Sir
William Smith, of whom it is recorded in *First-days Meetings*, p. 117:
"1683. 6 mo. 12. Ratcliff. Within ye house morning & afternoon, Quiet
& undesturbed the Con^bles being told to Trouble themselves no farther
till Sir William Smiths order"?

100   2   James Strutt, Senr. (*c.* 1619—1700), and James Strutt, Junr. (*c.* 1649
—1698), were both mariners, resident at Ratcliff and Wapping. "James
Strutt of Wappin" married Mary, daughter of John Meakins (122. 2),
in 1676. There is no indication whether this marriage was of father or
son. "Old Mary Strut" is mentioned on p. 171, *anno* 1687. She was
probably the Friend of that name who with others, men and women,
was appointed by Ratcliff M.M. to attend marriages and see them
properly conducted (*Sundry Ancient Epistles*, p. 41).
MSS. in D.

100   3   For Susanna Fell, *aft.* Ingram, see vol. ii. p. 451.

100   4   For John Rous see vol. ii. p. 385, and for his wife, Margaret, see vol.
ii. p. 421. The four of their children who survived their father were

Bethia (126. 1), Margaret (89. 5), Anne (pp. 196, 197, 208), and Nathaniel (p. 134). For the will of John Rous see *Jnl. F. H. S.* iv.

Nathaniel Rous (1670—1717) was a merchant of the parish of St Mary Bothaw, Cannon Street. He married Hannah Woods (—1714), of Guildford, in 1696. Beyond their immediate family no descendants are known. His attack of small-pox is mentioned on p. 134. He was a scholar at Richard Scoryer's writing school when the attack began (letter from John Rous, 20 i. 1685/6, printed in Webb, *Fells of Swarthmoor Hall*, 1865).

Anne Rous (1671—1709) married Benjamin Dykes, of Colchester, merchant, son of Edward Dykes, in 1698, and died *s.p.* Dykes's first wife was Mary Talcot, of Colchester, who died in 1696. See 237. 1.

Jnl. F. H. S.; Swarth. Account Book.

100   5   Fox's "own busyness" about which he consulted Attorney Vaughan (p. 93) is described in full in Ell. Text, ii. 355—358. The date is given loosely "about this time," but the affair appears under 1681. That 1684 is the date is clear from the mention of the "eight poor men from the North" in the same paragraphs, whose letter to Y.M. is dated 1 iii. 1684. Fox writes: "My wife and I and several other Friends were sued in Cartmel-Wapentake Court in Lancashire for small tithes and we had demurred to the jurisdiction of that court." Contrary to expectation Fox was not taken into custody. As with the doctors (80. 8) so with the lawyers Fox had advanced from the position he took up in 1649— "He shewed me also that the lawyers were out of the equity, and out of the true justice, and out of the law of God," but adding: "The lawyers might be reformed and brought into the law of God" (Tercent. Text, pp. 17, 18).

Crosfield, *Margaret Fox*, 1913, pp. 178—181—the letter printed on p. 179 should be dated 1684.

100   6   For William Penn see vol. ii. p. 419. He is frequently mentioned in the Itinerary Journal and the Haistwell Diary. He was visited by Fox at his lodgings at Charing Cross (pp. 100, 123), and at Holland House, Kensington (p. 115). At an earlier date he was visited by Fox at his lodgings at William Hages (p. 258). He was also to be found at the house of his brother-in-law, Daniel Wharley, in George Yard (pp. 122, 177). In Seventh Month, 1689, Fox met Penn "who was y^n under ye Messingers hand in picadilly" (p. 199).

Graham, *William Penn*, 1917.

100   7   Giles Fettiplace (—1702) "became a Friend in the early days and used to drive to Cirencester meeting in the style of a county magnate in his coach and six....He lived at Coln St Alwyns, in Gloucestershire...possessed considerable landed property and came of an old family" (*The Friend* (Lond.), 1905, p. 842). In the Life of Bishop Frampton (who succeeded Dr John Prichard in the see of Gloucester in 1680) it is related that Giles Fettiplace, "the Quaker Esquire, son of him who had defended Cirencester for the Parliament [Col. John Fettiplace], having gone in his coach and six to call upon the Dean and Chapter *re* renewal of leases, was received in much state and with great deference until the churchmen found the Quaker would not take off his hat to them. Then they irritably rammed their own on their heads, intimating to Giles that they were quite prepared to treat him and his friends with equal discourtesy. They even demurred to renewing one of the leases until the Dean recalled that the Esquire's father had dealt very liberally with the Church in its depressed days, which led to a better understanding of each other all round and an amicable settlement of the matter" (quoted in the Life of John Roberts

—*A Quaker of the Olden Time*, 1898, p. 36). Frances, daughter of Giles and Elizabeth Fettiplace, married, in 1686, John Bellers (1654—1725), who succeeded to the Fettiplace estate. They had a son, Fettiplace Bellers, philosopher, playwright, and Fellow of the Royal Society. Theophila, another daughter, married Thomas Church in 1693.

Jnl. F. H. S. xii. xvi.

101   1   This may have been the address *To the King, and Both Houses of Parliament, The Suffering Condition of the Peaceable People called Quakers*, etc., 1685.

102 1, 2   For Thomas Lower, the step-son-in-law of George Fox, see vol. i. p. 440, and for his wife, Mary Lower, see vol. ii. p. 421 (corrected by *Jnl. F. H. S.* ix. 153, as to date of birth). There is an interesting personal letter from Mary Lower to her mother in 1701 (see *Jnl. F. H. S.* ix. 185).

Quaker Post-Bag, 1910, p. 161 ; *Swarth. Account Book.*

102   3   Martha Hull signed the General Testimony to Anne Whitehead (148. 2) in 1686. She lived in Bethnal Green and for some reason unknown is associated here with Mary Stott, a neighbour (89. 3). Further information is lacking.

103   1   It is clear that a Quaker family of Birkett lived South of the Thames about Lambeth, but particulars are lacking. William Birkett was visited in the First Month (not "3ᵈ" as written), 1684/5 and about six months later Gulielma Penn accompanied Fox on a visit to "Widdow Berkit," she being visited also at later dates, and her name being, apparently, Eleanor (p. 193). There was a Mary Birkett living "near Lambeth" (p. 156).

103   2   It has not been found possible with our present knowledge to piece together with any certainty scattered information respecting Anne Travers (see vol. ii. p. 451). She was a widow when caring for Thomas Ellwood in 1662. She appears to have been of Hackney in 1665 and to have removed to Horslydown, where Ellis Hookes lodged with her from 1665 to his death in 1681. (Webb, *Fells of Swarthmoor Hall*, 1865 ; *Jnl. F. H. S.* i.) Here, at Newington, Fox visited her. In Eighth Month, 1685, Fox, with Nathaniel Wilmer, and Anne Travers and her daughter, went to Chiswick to prospect for a house in which to conduct a "Womens School" and had a look at the house in which William Loddington (123. 4) had kept school (p. 123). Anne Travers removed to Chiswick a few months later where Fox was a frequent and welcome visitor for longer or shorter periods. The Registers record the death in 1688/9 of Anne Travers, of Bermondsey, widow, aged about sixty.

Sarah Travers, spinster (probably the daughter mentioned on p. 123, who also sent messages to Friends *per* letters of Ellis Hookes, see Swarth. MSS.), married Jasper Robins in 1675, and was the Sarah Robins of pp. 198, 208.

103   3   The Marshalsea Prison was in the borough of Southwark. Imprisonments of Friends are referred to in many places, *e.g. Christian Progress*, pp. 319—321 ; *First-days Meetings*, p. 177.

103   4   The Lord Mayor who occupied the office in 1684—5 was Sir James Smith.

103   5   For a short note on Informers under the Conventicle Act of 1670 see vol. ii. p. 417. George Whitehead gives a list of forty-one of these troublesome people in his *Christian Progress*, p. 596, which list includes

fifteen women, adding : "John Hilton (called Captain), George Hilton, Christopher Smith and Elizabeth his wife, Esther Collingwood, Gabriel Shadd [86. 2], John Brown were some of the chief of that Society." Masters and servants, husbands and wives were engaged in this nefarious business. A monograph on the subject is much to be desired.

Christian Progress, pp. 327, 350, 484, 500, 501, 513, 521, 541, 570, 577, 591—609, 618; *Jnl. F. H. S.*

104   1   Information respecting John Belhouse is not forthcoming or the nature of the "difference" betwixt him and John Rous.

104   2   John Osgood (*c.* 1634—1694) was a linendraper, of Cheapside, when he married Rebecka Travers (97. 1) in 1667. His second wife was Mary, daughter of William Welch (233. 4), whom he married in 1674. She died at Hornchurch, Essex, in 1695/6, aged fifty years. His London house was one of those built by several Friends in White Hart Court, after the Fire (*London Friends' Meetings,* p. 145). His country-house was at Mortlake (pp. 124, 127, 134). He was on numerous committees and appointments of "London" M.M. and other Meetings (*Sundry Ancient Epistles,* pp. 35, 40, 41). He presented a petition to the King in 1679 and was called before the Grand Committee of the House of Commons in connection with the Toleration Bill (*Christian Progress,* pp. 374, 635). Osgood was engaged with William Meade in arrangements for supplying poor Friends with flax for spinning (*Jnl. F. H. S.* xii. 122). Some money transactions between Roberts, Osgood and Meade and Algernon Sidney are reported in *Jnl. F. H. S.* xi. 68. The family became allied with that of Hanbury (*The Hanbury Family,* 1916, p. 245; *Jnl. F. H. S.* xiv.).

104   3   Nathaniel Bland was a linendraper, living in Lombard Street (vol. ii. p. 488). In 1681 he married Elizabeth, daughter of Martha Fisher (93. 1). Fox repeatedly visited the Bland home and sometimes dined there ("Eate something to dinner," p. 133, seems to imply a hurried repast). The visits to mother and daughter recorded on pp. 163, 173 were doubtless paid at the home of the daughter. G. Fox states that some of his epistles "may be found in a Book yᵗ Eliz : Bland hath of her Mothers" (vol. ii. p. 350).

104   4   In *The Carriers' Cosmography, or a Brief Relation of the Inns, Ordinaries, Hostelries and other lodgings in and near London; where the Carriers...do usually come,* etc., by John Taylor, London, 1637 (reprinted in *An English Garner,* 1903, vol. i. p. 223), we find several notices of the Swan with Two Necks (*i.e.* Nicks), in Lad Lane : "The Carriers of Manchester do lodge at the two neck'd Swan in Lad Lane betweene great Woodstreet and Milkstreet end. They come every second Thursday : also there do lodge Carriers that doe passe through divers other parts of Lancashire." The inn was a coaching-centre also. For inns see Index.
Perhaps "yᵉ seedmans in Byshopgate street" was another coaching-centre. Fox was frequently at this place, see Index.

105   1   For Richard Pinder see vol. ii. p. 431. Tracts written by him, *c.* 1660, are in D. He wrote Testimonies concerning Francis Howgill, 1676, and William Dewsbury, 1689.

105   2   Elizabeth Dry, widow, of Enfield, was frequently favoured with the entertainment of George Fox. It was here that Fox spent that sad winter of 1670—1, of which he writes : "In my deepe misery I saw thinges beyonde wordes to utter, & I saw a blacke Coffin but I past over it" (vol. ii. p. 169).

105   3   Thomas Hart (*c.* 1629—1704) was of Swan Alley, in Coleman Street, in 1658 (*Jnl. F. H. S.* xvi. 63). In 1662 we read of his wife and him in Barbados (Swarth. MSS. iii. 120). In 1671, described as "late of Barbadoes," he married, at Devonshire House, Priscilla, widow of Richard Eccleston (160. 2). Their home was Enfield where Fox was frequently their guest and M.M. was held at their house (pp. 131, 148). Hart represented Friends of Yorkshire and Barbados in the Meeting for Sufferings in 1676. Was he the Thomas Hart, master of the ship that took John Taylor to Barbados in 1666 (*John Taylor*, 1710, p. 29)?

Priscilla Hart (1627—1694) was the mother of Mercy Eccleston, who married Walter Benthall (131. 2). She died at the house of her son-in-law in London "of an oppression at the stomach."

Christian Progress, pp. 594, 647; *London Friends' Meetings*, p. 301; Smith, *Cata.*; MSS. in D.

105   4   The name Thomas Robinson appears in the Itinerary Journal from 1685, as companion of Fox and Friend in the ministry. He does not figure as a London Friend. A Friend of the same name was appointed with well-known Friends to collect the writings of Fox (vol. ii. p. 348). It is presumed (vol. ii. p. 487) that Thomas *Robertson* is intended—a well-known Friend (see vol. i. p. 442), and it may be that *Robinson* should read *Robertson* here. Thomas *Robertson* appears among country Friends visiting London 1682 (*First-days Meetings*). Thomas *Robertson* wrote a Testimony *re* George Fox. Thomas *Robertson* is named on p. 260.

105   5   Thomas Bennett (*c.* 1630—1705), of Waltham Abbey, appears frequently in the Itinerary Journal. Fox was often at his house and in attendance at the weekly meeting at Waltham, held on a Wednesday. There is an entry in the Marriage Registers: "Bennett, Thomas, of Ratcliff, Baker, and Elizabeth Constable of Ratcliffe, 11 xi. 1671." For Elizabeth Bennett see 162. 2. A certain Mary Bennett "devised to Edward Mann, for the use of Friends as a burial ground, an orchard situated in East Street, Waltham Holy Cross, for a thousand years at a pepper corn rent, if demanded" (*London Friends' Meetings*, pp. 296, 297).

105   6   Benjamin Freeman is frequently mentioned in *First-days Meetings*. He was an apothecary in Westminster. He was frequently fined for attending meetings and preaching. In 1682 he had "all his Shop-Goods, being eight Porters Loads, valued at £30," taken off (*Suff.* i. 451). The death of Benjamin Freeman has not been found in the London Registers. There was a family of Freeman seated at Woodbridge, Co. Suffolk, and a Benjamin, apothecary, was married there in 1703 (*Jnl. F. H. S.* i. 34) and a Benjamin died during a small-pox epidemic at Woodbridge in 1719 (*ibid.* xviii. 45, 46).

105   7   Elizabeth Bathurst (*c.* 1655—1685) was the eldest daughter of Charles and Frances Bathurst (93. 7) and was always in delicate health. Her convincement, as that of the other children of Charles Bathurst, seems to have been due to the influence of Charles Marshall (see his Testimony) and took place about seven years before her death. Despite bodily weakness she undertook a preaching tour which included Windsor, Reading and district, and Bristol. She was imprisoned in the Marshalsea in Southwark, presumably for addressing the congregation of Samuel Ansley (30 viii. 1678), to the members of which she wrote *An Expository Appeal* in 1678: "Whether or no you will all justifie that Action of haling of me (and my sister who stood by me) out from amongst you." It is said that the justices that committed her thought her a person of great learning and education. There is an addendum

to the *Appeal*, signed by Anne Bathurst, who may have been the sister who stood by. Elizabeth also wrote an article on *The Sayings of Women*, taken from the Bible—twenty-one from the Old Testament and thirteen from the New. E. Bathurst's principal writing was called *Truth's Vindication*, a refutation of numerous misrepresentations of Quakerism, under headings, *e.g.* Scriptures, Humanity of Christ, Perfection, etc. Of this George Whitehead wrote that some would not believe "it was of her own Indicting," but he had seen it in her own handwriting. This book, preceded by Testimonies by her father and stepmother (93. 7) and by George Whitehead and Charles Marshall, was first printed in 1691 and was reprinted six times to 1788 (Smith, *Cata.* i. 210).

Whiting, *Memoirs*, pp. 154—157.

Anne Bathurst, of Bishopsgate, spinster, married William Kent (93. 6), at Devonshire House in 1679.

106   1   For Robert Barclay see vol. ii. p. 457. A letter from Barclay from Aberdeen Prison addressed to Jane Woodcock and Martha Fisher is referred to in MS. in D. A sermon preached by him in Gracechurch Street, 16 iii. 1688, appears in *Concurrence and Unanimity*, 1711.

Christian Progress, pp. 570, 575, 580; Cadbury, *Robert Barclay. His Life and Work*, 1912; *Friends' Intelligencer*, 1922, article by Elbert Russell, "The Quakerism of Robert Barclay."

106   2   Many visits were paid to Winchmore Hill Meeting in the N.E. of Middlesex. Richard Chaire usually received a visit after meeting. A meetinghouse was built here in 1687 and another in 1790 (*London Friends' Meetings*, esp. p. 299).

106   3   James Parke (Park, Parks) (1636—1696) lived in Horslydown, South of the Thames. He had formerly lived in North Wales. In 1666 he was one of the signatories to a long epistle "Ag^t Loose spirits denying ministry &c." (*Sundry Ancient Epistles*, pp. 93—97), and in 1689 his name is placed first among Friends signing an epistle *re* "Corruptions Creeping in abo^t Marriges" (*ibid.* p. 100). His name occurs twenty-six times in *First-days Meetings*. He spoke at the burial of George Fox. Bugg calls Parke to account about some money in his hands (*The Painted Harlot Both Stript and Whipt*, by Francis Bugg, 1682, p. 79). He was a useful man in the examination of manuscripts in the Morning Meeting (*Jnl. F. H. S.* xiv. 3, xviii. 3). He himself wrote numerous pamphlets. Parke married Frances Ceele (*c.* 1634—1696), a widow, of Horslydown, in 1667. He took part in disputes with John Wigan, as given in J. W.'s *Antichrists Strongest Hold Overturned*, 1665.

Davies, *Account of Convincement*, 1710, p. 101; *Concurrence and Unanimity*, 1711, p. 178; *Premonitory Extracts*, 1809, p. 208; *D. N. B.*; original letters and MSS. in D.

107   1   In the London Registers there is an entry of the marriage of John Dew to Susanna Twinn in 1668 at The Peel, in which he is described as "citizen and joiner." At the birth of his son, John, in 1682, he was of "Gregorys by Pauls London." In 1677, at a meeting at the Bull and Mouth, it was "Ordered that John Dew doe forthwith make two boxes for the use of the poore to be set up by him in some convenient place one at Devonshire House & the other at the Bull & Mouth and after they are set up that he give publick notice of them at the next mens meeting that ye keys of the said Boxes be kept by William Mackett & Ezekiell Wooley for Devonshire House and John Dew and John Osgood for the Bull & Mouth" (MS. in D). The Morning Meeting minutes give evidence of the active service of John and Susanna Dew. John Dew had, apparently, been released from prison a short time

before he appears in the Itinerary Journal. At the settlement of the
Meeting for Sufferings in June, 1676, Dew was a representative, with
Philip Ford, of Friends of Herefordshire and Shropshire (MS. in D).
His wife had, with others, the care of prisoners in the Fleet (*Sundry
Ancient Epistles*, p. 40).

Christian Progress, pp. 594, 595, 601 ; MSS. in D.

107   2   Josiah Ellis (*c.* 1631—1713) was described as a "salesman" in the
Register of his marriage with Sarah Sawyer, widow, in 1675, at the
Bull and Mouth. "Sarah Sawyer's meeting house" was well known in
the early days in London. It was situate in Rose and Rainbow Court
in Aldersgate Street (*London Friends' Meetings*, p. 196). Ellis's house
was at the sign of the Golden Key at the Savoy (p. 191). Sarah Ellis
died in 1695, aged "about fifty," and in 1697 Josiah Ellis married Mary,
widow of Thomas Wilcox, of the Savoy. Records of visits by Fox are
the only notices of Ellis in the Itinerary Journal.

Jnl. F. H. S. v. 178.

From the West G. Fox frequently went by water and landed at
"Salsbury Change" (pp. 134, 146, 169) in order to visit Josiah Ellis at
the Savoy. Is this landing-place the same as described in Wheatley's
Pepysiana, 1899, p. 204 : "Ivy Lane was the landing-place for the New
Exchange which was built on the site of the gardens of Durham House
and for Salisbury House, which stood on the site of the Hotel Cecil" ?
Another landing-place mentioned is "Cupit Stares" on the South side
(p. 118). Fox went frequently by water both along and across the
Thames—along to Ratcliff in the East (pp. 113, 135, 136) and Hammersmith, Chiswick, Mortlake, Putney, in the West, and across the
river to the Birkets' house, Horslydown, Lambeth. See Thames, The,
in Index.

Boats were always ready for hire at the various landing-stages on
the Thames, but, with the more frequent use of road-transportation,
the river water-men lost much of their custom. John Taylor (1580—
1653), the Water Poet, was a great opponent of coaches—"this is a
rattling, rowling and rambling age. The World runs on wheels," he
exclaimed. London Bridge alone spanned the river and it was not
usual for boats to pass through its narrow arches. The two Cities of
London and Westminster lay along the northern bank of the river,
connected by the Strand, with a narrow inhabited hinterland, bound, as
to London, by the City walls.

Wheatley, *Diary of Samuel Pepys*.

107   3   Philip Ford (*c.* 1631—1701/2) lived at the sign of the Hood and Scarf
in Bow Lane, Cheapside. At the Bull and Mouth, 24 viii. 1672, he
married Bridget Gosnell. There were two daughters, Bridget and
Ann, a son, Philip, who died, and another Philip, born 1679. At the
first settlement of the Meeting for Sufferings, in 1676, Ford was
appointed to represent Herefordshire and Shropshire Friends (MS. in D).
A letter from Fox to Penn, from Worcester Prison in 1676, is sent to
the care of Philip Ford (copy in D), as also a letter from Thomas Ellis
to George Fox in 1685 (original in D). See *Jnl. F. H. S.* vi. vii.). Fox
visited Ford, and dined with him alone on one occasion, and on another
with several other Friends. In 1685 and 1686 Ford was one of several
London Friends appointed by Y.M. to receive moneys collected for
captive and suffering Friends. He wrote *A Vindication of William
Penn, Proprietary of Pennsylvania, from the late Aspersions spread
abroad on purpose to Defame him*, which was printed in folio in 1683.
At the close of a letter from William Penn, reprinted in *Narratives of
Early Pennsylvania*, etc., edited by Albert Cook Myers and published

in 1912, we read : "Whoever are desirous to be concern'd with me in
this Province, they may be treated with and further satisfied at Philip
Fords in Bow Lane in Cheapside and at Thomas Rudyards or Benjamin
Clarks in George Yard in Lumbard-street" (p. 215). There is this
editorial note : "Philip Ford, Penn's steward, who later brought the
Founder into financial difficulties." (For a review of this book see *Jnl.
F. H. S.* ix. 157.)

The trouble between William Penn and his agent first came about
with Ford's loan to Penn in 1699 of £2800. J. W. Graham in his
chapter on "The Fords" in his *William Penn*, 1917, writes : "Penn's
affairs had for many years been in the hands of Philip Ford, a Friend
of Bristol, as lawyer and land agent. This man, who had a good reputation and manner, had developed into a first-class rogue....In 1702
Philip Ford died. Immediately his widow, Bridget, a terror of a woman,
though always confined to her bed, and her son Philip [b. 1679], who
did what she told him, presented her husband's astonished employer
with an account for £14,000, for immediate payment, on pain of losing
his whole property in Pennsylvania" (p. 291). Penn had been for
eleven months in a debtors' prison, when in December, 1708, the matter
was settled, and he was liberated. We do not find any connection
between Philip Ford and Bristol. In *London Friends' Meetings* there
is a notice of a long-standing case of appeal to the Six Weeks Meeting
between Philip Ford and Samuel Waldenfield in 1695 and between
Ford and Nathaniel Markes in 1699 (p. 120, see also p. 113).

Bridget Ford (*c.* 1636—1710) was among the prominent women
Friends of London. She wrote a Testimony respecting Anne Whitehead
in 1686 (148. 2), and signed, with other women, a letter to Margaret Fox
in 1695 (179. 1). A lurid light is thrown upon her subsequent career
and that of Philip, Junr., in J. W. Graham's *William Penn*, chap. xxii.
She was a daughter of Henry Gosnell, of London and Shropshire.

107	4	We have not been able to discover any information touching Edward Dyhey. He appears as Dyley on p. 142 ; Fox saw him in his shop.
108	1	John Bowron appears in vol. ii. p. 476.
108	2	For a brief sketch of the life of Leonard Fell see vol. i. p. 409 ; also *Swarth. Account Book*, p. 534. There are many references to Fell in vol. ii. and in *Swarth. Account Book*. As with many others in the Itinerary Journal who come suddenly upon the scene and as suddenly disappear, Fell meets us firstly in Samuel Boulton's shop (p. 108), in 1685, and then again in 1687 in a coach with Fox going out to Edward Mann's (p. 178). He accompanied Fox on his journey South from Swarthmoor in 1677 (pp. 226—231). He died in 1701 not 1699.
108	3	In the Friends' meetinghouse at Nottingham there is preserved a letter written by George Fox "To Suffering Friends," dated 31 iii. 1685, which was, no doubt, one result of the work of his secretaries on this Sunday.
108	4	Andrew Sowle (1628—1695) was a son of Francis Sowle, of the parish of St Sepulchre's, Holborn. He was apprenticed to Ruth Raworth for seven years from the 6th July, 1646 (*Jnl. F. H. S.* iv. 4). He practised his art in Devonshire New Buildings, at the Crooked Billet in Holy-well Lane, Shoreditch, and at the Three Keys in Nag's Head Court, Gracechurch Street. Many seizures were made by the authorities of paper, printing presses, type, etc. He married Jane —— and had two daughters, Elizabeth, who married, in 1685, William Bradford (*c.* 1658 —1752), who became Friends' printer in the American colonies, and

Tace (1666—1746), who was a practical printer, and who married Thomas Raylton (1671—1723) in 1706. See *Quaker Post-Bag*, 1910. *Piety Promoted*; *Antiquarian Researches*, 1844; *Jnl. F. H. S.* iv. xviii.; Penney, *My Ancestors*, 1920.

108 5   Pieter Hendricks, a native of Amsterdam, was one of the principal Friends in Holland. He was imprisoned at Leyden in 1661. His trade was button-making. His wife, Elizabeth, and he were the authors of pamphlets in Dutch (Smith, *Cata.*). Several of Fox's letters to P. Hendricks are given in Ell. Text (ii. 326, 483, 486). His wife's preaching was made the subject of Fox's letter to the Duke of Holstein (*ibid.* ii. 404 and see note 95. 2). He accompanied Fox in part of his tour in Holland in 1677.
Thompson, *Writings of Early Friends*, 1692, p. 328 (MS. in D); *Collectitia*, 1824; *Bulletin F. H. S. Phila.* iv.; MSS. in D.

108 6   Dr William I. Hull, of Swarthmore College, Pa., an authority on Dutch Quakerism and a writer of a history of Friends in Holland (still, alas! in manuscript), thinks that this curious name Mungumtongrum represents Barend van Tongeren, who planned to attend London Y.M. in 1685 with Pieter Hendricks (108. 5). "Barend van Tongeren was evidently one of the wheel-horses of the Amsterdam Y.M. for many years." His name is found at the foot of various documents from 1676 to 1698. He was one of the six trustees appointed to care for the fund of £364 left by Gertrude Diricks (Nieson), 11 vii. 1688. He is quoted by J. R. Markon in a controversial pamphlet against the Friends, published in Amsterdam in 1684, as having advised the Friends to "answer a fool according to his folly"; he is then charged with having committed "an even greater folly," and the Friends are quoted as replying (among many other things): "As our dear and worthy Friend, Barend van Tongeren, says, to our strength and comfort: 'Whatever we bind on earth is bound in heaven, and whatever we loose on earth is loosed in heaven'"!
Fell-Smith, *Steven Crisp*, 1892, pp. 15, 24.

109 1   William Taylby (Tileby—he signs himself *Taylby* in original MS. in D) lived in the district of "Leonards, Eastcheap." In 1672 he signed, with other Friends, *A Salutation or Testimony of True and brotherly Love* (*Gilbert Latey*, p. 88). William Taylby, "Clement Danes, co. of Middx, Tailor," married Elizabeth Hayeland in 1668.

109 2   This is the first notice in the Itinerary Journal of a Yearly Meeting (1685), but we know from the Ell. Text that George Fox was present at the Y.M. in 1681, 1683 and 1684. For reference to the Y.M. of 1686 see 142. 3, for 1687 see 176. 1, for 1689 see 195. 2, 3, and for 1690 see 210. 1. The Y.M. of 1688 is mentioned in Ell. Text (ii. 473). These accounts add freshness to the official records contained in the minutes of proceedings preserved in D. The 1685 Y.M. was held when the country was disturbed by the Monmouth Rebellion and Fox was much concerned for the safety of Friends who came up (Ell. Text, ii. 409). The Y.M. of 1677 is referred to in the Haistwell Diary (p. 233), also Y.M. 1678 (p. 270).
In 1679 Fox was at Swarthmoor and wrote a letter to the Y.M.; in 1680 he was in attendance (Ell. Text, ii. 337, 345).

110 1   Daniel Wharley (Whirley) was a woollen-draper in George Yard. In 1686 he married Mary, the only daughter of Isaac and Mary Penington, and so became brother-in-law to William Penn. Mary Wharley died in 1726 (Penney, *Experiences in the Life of Mary Penington*, 1911, p. 63 and genealogical table). Daniel Wharley's house and shop being

but across the road from the meetinghouse and Chamber, George Fox often resorted thither and met William Penn and other Friends in both the shop and house, at times remaining to the midday meal. Wharley's death took place 3 ii. 1721 at his country home and his burial at Jordans.

There is a reference in *Jnl. F. H. S.* i. 33 to "Daniel and *Sarah* Wharley (of Isaac Peningtons family)," present at a wedding at the Bull and Mouth in December, 1685.

110 2 In the Ell. Text, after giving a letter, 11 iv. 1685, "to caution all to keep out of the spirit of the world," we read : "Several other letters also I wrote at this time to Friends in divers foreign countries" (ii. 411). We find from his *Collection of Epistles* that on the tenth he wrote to Friends in Holland and in the same month to Pennsylvania (*Register of George Fox's Letters*, MS. in D).

111 1 For Charles Lloyd, Junr., see vol. ii. p. 407. The statement that his son, Charles 3rd, was born while both parents were in prison has been questioned, though it appears in numerous books relating to the family. The date of the birth is given as 18th August, 1662 (Lowe, *Farm and its Inhabitants*, 1883, p. 12), and Besse states that the apprehension of Lloyd took place in the middle of December, 1662 (*Suff.* i. 749). See *The Quaker Seekers of Wales: A Story of the Lloyds of Dolobran*, told by Anna B. Thomas, of Baltimore, Md., and published 1924. It is more probable that the second son, Sampson (1664—1724), was born while his parents were in some measure of imprisonment.

Memorials of the Old Square (Birmingham), 1897; Richards, *Religious Developments in Wales*, 1923.

111 2 As with others mentioned Richard Davies (1635—1707/8) suddenly appears and disappears without any hint of the circumstances surrounding his appearance. Davies was a hatter of Cloddiau Cochion, near Welshpool, Montgomeryshire, and was one of the most interesting characters of early Quakerism. His autobiography entitled *An Account of the Convincement, Exercises, Services and Travels...of Richard Davies*, first published in 1710, has been reprinted about a dozen times, and there are numerous references to him in literature of various periods. He was apprenticed to a felt-maker at Llanfair and later, in 1658/9, he settled in London as a felt-maker and in 1659 he married Tace —— (*c.* 1618—1705), "at Humphrey Bates's house, at the sign of the Snail, in Tower Street in the morning and in the afternoon at Widow Webb's in Horslydown" (*Jnl. F. H. S.* xiii. 169). There was a daughter, Tace, who married Jacob Endon, of Welshpool. Davies returned later to Welshpool. It was at his instigation that, in 1681, the Y.M. for Wales (including Monmouth and Salop) was set up. It functioned from 1682 to 1797 (*ibid.* x. 82). For his association with Counsellor Corbett see vol. ii. p. 450. He was friendly also with other prominent people in his native county and was able to bring about some damping of the fires of persecution. Once, on meeting Lord Herbert of Cherbury, the latter asked who he was and was told: "A Quaker, and Haberdasher of Hats," to which Lord Herbert replied: "Oh! I thought he was such an One, he keeps his Hat so fast upon the Block" (*Account*, p. 96).

Piety Promoted; *John Gratton*, 1720, p. 123; *The Friend* (Lond.), 1861, p. 42; Budge, *Annals of Early Friends*, 1877; Southall, *Prichards of Almeley*, 1893; Williams, *Montgomeryshire Worthies*, 1894, p. 44; Allen, *A Son of the Morning*, 1894; *D. N. B.*; Norris, *John ap John*, 1907; *Quaker Biographies*, vol. ii. 1909; *The Friend* (Phila.), 1909, p. 211; *F. Q. E.* 1912, pp. 482, 486; Danielowski, *Die Journale der frühen Quäker*, 1921, p. 32; Richards, *Religious Developments in Wales, 1654—1662*, 1923; Thomas, *The Quaker Seekers of Wales*, 1924; MSS. in D.

111   3   For Gravel Pits in Kensington see 115. 5.

111   4   This was, probably, John Edridge, citizen and haberdasher, son of Thomas Edridge, of Buntingford, in Hertfordshire. In 1683 he married Constance Moore, of Love Lane, distiller, widow of Francis Moore. For three years in succession, 1686, 1687, 1688, he was appointed by Y.M. to inspect charitable accounts. For his connection with West Jersey see *Penna. Mag.* v.

          There was another John Edridge, a tanner, of Ratcliff M.M. *Suff.* i. 482, 484; *First-days Meetings.*

111   5   For Bridget Austill see vol. ii. p. 491. Her school was at South Street in North Middlesex (p. 194) and was removed to Tottenham High Cross *circa* 1689 (p. 219). There was an interesting colony of Friends at South Street (now called Southgate, see pp. 187, 194).

112   1   James Harding, "a young man, well respected, was banished to Jamaica [in 1665] with Edward Brush [152. 1] and one other [Robert Hayes]....James Harding whilst he abode there, took to wife a young woman who before they left this island, was delivered of three daughters at a birth, all of which were brought alive to England well and in health" (Crouch, *Posthuma Christiana*, 1712, p. 82). But the return of Harding was longer delayed than implied by Crouch, for in July, 1685, when visiting Fox at Ford Green, he is still "of Jamaica," and in the same year, in a letter quoted by John Boweter, Harding writes of "our island" (MS. in D; see vol. ii. p. 408).

          John Taylor, 1710, p. 23; *Suff.*; *Second Period.*

          There was a John Harding, living on the borders of Essex, who had a meeting at his house, frequently attended by Fox and other Friends. See Ell. Text, ii. 456. There are references in *London Friends' Meetings* to a David Harding who held meetings at his house at Harold's Wood (pp. 278, 280).

112   2   Margaret Sefton-Jones found recently in the British Museum (Add. MSS. 19408) a certificate of the marriage at the Bull and Mouth, 17 vi. 1682, of Michael Russell, citizen and weaver, of London, son of Michael Russell, late of Aylesbury, and Mary, daughter of Thomas Forster (81. 4), late of Middlesex. Among the signatories to this marriage were Gulielma Maria Penn, George and Anne Whitehead and other well-known Friends. This was doubtless the Friend, living in White Hart Court, to whose house Fox often went after a meeting at Gracious Street and dined, and one Sunday, "being Weary he Lay downe to Rest him upon their Couch" (p. 188). His wife and sister are mentioned on p. 165. Michael Russell, with others, signed a petition to the House of Commons on the subject of oaths, 1695. The Registers record the sudden death in 1702 of M. Russell, of White Hart Court, parish of Allhallows, Lombard Street, citizen and weaver, of apoplexy at the age of fifty-four. There is a full account of his death in Gracechurch Street meetinghouse, in *Quaker Post-Bag*, 1910, pp. 187, 188.

          There was a Michael Russell (1674—1747), of the same parish of Allhallows, whose daughter Mary married Peter Collinson (*Jnl. F. H. S.* vi. 178).

112   3   There is a considerable account of John Field, the younger, in vol. ii. p. 486, and hints of others of the same name. He was a schoolmaster and had rooms over the meetinghouse at the Bull and Mouth, about

1671 (*London Friends' Meetings*, pp. 143, 360). In 1678 John Field "of the parish of Ann and Agnes Aldersgate" was prosecuted for keeping school without a licence (*Suff.* i. 443) and was committed to Ludgate Prison. Apparently Elizabeth Fry, who married Richard Marchant in 1692, had been an assistant in the school (*Jnl. F. H. S.* viii. 82). J. F. married Margery Saunders, of Shacklewell, in 1675, who died in 1700, aged 55. Field at this time is described as "haberdasher." In 1705 he married Mary Wyan, widow, as "citizen and blacksmith," of George Yard. In 1706 his daughter Mary married Thomas Crawley, and became the mother of Sarah Crawley (1717—1799) the noted Minister for sixty years. See *Jnl. F. H. S.* xii. 13 n. There is facsimile of his signature, "John Feild jun.," reproduced *Jnl. F. H. S.* v. 202, *anno* 1680. He was a great preacher as well as writer (*First-days Meetings*).

John Field, Senr., died in 1692, aged sixty-seven.

112   4   The marriage of Thomas Bowls, proposals for which were before Enfield M.M. 29 v. 1685, "to the Glading of fr^{ds} there generally," has not been found in the Registers of London and Middlesex.

113   1   This was probably Elizabeth Groom (*c.* 1626—1703), widow of Samuel Groom, the elder, of Limehouse, mariner.

114   1   Roger Longworth (*c.*1630—1687) was born at Longworth, Bolton, Lancs. In pursuit of his labours as a Minister "he passed six times through Holland, also part of Germany, five times through Ireland, once through part of Scotland, twice at Barbadoes, once through New England and Virginia, twice in Maryland and the Jerseys, and twice in Pennsylvania; having travelled by land above 20,000 miles and by water not much less" (*Phila. Memorials*, 1824, p. 11). In Brown's *History of Great and Little Bolton*, 1824—5, we read a story told to the author, but which the author could hardly have believed, "of a troublesome fellow of a Quaker, named Roger Longworth, who used to tell his neighbours of their faults, and how they, not liking him, got rid of him. A chap got secretly into Roger's shippon and hid himself in a hogshead that lay there. When Roger came in the evening to fodder his cattle, the man exclaimed in a hollow voice, 'Stay not here, but go thou and all that belongeth to thee, to America.' And taking it as a solemn warning, Roger soon after sold off and departed." Longworth went to America in 1684 and visited Europe in 1685—1687 ("List of Friends Crossing the Atlantic on Religious Visits," MS. in D). His visit to Holland, in or about 1676, was not much of a success—in a letter printed in *Steven Crisp and his Correspondents* we read: "His labours to enforce on them silent meetings are unavailing....They love the works of Jacob Behme, whereas Roger says though a candle was lighted in him at the beginning yet he hunted before the Lord, and those who have Behme's books are puffed up in their knowledge" (p. 38).

Whiting, *Memoirs*; *The Friend* (Phila.), vol. 27 (1854), pp. 148, 156; *Jnl. F. H. S.* v. viii. x. xii.; *Bulletin F. H. S. Phila.* v. 15.

114   2   John Casimir (*c.* 1634—1709) was of Pearl Street, Spitalfields. He was interested in Friends on the European Continent. Fox met at his house some German Friends who were going to Pennsylvania.

Fell-Smith, *Steven Crisp*, 1892, p. 17.

115   1   For a brief note on the Rebellion of the Duke of Monmouth see vol. ii. p. 454. Other references include Tanner's *Lectures on Friends in Bristol and Somersetshire*, 1858, pp. 105—110; *Jnl. F. H. S.* iv. v. viii. xi. xii. xv. xvi.; *The Western Rebellion*, by Richard Locke, 1782, reprinted 1912 (for reference see *Jnl. F. H. S.* xvi. 134); *Second Period*; MSS. in D.

The Chief Justice was George Jeffreys (1648—1689), who conducted "the bloody Assizes," 1685. "As a criminal judge he was notorious for his brutality" (*D. N. B.*). Jeffreys cleared Richard Vickris (95. 1) of his sentence of death, on recording which Whiting exclaims: "Few so bad but they may do some good Acts" (*Memoirs*, p. 120).

The Bloody Assizes: or, A Complete History of the Life of George Lord Jefferies...his unheard of Cruelties and Barbarous Proceedings, etc., 1689.

115   2   Mariabella Farmborough (1626—1708) was a native of Warminster, in Wiltshire. She married, *c.* 1662, Thomas Farmborough, of London. Her convincement of the Quaker way of life and thought took place about the year 1682. "She was a tender & servisable woman...and in hir old age (by ye hardships she met in prisons &c) she was afflicted with lameness" (Howard, *Eliot Papers*, 1894, ii. 3). Despite her physical disability, requiring much resting at home, she attended the women's meeting having care of the poor and would visit, with Mary Elson, the sick and afflicted "tho' it was with crutches." Her lameness, however, was cured when she was nearly eighty years of age. She suffered imprisonment in Newgate (Bristol) and Newgate (London). In the latter place, in 1684, "she lay in a little naisty place they called ye Ladys hole, where condemned persons lay." Her daughter of the same name (p. 138) married Peter Briggins (1666—1717) and the unusual name Mariabella has descended through nine generations to the present time in the Eliot, Howard, Fry and Lloyd families (*Jnl. F. H. S.* ix. 185).

Whiting, *Memoirs*, p. 77; *Piety Promoted*; *Jnl. F. H. S.* xvi.

115   3   Edward Brooks (*c.* 1618—1698) resided in the parish of "Giles in the Fields, Mdx." at his marriage with Martha Hill in 1665. He was a grocer and in 1670 had shop goods taken away to the value of £7 for fines for meeting at Westminster.

Christian Progress, p. 521; *Suff.*

115   4   William Beech (*c.* 1647—1725), wine-cooper, lived in the parish of St Martin's in the Fields and was visited by Fox on several occasions—once when the former was sick (p. 166). In 1708 John Vaughton and he were appointed "to search the books and papers of our ancient Friends & brethren and to mark such as may be suitable to read to our children and servants" (*London Friends' Meetings*, p. 253). He was buried in Long Acre Burialground, the cause of death being "Gravel & Stone."

See vol. ii. pp. 299, 453.

115   5   There were several Friends of the name of Kirton living in and around London. Richard Kirton and John Kirton (124. 2) were resident at Kensington Gravel Pits. William Kirton (—1706), son of Richard and Sarah, of West Town, in the parish of Kensington, received some notice in *Piety Promoted*. Richard Kirton departed this life in 1719, aged 76, "by being ridden over when crossing the road." *Jnl. F. H. S.* i.

115   6   For Gulielma Maria Penn see vol. ii. p. 425.

Graham, *William Penn*, 1917.

115   7   For Widow Birkett see 103. 1.

116   1   In the Diary of John Kelsall (*c.* 1683—1743), of Wales, under date of 1727, there is a reference to Walter Newberry, of Fenchurch Street (MS. in D, vol. iv. p. 213*). The name appears in the *Book of Ministering Friends*, 1 mo. 24, 1722/3 (*Jnl. F. H. S.* i. 25).

There was a Walter Newberry of colonial fame. Query the same. See *Jnl. F. H. S.* xii. 176, 177; *Quakers in American Colonies*, 1911.

The Newberry family is included among the "highest families" of English Friends in the middle of the eighteenth century (*Jnl. F. H. S.* xix. 26).

116 2   Edward Haistwell (*c.* 1658—1708/9) was a son of Thomas Haistwell, of Orton, Co. Westmorland, and a merchant living in Scotts Yard, St Mary Bothaw, Cannon Street. In 1687 he married Rachel Marsh, daughter of Richard Marsh, of London. He was employed by George Fox as an amanuensis from March, 1677, to June, 1678. The Itinerary Journal records several visits to Scotts Yard and on one occasion Fox, with Lower, Parker and Robinson, dined at his house (p. 154, where however there is some correction in the MS.). In 1695/6 a son was born to E. and R. Haistwell and named Edward. It was probably this son whose ex-libris book-plate was offered for sale in a catalogue sent out by Puttick in 1911—"Edward Haistwell of the Middle Temple, 1718." "On 16 January, 1744, died Edw: Haistwell, Esq., a Director of the SS. Company" (*Gent.'s Magazine*); in 1781, "Mr Benjamin Bartlett, Dr J. C. Lettsom and Edward Haistwell, Esq., were admitted Fellows of the Society of Antiquaries" (*Gent.'s Magazine*, quoted *Jnl. F. H. S.* xiii.).

In the will of Richard Marsh (MS. in D), dated 20 November, 1703, are the following bequests: "To my two grandchildren Rachel Jones and Edward Haistwell £1000 apiece at Marriage or 21; to Thomas Haistwell and Anthony Haistwell £10 apiece; to every servant living with my son and daughter Haistwell at my decease 40/s. apiece; the residue to my daughter Rachel Haistwell." Overseers of the will included "Edward Haistwell my son in law." Edward Haistwell, Senr., died 4 xi. 1708/9, aged 50, and was buried in Schoolhouse Lane, Ratcliff.

116 3   Richard Chaire lived at Winchmore Hill, North Middlesex. He was among "suffering Friends" mentioned by Whitehead in his *Christian Progress, anno* 1686 (pp. 594, 595). He was frequently visited by Fox when in the neighbourhood attending the Winchmore Hill meeting. At his marriage with Mary Lover, in 1680, he is styled a blacksmith.

116 4   For William Bingley see vol. ii. p. 496, and *Jnl. F. H. S.* v. vi. x. John Whiting records that when in Bristol, "going to the Meeting at the Friers in the afternoon, there was William Bingley standing on the Floor, in the middle of the Meeting, declaring to Friends, the Galleries being all broke down and not then repaired; but the Meeting was quiet at that time" (*Memoirs*, p. 92). Several pamphlets written by Bingley are noted in Smith, *Cata.*
Christian Progress, pp. 594, 595, 647, 659.

117 1   Benjamin Lindley (—1723), son of Isaac Lindley, of York (bapt. 1624, died 1705 at Yarm), lived at Yarm, N.R. Yorkshire. He was the author of several books, 1678 to 1713. The book referred to is doubtless *Truth Exalted...in Answer to...Edward Nightingale, Thomas Dennison, John Winnard and John Cox*, 1685. The Preface to this 28-page pamphlet is signed by *Isaac* Lindley and others; his son's name does not appear. See next note, and 228. 1.

117 2   There is a considerable account of the Separation in York connected with the names of Edward Nightingale, John Cox, John Hall, and others, in *Second Period*, pp. 475—478. See also vol. ii. p. 496. The Separation arose in 1682 over the question of re-marriage within a year;

later, according to Smith, *Cata.* i. 457, it "was occasioned by these individuals taking offence because Friends met together twice on First day."

See 196. 1.

A Paper of Condemnation Past at York, 1684, signed by 75 Friends, and answer thereto; Myers, *A Serious Examination...Yorke*, 1686; John Taylor, 1710, p. 39; Rowntree, *Hist. York Q. M. c.* 1900, pp. 7 ff.

117   3   Hannah Marshall was the wife of Charles Marshall (1637—1698). They lived in Bristol until the latter was committed to the Fleet Prison, when the family removed to London, *c.* 1683, and settled in Aldersgate Street.

Charles Marshall was convinced during the Camm and Audland mission to Bristol in 1654. In his turn he was the means of influencing John Whiting of Somerset (1656—1722). Whiting wrote a Testimony to Marshall in 1703. He was one of the ninety-four Friends who signed the marriage certificate of George Fox and Margaret Fell in 1669 and he signed with others the Testimony to George Fox prepared by the Morning Meeting, 26 xi. 1690/91. Of his funeral, 17 ix. 1698, it is said: "Its thought to be the greatest appearance of Friends at his buriall [at Bunhill Fields] as of any yet, exceeding in number either G. F's, S. C. or F. S." (G. Fox, Stephen Crisp, Francis Stamper). See *Jnl. F. H. S.* viii. 8, quoting *Quaker Post-Bag*, 1910, p. 146.

A Testimony to the religious character of Charles Marshall was signed, in 1703, by the following Friends mentioned in the Itinerary Journal: John Field, John Vaughton, John Butcher, Edward Bourne, John Boweter, Theodor Eccleston and Samuel Waldenfield.

Works, 1704, containing Testimonies by George Whitehead, John Freame, John Whiting, six Friends of Bristol, and the widow, all dated 1703; Whiting, *Memoirs*; *Piety Promoted*; Smith, *Cata.*; *Beginnings.*

118   1   George Ayres (*c.* 1620—1697), of East Smithfield, was a haberdasher of hats. He appears to have married two widows in quick succession, Ann Rowles, of Bishopsgate, 23 v. 1685, and Mary Bowman, 1689. It may have been a bridal visit that Fox and his three companions intended to pay; the bridegroom not being at home, the bride provided dinner for the callers and they remained some time at the house.

118   2   This epistle is given in Ell. Text, ii. 415—417, dated 15th of Seventh Month, 1685, and introduced by the words: "Finding my health much impaired for the want of fresh air, I went to Charles Bathurst's country-house at Epping Forest, where I stayed a few days."

118   3   Information respecting James Matthews is not forthcoming, save that he lived at Plaistow, East of London City. See 147. 1.

119   1   Lady Lawson is mentioned twice in the Itinerary Journal. In vii. 1685 she suddenly appears in a coach with Fox travelling from James Matthews's at Plaistow to Charles Bathurst's house "upon the forest a Mile from Wanstead." In v. 1687 Fox called "at Lady Lawsons & another frds house" and afterwards went to meeting at Wanstead. The meeting concluded, he returned to Lady Lawson's and many Friends came to him there, and then he returned to Gooseyes (p. 181). Lady Lawson was, in all probability, Isabella, daughter of William Jefferson, of Whitby, who became the wife and widow of Sir John Lawson, vice-admiral of the fleet, who died in 1665. Both Sir John and his Lady were of Yorkshire origin, and there is no intimation of any connection with Essex in either Pepys's *Diary* or *D. N. B.* But in W. A. Shaw's *Knights of England*, 1906, ii. 231, we read that on the 24th September, 1660, "John Lawson, vice-admiral, of Ashford, *Essex*" was knighted.

Notes

A further confirmation of the association of the Lawsons with Essex is to be found in the State Papers Domestic. In *Calendar*, 1663—4, p. 374, there is a letter from Stephen Furly, of *Colchester*, stating that he had been recommended for a favour by Sir J. Lawson; and in the volume for 1658—9, p. 351, "John Lawson" is mentioned among "modderat men" in *Essex*. Sir John Lawson was a naval colleague of Sir William Penn, who lived at Wanstead, and in 1653 Lawson succeeded Penn as vice-admiral of the fleet. Parliament was moved to present gold chains, worth £100 each, to both Penn and Lawson as a mark of favour for their services against the Dutch. In 1654 there is a record in S. P. D. of the illness of both John Lawson and his wife. On the 4th June, 1665, during the Dutch war, Sir John damaged his knee, and on the 29th June, 1665, he died. Shortly after, from *Wanstead*, a copy of the will was sent to London—"her ladyship hopes that respect for her late husband will encourage kindness to the fatherless." Lawson had been an Anabaptist, and also was in sympathy with Fifth Monarchism, hence we may judge that his Lady would be in sympathy with Nonconformity and interested in Quakerism. She had three daughters, of one of whom Pepys wrote, January 7, 1663/4: "A very pretty lady and of good deportment; with looking upon whom I was greatly pleased" (see also Jan. 23, 1662/3, Aug. 29, 1666—"Mr Norton that married Sir J. Lawson's daughter is dead....She is in a condition to help her mother, who needs it"). The date of the death of Lady Lawson does not appear, nor have we found further notice of her in quakeriana.

With assistance from Edward Bensly, 1924.

120   1   Thomas Whitehead (—1691) lived at South Cadbury and Bruton, in Somersetshire. In 1664 he married Jane Waugh (d. 1674), one of the two sisters who were servants in the Camm household at Preston Patrick, Westmorland. See vol. ii. p. 467.
F. P. T.

122   1   Henry Snooke (*c.* 1637—1705) was of the parish of St Olaves, Southwark. In 1669 he married Rebekah Field, of Southwark, at Horslydown. He belonged to the Horslydown Meeting and frequently acted on its behalf. Ellis Hookes (233. 1) left him a sum of money by his will and to Snooke was handed a balance of money due to Hookes at his death in 1681 (*Jnl. F. H. S.* i. 21, 22).

122   2   Margaret Meakens (*c.* 1622—1692) was the wife of John Meakens (*c.* 1622—1694), dyer, of Cripplegate. Their daughter Mary married James Strutt (100. 2) and their daughter Martha married William Dry (171. 1). Margaret was a member of the Six Weeks Meeting in 1671. She was one of the signatories to *A Testimony to Young People*, sent out in 1685 by the Women's Meeting at the Bull and Mouth. She wrote a Testimony to Anne Whitehead in 1686. For her action in remaining in town during the Great Plague see *Jnl. F. H. S.* x. 15. George Fox wrote a letter to the Women's Meeting in London, dated from Swarthmoor, 28 ii. 1676 (the same date as that of a very long letter to the Y.M., printed Ell. Text, ii. 235 ff.), and addressed to Rebecka Travers, Mary Elson, Anne Travers, Mary [?Marg.] Meakens, Jane Woodcock, Anne Whitehead and Martha Fisher.

122   3   John Staploe (*c.* 1638—1717) was of "near the Three Cups, further end of Aldersgate Street" in 1666 and at the Harrow in the same street in 1682. He was a member of Peel M.M. and active in its administration. In 1666 he married Grace Russell. Of their daughter, Anne Mercy (d. 1700), there is a short life-history in *Piety Promoted*. The

names of other children appear in the Marriage Register. Grace Staploe died in child-bed in 1691, aged 44.

The name Hester Staploe appears on the minutes of Peel M.M. *anno* 1712.

Sundry Ancient Epistles, pp. 35, 40, 41, 178; Kelsall, *Diaries*; *Christian Progress*, p. 647.

122   4   Nicholas Cooper may have been connected in some way with the Meakens family (122. 2). John Meakens named his son-in-law Edward Cooper and his grandson John Cooper executors of his will (*Jnl. F. H. S.* x. 16). The London Registers record the death of Nicholas Cooper, of St John Street, in 1701, who died "of a fever & fitts," aged seventy-one years.

123   1   No further information is at hand respecting John Collit or his wife, of the Bull's Head Tavern, at Charing Cross. Other Friends were inn-keepers—see *London Friends' Meetings*, p. 127 and Index to this volume.

123   2   Nathaniel Wilmer (*c.* 1650—*c.* 1711) was a son of Capt. Nathaniel Wilmer, citizen and armourer (1621—1654) and of Constance Sherwood, daughter of Edward and Constance Sherwood, of West Hendred, Berks. Constance Wilmer and her sons John (1647—1723) and Nathaniel joined Friends. Nathaniel was a merchant and ship-owner and evidently a prosperous man. Apparently he never married. He lived in the neighbourhood of the Chamber and Fox was several times at his house —once (p. 177) with William Penn "& a great many Country ffri^{ds}," all of whom appear to have dined there! In 1700 the City M.M. issued a Testimony against Wilmer "for his conversation being a scandal to Friends and a great hurt to his own soul, and denying his fellowship with them." He appears to have died on board ship.

Christian Progress, p. 595; Foster and Green, *History of the Wilmer Family*, 1888; *Jnl. F. H. S.* xi.; *Trans. Cong. Hist. Soc.* iv.

Constance (Sherwood) Wilmer removed to Ireland after her husband's death. She wrote a letter to Archbishop Fuller in 1661, which was printed (copy in D). In 1666 she married Thomas Starkey, son of George and Ann Starkey, of Wrenbury, Cheshire. They died *c.* 1691, and were buried at Mountrath (minutes of Mountmellick M.M., *per* favour of William R. Wigham, registrar, Dublin, 1924).

123   3   Peter Prince (—1694) lived at Hammersmith. The name was written *Prise* (p. 127) and then the *n* was inserted—the writer was probably thinking of Peter *Price*, the old man who is mentioned in vols. i and ii. Peter Prince built Stone Dean in the Jordans district of Bucks in 1691 (*Jnl. F. H. S.* iv. 138); the house was, later, occupied by his niece, Rebekah Butterfield, and her husband, Abraham Butterfield, and their son, Prince Butterfield.

The Diary of Rebekah Butterfield (MS. in D); Littleboy, *Jordans*, 1920, pp. 17, 23; *Bulletin F. H. S. Phila.* ix. 101, 102.

In 1684, at the Jordans meetinghouse there was a marriage of Peter Prince, son of Peter and Mary Prince, citizen and tallow-chandler, of London, and Mary Odingsells, of "Peters Chalfont." The name Mary Odingsells appears among those of women Friends in Bucks in 1678 (*Jnl. F. H. S.* vii. 64).

123   4   On the 22nd of Eighth Month, 1685, a little company of Friends was prospecting for a suitable site for a "Womens School." They visited Chiswick, and then called on Peter Prince at Hammersmith. After a rest they went to see the house where William Loddington (*c.* 1626—1711) had kept school, and after dining at the Goat Inn, they separated. In

a list of schools to be found in the Y.M. Minutes, under date 1691, is a school "near Watford for boyes Wm Loddington M^r" (*Jnl. F. H. S.* xiii. 87). Loddington may have moved his school thither from the Hammersmith district. Loddington, *inter alia*, signed a fire-brief, dated at the Q.M. at Weston Turville in Bucks, 29 iv. 1692 (MS. in D in handwriting of Thomas Ellwood, printed in *Jnl. F. H. S.* iii. 111). He was appointed with others to draw up some account of the rise of Friends in Hertfordshire, ix. 1704 (*F. P. T.* p. 342). Joseph Smith states that Loddington had been a Baptist preacher (*Cata.*). He wrote various short pieces, 1674—95, on emigration to the English Planta-tions, on Women's Meetings and marriage, on tithes, etc. (*ibid.*).

123 5 Widow Symmons has not been definitely identified. There was a Mary Simmons, widow, of Wheeler Street, who died 3 xii. 1721, aged seventy, noted in the Burial Registers, but it appears as though the widow here visited was living in the West and not the East.

124 1 This was, presumably, William Kemp, the elder (*c.* 1628—1708). He had a son of the same name who predeceased his father (*c.* 1657—1706). Both resided in Chelsea. Others of the same name, Kemp, resided in or near London.

124 2 John Kirton (*c.* 1650—1715) lived at "Kensington Gravell Pitts." His brothers were Richard (115. 5) and William. Damaris Kirton (268. 7), widow of John, died in 1716, aged 62. Patrick Livingstone (1634—1694) died at John Kirton's house (Whiting, *Memoirs*, p. 234).

125 1 John Thorp (*c.* 1637—1712) appears to have lived in the parish of St Bartholomew the Great, Smithfield, and been a member of Peel M.M. Besse tells us that in 1670 he was badly injured by a soldier when attending Peel meeting, so much so that his life was despaired of. He appears in the Itinerary Journal shortly after liberation from prison. In 1672 he signed, with others, *A Salutation of...brotherly Love* (*Gilbert Latey*, 1707, p. 88).

126 1 Bethia Rous (1666—   ) was the eldest surviving daughter of John and Margaret Rous. She married David English, of Pontefract, York-shire, in 1692, and had, *inter alia*, a son Nathaniel, *a quo* Hoyland, of Sheffield and Waterford.
  Webb, *Fells of Swarthmoor Hall*, 1865; *Jnl. F. H. S.* xii.; *Swarth. Account Book.*

127 1 John Fielder (*c.* 1621—1677) and Anne Fielder (d. 1686), of King-ston-on-Thames, were prominent Friends and held a meeting at their house. This meeting being near Hampton Court, its influence was felt in the Protector's household (*Gilbert Latey*, 1707, p. 12; *Beginnings*, p. 441). Latey (87. 1) was their son-in-law. John Fielder was liberated from the King's Bench Prison by the "General Pardon" of 1672. By business he was a mealman.
  Christian Progress, pp. 523, 613; *Suff.*; *London Friends' Meetings.*

127 2 For *William Mucklow* see vol. ii. p. 448.

127 3 The name of Christopher Ward (*c.* 1611—1686), of Hammersmith, is mentioned but once in the Itinerary Journal, when visited by Fox among other Friends of the district in which he lived.

128 1 The name of Richard Whitpain (*c.* 1631—1689) occurs thrice in the Itinerary Journal (pp. 128, 136, 137). There are records of his sufferings for conscience sake from 1660 to 1686. He was liberated, after a year and nine months' incarceration, on 2nd June, 1686 (*Suff.* i. 482), but

he could not have been in close confinement as, apparently, he was available for consultation in April of that year (pp. 136, 137). His burial certificate describes him of "Leonard, Eastchip, Butcher."
Jnl. F. H. S. v.

129　1　Ell. Text states: "I continued at London till the latter end of the 11th month; save that I went to visit an ancient Friend at Bethnal Green, with whom I tarried three or four days" (ii. 419). A long writing on the "backsliding Jews" came from his pen, as other papers alluded to in note 89. 3.

129　2　The great doctor from Poland has not re-appeared in any place in which we have searched for him.

A few days after the interview Fox wrote a letter to the King of Poland, John III, which is printed in Ell. Text, ii. 422. Previous letters are referred to in vol. ii. p. 466 and in Ell. Text, ii. 321. See *Christliches Sendschreiben an Johannes III, König in Pohlen*, etc. Amsterdam, Gedruckt vor Jacob Claus, Buchhändlern, 1678; Tercent. Text, p. 344.

130　1　For Samuel Waldenfield see vol. ii. p. 497. A sermon preached in 1693 appears in *Concurrence and Unanimity*, 1694, and in *The Harmony of Divine and Heavenly Doctrines*, 1696. A Testimony concerning him was issued by Enfield M.M. (MS. in D). See 184. 2.

Quaker Post-Bag, 1910, pp. 67, 130, 141, 149, 150, 157, 173, 180, 187; MSS. in D.

131　1　For George Whitehead see vol. i. p. 421. In the Itinerary Journal and Haistwell Diary occur frequently the initials "G. W." which refer to either George Whitehead or George Watts. See 87. 1. For his trial with Thomas Burr see 179. 3. In connection with this trial Whitehead handed in a certificate signed by Common-council men, Church Wardens and others but not allowed to be read, as follows: "These are to certifie all whom it may concern, That George Whitehead, of the Parish of St Butolph Bishopsgate, London, both lived in the same Parish for about Ten years last past, in Good Repute, and is esteemed a man of a Competent Estate, and hath Fined for all Offices in the Parish, save Church-Warden, and hath demeaned himself Peaceably in his conversation; and hath never been accounted nor reputed to be Jesuit or Papist, nor any way Popishly affected" (*Due Order of Law and Justice Pleaded*, 1680, p. 36; *Christian Progress*, p. 417). Sermons by him appear in *Concurrence and Unanimity*, 1711, and *Harmony of Divine and Heavenly Doctrines*, 1696. At his death in 1723 the first generation of Friends came to an end.

Fell-Smith, *Steven Crisp*, 1892; *Quaker Post-Bag*, 1910, pp. 58, 65, 102, 119, 123, 128, 136, 137, 148, 169.

131　2　Walter Benthall (*c.* 1644—1709) is described in the record of his marriage: "Late of the Island of Barbadoes, merchant, son of John and Ann Benthall." He married Mercy Eccleston, of Enfield, at Devonshire House, 6 i. 1683/4. They lived in George Yard. Benthall was committed to Newgate, 3 ix. 1662, at the age of about eighteen, for refusing to take an oath but was liberated shortly afterwards. He was appointed by Y.M. 1689 and 1690 on a committee of finance. Mercy Benthall died in 1717, aged about sixty-five years. See 105. 3.

Christian Progress, p. 647; *Extracts from State Papers*, p. 162—*Cal. S. P. Dom.* 1662—3, p. 1.

The excursion from London into the Enfield district is epitomized in Ell. Text, ii. 424—"After this I went to Enfield, where, and in the country around, several Friends had country-houses, among whom I tarried some time, visiting and being visited by Friends, and having meetings with them."

132   1   Cotten Oades (*c.* 1617—1697) was a member of Peel M.M. (*Jnl. F. H. S.* xii. 145—Cotton *Gadd*). His name occurs in connection with the closing scenes of the life of Matthew Hide, for many years a persecutor but finally repentant (Penn, *Saul Smitten*, 1675, p. 3). His death, "of age," took place in the parish of "Gules Cripplegate."

Sundry Ancient Epistles, pp. 35, 41 (MS. in D).

There was a Lydia Oades, a travelling Minister (*c.* 1617—1697), whose name is to be found in *John Taylor*, 1710, p. 20; *Suff.* (London section); and *Jnl. F. H. S.* x.

133   1   The Attorney General was Sir Robert Sawyer (1633—1692). He formed an important link in the chain of officials whose services were needed before Friends' liberation could be effected. In Latey's *Life* we find that the King's commission for liberation and remission of fines went to the Lord Treasurer, Attorney General, two Secretaries of State, King in Council, Lord Privy Seal, Clerk of the Pipe, "much time being taken in sollicitingand attending" (p. 110). On one occasion, so urgent was the matter that G. Whitehead and John Edge, accompanied by Rowland Vaughan, travelled down to Sir Robert's country-house at Highcleare in Hampshire, to obtain his signature to warrants prepared by Attorney Vaughan. The journey occupied 4 or 5 days (*Christian Progress*, p. 589, see also pp. 570, 587). Sir Robert vacated his position in 1687 (*D. N. B.*).

Gilbert Latey, 1707, pp. 112 ff.

133   2   The records of Elias Simms which have been brought to light refer mainly to his sufferings. In 1673 he had "3 Turky-work-carpets" taken "for not sending out a man on ye trained bands" and in 1683 there is a full account of a distress made at his house at the Harrow in Witch Street, parish of St Clement Danes, for £50, for being five times at the Savoy meeting "though I was absent 2 of ye days mentioned in the warrants." A list of the goods taken is extant, with this record of persecution, in *Record of Sufferings, London and Middlesex, 1654 to 1753* (MS. in D). The date of his death has not been found; his wife, Mary Simms, died in 1720, aged 87, "at their home Chiswick near Hammersmith."

Christian Progress, pp. 594, 595; *Suff.*

134   1   For Stephen Crisp see vol. ii. p. 485.

Collectitia, 1824.

135   1   For *Colonel Christopher* Codrington, governor of Barbados, see vol. ii. p. 432. Was there a Sir *William* Codrington, also governor of the island, or has the writer confused the Friend William Coddington (vol. ii. p. 377), sometimes called Codrington (vol. ii. p. 5), with Colonel Christopher? Six a.m. would now be considered an early hour to call on a great man!

135   2   The reference to Friend Hull is not definite enough to enable us to identify the Friend visited by George Fox.

135   3   There was a Thomas Winnington (*c.* 1615—1699), of St Martin's in the Fields, a hosier.

135   4   Jan Roeloffs was the son of a Mennonite preacher in Hamburg. He became a Friend in 1659 and was prominent in Dutch Quakerism. His wife was Deborah. They were in England in 1686 and lodged at the house of William Crouch (pp. 135—137). Roeloffs was one of the trustees of the Amsterdam property in 1682. He wrote in Dutch *A Looking-Glass for the City of Embden*. He is mentioned in Ell. Text (ii. 285, 483).

Pennsylvania Magazine, vol. ii. (1878), p. 250; Fell-Smith, *Steven Crisp*, 1892; MSS. in D.

136   1   Richard Mew (*c.* 1620—1690) was a baker, of Limehouse. As a widower he married Mary Smart (*c.* 1618—1680), widow, of Stepney, at the house of James Brock, Mile End Green, Stepney, in 1667. Richard Mew was one of the purchasers of the colony of East New Jersey in 1682 (*Jnl. F. H. S.* xiii. 76). He died "of a hectic fever" and his wife "of a cancer in side."
Second Part of the Peoples...Liberties Asserted, 1670.

136   2   Elizabeth Fullove (*c.* 1638—1688) was the wife of Lawrence Fullove (96. 3). As Elizabeth Edwards, she was married at the Bull and Mouth in 1678. Besse states that in 1684 she and others were convicted for meeting together and fined four nobles each (*Suff.* i. 472). She died of consumption at her home in Wood Street, 12 iii. 1688, aged fifty. Fox's two recorded visits found her out of health.

136   3   Henry Gouldney (*c.* 1657—1725), son of Adam Gouldney (263. 5), of Chippenham, in Wiltshire, is best known as the Friend at whose house in White Hart Court George Fox died (p. 222). With John Field and Theodor Eccleston he signed, in 1696, a letter respecting the due time for attendance at meetings (*Sundry Ancient Epistles,* pp. 152, 159). He was a trustee of Yoakley's Charity, 1724. He was concerned in the William Gibson controversy (see *Jnl. F. H. S.* i.; *Bigottry and Partiality,* 1705). Gouldney married Elizabeth Forster, of White Hart Court, daughter of Thomas Forster, in 1681, when he is described as linendraper, of Cheapside. His wife died in 1717, aged fifty-nine, and in 1719 he remarried, Ruth Munday, widow (*c.* 1675—1733), becoming his second wife. Relations of his married into the family of Michael Russell (112. 2).
See especially *Quaker Post-Bag,* 1910, where we read of Gouldney: "He has such Power over his friends (as I know none has the like) because of his loving disposition" (p. 117); vol. ii. p. 425; *Jnl. F. H. S.* iv. vii. viii. xi. xii. xviii.; MSS. in D.

136   4   John Bringhurst was a printer for Friends from about the year 1680. He lived at the sign of the Book in Gracechurch Street and later, *c.* 1683, at the sign of the Book and Three Blackbirds in Leaden-Hall-Mutton—Market (Smith, *Cata.*). He was an apprentice of Andrew Sowle (108. 4). It is not evident why Bringhurst's wife was to be interviewed, as her husband was living. Bringhurst suffered the pillory and imprisonment for re-printing a book by Fox and he was also reprimanded by Friends, in 1680, for having printed "an ungodly & pernitious booke" (*Jnl. F. H. S.* xviii. 7, 8). The date of his death has not been found in the London district Registers.
Antiquarian Researches, 1844; Plomer, *Dict. of Printers and Booksellers from 1668 to 1725,* 1922.
The book associated with the name of John Blaykling is entitled *Anti-christian Treachery Discovered and Its Way Block'd up.* The book (before us as we write) is a folio of 215 pages, written in opposition to the Separatists, William Rogers, John Wilkinson and John Story. Various Friends collaborated in its production. Copies of minutes of official bodies are given with names of signatories. The book was printed by Bringhurst, after having been examined by committees of the Morning Meeting (Minutes, pp. 64, 68, 75).

137   1   The book in question, by Thomas Budd, is (according to advices from Haverford, Pa.) *A True and Perfect account of the disposal of the one hundred Shares or Proprieties of the Province of West-New-Jersey, by Edward Bylling,* dated the 13th of July, 1685. Thomas Budd, the younger, was born in Somersetshire and emigrated to America. In 1685 he

wrote a valuable book on education entitled *Good Order Established in Pennsilvania & New Jersey*, etc. About the year 1692 Budd joined himself to the George Keith party and wrote much in defence of this schism. Sermons preached by him in 1694 in London are reported in *The Great Doctrines of the Gospel of Christ...Sermons preached by Sundry Servants of Christ of the Society of Christian Quakers*. Sermons by George Keith, Charles Harris and John Raunce, delivered at Devonshire House, Gracechurch Street and Harp Lane, are included. There are no prayers; see 90. 1.

Jnl. F. H. S. ix.; Jones, *Quakers in American Colonies*, 1911; *Second Period*; Woody, *Early Quaker Education in Pennsylvania*, 1920, *Quaker Education in the Colony and State of New Jersey*, 1923.

138   1   Anthony Elwood, of Gray's Inn Lane, was a blacksmith. He suffered loss of goods for attending meeting at The Peel—the Informer Gabriel Shadd "broke into ye house, without being commanded thereto by the Constable, and when he was in, he called to one of the red coat souldiers, who came with them, to give him a sword (who did so) ffearing he should be opposed by ye people in ye house" (*Record of Sufferings* (MS. in D) under date 1684).

139   1   It is to be regretted that of several Friends mentioned in the Itinerary Journal the record of death only is found by research. Job Netherwood (*c.* 1643—1688/9) is described at his decease: "Late of Long Lane, died in psh. of Dunstans in the West, buried Checker Alley near Bunhill Fields."

139   2   There was an Abel Wilkinson living in Cheapside in 1682 at the death of a son (Registers).

139   3   John Edge (*c.* 1634—1704) is mentioned six times in *Christian Progress* (pp. 542, 589, 595, 618, 640, 659). He accompanied Whitehead and Rowland Vaughan on their hurried visit to the Attorney General (133. 1) and was, in other ways, helpful to suffering Friends. The Y.M. of 1684 and 1685 appointed Edge one of the receivers for money collected for ransom of Friends captives in Algiers. He was a member of Peel M.M., living in the parish of St Andrew's, Holborn.

John Edge (? his son) and his wife Jane emigrated from St Andrew's, Holborn, to Pa. about the year 1685 (*Pa. Gene. Soc.* iv. (1909), 285). *First-days Meetings*; Kelsall, *Diaries*, i. 30.

139   4   For William Dewsbury see vol. i. p. 399. He was at this time near the end of his long imprisonment in Warwick Jail, "in all 19 years from first to last in this town of Warwick," writes John Whiting (*Memoirs*, p. 12).

140   1   The suffering of Barbadian Friends is described in *Second Period*, pp. 618 ff. It was mostly on account of refusal to join the Militia. See 187. 1.

140   2   For Francis Stamper see vol. ii. p. 496. During the visit of William Penn to Bristol in 1687, "he and Francis Stamper had a great Meeting at Chew, under Richard Vickris's great Oak in his Close, a Large and Heavenly Meeting it was" (Whiting, *Memoirs*, p. 172). *Christian Progress*, pp. 594, 595.

142   1   Daniel Skinner (*c.* 1651—1724), of Gracechurch Street, linendraper, son of William Skinner, of Barking, Essex, married Elizabeth Bowman in 1681.

142   2   This paper on marriage has not been found among Fox's literary remains.

142   3   The Y.M. of 1686 "for the Service of Truth and Friends in Sufferings" was held on the 24th and 25th of Third Month. Note the frequent recurrence of the statement : "many fri^{ds} Came to him," making a full time out of meeting as well as in it. King James's "General Pardon" released many Friends from bondage in time for them to attend. "This caused great joy to Friends to see our ancient, faithful brethren again at liberty in the Lord's work after their long confinement" (Ell. Text, ii. 432).

145   1   For Dr Edward Bourne, of Worcester, see vol. ii. p. 384. He accompanied Fox and took part in meetings they attended, in the years 1686 to 1688. Apparently he was not the "E. B." mentioned in vol. ii. p. 293; the initials should represent Edward Brookes of Oxfordshire (*Jnl. F. H. S.* xi. 101).

146   1   William Ingram (1639—1706) was a citizen and tallow-chandler of Fenchurch Street. In 1676, when the Meeting for Sufferings was set up, he was appointed to act on behalf of Hertfordshire Friends, his country correspondent being Henry Stout (179. 2). In vol. ii. p. 452 it is stated that Ingram had descendants through his first marriage— we can now give more information. Ingram's first wife was Susanna Robins (1648—1688), daughter of Jasper Robins, of Godmanchester. Joseph Ingram (1686—   ), son of William and Susanna (Robins) Ingram, married, in 1710, Mary Bellers (c. 1689—1751), elder daughter of John Bellers, and inherited Coln St Alwyns (*Jnl. F. H. S.* xii. 103; *Second Period*, p. 572). He was a trustee of Yoakley's Charity, 1731. Frances, daughter of Joseph, of Cheapside, married in 1737, at the Bull and Mouth, Joseph Vandewall (*Jnl. F. H. S.* xiii. 27). Hester Ingram (1674—   ) married, in 1697, John Ayre (1664—1713), *a quo* Vaux family (information from George Vaux, Junr., of Philadelphia, Pa., 1924).
For the Ingram family in America, headed by Isaac Ingram (d. 1682), see *Jnl. F. H. S.* iv. 5; *Genealogy of the Baily Family*, 1912.

146   2   Information is, at present, lacking respecting William Phillips. Perhaps he was father of the lad mentioned 166. 2. Besse has a reference to William Phillips of Pudding Lane and the name occurs among lists of names of sufferers (*Suff.* i. 366, 460, 474, 480, 484).

146   3   George Coale (c. 1648—1682) was a son of Robert Coale and nephew of Josiah Coale of Winterbourne, near Bristol. John Whiting gives a very loving tribute to his service in his *Memoirs*, p. 80. Whiting and Coale were mutually helpful to one another, the former about sixteen, the latter twenty-four. In 1673 "Cristable," daughter of William Jennings, of Bristol, was united to him in marriage and their only daughter, of the same name, married Robert Ingram, merchant, of London. Coale travelled considerably, as both trader and preacher, in America. His wife died while they were in Jamaica, and he departed this life in London, 17 x. 1682, aged about 34. Probably on account of his business affairs in foreign countries his estate was not settled three and a half years later. William Ingram, who was called to consult (p. 146), was probably the father-in-law of Coale's daughter.
Smith, *Cata.*; *Jnl. F. H. S.* iv. 9, x. 120.

146   4   Sir Robert Geffery was elected Lord Mayor in 1685.

147   1   John Matthews was a member of Peel Meeting and suffered for his attendance (*Suff.* i. 416, 461). Despite the correction on page 128, it is probable that *John* Matthews was intended, his residence being near that of John Elson, and not *James* Matthews who lived away to the East (118. 3).

148   1   James Lowrey (*c.* 1653—1725/6) lived at South Street. He placed his coach at the service of Friends. He married Mary Eames in 1674. At his marriage he is described as "merchant" and at his death as "Coachman."

148   2   Anne Whitehead (1624—1686), the first wife of George Whitehead, was widow of Benjamin Greenwell, and daughter of Rev. Thomas Downer (vol. ii. pp. 421, 441). The little volume *Piety Promoted by Faithfulness,* issued in the year of her death, contains Testimonies by her husband, Mary Elson, Margaret Meakens, Rebecka Travers, Mary Stout of Hertford, Grace Bathurst, Mary Woolley, Bridget Ford, Charles Bathurst, Bridget Austill, Ruth Crouch, John Staploe, William Ingram, Mary Forster, Anne Travers, Benjamin Antrobus (in verse), Jane Sowle, Susanna Dew, Ann Mackett, and Elizabeth Camfield, and a General Epistle, signed by, among others, the following, who appear in the Itinerary Journal, or perhaps wives of such: Mary Stott, Martha Hull, Mariabella Farmborough, Priscilla Hart, Patience Ashfield, Elizabeth Mann, Martha Matthews, Sarah Meade, Margaret Drinkwell, Elizabeth Fullove, Sarah Edge, Mary Whitpain, Elizabeth Vaughton, Grace Staploe, Joan Perkins, Susanna Ingram, Mary Antrobus, Grace Pinder, Elizabeth Collit, Mary Simms, Mary Wasse, Ann Cox, Mary Latey, Elizabeth Brassey, Anne Eccleston, Elizabeth Gouldney, Mary Oades, Margery Field, Elizabeth Baker, Dorothy Langhorne, Elizabeth Skinner, Mary Quare, Elizabeth Grice. The day and hour of decease agree with those given by George Whitehead in his Testimony. The Friends present included her husband, her sister Ann-Mary Freeman, Ann Cox, Mary Stout and Bridget Austill. The women may be among the "several women fri⁴ˢ" who accompanied G. F. in the coach to Edward Mann's (p. 148).

        Whiting, *Memoirs,* p. 165; Brailsford, *Quaker Women,* 1915.

149   1   There is a note on Gerard Roberts in vol. i. p. 434. He was convinced at the Glasiers' Hall Meeting in Thames Street (*Gilbert Latey,* 1707, p. 8). At the first settlement of the Meeting for Sufferings Roberts was entrusted with the interests of Friends in the shires of Worcester and Gloucester, along with Ezekiel Woolley, and he also took charge of Friends in the island of Barbados. His home in "Thomas Apostles" was a general meetingplace for Friends until his removal in 1666. Robert Fowler consulted him and other heads of the Church on his proposed voyage to America in the *Woodhouse,* 1657. He attended the wedding of George Fox and Margaret Fell in 1669. He married, in 1661, Milbrow Davies (*c.* 1617—1697).

        F. P. T.; Jnl. F. H. S. i. ii. vi. ix. xi. xvii.

149   2   William Shewen (*c.* 1631—1695) was at this time living at Enfield, Middlesex. In 1656 his dwelling was "in A yard in at ye signe of ye 2 bruers at ye uper end of Bermonsey streett" (*F. P. T.* p. 166). At a meeting "on account of sufferings," held at James Claypoole's, 12 iv. 1676, William Shewen was appointed on behalf of Southwark Friends (MS. in D). In 1680 he was appointed to act as umpire to compose the difference between Ellis Hookes, Recording Clerk, and Andrew Sowle, printer (*Jnl. F. H. S.* xviii. 7). Hookes left Shewen some money in his will, proved December, 1681, and in the will of Amy Fleetwood, proved August, 1684, £10 was left to "William Shewen of the Parish of Magdalens Bermondsey, Pinmaker, and Ellis Hooke of the Parish of Newington Butts, Scrivener" (*Jnl. F. H. S.* i. 22, ii. 4). Shewen removed to Enfield in 1686. His widow, Ann Shewen, gave £100, in 1696, towards building a meetinghouse (*London Friends' Meetings,* pp. 215, 235, 301). She also gave a meetinghouse in Baker Street,

Enfield, in 1700 (Note Book i., MS. in D). His most popular writings were entitled : *The True Christian's Faith and Experience*, printed 1675 to 1840, and *Counsel to the Christian Traveller*, printed 1683 to 1838. Whiting, *Memoirs*, p. 239.

150   1   Jan Claus was a merchant of Amsterdam, who settled in England where he became a Friend. In 1664 he was arrested and sentenced for transportation for seven years to Jamaica. He lived to return to Holland but did not return to England to live, though he was in this country in 1686. He acted as interpreter to the Friends visiting Holland in 1677. His wife and her father are mentioned 241. 1.

William Crouch, 1712, pp. 88, 89 ; *Collectitia*, 1824 ; *Penna. Mag.* ii. (1878); Fell-Smith, *Steven Crisp*, 1892 ; *Bulletin F. H. S. Phila.* iv.; MSS. in D.

151   1   Ezekiel Woolley (*c.* 1625—1693) was among the first members of the Meeting for Sufferings and represented Worcestershire and Gloucestershire (the country representative being "Edward Bourne, Physician, Worcester") and also Bristol. In 1668 he was asked to represent Wheeler Street Friends in the matter of registering births, marriages and burials (*Sundry Ancient Epistles*, MS. in D). He was a weaver, of Spitalfields, and a very active Friend. Fox was frequently at his house. Woolley is placed by Francis Bugg, ex-Quaker, in his "Cage of Unclean Birds" (*Picture of Quakerism Drawn to the Life*, 1697, p. 70). Ezekiel, the younger (1668—   ), was at Christopher Taylor's school at Edmonton in 1680 and was one of the children who wrote their appreciations of their late master, John Matern (*Testimony of that Dear and Faithful Man, John Matern*, 1680, p. 22).

152   1   Edward Brush (*c.* 1603—1696) is described by William Crouch as "a man of good repute, an inhabitant and housekeeper in Bearbinder Lane near Lombard Street" (*Posthuma Christiana*, 1712, p. 82). In his pamphlet *The Invisible Power of God known in Weakness, with a Christian Testimony of the Experience and Sufferings of Edward Brush, Aged Ninety One Years*, etc., London, 1695, he gives a few details of his life. He was twelve when he went to London. "I Kept House and Servants Twelve Years before I took a Wife and the Fear of God in my Soul preserved me from gross Evils." In 1665 he was one of the few whom the authorities succeeded in banishing. He was sent to Jamaica for seven years and arrived on the island in June. "After a while the Governor received an Express from King Charles the Second to send me home." He arrived in London, 1st May, 1669. His wife Sarah and son Isaac had been left in London. He wrote a letter to Jamaican Friends, dated at the Bull and Mouth, 15 vii. 1688. For his connection with the Great Plague see vol. ii. pp. 397 f. He suffered further persecution after his return. At the first settling of the Meeting for Sufferings, iv. 1676, Brush was appointed to represent Jamaican Friends (MS. in D). Sarah Brush died in 1687, aged 77.

Christian Progress, pp. 397 f.; *Extracts from State Papers; Second Period*.

154   1   See 80. 8.

156   1   For Mary Birkett see 103. 1.

157   1   Jacob Camfield (d. *ante* 1704 in which year his widow, Ann, remarried) was a tobacconist, of St Bartholomew the Great, probably son of Francis Camfield (87. 4).

157   2   There is a considerable note respecting John Taylor in vol. ii. p 496. At the date of his appearance in the Itinerary Journal he was resident

in York, combining preaching tours with business calls. Fox visited Taylor in York in 1677 (page 228). Whitehead records that "my ancient Companions in Sollicitation, Gilbert Latey, Thomas Lower (the Doctor), John Tayler of York (my late Brother-in-Law) and our Friend Daniel Quare" appeared before King William III to present to him the sufferings Friends had still to undergo in the matter of tithes, oaths, "contempts," etc. (*Christian Progress*, pp. 637, 639, 643). John Taylor's life-story of travel and travail is well worth perusal, dated 1710, reprinted 1830.

157   3   For John Blaykling see vol. i. p. 403, etc. See 136. 4.

Rogers, *Christian Quaker*, 1680, pt. v. pp. 36, 76; *Swarth. Account Book.*

158   1   Of this selfsame Lord Mayor's Show John Evelyn (1620—1705/6) wrote in his *Diary*: "There was a triumphant shew of the Lord Maior both by land and water, with much solemnity," thus giving a different view of the occasion from that of Fox. It is not evident in what manner Fox would be able "to still yᵉ people." The Lord Mayor's Day was the 29th of October until 1752, when it was altered by Act of Parliament to the present date, the 9th of November. The Lord Mayor taking office was Sir John Peake. Samuel Pepys (1632—1703) styled the pageants "good for such kind of things but in themselves but poor and absurd" (Oct. 29, 1660), "the pageants were very silly" (Oct. 29, 1663). Lady Springett writes that she "was burdened with the vanity of their show" (*Experiences in the Life of Mary Penington*, 1911, p. 33).

Pepys, *Diary*, ed. Wheatley, Oct. 29, 1660, note.

159   1   Daniel Quare (1648—1723/4) was a noted watch and clock maker. At the time of his marriage with Mary, daughter of Jeremiah Steevens, maltster, of High Wycombe, Bucks, in 1676, his address was "Martins-le-Grand in the liberty of Westminster" (*Jnl. F. H. S.* i. 56). Later he removed to Aldersgate Street, then to Lombard Street, and later still to "Kings Arms" in Exchange Alley. He had a country-house at Croydon. He was admitted a brother of the Clockmakers' Company in 1671, when twenty-three years of age and he became Master in 1708. He made a clock for King William III which required winding but once a year, and invented a portable barometer "which may be removed to any place, though turned upside down, without spilling one drop of quicksilver or letting any air into the tube" (*Cal. S. P. Dom.* 1694—5, p. 395, quoted *Jnl. F. H. S.* xiv. 44). George I was on very friendly terms with Quare and he was allowed special access to him "at the Back Stairs." Quare's professional connection with royalty was of use to Friends when appealing to the throne (*Christian Progress*, pp. 637, 642, 643). He moved in the highest social circle of the day, and the marriages of his daughters—Anne with John Falconar in 1705, Sarah with Jacob Wyan in 1712, Elizabeth with Silvanus Bevan in 1715 (of which marriage there is a reproduction of the certificate in D)—were attended by many members of the Court and diplomatic circles (see *F. Q. E.* 1900). In the Book of Cases (MS. vol. in D) there is a reference to "Danial Quare's Paper seting forth his Refusal of a Pension of 300 per Annum to be the Kings Watchmaker &c. Because for Conscience sake he could not Qualifie himselfe, as yᵉ Law directs by taking yᵉ Oath," dated 4 xii. 1714. In the same year Quare wrote to Thomas Aldam, the younger, on a printed copy of the new solemn affirmation of loyalty to George I, quoting the opinion of the King's Solicitor General that it contains the effect of the Oath of Abjuration and would legalize Friends as voters at the poll. He recommends Friends to use their vote and

not "by timorousness disfranchise themselves...but modestly give their assistance to Chuse Prudent men principled to preserve us in our Religous & Civil Liberties..." (original in Pease MSS. in D).

F. Q. E. 1900—a valuable article by Isaac Sharp; *Jnl. F. H. S.* viii. xv. xvi. xix.; *D. N. B.*; Williamson, *Cata. of Collection of Watches, the Property of J. Pierpont Morgan,* c. 1912, *Behind my Study Door,* 1922 ; Gamble, *Bevan Family,* 1924.

160   1   For Nathaniel Coleman see vol. ii. p. 446. Further reference to Coleman's Separatist activity may be found in *Jnl. F. H. S.* ix. 190, xvi. 143.

160   2   Theodor Eccleston (1650—1726) was son of Richard and Priscilla Eccleston, Seekers who became Friends. Richard died in 1665 and his widow married Thomas Hart, of Enfield (105. 3), in 1671. The descent of Theodor Eccleston is traced to its end, in *Jnl. F. H. S.* vi. 94. William Sewel (1654—1720), the Dutch historian, writes: "I cannot well omit here publicly to acknowledge the signal kindness and diligence of my well-beloved and much esteemed friend Theodor Eccleston, of London, who hath furnished me with abundance of materials...for the compiling of this work" (Preface to *History of the Quakers*). Eccleston's address was Crown Court, Gracechurch Street. He was prominent and active in the affairs of the Quaker Church. His mother was among the "7000 Handmaids," who petitioned in 1659 for the abolition of tithes.

Y.M. Epistles, 1684, 1685 ; *Christian Progress,* pp. 590, 647, 659, 695 ; *William and Alice Ellis,* 1849 ; *London Friends' Meetings,* 1869 ; *House of Lords MSS.* 1695—97; *Jnl. F. H. S.* i. ii. vii. xii. xviii.; MSS. in D.

160   3   See 104. 3.

160   4   The marriage of a daughter of Thomas Cox in 1686 has not been found on the Registers. See 96. 1. It would have been interesting to know who the couple was who accompanied Fox in a coach to South Street.

162   1   This was probably Mary Tyler, of Waltham Abbey, shopkeeper, who died in May, 1693 (Friends' Registers). She is mentioned in conjunction with Elizabeth Bennett (162. 2).

162   2   Elizabeth Bennett, *née* Constable, was the wife of Thomas Bennett (105. 5). The references represent her accompanying George Fox in a coach several times to meetings. She died 10 viii. 1704, aged ninety, evidently much older than her husband.

163   1   It seems strange, from our modern point of view, to read of George Fox instructing a young "innholder" how to carry on his business at his newly acquired White Lion Tavern in Cornhill, but "we must remember that when everyone went to the taverns, these were very superior resorts to the public houses which have taken their place, and the taverners were men of substance and repute" (Wheatley, *Pepysiana,* 1899, p. 190). Friends met for conference at several inns—in 1686 at the King's Head in Pudding Lane (*London Friends' Meetings,* p. 233) ; see also pp. 96, 137, 147, 185.

In a map of part of London, 1765, the White Lyon Tavern is shewn with entrances from Bishopsgate Street and Cornhill, with White Lyon Court at the rear.

165   1   Patience Ashfield (*c.* 1627—1708) was the relict of Richard Ashfield (vol. i. p. 453). The Friends' Meeting at Staines met in the house of Patience Ashfield before a meetinghouse was built. She was paid forty shillings a year for the accommodation (*London Friends' Meetings,* p. 284). She wrote an account of her husband's life and death which

appeared in Besse's *Sufferings,* vol. i. p. 440, the editor adding: "The conscientious Widow patiently endured the Spoiling of her Goods for the same testimony for which her husband had before cheerfully suffered the Loss both of his Liberty and his Life."
Christian Progress, p. 594.

166   1   Francis Dove (*c.* 1627—1707) lived in "Lesterfields" (p. 166), and in "Martins Lane Nigh Charing Cross" (p. 192), probably two addresses for the same house. There are several notices of George Fox's passing a night at his house. In 1665 Dove was committed to the Gatehouse Prison in Westminster by warrant from the Duke of Albemarle, for "attending an illegal meeting in St Johns."
MSS. in D.

166   2   Timothy Emerson (*c.* 1634—1712) was an oilman in Gerard Street. With William Crouch and Samuel Boulton and others, Emerson signed, *c.* 1686, an address to King James urging him "to put a Stop to the ruinous Prosecutions and Persecutions of the mercenary and merciless Informers." So wrote George Whitehead in his *Christian Progress* (p. 591). He had a "servant and apprentice," named William Phillips, who died in 1694, aged twenty, of small-pox. See 146. 2.

167   1   See 80. 5.

168   1   Stephen Hubbard (—1704) is mentioned in *London Friends' Meetings* (p. 318) as one of the "worthies" of Kingston Meeting. Ruth Lilley (168. 2) lodged at his house. He was a shoemaker. A minute of Kingston M.M. in 1690 "ordered" Francis Holden, Stephen Hubbard, and John Brown to "take care and draw up a writing against next M.M. in settling the Burying Ground, According to the uses intents and purposes as it was purchased for, and let the paper be entered in the book." Hubbard seems to have advanced money for the purchase of the ground; it was bought in his name and conveyed to trustees.
MSS. in D.

168   2   The Burial Registers contain the entry: "Ruth Lillay, parish of Kingston, widow of William [236. 1], of Hassam, Kingston, 1691/2 i. 4." It is stated in *London Friends' Meetings*: "In 1693 Ruth Lilley left £40, which was put out to interest till 1730, at which time land was bought to the amount of £70" (p. 314). George Fox called to see her when visiting his relations early in 1687. She was lodging at Stephen Hubbard's and out of health. In 1690, on his last visit to Kingston, he called again, and may have made other unrecorded visits to his friend.

169   1   This six-weeks' visit to Kingston produced several papers. Ell. Text (ii. 440): "Towards the latter end of this year I went to Kingston and stayed some time at my son Rous's." The papers occupy eight and a half pages of the Ell. Text.

170   1   The only notice found respecting Robert Scotting is in Besse (*Suff.* i. 483). He lived, presumably, at or near Ratcliff.

171   1   Martha Dry lived at Wapping, to the East of London. She was a daughter of John and Margaret Meakens (122. 2) and married William Dry in 1678. Her sister, Mary, married, in the same year, James Strutt, of Wapping (100. 2).
Jnl. F. H. S. x. 16.

171   2   John Patterem was among Friends tried at Guildhall in 1684, for meeting at White Hart Court "with Force and Arms, routously, tumultuously, and unlawfully assembled to the Breach of the Peace, etc." (*Suff.* i. 465, see also p. 470).

171   3   This was probably William Briggins (*c.* 1628—1688), about whose
son Joseph (*c.* 1664—1675) a small octavo tract was issued under the
title: *The Living Words of a Dying Child*, etc., 1675 and 1677.
Piety Promoted.

173   1   Not only did many Friends visit Fox at Gooseyes but he found time
to write letters and papers. Ell. Text (ii. 450) gives the reason of this
visit: "By reason of the many hardships I had undergone in imprisonments and other sufferings for Truth's sake, my body was grown
so infirm and weak that I could not bear the closeness of the city long
together, but was obliged to go a little into the country for the benefit
of the fresh air." (How did these personal remarks get into the Ell.
Text?—from some Fox original? or did Ellwood put the statement into
Fox's mouth?) A paper "A Distinction between the True Offering and
the False," written 28 ii. 1687, is given in Ell. Text, and an important
letter, dated the same day, was sent to Thomas Lower, respecting the
use of Fox's property known as "Pettys." See *Swarth. Account Book.*

174   1   Elizabeth Grice was one of the Friends who signed the General
Testimony to Anne Whitehead (148. 2). She was fined, with others,
including Elizabeth Fullove, four nobles for meeting, in 1684 (*Suff.*
i. 472).

175   1   Jasper Batt (—1702) lived at Street, in Somersetshire. The
Bishop of Bath and Wells described him as "the greatest seducer in
all the West, and the most seditious person in the county, and that
he would make Somersetshire too hot for him" (Whiting, *Memoirs*,
p. 108). His gift in the ministry was exercised in many parts of the
country. He preached at the funeral of George Fox.

176   1   The Y.M. of 1687 convened the 16th, 17th and 19th of the Third
Month. The veteran leader was in attendance though weak in body
and troubled with "great horstness." The Meeting was very large,
"Friends having more freedom to come up out of the counties to it by
reason of the general toleration and liberty now granted" (Ell. Text, ii.
453). This was the Declaration of Indulgence of King James which
appeared on the 4th April, 1687—"a high-handed act of authority,
which undoubtedly violated the whole spirit of English Institutions"
(*Second Period*, p. 131).
  For *1ˢᵗ mo:* read *3ᵈ mo:*

176   2   For Ambrose Rigge see an informing sketch in vol. ii. p. 470. He
signed a Testimony to Charles Marshall in 1703.
Marsh, *Early Friends in Surrey and Sussex*, 1886, chap. viii.

176   3   Samuel Watson (*c.* 1620—1708) lived at Knight Stainforth, near
Settle, Co. York. He was convinced in York Castle by some Friends
confined there, he having been sent to prison on account of some demand
on his estate in or about 1654. He travelled in the ministry in Scotland
with Roger Hebden (—1695) (*F. P. T.*; *Jnl. F. H. S.* xii. 83).
Later, Samuel Watson wrote: "For being at Three Meetings of the
People of God, and bearing my Testimony in a measure of the Spirit
of Truth...for which being called an offence according to the Act
against Conventicles, a fine was laid upon me for 120 l for those three
meetings. And the officers came in one Day and took away most of
my Cattle, to the Value of 150 l, the last Day of the 4th Month, 1670."
Watson wrote various pieces, longer and shorter—one was "To the
Mountebanks of Settle," 16 xii. 1696, whom he describes as a "Lofty
and Highly set up sort of Inchanters to Evil, who in their Serpentine
Subtility Bewitch People into vain Laughter, Madness and Folly by
their Ungodly Actings and Lying Wonders." He wrote letters from

PAGE NOTE

York Castle in 1661, 1682 and 1685. In 1664 Samuel Watson married
Mary Monk, widow of Thomas Monk, of Co. Notts, who brought two
daughters, Mary and Elizabeth, with her. Samuel and Mary had a
daughter, Grace (1668—1688), who died at the house of Benjamin
Antrobus in London, 20 vi. 1688. Mary Monk married at the house of
her step-father, in 1679, Isaac Moss, Junr., of Manchester, and died in
1691. Elizabeth Monk (*c.* 1663—1702) married Thomas Moss, of Manchester, in 1685. In 1680 appeared a tract : *A Narrative and Testimony
concerning Grace Watson,* containing appreciations by her parents, her
two half-sisters, Benjamin Antrobus and Charles Marshall. Other
Testimonies appear in *A Short Account of the Convincement of...Samuel
Watson,* being a Collection of his Works, 1712. Mary Watson died in
1694. Her husband removed to the neighbourhood of Chester, to the
home of his son-in-law, where he died.

> *F. P. T.*; *Jnl. F. H. S.* x. xii.; Watson mss. in D. For Elizabeth
> Moss, and Samuel, Mary and Grace Watson, see *Piety Promoted.*

176   4   John Gratton (1641—1712) was one of the Ministers who exercised
their gifts at Y.M. 1687. There is a valuable account of John Gratton,
written by Emily Manners and printed in *The Friend* (Lond.), 1921,
pp. 603, 618. He was born at Bonsall in Derbyshire and lived during
most of his married life at Monyash in the same county. He travelled
extensively as a preacher, principally in the Midlands, and has been
termed "The Quaker Apostle of the Peak." In 1680 he was cast into
Derby Jail and released in March, 1685/6. "Dʳ [Dear] J. G." appears
frequently in *A Quaker Post-Bag,* 1910. In 1707 the Monyash home
was given up and John and Mary his wife went to reside with their
daughter, Phebe Bateman, at Farnsfield in Notts. Gratton was buried
in the graveyard there. Mrs Manners writes : "No trace of the meetinghouse remains, and the burying place is now almost a legend ; but it
is said that a garden in the rear of a house on the village street is the
old Quaker burying place."

> *Journal,* first printed 1720, last reprint dated 1845 ; *Piety Promoted* ;
> *D. N. B.* ; Hall, *John Gratton, the Quaker Preacher,* 1885 ; *The Friend*
> (Phila.), vol. 80 (1907) ; Norris, *John ap John,* 1907 ; *Jnl. F. H. S.*
> iii.—vi. ix. xii. ; Danielowski, *Die Journale der frühen Quäker,* 1921,
> p. 41 ; Matthews, *Congregational Churches of Staffordshire,* 1924, p. 81.

176   5   This was, probably, George Myers (*c.* 1653—1714), of Farrfield, in
the parish of Addingham, in the Craven district of Yorkshire. He
wrote several pamphlets, one, *A Serious Examination,* relating to the
Separatists in York (117. 2). In the end of his little book on *Spiritual
Worship,* 1721, there is a record, by his children, George and Hannah
Myers, of some of his dying sayings. If the same George Myers is the
Friend of that name who appears in *William and Alice Ellis,* 1849,
then the report of his death in 1698 was not correct (pp. 28, 91, 105).
He married Mary Hardcastle in 1682/3. John Gratton (176. 4) visited
him several times (*John Gratton,* 1720, pp. 121, 126).

> *John Taylor,* 1710, pp. 45, 54.

176   6   See vol. ii. p. 412 for an account of Robert Lodge.

> *John Taylor,* 1710, p. 45 ; *Jnl. F. H. S.* x.

176   7   Among the ministering Friends who attended Y.M. 1687 was Thomas
Gilpin (1622—1702), of Warborough, Oxon. He was the youngest son
of Thomas Gilpin, of Millhill, in the parish of Caton, Lancs. He was
apprenticed to a tallow-chandler in London and joined the army during
the Civil War. In 1653 he was arrested by the preaching of Ambrose
Rigge and others in Oxfordshire and in London he was convinced by

the ministry of Burrough and Howgill. After his marriage with Joan, daughter of Thomas Bartholomew, he lived some years under his father-in-law's roof and then took a house at Warborough, which he opened for worship. There is a remarkable story of the way Friends persisted in holding meetings at Gilpin's house till almost all the men Friends were in jail (*F. P. T.* p. 217). He underwent various imprisonments and was liberated by the "Pardon" of 1672. His death is referred to in *Quaker Post-Bag*, 1910, p. 188.

First-days Meetings; *Piety Promoted*; *Gilpin Memoirs*; *F. Q. E.* 1912, p. 482; Hirst, *Quakers in Peace and War*, 1923, p. 528; *Biog. Memoirs*, iii. 445; a volume on the Gilpin family is in preparation by Alfred R. Justice.

177 1   William Penn writes of Fox in the Preface to the *Journal*: "He was often where the records of the affairs of the Church are kept and the letters from the many meetings of God's people, over all the world, where settled, come upon occasions, which letters he had read to him." Many letters are extant, endorsed by him in his bold, laboured handwriting.

179 1   Ann Cox (c. 1644—1716) was the wife of Thomas Cox (96. 1). Her maiden name was Hind. She married in 1682. She signed, with many other women Friends of London, a letter to Margaret Fox in answer to a letter from her to the Women's Q.M. It is dated 30 vii. 1695 and concludes: "We dearly salute thee in the fresh remembrance of thy dear husband and our honourable Friend and Father, whose travels were known to the Lord from the beginning." Other Friends, mentioned in these notes, who signed, are Ruth Crouch, Mary Elson, Mary Woolley, Grace Bathurst, Susanna Dew, Bridget Ford, Margaret Rous, Sarah Meade, Mary Lower, Susanna Ingram, Margaret Drinkwell, Ann Eccleston, Anne Whitehead, Mary Wharley, Elizabeth Vaughton, Mary Russell, Elizabeth Couldney, Anna Hutson (original letter in D).

179 2   Two visits to Hertford are recorded (pp. 179, 216) during both of which George Fox was entertained by Henry Stout (1631—1695). In 1664 Stout married Mary Saunders, of Cromwell's household (vol. i. p. 444; *Quaker Women*, 1915, pp. 249, 262, 263, 269). "He was the first called a Quaker who suffered imprisonment in Hertford gaol for the testimony of truth. He was sentenced to banishment and continued in prison nearly eight years" (*Piety Promoted*, quoted *F. Q. E.* 1916, "The Hertford Trials of 1664"). He entered into the Hat Controversy, and appears in Penn's *Alexander the Coppersmith*, 1673, p. 24, and Penn's *Judas and the Jews*, 1673, p. 90.

Sarah Stout, whose sudden death produced great sensation and much enquiry, was their daughter. John Tomkins (c. 1663—1706), writing to Sir John Rodes, 18 i. 1698/9, records the event: "I was last first day at Hartford and on 2d day comeing out of the Town I saw Sarah Stout wel in health, who the next morning was found drownd in a River near that Town. She left her mothers House (or rather her own for she was Mrs of that house and much riches besides) about 11 at night, another person [Spencer Cowper] was with her at that time who says he left her there at home but just about one time her Mother and servants found them both gone and sat up all night expecting her returne, when next morning soon as day, news was brought of her death. She was found without her Gown and Apron, close to the Grates of a Mill, her stayes and Petycoats on, some Gold and Silver in her pockets, and all her buttons &c. of gold and silver in her Sleeves and shoes.... The man that was with her has a wife and children: he did sometimes place mony out to Interest for her but the Juges verdict was that she drownd her self being non Compus mentes. She was, poor lass, grown very high, haveing litell regard to Truth nor her aged Mother, who is a good Woman" (*Quaker Post-Bag*, 1910, pp. 160, 161; we have not seen the original letter).

Trial of Spencer Cowper, 1699; *Some Observations*, 1702; *Sarah the Quaker to Lothario lately Deceased, on meeting him in the Shades*, 1728; *Lothario's Answer*, 1729; *D. N. B.*, under Cowper, Spencer (1669—1728).

179   3   Records of the life of Thomas Burr which have come down to us deal mainly with the sufferings this good man had to meet and endure for conscience sake. In 1659/60 he was taken from a meeting at Baldock and imprisoned. In 1664 he was among the prisoners sentenced to banishment to Jamaica but remained in prison till the King's "Pardon" of 1672, during which imprisonment he suffered the loss of £130 in goods for meetings at his house. At this time he lived at Baldock. When travelling in East Anglia he was arrested, with George Whitehead, and inhabited the City and County Jail, Bristol, from March, 1679/80, to the following July. The proceedings connected with the trial and imprisonment are given fully in *Due Order of Law and Justice*, 1680, a tract reprinted in *Christian Progress*, pp. 377 ff. A certificate respecting Burr, dated 14 April, 1680, contains the following information: "Thomas Bur of Ware in the County of Hartford, Malster, hath lived, and been a Trader in Malt for about fourteen Years past; and is a Man whom we judge of a Good Competent Estate, and of Good Credit and Reputation among his Neighbours in this Place, and hath never been accounted a Jesuit or Papist." Signed by Churchwardens, Constables and others. Between Fox's visits in 1687 and 1690 Burr had spent some time in Hertford Prison for non-payment of tithes. In 1681 he wrote a Testimony to his friend Giles Barnardiston.

Other Friends bearing the name of Burr lived in the neighbourhood. For later members of the family see *Memorials of the Old Square* (Birmingham), 1897; MSS. in D.

180   1   William Baker (*c.* 1642—1727), of Waltham Abbey, married Hannah, daughter of Francis Camfield (87. 4), at the Bull and Mouth in 1672. We do not know the circumstances connected with this "difference." Ell. Text reads: "Next day went to another place to compose a difference which, for want of a right understanding of each other, had happened between some Friends" (ii. 456). The name William Baker occurs in *Sundry Ancient Epistles*, p. 35 (MS. in D), among Friends representing London (*i.e.* City or Bull and Mouth) Meeting, in the matter of registers of births, etc., *anno* 1668. Hannah (Camfield) Baker died in 1705, aged fifty-five.

182   1   Fox writes (or perhaps we should say Ellwood wrote in his name) of this visit: "Here I stayed some weeks, yet was not idle....Between meeting and meeting I wrote many things for the spreading of truth." Several papers are printed in Ell. Text (ii. 456—463). A letter to Thomas Robinson (Robertson) was written on the day after arrival "concerning John Cox, who preaches in the meeting [Bristol] without orders." Attached to the letter is copy of the reply of Cox's sympathisers complaining of Robertson's preaching, while six months in and around Bristol! See Bristol MSS. (*Jnl. F. H. S.* ix. 191).

182   2   There is a hiatus here in the Journal from the 8th of the Seventh Month, 1687, to the 23rd of the Fourth Month, 1688, nearly ten months. From Gooseyes Fox returned to town where he remained three months, "being almost daily at public meetings and frequently taken up in visiting Friends that were sick and in other services of the church."

Then, his "body much stopped for fresh air," he went down to King-ston, returning to London towards the close of the Eleventh Month and continuing in the City till the middle of the First Month, 1687/8, when he passed to the northward, remaining in the Enfield district till the Yearly Meeting, which began early in the Fourth Month, 1688. Y.M. over, Fox went again into Essex where we find him at the open-ing of the next volume of the Itinerary Journal. See Ell. Text, ii. 463—475, and *Register of George Fox's Letters* (MS. in D).

183   1   For John Butcher see vol. ii. pp. 370, 497. With others he put his hand to a petition to Parliament *re* oaths in 1695 (*Christian Progress*, p. 647), and in 1715, after the rebellion of the Old Pretender, he accompanied George Whitehead into the King's presence, presenting George I with an address (*ibid.* p. 685).

A sermon preached by him at Gracechurch Street, "March 11th, 1693," was printed in *Concurrence and Unanimity*, 1711.

Quaker Post-Bag, 1910, pp. 149, 151, 182.

183   2   From this date we find fuller reference to subjects which formed bases of Fox's sermons. They were of great variety. See Introduction.

184   1   This would be Springett Penn (1675—1696/7), the elder son of W. and G. M. Penn—a son after the father's own heart. "He was a lad of noble parts and of a spiritual nature like his parents. He lingered under slow consumption till February, 1696/7, and died in his father's arms" (Graham, *William Penn*, 1917, p. 235). Mary Penington wrote a valuable letter to her grandson in 1680 "to be delivered to him after her decease."

Marsh, *Early Friends in Surrey and Sussex*, 1886; Jenkins, *The Family of William Penn*, 1899; *A Quaker Post-Bag*, 1910, p. 130 n.; Penney, *Experiences in the Life of Mary Penington*, 1911, p. 72.

184   2   For Mary Waldenfield, wife of Samuel (130. 1), see vol. ii. p. 497. The following incident of her early life is recorded: "George Fox was walking along Cheapside at the instant a coach stopp'd and a little woman in very gay apparel stepp'd out of it. He, laying his hand upon her head, said, 'Woman, mind the light within thee.' She became effectively convinced and was afterwards the wife of Sam¹ Waldingfield and a respectable member of our Society" (*Jnl. F. H. S.* vii. 39).

185   1   For Isabel Yeamans see vol. ii. p. 492. She was at this time the widow of William Yeamans, but in the following year (1689) she married Abraham Morrice, of Lincoln. Before this re-marriage there was an *affaire de cœur*, which is described in *Jnl. F. H. S.* xii.

Of the many Friends mentioned in the Itinerary Journal as speakers in the meetings attended by G. Fox, the men far outnumber the women. The women-preachers mentioned are Elizabeth Bathurst (p. 105), "a woman friend" (p. 114), Mariabella Farmborough and Isabel Yeamans (p. 185), "2 or 3 Women" (p. 198), Joan Cook (p. 200), Margaret Fox (p. 206).

186   1   Fox wrote, about the year 1687, a long paper entitled "Concerning the Church being clothed with the Sun, and having the Moon under her feet," given in Ell. Text, ii. 437—440—"all changeable things, re-ligious worships, ways, fellowships, churches and teachers in the world are as the moon; for the moon changes, but the sun does not change. Rev. xii. 1."

187   1   In the Barbados section of Besse's *Sufferings* there are several re-ferences to the sufferings undergone by Richard Sutton. In 1677 he was arrested for allowing thirty Negroes to be present at a meeting. In 1673 he was fined, "for refusing to pay Priest's wages, 1706 lb. and for Defaults of sending to the Troop, 1566 lb. In all 3272 lbs." of

sugar. He is described as "formerly a Captain." After his return from Europe he was fined again—"for Priest's Maintenance 1 l. 6 s." See Bowden, *Hist. of Friends in America*, 1854, ii. 192.

For Quakerism on the island of Barbados see vol. ii. p. 412. See note 140. 1.

190 1   Among the "great deal of many things" written during this six weeks' stay at the Meade home in Essex, we have on record papers "concerning the worlds teachers and the emptiness of their teaching"; another to shew that "many of the holy men and prophets of God and apostles of Christ were husbandmen and tradesmen"; and another "to shew the vanity of hearing and telling news" (Ell. Text, ii. 479—483). See also *Register of George Fox's Letters* under 1688 (MS. in D).

190 2   The revolution which brought William and Mary to the Throne ushered in a new era of tolerance for nonconformists. In Part IV of his *Christian Progress*, George Whitehead introduces this period thus: "Altho' for the space of about Twenty Five Years (from 1660 to 1684) we had but small Respite from some Kind of Persecution or other, yet the Truth lost no Ground but gained through all: The Persecution Time was a Seed-Time for the Truth and Gospel of Christ Jesus, which we suffered for, and the Faithful grew and multiplied....In order to give his Churches (among us) Rest from open Persecutions the Lord our God prepared the Heart of the Government (*after the Revolution*) to allow us the Sanction of a Law for our Liberty...respecting our Religious Exercise in our Publick Assemblies" (pp. 631 ff.). The bill before the Parliament was carefully examined by able Friends and "a chamber near yᵉ parliament house," "adjoyning to Westminster hall" (pp. 190, 191, 193, 194), was taken as a consultation-centre. G. Fox took a share in this work, coming up to London on purpose "and attending continually for many days, with other Friends at the parliament house" (Ell. Text, ii. 483). G. Whitehead, William Meade and John Osgood appeared before the Grand Committee on the bill. "After much Labour and attending on our Parts, the Bill was passed." It is generally called the Toleration Act (1 Gul. and Mar. cap. 18).

Second Period, pp. 153 ff.; *Jnl. F. H. S.* ix. 177.

190 3   Probably intended for Sir Robert *Napier* (c. 1642—1700). He was M.P. for Weymouth and Melcombe Regis in 1689—90. When High Sheriff of Dorset in 1681 he was knighted and he was created a baronet in 1682.

Hutchinson, *Dorset*, where the name *Napier* is occasionally given as *Napper*; *D. N. B.*

Several persons of the name Honywood appear in *The Diary of Samuel Pepys*. There was a John Manley, a major in Cromwell's army (*D. N. B. s.v.* Manley, Sir Robert, elder brother), M.P. for Bridport.

For the relationship between masters and apprentices see Coate, *Social Life in Stuart England*, 1924, chap. viii.

191 1   Sir John Vaughan, Lord Vaughan, third Earl of Carbery (1640—1713), is doubtless the person mentioned (the second Earl having died in 1686). George Whitehead writes: "Sir John Vaughan, a young man, appeared also for us [in Parliament], and afterward was convinced of the Truth, and went to our meetings and was imprisoned in Newgate under the Conventicle Act....He continued afterward among our Friends...and though at length some of his relations drew him aside, to his great prejudice, yet he retained a kindness, even when he came to be Earl of Carbery, and continued friendly to us...until his latter end" (*Christian Progress*, pp. 270, 652).

194   1   These letters to Peter Hendricks and Friends in Dantzig, and to the Magistrates of this town, are given in Ell. Text, ii. 483—486, dated Southgate, 28 ii. 1689. At the close is the suggestion: "Peter, thou mayst translate this into high Dutch and send them; and you may print it, if you will, and send it abroad; and translate that part of the letter that is to Friends into high Dutch, and send it to them."

195   1   See 190. 2.

195 2, 3   The Y.M. of 1689 occupied the 20th, 21st and 22nd of Third Month. It was Fox's practice for several years to write postscripts to the Epistles sent down into the country and these are printed with the Epistles. The addendum of this year contained about 500 words. It is printed in Ell. Text (ii. 487).

196   1   See 117. 2. As late as 1689 effects of the Separation in York were still felt. We find in Ell. Text, ii. 488, that, "inasmuch as there had been some hurt done in that place by some that were gone out of the unity of Friends," Fox was drawn to write a few lines of encouragement to true unity.

196   2   This was Margery Lower (1675—1706). She married Benjamin Robinson, of London, in 1700/01. There are numerous references to her in *Swarth. Account Book*—a penny rattle was bought for her in 1676—and to her marriage and after-life in Webb's *Fells of Swarthmoor Hall*, 1863—"many great persons and some members of parliament" were present at the wedding. Her husband settled "two hundred pounds yearly upon her in houses, groundrents and freehold."

197   1   Francis Holden (—1696) is mentioned in association with Stephen Hubbard (168. 1) as among the worthies more or less connected with Kingston Meeting (*London Friends' Meetings*, p. 318). A Meeting appointment in which he figures is referred to under Stephen Hubbard (168. 1). Mary, wife of Francis Holden, of Hampton Wick, died in 1687; her husband followed in 1696—"yeoman, of Hampton Wick."

        A second edition of William Caton's *Abridgment of Eusebius's History*, dated 1698, bears the imprint: "London: Printed for Francis Holden, in the Passage going into White-Hart-Yard in Lombard Street," but this must refer to a later bearer of the same name (Smith, *Cata.* i. 394).

197   2   We should be glad to know who was "yᵉ Kings Chirurgion" who visited Fox, but cannot, as yet, name him. He may have come over with William III from Holland. Dutch doctors were famous at this epoch.

        See 80. 8.

198   1   Sarah Robins (*c.* 1654—1710) was the daughter of Anne Travers (103. 2). She married Jasper Robins in 1675. He died in 1682, aged 32—a cheesemonger, of Laurence Pountney. In 1693 Sarah (Travers) Robins married Benjamin Crawley. They appear to have had a son, Joshua, who died at seven weeks "from being overlaid."

199   1   See 100. 6.

200   1   Joan Cook appears to have been a Minister, but no further information is forthcoming save the record of the death of a Joan Cook, of the parish of St Magdalene, Bermondsey, in 1711, aged 63. Was she akin to Richard Cook (202. 1)?

201   1   Charles Ker, second Earl of Ancrum, interested himself on behalf of Friends. He obtained the release of Isaac Penington in 1666 and Thomas Ellwood and others in the same year (Webb, *Penns and Peningtons*, 1867, pp. 155, 173; Ellwood, *History of Life*). A letter to his

lordship from Margaret Fox, dated 1685, contains valuable notes respecting her family (MS. in D, quoted *Beginnings*, p. 99). He died unmarried.

We may note a change of attitude towards "the worlds people," comparing this company at Bridget's table in 1689 with Fox's refusal to take money for his dinner in 1651 (Ell. Text, i. 92) or to dine with Esq. Marsh and others in 1668. See also pp. 238, 241.

Whiting, *Memoirs*, p. 24; Hist. MSS. Com.—*Manuscripts of J. Eliot Hodgkin*, 1897, p. 10.

202   1   Little is known respecting Richard Cook, innholder. We are told that, in 1701, "Richard Cooke has given up innkeeping, and a stable and man are to be sought" (*London Friends' Meetings*, p. 127). Did he turn to agriculture? There is a record of the decease of Richard Cooke, husbandman, at Hanworth, Middlesex, in 1709, aged 69.

205   1   The name of Robert Langhorne appears frequently in *First-days Meetings* (1682—3). He was a constant visitor at the London meetings. He is named in *Suff.* (i. 484) among "worthy and valiant Sufferers and Testimony Bearers," 1686. From the Marriage Registers we glean that Robert Langhorne, of Potton, Beds, milliner, son of Robert, of the same, married Dorothy Gunter, at Ratcliff in 1681. Dorothy Langhorne (148. 2) died in 1693, aged 58. There is a record of the burial of a Robert Langhorn, of Grays, Essex, 14 vi. 1704, aged 50, who "cut his own Throat being Lunatick."

206   1   For this winter's visit to Gooseyes see Ell. Text, ii. 491—497: "I stirred not much abroad, unless it were sometimes to the meeting to which the family belonged, which was about half-a-mile from thence, but I had meetings often in the house with the family and those Friends that came thither"; see also *Register of George Fox's Letters*, 1689 and 1690.

The complaint of William Rogers (*Christian Quaker*, 1680, pt. v. p. 28), referring to an earlier visit, probably to Gooseyes, certainly does not apply here: "Thou hast taken Liberty to stay almost a Quarter of a year from Meetings, or at least a considerable time, though held in the House of thy Residence."

207   1   Christ as Ensign, Isai. xi. 12, was much on Fox's mind at this time. He wrote a paper on the subject at Gooseyes on the 14th of Second Month, 1690 (Ell. Text, ii. 494), and preached on the subject at Tottenham on the 27th.

208   1   Probably Richard *Almond*, of Wandsworth. In 1698 Kingston M.M. "agreed that Richard Almond be desired and impowered to provide some wine for the refreshment of Labouring Friends after meetings; and that this meeting do reimburse him his charges again" (*London Friends' Meetings*, p. 321). Almond is also mentioned in *First-days Meetings*, as Richard *Ammon*.

210   1   From the official minutes of the proceedings of London Y.M. 1690, and from the personal side as revealed in the Itinerary Journal, we may present a brief sketch of this gathering, the last in the life-time of George Fox.

The name of George Fox does not appear in the minutes but it is probable that the addresses he gave coloured largely the Epistle sent out from the Meeting and his own addendum. The Y.M. was held on the 9th, 10th and 11th of the Fourth Month, the 9th being the second day of the week. Eighty-two Friends were present as representatives "from the counties." It appears that the mornings were set apart for meetings for worship, perhaps for Ministers only. G. F. was at the morning meeting at the Bull and Mouth, where he "Declared touching severall things & went to prayer." He also attended the business-meeting in the afternoon when a list of counties and Friends represented was recorded and also cases of suffering. "This meeting adjourns to Devonshire House at 3ᵈ hour afternoon tomorrow." Benjamin Bealing, secretary to Friends, would be acting as "clerk" for the second time. The meeting for worship convened at Wheeler Street the next morning, where Fox spoke on the subject of fashions (going without aprons), of the Jewish feasts and of the resurrection, exhausting himself to such an extent that he had to retire and take coach to Ezekiel Woolley's in Spitalfields near-by, where he rested on a bed till it was time to drive to Devonshire House for the next business session, at three o'clock. Various subjects were introduced—a paper was read from John Raunce and Charles Harris, querying whether Thomas Ellwood's books had been paid for from "the Publick Stock"—answer "no," and the paper was handed to Ellwood, as the Meeting did not think well to take notice of such papers from those out of unity. Epistles were read; the question of the clerkship of B. Bealing and John Lynam was referred to the Meeting for Sufferings and the meeting was adjourned to the next afternoon "at Bull above Stairs." The meeting done a coach conveyed G. Fox to the Plough and Harrow in Cheapside and he slept there under the watchful care of Benjamin and Mary Antrobus. On the morning of the 11th he attended the meeting at Gracechurch Street and recapitulated some portions of his previous day's sermon, leaving the meeting overdone and resting on a bed at Henry Gouldney's. In the afternoon he coached again to the Bull and Mouth where he "advised touching severall things & went to prayer." The business included the question of relief for Friends in Ireland and sufferers at Dantzig; accounts were audited and signed; and it was decided to request "Friends in the City not concerned in the business of the meeting to be spoken to not to croud this meeting for the Time to come." Other business concluded Fox drove to Fenchurch Street and passed the night at his son-in-law Meade's. The next day he was at the "Generall Womens Meeting," and by the end of the week he had attended nine meetings—"yᵉ first Day Morning Meeting, the Generall Meeting of fridˢ in yᵉ Ministry at yᵉ Bull & Mouth, yᵉ Generall Meeting at Wheeler street, 3 Generall Meetings abᵗ yᵉ Nationall Busyness, the 4ᵗʰ Dayes Meeting at Grace Ch: Street, the Generall Womens Meeting & yᵉ Meeting for Sufferings, besides much other Busyness with ffriends" (p. 211).

George Fox's name does not appear among those of Representatives to any Y.M. He did not belong to any definite Meeting in the country.

211   1   Aprons were in high favour when the Quakers arose and became the dress of women Friends, but they were to be of certain colours—*Green* aprons were almost regarded as a badge of Quakerism. Satires are plentiful in the shape of broadsides or pamphlets all making allusion to green aprons, as *e.g.*

> "When she to silent meeting comes,
> With apron green before her,
> She simpers so like muffle plums,
> 'Twould make a Jew adore her,"

which is from an old verse quoted in Gummere, *The Quaker*, 1901, p. 121. In a MS. in D, Fox to Friends, he writes: "Away with your short black aprons and some having none—away with vizards whereby you are not distinguished from bad wimon" (cp. vol. i. pp. 175 ff.). (Fox's stepdaughter, Sarah Fell, bought a "vizard maske" for herself in 1674 and two for her sister Rachel and herself in 1676 (*Swarth. Account Book*, pp. xx, 145, 367), perhaps for some necessary purpose.) In 1698 an Aberdeen Meeting wrote: "Let none want [*i.e.* lack] aprons at all, and that either green or blue or other grave colour and not white upon the street or in public at all, nor any spangled or speckled silk or cloth or any silk aprons at all." William Penn, in his *Alexander the Coppersmith*, 1673, writes: "It is a Wonder to me, that the Costly Clothes and Prodigal Feast (to Excess and Derision) of that exalted J. Penniman [259. 4] and his Beloved Mary Boreman who (in Token of her Self-Denial and Attainment to a more excellent Administration) exchanged her Cloth Waste-Coat for a silk Farendine Gown, her Blew Apron for one of Fine Holland and her ordinary Bodice for Rich Sattin it self, to say little of her Riding Fine Coaches, and several other things (once accounted by her self-righteousness Abomenable things), did never offend this author's nice and squeamish Stomach" (p. 73). The Lincolnshire Q.M. in 1721 stated: "We think green aprons are decent and becoming to us as a People." Ann Moore had a green apron with her when she crossed the Atlantic in 1761 on a religious visit to Great Britain (Comly, *Friends' Miscellany*, vol. iv. (1833), p. 350). In 1774 Sophia Hume, a Quaker Minister, dealing with a young man about his dress, queried: "How canst thou be so inconsistent as to wear a green waistcoat?" He replied: "I wear it with the same consistency as thou wears thy green apron." Of a Friend who died in 1804 we read: "With her, green aprons disappeared in our Meeting of Devonshire House" (*Jnl. F. H. S.* xvi. 15).

Gummere, *The Quaker, a Study in Costume*, 1901; Earle, *Two Centuries of Costume in America*, 1903, chap. xxiii.; *John Wilhelm Rowntree*, 1906, p. 60.

212   1   George Fox writes, at the conclusion of his epistle to Friends in Ireland (222. 1), that he had "ordered Nathanaell Willmour" to send over the heads of what he spoke at Y.M. to "his ffather in Law [stepfather] Thomas Starkey," but he had not heard that they were received (MS. in D). Thomas Starkey was one of several eminent persons who frequently solicited the Government in Dublin on behalf of sufferers (*Suff.* ii. 483). See 123. 2.

Fox refers to a collection of his "Speeches att yᵉ yearly Meetings" in his testamentary papers (vol. ii. p. 348).

213   1   See 97. 5.

215   1   Thomas *Sternhold* (d. 1549) was joint versifier of the Psalms with John Hopkins (d. 1570). The singing of hymns in public worship, apart from psalm-singing, had not by this time been introduced or become a source of much controversy; the date generally given is 1691 (*The Baptist Quarterly*, July, 1924).

There is a valuable article by Georgina King Lewis in *F. Q. E.* 1919 —"Puritan Singing in the Seventeenth Century."

Cooke, *Some Considerations...to all that sing David's Psalms*, 1670; *American Friend*, 1907, pp. 552 ff.; *D. N. B.*

216   1   Richard Thomas "was a member of the town corporation of Hertford, and also, I believe, a magistrate. His name figures prominently in the early minute books of Hertford M.M. and Q.M. That he was a man of good education with a thorough understanding of the law, is evidenced by his bold stand before the magistrates. He was a pillar of strength to Quakerism in Hertfordshire" (Samuel Graveson on "The Hertford Quaker Trials of 1664," in *F. Q. E.* 1916). Thomas, with others, wrote several replies to accusations of William Haworth, an

Independent preacher, that "Jesus of Nazareth was *not* the Quaker Messiah," 1676—1678. He subscribed £25 to the building fund of Hertford meetinghouse, 1670.

A. R. B. MSS. in D, no. 206.

216   2   For Thomas Dockray see vol. ii. p. 488. He was in London in 1678 (pp. 272, 273). We presume his residence in Ware was only temporary. Robert Barrow's letter on the death of George Fox (see vol. ii. p. 495) was addressed to Dockray among other *north-country* Friends (*The Friend* (Lond.), 1902, p. 136), and Fox left word that he was to "Come up to London to assist ffriends in Sorting of my Epistles & other writeings & Give him a Guiney" (vol. ii. p. 349). He is given as "of Lyndeth in the County of Lancaster" (vol. ii. p. 361).

Swarth. Account Book, many reff.

217   1   Of Benjamin Brown (1634—1704) there is a long account in *F. P. T.* (pp. 288, 289). He was convinced of the tenets of Quakerism by Christopher Knapton (for whom see *F. P. T.* pp. 286—288) and soon began to spread abroad the truth as he saw it. He visited Ireland in 1669, 1687 and 1693 (*Jnl. F. H. S.* x. 159, 161) and Scotland in 1692 —"a deep man of experiences" (*ibid.* xii. 141), and several of the plantations in America. "He was of the Apostles mind, not haveing much Outwardly to Live upon, wrought with his hands [as a shoemaker] in Severall Places when in Travells upon Truths account. He was much troubled with a Cough, which he thought he got in America with Lyeing in the woods all night and Wadeing in the Rivers." He travelled in England with John Taylor (*John Taylor*, 1710, pp. 49, 61). He was taken ill at the house of John Burleigh at Wetherby and was buried at Tadcaster.

217   2   Charles Harris and his father-in-law, Dr John Raunce, were the leading Friends in the Wycombe Separation. In 1687 Upperside M.M., in Bucks, wrote to the Second Days Morning Meeting in London "of the very immodest & obscene Carriages" of Charles Harris, "he is joyned to the separate Meeting his ffather Raunce hath set up," a minute signed by eighteen Friends (copy by Thomas Ellwood, in Bristol MSS., reprinted *Jnl. F. H. S.* ix. 196). In 1703 there is in the same MSS. a letter describing Harris as "a man disowned by ffriends many years ago for his work of separation" and in 1705 a minute was made by Bucks Q.M. and sent to Bristol respecting Harris, signed by twenty-four Friends. Before the time of his declension, presumably, he wrote several short pieces dated 1669 and 1670. Later, in collaboration with Dr Raunce and Benjamin Coale, he produced articles adverse to the general body of Friends.

Second Period, pp. 307, 475, 485.

217   3   John Hart appears in a list of Friends of Nottingham Meeting in 1668 (*Jnl. F. H. S.* xvii. 46). He was a tallow-chandler. He was one of the first trustees of the Almshouses built and endowed by Elizabeth Heath, of Mansfield, *circa* 1687 (*ibid.* x. 63). He signed a M.M. Document at Nottingham in 1707.

For Hart of Nottingham see Smith, *Smith of Cantley*, 1878, p. 69 ; *Jnl. F. H. S.* viii. 6.

218   1   The "Coffy house" is probably connected with the Chamber adjoining Westminster Hall referred to earlier (80. 10). "Coffee was first sold in England at a Coffee House in an alley adjacent to Lombard Street in 1652" (*Old Lombard Street*, 1912, p. 33). It was advertised as "a simple Innocent thing, incomparable good for those that are troubled with melancholy." We would fain know more of this coffee-house used by Friends.

PAGE   NOTE

219   1   Joan Perkins was one of the Friends who signed the General Testimony to Anne Whitehead (148. 2). Further knowledge respecting her or her son-in-law is lacking.

222   1   This last writing of George Fox is given in Ell. Text (ii. 503) with the following preamble: "The sense of the great hardships and sore sufferings that Friends had been and were under in Ireland, coming with great weight upon me, I was moved to write the following epistle, as a word of consolation unto them." Fines and imprisonment were the order of the day. The former are said to have amounted in one year (1689) to £100,000 (note to Ell. Text).

222   2   Letters respecting the illness, death and burial of George Fox were: (1) William Penn to Margaret Fox (Tercent. Text, p. 346, original in D, facsimile in Graham, *William Penn*, p. 192); (2) Robert Barrow to some Friends in the North (Tercent. Text, p. 347); (3) Anon. to John Airey (vol. ii. p. 369); (4) Henry Gouldney to Sir John Rodes (*Quaker Post-Bag*, 1910, p. 51, see *Jnl. F. H. S.* i. 54); (5) Robert Barrow to John Vaughton (Reynolds MSS. in D, copy).

222   3   The Friends who spoke at the meetinghouse were James Parke, Robert Barrow, Ambrose Rigge, Jasper Batt, William Penn, Francis Camfield, Charles Marshall, Stephen Crisp, John Taylor, Francis Stamper and George Whitehead, and Thomas Green ended in prayer.
Vol. ii. p. 495; *The Friend* (Lond.), 1902, p. 136.

222   4   Testimonies to Fox at the graveside at Bunhill Fields were given by William Penn, Jasper Batt, George Whitehead, John Vaughton and William Bingley. The Bunhill Fields belonging to Friends was and is separate from the general burialground of that name.
Vol. ii. p. 495; *The Friend* (Lond.), 1902, p. 136.
Testimonies respecting George Fox were penned by Luke Howard, Ambrose Rigge, John Taylor, Richard Robinson, John Boweter, Edward Bourne, Leonard Fell, Thomas Robertson, Stephen Hubbersty, Robert Jones, Friends in Berkshire and in Oxfordshire, by Margaret Fox and her children, the Second Days Morning Meeting, Thomas Ellwood. See Ell. Text, ii. 525.
The Friends requested by Fox to see to the printing of his Journal and other writings were John Blaykling, George Whitehead, Thomas Dockray, William Meade, John Rous, John Vaughton, Stephen Crisp, John Whitehead, Thomas Robertson, Benjamin Antrobus, Thomas Lower, Thomas Ellwood and John Field. They made an appeal for assistance through the medium of the Epistle of Y.M. 1691.

225   1   For Rachel Fell, afterwards Abraham, youngest of the children of Thomas and Margaret Fell, see vol. ii. p. 452.

225   2   This was the *Westmorland* Thomas Pearson. He signed various early epistles sent from the North (*Epistles of London Y. M. 1681 to 1857*, vol. i.). He died in 1691; his wife, Agnes, died in 1687. The burial-ground was Height. Powbank (also called Poolbank) was a considerable Meeting; its contributions to the Swarthmoor Fund are recorded in Swarth. MSS. vol. i. The house is still owned and inhabited by a descendant of Thomas Pearson (*Westmorland Quaker Records*, cuttings from the *Kendal Mercury and Times*, 1902).
There was a Thomas Pearson and wife Margery, from *Cheshire*, who went to the New World in 1682, and another Thomas Pearson and wife Grace, of *Lancashire*, who emigrated in 1698.

225   3   For Thomas Camm see vol. ii. p. 388 and Ell. Text, ii. 255 n. Thomas Camm and his wife, Ann Audland, had a daughter Mary, born 1669,

who married John Moore, of Eldroth, in 1691. The statement in vol. ii. p. 388 is incorrect.

226   1   "Richard Robinson, of Countersett in Wenslaydale, who was born at Preston, in the said dale, in the year 1628, was the first person that was convinced...in those parts" (*F. P. T.*). He travelled in the ministry in many places in his home district and spoke in "many Steeplehouses & in Markit places." There is a record in the State Papers (*Cal. S. P. Dom.* 1663—4, p. 338) of a business visit to London. His house is still standing on the edge of the beautiful lake of Semerwater. He deceased in 1693. He wrote a useful pamphlet on local persecutions named *A Blast blown out of the North*...1680, and also wrote *A Warning to the inhabitants of the whole Earth*, 1679. For a view of Counterside meetinghouse see *Early Friends in the North*, by John William Steel, 1905.

For Richard Robinson of Brigflatts see vol. i. p. 403.

226   2   Widow of James Tennant (vol. i. pp. 41, 403). The record of this visit here has been incorporated into the Ell. Text (ii. 256).

Elizabeth Tennant, of Bentham in Settle M.M., widow, died 28 viii. 1683, perhaps widow of James Tennant, who also belonged to Settle M.M.

227   1   Marmaduke Beckwith (—1704) lived at Burton-on-Ure. The following reference to ill-treatment is culled from Richard Robinson's tract (226. 1): "Marmaduke Beckwith (now of High Burton) going in the Town to get his Horse, a Man in great Rage said, 'Thou Dog, cannot thou speak?' and took him off the Ground by the Hair of the Head, and cast him down at his Feet, and then Fudded him sore with his Foot or Feet on his Head, both before and behind, that it swelled, and much Hair came off; and also fudded him in like manner on his back" (p. 8). Beckwith married Elizabeth Theakston, of Ellington, in 1666. In 1692 was printed *A True Relation of the Life and Death of Sarah Beckwith* [*c.* 1671—1691], *Daughter of Marmaduke and Elizabeth Beckwith of Audbrough near Masham in York-shire*. This little tract is composed of Testimonies by Sarah's parents, sister, and friends. See also *Piety Promoted*.

227   2   George Robinson lived at Borrowby in the North Riding of Yorkshire. He signed several early epistles sent out from the North (*Epistles of Y.M. 1681 to 1857*, 1858, vol. i.). The incident of the "cunning Justice" is made more clear in Ell. Text, ii. 256. The statement made by the justice was intended to provoke a denial that it was a silent meeting and a confession that Fox had spoken. He then could have fined them on their own confession, "but Friends standing in the wisdom of God did not answer him according to his desire and so escaped his snare." Ell. Text follows the Diary very closely.

227   3   Richard Watson, of Norton, near Stockton, Co. Durham, is several times mentioned in *Suff.* In 1666 he married Jane Townsend (*c.* 1647 —1690). In 1676 he had six cows taken from him for preaching in a Darlington meeting. Richard Watson and another were appointed, *c.* 1672, to speak to a Friend "about his intention of taking of a woman of the world to wife" (Steel, *Early Friends in the North*, 1905, p. 26). Richard Watson was a son of Thomas and Esther Watson.

227   4   Robert Linton (*c.* 1633—1716) lived at South Shields, Co. Durham. His wife was Joan Perrot (*c.* 1631—1715). Both Robert and Joan Linton sent presents of wine to Swarthmoor Hall in 1676 (*Swarth. Account Book*, pp. 315, 568). They were useful members of the Quaker Church at Gateshead (*Friends in Newcastle and Gateshead, 1653—1898*,

PAGE NOTE

p. 39, see pp. 8, 12, 20). "Robert Linton was one of the chief salt-pan owners in South Shields. In 1667 he had five pans, according to the Assessing List" (Steel, *Early Friends in the North*, 1905, p. 19, see also pp. 5, 18, 47).

Whitby and Scarborough Register, p. 22 (MS. in D).

228   1   Isaac Lindley (bapt. 1624, died 1705) lived at Yarm on the South (Yorkshire) side of the River Tees. He wrote a letter to Fox in 1669, which is mentioned in Camb. Text (vol. ii. p. 134) and printed in Ell. Text (ii. 105). *A Testimony from the Yearly Meeting at York*, 16 iv. 1686, addressed to the M.M.s in the county was signed by Mary Lindley, Isabel Yeamans, Frances Taylor, Elizabeth Leaper, Mary Wayte, and others.

F. P. T.

228   2   Thomas Wayte (d. 1695) was a prominent York Friend and a bookseller and printer, also a local agent for the publications of Friends (*Jnl. F. H. S.* ii. v.). In 1677 we find him sending to Swarthmoor for juniper berries (*Swarth. Account Book*, p. 419). His printing office was in the Pavement. His name appears in a list of booksellers and printers prepared by Henry R. Plomer and printed in 1907.

Wayte married Mary Smith (d. 1689), a Minister "who laboured much in the Ministry & in laying frds sufferings before such as were in Authority" (*F. P. T.* p. 318). Her name appears in *First-days Meetings*, pp. 138, 140. She signed, with other women, documents issued by York Friends—in 1686 (228. 1) and in 1688, with Elizabeth Beckwith, Mary Lindley and others (*Jnl. F. H. S.* ii. 42).

Davies, *Memoirs of the York Press*, 1868; Rowntree, *Hist. of Yorkshire Q.M.*, c. 1900, p. 4; Cooper, *Literary Associations of York*, 1913, p. xliv.

228   3   Edward Nightingale was a merchant living in Ousegate, York. At this time he seems to be in good esteem. Later he joined the Separatists in York (117. 2). In 1675 he consigned a box to George Fox at Swarthmoor Hall, the carriage of which from Lancaster cost two-pence (*Swarth. Account Book*, p. 243, see p. 564).

Suff.; *William Dewsbury*, 1836, p. 316; *F. Q. E.* 1892, "Friends in York and Neighbourhood in the Olden Time"; Rowntree, *Hist. of Yorkshire Q.M.*, c. 1900, p. 7, etc.

228   4   William Siddall (d. 1687), of Tadcaster, appears among Friends belonging to Tadcaster Meeting in 1668/9 (*Jnl. F. H. S.* ii. 32). Ell. Text (ii. 259) gives the names of places but not of Friends at Tadcaster, Knottingley and Doncaster.

228   5   The name of Samuel Poole appears with others in a very long list given by Besse (*Suff.* ii. 102), of Friends (229 in number) arrested in the West Riding on various charges in 1660. In 1662 Poole and two others received the severe sentence of premunire—put out of the King's protection, lands and goods forfeited to the King, and a prisoner at the King's pleasure. His wife, Baptista, died in 1692.

228   6   Henry Cooke (d. 1686) was of Sikehouse, in Balby M.M. Neither person nor residence is mentioned in Ell. Text.

228   7   For John Killam see vol. i. p. 461, and note 56. 1.

228   8   Thomas Aldam (1649—1722/3) was son and heir of Thomas Aldam (11. 1), of Warmsworth (d. 1660). He was repeatedly imprisoned in York Castle. He erected a meetinghouse on a portion of his estate (11. 1). He had considerable knowledge of Latin, Greek and Hebrew. He married Ann Stacy, daughter of Robert, of Ballifield, in 1671. She died in 1735.

Abraham de la Pryme (1672—1704), *Diary*, Surtees Society, vol. liv.;
John Taylor, 1710, pp. viii, 46, 49, 51, 64; *Piety Promoted*; *John
Gratton*, 1720, pp. 124—126; *William and Alice Ellis*, 1849; *Smith of
Cantley*, 1878.

228   9   In *Jnl. F. H. S.* xix. there is a full account of Jackson of Mealhill and
Wooldale, Yorks. Henry Jackson here mentioned (1633/4—1710), son
of Henry Jackson (1593—1667), became a Friend and a Minister. He
was a man of influence and wealth, and about 1682 he built Totties Hall,
Wooldale. He suffered imprisonment at Lincoln, Warwick and York.
In 1661 he was taken from an inn in Warwickshire and committed to
prison, "their giving thanks before Supper being called preaching at a
Conventicle" (*Suff.* i. 174; for a similar arrest see vol. ii. p. 168).
His wife was Katherine Cooke (d. 1695). His son, Henry Jackson
(1680—1727), was also a prominent Friend and travelling Minister.
Clay, *The Family of Jackson of Wooldale*, 1920.

228   10   For Thomas Killam see vol. ii. p. 465.

228   11   For Thomas Stacy see vol. i. p. 423. His estrangement from Friends
seems, according to later information, to have been ended at this time
(see footnote p. 229). Ell. Text refers impersonally to the difference
between them and adds that "they were reconciled." In earlier days
Stacy was one of the Publishers of Truth who visited Bedfordshire
(*F. P. T.*).

229   1   John Fox (d. 1716) was a mercer, of Wymeswold near Loughborough.
In 1680 he married Elizabeth Wells, probably daughter of William
Wells, of Knighton (230. 2). Fox and family were subject to severe
and sad suffering. In November, 1684, after repeated finings, a
carpenter was engaged to take down the bedsteads, etc., except the bed
which his sick wife occupied. "They took away their Meat and Drink,
and the Casks their Beer was in. They also took the Matting that was
nail'd to the Floor...." Later, "having heard that the poor man had
got some Bedding again, they came and swept away all they could find.
In the evening the Weather being cold, his whole family, viz. his Wife,
four small Children, the eldest not four years old, and two Maid-
Servants, were constrained to lodge at other Houses" (*Suff.* i. 344).
Despite his spoliation, Fox seems to have prospered financially as he
was able to lend £10 for Meeting purposes (*Jnl. F. H. S.* vi. 73).

229   2   For William Smith, of Sileby, in Leicestershire, see vol. i. p. 433.
His death took place, probably, in 1708.

230   1   Samuel Browne (*c.* 1648—1722) was a physician and apothecary, of
Leicester. He is known to bibliographers by the little book he wrote,
*An Account and Testimony of Samuel Browne, Concerning his dear
Mother, Sarah Browne*, 1693 (see vol. ii. p. 383). There are two refer-
ences to Samuel Browne in Besse (*Suff.* i. 340, 344). He married
Edith Elton, of Atherstone, in 1670. A son, Samuel, died in 1683. His
name is omitted from Ell. Text (ii. 259).

230   2   William Wells and his wife Ann lived at Knighton, near Leicester.
It was probably their daughter Elizabeth who married John Fox
(229. 1) in 1680 "at the house of Widow Wells." William Wells died
in 1678 and his wife died in 1690. They were buried in their own
garden-ground.
There is little to be recorded of many of these Friends visited by
Fox on his journey South They lived lives apart from the constant
movement of "publick friends," but they valiantly upheld the light of
Truth in the places where they lived and suffered. We honour them
though we know little of them.

230   3   "One of the first Sufferers in this County [Leicester] was Edward Muggleston, an ancient Man of Swanington, who was twice obliged to appear at London, ninety Miles from his Dwelling, before a Committee of Parliament appointed to enquire into the State of such Preachers as had been plundered during the Civil Wars; While he was attending on them at that Distance, a Seizure was made of his Goods...for Tithes" (Besse, *Suff.* i. 330, see also pp. 331—334, *anno* 1652). In 1664 Edward Muggleston married Jane Walker. His name is omitted from Ell. Text.

230   4   Samuel Fretwell's name has not been found among Quaker data. His place of residence, Hartshorn, is near Burton-on-Trent.

230   5   There are two notices of Henry Sidon (Siddons, Siddin) in White's *Friends in Warwickshire* (3rd ed. 1894, pp. 26, 97). Baddesley Ensor, sixteen miles from Birmingham, was, perhaps, about 1660, the largest gathering of Friends in the county and Henry Sidon one of the principal Friends (*ibid.* p. 97). The visit was paid on the 5th of May; on the 25th Fox wrote to Sidon: "Now concerning the thing thou speakst to me of, that Sarah Harris should say to the that Wm Mead & Wm Penn did ware Perrywiggs & call them Perriwig men—first concerning Wm Mead he bid me putt my hand upon his head and feel and said he never weare Perriwig in his life & wonder'd at it, and as for Wm Penn he did say that he did ware a little civil border because his hair was Come of his head...." For remainder of letter, which is in the handwriting of William Penn, in D, see *Jnl. F. H. S.* vi. 187; *Second Period*, p. 58 n. Fox concludes with a message of "love to thee & thy wife & father & N. Newton."

230   6   Richard Baal, of Whittington, has not been found among quakeriana searched. The name is given as *Ball* in Ell. Text (ii. 260).

231   1   Nathaniel Newton (—*c.* 1711) was of Hartshill, near Atherstone (vol. ii. p. 416). He was a man of property, and resided at the fine old Elizabethan mansion still standing at Hartshill (White, *Friends in Warwickshire*, 3rd ed. 1894, p. 26, see also pp. 32, 89, 90, 97—99; *Jnl. F. H. S.* ii. 43). Nathaniel, the younger, was the founder of the Hartshill Friends' school.

231   2   John Elliott, of North Kilworth, is described by Besse as a "husband-man." He passed some years in prison in Leicester (*Suff.* i. 332, 340, 345).
Ell. Text omits several places and names. From Hartshill Fox "passed on, visiting Friends in divers places till I came to Dingley" (ii. 260).

231   3   There is an interesting document among State Papers Domestic (*Cal.* 1655—6, pp. 64, 65—*Extracts from State Papers*, pp. 6—10), which contains lists of names of Friends considered as suitable for appointment as Justices of the Peace in different districts and of non-Quakers friendly and unfriendly. The first name under Northampton-shire in the list of "ffreindes Names that have estates in this County and judged to be fitting men to Rule for god" is that of "Thomas Allen, of Dingley, a man of about one hundred pound A yeare, one that were one of the first that owned truth 4 yeares agoe and hath beene servisable for truth ever since."
Thomas Allen was one of the 491 persons liberated from jail by the "General Pardon" of 1672. (*Extracts from State Papers*, p. 346—*Cal. S. P. Dom.* 1671—2, p. 489.)
His name is omitted from Ell. Text, ii. 260. His dates have not been found.

PAGE   NOTE

231   4   Thomas Charles, of Adingworth, that is *Arthingworth*, is mentioned in Ell. Text, ii. 260, but more respecting him does not appear.

231   5   Benoni Bradshaw, of Northampton, and Elizabeth, his wife, were sent to Northampton Town Prison out of a meeting in the town in 1660 (*Suff.* i. 532, 533). *Benjamin* Bradshaw died in 1688. His name is not given in Ell. Text, ii. 260.

231   6   Edward Cowper (*c.* 1638—1706) has a record in *F. P. T.* He was "Wise, grave, Meek, and Vertuous in his deportm^t among friends & towards all People, which well became his Hoar Head as ye servant of ye Lord....He is missed dearly" (p. 195, written in 1707). He married Ann Meakings. See 122. 4.
            Suff.

231   7   James Briarly, of Olney, is included in Besse's great books of *Sufferings* (vol. i. pp. 76, 77, 79, 81). He married Thomasin Knight, of Olney, and died in 1691.

231   8   William Richardson's name is not given in Ell. Text, ii. 260, in connection with Fox's visit to Turvey. Further respecting him is yet to be discovered, save his death in 1685.

232   1   John Rush, Senior and Junior, lived at Kempston Hardwick, about four miles S.W. of Bedford. John, Senior, died in prison in 1661 (*Memory of the Faithful Reviv'd*, MS. in D). The son was released from Bedford Jail by the "General Pardon" of 1672, as was also Tabitha Rush, his mother, and John Bunyan. He married Hannah Dewsbury, of Burton, Yorks, in 1666 (*c.* 1646—1707). See vol. i. p. 434.

232   2   The name Gamble occurs in connection with that of Rush (232. 1) in *F. P. T.* John Rush, the elder, and Henry Gamble of Pollockshill, were among the first entertainers of travelling Ministers. Thomas Gamble "now Liveing in y^t Parish," *anno* 1704/5, was the grandson of Henry Gamble.

232   3   George Sawyer's name does not appear in Ell. Text, ii. 260, in connection with Market Street.
            This is the first mention of Leonard Fell in Ell. Text since he joined Fox at the outset of his journey southward; the Haistwell Diary records much of his doings between the two events.

232   4   Edmund How's name does not appear in the Ell. Text, ii. 260. Notice that the Diary gives "*S^t* Albaines," here and on p. 269, which later, in more formal times, was reduced to "Albans." See *S^t* Ives (p. 43) and cp. Ell. Text, i. 267.

232   5   For Thomas Rudyard see vol. ii. p. 420. He is mentioned twice in Camb. Text and numerous times in the Haistwell Diary but not in the Itinerary Journal. It is said that he divested himself of his Quakerism, hence, probably, he is not mentioned in the Ell. Text (ii. 261). The unhappy ancient custom of crossing out the names of Seceders where they occur in writings of various kinds (see *e.g. F. P. T.* pp. 218 f.) has been adopted once in the Haistwell Diary (p. 257), where, in line 11, his name has a stroke through it. Rudyard was in Holland in 1671 with William Penn (Penn, *Travels*, 1835 ed. pp. 88, 90, 114) and again in 1677, associated with Isabel Yeamans (pp. 247—249), though he is not mentioned in the list of the party going over or coming back. His name occurs with those of Richard Mew, Job Bolton and others, in a pamphlet named *The Second Part of the Peoples...Liberties asserted...Trials*, etc., 1670. He was "fined one

hundred pounds, being convict of several Trespasses and Contempts" (p. 31). His will was proved in 1698 (*The Friend* (Lond.), 1860, p. 224). *Richard Davies*, 1710, p. 191; Myers, *Narratives of Early Pa.*, 1912; *Jnl. F. H. S.* x. xi. xiii. xviii. xix.

233   1   There is a full note to Ellis Hookes, the first Recording Clerk or general secretary, in vol. ii. p. 402.

233   2   For Jane Woodcock see vol. ii. p. 453 and note 93. 1.

233   3   The Epistle of the Y.M. of 1677 is dated 12 iv. 1677 and issued by "a Meeting held at Ellis Hookes his chamber." (This meeting is noted on p. 234, par. 4.) It is signed by 66 Friends, among them being Thomas Taylor, Henry Jackson, Giles Barnardiston, Roger Longworth, Richard Davies, Leonard Fell, Stephen Smith, Ambrose Rigge, William Gosnell, Benjamin Antrobus, Richard Pinder, Richard Vickris, James Claypoole, Jasper Batt, John Burnyeat, John Elson, John Dew, John Vaughton, Ezekiel Woolley, Charles Marshall, John Blaykling, William Penn, Francis Moore, William Gibson, Christopher Taylor, Bray D'Oyly, Thomas Burr, Richard Snead, Thomas Ellwood, Thomas Robertson. It was a gathering for Ministers only (*Jnl. F. H. S.* ii. 63).

233   4   William Welch was a merchant of Rotterdam in 1663 (*Extracts from State Papers*, p. 181—*Cal. S. P. Dom.* 1663—4, p. 366). He appears to have been led away for a while in sympathy with the Hat-men, 1669 (*Steven Crisp and his Correspondents*, 1892, p. 24). About 1669, with William Penn, William Meade, William Shewen, John Osgood, Samuel Newton, Stephen Crisp, Francis Moore, he signed a petition to the King against convictions as Popish Recusants, etc. (*Jnl. F. H. S.* xi. 136), and in 1672 his signature is appended, with those of G. Whitehead, Gerard Roberts, John Osgood, Thomas Moore and Ellis Hookes, to a letter to Friends in Colchester (*Steven Crisp*, p. 8, see p. 17). Welch held appointments among London Friends in 1668 and for London M.M. in 1672 (*Sundry Ancient Epistles*, pp. 35, 41). In 1680 Welch wrote from Stoke-by-Nayland, Co. Suffolk, a Testimony to Giles Barnardiston (237. 3), see *The Life of Christ*, etc., 1681.

William Welch, presumably the same, was in Scotland in 1657. The statement in vol. i. p. 297, that "Will: Welchs wiffe" was convinced is verified by the extract of a letter among Thurloe Papers, dated Leith, 19 Sept. 1658, which states: "This day Mr William Welch could mee that his wife, Sarah Welch, who is one of the cheefe of the Quakers tould him," etc. (*Jnl. F. H. S.* viii. 165). In a letter from Penn to Margaret Fox, among the Thirnbeck MSS. in D, dated London, 29 viii. 1684, we read: "yᵗ day Wᵐ Welch was to leave yᵉ place yᵗ in regard to his low estate I had putt him in to go to Jersy, he fell sick & in 3 or 4 days departed this life" (*Jnl. F. H. S.* ix. 143).

There was a William Welch, perhaps the same Friend, belonging to Horsham M.M. 1668, who contributed towards an early Loan Fund (*Jnl. F. H. S.* iv. 163) and for whom the King signed a release, *c.* 1668, from a sentence of premunire while lying in Horsham Jail (*Extracts from State Papers*, p. 295—*Cal. S. P. Dom.* 1668—9, p. 323), and William Welch was released from the Fleet Prison by the "General Pardon" of 1672 (*ibid.* pp. 343, 353—*Cal.* 1671—2, p. 489).

In 1682 William Welch, of Stoke-by-Nayland, was convicted and imprisoned ("The Norwich Case" by Arthur J. Eddington, in *Norfolk and Norwich Archae. Soc.* vol. xxii. (1924), 17—44).

233   5   Could "one Dʳ Moor" be Doctor Henry More (1614—1687), the great Cambridge Platonist? We know that Dr More was distressed when the

Countess Conway (267. 1) was perverted to Quakerism and he had
much to say and write against Friends, including a long letter addressed
to William Penn, who had called upon the doctor " at my lodging in
Paul's Church-yard when I was last in London." Richard Ward in his
Life of Dr More, 1710, writes : "He wrote to Mr. Pen a very excellent
Letter concerning Baptism and the Lord's Supper....And for their
great Leader (as most account of him) George Fox himself, he hath
said to some : *That in conversing with him, he felt himself, as it were,
turn'd into Brass.* So much did the Spirit, Crookedness, or Perverseness
of that Person move and offend his Mind," adding : "See also what he
farther speaks of him. *Schol. in Dial.* 5 *Sect.* 5" (p. 197). In one of
More's letters, advising "how to keep a perpetual Calmness," he writes :
" A Soul so well awakened into the Sense of the Best Things can scarce
want any External Director or Monitor. The Quakers Principle is the
most Safe and Seasonable here, *to keep close to the Light within a Man*"
(p. 247). (Italics are as printed in the *Life*.)

Smith, *Adv. Cata.*; *Jnl. F. H. S.* vii. xviii.; *F. Q. E.* 1889, 1921.

234   1   These initials represent Robert Barclay and William Rogers. The
Yearly Meeting of Ministers in June, 1677, provided the occasion for a
debate between Rogers and Barclay, which was attended by Fox and
some thirty-six others, and arranged by the Morning Meeting (called
by Rogers "a Company of Nameless Meeters" !). The date given in
Rogers's outstanding work, *The Christian Quaker Distinguished from the
Apostate and Innovator*, in eight parts, 1680—1682, pt. iii. p. 128, is
7th June, exactly the date given by Haistwell, though his reference to
the important conference is very brief. See *Second Period*, p. 347.
Rogers was a Bristol merchant and before his defection he was a helpful Friend. He signed the Fox-Fell wedding certificate (*Jnl. F. H. S.*
ix. 100) and recorded some of the Testimonies spoken on this occasion.
In February, 1675/6, he was yet among Friends (*ibid.* iv. 119, ix. 189,
xi. 151) but shortly afterwards he joined the Separatist body. "He
scornfully reviled his quondam brethren in paltry verses, stating that
some sustenance had been given from the public cash to indigent
preachers....To this it was answered that if it pleased God to call to
His ministry persons of mean estate, the Church was not warranted
to hinder it and let such suffer want" (Sewel, *Hist., sub anno* 1683).
His wife was Elizabeth.

There was a "Francis Rogers, of Bristol, part owner of the *Duke*
and *Duchess*, privateers that picked up 'Robinson Crusoe'" (*Jnl.
F. H. S.* vi. 4, ix. 102).

234   2   For Col. Kirkby see vol. ii. p. 390. For a brief notice of his funeral,
10 Sept. 1681, see *Jnl. F. H. S.* xi. 21. He had expressed friendship
with Fox but did not act on it (vol. ii. pp. 38, 47). It is to be hoped
that now his friendship went deeper.

234   3   William Gosnell's place of residence has not been found or his dates.
He was associated with other Friends in the Hat Controversy against
the "Hat-men," being named in Penn's *Alexander the Coppersmith*, 1673,
and *Judas and the Jews*, 1673, with Samuel Newton, James Claypoole,
John Osgood, John Swinton, Henry Stout, Solomon Eccles, Rebecka
Travers and Ellis Hookes.

Bridget Gosnell married Philip Ford (107. 3).

234   4   For Thomas Corbett see vol. ii. p. 450.
Jnl. F. H. S. xi. 190.

235   1   For Isaac Penington see vol. i. p. 445. In the life of William Penn,
by John William Graham, 1917, there is a reproduction of the marriage
certificate of William Penn and Gulielma Maria Springett, Penington's

stepdaughter, 1672, probably in the handwriting of Thomas Ellwood, to which are attached forty-six signatures, among them being those of the following, mentioned in these notes: Isaac Penington, wife Mary, daughter Mary, Alexander Parker, George Whitehead, Samuel Newton, William Welch, Gerard Roberts, James and Helena Claypoole, Thomas Rudyard, Charles Harris, Edward Mann, Thomas and Mary Ellwood, Jane Bullock, Sarah Welch, and Mary Welch, Mary Newton and Mary Odingsells. The signatures are in the same writing as the certificate.

Rogers, *Christian Quaker*, 1680, pt. v. pp. 34, 43, 44, 46, 53, where Fox is charged with encouraging Mary Penington to secure her husband's and her own estates "against the spoiler."

235   2   For George Keith see vol. ii. p. 455—a full account. For his wife, Elizabeth Keith, see 237. 2. There is a useful account of the Keithian' Controversy as it affected Byberry Meeting, Pa., in Comly's *Friends Miscellany*, vol. vii. (1835), pp. 103 ff.

235   3   For Stephen Smith see vol. ii. p. 446. For his widow see 78. 4.

235   4   For a long note on Roger Williams see vol. ii. p. 438. Williams's "very envious and wicked book" (Ell. Text, ii. 264) was *George Fox Digg'd out of his Burrowes* and the reply was entitled *A New England Fire-Brand Quenched*.

Jones, *Quakers in American Colonies*, 1911; *The Holborn Review*, July, 1924—"George Fox's Missionary Labours"; *The Friend* (Lond.), 1924, p. 685.

236   1   Of William Lilley no information is forthcoming, save that which appears in a note to his widow (168. 2).

236   2   A very careful record of this visit to Holland and Germany was kept by Edward Haistwell (116. 2), while travelling with "his Esteemed and wel-beloved Friend and Master," and when ill at Embden his Master "took an Account of his passages till hee came to Embden again" in about three weeks' time (pp. 241, 247). This Account was probably revised by Haistwell, who inserted it in its place in his own record. The Ell. Text gives 46 pages to the journey and the papers written the while. For William Penn's journal see 239. 2. For Fox's later visit to Holland see 93. 2. For Holland see vol. ii. p. 411. For the condition of Holland at about this period see *The Dutch drawn from the Life*, London, 1664.

While her father was in Holland business-like Sarah Fell sent him from Swarthmoor some specimens of iron-ore (*Swarth. Account Book*, pp. xxiii, 411, 413); later a box arrived at Swarthmoor containing maps and cheeses from Holland (*ibid.* pp. 443, 459); and Mrs Yeamans brought back with her a Dutch spinning-wheel (*ibid.* p. 477).

A multitude of flying visits were paid to Holland during many years, but despite these and the work of Dutch Friends the Quaker Church dwindled. Many Friends emigrated to America. Jan Claus described the depleted condition even in 1686, in a letter to London (*Bulletin F. H. S. Phila.* iv. 55). In 1845 John Stephen Mollet (1768—1851) was said to be the last survivor, or, as Peter Bedford (1780—1864) put the case, speaking to William Tallack in Mollet's presence: "William, thou seest before thee the whole Monthly, Quarterly and Yearly Meeting of Friends in Holland" (*Jnl. F. H. S.* v. 125 n.). There has, however, been some revival of late years.

In the portion of the Diary relating to the Low Countries we have had the valuable assistance of Rev. D. Mulder, of Westwoud, Holland, a former Woodbrooke student.

PAGE NOTE

"Searches and Researches for the Friends of Holland," articles by Dr William I. Hull in *Friends' Intelligencer*, 1908; *Bulletin F. H. S.* *Phila.* iii. iv. vii.

236   3   John Furly, the elder (1618—1686), was a son of John Furly (c. 1590—1673) who was Alderman of Colchester in 1637 and Mayor in 1650 (*Steven Crisp and his Correspondents*, p. xliv). His wife's name was Anna. His eldest son was John (255. 1) and there were other children.

236   4   John Vandewall (1646—1707) lived at Harwich, and was a baker and merchant. He was the eldest son of John Vandewall (c. 1621—c. 1657) and Mary his wife (d. *post* 1670). He married, 1669, Hannah Mace, Junr., of Harwich, in 1679, Susanna Cottesford, and in 1682 Mary Dove, probably of the same family as Francis Dove (166. 1). He was an active Friend and sufferer for the cause.
            Steven Crisp and his Correspondents, 1892; J. J. Green, *Hist. of the Vandewall Family*, 1902 (in MS.).

237   1   William Talcot (Taylcoat) was born about 1622, became a wealthy tradesman and died at his home at Colchester in 1697. His wife Ann died in 1709, aged 84. She is mentioned in *Steven Crisp and his Correspondents*, 1892. A daughter, Ann, married John Furly, Junr. (255. 1), in 1669, and another, Mary, married Benjamin Dykes (100. 4). The name Talcot is widely spread in U.S.A.
            Fell-Smith, *James Parnell*, 1907, where we should probably read *William* for *Thomas*, see Besse, *Suff.* i. 192.

237   2   "George Keith's wife" is the usual description of this Friend and for long we searched in vain for the baptismal name. In vol. ii. p. 455 it is given as Anna, following *Quakers in the American Colonies*, 1911, p. 369, *but this is incorrect*. William Penn in his journal (239. 2) writes *Elizabeth* Keith. George Keith married Elizabeth, daughter of Dr William Johnston and Barbara Forbes and widow of Dr Alexander White, professor in Marischal College, Aberdeen. She became a Friend after the death of her husband as also her mother Barbara Forbes. "Elizabeth Johnston, being a faithful and enlightened woman, became 'a succourer of many' and a considerable 'helper in Christ'" (Jaffray, *Diary*, p. 201). In Dr John Davidson's history of *Inverurie and the Earldom of the Garioch*, p. 341, he writes, in a chapter on Quakerism: "Among those seduced into Quakerism at that time [1663] were the widow of Dr William Johnston, the Professor of Mathematics, and his daughter Elizabeth, whose second husband, Mr George Keith, was a ringleader in the new sect." Friends of Aberdeen address a touching appeal to "our ancient Friends George and Elizabeth Keith," 23 iii. 1694, pleading for the restoration of love and unity and reminding George Keith of his early writings when in accord with the principles of early Quakerism (Jaffray, *op. cit.* p. 418, note H).
            Information from Thomas Davidson, Fritchley, Derby, 1924.

237   3   Giles Barnardiston (c. 1624—1680) came of an ancient and honourable family, and received a university education lasting six years, his parents designing him for the ministry. Not feeling himself spiritually qualified therefor, he entered the army, but he had no soul satisfaction as a soldier, so retired to Wormingford Lodge. About 1661 he invited the company of some Friends and was visited by George Fox, Junior, and George Weatherley, and was convinced. In 1669 he came forth as a Minister and took up his residence at his native place of Clare, in Suffolk. In 1672 his house at Clare was licensed for Presbyterian worship (*Cal. S. P. Dom.* 1672, p. 299). He was the means of the convince-

ment of Samuel Waldenfield (130. 1; see vol. ii. p. 497). His wife was Frances Waldegrave; they had no children. He came into local prominence by defending Samuel Cater in his dispute with Francis Bugg, ex-Quaker (Bugg, *The Painted Harlot Both Stript and Whipt*, 1682; see, by the same author, *Jezebel Withstood*, 1699). Ann Docwra (*c.* 1624 —1710), of Cambridge, replying in her book, *An Apostate Conscience Exposed*, 1699, to a work by Bugg, writes: "I heard this story [that 'George Fox had in one Nights time 24 Languages given to him by Devine Inspiration'] many years ago & spoke of it to my Brother G. Barnardistone of Clare [? outward or spiritual relationship], a Man well known to be a Wise and Honest Man; I told him, that we had some Shatter-brained People amongst us, and if they went on so, we should want a Religious Bedlam for such Mad Folks; my Brother Replied, that...the best way was to use them kindly so long as they were morally Honest, for some had recovered, being sincerely Honest, but they were not to be disturbed, for that would make them worse" (p. 18). Barnardiston was in prison in Chelmsford "many years" (Whiting, *Memoirs*, where there is a good *résumé* of his life, p. 53). He undertook many preaching tours and was in Holland with John Furly. Testimonies to the value of life and work were written by John Furly, Thomas Burr, Samuel Waldenfield, William Welch, George Whitehead and others (*The Life of Christ Magnified in his Minister...Giles Barnardiston*, 1681). An abstract of his will is printed in *Jnl. F. H. S.* vii. 43. He styled himself Giles Barnardiston, Junr.

Piety Promoted; Evans, *Friends' Library*, vol. iv. (1840); Davids, *Nonconformity in Essex*, 1863, p. 293; Gardiner, *Hist.* iv. 61, 68; *Report of Hist. MSS. Com. on Rydal MSS.* p. 51.

237　4　For Robert Duncon see vol. i. p. 431.

237　5　George Weatherley lived at Colchester, Essex. He was helpful in the convincement of Giles Barnardiston (237. 3). He was committed to the Moot Hall, in Colchester, in 1660, for refusing the oath of allegiance. Messages of love from various Friends in Holland are noted in *Steven Crisp and his Correspondents*, 1892. His occupation was that of maltster (Fell-Smith, *James Parnell*, 1907, p. 52). In 1666 he married Mary Reed, of Colchester, widow. He died in 1686, aged 62, and his wife in 1697, aged 60.

237　6　Job Bolton belonged to the parish of St Edmunds, Lombard Street. Besse records several instances of suffering, on one occasion caused by Dr Bradford, the clergyman of the parish.

237　7　Arent (Aaron) Sonemans was a merchant of Rotterdam where he was living when the English party breakfasted at his house (Penn, *Travels*, 1835, p. 3, see also pp. 148, 152). The question of the marriage to Aaron Sonemans of Frances, widow of John Swinton, is discussed by William F. Miller in *Jnl. F. H. S.* ii. 29. Sonemans resided later in Edinburgh. The Cambridge and Hunts Burial Registers record the sad end of this Friend: "Buried 16 vi. 1683—A Dutchman was shot by a Highwayman near Standgate, Huntingdon M.M." Jaffray relates the incident under date 8 August, at Stonegatehole, Robert Barclay being with Sonemans at the time (*Diary*, p. 342).

Miller, *Dict. of Scotch Friends, 1656—1790*, MS. in D.

237　8　Simon Johnson lived at Rotterdam. Farewells were said at his house, Friends gathering there at seven a.m. (Penn, *Travels*, 1835, p. 152). Further information is not at hand.

238　1　More than here told and on p. 251 is not known respecting Dirick

Klassen of the city of Haarlem. George Fox, Peter Hendricks and Gertrude Diricks lodged a night at his house.

The journey from Rotterdam to Leiden, and probably onward to Haarlem, was by means of "a boat drawn by a horse that went on the shore"—this picturesque touch is in the Ell. Text, ii. 267. The boat was probably the famous Dutch trekschuit (drawn by horses).

238   2   Gertrude Diricks Nieson (so named in Ell. Text) (d. 1687) was one of three sisters, living, in a good position, in Amsterdam. The eldest sister, Niesy, died about 1662; the youngest, Annekin, married William Caton (c. 1635—1665) in 1662. Gertrude, the middle sister, married a wealthy Dutchman, Adrian Van Losevelt, who was said to be "inconsistent & fickle, little as yet seasoned with truth." He died, presumably, prior to Fox's visit, leaving two children, Cornelis who married Abigail Furly, daughter of John Furly, the younger (255. 1), in 1686, and another. Gertrude Diricks and her two children crossed to Harwich with the returning party. The voyage was a stormy one and Gertrude succumbed to sea-sickness (letter from Fox to Friends in Holland, original in D, printed *Bulletin F. H. A.* 1924). She and her children went to the home of Stephen Crisp, whence, 29 ix. 1677, she wrote *An Epistle to Friends.* Another visit to England followed, and she was probably in Colchester at the time of the death of S. Crisp's wife Dorothy in 1684. On the first of October, 1685, as "Gertrude Diricks Nieson," she married Stephen Crisp, and two years later died, after a short illness.

Stephen Crisp, 1694; Penn's *Travails,* 1694; *Steven Crisp and his Correspondents,* 1892; Tanqueray, *The Royal Quaker,* 1904 (fiction); *Bulletin F. H. S. Phila.* vol. iv. (1912), pp. 83, 97; Brailsford, *Quaker Women,* 1915, chap. xi.

238   3   In fifteen numbered paragraphs William Penn sets out the decisions of this General Meeting, beginning "1. Be it known to all men that the power of God, the Gospel, is the authority of all our men's and women's meetings, and every heir of that power is an heir to that authority." He also gives a report of the proceedings at the "more select meeting," held at the house of Gertrude Diricks (*Travels,* 1835, pp. 4—10).

238   4   There are two notices of John Lodge in *Steven Crisp and his Correspondents,* 1892. He wrote to Stephen Crisp, from Amsterdam, 11 March, 1668/9, confessing that he had been led astray in the Hat Controversy—"thou art he against whom I had prepared myself against the day of battle....I did think the foundation of my house stood sure, but soon after was I made to feel that I was but as an old tottering wall. I felt the overgrown oak in me to bow like a young twig...all my armour broken to pieces and my spears turned into pruning hooks" (p. 24; see also *Collectitia,* p. 151). Another letter (p. 61) mentions Lodge being at great charges in teaching a Friend how to make combs. Lodge is mentioned in several of William Penn's letters to Friends in Holland, c. 1677, printed in *Bulletin F. H. S. Phila.* vol. iv. (1911).

239   1   Sir William J. Collins, M.D., in a lecture, in 1916, on "The General Baptists and the Friends" (*Trans. Bapt. Hist. Soc.* vol. ii.), stated that "Fox was consciously or unconsciously the exponent of an existing faith rather than the originator of a new one," many of the truths expounded by him having been held by General Baptists, Waterlander Mennonites and Collegiants, etc. As the meeting here recorded "ended in peace" we may suppose that the bearers of "severall opinions" agreed, at least, in general with what they heard. For these

bodies see *Short Hist. of Quakerism*, by Elizabeth B. Emmott, 1923. The Collegiants may be described as the Seekers of Holland. Without approved ministry or pre-arranged service their Collegia (or gatherings) met, men and women being on an equality as regards public ministry —Sacraments not essential, objection to oaths and fighting, believing in simplicity of life, mark of fellowship being brotherly love, and an attempt to carry out literally the Sermon on the Mount (*ibid.*).

239   2   William Penn's *Account of Travails in Holland and Germany, in 1677*, remained long in manuscript before publication. Penn tells us in his Preface: "A copy that was found amongst the late Countess of Conway's papers, falling into the hands of a person who much frequented that family [perhaps her friend, Francis van Helmont], he was earnest with me to have leave to publish it." The *Account* appeared first in 1694; the fourth edition appeared in 1835 in Barclay's Select Series, badly edited. It was also printed in the volumes of Penn's *Works* in 1726. The reference here must be to the manuscript. For a history of a manuscript (which is now in possession of the Hist. Soc. Pa., in Philadelphia) of the *Travels* see *The Friend* (Lond.), 1890, p. 40. A discourse on the *Travels* is reported in the *Pa. Mag.* vol. ii. (1878); extracts are given in *Collectitia*, pp. 389 ff.

Penn had paid a short visit to Holland and Germany in 1671. He added "two of our servants" to the list of persons going over in 1677 (*Travels*, p. 2), and wrote: "The best accommodation was given us by special favour of the master (he having formerly served under my father)."

239   3   Elizabeth, Princess Palatine of the Rhine (1618—1680),was a daughter of Frederick, King of Bohemia, her mother being a daughter of King James I of England. She was Abbess of Herford from 1667 to 1680 and a friend of many noted religious leaders. William Penn gives a long account of his visits to Herford in his *Travels*, ed. of 1835, pp. 19—30, 53, 88, 119, 153. Largely owing to enquiries at Herford, in Hanover, instituted in 1920 by M. Christabel Cadbury, author of a life of Robert Barclay, fresh interest has been evoked in that district in the life-history of the Princess (*Jnl. F. H. S.* xviii. 35). In *Descartes, His Life and Times*, by Haldane, 1905, there is a portrait of Elizabeth from a painting by Gerard Honthorst.

Stephen Crisp, works, 1694, p. 406; Sewel, *Hist.*; Jaffray, *Diary*, p. 437, note W; *Beginnings*; Cadbury, *Robert Barclay*, 1912; *Second Period*.

239   4   Willem Willems, of Alkmaar, is mentioned in Ell. Text in connection with both visits to Holland—in 1677 (ii. 273) and 1684 (ii. 402). There was, apparently, a Meeting of Friends in this "pretty city." Besse has handed down the statement that "William Williams, because he kept his Shop open on a Fast-day in 1665, appointed for Success of the War then against England, was fined three Guilders, which he refusing to pay, an Officer with seven Assistants came to his House, and took away his Household Goods and Bedding to the Value of 150 Guilders" (ii. 456). This sum would be equal to about £100 in the money value of the present day.

240   1   Two visits were paid to Hesel Jacobs's house at Harlingen, on the coast of Friesland. On the latter occasion (p. 248) William Penn and party were welcomed back from Germany. Penn tells us that a M.M. was settled for Friesland, Groningen and Embden (*Travels*, 1835, p. 90).

PAGE NOTE

240 2   More does not appear respecting Sijbrand Dowes, of Leeuwarden, than recorded here and on p. 247 and in Ell. Text, ii. 275, 282.

Willem Fredrik was stadtholder of Friesland till his death in 1664. He was succeeded by his young son, Hendrik Casimir II, under the regency of his mother.

241 1   We are told in the *Travels* of William Penn that the wife of Jan Claus (150. 1) was the fourth sister of Dr John William Hasbert, of Embden, whose family was the first to receive Truth in this city, which occurred shortly after Penn's visit in 1671 with B. Furly and T. Rudyard. Stephen Crisp visited the family in 1673 (works, 1694, p. 40). Here we learn that " Jhon Claus wifes ffathers name was Claes Jhon foeldricks." Our knowledge of Dutch Quakerism or Dutch relationships is insufficient to explain the apparent discrepancy. He is nameless in Ell. Text.

Embden, in the province of Ost Friesland, was one of the centres of early continental Quakerism. Great persecution befell Friends in this city, led, perhaps, by the burgomaster André in this year of 1677. Many protests were made, but only in 1686 did "the magistrates begin to see their true Interest, and directed their Councils another Way. Having found the decay of their trade, they set open a Door for admitting the Quakers peaceably to reside there." They desired Magdalena Van Loar and her daughter Magdalena Hasbert, local Friends, to invite Quakers to settle in the city from England and Holland!

Sewel, *Hist.*; *Suff.* ii. 443; *Steven Crisp and his Correspondents*, 1892.

242 1   After the death of Count Anton Günther in 1667, the duchy of Oldenburg was governed jointly by Frederick III, King of Denmark, and Christian Albert, Duke of Holstein, until the year 1702 (*Encyc. Brit.*).

242 2   "Münster is a town in Westphalia, the seat of a bishop, walled round, with a noble cathedral and many churches" (*Germany*, in the Story of the Nations, 1886, p. 211). Münster was long governed by independent bishops, in whom a warlike was often much more conspicuous than a Christian spirit.

243 1   For a full account of John Perrot see vol. ii. p. 375. He was a leader of the "Hat-men," those who refused to remove their hats during public prayer, thus causing a schism in England and America (see vol. ii. p. 483).

243 2   Fox's editors have carefully expunged many of Fox's statements regarding himself and thus endangered the knowledge of an interesting trait in his character. Many omissions from the Camb. Text were made when the Ell. Text was prepared; see vol. i. p. xl. See pp. 244, 246.

The omission of the reference here to Fox in the character of Moses may have been found desirable owing to William Rogers's statement that it was said: "The Lord ordained G. F. to be in that place amongst the Children of Light in this our day, as Moses was among the Children of Israel in his day" (*Christian Quaker*, 1680, pt. i. sect. 2).

243 3   The earl and his monument seem alike to have disappeared. We have failed to obtain any information respecting either of them. Ell. Text has *Rantzow*.

243 4   William Poole, living at Friedrichstadt, the furthest point reached by George Fox, has not been identified. Ell. Text has *Paul*.

244 1   For the Duke of Holstein see 95. 2.

PAGE	NOTE	
245	1	Ell. Text (ii. 279) informs us that John Hill was "an English Friend who had been travelling in Germany" but does not favour us with further particulars. He travelled a while with Fox and shared with him the tragic crossing of the "great water." He left the party at Leeuwarden on the 7th September and travelled to Amsterdam viâ Harlingen, arriving at Amsterdam on the evening of the 8th at the house of Gertrude Diricks (Penn, *Travels*, 1835, p. 89).
245	2	Probably Duke of Lüneburg. The city may have been Lüneburger-heide.
246	1	The game of shovel-board was very popular at this period with rich and poor. Discs were shot by hand across a table to stop at certain lines drawn on the table. A variation of the game is still played on ship-board with discs attached to handles. Fox wrote of the followers of Rice Jones: "ther meetinges scaterd except som of them met together on the first day to play at shovell bord" (vol. i. p. 397).
246	2	The prince and the prince's country seem too indefinite to individualize and describe. After the Thirty Years' War the several German princes were made almost wholly independent, so that the empire as a unity was reduced to a shadow (*Germany*, in the Story of the Nations, 1886, p. 258). This condition of Germany is made very clear on a map in a History-Atlas published in Gotha—"Deutschland nach dem Westfälischen Frieden, bis 1742," kindly lent by D. Mulder, of Westwoud, Holland, 1924.
247	1	See 241. 1. The name of the goldsmith does not appear. Ell. Text adds: "Leaving them neither place to come to nor anything to subsist on. We comforted and encouraged him in the Lord, exhorting him to be faithful and stand stedfast in the testimony committed to him. When we had taken leave of him we took boat..." (ii. 282).
247	2	Of Cornelis Andries, of the city of Groningen, we have not been able to glean any particulars. At this time, apparently, there was less persecution in this northern portion of Holland. In 1669 Stephen Crisp wrote *A Lamentation over the City of Groninghen*, in answer to two papers written by two magistrats against Friends and "two lies sung in the street by the wild and ungodly Ballet singers." One ballad was entitled *The Loose Sect of the Quakers*. "The anonymous author upbraids us about the death of the King of England and shews his knowledge to be as little as his honesty, for there was not the name of a Quaker in England when King Charles died."
249	1, 2	At Gertrude Diricks's house Fox wrote, 14 vii. 1677, a few lines to Friends "with relation to those seducing spirits...that endeavoured to insinuate themselves into the affectionate part" (Ell. Text, ii. 285—some decisive words). On the 18th he wrote a long epistle to suffering Friends at Dantzig (*ibid.* p. 286), and on the 19th other letters.
250	1	Before attending M.M. and early in the morning Fox wrote a long letter to Friends respecting "division and separation, the way, work and end whereof the Lord opened to me" (Ell. Text, ii. 288—290).
250	2	See Ell. Text, ii. 288, 291.
252	1	Of the writings mentioned in this paragraph Ell. Text gives, in full, Fox's "Warning to the City of Oldenburg," and "A Warning to the City of Hamburg," both dated the 19th of the Seventh Month; also an address to the Ambassadors met at Nimeguen, dated 21st. These are followed by a very long epistle dealing with fasting, prayer, persecution, observance of days, etc., dated Harlingen in Friesland, 11 vi. 1677 (ii. 292—310).

252   2   Fox's "Epistle to the Ambassadors that are met to treat for peace at the City of Nimeguen in the States' dominions" is printed in Ell. Text, ii. 298 ff., dated 21 vii. 1677. It was presented in Latin. Robert Barclay also addressed the ambassadors, and with his address, which was in Latin, was delivered to them copies of his *Apology* in Latin, 1676. The address was published in English in 1679 and entitled: *An Epistle of Love and Friendly Advice to the Ambassadors...* "wherein the Cause of the present war is discovered and the right Remedy and Means for a firm and settled Peace is proposed."

"The peace of Nimeguen, 1678, terminated the wars of Louis XIV against the Dutch Republic, Spain, and the Empire. While it failed to satisfy Louis' ambition to destroy the United Provinces of the Netherlands, it yet marked the zenith of his ascendancy in Europe, and greatly strengthened France territorially, chiefly at the expense of Spain. Against the strong desire of his Parliament, which wished to enter the war on the side of Protestant William of Orange, Charles II contributed to the triumph of France by keeping England out of the Allied cause, in return for which he received large subsidies from the French King" (note by John L. Nickalls, B.A., 1924).

253   1   Galenus Abrahams is described by William Penn as "the great father of the Socinian Menists [Mennonites]. He affirmed that there was no Christian Church, ministry, or commission apostolical now in the world" (*Travels*, 1835, p. 141, see pp. 90, 144, 157). He was born in 1622 (*Steven Crisp and his Correspondents*, 1892, pp. xlii, 64). Fox writes during his second visit to Holland (1684): "I had been with him when I was in Holland about seven years before....He was then very high and shy, so that he would not let me touch him, nor look upon him but bid me keep my eyes off him for they pierced him. But now he was very loving and tender, and confessed in some measure to truth; his wife also and daughter were tender and kind, and we parted from them very lovingly" (Ell. Text, ii. 401).

Sewel, *Hist.*, anno 1677; Penn, *Travels*; Emmott, *Short Hist. of Quakerism*, 1923, p. 63.

253   2   Cornelis Roeloffs lived at Amsterdam. The relationship with others of the name—Barent, Deborah, Edward, Jan (135. 4) and Pieter—is not evident.

253   3   Jan and Cornelis De Witt were imprisoned on a false accusation; the Orange mob attacked the prison, dragged the brothers out and murdered them, 1672.

In the Thirnbeck MSS. in D is a letter from John Rous to his mother-in-law, Margaret Fox, in which he sends her (lest she had not seen it in the "Gazet") a description of the murder of the De Witts— "stript y^m starke naked cut of their fingers & toes & flesh of their bodies & sold them at severall prizes wch many bought untill neer their whole bodies were Consumed."

A graphic description of these times may be read in the powerful novel of Marjorie Bowen, *I Will Maintain*.

253   4   Ell. Text gives simply "one of the judges of Holland" (ii. 311). Penn has a paragraph on the visit to "a judge of the chief court of justice in that republic. He made his observations, objections and queries...and declared himself satisfied. He brought us to his street door, and there we parted with dear love to him" (*Travels*, 1835, p. 146).

254   1   According to William Penn's *Travels* (1835, pp. 135, 151, 152), the name of the Resident was Docemius and his place of abode was

Cologne. He was among the Friends who accompanied, as far as the Brielle, the party returning to England. Though no name is given it was doubtless the same man mentioned, *ibid.* p. 65, as "the resident of several princes, a serious and tender man."

254   2   Ell. Text has, simply, "several Friends of Rotterdam." Penn mentions "M. Sonnemans" (*Travels*, pp. 148, 152), who would be the brother mentioned in the Diary.

254   3   After landing at seven p.m. and before retiring to bed at the house of John Vandewall, Fox wrote, with his own hand, a letter to Friends of Holland, dated "Harag 23 day 8 mo 1677." The letter is printed in *Bulletin F. H. Association*, tercent. no., 1924. The original is in D; for the history of the MS. see *Jnl. F. H. S.* ii. xxi.

255   1   John Furly, the younger (1644—   ), was the eldest son of John and Anna Furly, of Colchester (236. 3). In 1669 he married Ann Talcot, daughter of William and Ann Talcot, of Colchester (237. 1). Their fathers—John Furly and William Talcot—accompanied George Fox to Holland in 1677; in Ell. Text (ii. 266) they are referred to as "John Furly and his brother, William Tallcoat." There were several children—Abigail married Cornelis Losevelt (238. 2) in 1686, and William married Anna Vandewall (of the Harwich family) in 1697.

255   2   It is curious that so much space should have been given to the story of the duplicity of a post-mistress. The account in the Ell. Text (ii. 313) is briefer and Penn's words thereon are briefer still (*Travels*, p. 161): "George Fox and the others, through the miscarriage of a letter about the coach, not being come to Colchester." There was evident pleasure in the Quaker party that the woman's schemes had failed and that "shee was right served"!

256   1   There is a slight reference in Besse's *Sufferings* to William Bunting, of Halstead, Co. Essex. There is no record of a burial under that name in Essex Registers—a William Bunting, of Buntingfield, Chesterfield, Co. Derby, was buried, 15 x. 1719, in that county. He is not named in Ell. Text.

257   1   For John and Ann Child see vol. ii. p. 401. John Child was one of the "Dispersers of Quakers Books" (*Extracts from State Papers*, p. 228—*Cal. S. P. Dom.* 1664—5, p. 142).

257   2   This is, in all probability, William *Bennit*, of Woodbridge in Suffolk (*c.* 1634—1684, died in Ipswich County Jail). He was one of the first preachers to visit the neighbouring county of Essex (*F. P. T.* p. 102). His several epistles and other papers were collected and printed in 1685 and a selection issued in 1838, with a brief memoir. He wrote a Testimony to his friend, Giles Barnardiston. Penn notes a meeting with these two just prior to the meeting with Fox (*Travels*, p. 161). Smith, *Cata.* i. 248.

257   3   Gawen Lawrie (—1687). In the Hertfordshire Sessions Rolls, 1581—1698, under date of 1682, "Gaven Lourdy, merchant and speaker," is said to be one of the wealthiest dissenters in the parish of Cheshunt. He is mentioned in *The Haigs of Bemersyde*, 1881, as a friend of William Haig, the Quaker, with whom he had business relations. Haig wrote to his brother Anthony in 1669 from London: "I am in order for my Virginian voyage buying goods. Gavin Lowry's son, Obed, goes partner with me. Gavin is very loving and says still if any man

will lend me one hundred pounds, he will lend me so much more....
Direct thy letter to Gavin Lowry's in Houndsditch at the Helmet."
In 1667 Lawrie was living in Three Kings Court. In 1672 his daughter,
Mary, married, *s.p.*, the aforementioned William Haig (1646—1688).
In 1682 William Penn and eleven associates bought East Jersey.
Robert Barclay was appointed governor and he appointed Lawrie as a
deputy on the death of Thomas Rudyard. He went over in 1684,
followed shortly by his daughter and son-in-law. They settled at
Elizabeth Town (Myers, *Narratives of Early Pennsylvania*, etc., 1912,
p. 181).
Jnl. F. H. S. iii. vi. vii. ix. xvi. xvii. xix.; *Quakers in American
Colonies*, 1911.

257   4   For Samuel Newton see vol. ii. p. 422. With others—William Penn,
William Meade, Francis Moore, William Shewen, John Osgood, William
Welch, and Stephen Crisp—he signed a petition to the King *re* popish
recusants (*Jnl. F. H. S.* xi. 136). Francis Bugg caged Newton among
his "unclean birds," and it appears that he had fallen from grace, as
on p. 257, l. 11, the name is struck through in the Diary and also the
three following "S. N."

257   5   William Crow (d. 1726/7) was of Bardfield, Saling, Co. Essex. He,
or another of the same name and district, was sent to prison in 1659
for refusal to pay tithe, and remained there for some years (*Suff.*
i. 194).

258   1   William *Hages* has not been found. Perhaps William *Hedges* was
intended. He was a combmaker; he died of fever, in the parish of
"Ann & Agnes," in 1700, aged fifty-six.

258   2   John Bolton (*c.* 1599—1679) was a goldsmith, resident in the parish
of Aldersgate. He was convinced quite early in the work in London
and soon became a front-rank Friend. In 1658, with Amor Stoddard,
Gerard Roberts, Thomas Hart and Richard Davies, he had the care
of money sent from the North for travelling Ministers (*Beginnings*,
p. 326, see also pp. 245, 246). Bolton was one of a numerous band of
Friends taken up "travelling" and lodged in Exeter prison in 1656, and
later liberated by order of the Protector (*Extracts from State Papers*,
p. 6—*Cal. S. P. Dom.* 1656—7, p. 192). He suffered several imprisonments
and finings at later times. Short pieces of his with long titles appear
in Smith, *Cata.* i. 294.

258   3   It is curious that a prominent Friend like William Gibson (*c.* 1629—
1684) should not have found place in Ell. Text or Camb. Text or in the
Itinerary Journal. His name occurs frequently in the Haistwell Diary
between the years 1677 and 1678, being introduced by the initials W. G.
Sewel mentions Gibson's convincement among instances of a sudden
change: "William Gibson, whom I knew well, and who at the time of
the civil wars, being a soldier at Carlisle, he and three others having
heard that a Quaker meeting was appointed in that city they agreed to
go thither and abuse the preacher whose name was Thomas Holms,"
but Gibson "who came to scoff remained to pray" and became a zealous
Minister. He resided in Lancashire till about 1670, when he removed
to London. His wife was Elizabeth Thompson, of Crossmoor, Co.
Lancaster; they were married in 1662. (His son of the same name was
the centre of a raging controversy, *circa* 1720, described *Jnl. F. H. S.* i.)
He took a prominent part with Fox and others in the Wilkinson-Story
Controversy, dealing especially with Raunce and Harris. In 8 mo. 1684,
he was reported "nigh death" (Penn's letter to M. Fox, *Jnl. F. H. S.*

ix. 143). It is said that more than a thousand Friends followed his remains from Lombard Street to Bunhill Fields (*London Friends' Meetings*, p. 154).

Piety Promoted; Whiting, *Memoirs*; *D. N. B.*; *Jnl. F. H. S.* i. v. x. xi. xiii. xviii.; *Second Period*.

258   4   Dr John Raunce lived at Wycombe, Co. Bucks. His first wife, Elizabeth, was "one of ye first, if not ye very first, yt declared the Truth" at Turville Heath, Oxfordshire (*F. P. T.*). The doctor and his wife nursed Thomas Ellwood through a serious illness. In 1668 Raunce was present at a meeting at Weston, representing "Wiccomb" (*Jnl. F. H. S.* xvi.). He appears to have been liberated from prison in Bucks by the "General Pardon" of 1672 (*Extracts from State Papers*, p. 345—*Cal. S. P. Dom.* 1671—2). Later, in 1676, Dr Raunce joined the Separatist party. He wrote several tracts both before and after his defection (Smith, *Cata.*).

Rogers, *Christian Quaker*, 1680, postscript, p. 22; *Second Period*.

258   5   Francis Moore was a useful London Friend. In a MS. in D we read: "ffrancis Moor of London having a testimony for yᵉ Lord in meetings & a good service in meetings, though he did not much travail abroad...." His residence in the Ratcliff district appears probable from an appointment in 1672 to assist prisoners, but his name is crossed through and marked "removed." Other offices in the Church were allotted him (*Sundry Ancient Epistles*, MS. in D). He also had a share in the work of providing spinning for poor Friends (see 104. 2); this was shortly before his decease, if the record of the death of Francis Moore, of Love Lane, merchant, 3 xii. 1678, referred to him. See 111. 4.
Suff.

259   1   In Ell. Text there is given a letter from George Fox to his wife, dated this day—"every day I am fain to be at meetings about business, and sufferings which are great abroad" (ii. 314).

259   2   Colonel David Barclay (1610—1686) resided at Urie, near Aberdeen, Scotland, a mansion which he purchased in 1648 and rebuilt. His wife was Catherine Gordon. He served under Gustavus Adolphus in Germany and later in the Covenanting Army during the Civil War. He met Quakerism in London and was convinced by the medium of John Swinton while imprisoned in Edinburgh (261. 5). For the committal order see *Jnl. F. H. S.* v. 199. Whittier's picture of the indignities he suffered on allying himself with the despised Quakers is well known—"Barclay of Ury."

Jnl. F. H. S. v. vii.—ix.; *Swarth. Account Book*; *Second Period*.

259   3   For Thomas Moore see vol. i. p. 435, etc. In vol. i. p. 200 we have the first reference (1655) to Thomas Moore, J.P., as a "freindely moderate man," the reference to his convincement and service being omitted from Ell. Text. There was probably some relationship or other connection between Moore and Rebecka Travers—in 1662 he was the means of her release from prison (*Extracts from State Papers*, p. 155—*Cal. S. P. Dom.* 1661—2, p. 569), and was at this time to be found at her house.

Marsh, *Early Friends in Surrey and Sussex*, 1886; *Jnl. F. H. S.* vii. x.; *Extracts from State Papers*, many reff.

259   4   For John Pennyman see vol. ii. p. 431. We cannot be sure to which of his numerous writings there is a reference here. John Pennyman's marriage with Mary Boreman in 1671 is probably the marriage referred to in *The Character of a Quaker in his True and Proper Colours*, 1672: "A Westminster Wedding must be kept at Merchant Taylors Hall, and

a Trumpet sounded to publish the Nuptials between Diotrephes and Gomer the daughter of Diblain, where Jews and Gentiles are jointly invited to a Feast, and Seven and Twenty Venison Pasties saw their stately walls in a moment levelled."

Extracts from State Papers, pp. 154, 224; *Quaker Women*, 1915, p. 138.

260   1   We have not found any record of these letters in the *Register of George Fox's Letters*, or elsewhere.

260   2   George Fox visited Sergeant Birkhead, at Twickenham, in 1659 and "had a meetinge where there was many considerable people & some of quality & a glorious meetinge it was...& Christ sett above all soe y^t one man amongst y^m admired & sayde: this man is a pearle" (vol. i. p. 340). Ell. Text omits "soe...pearle." The use of the military title is noticeable. See also "Capt Stodart" (vol. i. pp. 186, 190 where "Capt" is inserted); "Captain Lawrence" (so named in Camb. Text and Ell. Text) ; "Captain Davenport" (vol. i. p. 307).

260   3   This visit to Kingston, and subsequent journeys into Bucks and Oxon, are recorded in Ell. Text, ii. 315 ff.

260   4   See 105. 4.

261   1   Further information respecting Thomas Tanner is not forthcoming.

261   2   For Christopher Taylor see vol. i. p. 410. In the *Diaries of Oliver Heywood* (1630—1702), vol. iv. p. 7, we read: "Antinomian Views. These were the principles of Mr. Taylor, the minister of Chapel-en-le-Brears, who became at length a professed Quaker." *Jnl. F. H. S.* i. ii. v. vi. ix. x. xvi.

261   3   For a sketch of the life of Bray D'Oyly see vol. ii. p. 446. He was one of the many substantial persons who joined the early Friends. Payment for the care of his horse and that of Stephen Smith at Ulverston is recorded in *Swarth. Account Book*, p. 239. (For such payments see *F. Q. E.* 1912, p. 482; *Beginnings*, p. 357.)

Rogers, *Christian Quaker*, 1680, pt. v. p. 42; *Jnl. F. H. S.* xi.

261   4   The slight reference here to a meeting at Hunger Hill "concerning differences" has been greatly expanded in Ell. Text (ii. 315, 316), but without reference by name to Raunce and Harris. "The meeting was in a barn there came so many that the house could not receive them....Most of their arrows were shot at me....The meeting ended to the satisfaction of Friends." From whence did Ellwood obtain these particulars? In the margin of the Haistwell Diary at this point there are several lines of shorthand, which may have been deciphered and incorporated in Ellwood's additional particulars.

261   5   George Salter, of Hedgerley, Co. Bucks, belonged to Chalfont Meeting (*Jnl. F. H. S.* xvi. 70). He entered into controversy with Roger Crab in answer to the latter's articles against Friends, 1659. "Roger Crab was an interesting character, a vegetarian and water drinker, the leader of some people called Rationals, and commonly reputed to be a prophet. He lived near Uxbridge" (*Beginnings*). Crab (*c.* 1621—1680) was a native of Buckinghamshire (*D. N. B.*). Though living quietly in the district Salter was repeatedly fined and imprisoned, but the numerous bequests in his will (in D), dated 1691, indicate some means despite fines and imprisonment. He had long disputes with the "priest" of Farnham Royal in whose parish he resided.

PAGE	NOTE	
261	6	There is a considerable note on John Swinton in vol. i. p. 466. See 237. 7 for a note respecting his widow. W. C. Braithwaite deals with Swinton in *Second Period*, pp. 335—337, where there is a fine bibliography.
262	1	The name of Henry Tredway (—1700) appears in a list of Bucks Friends in 1668; he belonged to Chalfont Meeting (*Jnl. F. H. S.* xvi. 70). With William Loddington, John Bellers, John White, Thomas Ellwood and others, he signed a fire-brief sent out by Bucks Q.M. 1692 (*ibid.* iii. 111). For fire-briefs see *Swarth. Account Book*; *Jnl. F. H. S.* iii. iv.

Suff.

There was a Margaret Tredway in 1678, also belonging to Chalfont Meeting (*Jnl. F. H. S.* vii. 64).

262	2	The paper prepared by these six prominent Friends for presentation to the King has not been found.
262	3	Jeremiah Steevens (—1688) belonged to Upperside M.M., Bucks (*Jnl. F. H. S.* ix. 196). He was a maltster. His widow, Ann Steevens, departed this life in 1712. A son, Jeremiah, died in 1682. In 1665 while several Friends, including Jeremiah Steevens, were carrying the remains of Edward Perrot to the graveyard at Jordans, Ambrose Benett, of Bulstrode, "rushed out of his inn...and having drawn his sword...with a forcible thrust threw the coffin off the bearers' shoulders, so that it fell to the ground in the midst of the street where it lay till evening." Steevens and others were taken prisoners (Besse, *Suff.*; Littleboy, *Jordans*, 1920). The Steevens family was, for several generations, prominent among Friends in Wycombe. The old oak table at which Steevens entertained Fox, Penn, Ellwood and others is still preserved (*Hist. of Life of Thomas Ellwood*, Graveson ed. 1906).
262	4	In *F. P. T.* we read: "George Fox setled ye meeting at Tirfield heath in ye year 1660 at ye Wid Weste houce whear it hath continued Ever since in heir time, heir Childrens, and now [1705] heir Granchildren" (p. 220). Elizabeth West, widow, was buried at Henley on Thames, 22 i. 1688.
262	5	For Thomas Curtis, of Caversham, see vol. i. p. 441. While on a business journey in Devonshire he was arrested as a vagrant and sent to Exeter Jail, but liberated shortly after, 1657 (*Extracts from State Papers*, p. 32—*Cal. S. P. Dom.* 1657—8, p. 156, see also *Extracts*, pp. 33, 45, 105, 196—198, 344, 351). After he left the main body of Friends, it was written of him by Reading M.M.: "Thomas Courtis said y^t Singing (or, Speaking Singingly) in Prayer or in Preaching or with a vocall voice, was abomination, & he Reflected upon Samuell Burgis at Oare, & said he had Sang them many a merry Jigg, but now he would seem to Excuse it & said he would as leif heare one Sing a Ballad, wch is noe better" (*Jnl. F. H. S.* xiii. 125).

Jnl. F. H. S. ix. xvii. xix. xx.

262	6	For George Lamboll see vol. i. p. 430. When Fox was at Reading in 1655 (vol. i. p. 185) the Sunday meeting was held in Lamboll's orchard, "almost all ye whole tounde came togeather...& people were mightily satisfyed." He was released from some years' imprisonment by the "General Pardon" of 1672.
262	7	William Austill figures in a disgraceful scene in the doings connected with the Wilkinson and Story Controversy in Berkshire. It is thus described by Howard R. Smith in *Jnl. F. H. S.* i.: "Benjamin Coale was clerk of the Q.M. and he had disseminated William Rogers's book, entitled *The Christian Quaker*. In Fifth Month, 1681, many Friends

resolved to supercede B. Coale and in Second Month, 1682, they appointed William Austill as clerk....Austill began to write the minutes, but Thomas Curtis tore the papers from him....As the Meeting for Sufferings refused to recognise B. Coale as clerk, the two parties held their Meeting at the same time in the same room, each with its own clerk."

262   8   For Bartholomew Maylin see vol. ii. p. 446.

263   1   William Hitchcock, of Marlborough, married Bridget Hitchcock, of Preshute in 1659, and had several children. Among "The Taylor Papers" in the possession of the Hist. Soc. Pa. is a letter from Hitchcock to John and Amy Harding, late of Wiltshire, then of Pennsylvania, dated at Marlborough, 28 vii. 1687. The letter conveys various items of news, including a visit of William Penn, Samuel Waldenfield and Francis Stamper—"hundreds of people stood to heare him [Penn] in ye street; ye rooms in my house being full, ye glass of ye windowes being taken down, freinds stood in ye Penthouse & spoke" (printed *Jnl. F. H. S.* iv.). William Hitchcock and Bridget Hitchcock were witnesses to the marriage of J. and A. Harding, 1672 (*ibid.*).

263   2   Israel Noyse (Noice) lived at Calne, N. Wilts. He married Margery Wallis, of Slaughterford in 1657 and had a considerable family. He was a "sergemaker." He died in 1708 and Margery Noyse in 1716. With other Wilts Friends he signed a Q.M. minute against "A sad & Lammenttabell sizem & devision...by John Story & John Wilkenson of westmorland" (*Jnl. F. H. S.* xvi. 143). A Friends' meeting at Calne has been held through the centuries until recent times.

263   3   Richard Snead (--1711) was a "Mercer at ye Blackmares head on ye bridg in Bristoll," in 1662 (*Cal. S. P. Dom.* 1661—2, p. 414). In 1680 he caused to be copied the Bristol Men's Meeting minutes beginning 1667, from a fear that the original might be appropriated by Rogers and his *confrères*. Both are still in the care of Bristol Friends. (In Wiltshire, a hot-bed of opposition, the Q.M. book was "Katched up & carried away & would not send it again nor return themselves," 1678 (*Jnl. F. H. S.* iv. 120).) Snead is frequently mentioned in the Bristol MSS. (*ibid.* ix.). When in jail in Newgate, Bristol, in 1683, "over the Anchor," he signed a certificate of liberation for a marriage, which was signed also in Bridewell, on behalf of women Friends there (*ibid.* ii. 15). In 1681 he wrote *A Letter in Recommendation of some Medicines prepared by Charles Marshall*, which was signed by Charles Jones, William Penn, John Staploe, Francis Stamper, Richard Whitpain, John Bellers, and Thomas Cox, and in the same year, with Richard Vickris, Charles Jones and another, he wrote *An Exalted Diotrephes Reprehended...William Rogers.*

Vol. ii. pp. 378, 384; *Suff.*; *Jnl. F. H. S.* vii. viii.; *Annals of the Harford Family*, 1909; MSS. in D.

263   4   For Laurence Steele see vol. ii. p. 465. His name occurs frequently in the Bristol MSS. (*Jnl. F. H. S.* ix.).

263   5   The name Gouldney (Goldney) appears in the Friends' Registers of Wiltshire from 1674 to 1761. There were at least four Adam Gouldneys in direct descent and it is probable that this Friend was the widow of the first Adam known to Quakerism. The family seat was Chippenham in the N.W. of the county. Adam, Junr., married, 1674, Mary Knight (d. 1716), who was a Minister; their daughter Jane (1680—   ) married Michael Russell (112. 2) in 1698. In the Bristol MSS. there is recorded a meeting at the house of "Widowe Goldneys" in connec-

tion with the Wilkinson and Story Controversy at which were present
Thomas Camm, Benjamin Antrobus, Samuel Boulton, Charles Marshall
and others, date 3 v. 1678 (*Jnl. F. H. S.* ix.).
Records of Chippenham, by Frederick H. Goldney, 1889.

263   6   The Registers for Wiltshire and the minutes of Q.M. and M.M.
reveal several families of Wallis, resident at Slaughterford and Chippenham. "Widow Wallis" was probably Elizabeth Wallis (d. 1685),
whose husband was John Wallis (d. 1660). There was a connection by
marriage with the Noyse family (263. 2). Slaughterford is a village
West of Chippenham; it was for long a Quaker centre. The meetinghouse is still standing.
    Three Wiltshire widows were visited in succession—Widow Hailes
(about whom nothing has been found), Widow Gouldney, and Widow
Wallis.

263   7   Little is known of Joan Hiley (Hely, Ely), of Bristol, widow. See
vol. ii. p. 385. She appears to have been the intermediary in the
matter of correspondence between Friends and the Separatists. See
Rogers, *Christian Quaker,* 1680, pt. v. pp. 18, 60.
    Suff. i. 50, 55; *Jnl. F. H. S.* ix.

263   8   For John Story see vol. i. p. 405, etc., and for the Wilkinson and
Story Controversy (1675—1686) see vols. i. and ii. In a letter to
William Penn in 1675 Fox writes on the controversy aroused by "y^e
2: Johns," and gives a relation of the principal points of divergence
between Friends and the Separatists: "They have vindicated fflyeinge
in times of Persecution and affirmed that ye paym^t of Tythes is not
Anti-christian, and womens Meetings are Rebuted Monsters, and
Recording Condemnations giveinge ye Devill Advantage; and singeinge
in Meetings whilst others are prayinge or speakeinge, Confusion &
delusion & calls Monthly & Quarterly Meetings Courts & sessions"
(printed *Jnl. F. H. S.* x. 146 from a contemporary copy of the letter).
    Further references to the controversy may be found in Sewel, *Hist.*;
Barclay, *Inner Life of the Religious Societies of the Commonwealth,* 1876,
chap. xix.; *Jnl. F. H. S.* i. iv. vii.—x.; *John Stephenson Rowntree,* 1908;
Second Period.

263   9   Thomas Jordan (d. 1688) was a grocer of Maryport parish, Bristol.
His wife was Lydia Jordan (d. 1685). They both signed the Fox-Fell
wedding certificate (*Jnl. F. H. S.* ix.).

264   1   The Bristol Registers contain the record of the death of John Batho,
of "James Parish—an antient friend," in 1679, and of Jane, his wife, in
1673. Jane was one of the Friends sentenced to banishment in 1664.
In 1669 she signed the Fox-Fell wedding certificate (*Jnl. F. H. S.* ix.).
Besse gives the following, under Bristol, 1670: "Last First-day M.
Bradshaw that was lately with the King beginning to speak was rudely
taken by the soldiers to the Guard and so were S. Pearson and
Jane Batho, and kept there till night, then sent to Bridewell and there
remain" (*Suff.* i. 53).
    The "S. Pearson" abovenamed was probably Susanna Pearson, of
Worcester, who is thus introduced in *Beginnings,* p. 391: "In February,
1657, a young man, convinced of Truth, became mentally unhinged and
drowned himself. After his burial, Susanna Pearson told his mother,
who was in great grief, that she would restore her son alive, and went
with another woman to the grave and took the corpse out, seeking to
raise it to life by imitating the action of Elisha when he raised the son
of the Shunammite woman. As this had no effect they went to prayer,
but with no better success, and so buried the body again."
    A Sad Caveat to all Quakers, Not to boast any more that they have

God Almighty by the hand when they have the Devil by the toe, with an account of the incident, "William Pool an apprentice & a known Quaker neer Worcester" being the young man, printed in black letter, 16 pages, in 12mo. 1657 (see Smith, *Adv. Cata.* p. 10); Baxter, *Reliq. Baxt.* 1696, pt. i. p. 77 ; *Suff.*; Barclay, *Inner Life of the Religious Societies of the Commonwealth*, 1876, p. 428 n. ; Brown, *Evesham Friends*, 1885, pp. 107, 112; *Jnl. F. H. S.* ix. xi.; for Susanna Pearson, Junr., see *Suff.* ii. 637 ; *Extracts from State Papers*, p. 228—*Cal. S. P. Dom.* 1664—5, p. 142. Mother and daughter signed the Fox-Fell marriage certificate (*Jnl. F. H. S.* ix.).

264   2   William Rogers, in his *Christian Quaker*, pt. v., refers to George Fox's visit to Bristol and to the abortive conferences at Simon Clement's and elsewhere in and about this city. Fox said in his book, *This is an Encouragement to all Womens-Meetings*, that Micah's mother was a Virtuous Woman—Rogers averred that she was an Idolatrous Woman ; see J. S. Rowntree's pamphlet, *Micah's Mother*, 1892, included in his memorial volume, 1908, pt. 1, chap. 2.

264   3, 4   There were two Friends living in Bristol at the same time named Charles Jones, father and son. Their trade was soap-making (*Suff.* i. 69 ff.). "Bristoll soap" appears in the *Swarth. Account Book*, p. 359—"halfe a hundred of Bristoll Sope" cost fourteen shillings. In 1663 Charles Jones and others were arrested and declined securities (*Extracts from State Papers*, p. 183—*Cal. S. P. Dom.* 1663—4, p. 428, see p. 477). Both names occur in the Bristol MSS. (*Jnl. F. H. S.* ix.). In 1681 George Whitehead, Charles Jones, Junr., and Laurence Steel appeared before Charles II to seek liberty for Friends in Bristol, but with little success (*Christian Progress*, pp. 504 ff.).

265   1   Hezekiah Coale was one of the Winterbourne family to which George Coale belonged (146. 3). He suffered for the faith that was in him.
Suff. i. 218, 223, 227.

265   2   Richard Gabell, of Sodbury, Gloucestershire, has not been found in the Registers or elsewhere.

265   3, 4   There is a lively account of the two Nailsworth Friends, Robert Langley and Richard Smith, in *F. P. T.* p. 106. The latter had been a soldier. "They married two sisters and thereby came to be Brother Laws. Pen would be to short here in this place to write the vallue of those two men and their wives. They were great entertainers of ffriends...all ways Lending a hand to help the weakons aLong in their Journey....Rob: Langley had a publick testimony."
Rogers, *Christian Quaker*, pt. vi. p. 5; *Suff.*

265   5   Should probably be *Stinchcombe*. It is also *Finchcombe* in Ell. Text (ii. 318), where there is a reference to the presence of "several of the opposite spirit." Stinchcombe would be about the eight miles stated in the margin, West of Nailsworth.

265   6   Richard Townsend was one of the Friends who signed the certificate respecting Giles Fettiplace (100. 7) which declares that he "is a Protestant Dissenter...commonly called Quaker," 25 March, 1692 (*Jnl. F. H. S.* xvi. 44). The author of the memoir of John Roberts—*A Quaker of the Olden Time*, 1898—suggests that Richard Townsend was a brother of Roger Townsend and that they were brothers of that woman "of great Understanding," as Besse styles her, Theophila Townsend, all of Cirencester. The last named suffered long and cruel imprisonments. Richard Townsend died in 1715.

PAGE NOTE

266   1   For Edward Edwards (Edward of Edwards) see vol. i. p. 448. He was with George Fox in Wales in 1657. We have here the additional information that Edwards lived at Stoke Orchard—above reference gives Gloucestershire only. He married Mary Surman (d. 1715). They were both much occupied in "industrious Travels and Pains for the Name and Power of the Lord, and Promotion of His holy Truth" (*F. P. T.* p. 323 n.).
Jnl. F. H. S. x. xvi. xix.

266   2   The name Joshua Cart appears once in the card-catalogue in D as a signature to a wedding certificate, 1696. It has not been found elsewhere.

266   3   There was a Baptist minister in Worcester, William Pardoe (1630—c. 1692), named in Brown's *Evesham Friends*, pp. 19, 20, styled "pastor of the General Baptist Congregation," who was a prisoner for nearly seven years, "a very useful man and blessed with great success in his ministerial work."
There was a Friend, of Worcester, named William Pardoe, who married Mary Amphlert, of Worcester, in 1664, and Margaret Handley, of Pontymoile, South Wales, in 1686, and died in 1712.
Were these father and son?
Letter from Dr W. T. Whitley, hon. sec. Bapt. Hist. Soc. 1924, see his *History of British Baptists*, 1923, p. 108; MSS. in D.

266   4   Robert Smith, of Worcester (d. 1705), became a Friend about 1655, and soon began to befriend travelling preachers. When Thomas Goodaire (vol. i. p. 399) was refused permission by the mayor to go to an inn Robert Smith "came & tooke him to his House, & gave him Intertainment & bid the people who were gathered aboute the door goe tell the mayor of it"! (*F. P. T.*). In 1662 a sentence of premunire was passed on Smith, and he lay in prison for ten years (Brown, *Evesham Friends*, 1885, p. 120, see also pp. 74, 83, 87).
For a list of 125 Friends lying under sentence of premunire see *Extracts from State Papers*, p. 351—*Cal. S. P. Dom.* 1672, p. 214.

266   5   Nothing further appears respecting Thomas Fuckes (?Folkes), of the city of Worcester.

266   6   "The Monthly Meetings of Worcestershire were 'settled' at a 'General Mens Meeting,' held at the house of Henry Gibbs at Pershore in 1667" (Brown, *Evesham Friends*, 1885, p. 141). Before that event took place Gibbs had been in prison with others "for having lately assembled themselves under the pretence of joining in a religious worship, to the great endangering of the publique peace and safetye and to the terrour of the people" (*ibid.* p. 113, see p. 180).
Suff. ii. 67, 68.
For the Meeting at Pershore see Brown, *op. cit.* p. 205.

266   7   John Woodward, of Evesham, was "a soldier in the service of the Commonwealth" (*The Cruelty of the Magistrates of Evesham*, 1655). Other sufferings followed, noted in Brown's *Evesham Friends*, 1885, pp. 57, 74, 84, 87, 111—113, 178, 196.
Joane Woodward's name occurs *ibid.* p. 111.
Suff.

267   1   A brief sketch only can be given in a note respecting Viscountess Conway and Kilulta (—1679). She was descended from an illustrious family, occupying a position of honour and responsibility in the affairs of the State and distinguished for its great intellectual power and administrative ability. She was the youngest daughter of Sir Heneage

Finch, of Kensington. Her eldest brother was Heneage Finch (1621—1682), afterwards Earl of Nottingham. In connection with his office as Lord Keeper, we read in Barclay's *Letters of Early Friends*, 1841, p. 199, that William Penn, writing to George Fox in Worcester Jail, ix. 1674, regarding Fox's release, complains that "it sticks with the Keeper and we have and do use what interest we can." See vol. ii. p. 298. Anne Finch married in 1651 Edward, Viscount Conway. "He had not his wife's taste for learning, and after their retirement to Ragley Hall [illustration in *Jnl. F. H. S.* vii. 49] he devoted himself to the ordinary pursuits of a country gentleman whilst she, 'deeply immersed in the stores of erudition imbedded in ponderous folios in the library,' strove to add to her already remarkable knowledge of ancient and general literature" (Brown, *Evesham Friends*, 1885, p. 128). There was only one child, Heneage, who died young, of small-pox in London in 1660. The exact date of Lady Conway's introduction to Quakerism is not known, but George Keith visited her in 1675 and she soon after made the acquaintance of Penn, Barclay, Fox and other front-rank Friends. She subscribed money to assist Barclay in building Aberdeen meeting-house. Her principal friendship was with Dr Henry More (233. 5), and Francis Van Helmont (see next note) was her medical adviser. She was in constant bodily ill-health. In the family vault at Arrow is a coffin upon which is scratched in the lead: "Quaker Lady."

Camb. Text, vol. i. p. 397, vol. ii. p. 453; Ell. Text, ii. 319; Pepys, *Diary*, May 18, 1668 (Sir H. Finch); Ward, *Life of Dr Henry More*, 1710, pp. 192 ff.; Dugdale, *Warwickshire*; Penington, *Letters*, 1829, p. 308; Penn, *Travels*, ed. 1835, Preface; *British Friend*, 1850—1852; *F. Q. E.* 1874, 1921; *Argosy*, vol. 30 (1880), pp. 378—387; Brown, *Evesham Friends in the Olden Time*, 1885, chap. v.; *D. N. B.*; *Gentleman's Magazine*, Nov. 1906, p. 464; *Jnl. F. H. S.* vii. xvii.; Malloch, *Finch and Baines: a Seventeenth Century Friendship*, 1917; *Second Period*, 1919. The "Lady Cardiff" of J. H. Shorthouse's *John Inglesant*, 1881, is said to be modelled on Lady Conway.

267   2   Francis Mercurius Van Helmont (—1699) "was the son of John Baptist Van Helmont, the famous Brabaçon physician. He held the doctrine of the transmigration of souls, and to his vain and speculative notions may be partly attributed the sad apostasy of George Keith" (Brown, *Evesham Friends*, 1885, p. 132 n.). See vol. ii. p. 455; Sewel, *Hist.*, *sub anno* 1692. He was Lady Conway's intimate friend and physician. Lady Conway wrote of him in 1675: "Monsieur van Hellmont is growne a very religious Churchman, hee goes every Sunday to the Quakers meetings" (letter in D, printed *Jnl. F. H. S.* vii.). After Lady Conway's death in 1679 Van Helmont removed to Hanover and died in Berlin.

Ward, *Life of Dr Henry More*, 1710, p. 209; *Jnl. F. H. S.* vii. x. xvi. xvii.; *F. Q. E.* 1921—"Henry More, Cambridge Platonist, and Lady Conway, of Ragley, Platonist and Quakeress."

267   3   John Stanley (bapt. 1646, died 1706) was of Cladswell in the parish of Inkberrow, Co. Worcester. He was one of the numerous persons of means and influence who joined themselves to the early Friends. His first wife was Mary Reading (d. 1693 *s.p.*). An ancient manuscript, once belonging to Stanley Pumphrey, gives a vivid picture of the sufferings of J. and M. Stanley in 1694, printed in *Jnl. F. H. S.* vi. Stanley's second wife was Elizabeth Chandless, née Somerford (d. 1732). "The descendants of John and Elizabeth Stanley are to be found in large numbers among Friends of to-day" (*ibid.*).

Vol. ii. p. 423; Brown, *Evesham Friends*, 1885, pp. 214—218.

267   4   We have not yet discovered the titles or authors of either the "German booke" or the book written by "ye priest of ye pish belonging to Ragley," answered by Fox, Keith and Van Helmont—a curious trio!

267   5   No further information is forthcoming regarding Richard Bromly, of Stratford-on-Avon.

267   6   William Lucas lived at Lamcote, South Warwickshire.

268   1   Edward Vivers, of Banbury, was convinced about the year 1654 and became one of the early entertainers of travelling preachers in "Bambury" (*F. P. T.* p. 208). George Fox to William Penn, from Worcester, 1674: "Heere is a ffreinde of Banbury with mee y^t saide If ye matter sticke with ye Keeper hee coulde improve some interest by some ffreindes of his to remove y^t obstacle....Hee may come upp about it" (copy in D, printed *Jnl. F. H. S.* vii. 75).

268   2   For John Halford see vol. ii. p. 447.

268   3   Joseph Harris (d. 1705) lived at *Sibford* Ferris, near Banbury, Oxon.

268   4   Nathaniel Ball lived at North Newington, near Banbury. In Ell. Text (ii. 319) place-names only are given. In the Haistwell Diary we learn the names of the Friends who were visited at these places.

268   5   Hiorne is probably *Hirons*—a name borne by Quakers in the Northants region. There was a Thomas Hirons, of Astrop and Northampton (d. 1664), and wife Alice.
Astrop is a hamlet a short way over the border of Oxfordshire into Northamptonshire.

268   6   Nothing further appears respecting William West save the entry of the burial at Meadle of William West, Senr., yeoman, of Long Crendon, 17 i. 1696. "Fox would leave Long Crendon by way of Thame and follow the main road to Risborough, diverging to the right (past Kingsey) to Ilmire, then on to Longwick, diverging to the left to Meadle, along the Lower Icknield Way, and following that way afterwards to Weston Turville, near Aylesbury" (letter from Richard Welford to the editor, 1901; see *Notes and Queries*, 9th series, viii. Nov. 2, 1901).

268   7   Thomas Sanders (died 1684, buried at Meadle) was an Ilmer Friend belonging to the Meeting at Meadle Farm (see next note). Damaris Sanders, of Meadle Meeting 1678, was probably the wife of Thomas. She and Ann Stevens (Steevens), probably the wife of Jeremiah, of Wycombe (262. 3), went to the Men's Meeting at Thomas Ellwood's in 1671 to suggest that the women "might meet together to feele there servis in the truth, and if they felt servis continew in it." They met a few times and then "the eye being to much outwards to outward buisness, and y^t not apearing," the Meeting was given up for a time ("Some Account concerning the Women's Monthly Meeting in the County of Bucks," from the Minute Book, printed *Jnl. F. H. S.* vii. 63, 64). In 1679 Damaris, daughter of Thomas Sanders, married John Kirton (124. 2).

268   8   John White (—1731) lived at *Meadle*, not Mendle as given in Ell. Text, ii. 319. A good example of local research is *A Visit to Meadle Farm in the Parish of Monks Risborough, Bucks*, by W. H. Summers, 1895. A meeting was held regularly at the farm, attended at times by Thomas Ellwood. "A curious feature in the old house is that in a small cellar, to which we descend by a flight of steps nearly opposite the front door, there is a spring of clear water." There is an orchard

attached which was once a burialground. Hannah, wife of John White, died in 1714. Descendants of "Quaker White" are known to-day but Meadle is now in others' hands.

Hist. of Life of Thomas Ellwood; *Suff.*; George Fox Note Book, folio MS.

268   9   For John Brown, of Weston Turville, see vol. ii. p. 410; *Jnl. F. H. S.* xvi.

269   1   The reason for the insertion of "points" here and elsewhere does not appear.

269   2   Robert Jones lived at Cholesbury, near Tring in Hertfordshire. His name appears once in Besse's *Sufferings* (i. 76), when he was imprisoned for refusing to take the oath.

269   3   George Belch, of Chorleywood, Bucks, belonged to the Chalfont Meeting (*Jnl. F. H. S.* xvi. 70). Besse states that he had three Geldings worth £23 taken from him by distraint and that when he appealed to the Quarter Sessions, his appeal, not being in Latin, was rejected and treble costs were given against him for which his Horse and other goods were taken away to the value of £40 (*Suff.* i. 83). His signature was attached to the letter sent to Samuel Boulton from Hunger Hill in 1687 (80. 5). Belch's son Thomas (d. 1741), of Cheapside, London, linendraper and clothworker, married Ann Owen (1677—1743), of Co. Surrey, in 1713/14. They had eight children, one of whom, Susanna, married into the Vaux family (*Jnl. F. H. S.* i. 75).

269   4   The statement in vol. i. p. 428 that John Crook had a house in Luton as well as a country-house at Beckerings Park seems to receive confirmation here, but the great meeting of 1658 was held at the latter not the former (see vol. i. pp. 180 n., 455).

270   1   Samuel Hodges, of South Mimms, a village lying North of Barnet, close to the Hertfordshire border, was a butcher by trade. In 1683 he was heavily fined for a meeting at his house.

The Meeting at South Mimms was discontinued in 1787 and the property was sold in 1820.

Suff. i. 482; *London Friends' Meetings.*

270   2   No further particulars are at hand respecting Henry Hodge of Barnet. Fox visited the Friends here in 1677 (p. 232). We read in *London Friends' Meetings*, under the head of Chipping Barnet, that in 1689 the house of John Huddlestone, of Chipping Barnet, was registered a place of worship for the Society of Friends, in accordance with the provisions of the Toleration Act. In 1743 this Meeting was laid down, its continuance being considered "disreputable to the Society" (p. 298).

270   3   The Pewter Platter was, apparently, kept by a Friend. In the chapter on the Six Weeks Meeting in *London Friends' Meetings* (p. 127), we read : "In 1682 an appointment is made 'to give notice to Friends in the country that the Friend at the Falcon is deceased, and that the Friend at the Platter can accommodate them.'"

270   4   The Y.M. of 1678 was composed of representatives. It was held on the 22nd to the 24th of the Third Month and mostly occupied with the subject of sufferings including "the often suffering of Friends by being impressed into the King's ships of war" (*Epistles, 1681 to 1857*, 1858, vol. i. p. xxiii). See the cases of Thomas Lurting (*Beginnings*) and Richard Sellar (*Second Period*).

PAGE	NOTE	

271 1   This was probably the book by Roger Williams: *Fox Digg'd out of his Burrowes.* See 235. 4.

272 1   See previous note and 235. 4.

273 1   There is a slight reference to Joseph Freeman in Barclay's *Letters of Early Friends*, 1841, p. 179: Ellis Hookes to Margaret Fox, 1671: "I saw a letter from John Hull who intends to come over in Wm Bailys or J. Freeman's ship."

   There is a record of the burial of Elizabeth Freeman, of Stepney, wife of Joseph, mariner, died 13 xi. 1673, aged fifty.

273 2   There is a long note on Solomon Eccles in vol. ii. p. 428. It is interesting to find him again, at the close of the Haistwell Diary. He was preaching in Ireland in 1669 and in Scotland in 1674 (*Jnl. F. H. S.* x. xii.). Further information of his visit to Barbados in 1671 may be found *ibid.* xiv. A minute made at a sitting of the Morning Meeting at the home of Anne Travers, 2 ix. 1674, reads: "Concerning S. Eccles his booke entituled The Soule Saveing Principle, &c., freinds have taken three daies to read it & their sense and judgment is that it is not safe to be published there being many things in it that are to be left out & others to bee corrected, both wch will require much labour & care and therefore it is referred to G. W., A. P., & W. G., & T. G., or any two or more of y^m to speak with Sollomon, the book in ye mean time to be left with E. H." No more has been heard of the book.

273 3   Was Edward Haistwell the "man" referred to in this extract from Rogers's *Christian Quaker*, written and printed against George Fox: "When he Travels, 'tis certainly known, he hath had such Attendance, which (considering the Work he is on) may be termed Great...and of late hath Travelled with a *Man* termed *George Fox's Man*" (1680, pt. iv. p. 64)?

ADDENDA

181 1   John Bowater (Boweter) (*c.* 1629—1704/5) is principally noted for his visit to America in 1677—8. "It appeared by the said John Bowater's own brief Relation, that he was more kindly used by the Poor Indians in America, than by some pretended Christians here in England, after his return" (Testimony issued by the Second Days Morning Meeting, 21 iii. 1705). He was for some time a prisoner in Worcester County Jail and also in the Fleet Prison in London. "He was low and poor in this World." His early home was at Bromsgrove in Worcestershire; he lived later in London.

   Christian Epistles...of John Boweter, with list of places visited in America, 1705; vol. ii. pp. 408, 426, 442, 444; *Bulletin F. H. S. Phila.* iii.

PAGE	LINE	

39 3   Of Cromwell, Richard Hubberthorne wrote, in 1657: "He spoke more against Friends than ever before he formerly expressed, saying that there was a good law against Quakers, and they did well to put it into execution and he would stand by them, for he said they were against both magistry and ministry." .

136 2   John Sellwood (*c.* 1634—1693) was a brewer, of Mile End, parish of Stepney. His widow, Elizabeth, of Schoolhouse Lane, died in 1717, aged 78.

   Suff.

PAGE LINE

222   2   In the Testimony to Fox, written by his friend, John Boweter, we read: "Not many Days before his Decease, to wit, the 5th of the 11th Month, 1690, about Eight Days before his Departure, at our 2d Days Morning-Meeting, I much minded his Exhortation to us, encouraging Friends that have Gifts, to make use of them, mentioning many Countries beyond the Seas that wanted Visiting, instancing the Labours and hard Travels of Friends, in the beginning of the spreading of Truth in our Days, in breaking up of Countries, and of the rough plowing they had in Steeple-Houses &c., but now it was more easie; and he complained of many Demases and Cains, who imbrace the present World, and incumber themselves with their own Businesses, and neglect the Lord's, and so are good for nothing; and said They that had Wives should be as tho' they had none; and who goeth a Warfare, should not entangle himself with the things of this World." See Preface to the volume of Fox's *Gospel Truth Demonstrated*, 1706; also *Bulletin F. H. S. Phila.* iii. 144.

234   21   An important event was passed over with but a slight mention: "And on y^e : 12 : day G ff : went to anoth^r Meeting at E : H^s." This meeting was called to prepare, or sign, a document addressed to the Separatist community, "From a Meeting held at Ellis Hook's Chamber in London, the 12th of the 4th Month, 77," respecting "false and pernicious Jealousies, Mutterings, and secret Smitings...more especially John Wilkinson and John Story." Sixty-six Friends appended their signatures, among them being many Friends beforementioned. See 233. 3.

The reply is signed by sixty-seven persons, of whom very few appear to have figured previously on the pages of the history of early Quakerism.

The above was printed as *A Testimony Against The 66 Judges call'd Quakers, who writ an Epistle (as they call it) against John Story and John Wilkinson*, etc., with introduction by Jeffery Bullock, of Sudbury, Co. Suffolk, "who was afterwards brought to see the delusion into which he had fallen, and in 1686 gave testimonies against his former conduct." The method adopted here of reproducing the letter or paper against which you are writing is of great value to the historian; see 27. 3; Rogers, *Christian Quaker*, 1680.

235   36   For John Burnyeat see vol. ii. p. 418.

239   37   Pastor D. Mulder writes from Werwoud, the "Long town called the Streik" (p. 240): "Old people of my village here tell me that going with the trekschuit from Alkmaar to Hoorn two changes were necessary —one at Rustenburg and one at Avenhorn." It seems probable therefore that the place-name Avenhorn may be substituted for the "———" on p. 239, where also there is evidence of a change of boat.

265   22   For Nathaniel Cripps see vol. i. p. 144.

INDEX

Figures in black type indicate main entries.
Figures within brackets represent anonymous references.

Aberdeen, 319, 351, 362, 371, 378
Abraham, Emma C., 280
Abraham, Rachel, 353
Abrahams, Galenus, 251, 253, **368**
Absom, *see* Topsham
Adderbury, 268
Adderstone, *see* Atherstone
Adingworth, *see* Arthingworth
Aikton, 282
Airey, John, 353
Albemarle, Duke of, 341
Aldam, Ann, 355
Aldam, Thomas, Senr., x, 11, 12, **278**
Aldam, Thomas, Junr., 228, [278], 339, **355**
Aldersgate Street, *see* Watts, George
Aldingham, 19, 283
Alexandretta, 297
Alexandria, 297
Algiers, 335
Alkmaar, 238, 239, 365, 382
Allen, Thomas, 231, **357**
Almond (Amon), Richard, 208, **349**
Amersham, 261, 269
Amphlert, Mary, 377
Ampthill, 232
Amsterdam, 238, 239, 245, 247–252, 254, 308, 312, 322, 333, 338, 364, 367
Anabaptists, 69, 329
Ancrum, Earl of, 201, 297, **348**
Anderigo, 248
André, Burgomaster, 366
Andries, Cornelis, 247, 367
Ansley, Samuel, priest, 318
Antrobus, Benjamin, 91–103, 105–108, 110–114, 116–130, 133–147, 150–160, 163–165, 167–179, 185, 188–196, **197**, 198–200, 202, 205, 209–213, 217–219, 221, 222, 258, 260, 269–272, 303, **306**, 337, 343, 350, 353, 359, 375
Antrobus, Elizabeth, 307
Antrobus, Joseph, 307
Antrobus, Mary, [173, 197 (and sister)], 219, **307**, 337, 350
Apen, 242
Appingedam, 241
Apprentices, 191, 341, **347**
Aprons, *see* Dress
Archdale, John, 76, 262, **294**
Armscott, 268
Arrow, 378

Arthingworth (Adingworth), 231, 358
Ashfield, Patience, 165, 337, **340**
Ashfield, Richard, 340
Ashford, Essex, 328
Astrop, 268, 379
Athenian Mercury, 310
Atherstone (Adderstone), xi, 13, 356, 357
Attorney General, *see* Sawyer, Sir Robert
Audland, Ann, 353
Audland, John, 286, 328
Austill, Bridget, 105, 106, 111, 116, 125, 132, 141, 150, 161, 162, 170, 179, 187, **194**, **200**, **201**, 207, 213, 215, 216, 219, 220, **324**, 337, 349
Austill, William, 262, **373**
Avenhorn, 382
Aylesbury, 324, 379
Ayre, Hester, 336
Ayre, John, 336
Ayres, Ann, 328
Ayres, George, 118, **328**
Ayres, Mary, 328

Baddesley Ensor, 230, 357
Bagworth, 12, 278
Baker, Elizabeth, 337
Baker, Hannah, 304, **345**
Baker Street, 337
Baker, William, 180, 304, **345**
Bala, 311
Balby, 228, 291, 355
Baldock, 345
Ball, Nathaniel, 268, 379
Ball (Baal), Richard, 230, 357
Ballifield, 228, 355
Banbury, 268, 379
Baptists, 31, 32, 55, 62, 65, 239, 243, 245, 248, 285, 312, 331, 364, 377
Barbados, 135, 140, 187, 298, 305, 318, 325, 332, **335**, 337, 346, **347**, 381
Barclay, David, 259, 261, 262, **371**
Barclay, Robert, xviii, xix, 106, 107, 111, 141–143, 174, 176, 181, 234, 235, 237, 238, 255, 295, **319**, 360, 363, 368, 370, 378
Bardfield, 370
Barker, Thomas, 97, 310, **313**
Barking, 181, 182, 185
Barnardiston, Frances, 363
Barnardiston, Giles, 237, 257, 345, 359, **362**
Barnet, 232, 270, **380**

Barr, Ann, 307
Barr, George, 92, 97, 110, 130, 136, 140, 141, 162, 179, 186, 215, 216, **307**
Barret, Thomas, [49], **289**
Barrow, Robert, 352, 353
Barrowe, Richard, mayor, 289
Bartholomew, Joan, 344
Bartholomew, Thomas, 344
Bartlett, Benjamin, 327
Bateman, Phebe, 343
Bates, Humphrey, 323
Batho, Jane, 375
Batho, John, 264, **375**
Bathurst, Anne, 309, 310, [318], **319**
Bathurst, Benjamin, 310
Bathurst, Charles, 93, 111, 118, 119, 182, 308–**310**, 313, 318, [319], 328, 337
Bathurst, Edward, 97, 118, 121, 129, 143, 151, 172, 178, 305, 309, 310, **313**
Bathurst, Elizabeth, 105, 118, 310, **318**, 346
Bathurst, Frances, 310, 318
Bathurst, Grace, [118], **310**, [319], 337, 344
Bathurst, Mary, 313
Batt, Jasper, 175, 176, 209, **342**, 353, 359
Battle-Door, The, 69, **292**
Bayly, William, 313, 381
Bealing, Benjamin, xxiv, 350
Beaumont, Viscount, [63], 277, **292**
Beaumorris (Blew Morrice), 51
Beckerings Park, **290**, 380
Beckwith, Elizabeth, 354, 355
Beckwith, Marmaduke, 227, **354**
Beckwith, Sarah, 354
Bedale, 227
Bedford, 358
Bedford Institute, 303
Bedford, Peter, 361
Bedfordshire, 40, 54, 65, 231, 356
Beech, James, Senr. and Junr., 77, 107, 111, **124**, 156, 166, 190, 191, 193, 208, 219, **295**
Beech, Widow, 156, 295
Beech, William, 115, 124, 166, **326**
Beemster, 239
Belch, Ann, 380
Belch, George, 269, **380**
Belch, Susanna, 380
Belch, Thomas, 380
Belhouse, John, 104, 317
Bellers, Fettiplace, 316
Bellers, Frances, 316
Bellers, John, 285, **316**, 336, 373, 374
Bellers, Mary, 336
Bellers, Theophila, 316
Belvoir, Vale of, 230
Bence, Martin, 80, 299
Bence, Philip, 80, 299
Benester, Elizabeth, 80
Benett, Ambrose, 373

Bennett, Elizabeth, 162, 180, 185, 186, 318, **340**
Bennett, Gervase, justice, 5, 71, **276**
Bennett, Mary, 318
Bennett, Philip, priest, [22, 23], 281, **282**
Bennett, Thomas, 105, 106, 149, 161, 180, 185, 186, 214, 215, **318**, 340
Bennitt, William, 257, **369**
Benson, Dorothy, [33], **285**
Benson, Gervase, 17, 18, 33, 225, **279**
Benthall, Ann, 332
Benthall, John, 332
Benthall, Mercy, xvi, 131, 318, **332**
Benthall, Walter, xvi, 131, 153, 310, 318, **332**
Bentham, 354
Berket, *see* Birkett
Berkshire, 76, 353, 373
Bermondsey, 337, 348
Berry Street, *see* Bury Street
Berwick, 53
Bethnal Green, 101, 102, 110, 316, 332; *see* Stott, Mary
Bevan, Elizabeth, 339
Bevan, Silvanus, 339
Beverley, 6
Bibles in use, 55, 63, 64, 290, **292**; *see* Scriptures, The
Bill of Indulgence, *see* Toleration Act
Bingley, William, 116, 176, 308, **327**, 353
Birkett, Eleanor, widow, 115, 118, 127, 193, **316**, 320, 326
Birkett, Mary, 156, 316, 338
Birkett, William, 103, 316
Birkhead, Sergeant, 260, **372**
Bishop, Elizabeth, 311
Bishop, George, 311
Bishopric (Durham), 34, 68, 227, 295
Bishopsdale, 227
Black Eagle, ship, 312
Blackhead, Thomas, 80
Blackley, James, alderman, [40], **287**
Bland, Elizabeth, 160, 163, 173, 308, **317**
Bland, Nathaniel, 104, 105, 111, 113, 114, 122, 124, 128, 133, 144, 154, 165, 170, 308, **317**
Blasphemy, *see under* Fox, George
Blatt, of Reigate, 75, 293
Blatt, John, 293
Blatt, Thomas, 293
Blaykling, John, 136, 157, 160, 225, 226, 334, **339**, 353, 359
Bletso, John, 297
Bletso, Sarah, 297
Blew Morrice, *see* Beaumorris
Boehme, Jacob, 277, 325
Bohemia, 365
Bolton, Lancs, 325
Bolton, Job, 237, 258, 358, **363**
Bolton, John, 258, **370**
Bolton-le-Sands, 283

Bonsall, 343
Books of Ministering Friends, **301**, 304, 326
Booth, Sir George, 291
Booth, Mary, 313
Bootle, 27, 284
Boreman, Mary, 351, 371
Bormerhaven (? Bremerhaven), 245
Borrat, 279
Borrowby, 227, 354
Boseth, *see* Market Bosworth
Boulton, Samuel, 80, 88, 92–96, 99, 105, **108**, 109, **113**, 120, 129, 167, 237, 259, 269, 270, **299**, 310, 321, 341, 375, 380
Bourne, Dr Edward, 145–147, 159, 176, 178, 179, 183, 266, 267, 300, 328, **336**, 338, 353
Bousfield, Miles, major, 17, **279**
Bow, 119, 300
Bow Lane, *see* Ford, Philip
Boweter, John, 181, 324, 328, 353, **381**
Bowles, Thomas, 112, 325
Bowman, Elizabeth, 335
Bowman, Mary, 328
Bowron, John, 108, 176, **321**
Boys, Priest, [14], 278
Bracey, *see* Brassey
Bradden, Captain, [45], **287**
Bradford, Elizabeth, 321
Bradford, William, 321
Bradshaw, Benoni, 231, **358**
Bradshaw, Elizabeth, 358
Bradshaw, M., 375
Braintree, 257
Brassey, Elizabeth, 137, 142–144, 146, 151, 152, 154–156, 159, 160, 163, 165, 167, 168, 170, 172–178, **308**, 337
Brassey (Bracey), Nathaniel, 92, 95, 98, 99, 104, 110, 114, 116, 117, 119, 122, 123, 125, 126, 128, 130, 134–136, **308**
Brassey, Nathaniel, Junr., 308
Brecknock, 50
Bremen, 242, 246
Bremerhaven?, 245
Briarly (Brearly), James, 231, **358**
Briarly, Thomasin, 358
Bridewell, Bristol, 374, 375
Brielle, The, 237, 254, 369
Brigflatts, 226, 279
Briggins, Joseph, 342
Briggins, Mariabella, 326
Briggins, Peter, 326
Briggins, William, 171, **342**
Briggs, Thomas, [65, 66], 292
Brigham, 285
Brighouse, 278, 286
Bringhurst, John, 136, **334**
Bristol, 47–49, 61, 62, 67, 141, **263–265**, 291, 310, 318, 327, 328, 335, 338, 345, 352, 360, 374–376
Brittain, Edward, 283
Broadbank, Elizabeth, 314

Brock, James, 334
Bromly, Richard, 267, 379
Bromsgrove, 381
Brookes, Edward, 336
Brooks, Edward, 115, 166, **326**
Brooks, Martha, 326
Broom House, 124
Brown, Benjamin, 217, **352**
Brown, James, 293
Brown, John (Bucks), 268, **380**
Brown, John, Informer, 317
Brown, John (London), 341
Brown, Ruth, 300
Browne, Edith, 356
Browne, Dr Samuel, 230, 300, **356**
Browne, Sarah, 356
Brownists, 239
Brush, Edward, 152, 176, 211, 324, **338**
Brush, Isaac, 338
Brush, Sarah, 338
Buckinghamshire, 40, 76, 231, 261, 268, 352, 372, 373, 379
Budd, Thomas, 93, 112, 137, 308, **334**
Bugg, Francis, xxvii, 292, 319, 338, 363, 370
Buiksloot, 239
Bull, John, 89, 305
Bull and Mouth, 77, 83, 84, 87–89, 93, 96, 98, 102, 117, 136, 138, 143, 152, 153, 155, 163, 174, 209, 211, 233, 234, 271, 272, **296**, 302, 304, 319, 324, 329, 350
Bullock, Jane, xv, 89, 91, **305**, 361
Bullock, Jeffery, 382
Bunhill Fields, xxvii, [222], 328, **353**
Bunting, William, 256, **369**
Buntingfield, 369
Buntingford, 324
Bunyan, John, 358
Burgis, Samuel, 373
Burleigh, John, 352
Burnyeat, John, 235, 272, 359, **382**
Burr, Thomas, 179, 214, 216, 332, **345**, 359, 363
Burrell, Mary, 307
Burrough, Edward, 275, 344
Burton on Ure, 227, 354
Bury Street, *see* Barr, George
Bushel, Thomas, [8], 276
Butcher, John, 183, 184, 206, 328, **346**
Butterfield, Abraham, 330
Butterfield, Prince, 330
Butterfield, Rebekah, 330
Buxtehude, 243
Byberry, Pa., 361
Bylling, Edward, 93–95, 97, 102, 103, 105, 112, **308**

Cader Idris, 289
Calendar (Old Style), 296
Calne, 263, 374
Calvinism, 53, 54, 240
Cambridge, 287

Cambridgeshire, 40, 64, 311, 363
Camelford, Gabriel, priest, 280
Camfield. Ann, 338
Camfield, Elizabeth, [180], **304**, 337
Camfield, Francis, 87, 91, 94, 97, 102, 104, 105, 107, 114, 122, 128, 131, 132, 136–138, 147, 157, 158, 163, 164, 169, 175, 176, **180**, 189, 192, 214, 216, 221, 234, 260, 272, 302, **304**, 307, 338, 345, 353
Camfield, Hannah, [180], 304, 345
Camfield, Jacob, 157, [176], 304, **338**
Camfield, Patience, 304
Camm, Ann, 353
Camm, John, 328
Camm, Mary, 353
Camm, Thomas, 225, **280**, **353**, 375
Cammsgill, 225, [329]
Carbery, Lord, 191, **347**
Cardigan (Kardiken), 49
Carlisle, 31, **285**, 370
Carlisle, Earl of, 285
Carlyle, Thomas, xxv
Carmarthen, 289
Carnarvon, 50
Carner, Edward, priest, [49], 289
Carolinas, 294
Carriers, 317
Cart, Joshua, 266, 377
Cartmel, 20, 22, 280, 281, 315
Casimer, John, 114, **325**
Castle, Thomas, 290
Cater, Samuel, 363
Caton, Lancs, 282, 343
Caton, William, 364
Caversham, 262, 373
Ceele, Frances, 319
Ceely, Peter, major, 42, 45, **287**
Chaire, Mary, 327
Chaire, Richard, 116, 149, 150, 161, 178, 319, **327**
Chalfont, 261, 294, 372, 373, 380
Chamber, The, Lombard Street, xv, xvi, 80, **88**, 103, **109**, 298, **300**, 330, etc.
Chamber, The, Westminster, 190, 191, 193, 194, **301**, **347**, 352
Chandler, Rebecca, 294
Chandless, Elizabeth, 378
Charing Cross, *see* Dove, Francis; Penn, William (residences)
Chariots, *see* Coaches
Charlcott, 263
Charles II, xxi, 56–59, 61, 64–66, 70, 262, 285, 299, 304, 317, 331, 338, 370, 373, 375, 376 ; *see* "Pardon"
Charles, Thomas, 231, **358**
Charter (Chater), John, 80
Chase Side, 105
Chatteris, 64, 292
Chelmsford, 257, 363
Chelsea, 124, 331
Cheltenham, 266, 311
Chesham (Chessum), 214, 269

Cheshire, 51, 353
Cheshunt, 369
Chester, 343
Chesterfield, 3
Chew Magna, 310, 335
Child, Ann, [257], 369
Child, John, 257, **369**
Chippenham, 263, 334, 374, 375
Chipping Barnet, *see* Barnet
Chiswick, xv, 197, 208, 320, 330, 333 ; *see* Travers, Anne
Cholesbury, 269, 380
Chorley, Thomas, 293
Chorley Wood, 76, 269, 294, 380
"Church," 3, 18, 29
Church, Theophila, 316
Church, Thomas, 316
Churches, Speaking in, x, xi, 1, 3, 4, 6–10, 12, 14, **27**, **28**, **34**, **56**, **284**, 287, 382
Cinder Hill Green (Sinderley), 35, **286**
Cipher, *see* Shorthand
Cirencester, 265, 315, 376
"City" Meeting, 296, 330
Cladswell, 267, 378
Clare, 362
Clark, Benjamin, 80, **300**, 321
Clark, —, of Oxon, 86
Claus, Jacob, 309
Claus, Jan, 150, 238, 239, 241, 243–245, 247–249, 251, 252, **338**, 361, 366
Claus, Jan, wife of, 241, 338, **366**
Claverham (Clarum), 264
Clawson, 230
Claypoole, Helena, 296, 361
Claypoole, James, **78**, 233, 234, 258, 260, 271, **296**, 337, 359, 360, 361
Claypoole, John, 296
Claypoole, John, Junr., 296
Clements, Simon, 264, 376
Cloddiau Cochion, 323
Closterseven, 242
Coaches, xvi, 87, 106, 197, 295, **305**, 337
Coale, Benjamin, 352, 373
Coale, Christabel, 336
Coale, Christabel, Junr., 336
Coale, George, 146, **336**, 376
Coale, Hezekiah, 265, 376
Coale, Josiah, 336
Coale, Robert, 336
Cockermouth, 29, 33
Coddington, William, 333
Codrington, Sir William (Christopher), 135, **333**
Coffee-house, 218, 301, **352**
Coins, 68, **292**, 342
Colchester, 236, 255, 256, 309, 315, 359, 362–364, 369
Colchester Post-mistress, 255, 369
Cole, Margaret, 309
Coleman, Nathaniel, 160, **340**
Collegians, 239, 240, 248, 364, **365**
Collingwood, Esther, Informer, 317
Collingwood, Richard, priest, 283

Collinson, Mary, 324
Collinson, Peter, 324
Collit, Elizabeth, 337
Collit, John, 123, 135, 330
Coln St Alwyns, 315, 336
Colne, 256
Colt, Dutton, M.P., 190
Comfort, Ann, 307
Committee of Safety, 55, **290**
Compton, Sir Henry, 283
Concord, ship, 296
Constable, Elizabeth, 318, 340
"Contempts," 339, 359
Conway, Viscount, 267, **378**
Conway, Viscountess, xxviii, 267, 360, 365, **377**
Cook, Joan, 200, 346, **348**
Cook, Richard, 202, 213, 348, **349**
Cooke, Henry, 228, **355**
Cooke, Katherine, 356
Cooper, Edward, 330
Cooper, John, 330
Cooper, Nicholas, 122, **330**
Cooper, Thomas, 308
Corbett, Counsellor, 234, 258, 323, **360**
Cornwall, 42, 48, 67, 152, **287**, 303
Cottesford, Susanna, 362
Counterside, 226, 354
Coventry, 41, 86
Cowper, Ann, 358
Cowper, Edward, 231, **358**
Cowper, Spencer, **344**, 345
Cox, Ann, 179, [194], 214, 221, [311], 337, **344**
Cox, Christian, 311
Cox, John, Separatist, 327, 345
Cox, Thomas, Senr., 311
Cox, Thomas, 96, 100, 110, 119, 125, 129, 137, 148, 154, 157, 159, 160, 164, 167, 170, 179, 194, **311**, 340
Cox, Thomas, 3rd, 312
Crab, Roger, 372
Cranswick, 277
Crawley, Benjamin, 348
Crawley, Joshua, 348
Crawley, Mary, 325
Crawley, Sarah (Robins), 348
Crawley, Sarah, 325
Crawley, Thomas, 325
Cripps, Nathaniel, 265, **382**
Crisp, Dorothy, 364
Crisp, Gertrude, 364
Crisp, Stephen, 134, 144, 176, 192, 193, 213, 218, 256, 306, 328, **333**, 353, 359, 364, 366, 367, 370
Cromwell, Elizabeth, 296
Cromwell, Oliver, 38, 43, 48, 54–56, 66, 71, 288, 290, 296, 331, 344, 370, 381
Cromwell, Richard, 55, 56
Crook, John, 148, 149, 180, 269, **290**, 380
Crosslands, 286
Crossmoor, 370
Crouch, Ruth, 300, 337, 344

Crouch, William, 80, 91, 102, 109, 113, 126, 134–137, 142, 144, 151, 175, **299**, 302, 308, 310, 341
Crow, William, 257, **370**
Croxton, xxii
Croydon, 339
"Crusoe, Robinson," 360
Cumberland, 27, 51, 68, 70
Cupid Stairs, 118, 320
Curses, The Priests', 53
Curtis, Thomas, 262, **373**
Curwen, Alice, 313

Dalston (Dolston), 83, 89, 95, 305
Dalton-in-Furness, 20
Danzig, 80, 194, 252, 253, 311, 348, 350, 367
Darlington, 354
Davenport, Thomas, [52], **290**, 293, 372
Daventry (Dentry), 41, 287
Davies, Milbrow, 337
Davies, Richard, 111, **323**, 359, 370
Davies, Tace, 323
Davies, Tace, Junr., 323
Dawes, Ellen M., xxiii
De Witt, Jan and Cornelis, 253, **368**
Death Sentence, 310
Deinum (Dinum), 240
Delft, 238, 253
Delfzijl, 241, 247
Delmenhorst, 242
Dendron, [20], **281**
Denmark, King of, 95, 242–244, 246, 253, 254, **366**
Dennison, Thomas, 327
Densbury, *see* Desborough
Dentry, *see* Daventry
Derby, 4, 5, 65, 305, 343
Derbyshire, xxix, 3, 4, 14, 36, 229, 230, 276, 296, 343
Desborough (Densbury), John, maj.-gen., 43, 46, **288**
Detern, 242
Devizes, 263
Devonshire, 67, 303, 373
Devonshire Buildings, 117, 321
Devonshire House, 75, 82, 88, 90, 99, 100, 103, 122, 127, 152, 154, 156, 160, 165, 174, 189, 191, 202, 211, 213, 217, 219, 221, 233, 258, **293**, 300, **304**, 319, 335, 350, 351
Dew, John, 107, 115, 139, 152, 153, 163, 312, **319**, 359
Dew, John, Junr., 319
Dew, Susanna, **319**, 337, 344
Dewsbury, Hannah, 358
Dewsbury, William, 139, 231, 232, 267, 317, **335**
Dickinson, Robert, 281
Dingley, 231, 357
Dinum, *see* Deinum
Diricks, Annekin, 364
Diricks, Gertrude, 238, 249–254, 256, 322, **364**, 367

Diricks, Niesy, 364
Docemius, the Resident, [254], **368**
Dockray, Thomas, 216, 272, 273, **352**, 353
Doctors, 80, 129, 135, 154, 197, 230, 248, **300**, 315, 332, 348, 374
Docwra, Ann, 363
Dokkum, 240, 247
Dolgelly, [50], 289, 311
Dolobran, 323
Doncaster, 10, 228, 276, 278, 355
Don-Rijp, *see* Dronrijp
Doomsdale, 45, **288**
Dorsetshire, 42, 67
Dove, Francis, 166, 192, 194, 199, 202, 209, 219, **341**, 362
Dove, Mary, 362
Dover, Widow, printer, 312
Dowes, Sijbrand, 240, 247, 366
Downer, Anne, [295], **337**
Downer, Thomas, priest, 337
D'Oyly, Bray, 261, 267-269, 359, **372**
Drawwell, 225
Drayton, Fenny, 36, 286
Dress, xxvi, 211, 277, 288, 290, 344, **350**, 351, 357
Drink, 16, 17, 312, 349
Drinkwell, Margaret, Senr., 96, 97, 119, 130, 174, 219, 221, **311**, 337, 344
Drinkwell, Margaret, Junr., 95-97, 311
Dronrijp (Don-Rijp), 240
Dry, Elizabeth, widow, 105, 112, 113, 131, 148, 149, 179, **317**
Dry, Martha, 171, 329, **341**
Dry, William, 329, 341
Duchess, The, ship, 360
Duke, The, ship, 360
Dunbar, 52
Duncon, Robert, 237, **363**
Dundee, [52], 290
Durham County, *see* Bishopric
Dyheys, Edward, 107, 142, 321
Dykes, Anne, 315
Dykes, Benjamin, 315, 362
Dykes, Edward, 315
Dykes, Mary, 315, 362

Eager, the apothecary, 88
Eames, Mary, 337
Eashing, 296
Eccles, Solomon, 273, 360, **381**
Eccleston, Anne, 337, 344
Eccleston, Mercy, 318, 332
Eccleston, Priscilla, **318**, 340
Eccleston, Richard, 318, 340
Eccleston, Theodor, 160, 172,173, 207, 304, 310, 328, 334, **340**
Edge, Jane, 335
Edge, John, 138, 139, 304, 310, 333, **335**
Edge, Sarah, 337
Edinburgh, 51, 52, 363, 371
Edmonton, 75, 91, 116, 148, 162, 307, 338

Edridge, Constance, 324
Edridge (Etridge), John, 111, 135, 143, 202, 310, **324**
Edridge, Thomas, 324
Education, *see* Schools
Edwards, Edward, 266, **377**
Edwards, Elizabeth, 334
Edwards, Mary, 377
Eider (Hyder), 243
Eldroth, 354
Eliot family, 326
Elizabeth, Princess, 239, **365**
Elizabeth Town, N. J., 370
Ellemensen, *see* Elmshorn
Ellington, xv, 90, 306, 354
Elliott, John, 231, **357**
Ellis, Josiah, 107, 111, 116, 118, 124, 134, 146, 169, **191**, 199, 203, 209, **320**
Ellis, Mary, 320
Ellis, Roland, 311
Ellis, Sarah, 320
Ellis, Thomas, 320
Ellwood, Mary, 361
Ellwood, Thomas, xix, 76, 261, 294, **295**, 316, 348, 350, 352, 353, 361, 371, 373, 379
Elmer, *see* Ilmire
Elmshorn (Ellemensen), 243
Elson, John, 303, 336, 359
  visited by Fox, 77, 96, 100, 101, 107, 114, 117, 121, 122, 125, 128, 130, 137, 138, 142, 144, 147, 151, 152, 155-158, 167, 169, 175, 189, 193, 198, 209, 213, 217, 232, 236, 258, 260, 270-272, **295**, [297]
  accompanied Fox, 112, 136, 155, 169, 181, 184, 193, 216, **295**, 312
Elson, Mary, [112], 134, 138, [155, 181], 189, 199, [216], **295**, 302, 312, 326, 329, 337, 344
Elton, Edith, 356
Elwood, Anthony, 138, **335**
Ely, Isle of, 64, 286, 292, 305
Embden, 241, 242, 247, 252, 333, 361, 365, **366**
Embs, river, 241
Emerson, Timothy, 166, **341**
Emigration, xv, 296, 311, 325, 331, 334-336, 353, 361, 370, 374
Endon, Jacob, 323
Endon, Tace, 323
Enfield, 91, 132, 150, 214, 215, 220, 273, **332**, 337, 346; *see* Dry, Elizabeth; Hart, Thomas; Watts, George
English, Bethia, 331
English, David, 331
English, Nathaniel, 331
Enkhuizen (Encusen), 240
Epping Forest, *see* Bathurst, Charles
Esom, *see* Evesham
Essex, xxx, 65, 155, 305, 328, 346
Etridge, *see* Edridge
Evesham (Esom), 40, 266, 377

Exeter, 47, 48, **289**, 370, 373

"Faculty," 57, 58
Falconar, Anne, 339
Falconar, John, 339
Fancy, *see* Fenchurch
Farmborough, Mariabella, 115, 138, 153, 185, 306, 312, **326**, 337, 346
Farmborough, Mariabella, Junr., 138, 312, **326**
Farmborough, Thomas, 326
Farnham Royal, 372
Farnsfield, 343
Fast Days, 240, 250, 269, 365
Fell, Henry, **xxi**, 288
Fell, Leonard, 108, 178, 179, 226–232, 269, 270, 284, **321**, 353, 358, 359
Fell, Margaret, *see* Fox, Margaret
Fell, Rachel, 225, 226, 350, **353**
Fell, Sarah, 281, 350, 361
Fell, Susanna, 100, 104, 126, 184, 285, **314**
Fell, Thomas, judge, xxi, 26, 27, **283**, 353
Felsted, 257
Fen Country, 65
Fenchurch (Fancy) Street, 155, 295, 326, 336, 350
Fettiplace, Elizabeth, 316
Fettiplace, Frances, 316
Fettiplace (Pettyplace), Giles, 100, 265, 266, **315**, 376
Fettiplace, Col. John, 315
Field, John, Senr., 325
Field, John, **xxiv**, 112, 161, 184, 296, **324**, 328, 334, 353
Field, Margery, 325, 337
Field, Mary, 325
Field, Mary, Junr., 325
Field, Rebekah, 329
Fielder, Ann, 127, 134, 260, 261, 272, 303, **331**
Fielder, John, 295, 303, **331**
Fielder, Mary, 303
Fifth-Monarchy Plot, 59, **291**, 329
Finch, Anne, 378
Finch, Sir Heneage, 378
Finchcombe (? Stiuchcombe), 265, 376
Firbank, 18, 279
Fire-brief, 331, **373**
"Firk," 44
Fischerhude, 242
Fisher, Elizabeth, 308, 317
Fisher, Martha, 93, 95, 96, 98, 101, 103, 107, 109, 111, 115, 116, 118, 123, 124, 127, 130, 133–135, 139, 141, 146, 153, 156, 159, **163**, 167, 169, **173**, 233, 234, 258, 260, 270, 297, **308**, 317, 319, 329
Fleet Prison, 296, 320, 328, 359, 381
Fleetwood, Amy, 337
Fleming, Daniel, justice, 68, 69, **292**
Flierden, of Lynn, 309
ffloyd, *see* Lloyd

Foeldricks, Claes Jhon, 241, [338], **366**
Forbes, Barbara, 362
Ford, Ann, 320
Ford, Bridget, 320, **321**, 337, 344, 360
Ford, Bridget, Junr., 320
Ford Green, *see* Mann, Edward
Ford, Philip, 107, 115, 117, 124, 139, 141, 142, 146, 155, 158, **320**, 360
Ford, Philip, Junr., 320, 321
Forster, Elizabeth, 334
Forster, Mary, 81, 103, 111, 114, 128, 130, 136, 141–143, 145, 151, 156, 159, 160, 164, **165**, **301**, 302, 337
Forster, Mary, Junr., 324
Forster, Thomas, 301, 324, 334
Forster, William, 280
Forster, William Edward, xxviii
Foster, Sir Robert, [58], **291**
Fowler, Robert, 337
Fox, Elizabeth, 356
Fox, George
  among the records, 177, 344
  attends business-meetings, xiv, xv, 298, 300, **350**, **371**
  autographs, ix, xxi, xxii, 275, 292, 314, 369
  "blasphemy," xi, xii, 4, 17, 27, 32, **279**, 283, 286
  busy days, **xv**, 80, **298**, 345, **350**
  care for sufferers, xv, 298, 371; *see* Guildhall; Hicks Hall
  changed attitude, xiv, **xxv**; towards doctors, 300; towards lawyers, 315; towards social life, 238, 241, 349
  death and burial, xxvii, 353
  declining health, xvi, xvii, 93, 94, 104, **106**, **144**–146, 159, 164, 168, 176–178, 180, 186, 188, 189, 192, 195, 211, 222, 301, 328, **342**, **350**
  entertained by his friends, xviii, xxv, **xxvi**, 87, 295
  escapes from injury or arrest, 8, 11, 15, 23, 53, 68, 83, 87, 303, 315
  false reports, xxvii, 4, 17, 18, 21, 25, 27, 363
  finances, 21, 307
  foresight, xiii, 22, 27, 35, 42, 56, 65, 82, 346
  in Holland and Germany, xxviii, 237–255, 308, 361–369
  imprisonments and sufferings, ix, x, xiii, **xxii**, 2, 4, 33, 44, 57, 59, 63, 71, **303**
  interest in Friends abroad, xv, xvii, 80, 114, 135, 137, 140, 218, 305, 323, 332; *see* New Jersey
  leaves meeting for church, 10, 12, 15, **275**
  letter-writing, **xvii**, 305, 323, 332, 341, 344–348, 353, 367
  meals—dinner, xxvi, 201, 238, 241, 349; supper, xxvi, 110, 238, 307
  nights in the open, 6, 7, 15–17

Fox, George—*continued*
  peace-maker, xv, 104, 124, 172, 180, 295, 317, 345
  personal appearance, xv, xxvi, 32, 84
  portraits, xxv, 293 : *see* Spence, Robert
  prayers, xvii, xxvii, 15, 90, 227, 289, **306**
  rapid recovery from injury, x, 11, 12, 24, 26, 27, **275**
  refusal to bear arms, 5, 65
  relations, xvi, xix, xxv, 4, 13, 17, 36, 38, 275; *see* Fox, Margaret; Meade family; Rous family
  remarkable cures, x, 3, 15, 27, 78, **275**
  secretaries, 381; *see* Haistwell, Edward; Richardson, Richard; Swanner, Mark
  sermons, x, xvii, **xxii**, **xxvi**, 84, **103**, **105**, 131, 212, 250, 271, 306, **346**, 351
  statements regarding himself, 243, 244, 246, **366**, 372
  at Swarthmoor, **280**, 282; *see* Swarthmoor
  testamentary papers, 295, 299, 352
  testimonies, **353**, 382
  travelling by coach, xvi, **305**; *see* Coaches
  travelling by water, 320
  visions, x, 11, 47
  visits to invalids, xiv, xv, xix, 15, 82, 89, 90, 100, 104, 105, 117, 125, 126, 136, 139, 147, 148, 156, 160, 163, 164, 167, 171, 174, 345; *see* vol. ii. p. 342
  visits to prisoners, 83, 91, 103, 104
  visits to schools, xv, 83, 91, 123, 134, 165, 169, 179, 194, 219, 259, 316, 330
  visits in shops, 108, 135, 142, 144, 321, 323
  wedding certificate, 308, 328, 337, 360, 375, 376
  work in London and district, xiv, xv, xxv, xxvii, xxviii, 77–222, 295–353
Fox, George, the younger, 362
Fox, John, governor, [43, 46], **287**
Fox, John, 229, **356**
Fox (Fell), Margaret, [xviii], xxi, [xxv], 97, 98, 100, 102, 104, **105**, 206, 208, 213, 225, 226, 280, 281, 291, 293, 310, 312, **313**, 321, 344, 346, **349**, 353, 359
Fox, Mary, 275
Frandley, 290
Franeker, 240, 248
Franklin, Jacob, [xv], 163, 217
Freame, John, 328
Freatling Parva, 230
Freckleton, Sarah, 167, **299**
Freeleven, Nicholas, jailer, 288
Freeman, Ann-Mary, 337
Freeman, Benjamin, 105, **318**
Freeman, Elizabeth, 381
Freeman, Joseph, 273, **381**
Fretwell, John, [4, 5], 229, **276**

Fretwell, Samuel, 230, 357
Friedrichstadt, 241, 243, 366
Friends
  banishment, 312, **314**, 338, 344, 345, 375
  books dispersed, 218, 275, 293, 355, 369, 381
  burials, 77, 186, 188, **222**, 328, 353, **373**
  care for the poor, **297**, **304**, 309, 317, 319
  carried to Justices, 63, 67, **292**
  disagreements, 172, 272, 295, 317, 321; *see* Separatists
  light within, xi, 19, 20, 29, **31**, 34, 39, 50, 53, 55, 284, 346, **360**
  marriages, xv, 75, 76, 112, **142**, **160**, 167, 199, 209, 219, 294, 297, 299, 312, 328, 331, 335, **354**, 371, 374; *see* re-marriages
  meetinghouses occupied by soldiers, 87, **304**
  meetings attended by notable persons, 156, 177, 201, 237, 243, 250, 252, 255, 266, **297**, 302, 308, 339, 348, 372
  meetings for Church business, **364**, 375
  meetings disturbed, **301**, 302
  offer to take places of others in prison, 54, 72, 285, **290**, 313
  opinions respecting, 3, 283, 285, 286, 296, 342, 360, 362
  prayers, 306
  public life and work, xv, 294, 339, 357
  " Quaker," 5, 70
  re-marriages, *passim* in Notes ; *see* 327
  " retired " and " threshing " meetings, 275
  women preachers, 3, **311**, **346**, 355, 365, 374
  women writers, 313, 319, 322
  women's meetings, 331, 375, 376, **379**
  women's work for the poor, 304
  See " Church"; Churches, Speaking in ; Dress; Emigration; Grace before Meat; Hat Controversy; Hat Honour ; Horse-hire ; Judgements ; London Y.M. ; Nudity; Oaths; Peace and War; Schools; Scriptures, The; Separatists; Silence in Worship; Singing; Soldiers become Friends ; Sunday Work ; Tithes; Vagrancy
Friends' Historical Association, v, xxxi
Friesland, 80, 240, 241, 247, 251, 365, **366**, 367
Fry family, 326
Fry, Elizabeth (*aft.* Marchant), 325
Fuckes, Thomas, 266, 377
Fuller, Archbishop, 330
Fullove, Elizabeth, 136, 156, **334**, 337, 342
Fullove, Laurence, 96, 101, 142, 174, **312**, 334

Furly, Abigail, 364, 369
Furly, Ann, Senr., 309, 362
Furly, Ann (Talcot), 369
Furly, Anna (Vandewall), 369
Furly, Benjamin, 93, 237-239, 251-254, 272, **309**, 366
Furly, John (d. 1673), 309
Furly, John, Senr., 236-238, 255, 256, 309, **362**, 363, 369
Furly, John, Junr., 255, 362, 364, **369**
Furly, Stephen, 329
Furly, William, 369
Furness, 281

G[?ouldney], T[homas], 265
Gabell, Richard, 265, 376
Gamble, Henry, 358
Gamble, Thomas, 232, **358**
Gandy, William, [51], 290
Gap, The, 291
Gardick, *see* Gorredijk
Garsdale, 17, 226
Gateshead, **286**, 354
Geffery, Sir Robert, [146], 336
George I, 339, 346
George Yard, 105, 108, 110, 116-118, 126, 129, 132, 133, 137, 144, 151, 153, 168, 271, 300, 306, 307, 313, 315, 325, 332
Germany, xv, xix, 114, 239, 248, 249, 251, 253, 254, 258, 267, 310, 325, 361, 365, **367**, 371
Gewen, Thomas, recorder, 288
Gibbs, Henry, 266, **377**
Gibson, Elizabeth, 370
Gibson, William, 258-260, 262-264, 359, **370**, 381
Gibson, William, Junr., 311, 334, 370
Gill, Henry, 78, **296**
Gilpin, Joan, 344
Gilpin, Thomas, Senr., 343
Gilpin, Thomas, 176, **343**
Glasgow, 52
Gleaston, 20
Glentworth, 277
Gloucestershire, 67, 315, 337, 338, 376, 377
Glynn, Sir John, Chief Justice, [44], **288**
Godalming, 296
Godmanchester, 336
Godowne, Abraham, 98, 130, **314**
Godowne, Benjamin, 314
Godowne, Jane, 314
Goodaire, Thomas, 377
Gooseyes, *see* Meade, William (Gooseyes)
Gordon, Catherine, 371
Gorredijk (Gardick), 248
Gosnell, Bridget, 320, 360
Gosnell, Henry, 321
Gosnell, William, 234, 359, **360**
Gotherby, Elizabeth, 174
Gouldney family, 374
Gouldney, Adam, 334, 374
Gouldney, Adam, Junr., 374

Gouldney, Elizabeth, 334, 337, 344
Gouldney, Henry, 136, 164, 175, 177, 187-189, 192, 198, 199, 203, 207, 211, 217-219, 221, 222, 293, **334**, 350, 353
Gouldney, Jane, 374
Gouldney, Mary, 374
Gouldney, Ruth, 334
Gouldney, Thomas, ?265
Gouldney, Widow, 263, 374
Gower, Sir Thomas, [69], **293**
Grace before Meat, 356
Gracechurch Street
  meetings attended, xxvii, 75, 77, 79, **82**, 83, 88, 89, 114, 128, 136, 140, 159, 160, 164, 168, 170, 175, 188, 217, 218, 221, **222**, 232, 257, 258, 270, **293**, 301, 306, 346, 350
  residential, 283, 293, 300, 307, 335, 340
Gratton, John, xxix, 176, 305, **343**
Gratton, Mary, 343
Grave, John, 285
Grave, William, 293
Gravel Pitts, 111, 124, 166, 324, 326, 331
Grays, 349
Green, Thomas, 353, 381
Green, Widow, 278
Greene, of Liversedge, 279
Greenwell, Anne, 337
Greenwell, Benjamin, 337
Greenwich, 307
Grice, Elizabeth, 174, 337, **342**
Groningen, 240, 247, 365, 367
Groom, Elizabeth, widow, 113, 135, 136, **325**
Groom, Samuel, 308, 325
Guildford, 78, 236, 315
Guildhall, 93, 99, 147, 313, **314**, 341
Gunter, Dorothy, 349
Günther, Count A., 366
Gurney, Edmund, 309
Gustavus Adolphus, 371
Guttershedge, 232, 312
Guy, Justice, xxv, 85, 303
Gwin, Paul, [48], **288**

Haarlem, 238, 250, 364
Hacker, Francis, colonel, 38, 66, **286**
Hacker, Isabel, 286
Hackney, 300, 305, 316
Hages, *see* Hedges
Hague, The, 253
Haig, Anthony, 369
Haig, Mary, 370
Haig, William, 369, 370
Hailes, Widow, 263, 375
Haistwell, Anthony, 327
Haistwell, Edward, xix, xxviii, xxix, 116, 151, 154, 158, 170, 172, 241, 247, [273], **327**, 361, 381
Haistwell, Edward, Junr., 327
Haistwell, Rachel, 327
Haistwell, Thomas, 327
Halford, John, 268, **379**

Halifax, 35
Hall, John, 327
Halstead, 256
Halton, 21, 23, 281
Ham, 118
Hamburg, **243-245**, 252, 253, 333, 367
Hammersmith, 77, 123, 124, 127, 134, 145, 146, 165, 166, 197, 208, 320, 330, 331
Hampshire, 42, 66, 76, 79
Hanbury Family, 317
Hancock, Edward, [42], **287**
Handley, Margaret, 377
Harborough, *see* Market Harborough
Hardcastle, Mary, 343
Harding, Amy, 374
Harding, David, 324
Harding, James, 112, **324**
Harding, John, 155, 173, 180–182, **324**
Harding, John, 374
Harlingen, 240, 247–249, 365, 367
Harold's Wood, 324
Harp Lane, 335
Harpson, Richard, 278
Harris, Charles, 217, 258, 261, 262, 269, 335, 350, **352**, 361, 370, 372
Harris, Joseph, 268, **379**
Harris, Sarah, 357
Hart family, 352
Hart, John, 217, **352**
Hart, Priscilla, xvi, 131, 179, [180], 186, **318**, 337, 340
Hart (Heart), Thomas, 105, 106, 112, 113, 131, 148, 149, 161, 179, 180, 214, 220, 308, **318**, 340, 370
Hartshill, 231, 357
Hartshorn, 230, 357
Hartshorne, Hugh, 308
Harwich, 236, 255, 256, 362, 364, 369
Hasbert, Dr J. W., 366
Hasbert, Magdalena, 366
Haselrig, Sir Arthur, 282
Hat Controversy, 309, 344, 359, 360, 364, **366**; *see also* Perrot, John
Hat Honour, xiii, 44, 49, 70, **288**
Hatt, Martha, 296
Hatton Garden, 100
Haverford College, xxiii
Haverfordwest, 50
Hawes, [17], 226, 279
Hawkins, Richard, 297, 303
Haworth, William, preacher, 351
Hawton, *see* Halton
Hayeland, Elizabeth, 322
Hayes, Robert, 324
Hayley, Ann, 96, 97, 107, 138, 232, 270, **312**
Heart, *see* Hart
Heath, Elizabeth, 352
Hebden, Roger, 342
Hedgerley, 261, 372
Hedges (Hages), William, 258, 315, **370**
Hegaroll, *see* Hunger Hill

Height, 353
Helmont, F. M. van, 267, 365, **378**, **379**
Hemel Hempstead, 269
Hempens Suameer, Lake, 248
Hendon, *see* Hayley, Ann
Hendricks, Elizabeth, 311, **322**
Hendricks, Peter, 108, 194, 250, 254, **322**, 348, 364
Henley, 76, 262, 373
Herbert of Cherbury, Lord, 323
Hereford, 67, 68
Herefordshire, 320
Herford, 365
Hertford, xxv, xxix, 179, 216, 337, 344, 345, 351
Hertfordshire, 40, 65, 310, 331, 336, 351, 369
Heywood, John, 308
Heywood, Oliver, 278, 372
Hicks, Sir Baptist, 307
Hicks Hall, 92, 94, 99, 102, 122, 128, 137–139, 147, 157, 304, **307**, 314
Hide, Matthew, 333
High Cross, Leics., 231
Highcleare, 333
Highgate, 232, 270, 295
Hightown, 14, 278
Hiley, Joan, 263–265, **375**
Hill, John, 245, 247, **367**
Hill, Martha, 326
Hilton, George, Informer, 317
Hilton, Capt. John, Informer, 317
Hind, Anne, 344
Hindelopen, 240
Hinkley, 230
Hirons (Hiorne), Mary, 268, 379
Hirons, Thomas, 379
Hitchcock, Bridget, 374
Hitchcock, William, 263, **374**
Hobart, *see* Hubbard
Hoddesdon, 185
Hodge, Henry, 270, 380
Hodges, Samuel, 270, **380**
Hodgson, Dr, 293
Hogenhorn (? Hohenhorne), 243
Holden, Francis, 197, 341, **348**
Holden, Francis, printer, 348
Holden, Mary, 348
Holderness, 6, **7**
Holker Hall, 69, 292
Holland, xv, xix, xxviii, 80, 91, 110, 150, 194, 236–255, 298, 305, **308**, 309, 311, 312, 322, 323, 325, 329, 333, 338, 348, 358, **361**, 363–369
Holland House, 315
Holland, a Judge of, 253, 368
Holme, Elizabeth, 289
Holme, Thomas, [50], **289**, 370
Holstein, Duke of, 95, 244, **311**, 322, 366
Honeywood, —, 190, 347
Hookes, Ellis, 233, 234, 257–260, 270–272, 316, 329, 337, **359**, 360, 381, 382

Hoorn, 239, 382
Hooton (Hutton), Elizabeth, 3, **275**
Hope, of Amsterdam, 309
Hope, Henry, 93, **309**
Hopegood, John, 297
Hopkins, John, 215, **351**
Hornchurch, 317
Horse-hire, 372
Horsham, 75, 293, 359
Horslydown, 75, 79, 88, 121, 122, 163, 234, 271, 272, **294**, 316, 319, 320, 323, 329
Hotham family, 277
Hotham, Durand, justice, [8], 277
Houndsditch, 104, 300, 307, 370
How, Edmond, 232, **358**
Howard family, 326
Howard, Luke, 353
Howgill, Francis, 275, 317, 344
Howkins, Thomas, 300
Hoyland family, 331
Hubbard, Grace, 310
Hubbard, Stephen, 168, **341**, 348
Hubbersty, Stephen, 353
Hubberthorne, Richard, [39, 57], 284, 286, 291, 381
Huddlestone, John, 380
Hull, 277
Hull, —, 135, 333
Hull, John, 381
Hull, Martha, 102, **316**, 337
Hume, Sophia, 351
Hunger Hill (Hegaroll), 75, 261, 294, 299, 372, 380
Husband Bosworth, 231
Hutchinson, George, 93, 308
Hutson, Anna, 313, 344
Hutson, John, 97, **313**
Hutton, *see* Hooton
Hutton, Thomas, [26], **282**, 283
Hyder, *see* Eider

Ilmire (Elmer), 76, 268, 379
Independents, 62, 65, 69, 285
Indians, American, 381
Infant mortality, 277, 303
Informers, 86, 88, 91, 103, 144, 145, 235, 303, **316**, 335, 341
Ingram, Christabel, 336
Ingram, Frances, 336
Ingram, Hester, 336
Ingram, Isaac, 336
Ingram, Joseph, 336
Ingram, Mary, 336
Ingram, Robert, 336
Ingram, Susanna (Fell), **314**, 344
Ingram, Susanna (Robins), **336**, 337
Ingram, William, 146, 310, **336**, 337
Inkberrow, 378
Innkeepers, xv, 147, 163, 311, 330, **340**, 349
Inns, xv, 96, 104, 118, 123, 129, 135, 137, 147, 163, 185, 202, 213, 270, **276**, 286, 289, 307, 311, **317**, 330, **340**, 377, 380

Insanity, xv, 2, 90, 171, 275, 349, 363
Ipswich, 312, 369
Ireland, 54, 80, 222, 227, 296, 325, 330, 350–**353**, 381
Itzehoe, 243

Jackson, Henry, Senr., 356
Jackson, Henry, Junr., 228, 229, **356**, 359
Jackson, Henry, 3rd, 356
Jackson, Katherine, [228], 356
Jacobs, Hesell, 240, 248, 249, 365
Jamaica, 52, 112, 260, **290**, 298, 312, 324, 336, 338, 345
James I, 365
James II, xviii, 101, 102, 107, 108, 140, 177, 197, 304, 336, 342; *see* "Pardon"
Jaques, John, priest, 27, **283**
Jefferson, Isabella, 328
Jefferson, William, 328
Jeffreys, George, Lord Chief Justice, [115], 311, **326**
Jenner, Sir Thomas, 313
Jennings, Christabel, 336
Jennings, William, 336
Jermyn, Emily, xxiii, xxxi
Jerseys, *see* New Jersey
Jews, 244, 250, 254, 293, 350
John III, 332
John, John ap, [49–51], **289**
Johnson, Simon, 237, 254, 363
Johnston, Elizabeth, 362
Johnston, Dr William, 362
Johnstons, *see* Perth
Jones, Charles, Senr., 264, 374, **376**
Jones, Charles, Junr., 264, 376
Jones, David, 297
Jones, Rachel, 327
Jones, Rice, 367
Jones, Robert, 269, 353, **380**
Jordan, Lydia, 375
Jordan, Thomas, 263–265, **375**
Jordans, 76, 261, **294**, 323, 330, 373
Judgements on Persecutors, xiii, 36, 54, 61, 80, 81, 244, 251, 286, 292, 298, 375
Justices of the Peace, **357**, 371

Kardiken, *see* Cardigan
Katenborough, 22, [282]
Keate, John, captain, [43, 44, 46], **287**
Keby, 246
Keith, Elizabeth, [237–239, 255, 309], 361, **362**
Keith, George, xix, 235, 237–239, 251, 252, 254–256, 261, 262, 267, 335, **361**, 378, 379
Kellet, 227
Kelsall, John, xxxii, 326
Kemp, William, 124, **331**
Kemp, William, Junr., 331
Kempston Hardwick, 232, 358
Kendal, xii, 19, 21, 226, **280**, 290
Kendall, John, mayor, xxii
Kensington, 111, 315, 324, 326, 378

Kensworth, 232
Kent, 39, 65
Kent, Anne, 309, 319
Kent, Edward, 309
Kent, Margaret, 309
Kent, William, 93, 213, **309**, 319
Ker, Charles (Lord Ancrum), 348
Kerton, *see* Kirton
Kett, of Norfolk, 309
Killam, John, 228, 291, **355**
Killam, Thomas, 228, **356**
Killingbeck, Humphrey, 75, **293**
Kingston, xxv, **301**, 348, 349; *see* Fielder, Ann; Fielder, John; Rous family
  meetings attended, 77, 78, 87, 100, 126, 168, 196, 208, 260, 261, 272, **301**, 348, **349**
Kirkby, Col. Richard, 69, 234, **292, 360**
Kirton, Damaris, [166], 331, 379
Kirton, John, 124, 166, 326, **331**, 379
Kirton, Richard, 115, 124, **326**, 331
Kirton, Sarah, 326
Kirton, William, 326, 331
Klasen, Dirk, 238, 251, 364
Knaper, *see* Napier
Knapton, Christopher, 352
Knight, Mary, 374
Knight Stainforth, 342
Knight, Thomasin, 358
Knighton, 230, 356
Knottingley (Nottingley), 228, 355

Lad Lane, 104, 317
Lambert, John, general, 55, **291**
Lambeth, 316, 320
Lamboll, George, 262, **373**
Lambourn Woodlands, 262
Lamcote, 267, 379
Lampitt, Widow, 282
Lampitt, William, priest, [19], 23, 25, 281, **282**
Lancashire, 22, 51, 56, 58, 68, 227, 317, 353
Lancashire Priests, 283
Lancaster, x, xi, xiii, 21, 26, 27, 57, 72, 283
Lancaster Castle, 57, 71, 281, **293**
Lancaster, James, 25, 26, **282**
Lancaster, Margaret, [25], 282
Landsmeer-in-Water-land, 249
Lane, —, constable, 88
Langhorne, Dorothy, 337, **349**
Langhorne, Robert, Senr., 349
Laughorne, Robert, 205, **349**
Langley, Robert, 265, **376**
Langstrothdale, 226
Larkham, George, priest, [29], **285**
Latey, Gilbert, 87, 122, 130, 133, 135, 143, 144, 153, 156, 202, 260, 272, 284, 302, **303**, 331, 339
Latey, Mary, 303, 337
Launceston, 44, 287, 288
Lawrence, John, 372

Lawrey, *see* Lowrey
Lawrie, Gawen, 257, **369**
Lawrie, Mary, 370
Lawrie, Obed, 369
Lawson, Sir John, 328
Lawson, Lady, 119, 181, **328**
Lawson, Thomas, 281
Leaper, Elizabeth, 355
Leaper, Esther, 282
Leaper, Margaret, 282
Leaper, Thomas, [22], **282**
Leavens, Priest, 8, 276, 277
Ledgerd, Thomas, alderman, 34, **285**
Lee, John, 296
Leer, 241, 246
Leeuwarden, 240, 247–249, 366, 367
Leeward Islands, 298
Leicester, 3, 63, 230, 356, 357
Leicesterfields, 166
Leicestershire, 3, 12, 13, 15, 36, 40, 63, 151, **152, 153**, 229, 231, 278, 291, 357
Leiden, 238, 253, 322, 364
Leith, 52, 359
Lely, Sir Peter, xxv
Lembachie, 242
Leominster, [55], 290
Lettson, Dr J. C., 327
Lewenbrog, *see* Lüneburg
Lilley, Ruth, 168, 208, **236, 341**
Lilley, William, 236, 341, 361
Lincoln, 346, 356
Lincolnshire, 36, 305, 351
Lindale, 20, 281
Lindley, Benjamin, 117, **327**
Lindley, Isaac, 228, 327, **355**
Lindley, Mary, 355
Line, John, constable, 80; **298**
Line, John; wife of, 298
Linton, Joan, 354
Linton, Robert, 227, 233, **354**
Littendale, 226
Liversedge, 278, 279
Livingstone, Patrick, 331
Llanfair, 323
Lloyd family, 326
Lloyd (ffloyd), Charles, Junr., 111, 176, **323**
Lloyd, Charles, 3rd, 323
Lloyd, Sampson, 323
Loar, Magdalena van, 366
Locke, John, 309
Lockington, 277
Loddington, William, 123, 316, **330**, 373
Lodge, John, 238, **364**
Lodge, Robert, 176, 227, **343**
Lombard Street, 77, 79, 88, 89, 272, 293, **298**, 308, 352
London
  fire of, 293, 296, 299, 300, 317
  Lord Mayors of, 82, 103, 146, 158, 302, 316, 336, **339**
  plague of, 313, 329, 338

London—*continued*
> visited by Fox, 38–40, 42, 54, 57, 63, 65, 75
> Yearly Meeting of, 291, **322**, 351; *1677*, 233, **359**; *1678*, 270, **380**; *1680*, xxix; *1681*, xxx; *1684*, 93, 308; *1685*, 109, 110, **322**; *1686*, 142, **336**; *1687*, xviii, 175, 176, **342**, 343; *1688*, 346; *1689*, 195, **348**; *1690*, xvii, 210, **349**
"London" Meeting, 296, 312, 317, 345; 359
Long Acre, xv, 166, 270, 326
Long Crendon, 268, 379
Long Lane, 335
Longford, 77, 261
Longworth, Roger, 114, **325**, 359
Losevelt, Abigail, 364, 369
Losevelt, Adrian van, 364
Losevelt, Cornelis, 364, 369
Lover, Mary, 327
Lower, Margery, 196, 197, **348**
Lower, Mary, [102], 104, 196, [213], **316**, 344
Lower, Thomas, 102, 104, 152–156, **213**, 275, 300, **316**, 327, 339, 342, 353
Lowrey (Lawrey), James, 148, 179, **337**
Lowrey, Mary, 337
Lucas, William, 267, 379
Lugmer Lake, 248
Lundy Island, 282
Lune, river, [16], 279, 281
Lüneburg (Lewenbrog), Duke of, 245, 367
Lurting, Thomas, 380
Luton, 232, 269, 380
Lutterworth, 231
Lynam, John, 350
Lyndeth, 352
Lynn, 40, 65

Mace, Hannah, 362
Mackett, Ann, 337
Mackett, John, 310
Mackett, William, 319
Makkum; 240
Mallett, Sir Thomas, judge, [58], 59, 291
Malquiring, *see* Molkwerum
Malton (Moten), 9, 278
Manchester, 71, 293, 317, 343
Manley, Major, 190, 191, **347**
Mann, Edward, 112, 215, 220, **306**, 318, 361
> visited by Fox at Ford Green, xvi, xxix, 91, 105, 106, 112, 113, 116, 131, 132, 141, 148–150, 161, 162, 178, 179, 186, 187, 194, 200, 214–216, 220, 258, **306**, 321, 337
> visited by Fox in George Yard, 105, **116**, 129, 132, 233, 234, 236, 257–260, 270–273, **306**
Mann, Elizabeth, [215, 220], 306, 337
Manner, Thomas, 80
Mansfield, x, 1, 12, 352

Mansfield Woodhouse, x, 12, 275
Marazion (Market Jew), 42, 287
Marchant, Elizabeth, 325
Marchant, Richard, 325
Marche (Marsh), Richard, "esq.," [59], **291**, 349
Markes, Nathaniel, 294, **321**
Market Bosworth (Boseth), xi, 13, 278
Market Harborough, 231
Market Jew, *see* Marazion
Market Street, 232, 269, 358
Marlborough, 262, 374
Marsh, *see* Marche
Marsh, Rachel, 327
Marsh, Richard, 327
Marshall, Charles, 108, 136, 140, 176, 197, 221, 233, 263–266, 306, 308, 318, 319, **328**, 342, 343, 353, 359, 374, 375
Marshall, Christopher, priest, [9], 278
Marshall, Hannah, 117, **328**
Marshall, William, priest, 26, **283**
Marshalsea, 103, **316**, 318
Marston (Marsdon), 231
Maryland, 260, 298, 305, 325
Matern, John, 338
Matthews, James, 118, 119, 128, 328, 336
Matthews, John, 147, 307, **336**
Matthews, Martha, 337
Maylin, Bartholomew, 262, **374**
Meade, Nathaniel, [91], 306
Meade, Sarah, [91, 102, 104], 181, 184, [232, 259], 285, **295**, [299], 306, 337, 344
Meade, William, **295**, 302, 305, 310, 317, 347, 353, 357, 359, 370
> visited by Fox in Fenchurch Street, 91, 97–103, 121, 122, 124–126, 128, 129, 131, 133, 134, 137, 139, 140, 155, 158, 159, 163–165, 167–169, 173–175, 177, 188–**190**, 191, 192, 195, 196, 198, 199, 206–208, 210–213, 259, **295**, 350
> visited by Fox at Gooseyes, xvi, xvii, xxv, 77, 155, 173, 180–**182**, 183–**185**, 188, **190**, 203, **206**, **295**, 328, 342, **345**, **349**
> visited by Fox at Highgate, 232, 270, **295**
Meadle, 268, **379**
Meakens, Ann, ? 358
Meakens, John, 314, **329**, 330, 341
Meakens, Margaret, 122, **329**, 337, 341
Meakens, Martha, 329, 341
Meakens, Mary, 314, 329, 341
Mealhill, 356
Meeting of Twelve, 128, **302**, 304
Menheniot, 287
Mennonites, 333, 364, 368
Merionethshire, 50
Metcalfe, Christian, 311
Metcalfe, Lascelles, 311
Mew, Mary, 334
Mew, Richard, 136, 308, **334**, 358
Micah's Mother, 376

Middleham, 227
Middlesex, 39, **140**
Middleton, Sir George, justice, 69, **292**
Mile End, 89, 381
Millar, James, 80, 299
Millhill, Lancs., 343
Milner, James, 284
Ministers' First Day Meetings, xvi, xxvii, 109, 142, 170, 174, 211, 296, **301**, 350
Molkwerum (Malquiring), 240
Mollet, John Stephen, 361
Monk, Elizabeth, 343
Monk, Mary, 343
Monk, Mary, Junr., 343
Monk, Thomas, 343
Monmouth, Duke of, 115, 322, **325**
Monyash, 343
Moor, Doctor, *see* More, Dr Henry
Moore, Ann, 351
Moore, Constance, 324
Moore, Francis, 258, 324, 359, 370, **371**
Moore, John, [65, 66], **292**
Moore, John (Eldroth), 354
Moore, Thomas, 259, 359, **371**
More, Dr Henry, 233, **359**, 378
Morning Meeting, Second Days, 81, 90, 92–94, 98, 100, 102, 103, 233, 295, 300, **301**, 312, 319, 352, 353, 360, 382
Morrice, Abraham, 346
Morrice, Isabel, 346
Mortlake, 320; *see* Osgood, John
Moses, 243, 366
Moss, Elizabeth, 343
Moss, Isaac, 343
Moss, Mary, 343
Moss, Thomas, 343
Moss-troopers, 33, **285**
Moten, *see* Malton
Mucklow, William, 127, **331**
Muggleston, Edward, 230, **357**
Muggleston, Jane, 357
Munday, Ruth, 334
Mungumtongrum, Francis (Tongeren, Barend van), 108, **322**
Münster, Bishop of, 241, 242, **366**
Myers, George, 176, **343**
Myers, George, Junr., 343
Myers, Hannah, 343
Myers, Mary, 343

Nailsworth, 265, 376
"Naked Bed," xxvi
Napier (Knaper), Sir Robert, 190, 191, **347**
Napkins, 288
Nayler, James, 9, **278**, 283, 312, 313
Negroes, 346
Netherwood, Job, 139, **335**
Nevis, 260, 298
New Chapel, 305
New England, 235, 284, 295, 298, 307, 325

New Jersey, xv, 93, 94, 97, 99, 102, 103, 105, 112, 137, **308**, 324, 325, 334, ?359, 370
New York, 298
Newberry family, 327
Newberry, Walter, 327
Newberry, Walter, 116, **326**
Newbury, 314
Newcastle, 34, 104, 227, 285
Newcastle Priests, 285
Newgate, Bristol, 326, 374
Newgate, London, 83, 86, 91, 104, 307, 326, 332, 347
Newington, Surrey, 103, 316
Newton-in-Cartmel, 19, 280
Newton, Mary, 361
Newton, Nathaniel, Senr., 231, **357**
Newton, Nathaniel, Junr., 357
Newton, Samuel, 257, 359–361, **370**
Nicholson, Joseph, [27], **284**
Niesen, Gertrude Diricks, *see* Diricks, Gertrude
Nightingale, Edward, 228, 327, **355**
Nimeguen, 252, 367, **368**
Noble, *see* Coins
"Noice" = common talk, public notice, 44, 46, 66, 68
Norfolk, **xxi**, 39, 311
North Kilworth, 231, 357
North Newington, 268, 379
Northallerton, 227
Northampton, 231, 358
Northamptonshire, 40, 268, 287, 357
Northscale, 281, 282
Northumberland, 34, 68, 295
Norton-on-Tees, 354
Norton, Humphrey, 290
Norway, 312
Norwich, 65, 297, 359
Nottingham, **x**, 1, 15, 229, 275, 352
Nottinghamshire, 12, 15, 36, 217, 343
Nottingley, *see* Knottingley
Noyse, Israel, 263, **374**
Noyse, Margery, 374, 375
Nudity, 290
Nuneaton, 231, 287

Oades, Cotton, 132, 133, 171, **333**
Oades, Lydia, 333
Oades, Mary, 337
Oare, 76, 262, 373
Oaths, xxi, 48, 60, 64, 70, 71, 173, 219, **292**, **293**, 295, 305, 311, 339, 346, 365
Odingsells, Mary, 330, 361
Oldenburg, 242, 246, 252, **366**, 367
Oldenburg, Earl of, 242, 366
Olney, 231, 358
Orange, Prince of, 253
Orton, Westmorland, 327
Osgood, John, 104, 124, 127, 134, 170, 197, 258, 313, **317**, 319, 347, 359, 360, 370

Osgood, Mary, 317
Osgood, Rebecka, 313, 317
Otway, George, [35], 286
Otway, Sir John, 286
Overdelend (? Obernenland), 242
Owen, Ann, 380
Oxfordshire, 76, 262, 353, 372

Palace Yard, 191, 301
Panes Place, 75, 293
Papists, 156, 311
Pardoe, Margaret, 377
Pardoe, Mary, 377
Pardoe, William, Baptist, 377
Pardoe, William, 266, 267, **377**
"Pardon" of Charles II, [61], 299, 331,
    344, 357-359, 371, 373
"Pardon" of James II, 336, 342
Park Meeting, The, 183, 304
Parke, Frances, 319
Parke, James, 106, 122, 163, 170, 174,
    308, **319**, 353
Parker, Alexander, **291**, 302, **307**, 308,
    361, 381
    Fox at his home, 92, 103, 104, 106, **108**,
        110, **114**, 271
    meetings with Fox, [61], 93, 105, 112,
        113, 132, 135-137, 149, 151, 154, 160,
        169-171, 176, 180, 186, 187, 233,
        259-262, 273, 290, **291**, 299, 308,
        327
Parker, Henry, justice, 268
Parker, Prudence, [232]
Parker, William, 304
Parliament, xv, 48, 54-57, 107, 190, 194,
    202, 219, 270, 301, 347
Pashur, *see* Pershore
Paterem, John, 171, **341**
Patrington, 6, 7
Paul, *see* Poole, William
Pavement, Oxon, 309
Peace and War, 5, **60**, **304**, 346, 365, 372
Peake, Sir John, [158], 339
Pearse, Philip, mayor, 288
Pearson, Agnes, 353
Pearson, Grace, 353
Pearson, Margery, 353
Pearson, Susanna, 375
Pearson, Susanna, Junr., 376
Pearson, Thomas (Cheshire), 353
Pearson, Thomas (Lancs), 353
Pearson, Thomas (Westmorland), 225,
    353
Peel, The, 79, 83, 89, 90, 96, 101, 114,
    120, 148, 158, 164, 169, 189, 193, 199,
    209, 217, 222, [258], 295, **297**, 329, 331,
    335 ; *see* Elson, John
Peel Collection Meeting, 171, 199, 213,
    297
Pendennis Castle, 43, 46, [287]
Pendle Hill, 279
Penington, Isaac, 235, 259, 261, 262, 269,
    299, 310, 322, 348, **360**, 361

Penington, Mary, 75, 76, [261, 262, 269],
    294, 310, 322, 339, 346, 361
Penington, Mary, Junr., 93, 95, 99, 129,
    259, **299**, **310**, 322, 361
Penn, Gulielma Maria, [115, 184, 192, 294],
    324, **326**, 346, 360
Penn, Hannah, [294]
Penn, Springett, [184], **346**
Penn, Sir William, 329
Penn, William, xviii, xx, 160, 184, 192,
    199, 235, 236, **237**-239, 248, 249,
    251-256, 258-265, **294**, 298, 299, 306,
    308, 313, **315**, 322, 335, **346**, 353,
    357-360, 364, 368, 370, 373, 374,
    378
    meetings with Fox, xix, 95, 105, 107,
        109, 120, 142, 143, 152, 153, 172, 177,
        184, 233, 234, 237-239, 249, 251, 253,
        258, 263, 264, 295, 311, 323, 330
    visited Fox, xvi, 115, 157, 160, 172,
        175, 192, 233, 248, 259, **260**, 261,
        269
    visited by Fox, xxx, 75, 78, 100, 103,
        115, 122, 123, 177, 199, **235**, 271, **315**
    residences, 100, 103, 115, 123, **315**
Penn, W., *Travels*, 358, **365**
Pennenbark (? Pinneberg), 244
Pennsylvania, xv, 114, 137, 311, 320, **321**,
    323, 325, 374
Pennyman, John, 259, 351, **371**
Pepys, Samuel, 296
Perkins, Joan, 219, 337, 353
Perrot, Edward, 373
Perrot, Joan, 354
Perrot, John, 243, 288, 309, 313, **366**
Pershore (Pashur), 266, 377
Perth (St Johnstons), 52, 290
Peterborough, 286
Pettie, John, 293
Pettyplace, *see* Fettiplace
Pettys, 342
Phillips, William, 146, **336**
Phillips, William, [336], 341
Pickering, [14], 278
Pietists, 304
Pinder, Grace, 337
Pinder, Richard, 105, 113, 157, **317**,
    359
Pinneberg, *see* Pennenbark
Pirbright, 297
Plaistow, 118, 273, 328
Plant, Elizabeth, 314
Plant, Ezekiel, 314
Plant, Humphrey, 314
Plant, John, 98, 116, **314**
Plots, 68, 69, **293** ; *see* Fifth-Monarchy
Plumpton, 282
Plumstead, Clement, 308, 311
Plumstead, Francis, 216
Plymouth, 42, 314
Poland, 129, 130, 251, 300, 332
Pollockshill (Pullockshill), 232, 358
Polsted, Hannah, 299

Pont-y-Moile, 67, 377
Pool, William, 376
Poolbank (Powbank), 225, 353
Poole, Baptista, 355
Poole, Samuel, 228, **355**
Poole (Paul), William, 243, 366
Pope, The, 156, 297
Porter, Henry, justice, 56, 57, **291**
Portsmouth, 71, 293
Potton, 349
Poulner (Pulner), 79, **298**
Powbank, *see* Poolbank
Prayers, 306
Premunire, 355, 359, **377**
Presbyterians, 69, 281, 362
Preshute, 374
Press-gang, 380
Preston, Yorks, 354
Preston Patrick, 18, 280, 286, 329
Preston, Thomas, justice, 69, **293**
Pretender, Old, 346
Pretender, Young, 304
Price, Peter, 330
Pricket, *see* Pritchett
Prince, Mary, 330
Prince, Peter, 123, 124, 127, **330**
Prisons, Condition of, xiii, 2, 33, 45, 326
Pritchard, Sir William, [82], 302
Pritchett (Pricket), Edward, 80, 299
"Proud People," 79, 83, **297**
Pullockshill, *see* Pollockshill
Pulner, *see* Poulner
Pumphrey, Stanley, 378
Purl House, 166
Purmerend, 239
Purse, Susanna, 297
Pursglove, Capt. Richard, [8], **277**
Putney, 233, 236, 320
Pyott, Edward, [43], **287**

Quare, Ann, 339
Quare, Daniel, 159, **339**
Quare, Elizabeth, 339
Quare, Mary, 337, 339
Quare, Sarah, 339

Radnorshire, 51
Ragley, 267, 378, 379
Rampside, 20, 26, 281, 282
Ranters, 8, 19, 276
Rantzow, Earl of, 243
Ratcliff (Ratliff), 83, 89-91, 100, 113, 114, 120, 126, 135, 170, 171, 234, 259, 271, **302**, 307, 314, 318, 320, 341, 349, 371
"Rationals," 372
Ratliffe, William, 8, **277**
Raunce, Elizabeth, 371
Raunce, Dr John, 258, 261, 262, 269, 335, 350, 352, 370, **371**, 372
Raworth, Ruth, 321
Rawthey, river, [16], 279

Raylton, Tace, 322
Raylton, Thomas, 322
Reading, 76, 262, 296, 318, 373
Reading, Mary, 378
Reckless, John, [2], 229, **275**
Recusants, 282, 286, 359, 370
Red Hill, 293
Redbourn, 232
Redruth, 43
Reed, Mary, 363
Reigate, 75, 293
Release, Charter of, *see* "Pardon"
Remington, Frances, 277
Rhode Island, 112, 284
Richardson, Richard, xxi, 80, 108, 119, 165, **300**, 303, 310
Richardson, William, 231, 358
Rickmansworth, 294
Rigge, Ambrose, 176, 299, **342**, 343, 353, 359
Ringwood, xxiv, **66, 79**, 292, 298, 299
Roberts, Abiah, 89, 305
Roberts, Gerard, 149, 153, 194, 233, 258, 260, 270, 293, 317, **337**, 359, 361, 370
Roberts, John, 315, 376
Roberts, Milbrow, 337
Robertson, Thomas, *see* Robinson, Thomas
Robins, Jasper (Godmanchester), 336
Robins, Jasper (London), 316, **348**
Robins, Sarah, 198, 208, **316, 348**
Robins, Susanna, 336
Robinson, Benjamin, 348
Robinson, George, 227, **354**
Robinson, Sir John, 302
Robinson, Margery, 348
Robinson, Richard (Brigflatts), 17, **279**, 354
Robinson, Richard (Counterside), 226, 353, **354**
Robinson (Robertson), Thomas, 105, 107, 111, 112, 118, 119, 122, 125, 133, 152, 154, 156, 216, 260, **318**, 327, 345, 353, 359
Rodes, Catherine, 277
Rodes, Francis, 277
Rodes, Sir John, **277**, 311, 344, 353
Roeloffs, Cornelis, 253, 254, **368**
Roeloffs, Deborah, 333, 368
Roeloffs, Jan, 135-137, 238, 249, 251, **333**, 368
Rogers, Elizabeth, 360
Rogers, Francis, 360
Rogers, Thomas, mayor, 289
Rogers, William, [234], 264, **360**, 373, 374
Romford, 306
Rosells, *see* Russell, William
Ross, 67
Rotterdam, 237, 238, 249, 253, 254, 309, 359, 363, 364
Rous family visited by Fox at Kingston, xvi, xxv, 89, **100**, 102, **126**, 168, **169**, 196, 208, 233, 236, **260**, 305, 341, **346**

Rous, Anne, 196, 197, 208, **315**
Rous, Bethia, 126, 181, 208, 315, **331**
Rous, Hannah, 315
Rous, John, 100, 102, 104, 126, 134, 168, 181, 184, 197, 208, 213, 260, 261, 305, **314**, 317, 331, 341, 353, 368
Rous, Margaret, xvi, 97, 104, 109, 152, 168, 196, [208], 233, 236, 305, **314**, 331, 344
Rous, Margaret, Junr., 89, 126, 149, 168, **305**, 315
Rous, Nathaniel, 134, **315**
Rouse, Anthony, colonel, [46], **288**
Rowles, Ann, 328
Royal Society, 316
Rudyard, Thomas, 232, 234, 247–249, 257, 258, 269, 271, 272, 308, 321, **358**, 361, 366, 370
Rush, Hannah, 358
Rush, John, Senr., 358
Rush, John, Junr., 232, **358**
Rush, Tabitha, 358
Russell, Elizabeth, 294
Russell, Grace, 329
Russell, Jane, 374
Russell, Mary, 324, 344
Russell, Michael, 324
Russell, Michael, Junr., 112, **165**, 168, 170, 172, 175, 188, 217, **324**, 334, 374
Russell (Rosells), William, 76, **294**
Rustenburg (Russlenborrow), 239, 382

Sacraments, 245, 286, 360, 365
Sadbury, *see* Sodbury
St Albans, 232, 269, 358
St Ives, Cornwall, 43, 358
St Johnstons, *see* Perth
Saling, 257
Salsbury Change, 134, 146, 169, **320**
Salt, William, [43, 45], **287**, 288
Salter, George, 261, **372**
Sanders, Damaris, 379
Sanders, Damaris, Junr., 379
Sanders, Thomas, 268, **379**
Sands, The, 23, **282**
Sauls Errand, 283
Saunders, Margery, 325
Saunders, Mary, 344
Savoy, The, xiv, 79, 82, **84**, **87**–91, 94, 98, 107, 125, 133, 153, 159, 169, 191, 199, 203, 209, 270, **297**, 301, 304, **308**, 333; *see* Ellis, Josiah; Fisher, Martha
  Yard and Entry, 86, 98, 107, 115, 125, 139, 160, 169, **297**, 304
Sawrey, John, justice, 23–26, **282**
Sawyer, George, 232, 269, 358
Sawyer, Sir Robert, [133, 141, 310], **333**
Sawyer, Sarah, 320
Sayes, John, mayor, [49], 289
Scarhouse, 226
Scarth (Scaife), Philip, [8], **276**, 277

Schools, 296, 305, 315, 316, 324, 330, 331; *see under* Fox, George
Scoryer, Richard, 315
Scotch Yard, *see* Haistwell, Edward
Scotland, xxxii, 51, 53, 54, 80, 262, 282, 284, 285, **290**, 325, 342, 352, 359, 381
Scotland Yard, 59, **291**
Scott, Thomas, 131
Scotting, Robert, 170, 171, **341**
Scriptures, The, xii, 1, 20, **33**, 34, 37, 51, 55, 84; *see* Bibles
Second Days Morning Meeting, *see* Morning Meeting
Sedbergh, xiii, 18, 35, 227, **279**
Seedsman, The, **xvi**, 105, 106, 111, 113, 116, 117, 131, 141, 147, [150], **317**
Seekers, 239, 279, 280, **284**, 285, 340, 365
Seething Lane, 97
Sellar, Richard, 380
Sellwood, Elizabeth, 381
Sellwood, John, 136, **381**
Semerwater, 354
Separatists, 117, 225, 228, 256, 264, 269, 271, **327**, 334, 348, 355, 356, 367, 372, 374, **375**, 376, 382; *see* Coale, Benjamin; Coleman, Nathaniel; Cox, John; Curtis, Thomas; Dennison, Thomas; Hall, John; Harris, Charles; Nightingale, Edward; Raunce, John; Rogers, William; Story, John; Wilkinson, John; Winnard, John
Sepulchre Close, 278
Settle, 285, 342, 354
Shacklewell, 83, 89, [91], 259, **305**, 325
Shadd, Dorothy, Informer, 303
Shadd, Gabriel, Informer, 86, **303**, 317, 335
Shaftesbury, Lord, 309
Sharman, Thomas, [5], **276**
Shaw, Thomas, priest, 283
Sheffield, 229
Sherwood, Constance, 330
Sherwood, Edward, 330
Shewen, Ann, 337
Shewen, William, 149, 161, 186, 220, 308, **337**, 359, 370
Shorthand, xxix, 271, 372
Shovel-board, 246, **367**
Shropshire, 320, 321, 323
Sibford (Sibbard), 268, 379
Siddall, William, 228, **355**
Sidney, Algernon, 309, 317
Sidon, Henry, 230, **357**
"Sign," *see* Nudity
Sikehouse, 355
Sileby, 229
Silence in Worship, xii, xvii, xxvii, 132, 137, 142, 159, 170, 174, **301**
Silesia, 310
Silverdale, 22, 282
Simmons, *see* Symonds
Simms, Elias, 133, **333**

Simms, Mary, 333, 337
Simpson, William, 288
Sinderley, *see* Cinder Hill Green
Singing, 33, 214, **351**, 373, 375
Six Weeks Meeting, 82, 88, 89, 98, 102, 272, 296, **302**, 329
Skegby, 3, 229
Skinner, Daniel, 142, **335**
Skinner, Elizabeth, 335, 337
Skinner, William, 335
Skipton, 227
Slaughterford, 263, 374, **375**
Smart, Mary, 334
Smith, Christopher, Informer, 317
Smith, Elizabeth, Informer, 317
Smith, Sir James, [103], 316
Smith, Justice, 100, 314
Smith, Mary, 355
Smith, Richard, 265, **376**
Smith, Robert, 266, **377**
Smith, Stephen, 235, 236, 261-263, 265-267, 297, 359, **361**, 372
Smith, Susanna, widow, 78, **297**
Smith, William (Sileby), 229, **356**
Smith, Sir William, 314
Smithfield, 147, 307, 331
Snead, Richard, 263, 264, 359, **374**
Snooke, Henry, 122, **329**
Snooke, Rebekah, 329
Socinians, 239, 248
Sodbury (Sadbury), 265, 376
Soldiers become Friends, 53, 343, 370, 376, 377
Somerford family, 378
Somersetshire, 67, 310, 329, 334
Sonemans, Arent, 237, 238, 253, 254, **363**
Sonemans, Frances, 363
Sonemans, M—, [254], **369**
South Mimms, 232, 269, 380
South Shields, 354, 355
South Street (Southgate), 111, 131, 148, 160, 161, 187, 194, 311, **324**, 337, 340; *see* Austill, Bridget
Southwark, 337
Soutwerke, Priest, [20], **281**
Sowle, Andrew, 103, 300, **321**, 334, 337
Sowle, Elizabeth, 321
Sowle, Francis, 321
Sowle, Jane, 321, 337
Sowle, Tace, 293, **322**
Spectacle-maker, xv, 115, 287
Spence, Robert, etchings, 276, 279, 285, 287, 288
Spitalfields, 75, 78, 98, 152, 168, 293, 302, 303, 313, 314, 338
Springett, Gulielma Maria, 360
Springett, Lady, *see* Penington, Mary
Stable, *see* Staveley
Stacy, Ann, 355
Stacy, Robert, 355
Stacy, Thomas, 228, **356**
Staffordshire, 296

Staines, 77, 340
Stainsby, 229
Stamper, Francis, 140, 176, 188 (Stamford), 220, 303, 306, 328, **335**, 353, 374
Stanley, Elizabeth, 378
Stanley, John, 267, **378**
Stanley, Mary, 378
Staploe, Ann-Mercy, 329
Staploe, Grace, 329, 337
Staploe, Hester, 330
Staploe, John, 122, 147, **329**, 337, 374
Starkey, Ann, 330
Starkey, Constance, 330
Starkey, George, 330
Starkey, Thomas, 330
Starkey, Thomas, Junr., 330, 351
Starling, *see* Sternhold
Stathes, [7], **276**, 277
Staveley (Stable), 19, 280
Stavoren, 240
Stebbing, 257
Steele, Laurence, 263, **374**, 376
Steevens, Ann, 373, 379
Steevens, Jeremiah, 262, 339, **373**, 379
Steevens, Jeremiah, Junr., 373
Steevens, Mary, 339
Stephens, Nathaniel, priest, [4], 36, **276**, 278
Stepney, 307, 314, 334, 381
Sternhold (Starling), Thomas, 215, **351**
Stickhausen (Strikehusing), 242
Stinchcombe (Finchcombe), 265, 376
Stirling, 290
Stoddard, Amor, 312, 370, 372
Stoke, 64, 292
Stoke-by-Nayland, 359
Stoke Orchard, 266, 377
Stokesley, 9, **278**
Stone Dean, 330
Story, John, 263, 265, 334, **375**, 382
Story, Thomas, 309
Stott, John, 305, 313
Stott, Mary, 89, 91, 95, 101, 102, 110, 111, 118, 125, 126, 129, 137, 143, 144, 146, 147, 151, 157, 159, 164, 167, 170, 182, **305**, 309, 313, 316, [332], 337
Stott, Mary, Junr., 313
Stout, Henry, 179, 180, 216, 336, **344**, 360
Stout, Mary, 337, **344**, 345
Stout, Sarah, 344
Stratford, Essex, 119
Stratford-on-Avon, 267, 379
Streat, John, capt., 80
Streek, De, 240, **382**
Street, 342
Strikehusing, *see* Stickhausen
Stroobos, 240, 247
Strutt, James, Senr., 314
Strutt, James, 100, 114, 120, 121, 126, 233, 234, 259, 271, 272, **314**, 329, 341
Strutt, "Old" Mary, xv, 171, **314**

Strutt, Mary, 314, 329, 341
Stubbs, John, 293
Stubbs, Thomas, 287
Sudbury, 382
Sufferings, Meeting for, xv, 79, 97, 113, 138, 158, **298**, 300, 303
Suffolk, 39, 65, 382
Sunbury, 77
Sunday Work, 108, 310, 321
Surman, Mary, 377
Surrey, xxix, 39, 42, 66
Sussex, xxix, xxx, 39, 42, 66
Sutton, Isle of Ely, [40], 286
Sutton, Richard, 187, **346**
Swan, Ann, 297
Swan, Thomas, 297
Swanington, 63, 230, 357
Swanner, Mark, 93–95, 97–100, 104, 108, 110, 165, 300, 308, **310**
Swarthmoor, xiii, xix, xxv, xxix, 19, 20, 23, 25, 26, 56, 68, 69, 93, 104, 225, **280**, 282, 283, 313, 321, 329, 354, 355, 361
Swarthmoor Fund, **280**, 282, 284, 290, 353
Sweden, 243, 245
Swinton, Frances, 363, 373
Swinton, John, 261, 262, 269, 360, 363, 371, **373**
Symonds (Simmons), Widow, 123, 331

Tadcaster, 228, 352, 355
Talcot, Ann, 362, 369
Talcot, Ann, Junr., 362, 369
Talcot, Mary, 315, 362
Talcot, William, 237, 238, 255, **362**, 369
Tallack, William, 361
Tanner, Thomas, 261, 372
Taylby, Elizabeth, 322
Taylby (Tileby), William, 109, 128, **322**
Taylor, Christopher, 261–263, 338, 359, **372**
Taylor, Francis, 355
Taylor, George, 283
Taylor, James, 280
Taylor, John (York), 157, 160, 228, 318, **338**, 352, 353
Taylor, John, water poet, 320
Taylor, Thomas (Brighouse), [36], **286**
Taylor, Thomas (Stafford), 359
Temple, The, *see* Vaughan, Rowland
Tenby, 49, **289**
Tennant, Elizabeth, widow, 226, **354**
Tennant, James, 354
Tenterden, 65, 292
Tetbury Upton, 265
Tewkesbury, 266
Thames, river, [103, 113, 115, 116, 118, 121, 124, 127, 134–136, 146, 156, 165, 169, 193, **305**], 312, **320**
Theakston, Elizabeth, 354
Theobalds (Tiballs), 214, **304**
Thetford, xxi
Thirsk, 228

Thomas, Richard, 216, **351**
Thompson, Elizabeth, 370
Thornton, 228
Thornton, James, 278
Thorp, John, 125, **331**
Three Kings Court, 88, 103, 172, 298, **300**, 370
Tickhill, 10, 11
Tileby, *see* Taylby
Tithes, 304, 315, 331, 339, 345, 346, 357, 370, 375
Tiverton, 67
Tobacco, 22, 304
Toleration Act, xviii, 195, 317, **347**
Tombes, John, priest, [55], **291**
Tomkins, Jane, 314
Tomkins, John, 311, 344
Tongeren, Barend van, *see* Mungumtongrum, Francis
Toovy, Elizabeth, 308
Toovy, John, 308
Topliffe, 278
Topsham, 48, 289
Tottenham (High Cross), 200, 207, 214–217, 219–221, 280, 324, 349
Totties Hall, 356
Toulnson, George, 283
Townsend, Jane, 354
Townsend, Richard, 265, 266, **376**
Townsend, Roger, 376
Townsend, Theophila, 376
Travers, Anne, 103, 121, 123, 127, 134, 145, 146, 165, 166, 169, 234, 259, 271, 272, **316**, 329, 337, 348, 381
Travers, Matthew, 313
Travers, Rebecka, xxv, 97, 155, 169, 233, 258, 259, 302, **312**, 329, 337, 360, 371
Travers, Rebecka, Junr., 313, 317
Travers, Sarah, **316**, 348
Travers, William, 312, **313**
Tredway, Henry, 262, **373**
Tredway, Margaret, 373
Tregrosse, Priest, 287
Trott, Elizabeth, 302
Turks, 250
Turvey, 231, 358
Turville Heath, 76, 262, 371, **373**
Twickenham, 372
Twineham, [75], 293
Twinn, Susanna, 319
Two Weeks Meeting, 82, **302**
Twycross, 15
Tyler, Mary, widow, 162, 180, **340**

Ullesthorpe, 231
Ulverston, xxii, 19, 23, 57, 281, 282, 372
Underbarrow, 19, 280
Urie, 371
Uxbridge, 76, 261, 269, 372

Vagrancy, **xxi**, 48, **288**, 370, 373
Vandewall, Anna, 369
Vandewall, Frances, 336

Vandewall, Hannah, 362
Vandewall, John, Senr., 362
Vandewall, John, 237, 255, **362**, 369
Vandewall, Joseph, 336
Vandewall, Mary, 362
Vandewall, Susanna, 362
Vaughan, Sir John, 347
Vaughan, Rowland, attorney, 93, 96, 100, 109, 115, 127, 130, 133, 140, 141, 153, 160, **310**, 315, 333
Vaughton, Elizabeth, 304, 337, 344
Vaughton, John, 87, 88, 111, 112, 127, 151, 160, 166, 188, 199, **304**, 326, 328, 353, 359
Vaux family, 336, 380
Vickris, Richard, 95, 265, **310**, 326, 335, 359, 374
Vickris, Robert, 310
Virginia, 298, 325, 369
Vivers, Edward, 268, 269, **379**

W——, G—— (Watts, George, or Whitehead, George), 123, 129, 137, 139, 145, 146, 170, 171, 176, 232, 259
Wager, Prudence, Senr., 299
Wager, Prudence, Junr., 299
Wakefield, [9], 278
Waldegrave, Frances, 363
Waldenfield, Mary, 184, **346**
Waldenfield, Samuel, 130, 308, 321, 328, **332**, 346, 363, 374
Wales, 49, 55, 67, 157, **289**, 306, 307, **311**, 319, 323, 377
Wales, Hist. of Friends in, 289
Walker, Jane, 357
Wallis, Elizabeth, widow, 263, **375**
Wallis, John, 375
Wallis, Margery, 374
Walney Island, 20, 25, **281**, 282
Waltham Abbey, 105, 131, 149, 150, 161, 162, 186, 215, 304, 340, 345 ; *see* Bennett, Thomas
Waltham Cross, 318
Wandsworth, [77], 295, 349
Wanstead, 181, 328
Wapping, 171, 314, 341
Warborough, 76, 343, 344
Ward, Christopher, 127, **331**
Ware, 216, 352
Warminster, 326
Warmsworth, 11, 278, 355
Warwick, 41, 335, 356
Warwickshire, xi, 13, 267, 285, 356, 357, 379
Wasse, James, 80, 117, 128, 140, 171, **300**
Wasse, Mary, 337
Waterland, 249
Watermen, 320
Waters, Thomas, 293
Watford, 76, 269, 331
Watson, Esther, 354
Watson, Grace, 343

Watson, Jane, 354
Watson, Mary, 343
Watson, Richard, 227, 228, **354**
Watson, Samuel, 176, **342**
Watson, Thomas, 354
Watts, Elizabeth, 304
Watts, George, 89, 93, 98–103, 105, 106, 108, 110, 112, 121, 131, 147–149, 151, 155, 158, 171, 175, 180, 237, 255, 272, **305**, 308, 309, 332 ; *see* W——, G——
Waugh, Jane, 329
Wayte, Mary, 355
Wayte, Thomas, 228, **355**
Weatherley, George, 237, 256, 362, **363**
Weatherley, Mary, 363
Webb, Mary, widow, 294, 323
Welch, Mary, 317, 361
Welch, Sarah, 359, 361
Welch, William, 233, 234, 262, 317, **359**, 361, 363, 370
Wellingborough, 231
Wells, Ann, 356
Wells, Elizabeth, 356
Wells, William, 230, **356**
Welshpool, 323
Wensleydale (Winsadayle), 17, 226, 279, 354
West, Elizabeth, 262, **373**
West, Robert, 308
West, William, justice, [26, 27], 72, **283**, 293
West, William, 268, **379**
Westminster, xv, 82, 89, 90, 96, 107, 109, 127, 156, 166, 193, 295, **302**, 303, 318
Westminster Hall, 58, 190, 193, 219, 270, **301**, 347, 352
Westmorland, xxix, 21, 34, 68–70, 226, 279, 353
Weston Turville, 268, 331, 371, 379
Wetherby, 352
Wharley, Daniel, 110, 111, 117, 120, 122, 126, 129, 131, 135, 151, 168, 177, 299, 310, 315, **322**
Wharley, Mary, 310, **322**, 344
Wheeler Street, 84, 88, 90, 92, 94, 119, 151, 172, 195, 259, 271, 293, **303**, 338, 350
Whispool Lake, 248
White, Dr Alexander, 362
White, Dorothy, 313
White, Hannah, 380
White Hart Court, 187, 293, 301, 317, 324, 334, 341
White, John, 268, 373, **379**
White Lion Prison, 296
Whitechapel, 96, 311
Whitehall, 46, 130, 290
Whitehead, Anne, 148, [232], 295, 301, 302, 313, 321, 324, 329, **337**, 342
Whitehead, Anne, 344
Whitehead, George, xxvi, 262, 263, 286, 297, 301–**303**, 304, 308, 310, 313, 319, 324, 328, **332**, 333, 337, 345, 347,

Whitehead, George—*continued*
353, 359, 361, 363, 381; *see* W——,
G——
  meetings with Fox, 106, 109, 122, 133,
  141, 144, 149, 167, 262, 264, 265, 295,
  299
  preached, 149, 150, 160, 162, 169, 191,
  194, 214, 215, 220, 353
  solicitations, 130, 133, 141, 202, 300,
  303, 310, 333, 346, 376
  travelled with Fox, xxix, 127, 192, 193,
  263, 270
  visited Fox, xvi, 107, 130, 131, 135, 143,
  149, 157, 160, 169, 175, 202, 233,
  260
  visited by Fox, 117, 122, 130, 154, 160,
  217
Whitehead, Jane, 329
Whitehead, John, 353
Whitehead, Thomas, priest, [21, 23], **281**
Whitehead, Thomas, 120, **329**
Whiting, John, 328, 336
Whitpain, Mary, 337
Whitpain, Richard, 128, 136, 137, 308,
  331, 374
Whitrow, Susanna, 313
Whittington, 230, 357
Widders, Jane, [225]
Widders, Robert, [22, 57], 225, **282**,
  291
Wigan, 277
Wigan, John, priest, 319
Wiggin, *see* Wigton
Wigs, 357
Wigton (Wiggin), 31, 285
Wilcox, Mary, 320
Wilcox, Thomas, 320
Wilkinson and Story Controversy, *see*
  Separatists
Wilkinson, Abel, 139, 335
Wilkinson, John, ex-priest, [29, 30, 33],
  285
Wilkinson, John, Separatist, 334, 382
Willems, Willem, 239, **365**
William III, 339, 347, 348
Williams, Roger, 235, 261, 272, **361**, 381
Wilmer, Constance, 330
Wilmer, John, 330
Wilmer, Capt. Nathaniel, 330
Wilmer, Nathaniel, 123, 154, 177, **199**,
  316, **330**, 351
Wilson, William, 293
Wiltshire, 67, 262, 374, 375
Winchmore (Winsmore) Hill, 106, 116,
  149, 150, 161, 178, 187, 188, 194, 215,
  216, 220, **319**, 327

Windsor, 318
Winnard, John, 327
Winnington, Thomas, 135, **333**
Winsadayle, *see* Wensleydale
Winterbourne, 265, 336, 376
Winthorpe, 277
Wise, Priest, 40, **287**
Withcote Hall, 286
Woodbridge, 318, 369
Woodcock, Jane, 233, 234, 258, 260, 270–
  272, **297**, 308, 319, 329, **359**
Woodcock, William, 297
Woodhouse, 286
Woodhouse, ship, 337
Woods, Hannah, 315
Woodside, Bucks, 294
Woodward, Joane, 377
Woodward, John, 266, 267, **377**
Woodwarde, Mary, 300
Wooldale, 356
Woolley, Ezekiel, 136, 140, 141, 151, 156,
  158, 172, 195, 211, 235, 259, 260, 271–
  273, 302, 319, 337, **338**, 350, 359
Woolley, Ezekiel, Junr., 338
Woolley, Mary, 82, 111, 125, 130, 141,
  150, 152, 168, 170, 178, 179, [260], **302**,
  337, 344
Worcester, 41, 66, 266, 267, 282, 336, 338,
  375, 377
Worcester Prison, 281, 320, 381
Worcestershire, 68, 337, 338, 381
Workum, 240
"World's People," 156, 166, 172, 177,
  297
Worminghurst, xxviii, xxx, 75, 235, 294
Worplesdon, 236, 297
Wray, Frances, 277
Wray, Sir John, 277
Wyan, Jacob, 339
Wyan, Mary, 325
Wyan, Sarah, 339
Wycombe, 76, 262, 294, 339, 352, 371
Wymeswold, 229, 356

Yarm, 327, 355
Yates, Informer, 303
Yealand, 282
Yeamans, Isabel, 185, 233, 237–239, 247–
  249, 255, 262, **346**, 355, 358, 361
Yeamans, William, 346
Yoakley Charity, 334, 336
York, 117, 227, 228, 327, 339, 348, 355
York Castle, 11, 12, 342, 343, 355, 356
York Separatists, *see* Separatists
Yorkshire, 6–11, 14, 16, 35, 55, 68, 69,
  140, 226, 229, 293, 318

CAMBRIDGE: PRINTED BY W. LEWIS AT THE UNIVERSITY PRESS

Lightning Source UK Ltd.
Milton Keynes UK
04 November 2010

162388UK00007B/1/P